Special Edition

USING
VISUAL
BASIC 5

Special Edition

Using
Visual
Basic 5

Written by

Mike McKelvy • *Ronald R. Martinsen* • *Jeff Webb* • *Bob Reselman*

Special Edition Using Visual Basic 5

Library of Congress Catalog No.: 96-70766

ISBN: 0-7897-0922-8

99 98 97   6 5 4 3 2

Interpretation of the printing code: the rightmost double-digit number is the year of the book's printing; the rightmost single-digit number, the number of the book's printing. For example, a printing code of 96-1 shows that the first printing of the book occurred in 1996.

Screen reproductions in this book were created using Collage Plus from Inner Media, Inc., Hollis, NH.

Credits

PRESIDENT
Roland Elgey

PUBLISHER
Joseph B. Wikert

PUBLISHING DIRECTOR
David W. Solomon

PUBLISHING MANAGER
Fred Slone

SENIOR TITLE MANAGER
Bryan Gambrel

EDITORIAL SERVICES DIRECTOR
Elizabeth Keaffaber

MANAGING EDITOR
Sandy Doell

DIRECTOR OF MARKETING
Lynn E. Zingraf

ACQUISITIONS EDITORS
Angela Kozlowski
Al Valvano

PRODUCT DIRECTOR
Erik Dafforn

PRODUCTION EDITOR
Mathew B. Cox

EDITORS
Kelli M. Brooks
Jim Bowie
Sherri Fugit
Aaron Gordon
Chuck Hutchinson
Sydney Jones
Jeannie Smith

PRODUCT MARKETING MANAGER
Kristine Ankney

ASSISTANT PRODUCT MARKETING MANAGERS
Karen Hagen
Christy M. Miller

STRATEGIC MARKETING MANAGER
Barry Pruett

TECHNICAL EDITORS
Mark Robinson
Joel Richard

TECHNICAL SUPPORT SPECIALISTS
Nadeem Muhammed

ACQUISITIONS COORDINATOR
Carmen Krikorian

SOFTWARE RELATIONS COORDINATOR
Susan D. Gallagher

EDITORIAL ASSISTANTS
Andrea Duvall

BOOK DESIGNER
Ruth Harvey

COVER DESIGNER
Dan Armstrong

PRODUCTION TEAM
Erin M. Danielson
Julie Geeting
Timothy Neville
Donna Wright

INDEXER
Eric Brinkman
CJ East
Chris Wilcox

Composed in *Century Old Style* and *ITC Franklin Gothic* by Que Corporation.

To my wife, Wanda, and my children, Laura and Eric, for their support, and for their patience with the long hours.

- Mike McKelvy-

To my FANTASTIC wife Karen for hanging in there during all the nights I missed with her while writing this book.

- Ronald R. Martinsen-

About the Authors

Mike McKelvy is the owner of McKelvy Software Systems, Inc., a software consulting firm in Birmingham, AL. Mike's firm specializes in the development of database applications for all types of businesses. Mike has been developing software for business and engineering applications for over 15 years and has recently started doing seminars on Visual Basic. Mike is also the author of Using Visual Basic 4 and Delphi 2 Tutor. Mike can be contacted on CompuServe at **71477,3513** or on the Internet at **mmckelvy@Traveller.Com** or at:

McKelvy Software Systems
P.O. Box 380125
Birmingham, AL 35238

Ronald R. Martinsen graduated Summa Cum Laude in Computer Information Systems Applications from Loyola University, and has been programming in Visual Basic since version 1.0. Ron is also proficient in C/C++ Win32 programming, and was the former president and founder of Martinsen's Software. Currently, he is employed as a Software Design Engineer by a major software development corporation. You can e-mail Ron at **RonMart@msn.com**.

Jeff Webb was a senior member of the Visual Basic team at Microsoft. Since then, he's written or contributed to a number of books including "Using Visual Basic for Applications" and "Using Visual Basic 4 Special Edition."

Bob Reselman is a Senior Software Engineer at Gateway 2000 and a part-time instructor at Western Iowa Tech Community College. In addition to his programming, writing and teaching activities, he also spends time thinking and making music. He presently lives in Sioux City, Iowa with his wife, Dorothy Lifka and his two daughters, Geneviève and Alix. He can be reached at, **reselbob@pionet.net** and viewed at, **http://www.pionet.net/~reselbob**. Oh yes, he likes motorcycles.

Acknowledgments

Mike McKelvy: Writing a book like this is always an effort by a large group of people. I have been fortunate to have an extremely good team working with me. Angela Kozlowski and Al Valvano, the Acquisitions Editors, have been great to work with and have had a number of ideas which have dramatically enhanced this book. The editing staff, headed by Matthew Cox, has also been very easy to work with and has helped me in clarifying many of the ideas that I put into words. I would also like to thank Fred Slone, who two years ago took a chance on a new author and started me on this great adventure of writing. Finally, I would like to thank Glenn Phillips of Forte, Inc., in Birmingham. Several of the sample programs and screens are from a program that I am writing for his company.

Ronald R. Martinsen: Thanks to Simon "Mr. Multimedia" Bernstein, Mike "The Wongman" Wong, Fred "The Fed" Nava (DDE Expert), Will Gregg, Evan C. Cacka, and Mike Willard for their technical advice. I'd also like to thank my family and friends (especially Dennis Dallimore) for their encouragement.

Jeff Webb: Thanks to everyone who has sent me suggestions and corrections over the last six months—most notably, Gettone Telephonico, I couldn't have done it without you, man.

Bob Reselman: Thanks to my friends, Elie and Brian who passed it on to me so that I could pass it on to others.

We'd Like to Hear from You!

As part of our continuing effort to produce books of the highest possible quality, Que would like to hear your comments. To stay competitive, we *really* want you, as a computer book reader and user, to let us know what you like or dislike most about this book or other Que products.

Please send your comments, ideas, and suggestions for improvement to:

The Expert User Team

Email: **euteam@que.mcp.com**

CompuServe: **72410,2077**

Fax: (317) 581-4663

Our mailing address is:

Expert User Team
Que Corporation
201 West 103rd Street
Indianapolis, IN 46290-1097

You can also visit our Team's home page on the World Wide Web at:

http://www.mcp.com/que/developer_expert

Thank you in advance. Your comments will help us to continue publishing the best books available in today's market.

Sincerely,

The Expert User Team

Contents at a Glance

I | **Visual Basic Fundamentals**

  1 Introduction to Visual Basic 9
  2 VB for COBOL Programmers 31
  3 Using Forms and Controls 43
  4 Understanding the Event Model 77
  5 Enhancing Your Program with Menus and Dialog Boxes 91
  6 Programming in Visual Basic 119
  7 Managing Your Project from Beginning to End 157
  8 Introduction to Classes 173

II | **Creating Database Applications**

  9 Introduction to Databases and the Jet Engine 197
  10 Applications at Warp Speed 221
  11 Designing and Creating a Database 247
  12 Doing More with Bound Controls 279
  13 Writing Programs with the Data-Access Objects 301
  14 Understanding Structured Query Language 335
  15 Multi-User Programming 369
  16 Accessing Other PC Databases 387
  17 Using the Remote Data Objects 403

III | **Using OLE**

  18 Controlling OLE Objects 417
  19 Programming OLE Containers 441
  20 Using Classes to Create Re-usable Objects 469
  21 Creating Remote Automation Servers 497
  22 Creating OCX Controls 511
  23 Debugging ActiveX Components 531
  24 Building and Distributing ActiveX Components 547

IV | **Integrating Visual Basic with Other Applications**

  25 Comparison of Visual Basic, VBA, and VBScript 557
  26 Integration with Excel 573
  27 Integration with Access and PowerPoint 609
  28 Intergrating Visual Basic with Mail, Schedule, and Exchange 645

29   Integration with Other OLE Applications   683

30   Creating Internet Applications with Visual Basic   713

31   Integrating Visual Basic with Internet Explorer and IIS   733

V | Optimization and Advanced Progra mming Techniques

32   Advanced Control Techniques   759

33   Advanced Form Techniques   787

34   Advanced Code Techniques   809

35   Accessing the Windows API   839

36   Designing Windows Applications   879

Index   899

Table Of Contents

Introduction   1

Fundamentals   2

Database Features in Action   3

How OLE Helps Your Programs   3

Working with Other Applications   3

Advanced Techniques   4

Special Help for COBOL Programmers   4

What's Special About the Special Edition   4

Parts of the Book   5

I | Visual Basic Fundamentals

1 Introduction to Visual Basic   9

Programming Basics   10

What Is a Program   10

Event-Driven Programming   11

Object-Oriented Programming   12

The Parts of a Program   13

A Few Definitions   14

New Features of Visual Basic 5   15

Types of Programs You Can Create in Visual Basic   16

Exploring the Visual Basic Interface   17

Using the Menu Bar   18

Accessing Functions with the Toolbar   19

Organizing Visual Basic's Controls   20

The Canvas of Your Programs   24

Controlling Your Forms and Controls   24

What's in the Project Window   24

Where Work Gets Done   25

Customizing your environment   25

Getting Help When You Need It   27

The Basic Help System   27

Context-Sensitive Help   28

From Here...   29

2 VB for COBOL Programmers   31

  Deciding to Make the Move to Visual Basic   32

  Exploring Visual Basic's Background   37
    The Code in Visual Basic   38
    The Graphical Nature of Visual Basic   39

  Having Fun While You Learn   40

  Learning Visual Basic   41

  From Here...   41

3 Using Form and Controls   43

  Exploring Properties, Methods, and Events   44
    Controlling Behavior Through Properties   44
    Taking Action with Methods   48
    Dealing with Actions   49
    How Properties and Methods Are Related   49
    Parts of a Form   50
    Setting Properties   51
    Displaying a Form   55
    Handling Events (Load and Activate)   56

  Using Controls   57
    What Are Controls   57
    Adding Controls to the Form   59
    Setting and Retrieving Property Values   59

  Finding Out What Controls Can Do   61
    Working with Text   62
    Making Choices   68
    Handling Lists   69
    Actions   74

  From Here...   75

4 Understanding the Event Model   77

  Living in an Event-Driven World   78

  Changing the Way You Think   79

  Handling Events in Your Programs   82
    Types of Events   83
    Writing Event Procedures   85
    Handling Multiple Controls with a Single Procedure   86

Understanding Event Sequences   87

Multiple Events for Each Action   88

Determining the Order of Events   88

From Here...   89

5 Enhancing Your Program with Menus and Dialog Boxes   91

Controlling a Program with a Menu Bar   92

Creating a Menu Bar   93

Code for the Menu Items   99

Optional Settings   100

Creating Pop-Up Menus   102

Creating the Menu to Be Displayed   102

Activating a Pop-Up Menu   103

Keeping the User Informed   103

Displaying a Message   104

Returning a Value from the *MsgBox* Function   107

Getting Information from the User   109

Setting Up the Input Dialog Box   110

Determining User Actions and Input   111

Using Built-In Dialog Boxes   111

The File Dialog Box   112

The Font Dialog Box   114

The Color Dialog Box   116

The Print Dialog Box   117

From Here...   118

6 Programming in Visual Basic   119

Working with Variables   120

Types of Variables   120

Variable Declarations   121

Using the Option *Explicit* Statement   124

What's Different About Constants   125

Writing Simple Statements   127

Using the Assignment Statement   127

Using Math Operators   127

Working with Strings   132

Making Decisions in Your Program   133
Using the *If* Statement   133
Working with the *False* Condition   135
Working with Multiple *If* Statements   137
Using *Select* Case   137

Working with Loops   140
For Loops   140
Do loops   142

Making Your Program Bug Free   144
How to Avoid Syntax Errors   145
What Happens When an Error Occurs   146
How the Debugging Environment Works   148
How to Determine the Value of a Variable   149
Running Commands   152
How Did I Get Here   154
Pausing the Program's Execution   154
Tracing Through Your Code   155

From Here . . .   156

7 Managing Your Project from Beginning to End   157

Working with Procedures and Functions   158
Why Use a Procedure   158
Creating Procedures and Functions   158
Determining the Scope of Procedures and Functions   162
Storing Procedures and Functions in a Module   163

Working with Multiple Forms   164
Adding New Forms to Your Program   164
Adding Code Modules to a Project   165
Accessing the Forms and Modules of a Project   166

Managing Components in Your Project   166
Managing Program References   166
Controlling Your Controls   167
Adding Forms, Modules, and Classes to the Project   168
Removing Pieces   168

Controlling How Your Program Starts   168
Setting the Startup Form   169
Using *Sub Main*   169

Creating Distributable Programs 169
Determining the Type of Program to Create 170
Compiling Your Program 170
From Here... 171

8 Introduction to Classes 173

Introduction to Classes 174
Understanding Object-Oriented Programming
Fundamentals 174
Implementing OOP with Classes in Visual Basic 175
Using Classes in Your Programs 175

Building a Class in Visual Basic 176
Creating a New Class Module 176
Adding Properties to the Class 178
Methods Let the Class Take Actions 181
Adding Events to Your Class 181
Accessing a Class from a Program 182

Classes in Your Programs 185
A Better Printer 185
Database Access 190

From Here . . . 193

II Creating Database Applications

9 Introduction to Databases and the Jet Engine 197

Understanding Databases 198
Flat-File and Relational Databases 198
Typical Databases You May Know 199
Definitions of Database Terms 199

Exploring How a Database Management System Works 201
The Advantages of a DBMS 202
The Parts of a DBMS 203

Understanding the Microsoft Jet Engine 203
Back in Time: A History of Jet 204
What Can I Put in a Database 205
Data-Access Objects 206
Introducing the Data Control 206

Explaining Database Integrity   207
   How Relations Work in a Database   207
   Keeping Relations from Falling Apart   211
   Accept No Duplicates   213
   Is the Data Any Good   214

Posing a Query   216
   Data-Manipulation Language (DML)   216
   Data-Definition Language (DDL)   218
   Avoid Repeating Yourself   219
   Queries on Non-Jet Databases   219

Making Copies of the Database   219

From Here...   220

10   Applications at Warp Speed   221

Understanding the Data Control   222
   What Is the Data Control   222
   Adding a Data Control to Your Form   223
   Two Properties are All You Need to Set   224

Getting Acquainted with Bound Control Basics   226
   What Do These Controls Do   226
   Adding Controls to Your Forms   227
   Data Display in Two Easy Properties   228

Creating a Simple Application   229
   Setting Up the Form   229
   Navigating the Database   230
   Essential Functions the Data Control Forgot   231

Creating Forms Automatically   232
   Setting Up the Data Form Wizard   232
   Getting to the Source of Your Data   233
   A Few Good fields   235
   What Does This Button Do   235

Designing Reports   237
   Starting Crystal Reports   238
   Selecting the Data Fields   240
   Previewing the Report   241
   Saving the Report   242

Running a Report   242
    Crystal Reports Control   243
    Setting Up the Control   243
    Taking Action   245
    Setting Properties at Runtime   245
From Here...   246

11   Designing and Creating a Database   247

Designing a Database   248
    Design Objectives   248
    Key Activities in Designing Your Database   248
    Organizing the Data   249
    Using Indexes   255
    Using Queries   257

Implementing Your Design   258
    Creating the Database   258
    Creating a Table   260
    Creating Indexes   265
    Creating Relations   267
    Creating Queries   268

Creating a Database with Other Tools   269
    Using the Visual Data Manager   269
    Using Microsoft Access   273
    Third-Party Database Designers   273

Modifying the Database Structure   273
    Adding and Deleting Tables   274
    Adding, Deleting, and Editing Indexes   274
    Adding, Deleting, and Editing Fields   275
    Deleting a Relation   275
    Using SQL to Modify the Database   275

Why Use a Program Instead of Visual Data
Manager   276

From Here...   277

12 Doing More with Bound Controls 279

Exploring the Data Control In-Depth 280
 What Are Its Advantages and Limitations? 280
 Using Other Databases 281
 Working Directly with Tables and Snapshots 283
 In the End (BOF And EOF Properties) 284
 Other Optional Properties 285

Programming the Data Control 286
 Changing Properties On-The-Fly 286
 Recordsets and the Data Control (Set Command) 287
 Programming the Data Control's Events 289
 Data Control Methods 290

Other Bound Controls 291
 Lists and Combo Boxes 292
 Data Bound Lists and Combos 293
 Data Bound Grids 295
 Other Visual Basic Controls 296
 Third-Party Controls 296

Further Enhancements 296
 Find and Seek Operations 296
 What About Options (Option Buttons) 297

From Here ... 299

13 Writing Programs with the Data-Access Objects 301

Opening an Existing Database 303
 Using Tables 304
 Using Dynasets 306
 Using Snapshots 309
 Using a Forward-Only Recordset 310

Placing Information On-Screen 310

Positioning the Record Pointer 312
 Using the *Move* Methods 312
 Using the *Find* Methods 314
 Using the *Seek* Method 317
 Using the *Bookmark* Property 320
 Using the *PercentPosition* and *AbsolutePosition* Properties 321

Using Filters, Indexes, and Sorts   322
   Setting the *Filter* Property   322
   Setting the *Sort* Property   323
   Setting the Current Index in a Table   324
   Creating an Index for a New Situation   324

Considering Programs that Modify Multiple Records   325
   Using Loops   326
   Using SQL Statements   327

Understanding Other Programming Commands   329
   Adding Records   330
   Editing Records   330
   Updating Records   331
   Deleting Records   331
   Incorporating Add, Edit, and Delete Functions in the Sample Case   332

Introducing Transaction Processing   333

From Here...   334

14   Understanding Structured Query Language   335

Defining SQL   336

Understanding the Parts of the SQL Statement   336
   Using *SELECT* Statements   337
   Using the *DELETE* Statement   357
   Using the *INSERT* Statement   358
   Using the *UPDATE* Statement   359

Using Data-Definition-Language Statements   359
   Defining Tables with DDL Statements   359
   Defining Indexes with DDL Statements   360

Using SQL   361
   Executing an Action Query   361
   Creating a *QueryDef*   362
   Creating Dynasets and Snapshots   362
   Using SQL Statements with the Data Control   363

Creating SQL Statements   363
   Using the Visual Data Manager   364
   Using Microsoft Access   366

Optimizing SQL Performance   366
    Using Indexes   366
    Compiling Queries   366
    Keeping Queries Simple   367

Passing SQL Statements to Other Database Engines   367

From Here...   368

15   Multi-User Programming   369

Controlling Data Access   370
    Using a Database Exclusively   370
    Denying Table Access to Others   371
    Using Read-Only Tables   372

Understanding Record-Locking Schemes   373
    Page-Locking Versus Record-Locking   373
    Pessimistic Locking   374
    Optimistic Locking   374
    Which Locking Method to Use and When   374
    Releasing Locks   375
    Using the Data Control   375

Exploring Jet Security Features   376
    Database Permissions   377
    Table Permissions   377
    Setting Up the Security System   377
    Encryption   378
    Application Passwords   379
    Using Network Security   379

Maintaining Data Currency   380
    Using Only Tables   380
    Requerying a Dynaset   380

Probing Performance Considerations   380
    Keep Dynasets Small   381
    Copy a Database or Table to a Local Drive   381
    Use Snapshots Where Possible   381
    Use Transactions for Processing Updates   381

Using Database Replication to Handle Multiple Users   381
    Making a Replicable Database   382
    Making Copies of the Database   382

Putting the Database Back Together   383
Handling Errors and Conflicts   383

From Here...   386

16 Accessing Other PC Databases   387

Accessing Data Directly   388
Using the Data-Access Objects with Other Databases   389
Using the Data Control with Other Databases   393

Importing Data from External Databases   394
Knowing When to Import Data   394
Using a Program to Import the Data   395
Using Microsoft Access   396

Attaching External Tables   396
Attaching a Table with the Data-Access Objects   397
Using the Visual Data Manager to Attach a Table   398
Using Access to Attach a Table   400
Using an Attached Table   401

From Here...   401

17 Using the Remote Data Objects   403

Introducing ODBC   404
Understanding ODBC Drivers   404
Setting Up an ODBC Data Source   404

Using the Remote Data Objects   409
Comparison of RDO to DAO   409
Accessing a Database with RDO   411

Using the Remote Data Control   412
Comparing the RDC and the Data Control   412
Setting Up the RDC   413

From Here...   414

III | Using OLE

18 Controlling OLE Objects   417

Creating OLE Objects at Runtime   418
Creating an Embedded Object   419
Using Class Types   419
Creating a Linked Object   420

Controlling the Display of OLE Objects   421
How the *SizeMode* Property and *Resize Event* Interact   421
Displaying Objects in a Sizable Window (Form)   422
Scrolling the Control for Large Objects   423
Scaling the Object to Fit the Control   427
Zooming an Object for the Best Fit   427

Moving and Sizing Embedded Objects During
In-Place Editing   429

Capturing the Object's Picture   431

Updating Linked Data   432

Controlling Object Activation   433
Activating an Object for Editing   434
Opening an Object Within Its Application   435
Deactivating an Object   435

Storing and Retrieving OLE Objects   436
Saving OLE Objects to Files   436
Reading OLE Objects from Files   437

Getting the OLE Automation Object from Linked or Embedded
Objects   437

From Here...   439

19   Programming OLE Containers   441

Understanding OLE and ActiveX Terminology   442

Designing Applications for Windows 95   443

Enabling OLE Drag-Drop   443
Handling Drop Events   444
Handling Drag Events   445
Dragging and Dropping Files   448

Creating an OLE Storage System   451
Storing Multiple Objects in a Single File   452
Retrieving Multiple Objects from a Single File   458

Registering Your Application   460
Associating a File Type with Your Application   461
Registering Program Manager Icons   462

Check Registration Entries at Start-Up   464

Handling OLE Errors and Timeouts   466
  Handling Trappable Errors from OLE Servers   467
  Polling for Errors   467
From Here...   468

20   Using Classes to Create Re-usable Objects   469

Choosing a Project Type   470

Creating Your First Class   471

Using a Class from Another Project   473

Using the Class Builder   474

Naming Classes, Objects, and Projects   476

Creating Methods and Properties   477
  Assigning the Default Method or Property   477
  Making Friends   478
  Creating Read/Write Properties   479
  Creating a Read-Only or Write-Only Property   480
  Creating Object Properties   481

Creating Public Constants as Enumerations   483

Creating Classes that Contain Collections   484
  Standard Collection Properties and Methods   485
  Creating a New Collection for Grouped Actions   485
  Using Collections to Organize Objects   487

Adding ActiveX Objects to Existing Projects   488
  Changing the Project Type   488
  Making Form Event Procedures Public   489
  Calling Form Events from a Class Module   489
  Running and Using the New ActiveX Object   490
  Refining the ActiveX Object   491

Documenting Objects, Properties, and Methods   495

From Here...   496

21   Creating Remote Automation Servers   497

Installing DCOM 95   498

Compiling Remote Applications   498

Registering a Remote Application   499

Using Remote Applications   501

Debugging Problems with Remote Applications   502

Improving Remote Automation Performance   503
   Optimizing Multi-Use Object Applications   504
   Understanding Multiple Threads   506
   Optimizing Single-Use Object Applications   507

From Here . . .   509

22   Creating OCX Controls   511

Creating Your First Control   512
   Starting a New .OCX Project   512
   Drawing a Control's Interface   514
   Writing Code for Resizing the Control   515
   Writing Code to Initialize the Control   516
   Writing Code to Respond to Changes   517
   Adding Public Properties, Methods, and Events   517
   Adding Design-Time Properties   519
   Running the Control Under Development   521
   Compiling the Finished Control   522

Using the Custom Control from VB and VBA   522

Using the ActiveX Control Interface Wizard   524

Understanding Property Pages   528

From Here. . .   530

23   Debugging ActiveX Components   531

Solving Problems Unique to Objects   532
   Watching Object Instances During Debugging   532
   Single-Use versus Multiuse Objects   533
   Single-Use Applications and Lost References   534
   Multiuse Objects and Initialization   536
   Multiuse Objects and Global Data   537
   Multiuse Objects and Subordinate Objects   538
   Problems with the Registration Database   539

Strategies for Debugging Objects   540
   Debugging In-Process (.EXE)   540
   Debugging In-Process (DLL)   542
   Debugging Cross-Process (.EXE)   542
   Testing on Target Platforms   544

Maintaining Compatibility with Released Versions   545

From Here...   546

24   Building and Distributing ActiveX Components   547

Adding Version Information to Objects   548

Creating New Versions   548

Creating New Editions   550

Installing Objects   550

Creating a Registration File   551

Registering a Registration File   553

De-Registering Objects   553

From Here. . .   554

IV   Integrating Visual Basic with Other Applications

25   Comparison of Visual Basic, VBA, and VBScript   557

Understanding the Differences between VB and VBA   558

Using Visual Basic for Applications   559

Type Libraries and the Object Browser   559

Introducing the Newest Visual Basic: VBScript   561

An Overview of VBScript   562

Using VBScript on a Web Page   565

A Quick Look at VBScript Programming in Outlook   568

Knowing When to Use Which Variety of Visual Basic   571

From Here...   572

26   Integration with Excel   573

Using OLE Automation with Excel   574

Using Excel's Macro Recorder to Write OLE Automation
Code   574

Tips for OLE Automation with Excel   576

Using the OLE Container Control with Excel   577

Using Your VB Application as a DLL for Excel   592

The Useful Class Object   592

From Here...   608

27 Integration with Access and PowerPoint 609

Integrating with Access 610
Jet Database Engine 610
Using Jet and DAO 610
Communicating with Access through OLE Automation 632

Integrating with PowerPoint 635
Understanding the *clsPowerPoint* Object 636
Using the *clsPowerPoint* Object 642

From Here... 644

28 Integrating Visual Basic with Mail, Schedule, and Exchange 645

Automating Microsoft Word 646
Tips for OLE Automation with Word 648

Using the OLE Container Control with Word 648
Optimizing Performance for Complex OLE Automation
Tasks 656

Automating Microsoft Outlook 664
Creating Items in Outlook Using a VB Form 667

Integrating with OLE Messaging (MAPI) 673
Creating a Generic SendMail Method 673
Handling Attachments 675
Using the MAPI Class Object to Send Mail 678

From Here... 681

29 Integration with Other OLE Applications 683

Connecting to OLE Automation Servers 684

Using Microsoft's OLE Miniservers 689

Using Other Microsoft Applications in Your Applications 693

Using Other Microsoft Applications that Don't Support OLE or DDE 696

From Here... 712

30 Creating Internet Applications with Visual Basic 713

Creating Your First Internet Application 714

Preparing Your First Application for the Internet 717

Using Your First Application over the Internet 722

Is It Safe   723

Moving Between User Documents   725

Passing Data Between User Documents   726

Passing Data to the Server   729

Creating a Remote Logging Service   729

Calling the Remote Logging Service   730

Installing the Remote Automation Server   731

From Here...   732

31   Integrating Visual Basic with Internet Explorer and IIS   733

Creating a Browser Application   734

Controlling Internet Explorer   736

Implementing the Browser as an Add-in   738

Using the Browser Add-In   739

Using the Internet Controls   741

Creating an FTP Browser   742

Creating a Chat Application   746

Accessing Databases over the Internet   749

Creating Applications that Run on IIS   751

Objects Provided with ASP   753

Using VB-Created Objects from ASP   754

From Here...   756

V   Optimization and Advanced Programming Techniques

32   Advanced Control Techniques   759

Using Control Arrays   760

Menu and Control Array Techniques   760

Option Button Techniques   764

Applying Windows Common Controls Techniques   765

Using a Progress Bar in Your Status Bar   765

The *TreeView* and *ListView* Controls   766

Writing Frankentrols   773

Brief Window Styles Background Information   774

Adding New Styles to a Control   774

Callbacks and Function Pointers Explained   777
Windows Hooks in Pure VB   779

From Here...   786

33 Advanced Form Techniques   787

Saving Window Positions   788

Simplifying MDI   791
The MDI Parent   792
The MDI Child   795

Creating Multimedia Forms   797
The Multimedia Form   798
Playing AVIs in a Picture Box   804
Playing Wave Files   806

From Here...   808

34 Advanced Code Techniques   809

Starting Simple   810
Taking Advantage of Variants   810
ParamArray: the King of Flexibility   815

Applying Computer Science Techniques in Visual Basic   816
Getting Started with Searching and Sorting   816
Going a Step Further with Linked Lists   825
Twiddling Bits in Visual Basic   833

From Here...   838

35 Accessing the Windows API   839

Calling Basic API and DLL Functions   840
Calling *GetVersionEx()*   840
Declaring API Functions   842
Calling Functions in Other DLLs   842

Getting Down to the Good Stuff   845
Warming Up with the Memory Class   846
Using the API to Overcome Visual Basic's Limitations   849
Going Graphical with the GDI API   862
Registry Revisited   867
Callbacks Revisited   873

From Here...   877

36   Designing Windows Applications   879

Implementing a "User Centered" Software Development
Process   880
    The Pre-Production Phase   881
    The Production Phase   882
    The Post-Production Phase   884

Creating Consistent and Effective Graphical Interfaces   885
    Making a Well-Designed Form   886
    Offering Choices   890
    Improving User Perceptions of Your Programs   892

Avoiding Programming Pitfalls   893
    Programming Readable Code   894
    Using Visual Basic Constants   894
    Commented Code   894
    Use Descriptive Naming   896

From Here...   897

Index   899

Introduction

Congratulations! You have decided to embark on learning Visual Basic.

This is an exciting time; there never has been a better time for Visual Basic programmers. While Visual Basic always made it easy to develop Windows programs, through the years it has progressed into a true professional development language and environment. You still can quickly create Windows programs with Visual Basic, but now you also can write enterprise-level client/server programs and robust database applications. While this is enough to get you hyped up about programming in Visual Basic, there's even more available in Visual Basic, version 5.

Unless you have been a hermit in a cave for the last several years, you know that the Internet promises to revolutionize computing. You also may have seen enough of Internet programming to think that it is reserved for only a select group of programmers. In version 5, Visual Basic gives you a number of tools that let you jump on the Internet bandwagon. There are tools that let you easily connect your programs to the Internet and include browser capabilities in your programs. In addition, you now can create ActiveX servers, ActiveX documents, and ActiveX controls from Visual Basic. Because ActiveX is the cornerstone of Microsoft's Internet strategy, this puts you right in the middle of the action. And the really good news is that all these ActiveX pieces can be used in non-Internet programs as well, extending the usefulness of any ActiveX components you create.

Excited yet? Wait, there's more! Microsoft also has integrated Visual Basic for Applications (VBA) into all the components of Office 97, Project, and other programs. Because VBA is the core language component of Visual Basic, this means that all your knowledge of Visual Basic can be applied to writing applications and macros for other products. And because Microsoft has licensed VBA 5.0 to over 40 other companies, you soon will be able to write applications and macros for those programs as well. All this benefit comes from your Visual Basic knowledge.

Okay, so now you are excited about learning Visual Basic. Your next question is, "What will this book do for me?" ■

Fundamentals

While this book focuses heavily on advanced Visual Basic programming, you can't just jump into these topics and expect to understand them. You need a good foundation from which to work.

In Part I of the book "Visual Basic Fundamentals," we cover the basics to get you started on your programming adventure. We start out by introducing you to the development environment of Visual Basic and discussing general programming concepts, such as the importance of good design. This is followed by a tour of forms and controls, which are the building blocks of every program you will create in Visual Basic. You will see how forms and controls are manipulated by their properties and perform tasks with their methods. We also examine the event model, which is the cornerstone of programming in a Windows environment.

After you grasp the basics of forms and controls, we show you how to make your programs perform all types of functions by using the BASIC language, which is built into Visual Basic. This programming language is rich in features and functions that let you write programs to handle any task.

We also look at how you can enhance your programs by using menus and dialog boxes. These program components give your users an interface that is familiar because of their using other Windows programs. Properly using menus and dialog boxes makes your programs more intuitive to the user.

Finally, we introduce you to classes and objects. These reusable pieces of code contain both data and procedures. By encapsulating the information and the means to process it in a class, you make it easier to reuse code in multiple places within your project and in multiple projects. This basic understanding of classes will be necessary when you start working with OLE Automation in Part III of the book, "Using OLE."

Database Features in Action

Database programs make up a large percentage of all programs built today. These programs range in complexity from a simple program for managing a mailing list all the way up to a program to handle the power bills for all major utility's customers.

In Part II, "Creating Database Applications," we take you through the process of building database applications to meet a variety of needs. We start by showing you how to quickly create applications using the data control, bound controls, and the Crystal Reports report writer. We then probe the depths of programming with the data-access objects, showing you how much programming power is available for creating your applications. We also show how to use the powerful commands of Structured Query Language to retrieve and modify information in a database.

While single-user, PC-based database applications are important, they are not the only database applications you will want to build. Therefore, we discuss some of the considerations required when implementing multi-user applications. Not to be left out, we show how to connect your programs to databases through ODBC. This will give you access to a wide range of PC, mini-computer, and mainframe databases.

How OLE Helps Your Programs

OLE—or ActiveX, as Microsoft is now calling it—provides a powerful means of allowing programs to work together. Using OLE techniques, you can embed Word or Excel documents in your applications, or, more importantly for many businesses, you can create your own multi-tier client/server programs. By building OLE Automation servers, you can have a server that handles the business rules while other programs handle the interface with the user.

Visual Basic makes it easy for OLE developers to write applications. You can add OLE features to Visual Basic applications with little or no code. In C, you have to deal with hundreds of functions in the OLE API and write thousands of lines of code to implement similar features. You can't do everything in Visual Basic that you can in C, but you sure can get further faster.

Therefore, you'll soon see thousands more OLE applications. Also, OLE-enabled applications will become the de facto industry standard, just as Windows did.

Part III, "Using OLE," tells you how to build applications by using OLE objects from other applications. We also explain how to create your own "parts" for use in your own applications, other Office applications, or within Visual Basic itself.

Working with Other Applications

As we mentioned, the VBA language that is the heart of Visual Basic also is included in Office 97 and a number of other products from many vendors. In addition, VBScript provides a subset of the VBA language to make developing Internet applications easier.

In Part IV of the book, "Integrating Visual Basic with Other Applications," we show you how to make Visual Basic work with Access, PowerPoint, Excel, Word, and Outlook. You also will see how to create applications that take advantage of the MAPI messaging capabilities. And because the Internet is such a big topic, we cover how to create some Internet applications with Visual Basic and integrate Visual Basic with both the Internet Explorer (IE) and Internet Information Server (IIS).

Advanced Techniques

Finally, in Part V, "Optimization and Advanced Programming Techniques," we expand on the fundamentals covered in Part I. We look at some of the more advanced techniques for working with forms, controls, and the Visual Basic programming language. We also look at how you can access Windows API functions to add even more capabilities to your programs.

Special Help for COBOL Programmers

Because a number of new Visual Basic programmers are coming from the mainframe world of COBOL programming, we added some information to help them make the transition. Chapter 2, "VB For COBOL Programmers," provides background information about the differences between programming in a COBOL environment and programming for a graphical user interface (GUI), event-driven environment. Then Chapter 4, "Understanding the Event Model," provides an in-depth look at how events work and how you write programs to respond to them.

What's Special About the Special Edition

This book covers a lot of material related to Visual Basic. We've tried to explain each topic, from the most basic to the most complex, in a manner that's easy to understand. We provide more than text about the topics; we also give you graphics to enhance your understanding, real-world examples that let you see how the concepts can be applied, and sample projects that show how we implemented the programming concepts.

In addition, we provide a number of notes with additional information. We include tips that show some of the cool shortcuts we have found and cautions that hopefully will help you avoid some common programming pitfalls. You also will find some other great things:

On the Web

While the hard-copy book is the main part of the package, we have also provided additional resource materials on the Internet. The book's Web site can be found at **http://www. quecorp.com/sevb5**. As you would expect, you will find complete code listings for all the projects presented in the book. In addition, here's a list of some of other great things you'll find there:

■ Articles related to some of the chapters.   These are short discussions of programming techniques that did not quite fit into the chapters of the book.

■ Full text of chapters from other Que books.   In several chapters, we point you to another book for related information, such as how to create a relation in a database using Access. For your convenience, we have included links to these books' home pages.

■ Sample controls.   There are a multitude of third-party ActiveX controls out there for you to use in your Visual Basic programs. With the permission of the vendors, we included sample controls and demo programs for some of the most popular third-party products.

Parts of the Book

To make it easier for you to work with the material in the book, we have divided the book into five major parts:

■ Part I, "Visual Basic Fundamentals," includes Chapters 1–8.

■ Part II, "Creating Database Applications," includes Chapters 9–17.

■ Part III, "Using OLE," includes Chapters 18–24.

■ Part IV, "Integrating Visual Basic with Other Applications," includes Chapters 25–31.

■ Part V, "Optimization and Advanced Programming Techniques," includes Chapters 32–36.

N O T E Because of the space limitations of this book's pages, a few code lines in this book's listings cannot be printed exactly as you must enter them. In cases where breaking such a line is necessary to fit within the book's margins, you'll find the following graphic:

➡

This character indicates that you must enter the line that you are reading as part of the line that precedes it. ■

Visual Basic Fundamentals

1 Introduction to Visual Basic   9

2 VB for Cobol Programmers   31

3 Using Forms and Controls   43

4 Understanding the Event Model   77

5 Enhancing your Program with Menus and Dialog Boxes   91

6 Programming in Visual Basic   119

7 Managing your Project from Beginning to End   157

8 Introduction to Classes   173

Introduction to Visual Basic

If you have visited a local computer store lately, you've seen that there are thousands of programs available for your computer. In fact, I recently read that there are over 4,600 programs that run under Windows 95, and this does not include programs written by companies for their own use. Looking through the software titles, you find game programs, productivity programs (such as word processors and spreadsheets), communications programs, databases, and many others. And if you have surfed the Internet, you've seen even more types of programs there.

In addition to all these commercial or publicly available programs, many companies need custom programs to handle their business. These programs can range from custom report writers that prepare expense statements (such as the one shown in Figure 1.1) to database programs for a single department, to complex client/server programs that handle billing and inventory using the information stored on a mainframe.

What kinds of programs can you write with Visual Basic

Visual Basic makes it easy for you to create standard Windows programs, as well as ActiveX documents, ActiveX controls, and Visual Basic Add-Ins.

What is object-oriented programming

You will learn the definition of object-oriented programming and see how Visual Basic uses object oriented techniques.

The basic parts of the Visual Basic interface

You will learn about the different pieces of the interface and how they help you develop your programs.

Where to find help

When you develop programs, you always need to have help readily available. You will see how the help system is organized and where else to turn for help with your programs.

FIG. 1.1
A simple program for preparing expense statements.

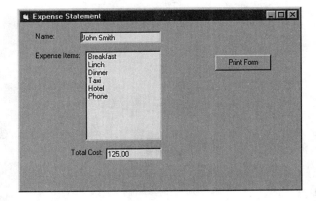

Not content just to use available programs, you have decided to embark on the adventure of creating your own programs. Well, you have come to the right place and chosen the right programming language. Visual Basic is capable of producing almost any program that your imagination can create. It can handle creating simple programs, database programming, games programs, client/server programs, and even Internet programs. And while there may be other programming languages that are better suited to a particular situation, Visual Basic is one of the most versatile *and* easy-to-use programming languages available. ■

Programming Basics

Before we dive into the details of Visual Basic, we will take a brief look at the history of programming, and some of the basic concepts that apply to programming in any language. This understanding of program basics will make it easier for you to write better and more efficient programs.

What Is a Program

To begin, you need to know the answer to the question, "Just what is a program?" A *computer program* is simply a set of instructions that tell the computer how to perform a specific task. You are probably familiar with many types of instructions, such as following a recipe to cook a particular food dish or following specific directions to get to an unfamiliar destination. Without these specific instructions, you could not perform the desired task.

Well, computers are the same way, except that they need instructions for every task they perform. They even need instructions for the simplest tasks, such as how to get a keystroke, how to place a letter on the screen, or how to store information to a disk. Fortunately, many of these instructions are contained on the processor chip or are built into the operating system, so you don't have to worry about them. Instead, you can concentrate on providing instructions for the tasks, such as calculating employee payroll, creating the mailing list for your neighborhood, or formatting text to display the information in the latest annual report.

While you and I read instructions in English, the computer must have its instructions in *binary code,* a series of on or off switches in the computer's memory and processors. There are languages, such as Assembler, that allow you to write this type of code directly. However, it is very difficult to write a program this way, so Visual Basic and other programming languages were written to allow programmers to write instructions in a way that is a little closer to their own language. However, even these instructions are limited and follow a highly defined structure. An example of these instructions is shown in Figure 1.2.

FIG. 1.2

A set of typical program instructions in Visual Basic.

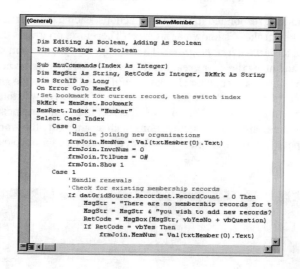

Event-Driven Programming

Visual Basic lets you create programs that respond to user actions and system events. This type of programming is known as *event-driven programming.* To get some insight into how event-driven programming works, take a look at how programs ran in the past and how things are different in the Windows environment.

Before the advent of Windows (back in the old days of DOS and the "prehistoric times"— before PCs), programs were written to be run in a *sequential fashion.* That is, once the program started, it proceeded, instruction by instruction, until it reached the end of the program or a fatal error occurred. The general steps for running a program were the following:

1. Create an input file.
2. Start the program.
3. Wait until the program finishes—often overnight, for large programs.
4. Examine the output file or printed report.

Even programs that most people take for granted, such as word processors, worked this way. For the early word processors, you would create your file with formatting codes embedded in the actual document (much like RTF or HTML codes today) and then run the file through a formatter to be printed. These programs got the job done, but they weren't nearly as easy to use as today's programs. They were, however, easier to write. This is because each program had a clearly defined task and little or no user interaction.

Then came Windows. Windows programs (and many later-generation DOS programs) provided the user with many more capabilities and with the ability to interact with the program to a much greater extent. The programs would now respond to mouse movements and clicks and would respond differently depending on where the mouse was located.

In these programs that responded to many user actions, each user interaction—such as a mouse click or a keystroke—is known as an *event*. Therefore, programs that respond to these events are known as *event-driven programs*. These programs provide almost immediate feedback to the user and allow the user great control over the activity of the program. For example, in the old word processors, a spelling checker would scan the entire file and print out a report of the possible errors, along with the line number where the error was found. By comparison, the spelling checker in Microsoft Word or WordPerfect highlights the possible error, provides suggested corrections, and lets you take actions such as changing the word, ignoring the error, or quitting the spelling checker. Figure 1.3 shows the interface for a typical event-driven program.

FIG. 1.3
Typical interface for an event-driven program.

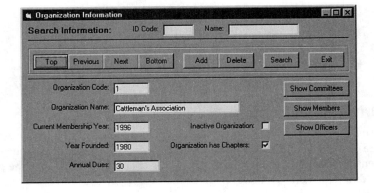

While event-driven programs were great for users, they were very difficult for developers to write. That is, they were difficult to write until the introduction of programs like Visual Basic made it much easier for people to create Windows applications.

Object-Oriented Programming

The key technology that made it easier to create Windows programs was *object-oriented programming,* or OOP. This technology made it possible to create reusable components that became the building blocks of programs.

What Is Object Oriented Programming OOP provides support for three basic principles: *encapsulation, inheritance,* and *polymorphism.* Take a brief look at these terms.

Encapsulation means that the information about an object (its *properties*) and the processes that are performed by the object (its *methods*) are all contained within the definition of the object. A real-world example of an object is a car. You describe a car by its properties, such as red convertible or black, four-door sedan. Each characteristic—color, number of doors, convertible or hardtop—is a property of the car. As for the methods, these are the things that a car does in response to an event. For example, you initiate an event when you turn the key to start the car. The car's "start method" takes over at that point, providing instructions such as "engage the starter gear, turn the starter, start fuel flow, initiate power to spark plugs, and disengage the starter." You don't have to tell the car how to start.

Inheritance means that one object can be based upon the description of another object. Continuing with the car example, I can define a car as something that has four wheels, an engine, and seats for passengers. I can then define a convertible as a car that has a retractable top. The convertible inherits the properties of the car and adds a new property, the retractable top. I don't have to redefine the car's properties for the convertible. Therefore, the convertible is said to inherit the properties of the car. In addition to properties, objects can also inherit methods and events from other objects.

Polymorphism means that many objects can have the same method, and appropriate action is taken for the object calling the method. For example, in your programs, you display text to the screen and output text to the printer. Each of these objects (the screen and the printer) can have a print or display method that tells the object to place text in a certain location. The method knows what to do, based on the object calling the method.

What OOP Does for You   The key element of OOP with which you will be working is reusable components, known as *controls*. The controls that you will use in building your programs are objects that have properties and methods and respond to events. You control the appearance and behavior of a control through its properties. For example, you specify how the text in a text box will look by setting its Font and Color properties. The controls you use have methods built into them that shield you from many of the tedious tasks of programming. Again look at the text box as an example: It knows how to retrieve a keystroke and display it in the edit region of the box in the proper format. You don't have to supply the details.

Each control also recognizes specific events. Most controls know if the mouse has been moved over them or a mouse button has been clicked. They even know which button was clicked. Components that handle text know when a key was pressed and which one it was. And for most events, you can write code that will take specific action when the event occurs.

The Parts of a Program

As you begin to create a program, there are two basic parts of the program that you need to consider: the *user interface,* the *processing of information.*

The user interface is the part of the program that your users see and interact with. This user interface is comprised of the forms you design using Visual Basic's forms and controls. A few key objectives for a good user interface are the following:

■ Present information in a neat manner.

■ Make instructions clear.

■ Make the appropriate parts of the interface (such as menus) consistent with corresponding parts of other programs.

■ Make key tasks easily accessible by providing menu shortcuts and Toolbars.

The processing of information is handled by the code that you write to respond to events in the program. One of your objectives here is to make the code as efficient as possible, to provide good response time to your users. A second objective is to make the code as easy to maintain as you can so that future modifications or updates to the code can be made with relative ease. There are two key components to making code easy to maintain: make it easy to read and use code modules to keep individual tasks small and simple. Making your code easy to read is done by formatting the lines of code and providing comments within the code to describe the functions.

A Few Definitions

Now for a few technical terms. You will hear these terms often in discussions of Visual Basic, so a basic understanding of the terms should be helpful to you.

Controls   Re-usable objects that provide the pieces of the visual interface of a program. Examples of controls are a text box, a label, or a command button.

Event   An action initiated by the user or by the operating system. Examples of events are a keystroke, a mouse click, the expiration of a specified amount of time, or the receipt of data from a port.

Methods   Program code that is embedded in the definition of an object, which defines how the object will work with information and respond to certain events. For example, database objects have methods that open recordsets and move from one record to another.

Object   A basic element of a program, which contains properties to define its characteristics, and methods to define its tasks and recognizes events to which it can respond. Controls and forms are examples of the objects used in Visual Basic.

Procedures   Segments of code that you write to accomplish a task. Procedures are usually written to respond to a specific event.

Properties   The characteristics of an object such as size, position, color, or text font. Properties determine the appearance and sometimes the behavior of an object. Properties are also used to provide data to an object and retrieve information from the object.

If you have written programs in a previous version of Visual Basic, all the new features and the new look may be a shock to you. But, you will quickly get over the surprise and be excited by all the things that you can do with Visual Basic. If you have never programmed in Visual Basic before, you will be pleased with how easy it is to get started programming. You will also be happy to know that this same easy-to-use development environment can help you develop very powerful programs as well.

New Features of Visual Basic 5

As with any new version of a product, Visual Basic 5 incorporates a number of new features that make it more powerful and easier to use than previous versions. One of the most requested features for Visual Basic was a native code compiler. Well, Microsoft has granted our wish. VB5 has a code compiler that will allow your programs to run much faster than before. In addition, a faster forms engine will greatly enhance the speed of loading forms. This is another feature that will make your programs run faster.

In addition to these two performance features, there are a number of other major features that were added to version 5 of Visual Basic. We will cover these features in functional groups in the next few sections.

Internet Features   Whether you are a seasoned Internet developer, or a neophyte, there are several features in Visual Basic that will help you with writing programs for the Internet. The first of these is the ability to create ActiveX controls. Creating ActiveX controls was formerly the domain of C++ programmers. Now you can quickly write controls from within Visual Basic. You can use these controls in your Visual Basic programs, or you can deploy them as part of an ActiveX document. These controls can work with any browser that supports ActiveX.

The other major feature is that you can create ActiveX documents. These are applications that run inside of Internet Explorer. You can also use ActiveX documents (whether created by Visual Basic or other products) within Visual Basic. This allows you to run programs such as an icon editor or HTML editor from within Visual Basic as if it were part of the development environment.

Finally, there are new controls that make it easier for you to create Internet enabled applications. There is a WebBrowser control that lets you incorporate browser features into your application and a WinSock control that makes it easier to connect your application to the Internet.

Development Environment Features   The most obvious new features are those that you see when you first start Visual Basic. This is the development environment. As old-timers will note, the development environment is completely different from the one in previous versions of Visual Basic. The environment is, however, consistent with the development environments of Microsoft's other programming languages. We will look closely at the development environment in the section entitled "Exploring the Visual Basic Interface," but let's take a brief look at the key features of the new environment.

First, the forms and code windows are handled in a full Multi-Document Interface (MDI) window. This means that each form and each control window are contained in separate child windows within the Visual Basic parent window. Each of these child windows is accessible from the main Window menu. As with other MDI applications, such as Word or Excel, you can also choose to have the child document fill the whole window or have multiple windows visible at the same time.

Next, you can edit multiple projects in the same Visual Basic session. This means that you do not have to close one project to open and make minor changes to another. This is very convenient for the professional developer, who may be working on several projects at the same time.

Another great feature is that all the toolbars and development windows are dockable and configurable. Being dockable means that you can have any toolbar or window floating on the screen, or you can drag it to the top, bottom, or sides of the Visual Basic window and park it there. Also, you can configure many of the toolbars and windows to your liking. This means that the toolbars will contain only the features you want, to make the interface match the way you work. These features allow a level of customization that has never been available in Visual Basic before.

Also, there is a great new feature in the code editor. Microsoft calls it "Auto Statement Builder"; I call it fantastic. What this statement builder does is present you with a list of the properties and methods that are available for an object. This makes it much easier to write code, since you don't have to constantly look up what the property names and methods are. Also, for a number of objects and functions, you can get lists of the VB constants that are used to define properties, such as color, fonts, or message box icons. This will speed up your development as you don't have to look in the help file to find out what constant to use to display an exclamation icon.

Control Features   What new version would be complete without a couple of new controls? We have already mentioned a couple of the Internet controls, but there are a few other noteworthy controls.

There is a new chart control that allows you to create many types of business charts in your programs. This control can create bar, pie, line, area, and scatter charts just to name a few. There is also a new MSFlexGrid control, which works like a regular grid, but allows formatting of individual cells. The MSFlexGrid also provides for other advanced features such as sorting and cell-grouping.

In addition to the new controls, several of the old controls have been enhanced to provide greater functionality. One significant new feature is in the Picture and Icon controls. These controls now have the ability to work with GIF and JPEG files. These formats are the ones most commonly used on the Internet.

Types of Programs You Can Create in Visual Basic

Visual Basic's version 5 lets you create all types of programs for the Windows operating systems. (I listed a few of these types of programs in the Introduction.) These programs can be run on either the Windows NT or Windows 95 systems. Programs created with Visual Basic 5 cannot be run on Windows 3.1 systems.

While you will most likely create stand-alone programs that are used directly by end users, Visual Basic 5 also gives you the ability to create libraries of functions that can be compiled into DLL (dynamic link library) files. These functions can be used by other programs to handle specialized tasks. In addition, Visual Basic 5 allows you to create ActiveX components, which can be used by your own programs, other programs, or even over the Internet.

Exploring the Visual Basic Interface

While I know you are anxious to just jump in and start programming, you might want to take a few minutes to acquaint yourself with Visual Basic's interface. You will find a lot of neat features in the interface that will help you with the development of your programs.

The first thing you will notice when you start Visual Basic is the New Project dialog, shown in Figure 1.4. This dialog allows you to choose a project type to create, or you can choose to open an existing project. The Recent tab in the dialog box contains a list of the project you have worked on most recently. The Existing tab is a file dialog box that allows you to open any project on your computer.

FIG. 1.4
The New Project dialog box lets you select from several types of projects to create.

New projects tab

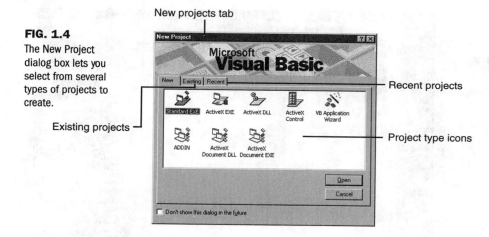

Recent projects

Existing projects

Project type icons

If you choose to create a new project, Visual Basic will create the appropriate project template for you, based on your selection from the project dialog box. You can choose to create one of eight project types:

- Standard EXE—This is the type of project you would use to create a standard Windows program.

- ActiveX EXE—This is a remote automation program that performs tasks as part of a multiple tier application. This used to be known as an OLE automation server.

- ActiveX DLL—This is a remote automation program that is created as a DLL. This program can only run when called from another program. It cannot be run alone.

- ActiveX Control—This is a control that you create that can be used in your Visual Basic programs or in any ActiveX application.

- VB Application Wizard—This choice runs a Wizard that builds the skeleton of an application for you.

- ADD-IN—This type of program is used to provide additional functionality to Visual Basic itself. An example of this is the Visual Data Manager.

■ ActiveX Document DLL—This type of project creates an application that runs in the Internet Explorer.

■ ActiveX Document EXE—This type of project creates an application that runs in the Internet Explorer.

For most project types, after you select the project type from the dialog box, you will be presented with the design environment. This is where you will do the work of actually creating your masterpiece application. The basic design environment is shown in Figure 1.5. This is probably what Visual Basic looked like when you started it for the first time.

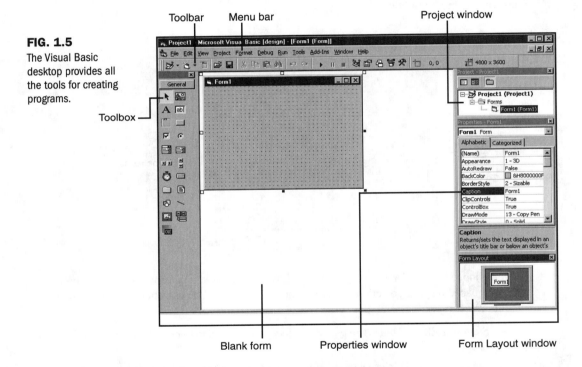

FIG. 1.5
The Visual Basic desktop provides all the tools for creating programs.

As you can see, Visual Basic shares a lot of elements with other Windows programs. There is a menu bar, a toolbar that contains buttons for the most commonly performed tasks, and a work area where you actually create your programs. Even a few of the menu items are the same: File, Edit, Help, and others.

Using the Menu Bar

The *menu bar* provides you with access to all of the functions that are available in Visual Basic. As with the menus on other Windows programs, you can access the functions in the menu by clicking the menu item or by using *hotkeys*. A hotkey is indicated by an underlined character in the item's name. To use a hotkey for the main menu, hold down the Alt key and press the key indicated by the underlined character. This provides you with quick keyboard access to most functions.

As mentioned earlier, there are several menu items in Visual Basic that should be familiar to you: File, Edit, and Help. Each of these menu items contain several familiar pieces. The File menu allows you to open, save, and close files. The Edit menu contains the cut, copy, and paste commands. The Help menu provides access to the Visual Basic help system. For many of the most commonly used functions, there is also another way to access the function. This is through the use of shortcut keys. A shortcut is a key combination, usually the Ctrl key plus another key, that starts the function directly, without having to go through the menus. Many of the shortcut keys that are familiar to you from other programs work the same in Visual Basic. A list of these keys is presented in Table 1.1. This similarity of menus and keystrokes makes it easier to learn how Visual Basic works.

Table 1.1   Shortcut Keys Provide Quicker Access to Functions than Menus

Menu Item	Shortcut Key	Description
Edit, Cut	Ctrl-X	Removes text or a control from its current location and copies it to the Clipboard.
Edit, Copy	Ctrl-C	Makes a copy of text or a control in the Clipboard.
Edit, Paste	Ctrl-V	Pastes the contents of the Clipboard to the form or code window.
Edit, Undo	Ctrl-Z	Undoes the last change.
Edit, Find	Ctrl-F	Finds a piece of text.
File, Open	Ctrl-O	Opens a project.
File, Save	Ctrl-S	Saves the current file.
File, Print	Ctrl-P	Prints the current form or module.

Accessing Functions with the Toolbar

As mentioned earlier, one of the pieces of the desktop is the *toolbar.* This provides you with quick access to some of the most often used functions in Visual Basic. Figure 1.6 shows the toolbar, with some of the individual buttons called out.

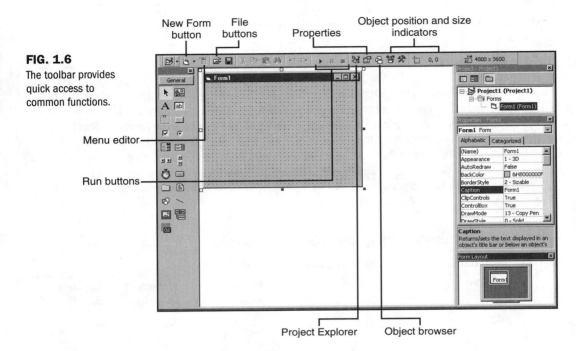

FIG. 1.6
The toolbar provides quick access to common functions.

New Form button · File buttons · Properties · Object position and size indicators

Menu editor

Run buttons

Project Explorer · Object browser

The toolbar in Visual Basic follows the standard used by the latest generation of programs in that it provides you with *ToolTips* to tell you what each button is. A ToolTip is a little yellow box with a description in it. These pop up if you leave the cursor on a button for a few seconds.

While most of the buttons on the toolbar are addressed later in the book, two other areas on the toolbar deserve special mention. At the far right of the toolbar are two blocks with a pair of numbers in each block. These two blocks show the position and size of the form or control with which you are working. The two numbers in the first block indicate the horizontal and vertical positions, respectively, of the upper-left corner of the current object. If you are working with a form, these positions are in relation to the top-left corner of the screen. If you are working with a control, the positions are in relation to the top-left corner of the current form. The two numbers in the second block show the horizontal and vertical dimensions, respectively, of the current object.

N O T E Both the position and dimension information is given in *twips*. Twips are used by Visual Basic for screen measurements. There are approximately 1,440 twips in an inch. A twip is also approximately 1/20 of a pixel, which is where it got its name. ▪

Organizing Visual Basic's Controls

The controls that are used in Visual Basic are the heart and soul of the programs that you create. The controls allow you to add functionality to your program quickly and easily. There are controls that allow you to edit text, to connect to a database, to retrieve file information from a user, or display and edit pictures. A list of the basic set of Visual Basic controls is contained in Table 1.2.

Table 1.2 The Toolbox Contains All the Visual Basic Controls

Icon	Name	Function
	Picture Box	Allows you to display and edit graphics images.
	Label	Displays text.
	Textbox	Allows you to display and edit text, numbers, and dates.
	Frame	Provides a method for grouping other controls.
	Command Button	Provides a means to start a program function.
	Check Box	Displays or allows input of a two-part choice, such as Yes/No or True/False.
	Option Button	Displays or allows a choice among multiple items.
	Combo Box	Allows the user to select an entry from a list or enter a new value.
	List Box	Allows the user to select an entry.
	Horizontal Scrollbar	Allows the user to input numerical information.
	Vertical Scrollbar	Allows the user to input numerical information.
	Timer	Provides a means for an action to be taken on a timed basis.
	Drive List Box	Displays and allows a user to choose from available disk drives on the computer.
	Directory List Box	Displays and allows a user to choose from available subdirectories on the computer.

continues

Table 1.2 Continued

Icon	Name	Function
	File List Box	Displays and allows a user to choose from available files on the computer.
	Shape	Displays geometric shapes on the form.
	Line	Displays lines on the form.
	Image	Displays graphics images.
	Data Control	Provides a link to database files.
	OLE Control	Provides you with a way to link to OLE servers.

Obviously, with all these controls available, you need a way to keep them organized. This is the function of the *control toolbox*. This toolbox contains all the controls available for use in your program. Figure 1.7 shows the basic control set that is available when you first start Visual Basic (the controls described in Table 1.2). The toolbox can be moved around on the screen to a location that is convenient to you. You move it by clicking and dragging the bar at the top of the toolbox.

You can add other controls to the toolbox by selecting the Components item from the Project menu. This brings up the dialog box shown in Figure 1.8. This dialog box allows you to choose any additional controls that have been installed on your system. If you choose to add a control to the toolbox, it appears after you close the Components dialog box.

 T I P You can also access the Components dialog box by right-clicking the mouse on the toolbox and then selecting the Components item from the pop-up menu.

By default, all the components for your project will appear in the toolbox at the same time. However, if you use a lot of controls, this can make it very difficult to manage all of them. To help with this problem, Visual Basic allows you to add tabs to the toolbox. (It has one tab, General, by default.) To add a tab to the toolbox, right-click the toolbox, select the Add Tab item from the pop-up menu, then give the new tab a name. You can then move controls from one tab to another and group your controls in a way that is most convenient to you. Figure 1.9 shows the toolbox with a Data Access tab added to it.

Part
I

Ch
1

FIG. 1.7
The control toolbox
provides you with the
pieces you will use to
create your user
interface.

Horizontal Scrollbar   Check Box   Label   Textbox   Option Button
     Combo Box   Frame   Picture Box   Command Button

Timer
Directory
Shape
Image
OLE Control
Data Control

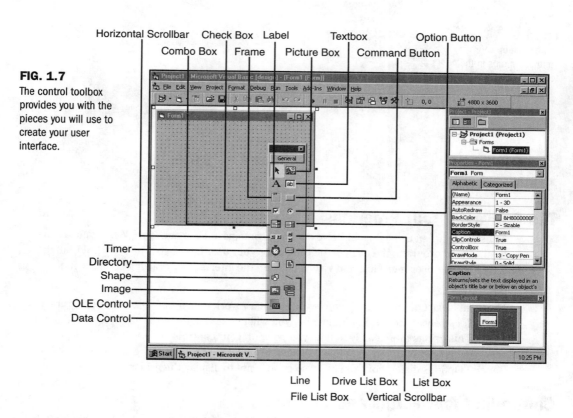

Line   Drive List Box   List Box
File List Box   Vertical Scrollbar

FIG. 1.8
Controls can be added
to the toolbox using
this dialog box.

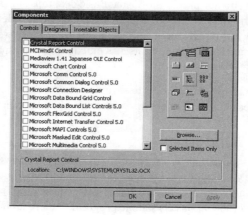

FIG. 1.9
You can group your
controls on tabs in the
toolbox.

The Canvas of Your Programs

As I stated earlier, every Visual Basic program contains at least one *form*. When you are de-signing your program, the form is the canvas for your user interface. The form holds all the pieces of your user interface. You visually design the interface by drawing controls on the form.

The form is part of the desktop and is your primary work area for creating your program. If you look closely at the form in Figure 1.5, you will notice that the form has dots on it that form a grid. This grid is there solely to help you position your controls on the form. When your program is run, the grid is not shown. You can control the spacing of the grid dots from the General Options dialog box. You can also choose not to display the grid at all.

Controlling Your Forms and Controls

The *Properties window* is another part of the Visual Basic desktop. This window shows all the available properties for the current form or control. These properties determine how a form or control will look and how it will perform in a program. Figure 1.10 shows the Properties win-dow with several key elements called out. (I discuss much more about properties throughout the book.)

You will notice in Figure 1.10 that the Properties window has two tabs on it. These tabs allow you to view the properties in either alphabetic order or grouped by logical categories.

What's in the Project Window

Another piece of the desktop is the *Project window*. This window shows all the forms and code modules that are used in your program. For many of your programs, you will have only a single form, and there will be only one entry in the project window. For other programs, such as the VISDATA program (one of Visual Basic's sample programs), there are a number of forms and code modules. Figure 1.11 shows an example of a simple project window and a more complex project window.

The Project window uses an outline list to not only show you the forms and code modules, but also any class modules or user defined controls that are part of your project. The window also shows multiple projects if you have more than one open at a time.

FIG. 1.10
The Properties window
lets you control the look
of a form or control.

Selected property—

Property description—

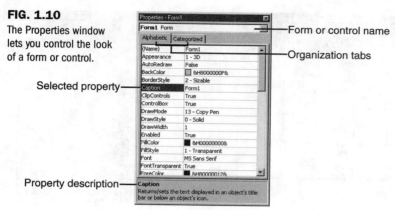

Form or control name

Organization tabs

FIG. 1.11
The Project window
shows you all the parts
of your program.

Part
I

Ch
1

Where Work Gets Done

The final piece of the desktop is the *code window*. The code window is where you do all the
entry and editing of program code that allows your programs to actually perform tasks. The
code window is not visible when you start Visual Basic. Instead, it is shown when you need to
edit your code. To access the code window, you can double click a form or any component of
the form, or you can choose the Show Code button in the Project window. An example of a
code window is shown in Figure 1.12.

Customizing your environment

Earlier in this section, in Figure 1.5, you saw how the development environment would look
when you start Visual Basic for the first time. You are not limited to using the environment this
way. Most of the windows and toolbars in Visual Basic can be docked at the edges of the main
program window, or they can float anywhere on the screen. You can also resize the windows to
suit your needs. In addition, there are other toolbars that you can add to the desktop. These
toolbars are accessible by choosing the Toolbars item of the View menu. Figure 1.13 shows
you one way the development environment can be rearranged.

FIG. 1.12
The code window lets you edit the program statements needed to respond to events.

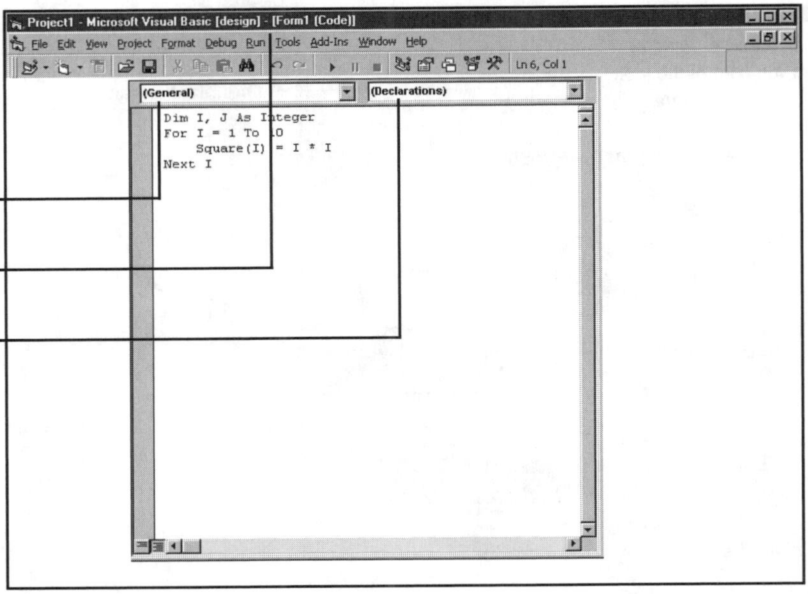

Object-selection box

Form name

Event-selection box

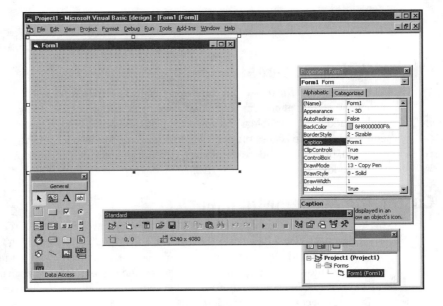

FIG. 1.13
The development environment can be customized to your needs.

Getting Help When You Need It

I cover most features of Visual Basic in this book; however, often you will need more details than I provide about a particular statement or control. For detailed information about every aspect of Visual Basic, refer to the online help system.

The Basic Help System

The easiest way to access the help system is through the Help menu. There are three choices available on the menu for Visual Basic help:

- Microsoft Visual Basic Help Topics
- Search Reference Index
- Search Master Index

The Contents item shows you the main table of contents for the help system, as shown in Figure 1.14. From here, you can choose topics of interest and navigate through the other parts of the system. You choose a topic by clicking one of the jumps (also known as links). You will also find jumps on many of the help pages that will take you to information on related topics.

FIG. 1.14
The Contents page of the help window lets you select topics to review.

To find help on a specific topic, you can select the Search Reference Index item on the Help menu. This brings up the help window with the Index page selected. To find an item, just type the name of the item in the text box in the window and then click the specific item in the list below the text box. The Index page of the help window is shown in Figure 1.15.

FIG. 1.15

The Index page of the help window lets you find specific topics.

Context-Sensitive Help

In addition to letting you look up information in the Contents and Index pages, Visual Basic provides you with *context-sensitive help*. This allows you to directly get the help you need for a particular control or code keyword. To get help for any control, simply select the control on your form and then press the F1 key. The help system displays the information for the control. This help page, such as the one shown in Figure 1.16, also provides links to detailed descriptions of the properties, methods, and events of the control.

FIG. 1.16

The help page for a control provides a description of the control and links to other pages.

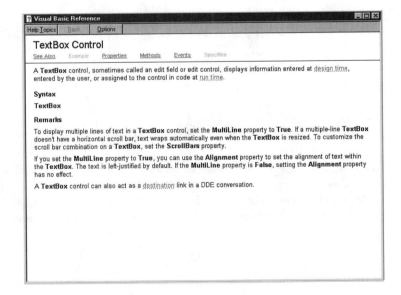

For code keywords, you simply select the word in the code window, as shown in Figure 1.17, and then press F1. The help system goes directly to the page for that command and provides you with the syntax of the command, as well as other information about it. In addition, for most commands, a link is provided that gives you an example of how the command is used.

FIG. 1.17

To get help for a command, select the word and then press F1.

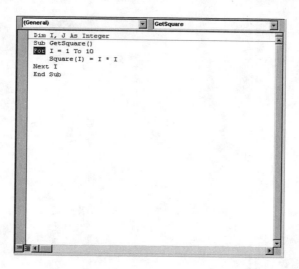

From Here...

This chapter introduced you to Visual Basic. To really learn the capabilities of the program, you will want to read further. A couple of good places to start are the following:

- Chapter 3, "Using Forms and Controls," explains forms and controls.
- Chapter 6, "Programming in Visual Basic," will teach you all about the programming language of Visual Basic.

CHAPTER 2

VB for COBOL Programmers

Many COBOL programmers come from a background rich in mainframe tools that provide comfortable environments for writing the "COBOL way." Today, most banks, corporations, and educational institutions use applications that contain COBOL code. Over the years, batch processing, aided by JCL (*job control language*, which did for mainframes what batch files now do for PCs), data access, transaction file processing, and almost every other business application, required the record-processing capabilities that COBOL offers.

Understanding the Visual Basic environment

See how writing programs in Visual Basic differs from writing programs in COBOL.

How programs work in a graphical environment

Learn about the unique aspects of writing programs for a graphical environment.

Why Visual Basic is so popular

Visual Basic's integrated development environment and component-based design make programming easy, without sacrificing power.

The history of Visual Basic

See where Visual Basic started and how it has evolved to version 5.

Why move to Visual Basic

Look at some of the reasons you might want to move to this new environment.

N O T E If you are already familiar with Visual Basic programming or have some experience developing Windows programs in other languages such as Delphi or Visual C++, you may want to skip this chapter. This chapter is primarily intended to provide information to programmers coming from a strictly procedural programming environment. ▨

If you are a traditional COBOL programmer, your programs have made a tremendous impact on the world. But now you are going to have to do an about-face, when you migrate from COBOL to Visual Basic. Moving to Visual Basic requires not only a change in the language but also a change in your approach to the language. The Visual Basic programming environment requires a new atmosphere that's completely different from the typical COBOL-based text editor. With Visual Basic, you'll design, create, and test programs differently.

This chapter introduces you to some of the differences between the programming environment to which you are accustomed and the "new world" of Visual Basic programming. Other chapters in the book provide the details of creating Visual Basic programs for all types of applications. For example, Chapter 3, "Using Forms and Controls," shows you how to create the visual interface to your programs and Chapter 6, "Programming in Visual Basic," shows you how to write program code to perform tasks in your programs.

N O T E While this chapter specifically mentions COBOL, the material is equally appropriate for programmers from other languages such as FORTRAN. ▨

Deciding to Make the Move to Visual Basic

One of the primary reasons you're making the shift to PC programming is obvious when you consider the sheer number of personal computers in use today. PCs are blanketing the home computer market and are installed within networked and distributed computing environments throughout every major company in the world. Technology has finally allowed the PC catch up with the demands of day-to-day business.

The PC's single CPU offers advantages over the distributed resources that a mainframe gives. The PC provides instant interaction with its user. A terminal connected to a centralized computer cannot respond to each user as fast as a PC can respond to its user. Therefore, mainframe and minicomputer terminals do not allow the graphical interaction provided by single-user PCs.

Since the development of today's powerful PCs—especially those PCs networked to other PCs and to larger computers—programmers see the tremendous opportunity for end-user interfaces that were never before possible. The PC's on-board CPU enables the user to interact instantaneously with the mouse and keyboard while background processing sends and retrieves data to and from other centralized sources. These new and powerful interfaces require different programming techniques from those needed in the past.

As you know, *COBOL* is an acronym for *COmmon Business-Oriented Language*. Although large-computer COBOL was the mainstream business language for almost 40 years, the PC has made tremendous inroads into the corporate environment in the last decade. The traditional, mainframe-based "programmer at each terminal" environment doesn't exist today. In its place is a variety of computers. Mainframes and minicomputers still exist, but often just as data repositories so that networked PCs can access the data through visual-based programming languages such as Visual Basic.

COBOL's Design

In 1958, the military, with the help of the late great Ms. Grace Hopper, designed COBOL to be a language that helped the military solve problems in ways that nonmilitary, business-oriented organizations could benefit from as well. (Yes, the military requires business-like programming. Think of the inventory nightmares incurred by tracking the military's supplies, clothing, and people, as well as the accounting requirements needed to keep accurate records of all movements and costs.)

Over the years, Ms. Hopper went on to become an admiral, and COBOL grew in stature and rank as well. Until the development of COBOL, there were no real programming standards. No methods existed that unified the programming process. With the help of the ANSI committee (the *American National Standards Institute*), which set in stone all COBOL standards, most COBOL-compiler vendors jumped on the bandwagon and offered ANSI-standard COBOL (called *ANSI COBOL*). The industry's adherence to the ANSI standard ensured that companies and programmers who used COBOL wouldn't find themselves in quick obsolescence, as was the case before COBOL came along.

Sure enough, COBOL remained the leading programming language in business for almost 40 years. It was only when technology surpassed everyone's wildest expectations, with the advent of fast PCs and graphical interfaces, that COBOL shops began to seek other tools for writing their programs.

COBOL's strength is its explicit language. A descriptive keyword is used in the place of a more cryptic symbol, as is the case with FORTRAN (and later, with C) programs. One of the goals of the original COBOL design team was to make COBOL a language for nonprogrammers. Before COBOL, there were many programming languages, lots of versions of each, and virtually no standards. COBOL's language is explicit and contains scores of keywords that describe exactly what each statement does.

With COBOL, a person who has never programmed before can look at a program and, in theory, decipher the code and understand what the program is supposed to do. Everyone agrees, that COBOL's wordiness makes the language approachable and less technical for the thousands of people who have used it over the years.

Where COBOL's strength is its wordiness, Visual Basic's strength is its *lack* of wordiness. Visual Basic relies on the visual elements that are so important in today's GUI world. Instead of typing text in a text editor, you'll be using the mouse to create and place components on the screen when writing programs with Visual Basic. There is a comprehensive Visual Basic programming language that you'll need to master, but a Visual Basic program relies much less on its language commands than other programming languages do. This is primarily because the programmer no longer has to write the code to present information to the user. The user interface is handled by the forms and components of the program.

Forms and components are covered extensively in Chapter 3, "Using Forms and Controls."

Microsoft Windows is the platform for which Microsoft developed Visual Basic. It's true that some mainframe programmers fight the shift from the traditional COBOL transaction-processing, text-based environment to a graphical user interface (GUI) environment such as Microsoft Windows. Obviously, you are interested in making this shift (or your boss is interested in your making it!), because you are reading this book to learn about Visual Basic.

Despite the fact that Visual Basic programs control data as well as complex graphical user interfaces, Visual Basic programs often require much less programming effort than equivalent COBOL programs. You will design your user interfaces much more quickly with Visual Basic than with COBOL. If you are accustomed to the four familiar COBOL divisions, ANSI standards, sequentially numbered labels, and page after page of readable, structured code, you may wonder how only a little programming effort with the mouse and keyboard can produce today's robust graphical programs.

> **CAUTION**
>
> The COBOL listings you see in this chapter have been modified to work with the author's PC-based COBOL compiler. Although standard COBOL is used, your ENVIRONMENT DIVISION details will vary slightly from the book's, depending on your hardware.

Listing 2.1 shows a very simple COBOL program that asks the user for an hourly rate and number of hours worked and then computes and displays the gross pay. As you know, even this elementary task requires a relatively long COBOL listing. The program performs simple I/O with the ACCEPT and DISPLAY statements. If the program instead contained typical READ and WRITE statements, the program would be even longer due to the record layouts necessary to support these statements.

 This book's Web site (at **http://www.quecorp.com/sevb5**) contains each complete code listing in the book. The file name for each program listing resides in an IDENTIFICATION DIVISION comment. If you use a COBOL compiler that requires a different file name extension, change the .COB extension to the extension required by your compiler.

Listing 2.1 COBOL.TXT—A COBOL Program Uses Lots of Text

```
IDENTIFICATION DIVISION.
PROGRAM-ID. EASY-GROSS-CALC.
PROGRAM-ID.    EASYCALC.
AUTHOR.
*************************************************************
* Computes simple gross pay
* Filename: EASYCALC.COB
*************************************************************
ENVIRONMENT DIVISION.
CONFIGURATION SECTION.
SOURCE COMPUTER. IBM-PS/2.
OBJECT COMPUTER. IBM-PS/2.
INPUT-OUTPUT SECTION.
```

```
*
* Send the output to the DOS console
* (the PC's screen) to keep things simple
*
  FILE-CONTROL.
      SELECT OUTFILE ASSIGN TO "CON:".
  DATA DIVISION.
  FILE SECTION.
  FD  OUTFILE.
  01  OUT-REC.
      02  FILLER       PIC X(48).
  WORKING-STORAGE SECTION.
  01  WORK-AREAS.
      02  RATE         PIC S9999     VALUE IS ZERO.
      02  HOURS        PIC S99       VALUE IS ZERO.
      02  GROSS        PIC S9(5)V99  VALUE IS ZERO.
  01  DETAIL-LINE.
      02  FILLER       PIC X(18) VALUE 'Your gross pay is '.
      02  FGROSS       PIC $$,$$9.99.
      02  FILLER       PIC X(21) VALUE ', enjoy your weekend!'.
*
  PROCEDURE DIVISION.
  Begin.
      OPEN OUTPUT OUTFILE.
      DISPLAY "What is the rate per hour? ".
      ACCEPT RATE.
      DISPLAY "How many hours did you work? ".
      ACCEPT HOURS.
*
* Calculate and print the Gross Pay
*
  MULTIPLY RATE BY HOURS GIVING GROSS.
  MOVE GROSS TO FGROSS OF DETAIL-LINE.
  WRITE OUT-REC FROM DETAIL-LINE.
  CLOSE OUTFILE.
  STOP RUN.
```

To see the equivalent Visual Basic program, examine Figure 2.1 and Listing 2.2. A Visual Basic program almost always requires both a graphically designed Windows interface and some code that controls the program's data flow. Don't worry about understanding the details of the Visual Basic program at this point. The important thing to note is the difference in approach between COBOL and Visual Basic.

FIG. 2.1

The interface screen is a key part of most Visual Basic programs.

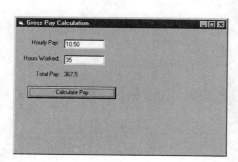

N O T E When you write a new COBOL program, you almost always make a copy of an existing
COBOL program and delete the portions that will change for the new one. A COBOL
program requires too much effort to begin typing a new program from scratch each time. While Visual
Basic programmers do reuse code, they take a different approach. Visual Basic encourages the use of
code modules, object classes, and forms that can be used in more than one project. Therefore, a
Visual Basic programmer may start a new project by assembling some of the pieces from other
projects and then adding the new features. ■

Listing 2.2   The Visual Basic Code that Augments the Window's Operation

```
Sub cmdGrossPay_Click ()
    lblGrossPay = txtRate.Text * txtHours.Text
End Sub

Sub cmdQuit_Click ()
    End    ' Exits the application
End Sub
```

N O T E Notice that a Visual Basic program consists of both the output screen and code. The
screen's window is an integral part of the program. By designing an application's window,
you eliminate a lot of tedious coding that you must do in a text-oriented language such as COBOL. ■

Figure 2.1's window title bar (the bar across the top of the window) contains a title that appro-
priately describes the running application. As you will learn in Chapter 3, in the section "Exploring Properties, Methods, and Events," this type of information is controlled by properties
of the forms and components used in your programs.

Visual Basic offers all kinds of tools that enable you to design program windows such as the
application shown in Figure 2.1. In the way that an artist uses a palette of paint colors, Visual
Basic programmers use window-design tools to design and add elements to their programs.
Figure 2.2 may look extremely busy (due to your newness to the Visual Basic environment);
however, it gives you a glimpse of the design screen and tools used to create the previous
gross pay application. (Your screen may appear slightly different from the one in Figure 2.2,
depending on your version of Visual Basic.)

FIG. 2.2

Visual Basic supplies
many screen-design
tools.

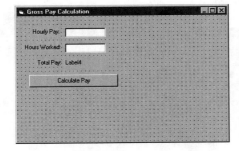

Visual Basic's Integrated Design Environment (IDE) is covered in detail in Chapter 1, "Introduction to Visual Basic."

 Later in the book, you will learn to create and run your own Visual Basic programs. If you want to take a look at the actual gross pay program described in Listing 2.2, you will find it on the book's Web site. The program consists of two files: EASYCALC.VBP and EASYCALC.FRM.

The first file, EASYCALC.VBP, is called a *project file* (perhaps you've heard of a similar term in the minicomputer world, *makefile*). The project file contains a listing of every file needed to produce the complete running application. All project files end with the .VBP file name extension. The other file, EASYCALC.FRM, is the *form file,* which contains a description of the program's window as well as the code used in the program. You'll learn more about the files that make up a Visual Basic program in Chapter 7, "Managing Your Project from Beginning to End."

Part

I

Ch

2

Exploring Visual Basic's Background

Visual Basic was created due to the need for a simple Windows programming tool. You can write Windows programs in virtually any programming language (even COBOL). Using a language other than Visual Basic, however, can be very difficult and extremely time-consuming. Although virtually all Windows programs share common elements, each program uses those elements differently. This difference in control usage gives traditional, text-based programmers nightmares.

As you'll see as you learn Visual Basic, users do not interact with a Windows-based program in the same way that they interact with text-oriented programs. Using a more traditional procedural programming language such as COBOL or FORTRAN to write a Windows program is akin to building a house with one arm tied behind your back.

The designers of Visual Basic moved away from the typical programming paradigm when they developed Visual Basic. They decided exactly which elements all Windows programs share. Visual Basic makes placing, using, and interacting with those Windows-programming, graphic-controlling elements extremely easy.

The most important advantage that Visual Basic offers is a set of graphical tools that you use to produce graphical programs. Traditional, text-based programming tools cannot adequately interpret the user's movements and interactions needed for Windows programs. Not only are text-based programming languages difficult for translating the needs of users into programs, but maintenance of such programs is virtually impossible. Where in the code do you look when the user's mouse movement over one part of the screen works properly, but not over another part of the screen? Visual Basic encapsulates the code for all possible mouse movements into specific areas of the program. The programmer can get to those areas with only a few keystrokes.

You may be more than a little confused at this point. This chapter refers to the visual tools in Visual Basic but also describes the code in a Visual Basic program. Where exactly does the code from Listing 2.1 fit with the graphical window portion of the program? How, and more importantly *when,* does this code execute?

Visual Basic's code is required to control underlying details that are specific to each application. If you could write every program solely by moving and clicking pictures, you would, because doing so is much easier than writing one line of code. However, there are just too many application-specific details that cannot be captured with graphical tools alone. The Visual Basic language augments the graphical interface by handling data manipulation and program control. The next section explains more about how Visual Basic's code orchestrates the application's details.

A Short Background of the BASIC Language

The *Basic* in Visual Basic comes from a programming language, BASIC, that's been around since the early 1960s. BASIC stands for *Beginner's All-Purpose Symbolic Instruction Code*. Although that acronym is almost as long as the language itself, the first word, *Beginner's,* is the focus of the language. Professors at Dartmouth College designed the language so that beginners and noncomputer types could master BASIC with relative ease.

BASIC was originally interpretive and never designed to be a compiled language. The authors of BASIC felt that the compilation process added an extra step that newcomers simply should not have to mess with. In eliminating compilation, however, they eliminated speed and power.

BASIC matured through the years, especially once Bill Gates and Microsoft started getting involved. BASIC was too slow and simple to be used for serious applications until Microsoft augmented the language and added powerful structured programming constructs and advanced data types. Microsoft has offered numerous BASIC interpreters and compilers over the years including MBASIC, BASICA, GW-BASIC, QuickBasic, QBasic, and now Visual Basic. Visual Basic was the first version used exclusively for writing Windows programs. (Microsoft sold a Visual Basic for DOS version a few months after releasing Visual Basic for Windows.)

The designers of Visual Basic could have used a language other than BASIC as the underlying control code. BASIC was a great choice, however, because of how quickly beginners can get up to speed with the language. There are other popular Windows programming tools on the market today that use C and C++ as the underlying control language, but these tools are almost out of reach for the introductory programmer. A programmer requires much more training before he or she can write Windows programs with C and C++, whereas a programmer can produce a Visual Basic program right away.

The Code in Visual Basic

Windows contains thousands of internal routines that Visual Basic uses to control I/O and common data manipulation. Sometimes, you need to tap into these routines. You can utilize the internal Windows routines through code written in the Visual Basic language.

When faced with a program requirement that cannot be described graphically, you'll have to resort to writing code. You write *a lot less* code using Visual Basic than you would otherwise write in another language. The code, written in an easy and structured BASIC-like style, interacts with the program's graphical elements and executes only when needed.

Calculations are excellent examples of why code is needed in addition to the program's graphical elements. There is no way to design graphical controls that handle every possible calculation needed in a program. Additionally, you need to manipulate and sort data in many different ways depending on the requirements of certain applications. The code handles these details.

TIP Actually, Visual Basic's code editor offers a few advantages over the COBOL code editors that you may have used before on the mainframe. You'll be able to utilize familiar Windows cut, copy, and paste operations and control those operations with your mouse. Also, you may be surprised to learn that the code editor actually writes some of the program's code for you and helps you with the syntax of the code!

Part
I
Ch
2

You can write Visual Basic code that is just as structured as the COBOL code you write. You'll just have less code to structure, because so much of a Visual Basic program is written without the traditional text. Every structured programming technique that you've mastered will pay off with Visual Basic, just as structured programming has paid off through the years with COBOL.

In a way, a well-written Visual Basic program is easier to follow and maintain than a program written in any other language; Visual Basic's programming interface keeps *routines* (similar to COBOL's *paragraphs*) separated. Each routine is a pocket of code that is easily accessible from whatever Windows graphical element the code controls. When you want to look at code that operates a pull-down menu, for example, you can use the mouse to move directly to that code without thumbing through page after page of a tedious listing.

CAUTION

You rarely can make a one-to-one comparison of a COBOL program and a Visual Basic program. The two environments are completely different.

The Graphical Nature of Visual Basic

Visual Basic programs almost always contain Windows elements such as command buttons, mouse selections, and pull-down menus that make up a true graphical Windows interface. COBOL's code, on the other hand, sequentially and specifically controls the order of actions that the user can do. Unless you purchase a third-party and nonstandard COBOL interface to Windows (none of which have done extremely well in the PC arena), COBOL's strength is best left to the text-based programs that perform traditional file processing and file-updating tasks.

To produce a program for Windows, you must find a tool that handles all the standard Windows I/O for you and frees you up for the more esoteric nature of Windows programming. In other words, you must use a programming tool designed to handle several possible user actions in several possible orders.

As you'll soon see, when your program needs a Windows push-button control (called a *command button,* in Windows terminology), you'll click a command button that the Visual Basic toolbox contains and then draw a command button on the screen in the size and location that you want. If you want a larger or smaller command button, use the mouse to resize the command button. If you want to change the command button's caption (the text on the button), you don't have to write code to change the text; instead, you set a property of the command button in the Properties window.

> **N O T E** Don't worry about standards. Although the ANSI committee probably will not adopt an ANSI Visual Basic standard any time soon, Visual Basic is in use by thousands of programmers all over the world. Tons of Visual Basic programs reside on electronic bulletin boards, the Internet, and commercial online services such as CompuServe. Microsoft has released several versions of Visual Basic since its introduction in the early 1990s. Each subsequent version has retained compatibility with the previous version while becoming even easier to use. ▪

Visual Basic has become a de facto standard by the sheer volume of Visual Basic programmers and the number of programs used every day all around the world.

Having Fun While You Learn

Here's a little secret about Visual Basic: Writing programs in Visual Basic can be really fun! You'll be creating a huge portion of Visual Basic programs just by clicking and dragging the mouse to create the graphical elements of your program. You'll be designing powerful and colorful user interfaces in minutes instead of scribbling on layout pads as programmers did throughout the last 40 years of mainframe programming. You'll be using Visual Basic to access vast databases without knowing or caring what the exact database schema design looks like.

Perhaps we should slow down, however, and warn you that Visual Basic is a serious programming tool with which you can design comprehensive and extremely powerful programs. Despite the easy interface and the enjoyable nature of Visual Basic, it is not a toy computer language. Some people from the mainframe world approach Visual Basic with a little distrust and lots of cynicism, and that's understandable. Visual Basic turns the entire programming paradigm topsy-turvy.

At first it's hard to focus on Visual Basic as a whole. When you design a Visual Basic program, you often work on one part, such as a data-entry form, and then move to a completely different part of the program, such as a report, before finally getting back to the rest of the original form. Visual Basic makes jumping from one program element to another easy. The nature of Windows programs often dictates a strange order of development. Always remain aware that you can write structured and well-written Visual Basic code without resorting to the time-tested top-down design that's worked so well in the COBOL world. Top-down design methodology is still a nice approach to breaking your problem into separate design components, but when you go to the keyboard to write the actual program, you'll find yourself building the program one part at a time, often in random order.

Part

I

Ch

2

What About Other Windows Programming Languages?

There's lots of debate right now among C, C++, and Visual Basic programmers as to which tool is the best to use for Windows program development. Here's a fact that even the C and C++ purists admit: While the debate rages on, Visual Basic programmers are cranking out complete, debugged, and productive programs, while the C and C++ programmers still are deciding what kinds of subroutines will best interact with certain mouse clicks.

It's true that Visual Basic programs often run more slowly than equivalent C and C++ programs. However, Visual Basic programs don't run much more slowly, and except in math-intensive and time-critical environments, most people never see the difference in speed. If the speed issue concerns you, however, keep the following in mind: Computers get faster all the time, not slower. As computers get faster, the differences in runtime speed become unimportant. The costly part of programming is development and debugging time, and Visual Basic races past other Windows development languages by making you a productive programmer rather than one who labors over long program listings late into the night.

Visual Basic is the champ when it comes to being a complete Windows development tool that beginners as well as advanced programmers can use to turn out production-quality code with flair and relatively little effort.

Learning Visual Basic

If you are coming from a procedural language, such as COBOL or FORTRAN, the biggest challenge you will face is not learning the Visual Basic language itself. In fact, many of the programming structures with which you are familiar have counterparts in Visual Basic. For example, Visual Basic contains loop and conditional structures just like COBOL and FORTRAN. You'll also find that Visual Basic contains variables that are nothing more than COBOL's DATA DIVISION's WORKING STORAGE items. Visual Basic also has a CALL statement for invoking other routines. This statement mirrors the functionality of COBOL's PERFORM statement.

The challenge, instead, will be to learn the new paradigm for programming and to understand how graphical elements are created and controlled. You will find that you not only can set up a graphical element in the design environment, but you also can control the appearance and behavior of many of these elements through code.

From Here...

This chapter introduced you to some of the challenges you will face as you start programming in Visual Basic. The good news is that the learning curve is shallow, so you can be creating useful programs in a short period of time. To learn about the actual workings of writing programs in Visual Basic, look at the following chapters:

- To learn about the Visual Basic development environment, see Chapter 1, "Introduction to Visual Basic."

- To learn about creating the visual interface of your programs, see Chapter 3, "Using Forms and Controls."

- To learn about Visual Basic's programming language, see Chapter 6, "Programming in Visual Basic."

- To learn how to create database applications, start with Chapter 10, "Applications at Warp Speed."

Using Form and Controls

Almost every Windows program has two main components. There is the *visual component,* which users see and with which they interact, and there is the *code component,* which actually allows the program to perform tasks.

The visual component of programs created in Visual Basic is created using *forms* and *controls.* The forms and controls allow you to handle user input, information display, and user decisions and to perform many other programming tasks. The nature of Visual Basic's design also allows you to extend the program's capabilities through the use of third-party controls and add-ins. This makes Visual Basic a very powerful system for creating Windows programs. ■

What forms do

Forms provide a container for the controls that make up the visual interface of your programs.

How to control the appearance and behavior of forms

You can change the appearance and often the behavior of forms through the use of properties.

How to use controls in your programs

You will see how to create an instance of a control on a form and how to set up the control using its properties.

What different controls can do

You will learn what functions some of the common controls can perform.

How control arrays can help you

Using arrays of controls can make it easier for you to change the properties of a group of controls using program code.

How to work with controls as a group

You will see how to select multiple controls on the form and manipulate their common properties.

Exploring Properties, Methods, and Events

While typically forms and controls are thought of as just the visual representations seen on the screen, their appearance and, especially, their behavior are controlled by three basic elements: *properties, methods,* and *events.* This discussion explains these elements in terms of how they define a form, but its principles apply to all controls that you might use in Visual Basic.

▶ **See** "Understanding the Event Model," **p.77**

Controlling Behavior Through Properties

When you look at a form, you see a rectangular window on the screen, like the one shown in Figure 3.1. But in reality, this window is defined by a series of properties. For example, the position of the form on the screen is controlled by the Left and Top properties, while the form's size is controlled by its Height and Width properties. The form title that you see in the title bar displays the contents of the form's Caption property. By setting properties, you can even determine which control buttons appear on the form.

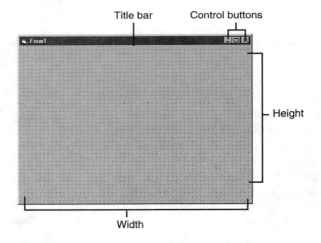

FIG. 3.1
A form's appearance is controlled by its properties.

To see how the form is defined by these properties, you can take a look at the .frm file that is created for each of your forms. This is a text file that contains the settings for all the properties used to determine the appearance of the form. Figure 3.2 shows a portion of an .frm file.

N O T E For many forms, you will also see a file with the .frx extension. This file is present if there are any graphics elements to the form that cannot be defined by text. These might include bitmaps, icons, and certain custom controls. ■

You can think of the properties of a form or control as descriptions of the object's characteristics. This is similar to describing a person. For example, how would you describe yourself? You would probably cite such characteristics as height, weight, hair color, and eye color. Each element of your description could be considered a property.

FIG. 3.2
The properties of the
form are stored in text
format in a .frm file.

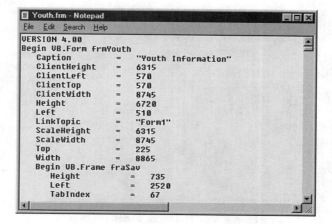

What Do Most Objects Have in Common   While each object in Visual Basic has its own set of properties (some objects have more properties than others), there are several properties that are common to almost all objects. The most important of these common properties are the following:

- Left
- Top
- Height
- Width
- Name
- Enabled
- Visible
- Index

Where Am I   The Left and Top properties of an object define its position on the screen or within its container. The Left property specifies the distance of the left side of the object from the left side of the object's container. The Top property specifies the distance of the top edge of the object from the top of its container. For forms, the distances are measured from the left and top of the screen. For Visual Basic controls, the distances are measured from the top and left of the form (or other container) that contains the object. By default, all distances are measured in a unit called *twips*. The Height and Width properties specify the size (again, usually in twips) of the object. These four properties are illustrated in Figure 3.3.

N O T E   A container is any object which can hold other objects. When controls are placed in a container, they can be moved or hidden as a group. ■

Part
I

Ch
3

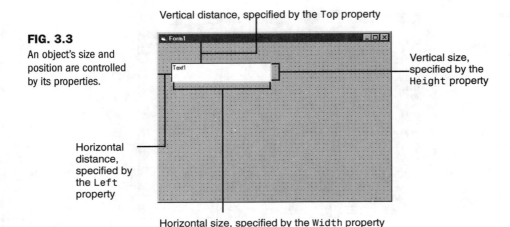

FIG. 3.3

An object's size and position are controlled by its properties.

Vertical distance, specified by the `Top` property

Vertical size, specified by the `Height` property

Horizontal distance, specified by the `Left` property

Horizontal size, specified by the `Width` property

N O T E   A twip is a unit of measure for objects. It is based on a logical inch. There are 1440 twips per logical inch, or about 20 twips per pixel. ■

Can You See Me Now   The `Visible` property and the `Enabled` property both have settings of either `True` or `False`. These properties determine whether an object can be seen by the user and whether the user can interact with the object. If the `Visible` property is set to `False`, the object is not shown, and the user will not know that the object is even there. Setting `Visible` to `True` allows the object to be displayed. If the `Enabled` property is set to `False`, the object is visible (provided that the `Visible` property is `True`), but the user cannot interact with the object. Typically, if an object is disabled, it is shown on the screen in a *grayed out* or *dimmed* mode. This provides a visual indication to the user that the object is unavailable.

What's in a Name   One other key property of every Visual Basic object is the `Name` property. The `Name` property defines a unique identifier by which you can refer to the object in code. Each form, text box, label, and so on must have a unique name.

N O T E   All forms in a project must have different names. However, control names have to be unique only for the form on which they are located. That is, you can have a `Text1` control on each form in your project. ■

Visual Basic provides a default name when the object is first created. For example, `Form1` is the name given to the first form created for your project, and `Text1` is the name given to the first text box that you place on a form. However, you usually will want to provide each object with a name that has some meaning. For example, `frmMain` might be used as the name of the main form for your application.

As you are naming your objects, it is a good programming practice to use a prefix to identify the type of object to which the name refers. This was the case with the `frmMain` name just shown. The prefix *frm* indicates that the object is a form. Table 3.1 lists the standard prefixes for many of Visual Basic's objects (forms and controls).

Table 3.1   Prefixes Identify the Object Type

Object Type	Prefix
CheckBox	chk
ComboBox	cbo
Command Button	cmd
Common Dialog	cdl
Data Control	dat
Data Bound ComboBox	dbc
Data Bound Grid	dbg
Data Bound ListBox	dbl
Directory ListBox	dir
Drive ListBox	drv
File ListBox	fil
Form	frm
Frame	fra
Grid	grd
Horizontal ScrollBar	hsb
Image	img
Label	lbl
Line	lin
ListBox	lst
Menu	mnu
OLE Container	ole
Option Button	opt
Picture Box	pic
Shape	shp
TextBox	txt
Timer	tmr
Vertical ScrollBar	vsb

Part

I

Ch

3

To set the Name property for an object, simply select the property in the properties window and then type in a new name. You can access the properties window by pressing the F4 key, clicking the Properties button, or selecting the Properties item from the View menu. The properties window is shown in Figure 3.4.

FIG. 3.4
The properties window allows you to set many of the characteristics of an object.

To quickly go to a specific property, hold down the Ctrl and Shift keys and press the first letter of the property name. This will take you to the first property starting with that letter. Additional key presses will take you to the next property with the same letter. For the Name property, you would press Ctrl+Shift+N until you came to the name property.

Taking Action with Methods

Forms and controls in Visual Basic are not just idle components that sit and look pretty. These objects are capable of performing tasks. Just as properties of an object define how it looks and behaves, methods of an object define the tasks that it can perform. The tasks can be simple, such as moving the object to another location, or they can be more complex, such as updating information in a database.

A method is really just a segment of program code that is embedded in the object. Using the embedded method, the object knows how to perform the task; you don't have to provide any additional instructions. This is like starting your car. When you start your car, you invoke the "start method" by turning the key. You don't have to specify to your car that it needs to start fuel flow to the engine, engage the starter gear, provide power to the spark plugs, and so on. Your car already "knows" to do all these things, because they were programmed into the car.

As with properties, each type of object can have different methods and different numbers of methods. A simple object like a label will have a minimum set of methods. Complex objects like a form or a data control may have a dozen or more methods.

While there are different methods for different objects, many objects have the following methods in common:

- ■ **Drag**   Handles the operation of the user's dragging and dropping the object within its container.

- ■ **Move**   Handles requests by the program to change the position of an object.

- ■ **SetFocus**   Gives focus to the control specified in the method call.

- ■ **ZOrder**   Determines whether an object appears in front of or behind other objects in its container.

> **N O T E**   *Focus* refers to the control that receives user actions, such as keystrokes. In your program, focus is indicated by the position of the edit cursor (for text boxes) or a dotted rectangle around the control (for check boxes, option buttons, and command buttons). ■

Dealing with Actions

In addition to performing tasks, the objects in your program can respond to user actions or other external actions. These actions are handled through the use of events. Part of the definition of an object determines to which events it will respond.

An event occurs whenever the user performs some action on a control, such as clicking a command button or changing the contents of a text box. Events also occur when the user exits a form or switches to another program. The key to having your program respond to events is to write program code in the event procedure.

Chapter 4, "Understanding the Event Model," delves into all the intricacies of events. In that chapter, you will learn how to write code to handle events and how multiple events are related.

How Properties and Methods Are Related

By now you know that objects have properties to define their appearance, methods that let them perform tasks, and events that let them respond to user actions. You might think that all these things happen independently of one another, but that is not always the case. Sometimes, the properties and methods of an object are related. That is, as you invoke a method of an object, the properties of the object are changed. Also, most times that you use the methods of an object or change its properties with code, you do so in response to an event.

You can see one example of the interdependence of methods and properties of an object when the Move method is used and the Left and Top properties are set. You can cause an object to change position either by using the Move method or by setting the Left and Top properties to new values. For example, the following two code segments accomplish the same task:

```
'*********************************************
'Move the text box by setting the properties
'*********************************************
txtMove.Left = 100
txtMove.Top = 100
'*************************************
'Move the text box using the Move method
'*************************************
txtMove.Move 100, 100
```

In addition, optional arguments of the Move method can change the size of an object. This has the same effect as setting the Height and Width properties to new values.

Similarly, the Show and Hide methods of a form have the same effect as changing the form's Visible property. When you invoke the Hide method, the effect is the same as setting the Visible property to False. (The effect, of course, is that the form disappears from the screen.) Likewise, the Show method produces the same effect as setting the Visible property to True.

For most Windows programs you create, you will have a visual interface that lets the program display information to the user and lets the user interact with the program. The key element of the visual interface for all Visual Basic programs is the form. The form provides a container that holds all the other controls (such as labels, text boxes, and pictures) that make up the user interface. All your programs (with a few rare exceptions) will have at least one form, and most will use a number of forms.

N O T E   It is possible to create a Visual Basic program that contains no forms; however, this is done only for very specialized programs. ■

The form is not just a simple container. Forms have properties that control their appearance and behavior and methods that allow them to perform tasks. Forms respond to events just as all other controls do. A form can even display text and graphics directly, without the use of other controls.

Parts of a Form

When you start Visual Basic or start a new project, you are presented with the development environment shown in Figure 3.5. Notice that the most prominent component of the environment is a blank form. This form is where you will do all your work on the visual interface of your program.

Caption (or title)   Close button

FIG. 3.5
A form lets you easily
create a visual interface
for your program.

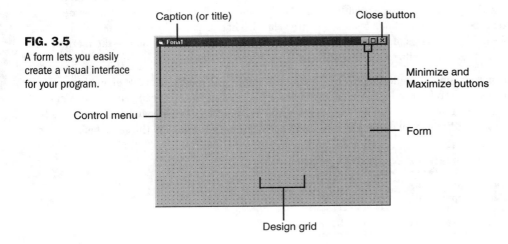

Minimize and
Maximize buttons

Control menu

Form

Design grid

As you can see in Figure 3.5, the form in Visual Basic contains all the elements you would expect to find on a window in a program. It contains a title, a control menu, and a set of Minimize, Maximize, and Close buttons. In addition, the form has a design grid that allows you to easily line up controls as you are designing your interface. You can control the behavior of the design grid through the Options dialog box, shown in Figure 3.6. The Options dialog box is accessible by choosing the Options item from the Tools menu. In this dialog box, you can change the size of the grid or even turn it off completely. You can also choose whether or not controls are automatically aligned to the grid. If this option is on (the default setting), the top left corner of each control is aligned with the grid point that's closest to the corner. Using the default setting makes it easier to precisely line up controls.

FIG. 3.6
You can control the design grid with the Options dialog box.

Grid-Display option

Align-to-Grid option

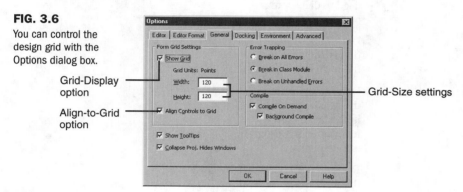

Grid-Size settings

Setting Properties

Forms, like most of the objects used in Visual Basic, have a series of properties that control their behavior and appearance. In the earlier section "Controlling Behavior Through Properties," you learned about some of the properties common to many objects. In this section, you will learn about several key properties of a form, as well as how those properties can be controlled during program design and while the program is running. Table 3.2 lists several of the key properties of a form and provides a brief description of the effect of each property. The table also identifies whether the value of the property can be changed while the program is running.

Table 3.2   Key Properties for Controlling a Form

Property Name	Description	Changeable at Runtime
BorderStyle	Determines the type of border that is used for the form.	No

continues

Table 3.2 Continued

Property Name	Description	Changeable at Runtime
ControlBox	Determines whether the control box (containing the Move and Close menus) is visible when the program is running.	No
Font	Determines the font used to display text on the form.	Yes
Icon	Determines the icon that is shown when the form is minimized.	Yes
MaxButton	Determines whether the Maximize button is displayed on the form when the program is running.	No
MDIChild	Determines whether the form is a child form for an MDI application.	No
MinButton	Determines whether the Minimize button is displayed on the form when the program is running.	No
StartUpPosition	Determines the initial position of a form when it is first shown.	Yes
WindowState	Determines whether the form is shown maximized, minimized, or in its normal state.	Yes

Now take a closer look at some of these properties. The BorderStyle property has six possible settings that control the type of border displayed for the form. These settings control whether the form is sizable by clicking and dragging on the border, they control the buttons that are shown on the form, and they even control the height of the form's title bar. The default setting provides a border that allows the user to resize the form while the program is running. This is the type of form that you find in most of the programs you use, such as Microsoft Word or Microsoft Money. However, you can change the BorderStyle setting to make the form look like almost any type of window that you would see in a program, including toolboxes and dialog boxes. Table 3.3 lists the possible settings of the BorderStyle property. The effects of these settings are shown on the forms in Figure 3.7.

Table 3.3 *BorderStyle* **Property Controls the Type of Window Displayed**

Setting	Effect
0 - None	No border is displayed for the form. The form also does not display the title bar or any control buttons.
1 - Fixed single	A single-line border is used. The title bar and control buttons are displayed for the form. The form is not resizable by the user.
2 - Sizable	The border appearance indicates that the form can be resized. The title bar and control buttons are displayed. The form can be resized by the user by clicking and dragging the border. This is the default setting.
3 - Fixed Dialog	The form shows a fixed border. The title bar, control box, and Close button are shown on the form. Minimize and Maximize buttons are not displayed. The form cannot be resized.
4 - Fixed ToolWindow	The form has a single-line border and displays only the title bar and Close button. These are shown in a reduced font size (approximately half height).
5 - Sizable ToolWindow	This is the same as the Fixed ToolWindow, except that the form has a sizable border.

Part I

Ch 3

FIG. 3.7
Changing the BorderStyle property can give a form many appearances.

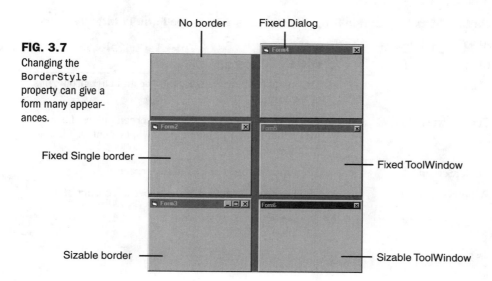

No border   Fixed Dialog

Fixed Single border

Fixed ToolWindow

Sizable border

Sizable ToolWindow

N O T E   The setting of the BorderStyle property affects only how the form looks while the program is running. It has no effect on the appearance of the form in the design environment. ■

In Table 3.3, several of the BorderStyle definitions indicate that a control box and the Close, Minimize, and Maximize buttons would be displayed in the title bar of the form. This is the default behavior. But even with these border styles, you can control whether these elements appear on the form. The ControlBox, MaxButton, and MinButton properties each have a True or False setting that determines whether the particular element appears on the form. The default setting for each of these properties is True. If you set a property to False, the corresponding element is not displayed on the form. These properties can be changed only at design time.

The Font property lets you set the base font and font characteristics for any text displayed on the form. The text is placed on the form by using the form's Print method. In addition, the setting of the form's Font property sets the font for all controls added to the form after you change the font.

TROUBLESHOOTING

I set the Font property of the form, but the font in the title of the form did not change. The Font property of the form has no effect on the form's title. Windows itself controls the font for a window title (remember, a form is a window). You need to change this font in the Windows 95 Control Panel.

One final property of note is the StartupPosition property. As you might guess, this property controls where the form will be located when it is first displayed. There are four possible settings for the property. These settings are summarized in Table 3.4.

Table 3.4   *StartupPosition* Property Controls Where the Form Is Initially Displayed

Setting	Effect
0 - Manual	The initial position is set by the Top and Left properties of the form.
1 - CenterOwner	The form will be centered in the screen unless it is an MDI child form, in which case it will be centered in the parent window.
2 - CenterScreen	The form will be centered in the screen.
3 - Windows Default	The form will be placed in the upper-left corner of the screen.

N O T E This is a really great feature. In previous versions of Visual Basic, you had to write code to center the form by setting the Top and Left properties or using the Move method. With the StartupPosition property, this is all handled for you. ■

Displaying a Form

If you write a program with just a single form, you needn't worry about displaying the form or hiding it. This is done automatically for you as the program starts and when you exit the program. However, if you have more than one form—as most of your programs will—you need a way to display and hide the different forms of your project. The showing and hiding of forms is controlled by two Visual Basic statements and two form methods: the Load and Unload statements and the Show and Hide methods.

The Load statement places a form in memory where it can be accessed and its properties can be set. The Load statement does not display the form. The following line of code shows how the statement is used:

```
Load frmMember
```

To display the form, you must use the Show method. The Show method works, whether or not the form was loaded previously into memory. If the form was not loaded, the Show method performs the load operation and then displays the form. Because the load operation is performed automatically, it is rarely necessary to use the Load statement with a form. The Show method is used as follows:

```
frmMember.Show
```

The Show method also has an optional argument that determines whether the form is shown as a *modal* or *modeless* form. If a form is shown as modal, then no other forms in your program can be accessed until the modal form is closed. (You can, however, access forms in other programs.) If the form is shown modeless, you can move at will between the current form and other forms in the program. The preceding statement displayed a form as modeless. To create a modal form, you simply set the optional argument of the method to 1, as shown here:

```
frmMember.Show 1
```

N O T E A modal form is typically used when you want the user to complete the actions on the form before working on any other part of the program. ■

After a form is displayed, you have two choices for getting rid of it. The Hide method removes the form from the screen but does not remove it from memory. This is useful when you need to temporarily remove the form from view, but you are not finished working on the form. More typically, you will remove the form from both the screen and memory. To remove the form from memory, you must use the Unload statement. If the form is still displayed when the Unload statement is issued, the form is first removed from the screen and then from memory. The Unload statement uses basically the same syntax as the Load statement, as shown here:

```
Unload frmMember
```

T I P If you are using the `Unload` statement from within the form you are removing, you can use the keyword `Me` to specify the form. This prevents errors if you later rename your form. In this case, the statement would be the following:

```
Unload Me
```

Using *Load* to Enhance Performance

Because the `Show` method automatically loads a form into memory, it typically is not necessary to use the `Load` statement in your program at all. However, some forms with a large number of controls display very slowly when they are shown. One way around this is to load the form into memory, using the `Load` statement, when the program is initially run. Then the `Show` method appears to perform much more quickly. If you use this trick, be careful of two things. First, when you remove the form from view, use only the `Hide` method; do not unload the form. You will, however, need to unload the form at the end of your program. Second, be aware of possible memory limitations. If you load too many forms in memory at once, you may see a decline in the overall performance of your program.

Loading the form into memory does increase the amount of time that it takes for your program to start, but you will save time whenever the form is shown. If you only show a form once during the program, there is no net time savings. However, if the form is shown more than once, there is an overall time savings. Also, users are typically more tolerant of time delays when a program loads than when they are performing a task.

Handling Events (*Load* and *Activate*)

In the section "Dealing with Actions," you learned that most objects respond to events or actions that are taken by a user, the program, or the operating system. With a form, there are four special events that occur in every program:

- ◼ **Load**   Occurs when the form is loaded into memory.
- ◼ **Activate**   Occurs when the form is displayed initially or when the user returns to the form from another form.
- ◼ **Deactivate**   Occurs when the user moves to another form or the form is hidden.
- ◼ **Unload**   Occurs when the form is unloaded from memory.

You can use program code in these events to set the properties of the form or any of its controls, set up databases or recordsets needed for the form, or run any other code that you might find necessary. The `Load` and `Unload` events each occur only once in the life of a form: when the form is loaded and unloaded from memory, respectively. On the other hand, the `Activate` and `Deactivate` events can occur many times. Therefore, you need to be careful which code is placed in which event.

The following code segments show you a couple of simple but useful things that you can do with code in the `Load` event. The first code segment shows how a form can be centered on the screen.

```
Private Sub Form_Load()
Dim LeftPos, TopPos As Integer
LeftPos = Int((Screen.Width - Me.Width) / 2)
TopPos = Int((Screen.Height - Me.Height) / 2)
Me.Left = LeftPos
Me.Top = TopPos
End Sub
```

This code is shown in the Load event of the form, but you could also use the code in the Resize event to make sure that the form stayed centered when the user changed the form's size.

It's also useful to maximize the form as it is displayed. This involves simply setting the WindowState property of the form when the form is loaded. This is done as follows:

```
Me.WindowState = 2
```

Notice in both of the preceding code segments that I used the keyword Me to refer to the form. This makes it easy to use the code for multiple forms. You could also write a procedure or class that took the form name as an argument and performed the center or maximize operation.

Using Controls

Forms provide the windows for your programs, but the Visual Basic controls do most of the work for the programs that you create. These controls let you display and edit text, display pictures, interface with a database, and perform many other tasks. Since version 1, controls have been one of Visual Basic's strongest features. Because of the Visual Basic design, you are not limited to using only the controls provided with Visual Basic. The design allows easy integration of third-party controls—which has led to a thriving market for these controls. With this amount of third-party involvement, chances are that you can find a control to perform almost any task you want. There are controls for handling word processing and for creating flowcharts, as well as controls for displaying graphics and creating business charts.

What Are Controls

Controls are objects in Visual Basic that are designed to perform specific tasks. Each control is, in essence, a miniature program that accepts input and provides output through its properties. For example, if you use a text box, you can set properties to determine the size of the text box, the font for the text that it displays, and the color of the display. The text box is coded to correctly size and display the text, based on the property values that you assign. Also, a text box has internal code that allows it to process keystrokes, so that it knows to erase a character when you press the Backspace key. If you wrote programs in earlier languages, particularly in the DOS and mainframe environments, you know that you may have had to write a significant amount of code just to accept and process keystrokes that allowed the user to enter input. Now you just drop a control on your form, and the rest is done for you.

Visual Basic comes with a standard set of controls that are available in all versions and that let you perform many types of programming tasks. These controls and their functions are listed in Table 3.5, and they are indicated in the toolbox shown in Figure 3.8. Many of these controls are discussed in detail in the section "What Can Controls Do"

Table 3.5   Standard Controls in Visual Basic

Control Name	Function
PictureBox	Displays graphics images. Also serves as a container for other controls.
Label	Displays text.
TextBox	Displays text and allows the user to enter and edit text.
Frame	Serves as a container for other controls.
CommandButton	Lets the user initiate actions by clicking the button.
CheckBox	Lets the user make True/False choices.
OptionButton	Lets the user choose one of a group of items.
ComboBox	Lets the user choose from a list of items or enter a new value.
ListBox	Lets the user choose from a list of items.
Horizontal ScrollBar	Lets the user choose a value based on the position of the button in the bar.
Vertical ScrollBar	Same as Horizontal ScrollBar.
Timer	Lets the program perform functions on a timed event.
Drive List Box	Lets the user select a disk drive.
Directory List Box	Lets the user select a directory or folder.
File List Box	Lets the user select a file.
Shape	Displays a shape on the form.
Line	Displays a line on the form.
Image	Displays pictures or graphics images.
Data Control	Provides an interface between the program and a data source.
OLE	Provides a connection between the program and an OLE server.
Common Dialog	Allows use of Windows standard dialog boxes to retrieve information such as file names, fonts, and colors.

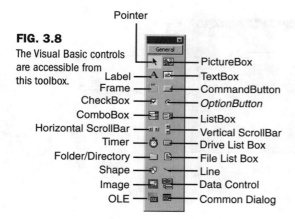

FIG. 3.8
The Visual Basic controls are accessible from this toolbox.

Pointer

Label
Frame
CheckBox
ComboBox
Horizontal ScrollBar
Timer
Folder/Directory
Shape
Image
OLE

PictureBox
TextBox
CommandButton
OptionButton
ListBox
Vertical ScrollBar
Drive List Box
File List Box
Line
Data Control
Common Dialog

Part
I

Ch
3

Adding Controls to the Form

To be able to use any of the available controls, you must first add them to your form. To add a control, you simply select the control from the toolbox and then draw it on your form by clicking the form and dragging the mouse to set the control's size. As you drag the mouse, you will see a "rubber band" box appear on the form, indicating the current size of the control. When you release the mouse button, the control is drawn on the form in the size and position that you want. This is indicated in Figure 3.9.

After you draw the control on the form, you can set the properties of the control using the Properties dialog box. Remember, you should always provide a unique name for each control.

Setting and Retrieving Property Values

Setting properties at design time using the Properties dialog box is one way that you can set properties. However, for the controls to be really useful in your programs, you need to be able to set the properties in code and, more important, retrieve the values of the properties. For example, you know that a user can enter text in a text box, but in order to be able to use the text, you need to be able to get it out of the control and into your code. Because the text is stored as a property of the text box, you can retrieve the text from the property.

FIG. 3.9
Drawing a control on a
form is similar to using
the Paint program.

Selected control

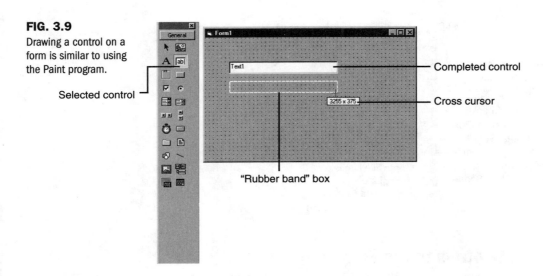

Completed control

Cross cursor

"Rubber band" box

When you are using a control's property in code, you can use it just like you would a variable or constant. You can use the properties in comparison statements to make decisions, and you can use them in assignment statements to set the value of a variable. You can also use an assignment statement to set the value of a property. The following code shows how the Text property of a text box is used to retrieve a name entered by the user, capitalize the first letter, and display the modified text back to the user:

```
Dim InptStr As String
InptStr = txtName.Text
Mid(InptStr, 1, 1) = UCase(Left(InptStr, 1))
txtName.Text = InptStr
```

To reference a property of a control in code, you must specify the name of the control (remember the Name property) and the name of the property. When specifying the names, the name of the control and the name of the property are separated by a period or dot. As seen in the previous code, the name of the control, txtName, comes first, followed by the dot; then the name of the property, Text, is specified. This notation can be used to reference any property of any control. Be aware, however, that some properties are read-only at runtime, and some are available only at runtime. To be certain, check the control's help files.

N O T E If you are referring to a control on a form other than the current form, you also need to specify the name of the form. The form name precedes the control name and is separated from it by a dot. For example:

```
frmMember.txtName.Text
```

It is good programming practice to always specify the name of the property, but many controls have what is known as a *value property*. This is a default property for the control and can be referenced simply by specifying the name of the control. For example, the Text property is the value property of the `TextBox` control. Therefore, the following two statements work exactly the same:

```
'**************************************
'Property name specifically referenced
'**************************************
txtName.Text = "Mike"
'**********************
'Property name omitted
'**********************
txtName = "Mike"
```

Table 3.6 shows the value property of a number of controls.

Table 3.6   The Value Property of Standard Controls

Control Type	Value Property
Check box	Value
Combo box	Text
Directory list box	Path
Drive list box	Drive
File list box	FileName
Horizontal scroll bar	Value
Image	Picture
Label	Caption
Option button	Value
Picture box	Picture
Text box	Text
Vertical scroll bar	Value

Finding Out What Controls Can Do

In the previous sections, you learned a little about what controls are and how to add them to a form so you can use them in your programs. You also learned how you can set property values of a control in the Properties dialog box and in code, and even how to retrieve the values of the properties for use in your code. In this section, you will learn what specific controls can do for you in your programs. For each of the controls covered, you'll learn some basic functions and how to set and use the properties. This is by no means an exhaustive discussion of everything that each control can do; rather, it's a way to get you started.

Working with Text

One of the most common tasks in programming is working with text. Now, *text* here does not just mean paragraphs and sentences like those you handle with a word processor. When you deal with text in a program, you also may want to display or retrieve a single word, a number, or even a date. For example, in a data-entry program, you may need to handle the name, address, phone number, date of birth, and other information about a member. Each of these pieces of information can be handled using the text-display and -editing controls of Visual Basic. Figure 3.10 shows a data-entry screen for a membership application.

FIG. 3.10

You can handle all types of information with text controls.

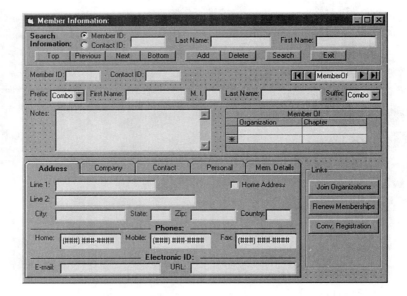

Visual Basic provides several controls that let you handle text. Three of the major controls are the Label, TextBox, and RichTextBox controls. These three controls can handle most of your text-editing and -display needs.

Using a Label to Display Text   The simplest control that displays text is the Label control. The most common use of the Label control is identifying different items on a form, such as the data-entry form shown in Figure 3.10. Each label identifies the information in the edit field next to it. Used in this way, each label typically is set up in the design mode, and the necessary text is assigned to the Caption property using the Properties dialog box.

However, you are not limited to using the Label control in this manner. In fact, you can use the Label control to display any type of information to the user. A label can display a date, a number, a single word, or even an entire paragraph of information. You can display up to 64,000 characters of text in the Label control, provided that your control and your form are large enough.

While the `Caption` property of the `Label` control contains the text to be displayed, there are other properties of the control that influence *how* the text is displayed. The most obvious of these properties are the `Font` and `ForeColor` properties, which determine the typeface and text color of the control, respectively. However, if you are going to use the label to display more than a small amount of text, the `AutoSize` and `WordWrap` properties are the ones that will be most important to you.

The `WordWrap` property determines whether the text in a label can occupy multiple lines of the control. If the `WordWrap` property is set to `False`, the text can appear only on a single line. If the text is longer than will appear on the one line, the end of the text is cut off the screen, even though the information is still contained in the `Caption` property. If the `WordWrap` property is set to `True`, and the control is tall enough to support multiple lines of text, the text wraps around to additional lines when the end of the control is reached. This is illustrated in Figure 3.11.

FIG. 3.11
The setting of the WordWrap property determines whether or not a label can display text on multiple lines.

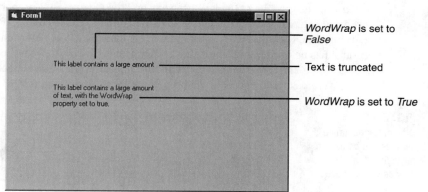

WordWrap is set to *False*

Text is truncated

WordWrap is set to *True*

If you know in advance what text is going to be displayed in the label, you can set the size of the label to accommodate the text. However, if different text will be displayed in the label at different times (for instance, in a database application), you need to be able to handle different lengths of text. The `AutoSize` property of the `Label` control determines whether or not the size of the control automatically adjusts to fit the text being displayed. How the control adjusts is also determined by the setting of the `WordWrap` property. If the `WordWrap` property is set to `False`, setting the `AutoSize` property to `True` causes the label to expand horizontally. If the `WordWrap` property is set to `True`, the width of the label remains constant, and the control expands vertically to accommodate the text. The effects of the different settings of the `WordWrap` and `AutoSize` properties are shown in Figure 3.12.

CAUTION

To preserve the original width of your `Label` control, you must set the `WordWrap` property to `True` before setting the `AutoSize` property. Otherwise, when you set the `AutoSize` property to `True`, the `Label` control adjusts to fit the current contents of the `Caption` property.

FIG. 3.12
Setting the AutoSize property to True lets the label adjust to fit the text.

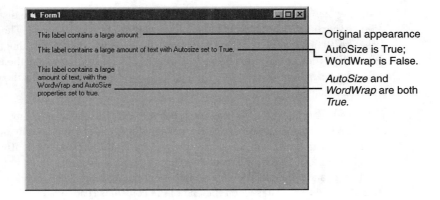

— Original appearance

— AutoSize is True; WordWrap is False.

— *AutoSize* and *WordWrap* are both *True.*

There are two other properties that, from time to time, you may need to use with the Label control. These are the Alignment property and the BorderStyle property. The Alignment property determines how the text is aligned within the Label control. The possible options are Left-Justified, Right-Justified, and Centered. The BorderStyle determines whether the Label control has no border or a single-line border around the label. With the BorderStyle set to Fixed Single, the Label control takes on the appearance of a non-editable text box. The effects of the Alignment and BorderStyle properties are shown in Figure 3.13.

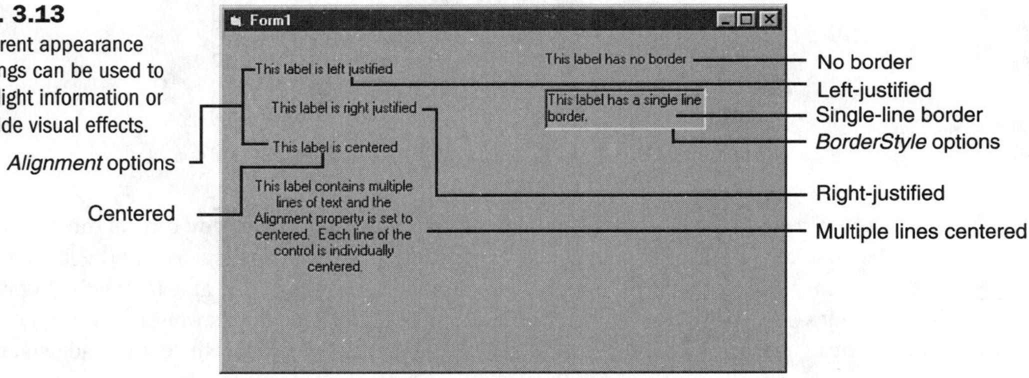

FIG. 3.13
Different appearance settings can be used to highlight information or provide visual effects.

Alignment options

Centered

— No border
— Left-justified
— Single-line border
— *BorderStyle* options

— Right-justified
— Multiple lines centered

N O T E The Alignment property also affects the text when the label is used to display multiple lines. The control aligns each line according to the setting of the Alignment property, as shown in Figure 3.13. ▪

Entering Text with a *TextBox* Because most of what programs do is retrieve and display text, you might guess (and you would be correct) that the major workhorse of many programs is the text box. The text box allows you to display text, but more important, it also provides an easy way for your users to enter and edit text and for your program to retrieve the information that was entered.

In many cases, you will use the text box to handle a single piece of information, such as a name or address. But the text box is capable of handling up to 64,000 characters of information. All the information displayed in a text box is stored in the Text property of the text box—the main property with which your programs will interact.

By default, the text box is set up to handle a single line of information. This is adequate for most purposes, but occasionally your program will need to handle a larger amount of text. The text box has two properties that are useful for handling larger amounts of text: the MultiLine and ScrollBar properties.

The MultiLine property determines whether the information in a text box is displayed on a single line or multiple lines. If the MultiLine property is set to True, information is displayed on multiple lines, and word-wrapping is handled automatically. The ScrollBar property determines whether or not scroll bars will be displayed in a text box, and if so, what type of scroll bars. The scroll bars are useful if more text is stored in the Text property than will fit in the text box. You can choose to have horizontal or vertical scroll bars, or both, in your text box. The ScrollBar property has an effect on the text box only if the MultiLine property is set to True. Figure 3.14 shows the effects of the MultiLine and ScrollBar properties.

Part
I
Ch
3

FIG. 3.14
You can use a text box to enter single lines of text or entire paragraphs.

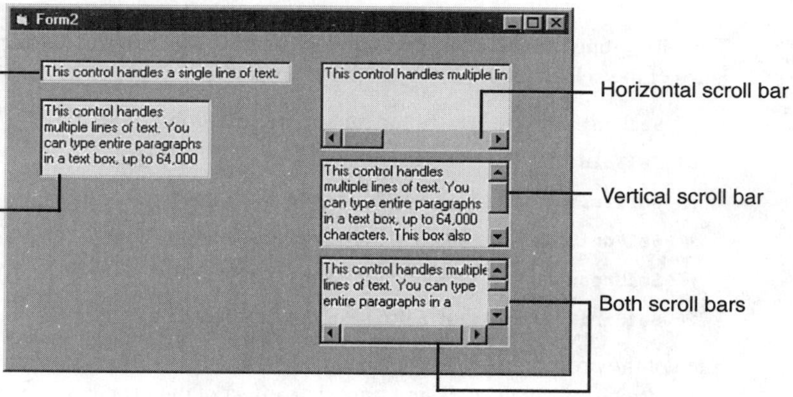

Single-line text box

Multiple-line text box

Horizontal scroll bar

Vertical scroll bar

Both scroll bars

TROUBLESHOOTING

The text box in my program will handle only 32,000 characters instead of the 64,000 specified in the documentation. When you use the default value of 0 for the MaxLength property, this corresponds to a limit of 32,000 characters. To allow more characters, set the MaxLength property to the desired value, but do not exceed 64,000.

Fancy Text with the *RichTextBox* Control   The text box is great for most of your editing needs. However, sometimes you need to edit even more information than the text box can handle. Or, more likely, you want to give your users more than one font with which to edit information, as would be available with a word processor. Because the text box allows only one font for all the text, what are you supposed to do? Well, help comes in the form of the RichTextBox control.

The `RichTextBox` control uses Rich Text Format (RTF) code to handle multiple formats within a single control. RTF codes are stored with the actual words of the text so that the format information is preserved. Figure 3.15 shows how some formatted text looks on the screen and how the RTF codes are stored to handle the formatting information.

FIG. 3.15
RTF information is enclosed in curly brackets ({}).

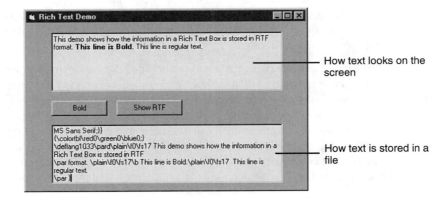

How text looks on the screen

How text is stored in a file

The formatting of the text is controlled by a series of properties that change the font characteristics of the selected text. Here are those properties:

- **SelFontName**   Changes the font of the selection.
- **SelBold**   Makes the selection bold.
- **SelItalic**   Makes the selection italic.
- **SelFontSize**   Changes the size of the selection's font.
- **SelUnderline**   Underlines the selection.
- **SelStrikeThru**   Shows the selection in strikethrough mode.

Each of the preceding properties can be set using an assignment statement in code. The properties are not available at design time. The effect of the property is determined by whether or not text is selected. If text is selected when the property is changed, only the selected text is affected. If there is no text selected when the property is changed, the new setting affects any text typed at the insertion point after the change. This works just like most word processors. Figure 3.16 shows a simple formatting program that makes use of the `RichTextBox` control. The code to handle the formatting is given in Listing 3.1.

Listing 3.1   Richtext.frm—Assignment Statements to Set Text Properties

```
'***********************************************
'This command button turns on the Bold setting
'***********************************************
Private Sub cmdBold_Click()
    rtbTextEdit.SelBold = True
End Sub
```

```
'***************************************************
'This command button turns on the Italic setting
'***************************************************
Private Sub cmdItalic_Click()
    rtbTextEdit.SelItalic = True
End Sub
'****************************************************
'This command button turns on the Underline setting
'****************************************************
Private Sub cmdUnderline_Click()
    rtbTextEdit.SelUnderline = True
End Sub
'*****************************************************
'This command button turns on the Strikethru setting
'*****************************************************
Private Sub cmdStrikethru_Click()
    rtbTextEdit.SelStrikethru = True
End Sub
'******************************************************
'This command button changes the font of the selection
'******************************************************
Private Sub cmdFontChange_Click()
    rtbTextEdit.SelFontName = "Times New Roman"
End Sub
'******************************************************
'This command button changes the size of the selection
'******************************************************
Private Sub cmdNewSize_Click()
    rtbTextEdit.SelFontSize = 14
End Sub
```

FIG. 3.16
You can format selected
text by clicking the
appropriate command
button.

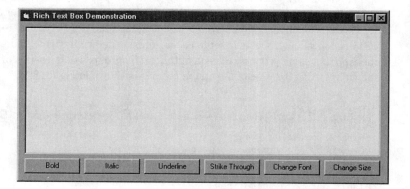

 The project containing this sample program is located on the book's Web site, **http://www.quecorp.com/sevb5**.

In addition to handling multiple fonts, the RichTextBox control handles text alignment and different forms of indentation.

Making Choices

While handling text is important for most applications, sometimes you just need to allow the user to make some simple choices. This may be a simple yes or no, or it may involve choosing among several possibilities. Two of Visual Basic's controls are designed to handle choices: CheckBox and OptionButton.

The CheckBox control allows a user to make a simple yes or no choice. When the user clicks the check box, the box toggles between the yes and no states. The yes state is indicated by a check mark in the box. The no state is indicated by an empty box. The state of the box is stored in the control's value property: 0 for an unchecked box and 1 for a checked box. These states are shown in Figure 3.17.

FIG. 3.17

A check box can be used to make simple choices.

N O T E   There is a third possible value for the check box: 2-Grayed. This is generally used to indicate that no choice has been made.

When you have a situation that requires more than a yes/no choice, you can use *option buttons*. These buttons are always used in groups to indicate one of a number of possible choices. When option buttons are placed on a form, they create an *option group*. Within this group, only one of the buttons may be selected at a time. When a button is chosen, all other buttons in the group are cleared. When an option button is selected, its value property is set to True. For the other buttons, the value property is set to False. You can determine which button was selected by checking the value property of each button in the group, using a series of If statements as shown in Listing 3.2. Use of the option buttons is shown in Figure 3.18.

Listing 3.2   OptDemo.frm—*If* Statements Determine Option Button Selection

```
If optGreen.Value Then
    MsgBox "Your eyes are green"
ElseIf optBlue.Value Then
    MsgBox "Your eyes are blue"
ElseIf optBrown.Value Then
    MsgBox "Your eyes are brown"
End If
```

FIG. 3.18
Option buttons can
handle a series of
possible choices.

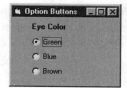

Handling Lists

While check boxes and option buttons are good for handling simple choices or small numbers of choices, there are many occasions that require your presenting the user with a larger number of choices. For this purpose, Visual Basic provides two controls that handle lists: the ListBox and ComboBox controls.

Both the ListBox control and the ComboBox control let you present the user with a list of choices from which to select an item. The key difference between the two controls is that a combo box allows the user to enter an item that is not on the list. Read a little further to take a closer look at these two controls.

Parts of a List Box   Figure 3.19 shows a simple list that you might use to let the user select a state abbreviation for a mailing label. As you can see, the ListBox control consists of the list of items and a scroll bar. The list is usually a group of related items; for example, state codes, job classifications, or cafeteria items. Typically, the items in a list are all text items. Lists are not typically used for handling numerical input.

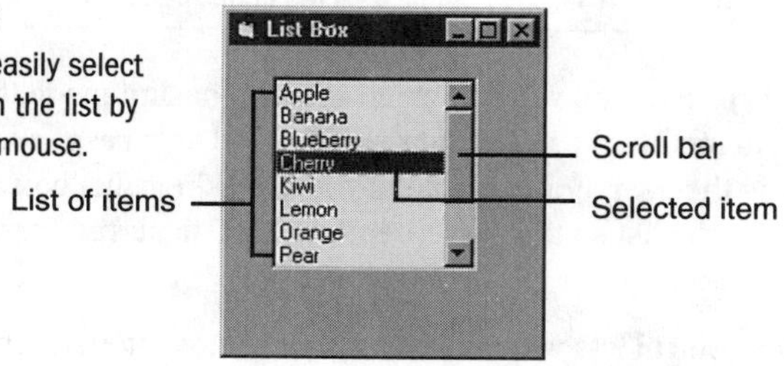

FIG. 3.19
A user can easily select
an item from the list by
clicking the mouse.

List of items ⎯⎯⎯⎯

Scroll bar

Selected item

To select an item from the list, the user can use the scroll bars to move about in the list and can then click the desired item with the mouse. The selected item is indicated by a *highlight bar,* which on most systems is a blue bar with white text. The user can also move the highlight bar up and down through the list by using the cursor keys.

Setting Up a *ListBox* Control   To set up a ListBox control, you first draw it on your form just as you would any other control. Initially, the list box contains no list items; it simply shows the name of the control in the list. You should, of course, name the control after you create it. After placing the control on the form and naming it, you add items from which the user can select.

Part
I

Ch
3

The list items are stored in a string array contained in the List property of the list box. Each list item is an element of the string array. To add items to the list, select the List property from the Properties dialog box and then click the arrow at the right of the field. This presents you with an edit area where you can enter items.

To add an item to the list, just type the item's name in the edit area and then press Enter to accept it. The list box then displays all the items you have added. If you have more items than will fit in the list box, the box also displays a scroll bar. Figure 3.20 shows a completed list in design mode.

FIG. 3.20
You create a list by adding items to the List property.

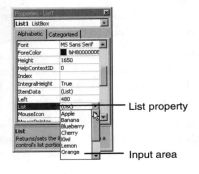

List items

List box

List property

Input area

 TIP To enter more than one item at a time, press Ctrl+Enter after typing each item to accept the entry and move to the next line of the input area. After you have finished entering all the items, press Enter.

Modifying the List from Code   Typically, you will set up your lists in design mode, but there may be occasions when you want to modify the items displayed in the list in response to events in the program or events caused by the user. For example, if you are using a list box to display food items, you might want to set up the list so that meat items are not displayed for a vegetarian user.

To accommodate this, the ListBox control lets you add items to or remove items from the list box as the program is running. You can place code to accomplish this in any control event. If you want, you can even place code in the Load event of your form to set up the initial list, instead of typing the entries in through the Properties dialog box. To add items to the list, you use the AddItem and RemoveItem methods.

Use the AddItem method to add a list item to a ListBox or ComboBox control. The AddItem method performs the same function that you do when you write a new item on your grocery list. The AddItem method is used as follows:

```
Listname.AddItem listitem [, index]
```

In the preceding statement, Listname refers to the control name of the list box or combo box to which the item will be added. AddItem is the name of the method. The word listitem refers to the particular item that you are adding. This can be a word, a number, a group of words, or any

other text. If the item is anything but a number, it must be enclosed in a pair of double quotes
(" "). The index is an optional entry that specifies the list position at which the new item will be
placed. (Note that the first item in a list has an index of 0.) For example, say that you had a list
consisting of Orange, Apple, Lemon, and Pear, and you entered the following line:

```
lstFruits.AddItem "Tangerine", 1
```

Tangerine would be placed in the list between Orange and Apple. If you include the index, it
must be separated from the item by a comma. If you do not include the index, the item is
placed at the end of the list, or in the proper sort order if the Sorted property is True.

To delete an item from the list (equivalent to using the eraser on your grocery list), you use the
RemoveItem method as follows:

```
Listname.RemoveItem index
```

In the case of the RemoveItem method, the index must be entered. This is the only way for the
program to know which item to remove. The following code removes the first item of the list.

```
lstFruits.RemoveItem 0
```

TIP If you want to remove all the items in a list, use the Clear method, (that is, lstFruits.Clear). In
essence, this method throws away your entire list.

Determining the User's Selection   In order to use the information that the user selected from
the list, you need to determine which item was selected. This is handled using the ListIndex
and List properties of the ListBox control. The ListIndex property tells you the index number of the item that was selected. You can then use the index number to retrieve the actual item
from the List property. If the ListIndex property is –1, no item was selected. The following
code displays the selected item in a text box.

```
idx = lstFruits.ListIndex
If idx < 0 Then
   txtChosen.Text = "No item was selected."
Else
   txtChosen.Text = lstFruits.List(idx)
End If
```

Allowing Multiple Choices   You have probably worked with lists that allow you to select more
than one item at a time. You can implement this in your list boxes, as well. To do this, you set
the value of the MultiSelect property. This property has three possible settings: 0 - None, 1 -
Simple, and 2 - Extended.

A setting of "0 - None" means that multiple selections are not allowed, and the list box can
accept only one selection at a time. This is the default setting. Both of the other two settings
allow multiple selections; the difference is in how they let the user make selections.

With a setting of "1 - Simple," you click an item with the mouse to select it or click a selected
item to deselect it. If you are using the keyboard to make your selection, use the cursor keys to
move the focus (the dotted-line border) to an item and then press the spacebar to select or
deselect it. Figure 3.21 shows a list with multiple items selected.

Part
I

Ch
3

FIG. 3.21

You can select multiple items from a list with the proper setting of the `MultiSelect` property.

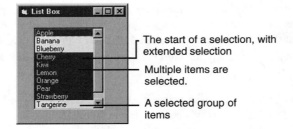

The start of a selection, with extended selection

Multiple items are selected.

A selected group of items

The final setting of `MultiSelect`, "2 - Extended," is the most complex. In this mode, you can quickly select a range of items. With the mouse, click the first item in the range and then, while holding down the Shift key, click the last item in the range. All the items between the first and last item are selected. If you want to add or delete a single item, hold down the Ctrl key while you click the item.

Retrieving Multiple Choices   If you give the user the option of selecting multiple items, obviously you want to be able to retrieve all the items selected. This is a little different and slightly more complicated than determining the selection of a single item. Because the `ListIndex` property works only for a single selection, it can't be used in this case. Instead, you must examine each item in the list to determine if it is selected.

Whether or not an item is selected is indicated by the `Selected` property. This property is an array that has an element for each item in the list. The value of the `Selected` property for each item is either `True` (the item is selected) or `False` (the item is not selected).

In addition, you need to know how many items are in the list, so you can be sure that all the items are checked. This information is contained in the `ListCount` property. The following code prints the name of each selected item on the form:

```
numidx = Fruits.ListCount
For I = 0 to numidx - 1
    If Fruits.Selected(I) Then Form1.Print Fruits.List(I)
Next I
```

How a Combo Box Differs from a List Box   The other control for handling lists is the `ComboBox` control. In many ways, the `ComboBox` control is similar to the `ListBox` control. Both controls use the `List` property to store the items in the list. Both let you use the `AddItem`, `RemoveItem`, and `Clear` methods to modify the list from code. And both let the user select an item in the list with the simple click of a mouse.

The key feature supported by the `ComboBox` control and not supported by the `ListBox` control is that the user can enter in the text area of the combo box an item that is not on the list. As an example of the usefulness of this feature, consider a personnel application requiring information about the college that a person attended. You could use a combo box to supply the user with a list of major universities. However, if the college attended was not on the list, the information could be entered in the text portion of the combo box.

N O T E   The drop-down-list style for a combo box does not allow the user to input other values. ■

The key feature of a list box that is not supported by a combo box is the capability to select multiple items. A combo box supports selection of only a single item at a time.

Styles of Combo Boxes   There are three combo-box styles that can be used in Visual Basic:

- ■ **DropDown Combo**   This is the default style for combo boxes. The ComboBox control contains an edit area and a list that drops down when the user clicks the arrow. After the user makes a selection, the list rolls back up, and the selected item is displayed in the edit area. Users can enter items that are not on the list.

- ■ **Simple Combo**   This style also contains an edit area and a list of items. However, the list does not drop down. The user still may select an item from the list or enter a new item. The default size for this style does not show any of the list. In this case, the user moves through the list using the cursor keys.

- ■ **DropDown List**   This style is similar to the DropDown combo, except that it does not allow the user to enter an item that is not on the list.

Setting Up the *ComboBox* Control   Setting up a ComboBox control is similar to setting up a ListBox control. You simply draw the control on your form and set its properties. You set the Style property to determine which type of combo box to display, and you will probably want to enter a series of items in the List property of the ComboBox control.

Depending on your application, you might want to set the initial item for a combo box. For example, if a program needed to know the user's citizenship, you could provide a list of choices but set the initial value to US citizen, because that would be the selection for most people in this country.

You set the initial value using the ListIndex property, as shown in the following code:

```
cboFruits.ListIndex = 3
```

The preceding statement causes the fourth item in the list to be displayed when the combo box is first shown. (Remember, the list indexes start at 0.) Setting the initial choice works with any of the three combo-box styles. If you do not set an initial choice, the first item in the list is displayed.

Retrieving the User's Choice   Getting the user's choice from a combo box is different from getting the choice from a list box. With a combo box, you must be able to handle the possibility of the user's entering a value that is not on the list. You can get the user's choice with the Text property of the combo box. The Text property holds any value typed in by the user, or the item selected from the list. The following line of code would store the user's selection to a variable for further processing:

```
SelFruit = cboFruits.Text
```

Actions

One final control important to most of the applications that you will develop is the CommandButton control. Typically, this control is used to let the user initiate actions in your program. The setup of a CommandButton control is quite simple. You draw the button on the form and then set the Caption property of the button to the text that you want displayed on the button's face. To activate the button, you simply place code in the Click event of the button. As with code for any other event, this code can consist of any number of valid Visual Basic programming statements.

While users most often will use command buttons by clicking them, some users prefer accessing commands through the keyboard versus using the mouse. This is often the case for data-entry intensive programs. To accommodate these users, you want your program to trigger command-button events when certain keys are pressed. You accomplish this by assigning an access key to the command button. When an access key is defined, the user holds down the Alt key and presses the access key to trigger the Click event of the CommandButton control.

You assign an access key in the CommandButton control's Caption property. Simply place an ampersand (&) in front of the letter of the key you want to use. For example, if you want the user to be able to press Alt+P to run a print command button, you set the Caption property to &Print. The ampersand does not show up on the button, but the letter for the access key is underlined. Figure 3.22 shows several command buttons with different access keys. The figure also shows the Properties dialog box, which shows the Caption property of one of the buttons.

FIG. 3.22
You can assign access keys to your command buttons to let the user trigger the button from the keyboard.

In addition to assigning access keys, you may set one command button on your form as the default button. This way, the user can simply press Enter on any control (except another command button) to access the default button. This triggers the Click event of the button, just as if the user had clicked the button with the mouse. To set up a button as the default button, simply set the Default property of the button to True. Only one button on a form may be the default button.

You can also set up a button that is triggered if the user presses the Esc key. For this button, you set the Cancel property of the button to True. There can be only one default and one Cancel button on any one form. As you set the value of the Default and/or Cancel property of one button to True, the properties of all other buttons are set to False.

From Here...

This chapter covered a lot of material about forms and controls, specifically how their appearance and behavior was controlled through property settings. You also saw how forms and controls could take action through their methods. If you want to learn more about related issues, refer to the following chapters:

- Chapter 4, "Understanding the Event Model," will teach you how events are handled by your programs.
- Chapter 6, "Programming in Visual Basic," teaches you how to write program code.
- Chapter 8, "Introduction to Classes," shows you how to use classes and objects in your programs.
- Chapter 32, "Advanced Control Techniques," and Chapter 33, "Advanced Form Techniques," gives you a more in-depth look at some of the capabilities of forms and controls.

Part
I

Ch
3

Understanding the Event Model

While the concept of an event-driven program may be fairly new to you, the idea of responding to events should not be. Most of the world is what we would call *event-driven*. For example, consider your TV. You can change the channel whenever you feel like it, and with today's remote controls, you can go directly to your favorite channel instead of having to scroll through all the channels on the TV. By the same token, you can change the volume of the TV whenever you want by as much as you want. You probably can also cut out the sound altogether by pressing the Mute button. This type of control exhibits event-driven programming. You, the user of your TV, initiate events (by pressing a button) that cause the TV to take actions. You also control when these events happen. ■

Programs that work the way a user thinks

Event-driven programs let the users execute tasks in almost any order. This lets them process information in the way they find most comfortable.

Common events you will encounter

Take a look at many of the events common to most of a program's graphical elements.

A new way to program

Event-driven programs are dramatically different from traditional procedural programs. See how these differences require a change in how you create the program.

Multiple events from a single user action

One action taken by a user may trigger a single event or a series of events. Learn about the sequence of events and how to plan for them.

Living in an Event-Driven World

If you have worked much with Windows programs, you probably have noticed that they work in a similar manner. In Microsoft Word, for example, you can easily change the font or style of a piece of text. You also can highlight a section of text and drag it to a new location. Each of these actions is made possible by the program's ability to take actions in response to user-initiated events.

As you create your own Windows programs, you will seek to model the program after the real-world tasks that the program is supposed to handle. This means that you will want to give the users command buttons or menu selections so that they can perform tasks when they want. Figure 4.1 shows an example of the interface for an event-driven program.

FIG. 4.1

Graphical user interfaces go hand in hand with event-driven programming.

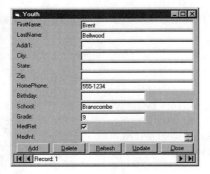

The other advantage of event-driven programming is that you can use the events to provide immediate feedback to the user. For example, you can program an event to verify a user's entry as soon as the user finishes typing. Then, if there is a problem with what the user entered, he or she knows immediately and can fix it. This type of feedback is handled by code such as that shown in the following code segment, which checks the age that a user has entered.

Listing 4.1   AgeCheck.txt—Code to Verify the Age Entered

```
Private Sub txtAge_LostFocus()
Dim InptAge As Integer
InptAge = Val(txtAge.Text)
If InptAge <= 0 Then
    MsgBox "You must enter an age greater than 0", vbCritical
End If
If InptAge > 120 Then
    MsgBox "Are you sure the person is this old?", vbCritical
End If
End Sub
```

Changing the Way You Think

If you are a programmer coming from a traditional procedural language such as COBOL or FORTRAN, you probably are eager to get into the specifics of Visual Basic's programming language. However, if you jump right into the Visual Basic code without understanding the event model, you quickly will be lost. This is because in Visual Basic—unlike more traditional languages—you cannot simply replace one command with another and expect to write programs in the new language.

It is true that all programming languages are different. Even more traditional languages such as COBOL and FORTRAN have different strengths and weaknesses. COBOL is great for business applications, and FORTRAN's strength is its scientific and mathematical capabilities.

Even though COBOL and FORTRAN are used to write different kinds of programs, a programmer who knows COBOL can pick up a FORTRAN manual and begin to write programs immediately. Where normally you would use COBOL's WRITE statement, you'd quickly see that FORTRAN also has a WRITE statement. Rather than defining the output format in a DATA DIVISION statement, FORTRAN defines the output with a FORMAT statement. Although you would not become a FORTRAN programming expert overnight, you could be productive in a matter of a couple of hours.

Even the brightest of programmers, however, have a much more difficult time making the programming transition to a GUI-based language such as Visual Basic. Programmers moving from COBOL to Visual Basic face the following two obstacles:

- The language differences between COBOL and Visual Basic.
- The philosophical differences between COBOL and Visual Basic. Programmers must approach a Visual Basic program differently than a more traditional language.

If Visual Basic were another more traditional, text-based language, programmers would face only the challenge of a language conversion. The dual problem of the language conversion combined with the paradigm shift adds an extra burden to anyone making the move.

In the past, how did your users inform your programs of their intent? In other words, if the user had the choice of adding, deleting, or printing records from a file, how did your COBOL program know what the user wanted to do?

One of the primary methods by which a traditional program provides the user a series of choices is with a menu. Look at the screen shown in Figure 4.2. The menu presents the user with a choice of five options. The program cannot know in advance which choice the user will make; however, the program does know that the user can and will select only one of the five choices.

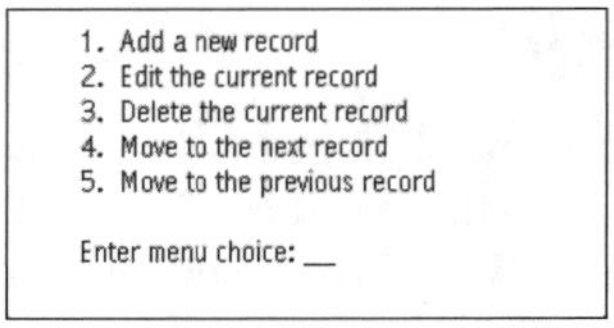

FIG. 4.2

There are several ways to code a user's menu selection using COBOL. Listing 4.2 shows one way, using a GO TO...DEPENDING ON statement.

```
1. Add a new record
2. Edit the current record
3. Delete the current record
4. Move to the next record
5. Move to the previous record

Enter menu choice: __
```

Listing 4.2   MenuSel.txt—One Way COBOL Can Handle the User's Menu Selection

```
GO TO PARA-ADD,
    PARA-CHANGE,
    PARA-DELETE,
    PARA-PRINT,
    PARA-END
DEPENDING ON USER-ANS.
```

There are other ways to handle the user's menu selection without the GO TO statement, however. Listing 4.3 shows the menu code handled with an IF statement and PERFORM statements, which call appropriate routines.

Listing 4.3   IFExampl.txt—The *IF* Statement Takes Care of the User's Menu Selection

```
IF USER-ANS = 1
    PERFORM PARA-ADD
ELSE IF USER-ANS = 2
    PERFORM PARA-CHANGE
ELSE IF USER-ANS = 3
    PERFORM PARA-DELETE
ELSE IF USER-ANS = 4
    PERFORM PARA-PRINT
ELSE IF USER-ANS = 5
    STOP RUN
ELSE PERFORM ERROR-RTN.
```

In a way, even this traditional, text-based menu shows an example of event-driven programming, albeit an example that is archaic in today's GUI world. An *event,* which in this case is the user's response, determines the course of action. Events are anything, including keystrokes, that determine a running program's next action. The user's response determines what the program does next; therefore, this program's event is the user's key press. The actual key pressed determines what the program executes.

When you shift to Windows programming, many more events in addition to keystroke events can occur. A Windows event also may be a mouse movement, a mouse click, a menu selection (using either the keyboard or the mouse), a window movement by the user, or even a programmed, internal clock timer hitting a preset time.

Not only are there more kinds of events possible in a Windows environment, but handling these events can be a difficult task. Fortunately, Visual Basic supplies programmers with all kinds of tools to work with events. Although scores of events may occur in a program at any given moment, Visual Basic enables the programmer to concentrate only on a subset of selected events required for the program's next course of action.

Figure 4.3 presents a programming scenario similar to the menu shown in Figure 4.2. Instead of a text-based environment, however, the menu routine has been converted to match a typical Windows-like environment. Study the figure and see if you can determine all the possible events that the user can trigger.

FIG. 4.3
Menus provide user choices in a windows program.

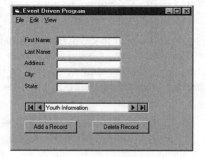

Here are the possible events that can be triggered in Figure 4.3:

- The user can edit text in one of the text boxes.
- The user can click one of the buttons on the data control.
- The user can click one of the command buttons.
- The user can select an item from the menu.
- The user can click or double-click the mouse button.
- The user can minimize the window.
- The user can move the program window.
- The user can close the program.

As you learn more about Windows, you'll see that there are several additional but less obvious events that also can take place. Many possible events aren't even triggered by the user, but for now we stick to the user-controlled events.

What is the user going to do after seeing the screen in Figure 4.3? You need to anticipate what events the user may trigger. For example, you cannot be sure that the user will select an option button before selecting from the menu. You know all the events that the user may do, but you don't know *if* the user will do any or all of the possible events.

N O T E Writing code to handle so many possible events becomes almost unmanageable unless you use the advanced programming tools provided by the Visual Basic programming environment. ▪

The traditional approach to programming is not suitable for all the possible events. If you wrote an extremely lengthy GO TO...DEPENDING statement that handled all possible events, you soon would find yourself in page after page of GO TO labels, and even the best-structured program rapidly would end up looking like spaghetti code. Perhaps a long, nested IF would be even worse.

When Windows senses an event taking place, it attempts to tell your running program about the event. Windows sends your running program a *message*; your program must interpret that message, determine which event the message refers to, and then act accordingly. A lot more work is required than simply checking a working-storage location for one of five values, as you can do with a text-based menu of five choices.

Visual Basic enables you to write routines (similar to COBOL's paragraphs) that execute *if and only if a certain event occurs*. Therefore, you'll write a routine that you want Visual Basic to execute only if the user clicks a certain command button or selects the first option. You'll write a routine for each menu option that Visual Basic executes only if the user selects that menu command.

Visual Basic eliminates the need for multiple-choice testing for events, which greatly improves the readability of programs, reduces the amount of code you have to write, and reduces the amount of debugging and maintenance time in the future. People often find that they are more productive when they write Visual Basic programs than they are with virtually any other programming language available.

N O T E When you first start programming in Visual Basic, you probably will use individual buttons and other controls to create the interface. As you progress to more advanced techniques, however, you're likely to use control arrays for some functions. In this case, you still will use multiple-choice testing to determine the program's course of action. ▪

Handling Events in Your Programs

As discussed, events in your Visual Basic program can be triggered by user actions, internal functions such as timers, or external factors such as receiving an e-mail message. There are hundreds—if not thousands—of events that can occur in any given program. You want your program to be able to isolate these events and take action for only specific ones. Fortunately, this is not as hard as it sounds.

You Never Check for Events

An event can happen at any time during a running Windows program's session. Without the aid of the Visual Basic event model, there would be almost no way for a programmer to handle the events that can occur.

One difficulty of Visual Basic programming that programmers from other environments face is that a programmer's program is not always in control of the user's next move. Windows is more than a pretty interface; it relieves you of the tedious burden of always checking for an event.

Concentrate your programming efforts on the user's interface and the data-manipulation needed. Windows lets your program know when an event takes place. When Windows notices an event, the program executes the code you wrote for that event. You never have to check for an event or directly execute specific, event-handling code. The event-handling may seem like magic to you at this point (it is magic compared to the old-fashioned ways), but soon you'll see how you set up a program so that Windows and Visual Basic work together.

With Visual Basic, each control or form in your program is capable of recognizing only a select group of events. However, the key to handling events is to write code for only the events where you want your program to take an action. This is done by selecting the particular control and event you want to handle and then writing some program code in the code window. If there is code written for an event, Visual Basic processes the code when the event occurs. If there is no code for an event, Visual Basic ignores the event. Figure 4.4 shows an example of an event procedure written for a specific control and event.

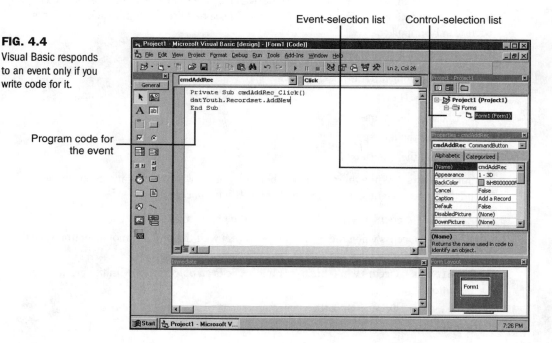

FIG. 4.4
Visual Basic responds to an event only if you write code for it.

Event-selection list   Control-selection list

Program code for the event

Part
I

Ch
4

Types of Events

There are two basic types of events that can occur in your Visual Basic program: *user-initiated events* and *system-initiated events*. Most often, you will program for the user-initiated events.

These events let your users control the direction of the program. That is, your users can take a specific action whenever they want, which gives them almost complete control over your program.

> **N O T E**   You can, of course, limit the actions that a user may take by hiding or disabling controls when you don't want the user to have access to them. This is covered in Chapter 3, "Using Forms and Controls." ▨

User-Initiated Events   User-initiated events are those that occur because of an action taken by the user. As you might guess, these events include keystrokes and mouse clicks, but there also are other events caused by the user, either directly or indirectly. For example, when the user clicks a text box to start editing the information in the box, a `Click` event is fired for the text box. What you may not realize is that several other events also are fired. One is the `GotFocus` event for the text box. This event occurs every time the user moves to the text box, either by clicking the mouse or using the Tab key. Also, if the text box gets the program's focus, another control must loose focus. This causes a `LostFocus` event to fire for the other control. The `GotFocus` and `LostFocus` events are caused by the user's action, just as the `Click` event is. As you will see in the section "Understanding Event Sequences," multiple events can occur for each action a user may take. You also will see that the order in which the events occur can be important.

Here are the main user actions that trigger events in your program:

- Starting your program
- Pressing a key
- Clicking the mouse
- Moving the mouse
- Closing the program

Common Events   While there are a number of events to which forms and controls can respond, there are several events that most controls have in common:

- **Change**   Occurs when the user modifies the text in a text box or combo box.
- **Click**   Occurs when the user clicks an object with the primary mouse button (usually, the left button).
- **DblClick**   Occurs when the user rapidly clicks an object twice with the primary mouse button.
- **DragDrop**   Occurs when the user drags a control to another location.
- **DragOver**   Occurs when an object is dragged over a control.
- **GotFocus**   Occurs when an object receives focus.
- **KeyDown**   Occurs when a key is held down while an object has focus.
- **KeyPress**   Occurs when a key is pressed and released while an object has focus.
- **KeyUp**   Occurs when a key is released while an object has focus.

- **LostFocus** Occurs when focus is transferred from one object to another.
- **MouseDown** Occurs when a mouse button is held down while an object has focus.
- **MouseMove** Occurs when the mouse cursor is moved over an object.
- **MouseUp** Occurs when a mouse button is released while an object has focus.

You may have noticed that several of the events seem to correspond to the same user action. For example, the Click, MouseDown, and MouseUp events all occur when the user clicks the mouse button. While some of the differences between the events are obvious—for example, the MouseDown event occurs when you press the mouse button—there are other differences between the events. In the case of pressing a mouse button, the Click event is fired only if the left mouse button is pressed; it does not respond to the click of any other mouse button. The MouseDown and MouseUp events respond not only to any mouse button, but the event also can tell you which button was pressed, so you can take appropriate action.

The KeyDown, KeyPress, and KeyUp events work in a similar manner. The KeyPress event tells you only which key was pressed, not whether a Shift or Ctrl key was held down when the key was pressed. If you need that information, you need to use the KeyDown or KeyUp events.

Writing Event Procedures

With all these events going on, how do you make your code respond to any of the events, and how do you filter out the events that you don't want? The answer to both questions is the same. To respond to any event, you write program code for the event. Any event that has no code written for it is ignored. So the next question is, how do you write code for an event?

To write code, you first need to access the code-editing window. Do this by double-clicking a control on your form, by clicking the View Code button in the project window, by selecting the Code item from the View menu, or by pressing F7. Any of these actions present you with the code window, shown in Figure 4.5.

Part

I

Ch

4

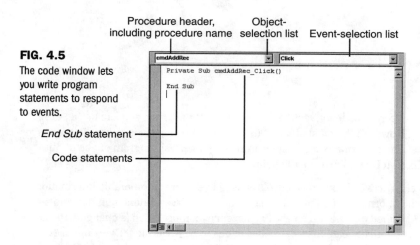

Procedure header, including procedure name   Object-selection list   Event-selection list

FIG. 4.5
The code window lets you write program statements to respond to events.

End Sub statement

Code statements

In the code window, you can select the object and event for which you want to write code. When you make a selection, Visual Basic automatically sets up the skeleton of a procedure with the procedure name and the End Sub statement. Notice that the procedure name for an Event procedure contains the name of the object and the name of the event. At this point, you can write program statements to take any actions you desire for the event. The following code shows how the program displays a second form in response to the user's clicking a command button:

```
Private Sub cmdShowDetail_Click()
    frmDetail.Show 1
End Sub
```

Handling Multiple Controls with a Single Procedure

We stated earlier that typically you would write separate procedures for each control on your form. There are times, however, when you will want to write one procedure to handle the same event for multiple controls. The first step to doing this is creating a control array, as described in Chapter 3, "Using Forms and Controls." After you have created a control array, open the code window for one of the controls. You will notice a slight difference between the procedure declaration for the control that is part of a control array and one that is not. For the control array, the procedure declaration contains a parameter called Index, as shown in Figure 4.6. This parameter tells you which element of the control array was accessed.

FIG. 4.6

The *Index* parameter identifies the element of the control array.

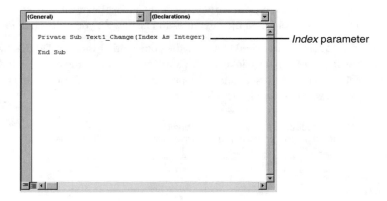

```
Private Sub Text1_Change(Index As Integer)

End Sub
```
— *Index* parameter

If you want to write different code for each of the elements of the array, you can use a Select Case block to do so. However, the most efficient use of the control array is to handle actions for groups of elements. The following two examples from a commercial program of one of this book's authors, Mike McKelvy, illustrate the point.

In the first example, an array of text box controls is used to display membership information from a database. The information includes a person's name, address, phone number, and so on. This information is verified on a periodic basis. When certain information is changed, the application needs to set a flag to indicate that the record needs to be re-verified. By using an IF statement to check the index of the control array, the program can determine whether or not to set the flag. This is illustrated in the following code:

```
Private Sub txtMember_Change(Index As Integer)
If Index >= 6 And Index <= 11 Then CASSChange = True
End Sub
```

In the second example, say that you want to change the foreground color of all text boxes to red whenever someone makes a change to any one of them. This indicates to the user that editing is in progress. Without a control array, you would have to write code in the Change event of every text box. By using the control array, you have to write the code only once. This code is shown here:

```
Private Sub txtMember_Change(Index As Integer)
Dim I As Integer
For I = 0 To 22
    txtMember(I).ForeColor = &HFF&
Next I
End Sub
```

You also could use a different event and change the color of the text box with focus. You would use the GotFocus event to change the color to red while the user is editing the text box, and use the LostFocus event to return the color to normal when the user leaves the text box. The following code shows how this could be done:

```
Private Sub txtMember_GotFocus(Index As Integer)
txtMember(I).ForeColor = &HFF&
End Sub
Private Sub txtMember_LostFocus(Index As Integer)
txtMember(I).ForeColor = &H80000008&
End Sub
```

Understanding Event Sequences

By now, you have an understanding of what events are and how Visual Basic handles them. You have seen how to write code to take action when an event occurs. But we need to take you just a little deeper into the world of events.

As stated, a user action or system event can trigger multiple events. This can be a good thing, because you can use these different events to handle different situations, as in the case of the MouseDown and Click events. However, there is a flip side (isn't there always). If you write code for multiple events that can occur, these procedures can interact in ways that you don't want. In the worst case, a sequence of events, each with a code procedure, can put your system into an infinite loop. There are several keys to avoiding these problems:

- Recognize that multiple events can occur.
- Determine which events occur for a user action.
- Understand the sequence in which the events occur.
- Test the interactions between multiple events in your code.

Multiple Events for Each Action

One of the problems of handling multiple events is that there are almost an infinite number of ways in which the user can interact with your program. For example, did the user move to the text box with a mouse or with the Tab key? Prior to the move, was the focus on another text box or was it on a command button? And what happens when you move from one form to another? As you can see, the possibilities can be almost overwhelming.

The good news, though, is that you will not write code for most events. Therefore, even though these events occur, your program ignores them—and they do not cause you problems.

While this simplifies the task of handling multiple events, it does not eliminate it. To get a handle on this, take a look at some simple sets of events that occur when a user performs an action.

First, look at the simple keystroke. Not all controls respond to keystrokes. But for the ones that do, every time the user presses a key, three events are fired: KeyDown, KeyPress, and KeyUp. If the keystroke happens to move the focus from one control to another, two additional events are triggered: LostFocus, for the current control, and GotFocus, for the new control.

Next, consider the innocent mouse click. This simple user action also fires three events: MouseDown, MouseUp, and Click. If the user double-clicks the mouse, two more events occur after the Click event: the DblClick event and another MouseUp event. That's five events for what would seem like a single user action! And, if the mouse causes the focus to move from one control to another, a LostFocus and GotFocus would also be triggered.

Finally, there also is the problem that different actions to achieve the same purpose cause different event sequences. For example, you know that to change the value of a check box, you can either click the box with the mouse or press the spacebar while the check box has the focus. But did you know that different events occur depending on how you check the box? Using the mouse triggers the MouseDown, MouseUp, and Click events. Using the spacebar triggers the KeyDown, KeyPress, KeyUp, and then the Click events. It can be confusing, can't it?

However, there are ways to determine what events will occur in your program and in what order they will occur.

Determining the Order of Events

In trying to figure out whether the interaction between events will cause a problem, the first step is to ignore every event that you don't need. If you write code for only the Click event, you don't care when or if the keystroke or mouse events occur. The only time you have to be concerned is when you have written code for multiple, related events.

N O T E   The GotFocus and LostFocus events are related to just about everything else. Because these events occur whenever the focus moves from one control to another, any action that can change the focus will trigger these events. The reason we bring this up is that many programmers use the LostFocus event to handle data validation. While this is the perfect place to handle this task, the event interactions can cause problems. ▪

The next step to determining the event interaction is to map the events with a program. The easiest way to do this is to write a simple program to display the event name in a text box for each event that is fired. Figure 4.7 shows an example of this type of program.

FIG. 4.7
A simple program can help you map events.

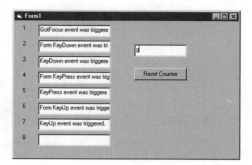

 The program uses an array of text boxes and keeps track of the index of the last box written to. Then, for each event of interest, you write a line of code to write to the next text box and increment the index. This way, the events map themselves. The code for one event is shown here. The entire program is on the book's Web site (at **http://www.quecorp.com/sevb5**), as EventSeq.Vbp. You can modify this program to handle any sequences you want.

```
txtSequence(SeqNo).Text = "Click event was triggered."
SeqNo = SeqNo + 1
```

Part
I

Ch
4

From Here...

This chapter focused on how Visual Basic handles events. But events are useful only in the context of forms and controls, because these are the objects capable of receiving events. Also, events can cause an action in your program only if some code has been written for the event. You can learn more about these related topics in the following chapters:

- Chapter 3, "Using Forms and Controls," will teach you the basics of creating controls and designing the visual interface of your programs.

- Chapter 6, "Programming in Visual Basic," will teach you about writing program code for the events.

- Chapter 32, "Advanced Control Techniques," and Chapter 33, "Advanced Form Techniques," explore forms and controls in more depth.

CHAPTER 5

Enhancing Your Program with Menus and Dialog Boxes

In Chapter 3, "Using Forms and Controls," you learned the basics of creating programs using the forms and controls that are provided with Visual Basic. You learned how controls such as the Label and TextBox controls are used to display and even edit information. You also learned how a command button can be used to let the user initiate an action. All these controls are very powerful tools, and you can create a number of applications by using just the forms and controls. However, there are other tools available in Visual Basic that can make your programs even more powerful and easy to use.

For example, consider a program menu. While it's true that a menu item provides the same functionality as a command button (a way for a user to start an action), menus are much better suited for handling large numbers of possible actions. For example, the word processor I am using has about 100 menu options. Can you imagine how the program would look if it used only command buttons? There would be no room left to enter text!

Creating a menu

You will see how to create a menu for your programs like the ones you would find in most Windows programs.

Implementing pop-up menus

Many programs have context menus that are displayed with a click of the right mouse button. You can have these in your program too.

Providing user information with a message box

Forms aren't the only way to display information. You can use a message box for providing small bits of information to the user.

Getting user decisions with the message box

If you need to have the user make a decision, the message box can handle this as well.

Getting input from the user

Just need one piece of information, the Input box may be just the thing you are looking for.

Working with dialogs your users will know

When your user needs to open or save a file, you can present them with the same dialogs that they see in other Windows programs.

In this chapter, I look at how to develop menus for your programs, as well as how to use message and input boxes to communicate with your users. I also tell you how to use some common dialog boxes for functions such as choosing file names and fonts and selecting a printer. ■

Controlling a Program with a Menu Bar

When you create a program, you provide a lot of functions for your users. For a number of programs, you will have file functions that let the user create, edit, and save files. You might also have edit functions that let users move information around. Then there are functions for tasks specific to your program. A program on which I'm currently working, for example, has functions for handling member information, organization data, conventions and events, and financial functions. In other words, lots of things the user can do.

One of the most important things in any program is enabling the user to easily access all the functions of the program. Users are accustomed to accessing most functions with a single click of a mouse—or at most, two clicks. And users want all the functions located conveniently in one place. You handle this in your programs by using *menus*. Visual Basic lets you quickly and easily create menus with the Menu Editor. With the editor, you create menu bars located at the top of a form, or pop-up menus that the user typically accesses by clicking the right mouse button. The menu bar from a membership program is shown in Figure 5.1.

FIG. 5.1

A menu provides a convenient location for a large number of functions.

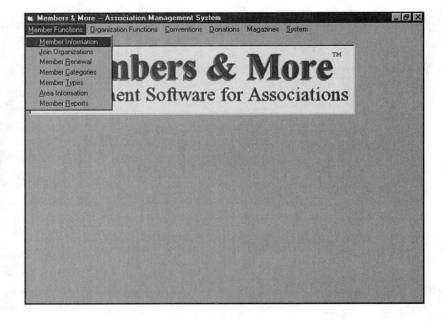

Creating a Menu Bar

The first step in creating a menu is determining what functions need to be on the menu and how these functions will be organized. Figure 5.2 shows Visual Basic's main menu. As you can see, the functions are organized into groups of similar items.

FIG. 5.2

Menu items are organized into functional groups.

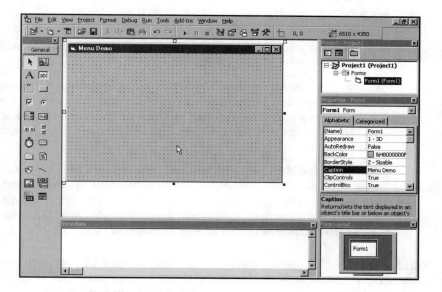

When you create your menu, you should group similar items. In fact, if possible, use groups with which your users are familiar. This way, users have some idea where to find particular menu items, even if they've never used your program. The following list describes some standard items you will find on many menus:

■ **File**   This menu contains any functions related to the opening and closing of files used by your program. Some of the typical menu items are New, Open, Close, Save, and Save As. If your program works extensively with different files, you might also want to include for quick access a list of the most recently used files. If you include a File menu, the program's Exit command is usually located in this menu.

■ **Edit**   The Edit menu contains the functions related to the editing of text and documents. Some typical Edit menu items are Undo, Cut, Copy, Paste, and Clear.

■ **View**   The View menu might be included if your program supports different looks for the same document. A word processor, for example, might include a normal view for editing text and a page-layout view for positioning document elements. A database program might have a view for looking at multiple records and a view for detailed examination of a single record.

■ **Tools**   This menu is a catchall for auxiliary programs. For example, a spelling checker, grammar checker, or equation editor might be included for a word processor.

■ **Window**   This menu typically is included if your program supports simultaneously editing multiple documents, databases, or files. The Window menu is set up to let users arrange the multiple documents or switch rapidly between them.

■ **Help**   The Help menu contains access to your program's help system. Typically, it includes menu items for a *help index* (a table of contents for help), a *Search option* (to let the user quickly find a particular topic), and an *About option* (providing summary information regarding your program).

You can use these six menus as a basis for creating your own menu system. Include any or all of them as needed by your program. If you need to add other menu groups, feel free; you are not bound to use only these options. I recommend, however, that if you need these functions, you place them in the menus as just identified. Otherwise, you might confuse and frustrate your users.

Setting' Up the Main Items   After deciding what functions to include in your menu and how these functions will be grouped, you can build the menu. To create a menu, first open the form where you want the menu located and then start the Menu Editor in any of three ways: Click the Menu Editor button on the tool bar, select the Menu Editor item from the Tools menu, or press Ctrl+E. The Menu Editor appears, as shown in Figure 5.3.

FIG. 5.3
The Menu Editor provides an easy way to create menus for your program.

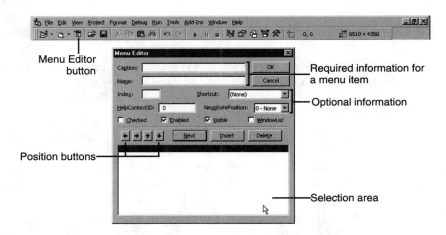

Once you are in the Menu Editor, you can start entering the items for your menu. For each item that you want to appear on your menu, you need to enter a value for the Caption and Name properties of the item. The Caption property determines what is displayed to the user in the menu. The Name property is used to identify the menu item in code. You need the Name property in order to assign code to the item, so that something happens when the user chooses the menu item.

After entering the information for one item, press the Enter key. Visual Basic then accepts the property values for the item and places it in the selection area indicated in Figure 5.3. Pressing Enter also clears the property edit areas and sets them up to accept the next item. When you're finished entering items, accept the menu by clicking the OK button on the Menu Editor. Your menu appears on the form, as shown in Figure 5.4.

FIG. 5.4
Exit the Menu Editor, and your newly created menu appears on the form.

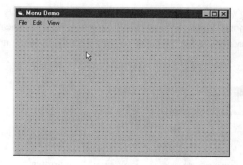

TROUBLESHOOTING

When I started to exit the Menu Editor, I got the message "Menu control must have a name." What has happened here is that you inadvertently left out a value for the Name property of one of your menu items. Each item in a menu must have a name. Fortunately, Visual Basic helps you track down your mistake by highlighting the offending item. Just enter a name for the item and continue on.

Multiple-Level Menus   If you entered several items in the Menu Editor and clicked OK, you probably noticed that you created a series of items on only the menu bar itself. You have no items appearing below the main item. This might be acceptable for a very simple menu, but if you place items only on the menu bar, you quickly run out of space. As you are probably aware, the key to creating successful menus with a large number of items is using *multiple menu levels*. The first level of a menu is the drop-down list of items appearing when you click an item on the menu bar. This is illustrated for the File menu in Figure 5.5.

FIG. 5.5
You can give your menu multiple levels of menu items.

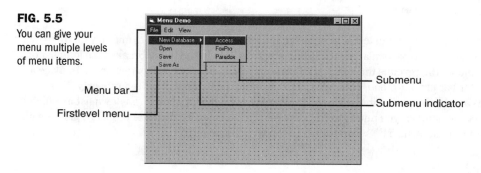

Menu bar

Firstlevel menu

Submenu

Submenu indicator

It is easy to create the items in different levels of a menu. You simply add the items to the menu and indent them in the Menu Editor. To indent an item, select the item in the selection area of the Menu Editor and then click the right-pointing arrow above the selection area. This indents the item one level and indicates to Visual Basic that the item is part of a *submenu* for the main item above it. Figure 5.6 shows the Menu Editor as it appears for the File menu shown in Figure 5.5.

N O T E When you create multiple menu levels, Visual Basic will provide the indicator that a submenu exists. Any other text in the menu item is part of the Caption property that you must enter. ▪

FIG. 5.6
Use the indent arrow to make an item part of a submenu.

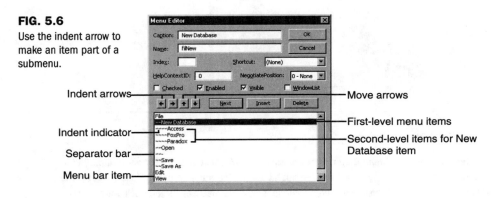

If you are entering new items, each one is automatically indented to the same level as the item directly above it in the selection list. To promote an item up to a higher menu level, click the Left Arrow button. This promotes the item one level.

 T I P Instead of clicking the arrow buttons, you can press Alt+R to indent a menu item or Alt+L to promote an item.

N O T E Typically, you will have no more than two levels in your menu, but Visual Basic lets you have up to four levels. ▪

In addition to using menu levels to organize the items of your menu, you might want to further separate items in a particular level. Placing *separator bars* in the menu breaks up a long list of items and further groups the items, without your having to create a separate level. To place a separator bar in your menu, enter a hyphen (-) in the menu item's Caption property. This causes a bar to be placed in the menu. The bar is the full width of the drop-down list in which it appears. Remember, you must give the separator bar a value for the Name property, just as with any other menu item. The separator bar is shown in Figure 5.6.

CAUTION

You cannot use a separator bar in the top level of the menu; it must be part of a submenu. If you do this, Visual Basic will inform you of the error as you try to save the menu.

Modifying the Menu   After creating your menu, you will probably find that you need to make some changes to the menu's structure. This also is easily accomplished with the Menu Editor. Table 5.1 lists some common editing needs and how they are accomplished.

Table 5.1   Editing a Menu with a Few Mouse Clicks

Editing Function	How to Do It
Move an item	Select the item and then click one of the Move arrows to move the item up or down in the list. The indentation level of the menu does not change as you move the item.
Add an item to the middle of the list	Select the item that should appear below the new item in the list and then click the Insert button. A blank item appears, and you can then enter the Caption and Name properties for the item. The new item is indented at the same level as the item below it.
Remove an item	Select the item and then click the Delete button. The item is immediately deleted, without any confirmation. (There is no Undo feature in the Menu Editor; whatever you delete is gone.)

TIP When moving menu items, you can use the Alt+U key combination instead of the Up button, or you can use the Alt+B keys instead of the Down button.

Part

I

Ch

5

Adding Hotkeys and Shortcuts for Quick Access   If you have been working in Windows for long, you probably have noticed that many menu items can be accessed by using a combination of keystrokes. You can let users access your menu items in the same way. There are two types of key combinations that can be used this way: *hotkeys* and *shortcuts*.

What is the hotkey for a menu item? The hotkey is indicated by an underscore beneath the letter in the item's *caption* (for example, the F in File). You create a hotkey by placing an ampersand (&) in front of the letter in the Caption property. For the File menu, the Caption property would be &File. You can create a hotkey for any or all of the items in your menu.

When you have hotkeys defined for your menu, the user can select a top-level menu item (the ones in the menu bar) by holding down the Alt key and then pressing the hotkey. This causes the submenu for that item to drop down, showing the items for that group. The user can then start the desired task by pressing the hotkey defined for the menu item. For example, the user could press Alt+F and then N for the New item of the File menu.

To create an effective set of hotkeys, you must specify a different key for each of the top-level menu items. Then specify a different key for each of the items in the submenu. Conceivably, you can have up to 36 hotkeys, one for each letter of the alphabet and one for each of the ten digits, but you will run out of screen space for the choices before running out of letters.

N O T E You can use the same letter for submenu items in different groups. For example, the Close item in the File menu and the Copy item in the Edit menu both can use C as an access key. However, if you use the same key for two items within a menu—for example, if you try to use C for both the Cut and the Copy items in the Edit menu—only the first item is accessed. ■

  T I P If possible, use the first letter of the menu item as the hotkey, because typically the user expects this.

In addition to the hotkeys just discussed, you can assign shortcut keys to some of the more commonly used functions in your program. Shortcut keys provide direct access to a function through a single key (such as Delete) or key combination (such as Ctrl+S). Users who know the shortcut keys can quickly perform the tasks assigned to the shortcut keys without having to walk through the menu items.

To assign a shortcut key to one of your functions, you simply select the menu item for which you want a shortcut key and then select the desired key from the Shortcut list in the Menu Editor. The key is assigned to that function, and the shortcut-key information appears next to the menu item in the menu, as shown in Figure 5.7. There are 79 shortcut keys that you can use.

FIG. 5.7

When you assign a shortcut key to a menu item, Visual Basic displays the information next to the item in the menu.

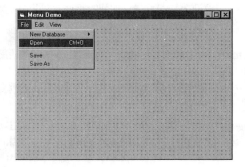

You can assign any shortcut key to any function, but there are a few "standard" keys used in most Windows programs. Some of these are listed in Table 5.2.

Table 5.2	Shortcut Keys Speed Access to Program Tasks	
Menu Item	**Shortcut Key**	**Description**
Edit,Cut	Ctrl+X	Removes text or a control from its current location and copies it to the Clipboard.
Edit,Copy	Ctrl+C	Makes a copy of text or a control in the Clipboard.
Edit,Paste	Ctrl+V	Pastes the contents of the Clipboard to the form or code window.
Edit,Undo	Ctrl+Z	Undoes the last change.
Edit,Find	Ctrl+F	Finds a piece of text.
File,Open	Ctrl+O	Opens a project.
File,Save	Ctrl+S	Saves the current file.
File,Print	Ctrl+P	Prints the current form or module.

T I P

As with hotkeys, try to have the shortcut key correspond to the first letter of the item name; for example, Ctrl+P for Print. This makes it easier for users to remember the shortcuts.

CAUTION

To avoid confusing your users, use the "standard" shortcut keys.

TROUBLESHOOTING

When I tried to save the changes to my menu, I got the error message "Shortcut key already defined." What happened? If you got this message, you inadvertently gave the same shortcut key to two or more functions. You need to look through the menu-item selection area to find the duplicate definition and then assign another key to one of your items.

Code for the Menu Items

After creating the menu's structure, you have to write code to let the menu items actually perform tasks. As with a form or the Visual Basic controls, you do this by writing code in the menu item's Event procedure. A menu item handles only one event: the Click event. This event is triggered when the user clicks the menu item or selects the item and then presses the Enter key.

N O T E A menu item's `Click` event is also triggered when the user uses a hotkey or shortcut to access an item. ◼

To add code to a menu item's `Click` event, first select the menu item on the form by clicking the item. This starts the Code Editor and sets up the `Event` procedure for the selected item. Then simply type in the code to handle the task. The following code could be used to create a new database in response to a menu selection.

```
GetFile.ShowOpen
newfile = GetFile.FileName
Set NewDb = DBEngine.WorkSpaces(0).CreateDatabase(newfile,dbLangGeneral)
```

The preceding code uses the `CommonDialog` control (covered later in this chapter) to obtain a file name from the user. It then uses this file name to create a new database.

Optional Settings

In addition to the required `Caption` and `Name` properties, each menu item has several optional properties that you might set either to control the behavior of the menu or to indicate the status of a program option. Three of these properties are `Visible`, `Enabled`, and `Checked`.

The menu item's `Visible` and `Enabled` properties work just like their counterparts on a form or control. When the `Visible` property is set to `True`, the menu item is visible to the user. If the `Visible` property is set to `False`, the item and any associated submenus are hidden from the user. You have probably seen the Enabled and Visible properties used in a word processing program (though you might not have been aware of how it was accomplished), where only the File and Help menus are visible until a document is selected for editing. Once a document is open, the other menu items are shown. Changing the setting of the `Visible` property allows you to control what menu items are available to the user at whichever point in your program. Controlling the menu this way lets you restrict the user's access to menu items that might cause errors if certain conditions are not met. (You wouldn't want the user to access edit functions if there was nothing to edit, right?)

The `Enabled` property serves a function similar to that of the `Visible` property. The key difference is that when the `Enabled` property is set to `False`, the menu item is *grayed out*. This means that the menu item still can be seen by the user but cannot be accessed. This is shown in Figure 5.8.

Both the `Visible` and `Enabled` properties can be set in the Menu Editor and from your program code. In the Menu Editor, the properties are set by using check boxes. The default value of the properties is `True`. In code, you set the property value by specifying the name of the menu item (from the `Name` property), the name of the property, and the value you want to set. This is shown in the following line of code for the Edit menu:

```
Mnu_Edit.Visible = False
```

FIG. 5.8
A disabled menu item still is visible to the user but is shown in gray tones, indicating that the item is unavailable.

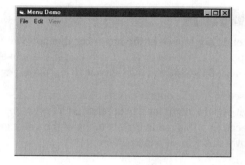

The Checked property of the menu item determines whether or not a check mark is displayed to the left of the item in the menu, as shown in Figure 5.9. The Checked property typically is used to indicate the status of a program item; for example, whether a tool bar or particular window is visible. The menu item is then used to toggle back and forth between two program states. The following code shows how you might use a menu item and the Checked property to control and indicate the visibility of a toolbox.

```
If view_ToolBox.Checked Then
    frmToolBox.Hide
    view_ToolBox.Checked = False
Else
    frmToolBox.Show
    view_ToolBox.Checked = True
End If
```

FIG. 5.9
The Checked property controls whether or not a check mark is placed to the left of the menu item.

Check mark

> **CAUTION**
> You cannot set the Checked property to True for an item on the menu bar. Doing so results in an error.

Creating Pop-Up Menus

So far, my discussion of menus has looked at the menu bar that appears along the top of the form. Visual Basic also supports *pop-up menus* in your programs. A pop-up menu is a small menu that appears somewhere on your form in response to a program event.

Pop-up menus often are used to handle operations or options related to a specific area of the form; for example, a format pop-up menu for a text field that lets you change the font or font attributes of the field. You can find this menu type in many of the latest generation of Windows programs. Figure 5.10 shows this type of pop-up menu.

FIG. 5.10

You can use a pop-up menu to handle tasks related to a specific form or control.

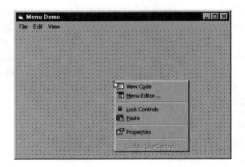

When a pop-up menu is invoked, the menu appears on the screen at the current mouse location. The user then makes a selection from the menu. After the selection is processed, the menu disappears from the screen.

Creating the Menu to Be Displayed

You create a pop-up menu in the same way that you created the main menu for your program—from the Menu Editor. There is, however, one extra step. The pop-up menu must be hidden, so that it does not appear on the menu bar. To do this, set the `Visible` property of the top-level menu item to `False`.

> **N O T E**   Typically, you will hide the menu item that is used as a pop-up menu, but you can use any of the top-level items of a menu bar as a pop-up menu. That is, a particular menu can appear both as a pop-up menu and a part of the main menu of a form. ■

Creating a pop-up menu is easy. The following four steps tell you how to create a pop-up menu to handle text formatting:

1. Create a top-level menu item with `Format` as its `Caption` property and `popFormat` as its `Name` property.

2. Set the `Visible` property of the menu item to `False` by clearing the Visible check box in the Menu Editor.

3. Create three submenu items under popFormat, with the Caption properties Bold, Italic, and Underline and the Name properties popBold, popItalic, and popUnder, respectively.

4. Click the OK button to accept the menu changes.

Notice that the Format menu does not appear on your form's menu bar. However, the menu is present.

The technique you must use to add code to the Click event of the items in a pop-up menu is also a little different. Because the menu is not visible on the form, you cannot just click the item to bring up the code-editing window. Instead, bring up the code-editing window by selecting the View Code button in the project window. You can then select the menu item in the Code Editor's Object list. This lets you enter code for the item.

Activating a Pop-Up Menu

To have the pop-up menu appear on your screen, you must invoke the menu using the PopUpMenu method. You do this by specifying the name of the form where the menu will be displayed, the PopUpMenu method, and the name of the menu to be shown.

While you can use this method from anywhere in your code, pop-up menus are used most often in response to mouse clicks, usually those using the right mouse button. The following code shows how the Format menu created in the last section would be called up by clicking the right mouse button anywhere on your form.

```
Private Sub Form_MouseDown(Button As Integer, Shift As Integer,
  X As Single, Y As Single)
If Button = 2 Then
    frmMain.PopUpMenu popFormat
End If
End Sub
```

In this code segment, the MouseDown event is used to take an action whenever a mouse button is pressed. The event passes a parameter, the Button parameter, that tells you which of the mouse buttons was pressed. Because you want the menu to appear in response to only a right-button click, you check for the value of the Button parameter. If it is 2 (the value for the right button), the code is run to display the pop-up menu.

N O T E You can create multiple pop-up menus and have them displayed in response to different mouse buttons or different areas of the screen. ▪

Keeping the User Informed

A big part of any programming project is providing information to the users about the program's progress and status. Whereas the forms and controls of your program provide the main interface to the user, they are not necessarily the best vehicles for providing bits of information, such as warnings or error messages, to the user. For providing this type of information, the *message box* is the way to go.

The message box is a simple form that displays a message and at least one command button. The button is used to acknowledge the message. Optionally, the message box can display an icon or use multiple buttons to let the user make a decision. Message boxes can be used in either of two ways, depending on your needs. You can use the message box to simply display information, or you can use the message box to get a decision from the user. In either case, you will use the MsgBox function to display the information to the user. The MsgBox function lets you produce a message to the user with only a single line of code. For example, the following code line produces the message box shown in Figure 5.11:

```
MsgBox "Please confirm the deletion of the record", 52
```

FIG. 5.11

A message box communicates with the user and accepts decisions.

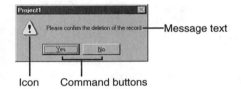

While the message box is a powerful tool, it does have a few limitations:

- The message box cannot accept input from the user. It can only display information.
- You can use only one of the four predefined icons or one of six predefined command-button sets in the message box. You cannot define your own icons or buttons.
- The message box requires a user to respond to the message before the program can continue. This means that the message box cannot be used to provide continuous status monitoring of the program.

Displaying a Message

The simplest way to create a message box in your program is to use the MsgBox function without returning a value. Using the MsgBox function this way, you simply specify the message text that you want to appear in the message box and then call the function. For the simplest message, only the OK button is shown in the message box. This enables the user to acknowledge the message. The following line shows how to create a simple message.

```
MsgBox "Please insert a disk in Drive A:"
```

This line shows the minimum requirement for producing a message box. When you specify the message text, you can use a *literal statement* (a string of text enclosed in quotes, as shown above) or a string variable.

The simple message box is acceptable for many types of messages, but you probably will want to dress up your messages a little more. There are two optional arguments that you can specify for the MsgBox function: the options argument and the title argument. The options argument is an integer number that specifies the icon to display in the message box, the command button set to display, and which of the command buttons is the default. The title argument is a text string that specifies a custom text to be shown in the title bar of the message box.

When you want to display an icon in the message box, you have a choice of four icons. These icons and their purposes are summarized in Table 5.3.

Table 5.3 Icons Indicate the Type of Message Being Shown

	Icon Name	Purpose
	Critical message	Indicates that a severe error has occurred. Often a program is shut down after this message.
	Warning message	Indicates that a program error has occurred that requires user correction or that might lead to undesirable results.
	Query	Indicates that the program requires additional information from the user before processing can continue.
	Information message	Informs the user of the status of the program. Most often used to notify the user of the completion of a task.

To tell Visual Basic that you want to use an icon in the message box, you set a value for the `options` argument of the `MsgBox` function. The `options` argument can be set to one of four values, as defined in the following table. You can use either the numerical value or the constant from the table.

Message Type	*options* Argument Value	Constant
Critical	16	vbCritical
Query	32	vbQuestion
Warning	48	vbExclamation
Information	64	vbInformation

The `options` argument can either directly specify the number or the constant (both shown in the following code line) or can reference a variable containing a number. To illustrate how icons and titles can be used in your message boxes, the following code produces the message box that is shown in Figure 5.12.

```
MsgBox "This message contains an icon", 64, "Icon Demo"
MsgBox "This message contains an icon", vbInformation, "Icon Demo"
```

FIG. 5.12
Use titles and icons to give the user visual clues to the nature of the message.

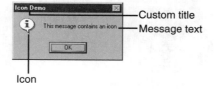
Custom title
Message text
Icon

If you are wondering how you are going to remember the syntax of the MsgBox function and the constants to be used for the options, don't worry. The new statement completion capabilities of Visual Basic's code editor will help tremendously with this. When you type the space after the MsgBox function name in the code window, a pop-up will appear that shows you the syntax of the command. This is illustrated in Figure 5.13.

FIG. 5.13

Syntax help assists you in setting up the message box.

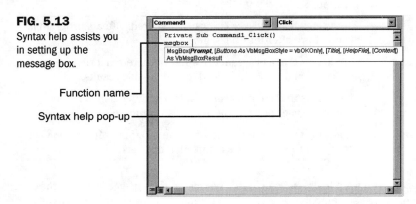

Function name ⎯

Syntax help pop-up ⎯

Then, after you enter the message to be displayed and enter a comma, Visual Basic will pop up a list of constants that can be used to add an icon to the message box, or specify the button set to be used. You can select one of the constants from the list or type it in yourself. This is one of the really great new features in the editor. Figure 5.14 shows the constant list in action.

FIG. 5.14

You no longer have to remember the options constants with the pop-ups available in the editor.

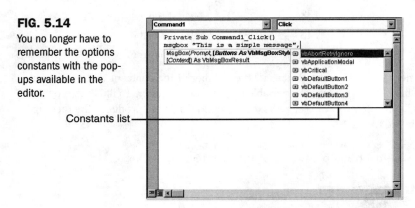

Constants list ⎯

Returning a Value from the *MsgBox* Function

The MsgBox function, as described above, works fine for informing users of a problem or prompting them to take an action. However, if you need to get a decision from the user, you need to return a value from MsgBox function. There are two key differences to using the MsgBox function this way – you assign the function to a variable, and you must enclose the arguments of the function in parentheses. This value determines which command button was pressed by the user. The following line of code shows how the value returned by the function is assigned to a variable for further processing.

```
Usrchc = MsgBox("The printer is not responding", vbRetryCancel)
```

There are six sets of command buttons that can be used in the MsgBox function:

- **OK**   Displays a single button with the caption OK. This simply asks the user to acknowledge receipt of the message before continuing.
- **OK, Cancel**   Displays two buttons in the message box, letting the user choose between accepting the message and requesting a cancellation of the operation.
- **Abort, Retry, Ignore**   Displays three buttons, usually along with an error message. The user can choose to abort the operation, retry it, or ignore the error and continue with program execution.
- **Yes, No, Cancel**   Displays three buttons, typically with a question. The user can answer yes or no to the question, or choose to cancel the operation.
- **Yes, No**   Displays two buttons for a simple yes or no choice.
- **Retry, Cancel**   Displays the two buttons that allow the user to retry the operation or cancel it. A typical use is to indicate that the printer is not responding. The user can either retry or cancel the printout.

To specify the command buttons that will appear in the message box, you need to specify a value for the options argument of the MsgBox function. The values for each of the command-button sets are listed in Table 5.4.

Part

I

Ch

5

Table 5.4   To Specify Which Set of Buttons to Use, the *options* Argument Can Be Set to One of the Following Values

Button Set	Value	Constant
OK	0	vbOKOnly
OK, Cancel	1	vbOKCancel
Abort, Retry, Ignore	2	vbAbortRetryIgnore
Yes, No, Cancel	3	vbYesNoCancel
Yes, No	4	vbYesNo
Retry, Cancel	5	vbRetryCancel

Because the `options` argument controls both the icon and the command-button set for a message box, you might wonder how you can specify both at the same time. You do this by adding the values of the constants together. The `MsgBox` function is designed so that any combination of the icon constant and the command-button constant creates a unique value. This value is then broken down by the function, to specify the individual pieces. The following code combines an icon constant and command-button constant to create a warning message that enables the user to choose an action. The results of the code are illustrated in Figure 5.15.

```
optval = vbExclamation + vbAbortRetryIgnore
retval = MsgBox("File does not exist", optval)
```

N O T E   When you are using the pop-up constants list, you can select a second constant by entering a plus sign (+) after the first constant. ■

FIG. 5.15

The `options` argument controls both the icon and the command buttons.

If you are using more than one command button in the message box, you can also specify which button is the default. The *default button* is the one that has focus when the message box is displayed. This button is the one that the user is most likely to choose or that will be the most benevolent if the user just automatically presses the Enter key. For example, if you display a message box to have the user confirm the deletion of the record, you probably should set up the default button so that the record is not deleted. This way, the user must make a conscious choice to delete the record.

To specify which button is the default, you need to add another constant to the `options` argument of the `MsgBox` function. There are four possible default button values, even though there are only a maximum of three buttons displayed at any one time. Go figure! These are identified in following table.

Default Button	Value	Constant
First	0	vbDefaultButton1
Second	256	vbDefaultButton2
Third	512	vbDefaultButton3
Fourth	768	vbDefaultButton4

There are seven buttons from which a user might choose, with the selection depending on the button set used in the message box. Each of these buttons returns a different value to identify the button to your program. These values are summarized in Table 5.5.

Table 5.5   Return Values Indicate the User's Choice

Button	Value	Constant
OK	1	vbOK
Cancel	2	vbCancel
Abort	3	vbAbort
Retry	4	vbRetry
Ignore	5	vbIgnore
Yes	6	vbYes
No	7	vbNo

Once you know which button was selected by the user, you can use the information in your program. The following code is used to confirm the deletion of a file.

```
trgtfil = "MYDATA.TXT"
msgtxt = "Do you really want to delete file: '" & trgtfil & "'?"
optval = vbExclamation + vbYesNo + vbDefaultButton2
ttlval = "Delete Confirmation"
retval = MsgBox(msgtxt, optval, ttlval)
If retval = vbYes Then Kill trgtfil
```

For completeness, there is one final setting that can be applied to the options argument of the MsgBox function. You can choose to have the message box be modal for your application, or for the entire system. By default, the message box is modal for your application. This means that the user must respond to the message box before continuing work in your application. The user can, however, work in any other application. If you specify that the message box is modal to the system, the user must respond to the message box before he or she can do any further work on the computer. This option should be used with extreme care. To use the default of modal to the application, you do not have to add anything to the options argument, or you can add the vbApplicationModal constant, which has a value of 0. To make the message box modal to the system, you need to add the constant vbSystemModal, which has a value of 4096, to the options argument.

Part
I

Ch
5

Getting Information from the User

Many times in a program, you need to get a single piece of information from the user. You might need the user to enter a person's name, the name of a file, or a number for various purposes. While the message box lets your users make choices, it does not allow them to enter information in response to the message. Therefore, you have to use some other means to get the information. Visual Basic provides a second built-in dialog box for exactly this purpose: the *input box.*

The input box works something like a bank-by-phone system. If you have ever used one of these, you know that it uses *prompts* (in this case, voice commands) to tell you what information to enter. This information might be an account number, password code, or amount. After the prompt, you enter the information using the phone buttons instead of a keyboard. When you've finished entering the information, you press the # button (or some other one) to indicate that you have finished—just as you click the OK button of the input box.

The input box displays a message to tell the user what to enter, a text box where the user can enter the data, and two command buttons—OK and Cancel—that can be used to either accept or abort the input data. A sample input box is shown in Figure 5.16.

FIG. 5.16

An input box lets the user enter a single piece of data in response to a message.

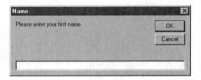

Setting Up the Input Dialog Box

The input box works very much like the message box with a return value. You specify a variable to receive the information returned from the input box and then supply the message and (optionally) a title and default value as arguments to the function. The syntax used for the input box function is the following:

```
userinput = InputBox(prompt[, title][, default])
```

In this statement, the word `userinput` represents the variable that contains the information input by the user into the input box. `InputBox` is the name of the function itself.

`prompt` represents the message that is displayed to the user to indicate what should be entered in the box. Like the message in the message box, the prompt can be up to about 1,024 characters. Word-wrapping is automatically performed on the text in the prompt, so that it fits inside the box. Also, as with the message box, you can insert a carriage return or line-feed character to force the prompt to show multiple lines or to separate lines for emphasis.

The `title` argument specifies the text that will be shown in the bar at the top of the input box. This is an optional argument and can be excluded.

The other optional argument of the function is the `default` argument. If this is included, it is used to specify an initial value for the text box in the input-box dialog. This value can be accepted by the user or modified, or it can be erased and a completely new value entered.

There is no option in the `InputBox` function to specify any command buttons other than the defaults of OK and Cancel.

Determining User Actions and Input

When you use the input box, the user can enter data in the box and then choose the OK or Cancel button. If the user chooses the OK button, the input box returns whatever text is in the input field. If the user chooses the Cancel button, the input box returns an empty string, regardless of what the user typed.

To be able to use the information entered by the user, you must determine whether the data meets your needs. First, you probably want to make sure that the user actually entered some information and chose the OK button. You can do this by using the Len function to determine the length of the returned string. If the length is zero, the user pressed the Cancel button or left the input field blank. If the length of the string is greater than zero, you know that the user entered something.

You also might need to check the returned value to make sure it is of the proper type. If you are expecting a number, which will be compared to another number, an error message occurs if the user enters letters. To make sure that you have a numerical value with which to work, you can use the Val function to get the numerical value of the string. If the string contains only numbers, the function returns the number. If the string contains anything else, the function returns zero. The following code illustrates the additional processing of the returned value of the input box.

```
inptval = InputBox("Enter your age")
If Len(inptval) = 0 Then
    MsgBox "You forgot to enter your age"
Else
    If Val(inptval) = 0 Then
        MsgBox "You did not enter a number"
    Else
        MsgBox "Congratulations for surviving this long"
    End If
End If
```

Using Built-In Dialog Boxes

For most of your programs, your users will need to be able to specify file names, select fonts and colors, and control the printer. While you could create your own dialog boxes to handle these tasks, there is no need to do so. Visual Basic provides you with the CommonDialog control, which allows you to easily display dialog boxes to obtain information from the user. And while the ease of setup is a great benefit, an even bigger bonus is that these dialog boxes are already familiar to the user. This is because they are the same dialog boxes used by Windows itself.

Using a single `CommonDialog` control, you have access to four Windows dialog boxes:

- **File**   Lets the user select a file to open or choose a file name in which to save information.
- **Font**   Lets the user choose a base font and set any font attributes that are desired.
- **Color**   Lets the user choose from a standard color or create a custom color for use in the program.
- **Print**   Lets the user select a printer and set some of the printer parameters.

To access the CommonDialog control, you first have to add it to your project by selecting it from the components dialog. This dialog is accessible by choosing the Components item from the Project menu. After the CommonDialog control is added to your toolbox, you can add the control to a form by clicking the control and drawing it on the form just like any other control. The CommonDialog control will appear on your form as an icon, as the control itself is not visible when your application is running.

In the following sections, we will discuss each of the types of dialogs that can be accessed with the CommonDialog control. For each of these dialogs, you will need to set properties of the control. You can do this through the Properties window, or you can use the Property Pages of the CommonDialog control. The Property Pages are a dialog which provides you easy access to the specific properties that are necessary for each of the common dialog types. You can access the Property Pages (see Figure 5.17) by clicking the ellipsis button in the Custom property of the CommonDialog control.

FIG. 5.17
The Property Pages
make it easy to set up
the CommonDialog
control.

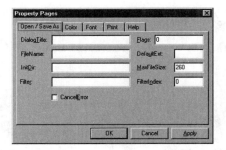

The File Dialog Box

One of the key uses of the `CommonDialog` control is to obtain file names from the user. The `CommonDialog` control can be used in either of two modes: file open and file save. The file-open mode is used to let the user specify a file to be retrieved and used by your program. The file-save mode is used to let the user specify a name for a file to be saved. This is the equivalent of the Save As dialog box for many programs.

The dialog boxes for the Open and Save functions are very similar. Figure 5.18 shows the dialog box with the major components indicated. These components are the following:

- **Drive/Folder list**   Where the current folder is indicated. You can move up the folder levels from this list.
- **File/Folder selection**   Where you select the file or folder to be used. The folders indicated in this area are the subdirectories of the folder in the Drive/Folder list. A folder can be selected either by double-clicking it or by highlighting it and then pressing Enter. This changes the display to show the files and folders contained within the new folder. A file is selected by clicking its icon. Its name is then displayed in the File Name text box.
- **File Name text box**   Where the user can enter a file name or where the name of the selected file is displayed.
- **File Type list box**   Where the user selects the type of files to display. These types determine the extension of the file, and the available types are controlled by the Filter property of the CommonDialog control.
- **Command buttons**   The buttons in the upper-right corner let the user move up one folder level, create a new folder, or switch the file display area between the list mode and the file-details mode. The buttons at the lower-right let the user process the selection or cancel the dialog box.

FIG. 5.18

The Open and Save dialog boxes share many components.

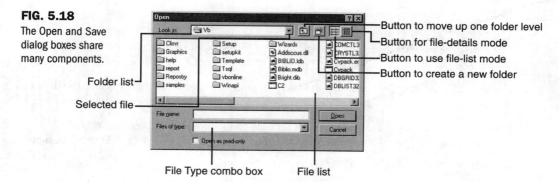

Button to move up one folder level
Button for file-details mode
Button to use file-list mode
Button to create a new folder

Folder list
Selected file

File Type combo box   File list

Opening and Saving Files   To open an existing file, you use the ShowOpen method of the CommonDialog control. This method displays the dialog box that was shown in Figure 5.16. You use this method by specifying the name of the CommonDialog control and the method name, as shown in the following line of code:

```
CdlGetFile.ShowOpen
```

Part
I

Ch
5

Running the `CommonDialog` control to get a file name to save is essentially the same as for opening a file. In this case, however, the name of the method is `ShowSave`. There are a few subtle differences between the dialog boxes shown for the `Open` and `Save` functions, such as the title of the dialog box and the captions on the command buttons.

Specifying File Types with the *Filter* Property   So far, I have explained only how to display the File dialog boxes with all files shown in a folder. You might, however, want to specify that only certain file types, such as text or document files, be shown. You can accomplish this with the `CommonDialog` control. The file types shown in the dialog box are specified by using the `Filter` property.

You set the `Filter` property either in design mode from the Properties dialog box, or at runtime with an assignment statement as shown here:

```
controlname.Filter = "description¦filtercond"
```

`controlname` is the assigned name of the `CommonDialog` control, and `Filter` is the name of the property. `description` is a text description of the type of files to be shown. Examples of the description are Text Files, Documents, and All Files. The vertical line is known as the *pipe symbol*. This symbol must be present. `filtercond` is the actual filter for the files. You typically express the filter as an asterisk followed by a period and the extension of the files that you want to display. The filters that correspond to the preceding descriptions are `*.txt`, `*.doc`, and `*.*`, respectively.

> **CAUTION**
>
> Do not include spaces before or after the pipe symbol, or you might not get the file list that you want.

If you specify the `Filter` property with an assignment statement, you must enclose the filter in double quotes. The quotes are omitted if you specify the filter from the Properties dialog box.

You can specify multiple `description¦filtercond` pairs within the `Filter` property. Each pair must be separated from the other pairs by the pipe symbol, as shown in the following example:

```
GetFile.Filter = "All Files¦*.*¦Text Files¦*.txt"
```

The Font Dialog Box

Setting up the `CommonDialog` control to show the Font dialog box is just as easy as setting it up for file functions. In fact, you can use the same `CommonDialog` control to handle file, font, color, and printer functions.

The first step in using the `CommonDialog` control to handle font selection is to set a value for the `Flags` property. This property tells the `CommonDialog` control whether you want to show screen fonts, printer fonts, or both. The `Flags` property can be set to one of the three constants listed in the following table:

Font Set	Constant	Value
Screen Fonts	vbCFScreenFonts	1
Printer Fonts	vbCFPrinterFonts	2
Both sets	vbCFBoth	3

> **CAUTION**
>
> If you do not set a value for the Flags property, you will get an error message stating that no fonts are installed.

You can set the value of the Flags property from the design environment, using the Properties dialog box, or from your program, using an assignment statement. Once the Flags property has been set, you can run the Font dialog box from your code, using the ShowFont method. This method has the same syntax as the ShowOpen method, described earlier. Figure 5.19 shows the Font dialog box that is presented to the user. This particular dialog box contains only screen fonts.

FIG. 5.19
The Font dialog box lets the user select fonts.

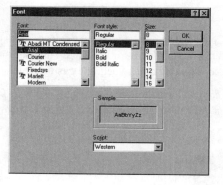

The information about the fonts chosen from the CommonDialog control is contained in the control's properties. Table 5.6 shows the control's properties and the font attributes that each controls.

Table 5.6   Control Properties Store Font Attributes

Property	Attribute
FontName	The name of the base font
FontSize	The height of the font in points
FontBold	Whether boldface was selected

continues

Table 5.6   Continued

Property	Attribute
FontItalic	Whether italic was selected
FontUnderline	Whether the font is underlined
FontStrikethru	Whether the font has a line through it

The font information can be used to set the font of any control in your program, or even set the font for the Printer object. The following code shows how the font information would be retrieved and used to change the fonts in a text box.

```
GetFont.ShowFont
txtSample.FontName = GetFont.FontName
txtSample.FontSize = GetFont.FontSize
txtSample.FontBold = GetFont.FontBold
txtSample.FontItalic = GetFont.FontItalic
txtSample.FontUnderline = GetFont.FontUnderline
txtSample.FontStrikethru = GetFont.FontStrikethru
```

The Color Dialog Box

The CommonDialog control's Color dialog box lets the user select colors that can be used for the foreground or background colors of your forms or controls. The user has the option of choosing one of the standard colors or creating and selecting a custom color.

Setting up the CommonDialog control for colors is basically the same as for fonts. You set the Flags property to the constant vbCCRGBInit and then call the ShowColor method. Figure 5.20 shows the Color dialog box.

FIG. 5.20
The Color dialog box lets your users choose a color to use in the program.

When the user selects a color from the dialog box, its color value is stored in the Color property of the control. The following code shows how to change a form's background color using the Color dialog box.

```
GetColor.Flags = vbCCRBGInit
GetColor.ShowColor
Myform.BackColor = GetColor.Color
```

The Print Dialog Box

The `CommonDialog` control's Print dialog box lets the user select which printer to use for a printout and specify options for the print process. These options include specifying all pages, a range of pages, or the selection to print. There is also an option to specify the number of copies to be printed, as well as an option to print to a file.

To run the Print dialog box, just call the `CommonDialog` control's `ShowPrinter` method. There are no flags to set prior to the call. The basic Print dialog box is shown in Figure 5.21.

FIG. 5.21
The Print dialog box lets the user select which printer to use and specify print options.

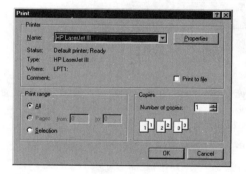

Once the Print dialog box is displayed, the user can select the printer from the Name list at the top of the dialog box. This list contains all the printers installed in Windows. Right below the Name list is the Status line, which tells you the current status of the selected printer.

If users want to change any of the printer's parameters (such as paper size and margins), they can click the Properties button on the Print dialog box. This brings up the Properties dialog box for the selected printer, as shown in Figure 5.22. This dialog box lets you control all the settings of the printer, just as with the Windows Control Panel.

The Print dialog box returns the information from the user in the dialog box's properties. The `FromPage` and `ToPage` properties tell you the starting and ending pages of the printout selected by the user. The `Copies` property tells you how many copies the user wants printed.

This is provided only as information. The Print dialog box does not automatically set up the desired printout. Your program must do that.

Part
I

Ch
5

FIG. 5.22

The Properties dialog box for the printer lets you control paper size, margins, and other printer attributes.

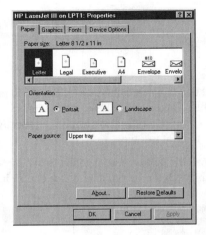

From Here...

This chapter introduced you to the basics of menus and dialog boxes. Several other topics were mentioned in the discussion, such as writing code for events. To review or learn more about related topics, refer to the following chapters:

- Chapter 3, "Using Forms and Controls," provides detailed information about forms and controls.
- Chapter 4, "Understanding the Event Model," provides you with more information about how events, such as a menu click, are handled by Visual Basic.
- Chapter 6, "Programming in Visual Basic," tells you all about the program code.

Programming in Visual Basic

Visual Basic's forms and controls provide the visual inter-face of your programs, but most of your program's actual work is done with program code. This code performs tasks in response to user and system events. Visual Basic provides a powerful programming language that is rela-tively easy to use. As you might guess, this programming language is based on the BASIC language, which has been around for a number of years.

However, Visual Basic's language has been extended so that you can easily control your programs through deci-sion and loop structures. The language also has been adapted in a way that lets programmers easily work with Visual Basic's objects and controls. In this chapter, I give you a look at some of the basic concepts of programming in Visual Basic. I start with a look at variables and then proceed to working with information and controlling your program with loops and conditional statements. ■

Performing math in Visual Basic

Visual Basic supports a variety of math operators which let you per-form many types of calculations in your programs.

Using variables in your programs

Variables store information in memory for further processing.

Understanding the differences between variables and constants

While variables and constants are similar in function, there are subtle differences in the way they are created and used.

Making decisions in your program

Often in your program, you will want to perform tasks only for certain conditions. If and Select statements allow your programs to selectively process blocks of code.

Repeating tasks

Many tasks in your programs will need to be performed repetitively. There are several types of loops in Visual Basic which handle this well.

Ridding your program of bugs

Visual Basic provides you with many useful tools to help you avoid errors and to track down the ones that do occur.

Working with Variables

In Chapter 3, "Using Forms and Controls," you saw how controls can be used both to let the user input data and to display data. But what do you do with the data while it is being processed in your program? The answer is that you temporarily store the information in the computer's memory, while your program operates on it. In order to store the information, you must specify where the information is stored, so that it can be retrieved. This is the function of *variables*.

Variables are used in all programming languages to give a name to a specific location in memory. Once a variable is defined, it continues to point to the same memory location until the variable is released. Now don't worry, you don't have to define where in memory the information will be stored (Visual Basic handles those details for you); you just have to provide a name so that you can refer to the memory location in other parts of your program.

In naming a variable, you have a tremendous amount of flexibility. Variable names can be simple, or they can be descriptive of the information they contain. For example, you may want to name a counter variable simply I, or you may want to use a more descriptive name, such as `NumberOfRecordsProcessed`. While you are allowed great latitude in naming, there are a few restrictions:

- The name must start with a letter, not a number or other character.
- The name cannot contain a period.
- The name must be unique.
- The name can be no longer than 255 characters.

 Make your variable names descriptive of the task in order to make your code easy to read, but also keep the names short in order to make the code easy to type. Many programmers will also use prefixes on their variables to indicate the type of data stored and the scope of the variable. For example, a prefix of gint- would indicate a global or program-level variable that stores an integer.

Types of Variables

Okay, you know what a variable does and how to name it. But what can you store in a variable? The simple answer is, almost anything. A variable can hold a number; a string of text; or an instance of an object, including forms, controls, and database objects. In this chapter, I look specifically at using variables to store numbers, strings, and logical values. Use of objects and database objects is covered later in the book.

▶ Objects are covered in Chapter 8, "Introduction to Classes," and database objects are covered in Chapter 13, "Writing Programs with the Data-Access Objects."

You can use a variable to hold any type of information, but different types of variables are designed to work efficiently with different types of information.

Table 6.1 shows the different types of variables available in Visual Basic. The table also shows the range of values that the variable can hold and the amount of memory required to store the information in the variable. The memory requirements are important in optimizing your code. Variables with smaller memory requirements should be used wherever possible to conserve system resources.

Type	Stores	Memory Requirement	Range of Values
Integer	Whole numbers	2 bytes	−32,768 to 32,767
Long	Whole numbers	4 bytes	(approximately) +/− 2 billion
Single	Decimal numbers	4 bytes	+/− 1E-45 to 3E38
Double	Decimal numbers	8 bytes	+/− 5E-324 to 1.8E308
Currency	Numbers with up to 15 digits left of the decimal and 4 digits right of the decimal	8 bytes	+/− 9E14
String	Text information	1 byte	Up to 65,000 characters for fixed length string and up to 2 billion characters for dynamic strings per character
Byte	Whole numbers	1 byte	0 to 255
Boolean	Logical values	2 bytes	True or False
Date	Date and time information	8 bytes	1/1/100 to 12/31/9999
Object	Pictures and OLE objects	4 bytes	N/A
Variant	Any of the preceding data types	16 bytes + 1 byte per character	N/A

Table 6.1   Variables Store Many Types of Information

Part

I

Ch

6

Variable Declarations

You know how to name a variable and what a variable can store, but how do you tell the program what you want to store? In reality, you do not have to tell Visual Basic what a variable will contain. Unlike other languages, Visual Basic does not require you to specifically declare a variable before it is used. If a variable is not declared, Visual Basic uses a default data type known as a *variant*. A variant can contain any type of information. However, using a variant for general information has two major drawbacks: It can waste memory resources, and the variable type may be invalid for use with some data-manipulation functions.

It is a good idea to declare your variables before they are used, so take a look at the two ways to declare a variable in Visual Basic: *explicit declaration* and *implicit declaration*.

Explicit Declaration   Explicit declaration means that you use a statement to define the type of a variable. These statements do not assign a value to the variable but merely tell Visual Basic what the variable can contain.

Each of the following statements can be used to explicitly declare a variable's type:

```
Dim varname [As vartype][, varname2 [As vartype2]]
Private varname [As vartype][, varname2 [As vartype2]]
Static varname [As vartype][, varname2 [As vartype2]]
Public varname [As vartype][, varname2 [As vartype2]]
```

`Dim`, `Private`, `Static`, and `Public` are Visual Basic keywords that define how and where the variable can be used. `varname` and `varname2` represent the names of the variables that you want to declare. As indicated in the syntax, you can specify multiple variables in the same statement, as long as you separate the variables by commas. (Note that the syntax shows only two variables, but you can specify any number.)

`vartype` and `vartype2` represent the type definition of the respective variables. The type definition is a keyword which tells Visual Basic what kind of information will be stored in the variable. The type must be one of those specified in Table 6.1. As indicated, the variable type is an optional property. If you include the variable type, you must include the keyword `As`. If you do not include a variable type, the default type is used.

N O T E   Unless otherwise specified, the default variable type is variant. ▨

The following code shows the use of these declaration statements for actual variables:

```
Private numval As Integer
Private avgval As Integer, inptval As Variant
Static clcAverage As Single
Dim inptmsg As String
```

Implicit Declaration   It is best to declare your variables using the `Dim` or other statements shown earlier, but you also can assign a type to a variable using an implicit declaration. With this type of declaration, a special character is used at the end of the variable name when the variable is first assigned a value. The characters for each variable type are shown in Table 6.2.

Table 6.2   Special Characters at the End of a Variable Name Can Identify the Type of Data Stored by the Variable

Variable Type	Character
Integer	%
Long	&
Single	!
Double	#
Currency	@
String	$
Byte	None
Boolean	None
Date	None
Object	None
Variant	None

Using implicit declarations, the preceding code could be rewritten as follows:

```
numval% = 0
avgval% = 1
inptval = 5
clcAverage! = 10.1
inptmsg$ = "Mike"
```

You may have noticed that the variable `inptval` didn't have a declaration character. This means that `inptval` will be of the variant type.

Fixed-Length Strings   Most strings that you use in your programs will be of the type known as *variable-length strings*. These strings can contain any amount of text, up to 64,000 characters. As information is stored in the variable, the size of the variable adjusts to accommodate the length of the string. Both the implicit and explicit declarations shown earlier created variable-length strings. There is, however, a second type of string in Visual Basic: the *fixed-length string*.

As the name implies, a fixed-length string remains the same size, regardless of the information assigned to it. If a fixed-length string variable is assigned an expression shorter than the defined length of the variable, the remaining length of the variable is filled with the space character. If the expression is longer than the variable, only the characters that fit in the variable are stored; the rest are truncated.

Part
I

Ch
6

A fixed-length string variable may only be declared using an explicit declaration of the form:

```
Dim varname As String*strlength
```

Notice that this declaration is slightly different from the previous declaration of a string variable. The declaration of a fixed-length string variable contains an asterisk (*) to tell Visual Basic that the string will be of a fixed length. The final parameter, `strlength`, tells the program the maximum number of characters that the variable can contain.

> **N O T E**   As with variable-length strings, you can use the Public, Private, or Static keywords in place of Dim. ▓

Using the *Option Explicit* Statement

I told you earlier that it's a good programming practice to declare the variables of your program before they are used. You can ensure that you do this by setting one of the environment options of Visual Basic. Figure 6.1 shows the Options dialog box that is accessible when you choose the Options item from the Tools menu. On this dialog box, you'll find the option Require Variable Declaration. Checking this box forces you to declare each variable before you use it.

FIG. 6.1
Requiring Variable declaration helps you prevent mistyping variable names.

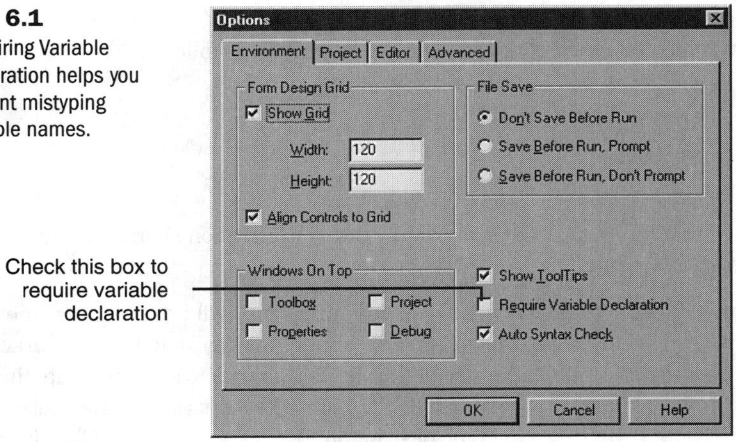

Check this box to require variable declaration

Setting the Require Variable Declaration option causes the `Option Explicit` statement to be placed at the beginning of each new code module or form that is added to your project, as shown in Figure 6.2.

FIG. 6.2
The *Option Explicit* statement is added to your program.

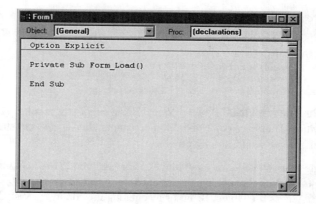

If you fail to declare a variable with this option set, you will receive the message `Variable not defined` when you try to run your code. The integrated debugger highlights the offending variable and halts the execution of your program. The benefit of this is that it helps you to avoid errors in your code that might be caused by typographic errors. For example, you might declare a variable using the following statement:

```
Dim myname As String
```

If in a later statement, you mistyped the variable name, Visual Basic would catch the error for you. For example, this statement would cause an error.

```
mynme = "Mike McKelvy"
```

> **CAUTION**
>
> If you set the Require Variable Declaration option after starting to create a program, the option has no effect on any forms or modules that have already been created. In this case, you need to add the `Option Explicit` statement as the first line of code in any existing forms or modules.

What's Different About Constants

Variables are just one way of storing information in the memory of a computer. Another way is to use *constants*. Constants in a program are treated a special way. Once you define them (or they are defined for you by Visual Basic), you cannot change them later in the program by using an assignment statement. If you try, Visual Basic generates an error when you run your program.

Constants are most often used to replace a value that is hard to remember, such as the color value for the Windows title bar. It is easier to remember the constant `vbActiveTitleBar` than the value—2147483646. You can also use a constant to avoid typing long strings if they are used in a number of places. For example, you could set a constant such as `FileFoundError` containing the string, "`The requested file was not found.`"

Part

I

Ch

6

Constants are also used a lot for conversion factors, such as 12 inches per foot or 3.3 feet per meter. The following code example shows how constants and variables are used.

```
Const MetersToFeet = 3.3
inpmeters = InputBox("Enter a distance in meters")
distfeet = inpmeters * MetersToFeet
MsgBox "The distance in feet is: " & Str(distfeet)
```

Constants Supplied by Visual Basic   Visual Basic supplies a number of sets of constants for various activities. There are color-definition constants, data-access constants, keycode constants, and shape constants, among others.

The constants that you need for most functions are defined in the help topic for the function. If you want to know the value of a particular constant, you can use the Object Browser, as shown in Figure 6.3. Access the Object Browser by clicking its icon in the Visual Basic toolbar. You can use the list to find the constant that you want. When you select it, its value and function are displayed in the text area at the bottom of the dialog box.

FIG. 6.3
The Object Browser shows you the value and function of most of Visual Basic's internal constants.

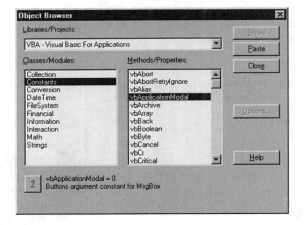

Creating Your Own Constants   While Visual Basic defines a large number of constants for many activities, there will be times when you need to define your own constants. Constants are defined using the Const statement to give the constant a name and a value, as illustrated in the following syntax:

```
Const constantname [As constanttype] = value
```

If you think this statement looks similar to the declaration of a variable, you are right. As with declaring a variable, you provide a name for the constant and, optionally, specify the type of data it will hold. The Const keyword at the beginning of the statement tells Visual Basic that this statement defines a constant. This distinguishes the statement from one that just assigns a value to a variable. In declaring the type of a constant, you use the same types as you did for defining variables (these types are defined in Table 6.1). Finally, to define a constant, you must include the equal sign and the value to be assigned. If you are defining a string constant or date constant, remember to enclose the value in either quotes or pound signs, respectively.

TIP While you can use the `Const` statement anywhere in a procedure, it is best to define all the necessary constants at the beginning of the procedure.

Writing Simple Statements

Now you know a little about variables and constants. You know what data they can store and how to initially set them up. But that is just the beginning of working with information in a program. You also need to be able to assign information to the variable and manipulate that information. Stay tuned—I am about to cover that.

Using the Assignment Statement

After setting up a variable, the first thing you need to do to use the variable is to store information in the variable. This is the job of the *assignment statement.* The assignment statement is quite simple; you specify a variable whose value you want to set and then place an equal sign after the variable name, and then you follow this with the expression that represents the value you want stored. The expression can be a literal value, a combination of other variables and constants, or even functions that return a value. There is no limit on the complexity of the expression you use. The only restriction is that the expression must yield a value of the same type as the variable to which it is assigned. The following statements illustrate different assignment statements.

```
NumStudents = 25
SumScores = 2276
AvgScore = SumScores / NumStudents
TopStudent = "Janet Simon"
ISpace = InStr(TopStudent," ")
FirstName = Left(TopStudent,ISpace)
```

You might have noticed that these statements look very similar to the ones used to set the properties of forms and controls in the section "Getting Down to Basics of Forms" in Chapter 3, "Using Forms and Controls." Actually, they are the same. Most properties of forms and controls are variables. They can be set at design time, but can also be changed at runtime using an assignment statement. You can also use a property on the right side of a statement to assign its value to a variable for further processing. For example, you could change one of the preceding lines to read the top student name from a text box:

```
TopStudent = txtTop.Text
```

Using Math Operators

Processing numerical data is one of the key activities of most computer programs. Math operations are used to determine customer bills, interest due on savings or credit card balances, average scores for a class test, and many other tasks. Visual Basic supports a number of different math operators that can be used in program statements. These operations and the Visual Basic symbol for each operation are summarized in Table 6.3. The operations are then described in detail.

Part

I

Ch

6

Table 6.3   Math Operations Are a Cornerstone of Many Computer Programs

Operation	Operator
Addition	+
Subtraction	-
Multiplication	*
Division	/
Integer division	\
Modulus	mod
Exponentiation	^

Addition and Subtraction   The two simplest math operations are addition and subtraction. You use these operations in such everyday chores as balancing your checkbook or determining how much change you should get back from a salesclerk. If you have ever used a calculator to do addition and subtraction, you already have a good idea how these operations are performed in a line of computer code.

A computer program, however, gives you greater flexibility than a calculator in the operations you can perform. Your programs are not limited to working with literal numbers (for example, 1, 15, 37.63, −105.2). Your program can add or subtract two or more literal numbers, numeric variables, or any functions that return a numeric value. Also, as with a calculator, you can perform addition and subtraction operations in any combination. Now take a look at exactly how you perform these operations in your program.

As indicated in Table 6.3, the operator for addition in Visual Basic is the plus sign (+). The general use of this operator is shown in the following syntax line:

```
result = number1 + number2 [+ number3]
```

`result` is a variable (or control property) that will contain the sum of the numbers. The equal sign indicates the assignment of a value to the variable. `number1`, `number2`, and `number3` are the literal numbers, numeric variables, or functions that are to be added together. You can add as many numbers together as you like, but each number pair must be separated by a +.

The operator for subtraction is the minus sign (–). The syntax is basically the same as for addition:

```
result = number1 - number2 [- number3]
```

While the order does not matter in addition, in subtraction, the number to the right of the minus sign is subtracted from the number to the left of the sign. If you have multiple numbers, the second number is subtracted from the first, then the third number is subtracted from that result, and so on, moving from left to right. For example, if you enter the equation

```
result = 15 - 6 - 3
```

the computer first subtracts 6 from 15 to yield 9. It then subtracts 3 from 9 to yield 6, which is the final answer stored in the variable result.

You can create assignment statements that consist solely of addition operators or solely of subtraction operators. You can also use the operators in combination with one another or other math operators. The following code lines show a few valid math operations:

```
val1 = 1.25 + 3.17
val2 = 3.21 - 1
val3 = val2 + val1
val4 = val3 + 3.75 - 2.1 + 12 - 3
val4 = val4 + 1
```

If you are not familiar with computer programming, the last line may look a little funny to you. In fact, that line is not allowed in some programming languages. However, in Visual Basic, you can enter a line of code that tells the program to take the current value of a variable, add another number to it, and then store the resulting value back in the same variable.

Multiplication and Division   Two other major math operations with which you should be familiar are multiplication and division. Like addition and subtraction, these operations are used frequently in everyday life.

Multiplication in Visual Basic is very straightforward, just like addition and subtraction. You simply use the multiplication operator, the asterisk (*) operator, to multiply two or more numbers. The syntax of a multiplication statement is almost identical to the ones for addition and subtraction:

```
result = number1 * number2 [* number3]
```

As before, result is the name of a variable used to contain the product of the numbers being multiplied, and number1, number2, and number3 are the literal numbers, numeric variables, or functions.

As a demonstration of how multiplication and division might be used in a program, consider the example of a program to determine the amount of paint needed to paint a room. Such a program could contain a form that lets the painter enter the length and width of the room, the height of the ceiling, and the coverage and cost of a single can of paint. Your program could then calculate the number of gallons of paint required and the cost of the paint. An example of the form for such a program is shown in Figure 6.4. The actual code to perform the calculations is shown in Listing 6.1.

Part

I

Ch

6

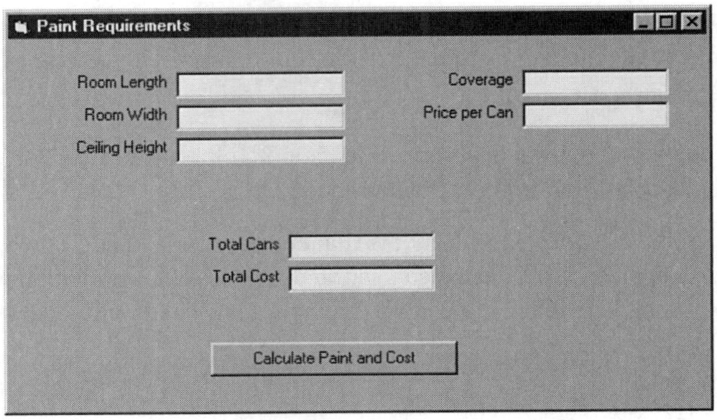

FIG. 6.4
Multiplication and
division are used to
determine the amount
of paint needed for
a room.

**Listing 6.1   CostEst.Txt—Cost Estimation Using Multiplication and
Division Operators**

```
rmLength = txtLength.Text
rmWidth = txtWidth.Text
rmHeight = txtHeight.Text
canCoverage = txtCoverage.Text
canCost = txtCost.Text
rmPerimeter = 2 * rmLength + 2 * rmWidth
wallArea = rmPerimeter * rmHeight
numGallons = wallArea / canCoverage
projCost = numGallons * canCost
txtGallons.Text = numGallons
txtTotalCost.Text = projCost
```

Division in Visual Basic is a little more complicated than multiplication. In Listing 6.1, you saw
one type of division used. This division is what you are most familiar with and what you will
find on your calculator. This type of division returns a number with its decimal portion, if one is
present.

However, Visual Basic supports three different ways to divide numbers. These are known as
floating-point division (the normal type of division, with which you are familiar), *integer division,* and *modulus* or *remainder division.* I'll give you a look at the syntax and then divide two
numbers to show the different results obtained with each.

Floating-point division is the typical division that you learned in school. You divide one number
by another, and the result is a decimal number. The floating-point division operator is the forward slash (/):

```
result = number1 / number2 [/ number3]
```

Integer division divides one number into another and then returns only the integer portion of
the result. The operator for integer division is the backward slash (\):

```
result = number1 \ number2 [\ number3]
```

Modulus or remainder division divides one number into another and returns what is left over after you have obtained the largest integer quotient possible. The modulus operator is the word mod:

```
result = number1 mod number2 [mod number3]
```

As with the case of addition, subtraction, and multiplication, if you divide more than two numbers, each number pair must be separated by a division operator. Also like the other operations, multiple operators are handled by reading the equation from left to right.

Figure 6.5 shows a simple form that will be used to illustrate the differences between the various division operators. The code for the command button of the form is shown here:

```
inpt1 = Text1.Text
inpt2 = Text2.Text
Text3.Text = inpt1 / inpt2
Text4.Text = inpt1 \ inpt2
Text5.Text = inpt1 Mod inpt2
```

FIG. 6.5
Visual Basic supports three types of division operators.

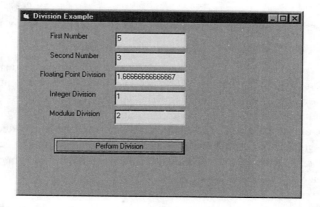

After setting up the form, run the program and enter **5** in the first text box and **3** in the second text box, and then click the command button. Notice that different numbers appear in each of the text boxes used to display the results. You can try this with other number combinations as well.

Exponents   Exponents are also known as *powers* of a number. For example, 2 raised to the third power is equivalent to 2 times 2 times 2, or 8. Exponents are used quite a lot in computer operations, where many things are represented as powers of 2. Exponents are also used extensively in scientific and engineering work, where many things are represented as powers of 10 or as natural logarithms. Simpler exponents are used in statistics, where many calculations depend on the squares and the square roots of numbers.

To raise a number to a power, you use the *exponential operator,* which is a caret (^). Exponents greater than 1 indicate a number raised to a power. Fractional exponents indicate a root. And negative exponents indicate a fraction. Here is the syntax for using the exponential operator:

```
answer = number1 ^ exponent
```

Part
I

Ch
6

The equations in the following table show several common uses of exponents. The operation performed by each equation is also indicated.

Sample Exponent	Function Performed
$3 \wedge 2 = 9$	This is the square of the number.
$9 \wedge 0.5 = 3$	This is the square root of the number.
$2 \wedge -2 = 0.25$	A fraction is obtained by using a negative exponent.

Working with Strings

Visual Basic supports only one string operator, the *concatenation operator.* This operator is used to combine two or more strings of text, similar to the way the addition operator is used to combine two or more numbers. The concatenation operator is the ampersand symbol (&). When you combine two strings with the concatenation operator, the second string is added directly to the end of the first string. The result is a longer string containing the full contents of both source strings.

The concatenation operator is used in an assignment statement as follows:

```
newstring = stringexpr1 & stringexpr2 [& stringexpr3]
```

In this syntax, `newstring` represents the variable that will contain the result of the concatenation operation. `stringexpr1`, `stringexpr2`, and `stringexpr3` all represent string expressions. These can be any valid strings, including string variables, literal expressions (enclosed in quotes), or functions that return a string. The & between a pair of string expressions tells Visual Basic to concatenate the two expressions. The & must be preceded and followed by a space. The syntax shows an optional second & and a third string expression. You can combine any number of strings with a single statement. Just remember to separate each pair of expressions with an &.

N O T E If you are working on converting programs from an older version of Visual Basic, you may find strings combined using the + operator. This was prevalent in versions of Visual Basic prior to version 4, as well as in older BASIC languages. While Visual Basic still supports the + operator, in case this operator is present in older code that you are modifying, I recommend that you use the & for any work that you do to avoid confusion with the mathematical addition operation. ▪

The following code (see Listing 6.2) shows how the concatenation of strings would be used in a simple program to generate mailing labels. The fields from the different text boxes are combined to create the different lines of the mailing label. The form for this program is shown in Figure 6.6.

Listing 6.2   Mailing.txt—String Concatenation Used in Mailing Labels

```
strFirst$ = txtFirst.Text
strLast$ = txtLast.Text
strAddr$ = txtAddress.Text
```

```
strCity$ = txtCity.Text
strState$ = txtState.Text
strZip$ = Str(txtZip.Text)
If optTitle1.Value Then strTitle$ = "Mr. "
If optTitle2.Value Then strTitle$ = "Mrs. "
If optTitle3.Value Then strTitle$ = "Miss "
If optTitle4.Value Then strTitle$ = "Ms. "
strLine1$ = strTitle$ & strFirst$ & " " & strLast$
strLine3$ = strCity$ & ", " & strState$ & "   " & strZip$
picOutput.Print strLine1$
picOutput.Print strAddr$
picOutput.Print strLine3$
```

FIG. 6.6
The mailing label application shows how strings are combined for display or printing.

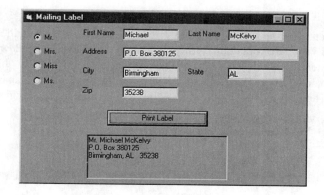

Making Decisions in Your Program

Most of the statements in your programs will be assignment statements, but there are other statements that are important for handling more complex tasks. These statements are known collectively as *control statements*. Without control statements, your program would start at the first line of code and proceed line by line until the last line was reached. At that point, the program would stop.

One type of control statement is the *decision statement*. These statements are used to control the execution of parts of your program, based on conditions that exist at the time the statement is encountered. There are two basic types of decision statements: If statements and Select Case statements. Each is covered in this section.

Using the *If* Statement

For many decisions, you will want to execute a statement (or group of statements) only if a condition is True. There are two forms of the If statement for handling True conditions: the *single-line* If statement and the *multiline* If statement. Each uses the If statement to check a condition. If the condition is True, the program runs the commands associated with the If statement. If the condition is False, the commands are skipped.

Part
I

Ch
6

The Single-Line *If* Statement   The single-line `If` statement is used to perform a single task when the condition in the statement is `True`. The task can be a single command, or you can perform multiple commands by calling a procedure. Here is the syntax of the single-line `If` statement:

```
If condition Then command
```

The argument `condition` represents any type of logical condition. The condition can be any of the following:

- Comparison of a variable to a literal, another variable, or a function.
- A variable or database field that contains a `True` or `False` value.
- Any function that returns a `True` or `False` value.

The argument `command` represents the task to be performed if the condition is `True`. This can be any valid Visual Basic statement, including a procedure call. The following code shows how an `If` statement would be used to print a person's name if his or her 40th birthday occurred during a particular year. This code is retrieving information from a database to perform the comparison and get the names. Figure 6.7 shows the output list that might be generated.

```
CompYear = Val(txtYear.Text)
BirthYear = Year(Members("BirthDate"))
If BirthYear = CompYear Then Form1.Print Members("FullName")
```

FIG. 6.7

You can use comparisons to print names of 40-year-olds.

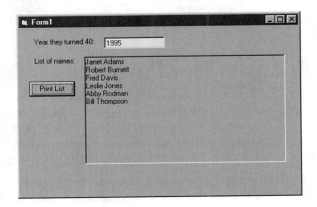

Multiple Commands for the Condition   If you need to execute more than one command in response to a condition, you can use the multiple line form of the `If` statement. This is also known as a *block* `If` statement. This form bounds a range of statements between the `If` statement and an `End If` statement. If the condition in the `If` statement is `True`, all the commands between the `If` and `End If` statements are run. If the condition is `False`, the program skips to the first line after the `End If` statement. The following code shows how a block `If` statement is used to credit an invoice in a membership program. The program asks the user if a credit should be issued and executes the block of code if the user answers yes (see Listing 6.3).

Listing 6.3 Credit.txt—Making Decisions in Code

```
If Retval = vbYes Then
    OrgCanc.Close
    Set OrgCanc = MemDb.OpenRecordset("Dues", dbOpenTable)
    OrgCanc.Index = "InvoiceID"
    OrgCanc.Seek "=", InvcID
    TotDues = OrgCanc("AmountDue") - TotDues
    If TotDues < 0 Then TotDues = 0
        OrgCanc.Edit
        OrgCanc("AmountDue") = TotDues
        OrgCanc("LastUpdate") = Date
        OrgCanc("UpdateBy") = UserID
        OrgCanc.Update
    End If
End If
```

TIP If you have a lot of commands between the If and End If statements, you may want to repeat the condition as a comment in the End If statement. This makes your code easier to read.

Working with the *False* Condition

Of course, if a condition can be True, it can also be False, and there may be times when you want code to execute only on a False condition. There may be other times when you want to take one action if a condition is True and another action if the condition is False. This section looks at handling the False side of a condition.

Using the *Not* Operator   One way to execute a statement or group of statements for a False condition is to use the Not operator. The Not operator inverts the actual condition that follows it. If the condition is True, the Not operator makes the expression False, and vice versa. The following code (see Listing 6.4) uses the operator to invert the value of the NoMatch property of a recordset. NoMatch is True if a record is not found in a search operation, and it is False if the search succeeds. Because the program can operate on a record only if it is found, the Not operator and NoMatch property are used as the condition of the If statement.

Listing 6.4 Falself.txt—Handling a False Condition

```
If Not OrgCanc.NoMatch Then
    OrgCanc.Edit
    OrgCanc("Renewed") = False
    OrgCanc("LastUpdate") = Date
    OrgCanc("UpdateBy") = UserID
    OrgCanc.Update
End If
```

Part
I

Ch
6

Handling *True* and *False* Conditions   The other way of handling `False` conditions allows you to process different sets of instructions for the `True` or `False` condition. You can handle this "fork in the road" in Visual Basic with the `Else` part of the `If  Else` statement.

To handle both the `True` and `False` conditions, you start with the block `If` statement and add the `Else` statement, as follows:

```
If condition Then
statements to process if condition is True
Else
statements to process if condition is False
End If
```

The `If` and `End  If` statements of this block are the same as before. The condition is still any logical expression or variable that yields a `True` or `False` value. The key element of this set of statements is the `Else` statement. This statement is placed after the last statement to be executed if the condition is `True`, and before the first statement to be executed if the condition is `False`. For a `True` condition, the program processes the statements up to the `Else` statement and then skips to the first statement after the `End  If`. If the condition is `False`, the program skips the statements prior to the `Else` statement and starts processing with the first statement after the `Else`.

N O T E   If you want to execute code for only the `False` portion of the statement, you can just place code statements between the `Else` and `End  If` statements. You are not required to place any statements between the `If` and `Else` statements. ■

The following code (see Listing 6.5) shows how both parts of an `If` statement are used to handle different handicap calculations for men and women in a golf handicap program.

Listing 6.5   Handicap.txt—Handicap Calculation Using Conditional Statements

```
If slope = 1 Then
    avgdif! = totdif! / bstscr
    hcidx! = Int(avgdif! * 0.96 * 10) / 10
    hcp% = Int(hcidx! + 0.5)
Else
    hcidx! = 0!
    avgdif! = Int(totdif! / bstscr * 100) / 10
    hcp% = 0
    Call Hcpchrt(avgdif!, hcp%)
End If
' Get member record
Get #1, pnt, mmbr
' Set maximum handicap for gender
If mmbr.gendr = "M" Then
    If hcp% > 36 Then hcp% = 36
Else
    If hcp% > 40 Then hcp% = 40
End If
```

Working with Multiple *If* Statements

In the previous sections, you saw the simple block If statements, which evaluate one condition and can execute commands for either a True or a False condition. You can also evaluate multiple conditions with an additional statement in the block If. The ElseIf statement lets you specify another condition to evaluate whether or not the first condition is False. Using the ElseIf statement, you can evaluate any number of conditions. The following code (see Listing 6.6) shows how a series of ElseIf conditions could be used to determine the grade distribution in a class.

Listing 6.6   GradesIf.txt—Grade Distribution with Multiple *If* Statements

```
For I = 0 To numstd
    If inpGrades(I) >= 90 Then
        GradeDist(4) = GradeDist(4) + 1
    ElseIf inpGrades(I) >= 80 Then
        GradeDist(3) = GradeDist(3) + 1
    ElseIf inpGrades(I) >= 70 Then
        GradeDist(2) = GradeDist(2) + 1
    ElseIf inpGrades(I) >= 60 Then
        GradeDist(1) = GradeDist(1) + 1
    Else
        GradeDist(0) = GradeDist(0) + 1
    End If
Next I
```

The preceding code works by first evaluating the condition in the If statement. If the condition is True, the statement (or statements) immediately following the If statement is executed, and then the program skips to the first statement after the End If statement.

If the first condition is False, the program skips to the first ElseIf statement and evaluates its condition. If this condition is True, the statements following the ElseIf are executed, and then control again passes to the statement after the End If. This process continues for as many ElseIf statements as are in the block.

If all the conditions are False, the program skips to the Else statement and processes the commands between the Else and the End If statements. The Else statement is not required.

Using *Select Case*

Another way to handle decisions in a program is to use the Select Case statement. This allows you to compare-run any of a series of statement groups, based on the value of a single variable. The Select Case statement identifies the variable to be evaluated. Then a series of Case statements specifies the possible values. If the value of the variable matches the value (or values) indicated in the Case statement, the commands after the Case statement are executed. If the value does not match, the program proceeds to the next Case statement. The Select Case structure is similar to a series of If/Then/ElseIf statements. The following lines of code show the syntax of the Select Case block.

```
Select Case testvalue
Case value1
```

```
statement group 1
Case value2
statement group 2
End Select
```

The first statement of the `Select Case` block is the `Select Case` statement itself. This statement identifies the value to be tested against possible results. This value, represented by the `testvalue` argument, can be any valid numeric or string expression, including literals, variables, or functions.

Each conditional group of commands (those are run if the condition is met) is started by a `Case` statement. The `Case` statement identifies the expression to which the `testvalue` is compared. If the `testvalue` is equal to the expression, the commands after the `Case` statement are run. The program runs the commands between the current `Case` statement and the next `Case` statement or the `End Select` statement. If the `testvalue` is not equal to the value expression, the program proceeds to the next `Case` statement.

The `End Select` statement identifies the end of the `Select Case` block.

N O T E   Only one case in the `Select Case` block will be run for a given value of `testvalue`. ▪

CAUTION

The `testvalue` and value expressions must represent the same data type. For example, if the `testvalue` is a number, the values in the `Case` statements also must be numbers.

The simplest form of the `Select Case` block uses only a single value for the comparison expression. You might use this type of statement to handle a payroll calculation where you have a single pay for each job grade. Figure 6.8 shows a form that could be used to calculate pay for hourly employees with various job classifications. The code to perform the calculation is shown in the following listing (see Listing 6.7).

Listing 6.7   Payroll.txt—Payroll Calculation with *Select Case* Statement

```
totpay = 0.0
paygrd = Val(txtGrade.Text)
payhrs = Val(txtHours.Text)
Select Case paygrd
    Case 1
        totpay = payhrs * 4.35
    Case 2
        totpay = payhrs * 4.85
    Case 3
        totpay = payhrs * 5.35
```

```
        Case 4
            totpay = payhrs * 5.85
    End Select
    txtPay.Text = totpay
```

FIG. 6.8
A payroll calculator can use a *Select Case* statement to handle different wages for different classes of employees.

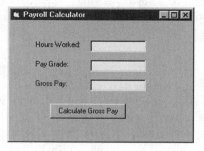

The preceding code works fine if your test variable matches one of the conditions in a Case statement. But, how do you handle other values that are outside the ones for which you tested? You can have your code do something for all other possible values of the test expression by adding a Case Else statement to your program. The Case Else statement follows the last command of the last Case statement in the block. You then place the commands that you want executed between the Case Else and the End Select statements.

You can use the Case Else statement to perform calculations for values not specifically called out in the Case statements. Or you can use the Case Else statement to let users know that they entered an invalid value. The following listing (see Listing 6.8) shows how to add a message to let the user know that an invalid code was entered in the payroll program shown earlier.

Listing 6.8   CaseElse.txt—Handling Invalid Input with *Case Else*

```
totpay = 0#
paygrd = Val(txtGrade.Text)
payhrs = Val(txtHours.Text)
Select Case paygrd
    Case 1
        totpay = payhrs * 4.35
    Case 2
        totpay = payhrs * 4.85
    Case 3
        totpay = payhrs * 5.35
    Case 4
        totpay = payhrs * 5.85
    Case Else
        MsgBox Str(paygrd) & " is an invalid pay code."
End Select
txtPay.Text = totpay
```

Part

I

Ch

6

Working with Loops

The other major type of control statement is the *loop*. Loops are used to perform repetitive tasks in your program. There are two main types of loops that are supported by Visual Basic: *counter loops* and *conditional loops*. Counter loops are used to perform a task a set number of times. Conditional loops are used to perform a task while a specified condition exists or until a specified condition exists. Each of these loops is discussed in this section.

For Loops

A counter loop is also known as a For loop, or a For/Next loop. This is because the ends of the loop are defined by the For statement and the Next statement. At the beginning of a For loop, you define a counter variable, as well as the beginning and end points of the variable's value. The first time the loop is run, the counter variable is set to the value of the beginning point. Then each time the program runs through the loop, the value of the counter is checked against the value of the end point. If the counter is larger than the end point, the program skips to the first statement following the loop.

> **CAUTION**
>
> If the beginning value of the loop is greater than the ending value, the loop will not execute at all. The exception to this is if you set up the loop to count backward, as is shown later.

The counter variable is changed each time the loop reaches the Next statement. Unless otherwise specified, the counter is increased by 1 for each loop.

 TIP For ease of reading your program, it is good practice to include the variable name in the Next statement. This is especially important in nested loops.

> **CAUTION**
>
> While you can use any numeric variable for the counter, you need to be aware of the limits of variable types. For example, trying to run a loop 40,000 times using an integer variable will cause an error during execution because an integer has a maximum value of 32,767.

The following code (see Listing 6.9) illustrates the use of several For loops to set the initial values of control arrays for a membership data-entry screen. The effect of the code is to create blank data-entry areas for a new member to be added. The form, after the code is run, is shown in Figure 6.9.

Listing 6.9   ForLoop.txt—Using *For* Loops to Initialize Variables

```
Dim I As Integer
For I = 0 To 22
    txtMember(I).Text = ""
```

```
Next I
For I = 0 To 1
    cboMember(I).ListIndex = -1
Next I
For I = 0 To 3
    mskPhone(I).Text = ""
Next I
For I = 0 To 1
    mskDate(I).Text = "  /  /  "
Next I
```

FIG. 6.9

A series of *For* loops is used to initialize control arrays.

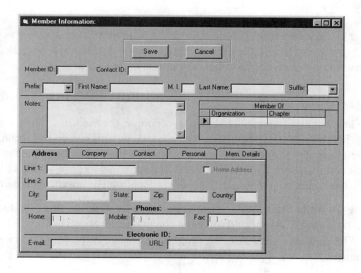

> **CAUTION**
>
> Never reset the value of the counter variable inside a `For` loop. Doing so may cause an infinite loop.

Typically, you will want your `For` loop to run through all the values of the counter variable. However, there may be times when you want the loop to terminate early. To do this, simply place an `Exit For` statement at the point in your loop where you want the loop to stop. The `Exit For` statement is typically associated with an `If` statement, as shown in the following code (see Listing 6.10).

Listing 6.10   ExitFor.txt—Exiting a Loop Early

```
Private Sub cmdSearch_Click()
txtResults.Text = "No match was found."
For Icnt = 1 To 30
    iloc = InStr(1, NameArray(Icnt), findstr, 1)
    If iloc > 0 Then
        txtResults.Text = NameArray(Icnt)
```

continues

Part

I

Ch

6

Listing 6.10   Continued

```
        Exit For
    End If
Next Icnt
End Sub
```

This code is used to search an array for a particular name. When the name is found, it is not necessary to continue searching the rest of the elements of the array. Therefore, the `Exit For` is used to terminate the loop.

> **N O T E**   As you have seen in this example and in others in the book, arrays and `For` loops are often used together. A `For` loop provides an easy way of looking at or processing each element of an array, because the counter variable can be used as the array index. ■

Do loops

The key feature of a conditional loop is, of course, the *condition*. The condition is any expression that can return either a `True` or a `False` value. This can be a function, such as `EOF`; the value of a property, such as the `Value` property of an Option button; or an expression, such as `numval < 15`. There are two basic types of conditional loops: a `Do While` loop, which repeats while the condition is `True`, and a `Do Until` loop, which repeats until the condition is `True`.

Using *Do While* Statements   The keyword `While` in the `Do While` statement tells the program that the loop will be repeated while the condition expression is `True`. When the condition in a Do While loop becomes false, the program moves on to the next statement after the Loop statement.

There are two forms of the `Do While` loop. The difference between the two is the placement of the condition. The condition can be placed either at the beginning or the end of the loop.

The first form of the `Do While` loop places the condition at the beginning of the loop, as shown in the following code. This code repeats the steps while there are available records in the recordset.

Listing 6.11   DoLoop.txt—Processing Database Records with a *Do Loop*

```
Do While Not OrgRenew.EOF
    OrgRenew.Edit
    If OrgRenew("Renew") Then
        OrgRenew("NumYears") = 0
        OrgRenew("Renew") = False
    Else
        OrgRenew("NumYears") = 1
        OrgRenew("Renew") = True
    End If
    OrgRenew.Update
```

```
        OrgRenew.MoveNext
Loop
```

By placing the `While` condition clause in the `Do` statement, you tell the program that you want to evaluate the condition *before* you run any statements inside the loop. If the condition is `True`, the repetitive statements between the `Do` statement and the `Loop` statement are run. Then the program returns to the `Do` statement to evaluate the condition again. As soon as the condition is `False`, the program moves to the statement following the `Loop` statement.

Both the `Do` and the `Loop` statements must be present.

With this form of the loop, the statements inside the loop may never be run. If the condition is `False` before the loop is run the first time, the program just proceeds to the statements after the loop.

To run the `Do While` loop at least once, the second form of the `Do While` loop must be used. This form of the loop places the condition in the `Loop` statement. This tells the program that you want the loop to run at least once and then evaluate the condition to determine whether to repeat the loop.

> **CAUTION**
>
> Do not put the `While` condition clause in both the `Do` and the `Loop` statements, because this will cause an error when you try to run your program.

N O T E If you are working on code that was developed by someone else, you may find a loop that starts with a `While` statement and ends with a `Wend` statement. This type of loop works the same as a `Do While` loop with the `While` clause in the `Do` statement. Visual Basic still supports a `WhileWend` loop, but I recommend that you use the `Do While` type of loop because it is more flexible. ■

Using a *Do Until* Statement The `Do Until` loop is basically the same as the `Do While` loop, except that the statements inside a `Do Until` loop are run only as long as the condition is `False`. When the condition becomes `True`, the loop terminates. As with the `Do While` loop, there are two forms of the `Do Until` loop: one with the condition in the `Do` statement and one with the condition in the `Loop` statement. If you place the condition in the `Do` statement, it is evaluated before the statements in the loop are executed. If you place the condition in the `Loop` statement, the loop is run at least once before the condition is evaluated.

A frequent use of the `Do Until` statement is in reading and processing data files. A loop starts with the first record of the file and processes each record until the end of file is reached. The following listing (see Listing 6.12) uses a loop to load all the authors from the BIBLIO.MDB sample database into a list box. Figure 6.10 shows the results of the program.

Part
I

Ch
6

Listing 6.12 Authors.txt—Using *Do Until* to Process a Database

```
Private Sub cmdListAuthors_Click()
Dim OldDb As Database, OldWs As Workspace, OldTbl As Recordset
Set OldWs = Workspaces(0)
Set OldDb = OldWs.OpenDatabase("C:\VB4\BIBLIO.MDB")
Set OldTbl = OldDb.OpenRecordset("Authors", dbOpenTable)
OldTbl.MoveFirst
Do Until OldTbl.EOF
    lstAuthors.AddItem OldTbl("Author")
    OldTbl.MoveNext
Loop
OldTbl.Close
OldDb.Close
End Sub
```

 T I P Indenting your code inside a loop or other structure (such as an `If` statement) makes the code easier to read.

FIG. 6.10
The list was set up using a *Do Until* loop.

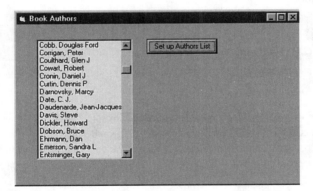

Making Your Program Bug Free

No matter how long you have been developing programs or how good you are at what you do, you'll still have errors crop up in your program. It's easy to make mistakes. All it takes is a simple typo to make your program crash. There are also logic errors, where your program runs but it just doesn't do what you want it to do.

Because you will make errors, one of the keys to successful program development is the ability to track down these errors, or bugs as they are often known, and kill them. Visual Basic provides you with a number of tools to help you find and eliminate bugs. These tools provide you with the following capabilities:

- Syntax checking which makes sure you enter commands correctly.
- Watches for variables which let you see the value of variables as your program runs.
- Code tracing which lets you see which program lines are being executed.
- Procedure call listing which tells you how your program got to a certain point.

How to Avoid Syntax Errors

One of the best ways to eliminate bugs is to prevent them in the first place. Visual Basic provides you with a syntax checker that checks each line of code as you enter it. If you have an error in the code, the checker alerts you to the problem as soon as you move to another line. The syntax checker looks for misspelled keywords and missing items in a statement, such as a parenthesis or a keyword. When you have a syntax error, Visual Basic shows the erroneous line in red and displays a message telling you the cause of the problem. Figure 6.11 shows how the syntax checker can alert you to a missing part of an If statement.

FIG. 6.11
The syntax checker looks for obvious errors in the commands you enter.

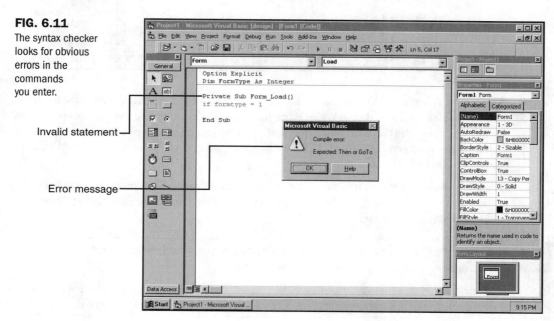

The syntax checker is usually turned on when you first install Visual Basic. However, if for some reason it has been turned off, you can activate it by checking the Auto Syntax Check box in the Editor Options dialog shown in Figure 6.12. The options are accessed by choosing Options from the Tools menu.

Part
I

Ch
6

FIG. 6.12

The Editor Options dialog box lets you turn syntax checking on and off.

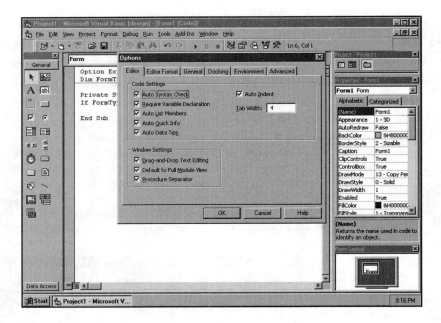

Another great feature of Visual Basic is the new code completion assistant. This assistant helps you by popping up the syntax of Visual Basic functions and by providing you with property lists for any object used in the code. While this feature is designed to help speed your coding, it also helps cut down on errors. Figure 6.13 shows how a property list for a form is displayed after you enter the dot in the code line.

The other thing that Visual Basic does for you in the Code window is it properly capitalizes keywords and displays them in blue. This gives you another visual indication that you have correctly entered a command.

TIP If you enter all your control names and properties in lowercase and spell them correctly, Visual Basic capitalizes them. This indicates that you didn't make any typos.

If you don't like the default colors that are used in the code editor, you can change them using the Editor Format Options dialog box. This is another tab on the same Options dialog box as the Editor Options.

What Happens When an Error Occurs

While you are running your code from the Visual Basic development environment, you may encounter errors in your program. These errors can be one of the runtime errors listed in the Help files or the program manuals. When you encounter an error, you are shown an error message like the one in Figure 6.14. The error message gives you the error number and a text description of the problem.

FIG. 6.13
The code completion
assistant helps
eliminate programming
errors.

FIG. 6.14
An error message
appears when you
encounter a runtime
error.

Error text

Error number

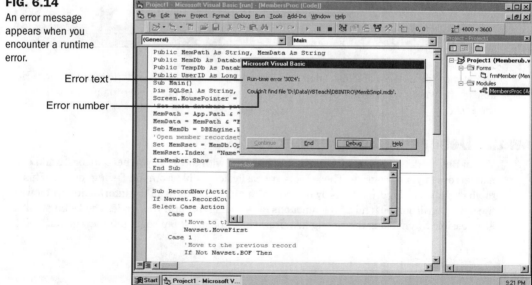

Part

I

Ch

6

Notice that the message box has several command buttons on it. One of these buttons, the Debug button, provides you with the first line of assistance in tracking down errors in your code. If you choose the Debug button, you are shown the Code Editing window with the offending line highlighted by a highlight bar and arrow as shown in Figure 6.15.

FIG. 6.15
Choosing Debug from the error message box shows you the line of code that caused the error.

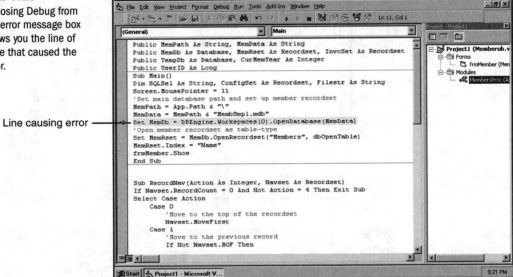

Line causing error ──→

Sometimes the error is obvious, such as mistyping a variable name or dimensioning the variable as the wrong type. Other times, though, you will need to dig deeper to find the source of the error.

How the Debugging Environment Works

Visual Basic's debugging environment provides you with the tools you need to locate and eliminate errors in your program. These tools are easily accessible from the Debug toolbar. This toolbar, shown in Figure 6.16, provides you with quick access to all the information windows of the debug environment and all the functions for stepping through your code. The Debug toolbar is accessible by choosing the Debug item from the Toolbars submenu of the View menu.

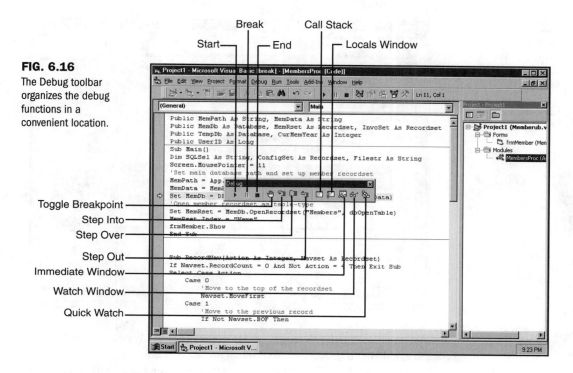

FIG. 6.16
The Debug toolbar organizes the debug functions in a convenient location.

Let's take a closer look at the tools at your disposal.

How to Determine the Value of a Variable

Often when you encounter an error, it is because a variable contains a value that you did not expect. It may be that a variable had a zero value and was then used in a division operation. Or a variable that was supposed to contain the name of a file somehow had a number stored in it. You can also see how a variable changes as the program runs. Watching the change in a variable's value, or the lack of a change, is one of the major factors in finding many program errors, including infinite loops.

To debug your program, you have to be able to determine the value of the variables that are used in the program at different points in the execution. Visual Basic provides you with three basic methods of checking the values of variables—the Watch window, the Locals window, and quick watches.

Using the Watch Window   One way to view the value of variables is with the Watch window. This window, shown in Figure 6.17, will show you the expression you are watching, the value of the expression, the type of watch, and the procedure where the expression is being evaluated. Using the Watch window allows you to look at only the variables or expressions which interest you. You can access the Watch window from the Debug toolbar or by selecting the Watch Window item from the View menu.

FIG. 6.17
The Watch window shows the value of variables and expressions you define.

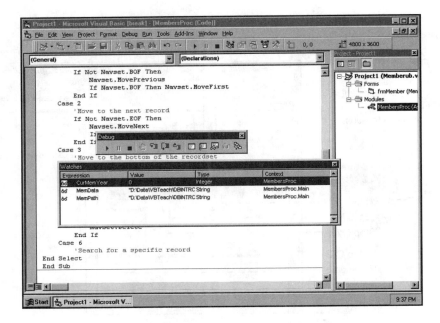

To set up a variable or expression for viewing, you have to add it to the Watch window. To do this, you choose the Add Watch option from the Debug menu. This brings up the Add Watch dialog box as shown in Figure 6.18. The dialog allows you to enter the name of the variable to observe in the Expression Field.

FIG. 6.18
The Add Watch dialog box lets you set up variables to observe during program execution.

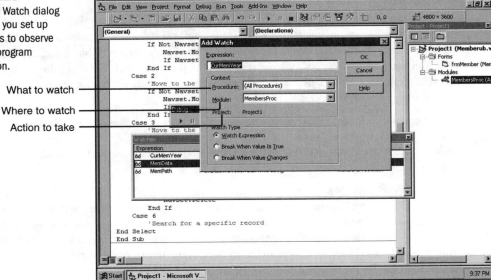

The Add Watch dialog box also allows you to specify where you want to observe the variable. These context settings let you observe the value of the variable during the entire program or just during a specific procedure.

The Watch Type options let you decide whether to just look at the value of the variable or to break (pause the execution of the code) when a specific condition exists. You can choose to have the program pause every time a variable changes or when the watch expression is True. This way, you can determine when a variable reaches or exceeds a specific value. To use this type of watch, the expression must be a Boolean variable or a logical expression.

If at a later time, you want to edit the watch expression, you can right-click the mouse in the Watch window and select the Edit Watch item from the pop-up window. This brings up the Edit Watch dialog box which is basically the same as the Add Watch dialog box, but adds a command button that allows you to delete the watch.

Using the Locals Window   Sometimes, it is easier to just check the values of all the variables in a procedure than to try to guess which variable has the problem. This is easily done with the Locals window. The Locals window, shown in Figure 6.19, lists all the variables declared in the current procedure along with their current values. Variables that are declared outside the current procedure are not shown.

FIG. 6.19
The Locals window lets you look at all the declared variables in a procedure.

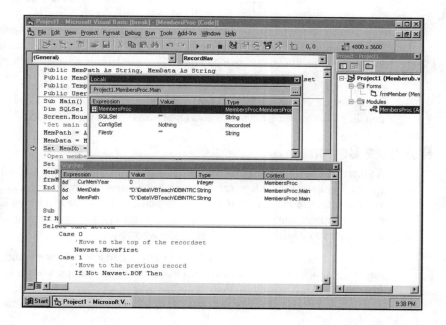

Part
I
Ch
6

Using a Quick Watch   If you need to find out only the current value of a variable, but do not need to track its value as the program progresses, you can use a quick watch. A quick watch displays a dialog box that shows the name of the variable, its current value, and the procedure in which it is currently being used. An example of the quick watch is shown in Figure 6.20.

FIG. 6.20

A quick watch provides a snapshot look at a variable.

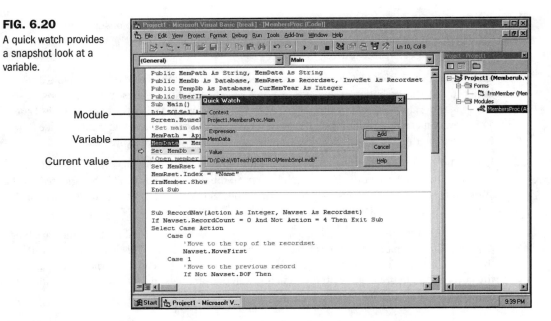

Module

Variable

Current value

To use a quick watch, highlight a variable in the Code window while the program is paused. Then you can click the Quick Watch button on the Debug toolbar or choose Quick Watch from the Debug menu to show the dialog box. You can also run a quick watch by pressing Shift+F9.

Another way to quickly view the value of a variable or an object property is to rest the mouse cursor on the variable in the code window. After the mouse sits for a few seconds, the value will pop up in a little box, similar to a ToolTip. This is shown in Figure 6.21.

Running Commands

Another part of the Debug environment is the Immediate window. This window allows you to enter program commands which are executed as soon as you press Enter. From this window, you can print the value of a variable, or even change the value of a variable, using an assignment statement. You can also use commands to change the environment of your program, such as the fonts on a form or the color of text in a text box.

The Immediate window allows you to enter any single line command. Loops and block statements (If blocks and Select Case blocks) are not allowed. If you issue the print command from the Immediate window, the results are printed on the line following the command. This provides another way to view the contents of a variable. Figure 6.22 shows how the Immediate window can be used to find the value of a variable or set a variable.

FIG. 6.21

You can find the value of a variable simply by resting the mouse on the variable in the code window.

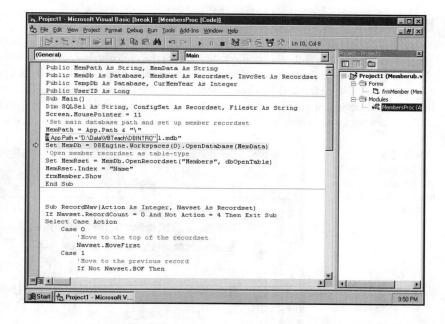

FIG. 6.22

You can run any code statement in the Immediate window.

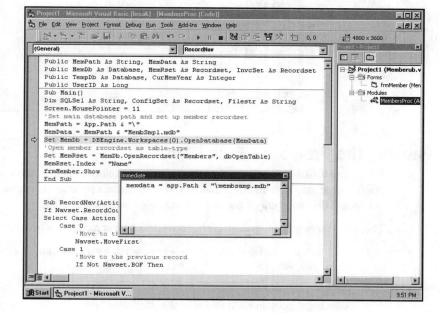

How Did I Get Here

One final item you may need in debugging is the Call Stack. This window tells you which procedure is currently executing. It also shows the entire string of procedure calls from the initial procedure to the current one. These calls are listed from the most recent procedure (at the top of the list) to the initial calling procedure (at the bottom of the list). This list helps you determine how you got to the current point. This way, you will know if a procedure is being accessed from an area that you don't want. The Call Stack is shown in Figure 6.23.

FIG. 6.23
The Call Stack shows you the procedures that led up to the current procedure.

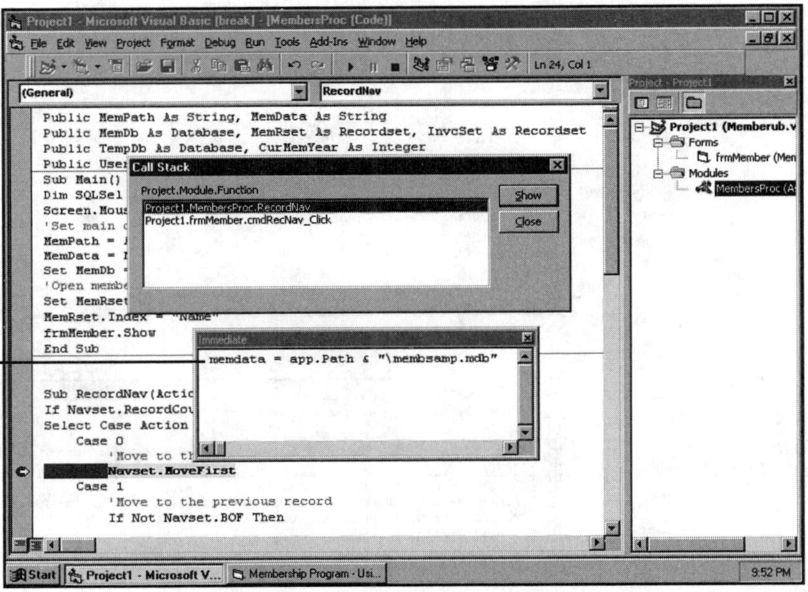

Current procedure

Pausing the Program's Execution

Whenever Visual Basic encounters an error, it automatically pauses the execution of the program. There may also be times that you want to pause a program when there is no error. You would do this to check the value of variables at a specific point.

There are three ways to pause a program without an error having occurred.

- Set a watch to pause the program, either when a variable changes value or when an expression is True.
- Click the Break icon on the toolbar.
- Set a breakpoint in code to pause at a particular line.

Setting a watch point to pause the program was discussed in the previous section, and clicking the Break icon is self-explanatory. Therefore, we will concentrate on setting a breakpoint in the code.

A breakpoint in code is set while you are in design mode. In order to set the breakpoint, you must have the Code window open and be in the procedure containing the statement where you want the break to occur. At this point, you can set the breakpoint in one of four ways:

- Click the mouse in the margin to the left of the statement.
- Select the statement on which to break and click the Toggle Breakpoint icon from the Debug toolbar.
- Select the statement on which to break and choose the Toggle Breakpoint item from the Debug menu.
- Select the statement on which to break and press F9.

When a breakpoint is set, the code statement is highlighted as shown in Figure 6.24.

FIG. 6.24
A breakpoint allows you to pause the code at a specific statement.

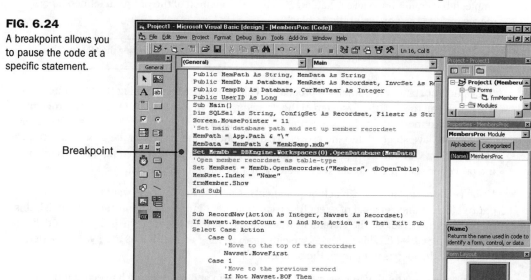

Each of the methods for setting the breakpoint actually toggles the breakpoint status of the line. This means that if the statement is not a breakpoint, it becomes one. Also, if it is a breakpoint, the breakpoint is removed.

Tracing Through Your Code

In the previous sections, we have discussed how to pause the code, but in order for debugging to be effective, you have to be able to execute program statements and watch their effects.

After the execution of the program has stopped, you have several options for continuing the execution. You can:

Part

I

Ch

6

- Execute a single statement
- Execute a group of statements
- Resume normal execution of the code

To execute a single statement or group of statements, you need to be in the Code Editing window. To execute the program one statement at a time, you can press the F8 key. This executes the statement currently highlighted by the highlight bar, and moves the box to the next statement. By repeatedly pressing the key, you move through the code a step at a time.

This method is extremely useful for determining which part of a conditional statement is being accessed. When the program encounters an If or Select Case statement, it evaluates the condition and moves immediately to the proper part of the block for the condition. For example, if the condition in an If statement is False, execution of the program immediately moves to the Else portion of the If block.

 TIP Clicking on the Step Into button on the Debug toolbar has the same effect as pressing the F8 key.

If the current statement contains a procedure call, pressing F8 or clicking the Step Into button will cause you to go to the first step of the procedure. If you want to run the entire procedure and return to the next line in the current program, press Shift+F8 or click the Step Over icon. Also, if you have stepped into the procedure and want to run the rest of the procedure, you can click the Step Out button or press Ctrl+Shift+F8. This will run the remaining lines of code in the procedure and pause again at the statement after the procedure call.

If you're fairly certain that a block of statements is error free, you may want to execute the entire block at once instead of executing each statement individually. You can accomplish this by placing the cursor on the statement where you next want to pause the program execution, and pressing Ctrl+F8. This method is useful for executing an entire loop after you have determined that the loop is not part of the problem.

Finally, when you think you have resolved the problem and want to finish executing the program, you can press the F5 key to allow the program to continue running normally. You can also do this by pressing the Continue icon (which also serves as the Run icon) on the toolbar.

From Here . . .

This chapter introduced you to a variety of program language pieces. Several of the examples also used programming elements that are covered in other chapters of the book. To learn more about related topics, see the following chapters:

- Chapter 3 "Using Forms and Controls," provides in-depth information about Visual Basic's forms and controls.
- Chapter 13, "Writing Programs with the Data-Access Objects," will teach you how to access databases.

CHAPTER 7

Managing Your Project from Beginning to End

In Chapter 6, "Programming in Visual Basic," you learned a little about writing code to make your computer programs accomplish various tasks. You saw how you could manipulate data and how control statements allowed you to execute repetitive tasks and to selectively execute statements. However, there is more to creating a good, maintainable program than just writing code.

One of the things you need to be able to do is create reusable pieces of code and reusable program pieces so you are not constantly reinventing the wheel (or the program, in this case). The second thing you need to be able to do is manage those various pieces of code and forms effectively. This chapter deals with both these aspects of project management. First, I discuss how you can use procedures to eliminate repetitive code in your programs. Then I show you how those procedures and other program components are managed using the project manager. Finally, I give you a brief look at compiling and distributing your programs for others to use. ■

Using the same code in multiple parts of your program

You will often find that several parts of your program perform the same function. It is easier to maintain your program if you only have the code for the function in one place.

Reusing forms that were created for other programs

You can use the same form in multiple programs, or you can create a form template to make it easier to create similar forms.

Managing custom controls in the program

As you work more with Visual Basic, you will probably add third-party controls to your set of tools. You will see how to add these controls to your project.

Keeping up with all the pieces

Your programs will typically consist of a number of forms, some code modules, class modules, and possibly some user defined controls. Visual Basic provides you with a set of tools to manage all these pieces.

Working with Procedures and Functions

If you have ever watched a machine such as a car being built, you know that the entire machine is not built in one place. Rather, different components of the machine are built and tested, and then the final product is assembled. This modular approach to manufacturing makes the entire production operation more efficient.

For years, computer programmers have used the same principal of modular construction that is used in manufacturing. Many parts of a program are written in modules known as *procedures* or *functions*. These are pieces of program code that perform a specific task. When the task needs to be performed, the procedure is called by another part of the program.

You have already been exposed to working with procedures, even if you didn't know it. Each time you enter code to be executed by a command button (or other control) in response to an event, you are building a procedure. These procedures are called automatically by the program when an event is triggered. You can build other procedures that you can specifically call from your program for other tasks. The procedures that you build will be referred to as Sub procedures to distinguish them from event procedures. These Sub procedures, along with functions, are the subject of this chapter. Many of the development principles also apply to event procedures (those specifically associated with a Visual Basic event).

Why Use a Procedure

Using procedures and functions provides you with several advantages over writing all your code in a single module. These advantages are the following:

- You can test each task individually. The smaller amount of code in a procedure makes it easier to debug.

- You can eliminate redundant code by calling a procedure each time a task needs to be performed instead of repeating the program code.

- You can create a library of procedures that can be used in more than one program, saving yourself development time in many of your projects.

Creating Procedures and Functions

The first step to creating a procedure or function is determining the task that you want the procedure to perform. Because a procedure is like a miniature program, this process is similar to the design of the program itself. You need to determine what task you want the procedure to perform, what information must be fed into the procedure, and what information will be returned by the procedure.

After you have determined the design of the procedure, you are ready to start building. There are two methods to start the construction of a procedure: using the Sub statement and using the Add Procedure dialog box.

All on Your Own   To create a procedure using the Sub statement, you first go to Visual Basic's code-editing window. This window is shown in Figure 7.1. In the code-editing window, select the (General) area from the Object list and the (Declarations) area from the Proc list. This places the cursor in an area that is not already part of a procedure.

FIG. 7.1
To start a new procedure, move to the (General) area of the code-editing window.

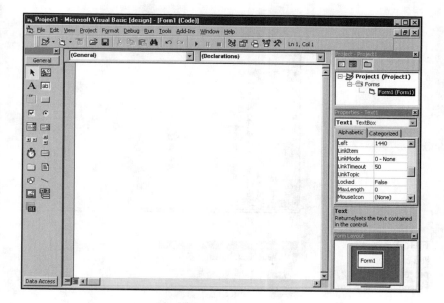

Start the new procedure by entering the keyword Sub and the procedure name at the cursor location. Procedures are named the same way that variables are named. (These naming conventions were summarized in Chapter 6 in the section, "Working with Variables.") When you enter the Sub keyword and the procedure name, three things happen: a set of parentheses is added at the end of the Sub statement, an End Sub statement is placed in the code window, and the current object in the Proc list of the code window becomes your new procedure name. This is shown in Figure 7.2 for a procedure named FirstProc.

You are now ready to enter any commands that you want to be run when the procedure is called.

With the Help of the Add Procedure Dialog Box   In the other method of creating a procedure, you first choose Add Procedure from the Tools menu. This brings up the Add Procedure dialog box, as shown in Figure 7.3. In the dialog box, perform the following steps:

1. Enter the name of the procedure.
2. Choose the type of procedure (Sub, Function, Property, or Event).
3. Choose whether the procedure is Public or Private.
4. Choose whether local variables are to be Static.

FIG. 7.2
The End Sub statement is automatically added when you define a new procedure.

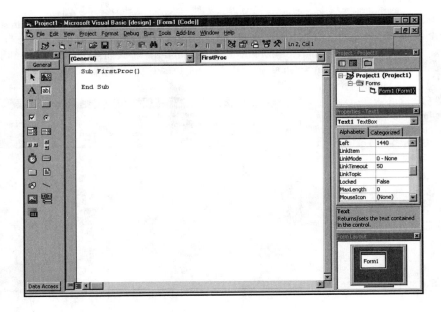

FIG. 7.3
You can create a procedure using the Add Procedure dialog box.

For most procedures, you will want to choose the Sub procedure type. This is similar to the procedures that are used in handling events in your code. A *function* type of procedure is one that returns a specific value. These procedures are covered later in this chapter. A *property* procedure is one used to set or retrieve the value of a property in a form or class module. An event procedure is one that is used to create an event in a form or class module.

After you have filled in the necessary information, you can choose the OK button on the dialog box. Visual Basic will then create the framework of a procedure in your code window.

If you choose to use parameters in your procedure, you will need to include them in the Sub statement at the beginning of the procedure.

Running the Procedure   Developing a procedure is only the first step to using one. You also need to be able to *run* (or call) the procedure from other parts of your program in order for it to perform its tasks. There are two methods for running a procedure: You can enter just the procedure name or you can use the Call statement. With either method, you simply specify the procedure name and any arguments that are required by the procedure. (The arguments are the ones specified in the Sub statement when you defined the procedure.)

> **CAUTION**
>
> If you specify parameters for your procedures, you must include the same number of parameters in the calling statement as were present in the definition of the procedure. Also, the parameters in the calling statement must be the same data type as defined in the procedure. Violating either of these conditions results in an error when your program is run.

 TIP   Including the Call keyword in all your procedure calls makes your code easier to read, because it immediately identifies a procedure.

Creating a Function   As with a procedure, a function can be created either with the Procedure dialog box or by entering the Function statement. Also as with procedures, a function can be public or private, and it can be stored in a form or in a separate module file. The syntax for a function is almost identical to that of a procedure. The following code shows how a function is created to calculate the maximum of two numbers.

```
Public Function Max(inptnum1, inptnum2)
    If inptnum1 > inptnum2 Then
        Max = inptnum1
    Else
        Max = inptnum2
    End If
End Function
```

As you can see, the declaration of the function—the first line—is very similar to the declaration of a procedure. The key difference between a function and a procedure is that a function returns a value. This value is assigned to the function name in one of the statements of the function. You can see this in the third and fifth lines of the preceding code.

While creating a function is very similar to creating a procedure, calling a function is quite different. A function typically does not stand alone in a statement. It is usually assigned to a variable or used in another type of statement. This is true of both the functions you create and Visual Basic's internal functions. To illustrate this, Listing 7.1 defines a simple function and shows two uses of the function in statements.

Part

I

Ch

7

Listing 7.1   FuncTest.txt—A Function Averaging Two Numbers

```
'*******************
'Define the function
'*******************
Public Function VarAverage(varavg1,varavg2)
    VarAverage = (varavg1 + varavg2) / 2
End Function
'********************************************
'Call the function in an assignment statement
'********************************************
newavg = VarAverage(25,15)
'********************************************
'Call the function from a decision statement
'********************************************
If VarAverage(num1,num2) > 25 Then
    NumSum = num1 + num2
End If
```

Determining the Scope of Procedures and Functions

When you create a procedure, it might be limited in where it can be used. The limitations are determined by where the procedure is stored and whether you include the Public, Private, or Static keywords in the definition of the procedure. Where a procedure can be used is referred to as the *scope* of the procedure.

Procedures can be defined in either of two ways: *public procedures* or *private procedures*. Which of these keywords you use in the Sub statement determines which other procedures or programs have access to your procedure.

Going Public   If you want to have your procedure or function available throughout your program, you need to use the Public keyword when you define the procedure. Using the Public keyword allows a procedure defined in one form or module to be called from another form or module. However, you have to be more careful with the names of public procedures, because each public procedure must have a unique name.

If you omit the keywords Public and Private from the Sub statement, the procedure is set up by default as a public procedure.

Keeping It Private   Using the Private keyword in the Sub statement lets the procedure be accessed from only the form or module in which it is defined. There are, of course, advantages and disadvantages to this approach. The advantage is that you can have private procedures of the same name in separate modules. The disadvantage is that the procedure is not accessible from other modules.

One thing you may have noticed in working with event procedures in other chapters is that they are, by default, private procedures. This is because, typically, controls are not accessed outside of the form on which they reside.

Preserving Variables   Typically, when a procedure is run, the variables it uses are created, used in the procedure, and then destroyed when the procedure is terminated. However, there may be times when you want to preserve the value of the variables for future calls to the procedure. You can handle this by using the Static keyword. This keyword can be applied to the declaration of the variables in the procedure or in the declaration of the procedure itself.

When Static is used in a variable declaration, only the variables included in the Static statement are preserved. If you use the Static keyword in the procedure declaration, all the variables in the procedure are preserved.

Storing Procedures and Functions in a Module

To create a procedure in a form file, you just need to choose the form from the project window and then access the code for the form. This is done either by double-clicking the form itself (or any control) or by choosing the View Code button in the project window, as indicated in Figure 7.4. Once the code-editing window is displayed, you create a procedure as described in the earlier section, "Creating Procedures and Functions."

FIG. 7.4
You can select a form for your procedure from the Project window.

If you want to be able to use a procedure throughout your program, and potentially in other programs, you need to store your procedure in a *module file*. This file is separated from the forms that you create for your program.

If you already have a module file in your project, you can create a new procedure by selecting the file, opening the code window, and then using the steps in the section "Creating Procedures and Functions" to build the procedure.

 Double-clicking the module name in the project window automatically opens the code window for the module.

If you don't have a module file in your project, or if you wish to use a new module, you can create a module by selecting Add Module from the Project menu. You can also create a new module by clicking the Add File icon in the toolbar. Either way, a new module is created, and you are placed in the code window to begin editing. When you go to save your project or exit Visual Basic, you are asked for a file name for the module file.

Working with Multiple Forms

While some programs you write will be simple enough that you can use a single form, most will be made up of multiple forms. One reason for this is the limitation of the amount of space on a single form. Another more important reason is that you will want to use multiple forms in your program to logically separate program tasks. For example, if you have a task in your program that is not performed often, it makes more sense to put it onto a separate form than try to squeeze it onto a single form with everything else. Also, loading and unloading forms as you need them saves system resources. In other words, your program takes up as little space as possible while running.

Adding New Forms to Your Program

When Visual Basic first starts a new project, typically it loads one blank form, as shown in Figure 7.5. As you design your program, you add controls to this form and write code to handle events that occur on the form.

FIG. 7.5
Visual Basic starts a new project with a single blank form.

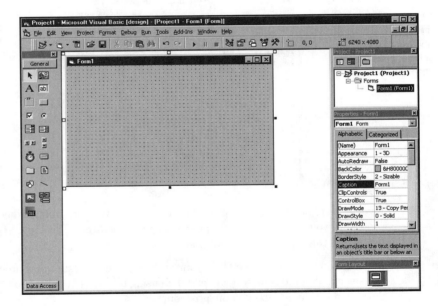

At some point in your design, you will decide that you need a second form (or third, fourth, and so on) to handle a new task or provide space to relieve the crowding on the initial form. Adding a new form is simple. You can either click the Add File icon or select Add Form from the Project menu. This places a new blank form on the screen, which looks just like your first form initially did. If you did not rename your first form from the default of Form1, the new form is named Form2 (or Form3, Form4, and so on). Otherwise, the new form is named Form1.

After you have added a new form, you can place controls on it and write code for its events, just like for the initial form.

Adding Code Modules to a Project

As you write more code to handle more events and more tasks, you will often find that you need to access the same procedure from a number of different places on a form or from multiple forms. If this is the case, it makes sense to store the procedure in a module file.

A module file contains only Visual Basic code. It does not contain any controls, pictures, or other visual information. When the time comes to add a module file to hold your procedures, you can do this either by clicking the Add File icon or by choosing Add Module from the Project menu. Either of these actions adds a new module to your project and places you in the code-editing window for the module, as shown in Figure 7.6.

FIG. 7.6
When you open a new module, you are placed in the code-editing window.

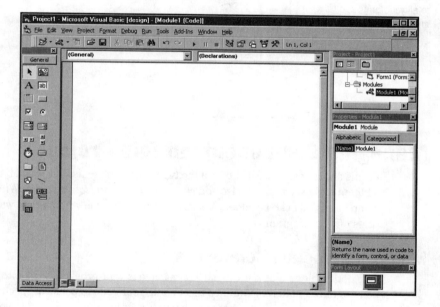

When you first open a new module, Visual Basic gives it the default name of Module1 (or Module2 for a second module, and so on). Like your forms and controls, it is a good idea to give the module a unique name. The module has a Name property, just as a form does. To change the name of the module, access the Properties dialog box and change the value of the Name property.

Part

I

Ch

7

Accessing the Forms and Modules of a Project

As you add forms and modules to your program, they are added to the project window. This window (see Figure 7.7) allows you to easily access any of the pieces of your program. You simply select a form or module by clicking its name in the project window. For a form, you can then click either the View Object button to work on the design of the form, or the View Code button to edit the code associated with the form. For a module, only the View Code button is enabled, because a module has no visual elements. Double-clicking the name of a form has the same effect as clicking the View Object button. Double-clicking a module name has the same effect as clicking the View Code button.

FIG. 7.7
The project window gives you easy access to all your forms and modules.

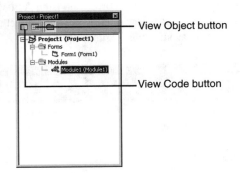

Managing Components in Your Project

Forms and modules are just two of the types of components that you can add to your project. In addition to these, you may also add *custom controls* and *class modules*. While there are a lot of components that can be added, Visual Basic provides you with an easy way to manage all the parts of your program.

Managing Program References

One of the things that you will have to manage is your program's *references*. The references point to different library routines that enable your code to perform specific tasks. For example, if you will be accessing databases with your programs, you will need to specify the Data Access Object library as one that is used by your code. Controlling references is quite easy in Visual Basic. The References dialog box, shown in Figure 7.8, lets you select the references required by your program by marking the check box to the side of the reference. Mark the ones you need and unmark the ones you don't need. You access the References dialog box by choosing the References item from the Project menu.

FIG. 7.8
The References dialog box lets you choose which libraries are used by your program.

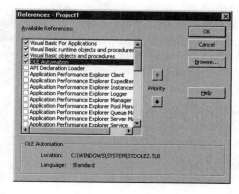

Controlling Your Controls

In a manner similar to that with the library references, you can add and remove custom controls from your project. Typically, when you loaded Visual Basic, a number of custom controls were loaded with the program. These controls are designed to perform specific tasks that are beyond the capabilities of the standard controls. You manage the custom controls in your project using the Components dialog box. You access this dialog box by choosing the Components item on the Project menu. As with the References dialog box, you choose the custom controls to add to your program by marking the check box next to the control name. After you exit the dialog box, your Control toolbox is modified to display the new controls. The Components dialog box is shown in Figure 7.9.

FIG. 7.9
The Components dialog box lets you add controls to your project.

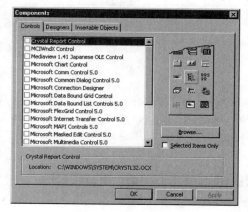

Adding Forms, Modules, and Classes to the Project

As you develop more programs, you may find that you have standard procedures or forms that can be used in many of your projects. You also may have developed custom procedures for getting the names and passwords of users, for opening files, or for any number of other tasks that are used in almost every program.

You could rebuild the form or rewrite the procedure for each program, but that would be a very inefficient way to do your program development. A better way is to reuse modules and forms that have been previously developed and fully tested.

Getting these modules and forms into your current project is a simple process. By selecting Add File from the Project menu, you bring up the Add File dialog box (shown in Figure 7.10). This dialog box lets you locate and select files to be added to your current project. Unfortunately, the Add File dialog box lets you add only a single file at a time. Therefore, if you have multiple files to add, you must repeat the operation several times.

FIG. 7.10

The Add File dialog box lets you select an existing form or module to add to your program.

N O T E   Files with a .FRM extension are form files. Files with a .BAS extension are module files. ■

Removing Pieces

To remove a module or form from your project, simply select the form or module in the project window and choose the Remove File item from the Project menu. Visual Basic asks you to confirm that you want to remove the file and then removes it from your project.

Controlling How Your Program Starts

When you first start a programming project, Visual Basic assumes that the first form created is the one that will be displayed as soon as the program starts. While this will be the case for many programs, for others you will want to start with one of the forms you create later in the development process. For some programs, you may not even want to start with a form at all.

Setting the Startup Form

If the first form is not the one you want to use to start your program, Visual Basic lets you choose which of your forms is shown initially by the program. This selection is made in the Project Properties dialog box, as shown in Figure 7.11. You access this dialog box by choosing Project Properties from the Project menu.

FIG. 7.11
The Startup Object list lets you choose which form is loaded when your program starts.

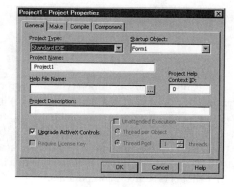

Using *Sub Main*

You may have noticed that, in addition to listing all the forms contained in your project, the Startup Object list includes the entry Sub Main. This is a reserved procedure name that lets your program start without an initial form. If you choose this option, one of your module files must include a procedure called Main.

One reason to start your program with the Sub Main option would be for security. The Main procedure could use an input box to obtain a user ID from the person running the program. If the ID was valid, the program could continue. Otherwise, the program would terminate.

The other reason to use Sub Main is if your program requires no user interaction. This type of program could be used to monitor a manufacturing process and record data.

Creating Distributable Programs

Obviously, when you write a program, you want to be able to distribute it so others can benefit from your work (and hopefully you can too). Since most of the people who will be using your program will not have Visual Basic on their machine, having them run the program from the development environment is not an option. Therefore, you will need to compile your program to make it available to others.

When you are planning to distribute your program, you will need to make several decisions. First, you will need to decide what type of program to create. And, second, you will need to decide how to compile your program. We will look at both of these decisions in this section.

Determining the Type of Program to Create

In Chapter 1, "Introduction to Visual Basic," in the section, "Types of Programs You Can Create in Visual Basic," you saw that there were several different types of projects that could be created in Visual Basic. Of these different project types, there are four basic types of distributable programs that can be created. These are:

- Standard EXE
- ActiveX EXE
- ActiveX DLL
- ActiveX Control

The standard EXE program is probably the most common type that you will create. This is the program that can run as a stand-alone application in a Windows 95 or Windows NT environment. The ActiveX EXE and ActiveX DLL are remote automation programs that are created as part of a multiple tier client server application. The difference between the two is that the EXE can be run on its own, while the DLL must be called from another application. The ActiveX control is a program component, like a text box or list, that can be used in Visual Basic programs or any other program that supports ActiveX components.

While you will typically make the choice of the type of program to create when you first start the project, you can change the program type later. You can do this in the Project Properties dialog that was shown in Figure 7.11. Simply select the new type from the Project Type list and click the OK button.

Compiling Your Program

When you are ready to compile your program, all you have to do is select the Make item from the File menu. This menu item will list the project name and the proper file extension for the type of program you are creating. For a Standard EXE or ActiveX EXE, the file extension will be .EXE. For an ActiveX DLL, the file extension will be .DLL, and for the ActiveX control, the file extension will be .OCX. After selecting the Make item, you will be shown the Make Project dialog, which allows you to specify the name and location of the executable file. Visual Basic then does the rest of the work.

While the actual compilation is quite easy, there are a few decisions you will need to make ahead of time. The key decision to make is whether to compile to P-code or native code.

P-code is the way Visual Basic programs have been compiled since version 1. These executables require a runtime DLL in order to run. The advantage of compiling to P-code is that the actual executable is small. This can be a real advantage if you have several programs which would require the same runtime DLL or are distributing over a network where the DLL can reside on the server machine.

Compiling to native code is an option that is new to Visual Basic 5. Native code runs faster than P-code, but produces a significantly larger executable file. If you choose to compile to native code, you will also need to make a decision about compiler optimization. You can choose to have the compiler try to create the smallest possible code, the fastest possible code, or not perform any optimization. You also have the option of compiling your program specifically for the Pentium Pro processor.

To choose the compiler options, you will need to go to the Compile tab of the Project Properties dialog. This part of the dialog is shown in Figure 7.12.

FIG. 7.12
The Compile options determine how your program will be compiled.

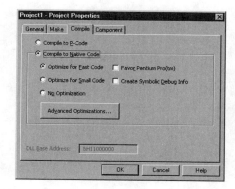

From Here...

In this chapter you have learned how to create procedures and functions to make reusing code routines easier. You have also seen how to add existing forms and modules to your programs to allow reuse of those components. And, finally, you have seen how to compile your program for distribution. For more information about other aspects of Visual Basic programming:

- See Chapter 3, "Using Forms and Controls," to learn more about creating the visual interface of your program.

- See Chapter 6, "Programming in Visual Basic," to learn more about writing code for your applications.

- See Chapter 8, "Introduction to Classes," to learn more about creating class modules.

Part

I

Ch

7

Introduction to Classes

The controls that you use in your Visual Basic programs are actually *classes* from which you create *instances* on a form. Until Visual Basic's version 4, you could not create a class from within Visual Basic. You had to use another program, such as Visual C++. Now, however, you can create your own classes to help make your programs more efficient and easily maintained. ■

What is a class

Classes are used to define reusable objects in your programs. A class contains data and procedures for manipulating the data.

How classes relate to controls

The Visual Basic controls that you use are classes with a visual interface. These classes contain properties, methods, and events.

How classes implement object-oriented programming

While the classes in Visual Basic are not 100% object-oriented, they do provide for encapsulation of data and methods and make it easier to create reusable code.

How to build a class

You will see how to create a class from scratch, and how to use the Class Builder to create new classes from existing ones.

How to access properties methods, and events of a class

Once a class has been defined, you still have to create an instance of the class to be able to use it. You will see how this is done.

Introduction to Classes

Programmers have always been concerned with efficiency in their programs. A programmer wants the program to run as quickly as possible, create the smallest possible executable file, and be as easy as possible to create and maintain. This last aspect of efficiency leads to using *reusable components*—pieces of code that can be used over and over in multiple projects. Most veteran programmers have a library of subroutines and functions that have been developed over time to handle various tasks. These components are then added to a new project as needed.

Since its inception, Visual Basic has supported the notion of reusable components. The controls you use to build the user interface of your programs are components that perform specific functions, such as getting a piece of text input or displaying a picture. These controls contain all the functions necessary to accomplish their tasks. This means that you do not have to add the code for these tasks to each of your programs. The controls are one form of object that can be used in your code. Visual Basic also has supported the use of *object linking and embedding* (OLE), which lets you access other programs to perform specific tasks.

Use of controls and OLE have greatly benefited programmers, but up to now, one thing was missing: the ability to create your own objects. Visual Basic now lets you create your own objects through the use of *class modules*.

Understanding Object-Oriented Programming Fundamentals

You have probably heard the term *object-oriented programming* or read about it in programming books or magazines. Even with the addition of the ability to create classes, Visual Basic is not a fully object-oriented programming language. To understand what Visual Basic can and can't do, you need to start with some basics of what OOP is.

OOP's key element is its use of reusable objects to build programs. These objects must be capable of supporting the following:

- **Encapsulation**   The information about an object and the manner in which the information is manipulated are all stored within the object definition.
- **Inheritance**   A new object can be created from an existing object and contains all the properties and methods of the *parent* object. This makes it easier to define new objects for specific needs.
- **Polymorphism**   While many objects can have the same methods, the method can perform differently for each of the objects. Through polymorphism, the program resolves the method call at runtime and runs the method appropriate for the current object. For example, almost all Visual Basic controls contain the Move method. When this method is called for a control, the program knows how to handle tasks for that particular control.

The controls that you use in Visual Basic support the concepts of encapsulation and polymorphism. However, they do not support the concept of inheritance. That is, you can't create a new control based on the definition of another control. There are, however, other programming languages that let you do this, such as Microsoft's Visual C++ and Visual FoxPro and Borland's Delphi.

Implementing OOP with Classes in Visual Basic

The classes that you can build in Visual Basic let you encapsulate the data and functions of an object. The classes let you define *properties* (the information or data in the object) and *methods* (what the object does with the information). But, as with the controls in Visual Basic, you can't use inheritance to create a new class from an existing one.

Even with this limitation, Visual Basic classes are powerful programming tools, as you will see in the rest of this chapter.

Using Classes in Your Programs

You can use classes in your Visual Basic programs in several ways. Each way provides you with programming capabilities that did not exist in Visual Basic prior to version 4. Visual Basic 5 has further enhanced the programmer's ability to work with classes.

First, you can use classes to encapsulate program segments to make them more easily reusable. The classes you create (to handle the program segments) define objects that can be created anywhere in your program. The advantage of using the objects to handle certain program functions is that it reduces the need for global variables and procedures in your programs. This is helpful because global variables are one of the most frequent causes of program errors, as well as one of the more difficult errors to trace. The classes that you define also can be added to other program projects to handle the same functions. Used this way, you can build up a library of useful classes for your development work. You can also create multiple instances of a class, with each object (instance) having its own set of property values. This modularity is something that can't be accomplished with global variables or routines.

The second use of classes is in building OLE Automation servers. Used in this way, the objects of a class provide functions to any of your programs, as well as to other programs that can serve as an OLE client. One use of OLE servers is to establish a program that enforces business rules on all data access to a database. This is the foundation of the three-tier client/server model.

Finally, you can use classes to build Visual Basic *add-ins*. These programs actually let you enhance the Visual Basic development environment itself. Add-ins can be used to build program wizards, such as the Data Form Designer; provide supplemental programs, such as the Data Manager; or provide tools for making your programming easier, such as a routine to automatically reset the tab order of all the controls on a form.

This chapter covers the development of classes for reuse in your programs. The creation of OLE Automation servers is covered in Chapter 21, "Creating Remote Automation Servers." However, the principles demonstrated in this chapter also are used in creating automation servers.

Building a Class in Visual Basic

Classes in Visual Basic are developed using the Class Module. This module contains only variable declarations and procedure code. There is no user-interface component of a class module. However, a class may take action using a form that is in the program. In the case of an OLE server, the forms can be included with the program that creates the server.

N O T E   You may add properties to forms and code modules using the same principals as those for adding classes. ■

A class module is a fairly simple program object. A class module has only three built-in properties and two native events. It has no methods of its own. Once a class module is created, you can add properties methods, and events to the class by declaring variables and by programming procedures and functions in the class module.

Creating a New Class Module

You start the process of creating a new class module by selecting Add Class Module from Visual Basic's Project menu. This starts a new class module with the default name of Class1 and opens the code-editing window for the class, as shown in Figure 8.1.

FIG. 8.1
The code-editing window opens when a new class module is created.

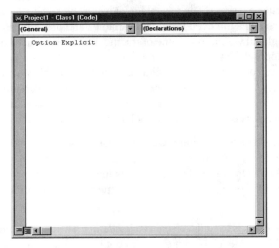

Once the new class is created for your project, you need to set the values of the three properties that define the class. These properties are Instancing, Name, and Public. Start with the easiest property, Name.

Choosing a Name You want to give each of your classes a unique name that is descriptive of the function it will perform. In addition, many developers like to preface the class name with the letter c to indicate in the programs that this is the name of a class. Using this convention, a class that provided improved printer functionality might be named cPrinter.

Going Out in Public The Public property of a class determines whether the class is available to other programs outside the current project. This property has only two possible settings, True or False. When Public is set to False, the class—and therefore the objects created from it—are available only to the program where the class is defined.

If the Public property is set to True, other applications have some access to the class. The type of access available is determined by the Instancing property, as defined in a moment. If you are creating an OLE Automation server, at least one class in the application must have its Public property set to True.

For Instance The final property of the class module is the Instancing property. This property has an effect only if the Public property is set to True; that is, when other applications can access the class. The Instancing property can be set to one of three values to define the type of access to the class that is available to other applications. These property values and their meanings are summarized in Table 8.1.

Table 8.1 Controlling Access to Your Class with *Instancing* Property

Value	Name	Description
0	Not Creatable	Instances of the class may be created only within the project that defines the class. However, other applications can control the class once it is created.
1	Creatable SingleUse	Other applications can create instances of the class. However, each time another instance of the class is created, a new copy of the OLE Automation server containing the class is started. The program that defines the class may create any number of instances of the class.
2	Creatable MultiUse	Other applications may create any number of instances of the class, and only one copy of the OLE Automation server is started.

In Any Event In addition to the three internal properties, the class module supports two events: Initialize and Terminate. When you create your class, you may want to include code in these events to cause your programs to take specific actions when an instance of the class is created and destroyed.

For example, if your class needs to know the current system date, you can include a code line in the `Initialize` event to set an internal variable to the system date. An example of use of the `Terminate` event would be to close an open database that was being used by the class.

Adding Properties to the Class

After defining the properties of the class, you need to start adding your own properties. The properties you add are the properties of the objects created from your class. These properties provide the way for the user to get information into the object. (You can also supply information to the object when you call a method, as you will see shortly.)

There are two ways to add a property to a class:

- Define a `Public` variable (you're probably familiar with this).
- Use a `Property` procedure.

Creating a Public Variable   You create a public variable using a declaration statement with the `Public` keyword, as shown in the following line of code. (The `Public` keyword takes the place of the `Global` keyword used in Visual Basic 3.)

```
Public str1 As String
```

The declaration statements can appear in the `Declarations` section of the class module or in any `Sub` procedure in the class.

> **N O T E**   You must explicitly declare public variables, but it is also a good practice to declare all variables. Therefore, you should require variable declaration by placing the `Option Explicit` statement as the first statement in the `Declarations` section of the class. You can require variable declaration throughout your program by checking the Require Variable Declaration check box on the Environment tab of the Options dialog box. This dialog box is accessible by choosing Options from the Tools menu. ▦

You can create properties for your class in this manner, but it is not the method recommended by most programmers. A public variable is visible to your application as soon as the object is created. Any part of your program can change the value of the variable without performing any checks on the data. Bad data passed to the object can then cause problems with operations done by the object.

Property Procedures   A better way to create properties in a class is to use the property procedures. These procedures provide the interface to the properties of the object, but they let you write code to verify that the proper data is passed to the class and perform other processing of the data. This protects the functions of your class from crashing as a result of bad data. Property procedures also provide you with the ability to create read-only properties, something that is not possible when using public variables.

There are three types of property procedures available: `Property Let`, `Property Get`, and `Property Set`. These procedures are defined in Table 8.2.

Table 8.2 Three Property Procedures Set and Retrieve the Values of Properties

Procedure Type	What It Does
`Property Let`	Accepts the value of a property from the calling program. Used to set the value of the property.
`Property Get`	Sends the value of the property to the calling program. Used to retrieve the value of the property.
`Property Set`	Special case of the `Let` procedure, used to set the value of an object variable.

To create a property procedure, you need to be in the code-editing window for the class with which you are working. Then choose Add Procedure from the Tools menu. This displays the Add Procedure dialog box, as shown in Figure 8.2.

FIG. 8.2
Create a property
procedure using
the Add Procedure
dialog box.

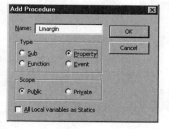

In the Insert Procedure dialog box, enter a name for the procedure. (This name will be the name of the property for your object.) Next, choose the Property Option button on the dialog box and then click the OK. This creates a `Property Let` and a `Property Get` procedure in your class module, as shown in Figure 8.3.

Setting a Property's Value   Notice that in Figure 8.3, the `Property Let` procedure automatically adds an argument to the procedure. This argument is the value that is passed from the calling program by the property-assignment statement. You can change the name of this argument to any valid variable name. You also can—and should—define the type of the variable by using the `As VarType` clause of the argument.

The code you place in the `Property Let` procedure typically takes the argument's value, performs data validation if necessary, and assigns the value to a private variable in the class module. When you use the private variable for any tasks in the class module, the information is protected from being inadvertently changed by other parts of the program. Also, because you can have multiple instances of an object, each object can have its own property values. An example of a Property Let procedure follows.

```
Private m_lmarg As Integer

Public Property Let LMargin(LMarg As Integer)
    If LMarg < 0 Then
        m_lmarg = 0
    Else
        m_lmarg = LMarg
    End If
End Property
```

Property Let procedure   Input value

FIG. 8.3

Both the Property Let and Property Get procedures are created with the Insert Procedure dialog box.

Property Get procedure

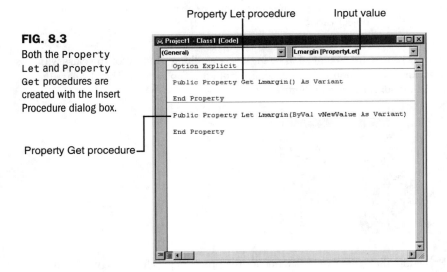

Retrieving a Property's Value The Property Get procedure lets your program retrieve the value of the property for the object. This is done by assigning the value to be returned to the name of the property, as shown here:

```
Public Property Get LMargin() As Integer
    LMargin = m_lmarg
End Property
```

You can also place other code in the procedure when a value for the property needs to be calculated or other actions need to be taken in returning the property's value. Notice that the Property Get procedure just shown includes the As Integer clause in the first line. This is optional, but if it is included, the type should be the same as that used for the argument passed to the Property Let procedure.

You can create a read-only property for a class by including only the `Property Get` procedure for the property. If the `Property Let` procedure is excluded, there is no way for the property value to be set other than by code within the class module.

Objects Are a Special Case   For some of your properties, you will want to be able to pass a database object, a control, or some other object to the class module. In this case, you must use the `Property Set` procedure instead of the `Property Let` procedure to give the property a value. When passing an object, the private variable you're using in the class module must be of the object type. This and the `Property Set` procedure are shown in the following code:

```
Private OutputTo As Object

Public Property Set OutputDev(inDev As Object)
    Set OutputTo = inDev
End Property
```

Notice in the code that the `Set` statement is used to assign the value of the object to the object variable. This is required any time you are setting the value of an object.

Methods Let the Class Take Actions

Because a class that could not perform actions would be practically useless, you need a way to create methods for your class. This is done by writing *public procedures* for the class. These procedures are just like the ones you write for other parts of your program. The procedures in a class can even have arguments passed to the procedures by the calling routines, just like other procedures. Passing arguments provides the final way to get information into the class. (Remember, public variables and property procedures were the other ways.)

Like all other procedures, the procedure in a class module starts with the declaration statement. If this statement uses the `Public` keyword, then the procedure becomes a method of the class and is accessible to any program that creates an object based on the class. If the procedure is prefaced by the `Private` keyword, the procedure may be called only from within the class itself. The following code shows a simple procedure in a class that prints a line of text to the printer in bold font. Because the procedure is public, it becomes a method of the class module.

```
Public Sub PrintBold(InText As String)
    curBold = Printer.Font.Bold
    Printer.Font.Bold = True
    Printer.Print InText
    Printer.Font.Bold = curBold
End Sub
```

Adding Events to Your Class

In Chapter 4, "Understanding the Event Model," you learned what events were and how to handle them in your code. An event is triggered when the user takes an action, such as a keystroke, or when a change has taken place, such as having a specific amount of time elapsing. Your classes can also initiate events as they are running. This is a new feature of Visual Basic 5 that enhances the capability of your classes.

To create an event in your class, you need to do two things:

1. Declare the event in the class.
2. Use the `RaiseEvent` statement to trigger the event.

To declare an event, you simply supply the name of the event and the variable passed by the event in a statement like the following:

```
Public Event QueryStatus(ByVal Completion As Single, _
ByRef Cancel As Boolean)
```

This statement is placed in the declarations section of the Class in which you want the event. The `Public` keyword is necessary to allow programs using the objects created from the class to respond to the event. The variables allow the event to pass information to the program using the class and to receive information back from the program. The event declared in the previous code could be used to keep the user informed of the status of a long query and to allow the user to cancel the query prior to completion.

After the event is declared, you can use the `RaiseEvent` statement to trigger the event anywhere in the code of your class. For the `QueryStatus` event, you might want to trigger the event after every 100 records that have been processed. This is illustrated in Listing 8.1.

Listing 8.1   Triggering an Event in Your Class

```
Public Sub ProcessData()
Dim MaxRecords, RecordsProcessed As Long
Dim blnCancel As Boolean
If ClsRset.RecordCount = 0 Then Exit Sub
ClsRset.MoveLast
MaxRecords = ClsRset.RecordCount
RecordsProcessed = 0
blnCancel = False
ClsRset.MoveFirst
Do While Not ClsRset.EOF
    If RecordsProcessed Mod 100 = 0 Then
        RaiseEvent QueryStatus(RecordsProcessed / MaxRecords, blnCancel)
        If blnCancel Then Exit Sub
    End If
    ClsRset.MoveNext
    RecordsProcessed = RecordsProcessed + 1
Loop
End Sub
```

Accessing a Class from a Program

After creating a class, you will of course want to use it in your program. In fact, you will probably want to use it in several places in your program and in multiple programs. After all, this is why programmers create reusable components in the first place.

Using a class is relatively easy, but it's a little different than using other program pieces with which you may be familiar. The main thing to remember is that a class cannot be used by itself. You must create an object from the class and then manipulate the object by setting its properties and using its methods. The creation of the object is the key part using the object, because you are already familiar with setting properties and using methods of other objects such as controls.

Creating the Object   There are two ways to create an object from a class that you have developed—using a declaration statement or using a Set statement. Once the object is created using either of these ways, you have access to its properties and methods and can use the object in your program. When the object is created using either method, the code in the Initialize event of the class module is run for the object.

Using a Declaration Statement   The first way to create an object from a class is to do it directly, with a declaration statement such as the following:

```
Dim EhnPrint As New cPrint
```

The declaration defines an object variable as being a new instance of the class (in this case, the cPrint class, shown in earlier code segments). Notice the use of the New keyword in the declaration statement. This keyword is required when you create an instance of an object.

Used in this way, the declaration statement immediately creates an instance of the object, and the properties and methods of the object are accessible to the program. As with any other variable-declaration statement, you may also use the Static keyword in place of the Dim keyword.

Using the Set Statement   The second way to create an object from a class is by using the Set statement. In this case, an object variable is declared, and then the Set statement is later used to create the instance of the object. The following code illustrates this method of creating an object:

```
Dim EhnPrint As Object
Set EhnPrint = New cPrint
```

Again, once the Set statement is used to create the object variable, the object's properties and methods are available to your program. The only difference from the previous method is that with this method, the object is not actually created until the Set statement is used. The preceding code can also be written as follows:

```
Dim EhnPrint As cPrint
Set EhnPrint = New cPrint
```

In this case, the type of object to be created is defined in the declaration statement, but because the New keyword is not present in the statement, the object is not actually created until the Set statement is issued.

If the object you are creating has events associated with it, you will need to use the Set method to create the object. You will also need to add one more keyword to the variable declaration statement. This is the WithEvents keyword. This keyword tells your code that the object will contain custom events that are available to be handled by your program. The use of the WithEvents keyword is shown in the following statement:

```
Private WithEvents mDataProc As DataProc
```

Setting and Retrieving the Property Values   Once the object has been created, you have access its properties. You can set and retrieve values of the properties in your code using assignment statements, just as you would do for the properties of a control. For example, the following code sets the left margin of the EhnPrint object:

```
EhnPrint.LMargin = 500
```

Because I previously defined LMargin in the class using a property procedure, this assignment statement causes the Property Let procedure of the class to be run. Similarly, to retrieve the value of the left-margin property, you use a statement like the following:

```
curmarg = EhnPrint.LMargin
```

As with properties of controls, you need to make sure that variables and literal values used in accessing the object's properties are of the same type as was defined for the property. Also, if you are going to be retrieving values of the property, it is a good idea to set a default value in the Initialize event of the class module.

When the property of an object is itself an object, you cannot use a standard assignment statement to set or retrieve the value. In this case, you must use the Set statement. The following code shows how the value of the OutputDev property of the EhnPrint object is set and retrieved.

```
'********************************
'Setting the value of the property
'********************************
Set EhnPrint.OutputDev = Printer
'***********************************
'Retrieving the value of the property
'***********************************
Set objvar = EhnPrint.OutputDev
```

As with any other properties, the variable or literal used in assigning or retrieving a property value must be of the same type as the property. In this case, the objvar variable must be defined as an object variable.

Using the Methods   Using the methods of the objects you create is like using the methods of Visual Basic's internal objects and controls. To execute a method, you supply the name of the object and the name of the method and provide any values that are required by the method as arguments. For the methods of your class, these arguments are defined in the argument list of the class module's procedure. The following line of code runs the `Output` method of the `EhnPrint` object.

```
EhnPrint.Output "This is a test."
```

Handling an Object's Events   Handling the events of an object you create is the same as handling the events of a form, control, or other object in your program. Basically, you write code for the events you want to handle and don't write code for the events you want to ignore. After you have declared an object using the `WithEvents` keyword, the object is added to the list of objects in the code window of your program. To handle an object's events, you select the object from the left drop-down list, and its event from the right °drop-down list, then write code for the event.

Getting Rid of an Object   After you've finished using an object in your program, you will want to get rid of it in order to recover the resources that it was using. You accomplish this by literally setting the object to nothing, as shown in the following code:

```
Set EhnPrint = Nothing
```

Note that an object created within a form or a procedure is usually released when the procedure terminates or when the form is unloaded. However, it's good practice to release the object when you're finished with it. When the object is released, any code that was in the `Terminate` event of the class is run.

Classes in Your Programs

Now that I've covered the basics of developing and using a class module, take a look at a couple of examples of using class modules in actual programs. These examples are relatively simple, but they demonstrate the power of classes. You can enhance these examples to provide powerful tools for your own programs.

A Better Printer

One of the biggest problems with sending data to the printer is that you don't know how long the line of print will be when you send it, and the printer itself isn't smart enough to perform word wrapping. The `cPrint` class shows a way to handle this problem by providing you with an object that does word wrapping. The object also provides properties that let you set the desired margins for the output. As an added bonus, the object lets you choose where to print the output of the code—to the printer, a form, or a picture box. Figure 8.4 shows the form used to run the example program.

The form has a text box for you to enter the string to be printed, as well as a picture box that is one of the output choices. In addition, three command buttons are placed on the form to let you determine where to direct the output. Also, text boxes and a command button are used to set new margin values for the output device. The code for this program is located in the CLASSEX.VBP file.

FIG. 8.4
User interface for the
print class sample case.

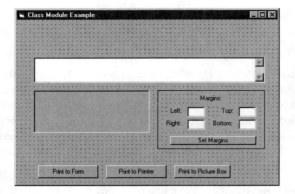

The CLASSEX.VBP project shows you how to create and use a class to print information to a
variety of objects. For this project, check the book's Web site at **http://www.quecorp.com/
sevb5**.

Setting Up the Class   The first step in setting up the class for the enhanced printer object is
to create the class module. You can do this by choosing Class Module from the Insert menu.
You then give the class module the name cPrint by setting the Name property. The Public
property of the class module is set to False, because this class is used only inside the current
program. At this point, all the properties of the class module have been set, and you're ready to
input code for the class.

Defining the Internal Variables   The next step is to define the internal variables that will be
used by the class module to store the values of the module's properties. These variables are
declared as private, so that they may not be directly manipulated by the calling program. The
code in Listing 8.2 shows the variable declaration for the cPrint class.

Listing 8.2   Declaring the Private Variables of the Class

```
Option Explicit

Private OutputTo As Object
Private m_lmarg As Integer, m_rmarg As Integer
Private m_tmarg As Integer, m_bmarg As Integer
Private objwid As Integer, objhit As Integer
Private txtht As Integer, endpos As Integer, txtlen As Integer
Private strtpos As Integer, endps2 As Integer
Private crlf As String, prntln As String
```

The first line of the code, the Option Explicit statement, indicates that all variables must be
declared prior to their use in the code. The next three lines declare the variables that will be
used with the object's properties. The OutputTo variable contains the object that is the destination of the printout. This variable is set to another object, such as the printer or the name of a

form or picture box. The four variables ending in marg will contain the values of the page margins input by the user. The other declaration statements set up the other variables that are used in the processing of the printout.

Creating the Properties   The cPrint class has an interface that lets the user set the desired output device and the page margins for the printout. This interface consists of the properties defined for the class. These properties are defined by the Property Let, Property Get, and Property Set procedures of the class. Listing 8.3 shows the procedures for the four margin properties and the output-device property.

Listing 8.3   Properties of a Class Are Defined by Property Procedures

```
Public Property Get LMargin() As Integer
    LMargin = m_lmarg
End Property

Public Property Let LMargin(LMarg As Integer)
    If LMarg < 0 Then
        m_lmarg = 0
    Else
        m_lmarg = LMarg
    End If
    objwid = OutputTo.Width - m_lmarg - m_rmarg
End Property
Public Property Get RMargin() As Integer
    RMargin = m_rmarg
End Property

Public Property Let RMargin(RMarg As Integer)
    If RMarg < 0 Then
        m_rmarg = 0
    Else
        m_rmarg = RMarg
    End If
    objwid = OutputTo.Width - m_lmarg - m_rmarg
End Property
Public Property Get TMargin() As Integer
    TMargin = m_tmarg
End Property

Public Property Let TMargin(TMarg As Integer)
    If TMarg < 0 Then
        m_tmarg = 0
    Else
        m_tmarg = TMarg
    End If
    objhit = OutputTo.Height - m_tmarg - m_bmarg
End Property

Public Property Get BMargin() As Integer
    BMargin = m_bmarg
End Property
```

continues

Listing 8.3 Continued

```
Public Property Let BMargin(BMarg As Integer)
    If BMarg < 0 Then
        m_bmarg = 0
    Else
        m_bmarg = BMarg
    End If
    objhit = OutputTo.Height - m_tmarg - m_bmarg
End Property


Public Property Set OutputDev(inDev As Object)
    Set OutputTo = inDev
    objhit = OutputTo.Height - m_tmarg - m_bmarg
    objwid = OutputTo.Width - m_lmarg - m_rmarg
End Property
```

Notice that to set the output-device property, a `Property Set` procedure must be used. This is because the output device is an object.

Supplying an Output Method   Next, because the object needs to be able to perform some function, a method must be created for the class. You can do this by creating a Public procedure in the class module. The method for the cPrint class performs the word-wrapping of the input text. This m ethod is defined by the code in Listing 8.4.

Listing 8.4   A *Public* Procedure Defines the *Output* Method of the *cPrint* Class

```
Public Sub Output(prntvar As String)
    crlf = Chr$(13) & Chr$(10)
    txtht = OutputTo.TextHeight("AbgWq")
    Do
        endpos = 0
        txtlen = 0
        prntln = ""
        Do
            strtpos = endpos + 1
            endpos = InStr(strtpos, prntvar, " ")
            prntln = Left$(prntvar, endpos)
            txtlen = OutputTo.TextWidth(prntln)
        Loop Until txtlen > objwid Or endpos = 0
        If endpos = 0 Then
            prntln = prntvar
            endps2 = InStr(1, prntln, crlf)
            If endps2 > 0 Then
                prntln = Left$(prntvar, endps2 - 1)
```

```
                        prntvar = LTrim$(Mid$(prntvar, endps2 + 2))
                Else
                        prntvar = ""
                End If
        Else
            prntln = Left$(prntvar, strtpos - 1)
            endps2 = InStr(1, prntln, crlf)
            If endps2 > 0 Then
                prntln = Left$(prntvar, endps2 - 1)
                prntvar = LTrim$(Mid$(prntvar, endps2 + 2))
            Else
                prntvar = LTrim$(Mid$(prntvar, strtpos))
            End If
        End If
        OutputTo.CurrentX = m_lmarg
        OutputTo.Print prntln
    Loop While Len(prntvar) > 0
End Sub
```

Initializing the Class Finally, because the user might call the method without first setting the properties of the class, it's a good idea to set initial values for the internal variables. This is done in the `Initialize` event of the class, as shown in Listing 8.5.

Listing 8.5   Setting the Initial Value of Variables

```
Private Sub Class_Initialize()
    m_lmarg = 0
    m_rmarg = 0
    m_tmarg = 0
    m_bmarg = 0
    Set OutputTo = Printer
End Sub
```

Using the Class As I said earlier, to use a class in a program, you must create an instance of the object defined by the class and then set the properties of the object and use its methods. For the `cPrint` class example, this is all done in the form that supplies the user interface for the example code.

First, the object is defined in the `Declarations` section of the form using a declaration statement, as shown here:

```
Dim EhnPrint As New cPrint
```

If the user chooses to set page margins for the output, values can be entered in the text boxes for the appropriate margins. The text-box values are then assigned to the properties of the object, using the code in the `Click` event of the Set Margins command button. This code is shown in Listing 8.6.

Listing 8.6   Setting the Margins of the Output Device

```
Private Sub cmdSetMargin_Click()
EhnPrint.LMargin = Val(txtMargin(0).Text)
EhnPrint.RMargin = Val(txtMargin(1).Text)
EhnPrint.TMargin = Val(txtMargin(2).Text)
EhnPrint.BMargin = Val(txtMargin(3).Text)
End Sub
```

As you can see, the properties are set using simple assignment statements. The Val function is used in the event that the user accidentally enters a text string instead of a number in the text box.

Finally, after the user has entered some text to be printed, the Output method of the object can be used to print the text. The following code shows how this is done to print the text to the picture box.

```
Private Sub cmdPicture_Click()
Set EhnPrint.OutputDev = picPrint
PrntStr = txtInput.Text
EhnPrint.Output (PrntStr)
End Sub
```

The code first uses the Set statement to tell the EhnPrint object to direct the output to the picPrint picture box. Next, the text to be printed is retrieved from the text box. Finally, the text string is passed to the object, and the Output method is invoked. The results of this operation are shown in Figure 8.5.

FIG. 8.5

The cPrint class can be used to output text to different output devices.

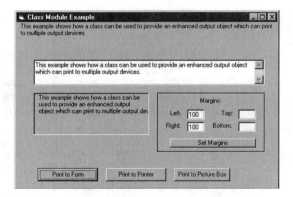

Database Access

Another use of classes is in database access. The class shown in this section's example is used to simply open a database and return the database object to the calling program. You're probably wondering why you wouldn't just use the database objects directly to perform this operation. The answer is that using a class lets you encapsulate the OpenDatabase method and all the associated error handling code that is required for it.

By using a class, you don't have to repeat this code multiple places in your program or in multiple programs. You simply create it once in a class module and then create an instance of the class any time that you need to open the database in your program. You can also easily add the class module to other programs, which keeps you from having to copy and paste code from one program to another. The final advantage is that if you find additional things that you need your open database routine to handle, you have to change the code in only one place—the class module. Then all your programs have the benefit of the changes. The example case is contained in the file CLSDBEX.VBP.

The CLSDBEX.VBP project shows you how to create and use a class to open databases.

 The _cDataAccess_ Class The cDataAccess class is fairly simple. The class consists of one method and one read-only property. To use the class, the name of a database is passed to the OpenDb method, and then the database object is retrieved using the OpenData property. The code for the class is shown in Listing 8.7.

Listing 8.7 The _cDataAccess_ Class Property and Method

```
Private m_ClsDb As Database

Public Property Get OpenData() As Database
Set OpenData = m_ClsDb
End Property



Public Sub OpenDb(dbName As String)
On Error GoTo DBErrHandle
Set m_ClsDb = DBEngine.Workspaces(0).OpenDatabase(dbName, _
False, False)
On Error GoTo 0
Exit Sub

DBErrHandle:

errnum = Err
Select Case errnum
    Case 3049
        'Corrupt database, attempt to repair
        msgstr = "Your database has been damaged.  Do you wish the "
        msgstr = msgstr & "program to attempt to repair it?"
        msgrtn = MsgBox(msgstr, 52, "Database Problem")
        If msgrtn = 7 Then Exit Sub
        RepairDatabase (dbName)
        Resume
    Case 3056
        'Couldn't repair database
        msgstr = "Your database could not be repaired.  You will "
        msgstr = msgstr & "need to restore the database from your "
        msgstr = msgstr & " latest backup!"
```

continues

Listing 8.7 Continued

```
            MsgBox msgstr, 48, "Database Problem"
            Exit Sub
    Case Else
        'Show any other messages
        msgstr = "The following error occurred while trying to open "
        msgstr = msgstr & "the database: "
        msgstr = msgstr & Error$(errnum)
        MsgBox msgstr, 48, "Database Problem"
        Exit Sub
End Select
End Sub
```

Notice that in the `Property Get` procedure, the property is defined as a `Database` object. This is to match the object that will receive the value of the property.

Using *cDataAccess* The case I'll use as a sample calls the object to open the BIBLIO.MDB database that comes with Visual Basic. The code then opens the Authors table of the database and displays a list of authors in a list box. The code for the example is shown in Listing 8.8.

Listing 8.8 Accessing the *cDataAccess* Object

```
Dim OldDb As Database, OldRc As Recordset
Dim o_Data As Object

Private Sub cmdAuthors_Click()
Set o_Data = New cDataAccess
o_Data.OpenDb "C:\VB4\BIBLIO.MDB"
Set OldDb = o_Data.OpenData
Set o_Data = Nothing
Set OldRc = OldDb.OpenRecordset("Authors", dbOpenDynaset)
Do Until OldRc.EOF
    lstAuthors.AddItem OldRc("Author")
    OldRc.MoveNext
Loop
OldDb.Close
End Sub
```

N O T E The code assumes that the database is located in the VB5 directory of your C: drive. If your Visual Basic directory is different, you will need to change that line of code in the example. ■

Figure 8.6 shows the results of the sample program.

FIG. 8.6
The cDataAccess object is used to handle the opening of the database.

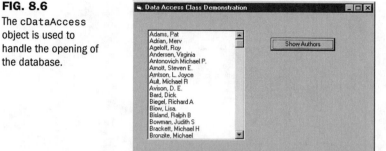

From Here . . .

This chapter provided you with an introduction to the creative class modules and the objects that can be created from them. To learn more about some of the topics covered in this chapter, see the following chapters:

- For more on using objects in your programs, see Chapter 20, "Using Classes to Create Re-usable Objects," and Chapter 22, "Creating OCX Controls."

- To learn about creating an OLE server, see Chapter 21, "Creating Remote Automation Servers."

Creating Database Applications

9   Introduction to Databases and the Jet Engine   197

10   Applications at Warp Speed   221

11   Designing and Creating a Database   247

12   Doing More with Bound Controls   279

13   Writing Programs with the Data-Access Objects   301

14   Understanding Structured Query Language   335

15   Multi-User Programming   369

16   Accessing Other PC Databases   387

17   Using the Remote Data Objects   403

Introduction to Databases and the Jet Engine

Databases and database applications are everywhere. In fact, the vast majority of new applications that are created these days are database applications. If you use a *personal information manager* (PIM), you are using one type of database application. Even if you look up the price of a computer or software on the Internet, you are using a type of database application. With all these databases and applications floating around, it stands to reason that at some point in your programming career, you will have to design an application to access a database. You may even have to design a database from scratch. But before I get into the actual programming of database applications, take a look at what a database really is and how Visual Basic helps you write database programs quickly and easily. ■

What is a database

You'll learn the concept of a database and examine some real world examples.

What are the parts of a relational database

Databases are made up of tables, records, fields, indexes, and other pieces. We'll explain all these concepts.

How does a database management System Work

You'll see how information is stored and how different pieces of data are related.

What database management features are supported by the Jet engine

Jet supports data manipulation, data definition, database security, and many other features.

What is Structured Query Language (SQL)

You'll see how simple query statements can be used to perform many programming tasks.

What is database replication

Now you can create and manage copies of the database.

Understanding Databases

In simple terms, a *database* is a collection of information, usually a series of records containing similar information. The most common example of a database is a phone book. The phone book is a collection of names, addresses, and phone numbers. Each line in a phone book is a record that contains the information for a single person or family. A phone book exhibits another characteristic of most databases: the information is presented in a specific order. In the case of the phone book, this is alphabetical order, by name.

Computer databases are similar in concept to the phone book. These databases provide a way to easily store and retrieve information. However, computer databases have a number of advantages over their noncomputerized counterparts. Here are a few of these advantages:

- It is easy to add new records or remove existing records.
- It is easier to edit the information in an existing record.
- You can quickly change the presentation order of the information (for example, listing people in order according to where they live).

Flat-File and Relational Databases

There are two basic types of databases used on computers: *flat-file databases* and *relational databases*. A phone book is an example of a flat-file database, where a single record stores all the information for each entry, and a single table contains all the records for the database. A number of computer database systems use this type of file management.

By contrast, a relational database stores the information in a number of tables that are related by key fields. In the example of a contact list (addresses and phone numbers), one table might contain the names, street addresses, and phone numbers of a person, while a second table would contain the city and state information for the person. These tables would be related by the ZIP code. Any one ZIP code refers to a single city. The advantage of this type of database system over the flat-file type is that with relational databases, information is stored more efficiently. In fact, one of the design goals of a relational database system is to eliminate redundant information. (You will learn more about design objectives in Chapter 11, "Designing and Creating a Database.")

▶ Eliminating redundant information is the goal of database normalization. You can learn more about this in the section, "Designing a Database" in Chapter 11, "Designing and Creating a Database."

N O T E A relational database contains not only the actual information that is stored in the tables but also information about the relations between the tables. ■

Typical Databases You May Know

You already may have used a number of database programs without even knowing it. In fact, you probably have used several. Most address book or contact management programs are a form of database program, even the simple Cardfile program that was included in Windows 3.1. Also, most check management programs, like the one shown in Figure 9.1, are database programs. In these programs, each check entry is a record in the database, and each of the entries for the check (for example, check number, payee, category, and amount) are fields in the record. These programs give you an idea of how a database program may be used.

Part

II

Ch

9

FIG. 9.1
You may use a
database to manage
your checkbook.

Fields—

Records—

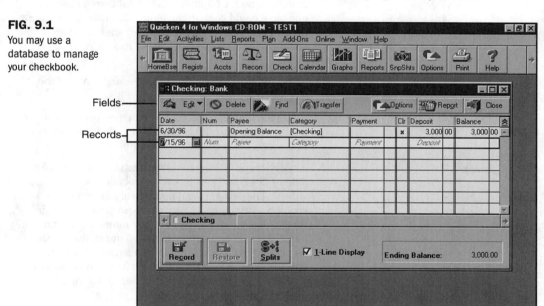

Definitions of Database Terms

In the discussion on the concept of a database, you saw a few of the terms, such as *record* and *field,* that are used to refer to the parts of a database. Before going further, I'll take a minute to formally define some database terms. Understanding these terms will help you in the rest of the database discussions. I define these terms with the Jet database system specifically in mind, but most terms apply to other database systems as well. Table 9.1 defines the key parts of a database.

Table 9.1   Elements of a Database

Element	Description
Database	A group of data tables that contain related information. Note that a Jet database may consist of only a single table. A membership list for a church would be one example of a database.
Table	A group of data records, each containing the same type of information. Continuing the membership example, one table could contain the information about the family name, address, and phone number; while another table could contain the names of family members.
Record	A single entry in a table; the entry consists of a number of data fields. In a phone book, a record is one of the single-line entries.
Field	A specific item of data contained in a record. In a phone book, at least four fields can be identified: last name, first name, address, and phone number.
Index	A special type of table that contains the values of a key field or fields and pointers to the location of the actual record. These values and pointers are stored in a specific order and may be used to present the data in the database in that order. For the phone book example, one index may be used to sort the information by last name and first name; another index may be used to sort the information by street address. If you want, you can also create an index to sort the information by phone number.
Query	A Structured Query Language (SQL) command designed to retrieve a certain group of records from one or more tables or to perform an operation on a table. Although SQL commands can be executed directly from a program, a query lets you name the command and store it in the database itself. This is useful for SQL commands that are used often, such as commands that retrieve records for a specific monthly report. In a phone book or membership list, you might use a query to retrieve the names of people that live on a specific street.

Element	Description
Recordset	A group of records created from one or more tables in a database. The records in a recordset are typically a subset of all the records in a table. When the recordset is created, both the number of records and the order in which they are presented can be controlled by the query that creates the recordset. Two examples of recordsets from phone book data are an alphabetical listing of all people who live on Main Street and the first ten people whose last names start with *S*.

Part
II

Ch
9

Exploring How a Database Management System Works

Most programs that you create must be able to retrieve, analyze, and store information. Before the advent of *database management systems* (DBMS), the developers (you) had not only to handle the user interface (input and output) and calculation portions of the program but also to develop the methods of storing and retrieving the data in sequential, binary, or random-access files. Developers also had to write program code to handle any searches required by the program, or indexes necessary to control the order of records. This type of processing is illustrated in Figure 9.2.

FIG. 9.2
Without a DBMS, data retrieval and storage was a major effort.

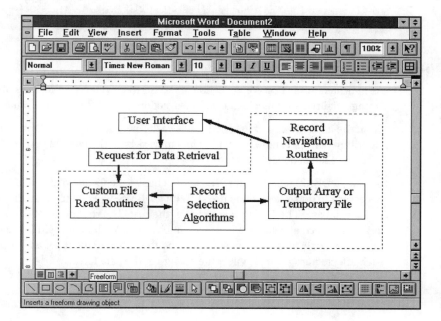

With a DBMS, the process is much easier. The main task in setting up a DBMS is initially defining the type of data to be stored. Then when data must be retrieved or stored, the program issues a request to the DBMS, and the DBMS automatically handles all the gory details of data management. The DBMS also handles searches and creates indexes as you instruct, without a lot of code. Figure 9.3 illustrates data handling using a DBMS.

FIG. 9.3

Data handling is much easier with a database management system.

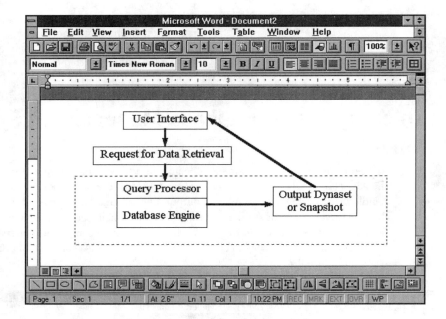

The Advantages of a DBMS

As indicated in the preceding section, a DBMS frees you from the tasks of defining the data storage and retrieval mechanisms. This freedom provides several advantages.

First, the initial design of the program is easier because you don't have to program search algorithms or read-and-write statements to work with the current record. This can speed a program's initial development.

Second, a DBMS makes it much easier to change the format of some of the data if it becomes necessary to do so (as it often does). With a DBMS, you change only the data definition stored in the database. The DBMS takes care of the rest. The routines in the programs that access an individual piece of data usually remain unchanged. Without a DBMS, you have to write a routine to port data files to the new format and then change the input and output statements in each affected program to reflect the change to the data format.

Finally, it is easier for users and other developers to create additional programs to access the data in the database. This is because they don't have to know the format in which the data was stored, only the names of the data fields and the types of data they contain. This information is easily found, because most DBMS systems contain methods to report the *structure* (field names and types) of the database.

The Parts of a DBMS

A DBMS consists of two major parts: the *programming interface* (which consists of the user interface and the data-retrieval requests) and the *database engine*. These two parts are shown in the DBMS block of Figure 9.3.

The Functions of the Programming Interface

The programming interface provides the commands that let a program tell the database engine what to do. The programming interface usually includes the following elements:

- A *data-definition language* (DDL) that tells the database engine the format of the data objects (tables, records, fields, and indexes). The DDL also defines the data-validation and data-integrity rules for the database.
- A *data-manipulation language* (DML) that tells the database engine the functions to perform on the data (retrieve, change, add, delete, and store).
- A *data-control language* (DCL) that tells the database engine what type of access is allowed to the data by various users.

The Functions of the Database Engine

The simplest form of database engine provides mechanisms for the physical storage of the data, retrieval and updating of data, and data search and index capabilities. A database engine may also provide methods for ensuring data validity, data integrity, and data security.

The design of the database engine also determines what data manipulation features are supported. For example, if you need to increase the price of every item in a retail sales table, one database engine may support the use of action queries that let a single program line perform the function. With a different database engine, you may have to use a program loop to retrieve each record, change the price, and store the changes.

Understanding the Microsoft Jet Engine

The Microsoft Jet engine provides the primary means for Visual Basic to interface with databases. The Jet engine is shared by Visual Basic, Microsoft Access, and other Microsoft products. The Jet database engine supports most of the functions described in the preceding section for database management systems. The data-definition features of Jet support the creation, modification, and deletion of tables, indexes, and queries. Jet also supports field-level and record-level data validation. Data integrity is supported in the form of primary keys and referential integrity between tables.

For data manipulation, Jet supports the use of SQL. SQL provides the means for a single state-ment to retrieve, add, delete, or update groups of records based on user-defined criteria. (The SQL supported by the Jet engine is close to but not fully compliant with ANSI SQL-89.)

Jet also provides support for security features. These features let the developer assign a user ID and password that must be given before the user can access the database. Jet also supports the use of *permissions,* or access levels (for example, read-only or read/write accessibility), for individual tables and queries. This lets the database administrator assign each user or group of users specific access to different parts of the database. For example, you can set up security so that everyone can look at the address and phone number information in an employee database, but only the department manager can view salary and performance information.

N O T E   In addition to the data manipulation and data definition tasks you can perform with the Jet engine, Jet has other capabilities that you will need during your database development tasks. These capabilities include database repair, database compacting (to eliminate unused space), and reindexing. ▓

Back in Time: A History of Jet

The Jet engine has not always been a part of Visual Basic. The first version of Jet was intro-duced with Microsoft Access, version 1. The first version of Visual Basic that could use the Jet engine was version 3. Before that, you had to work directly with the Open Database Connectiv-ity (ODBC) application program interface (API), use a third-party database library, or write your own routines to access databases. There was also no native database that was used with Visual Basic.

When first introduced, Jet provided the Visual Basic programmer with a native database to use in program development. The Jet engine stores all the tables and other information about a database in a single file. The initial version of Jet also let the programmer work with records from multiple tables as part of a single recordset.

With version 1.1 of the Jet engine, programmers were able to more easily connect to other databases through ODBC drivers. This made it easier for programmers to work with multiple database formats. Also, the maximum database size was increased from 128 megabytes to 1.1 gigabytes.

Version 2 of the Jet engine provided some significant enhancements over its predecessors. First, there was increased support for referential integrity and data validation at the engine level. Next was the support for cascading updates and deletes. Finally, Jet 2.0 increased the performance of queries through the use of Rushmore™, which Microsoft gained when it merged with Fox Software. Version 2 of the Jet engine was introduced with Access 2.0. The engine was accessible to Visual Basic programmers through the VB3/Jet2 compatibility layer.

N O T E Rushmore™ technology is a high-speed indexing method first used in FoxPro, then later added to the Jet engine as well. ■

Finally, version 3.0 of the Jet engine moved the Jet database system to full 32-bit implementation. The engine was introduced with Access 7.0 (95) and the 32-bit version of Visual Basic 4. The main feature of the engine, other than 32-bit capability, was support for database replication. This lets copies of a database be created; then the copies can be modified by multiple users and the information in each copy synchronized back to the master database.

Jet 3.5 is the current version of the engine that comes with Visual Basic 5. This version includes the capability of partial database replication and some enhanced features for dealing with ODBC data sources.

What Can I Put in a Database

The Jet engine supports a wide variety of data types, including several types of text and numeric fields. These different data types allow the developer a great deal of flexibility in designing a database application. Table 9.2 shows the more common data types used with the Jet engine.

Table 9.2   The Data Types Available with the Jet Engine

Name	Information Stored	Size or Range
Text	Character strings	255 characters maximum
Memo	Long character strings	Up to 1.2G (gigabytes)
Byte	Integer (numeric data)	0 to 255
Integer	Integer (numeric data)	–32,768 to 32,767
Long	Integer (numeric data)	–2,147,483,648 to 2,147,483,647
Single	Real (numeric data)	-3.4×10^{38} to 3.4×10^{38}
Double	Real (numeric data)	-1.8×10^{308} to 1.8×10^{308}
Currency	Real (numeric data)	-9.0×10^{14} to 9.0×10^{14}
Boolean	Contains a value of True or False	
Date	Date and time values	Dates from 1/1/100 to 12/31/9999
Binary	Binary data	Up to 1.2G
OLE	OLE objects	Up to 1.2G

Data-Access Objects

Visual Basic accesses the capabilities of the Jet engine through a series of *data-access objects* (DAOs). These objects let you create new databases, tables, queries, indexes, and relations or to modify existing parts of the database. The DAOs also let you easily access the actual data in the database to add, edit, or delete records. The DAOs let you manipulate information in the database by setting the properties of the objects and executing the methods attached to the objects. Table 9.3 lists these objects and gives a brief description of their functions.

Table 9.3   Visual Basic's Data-Access Objects

Object	Description
DBEngine	The object referring to the Jet database engine.
Workspace	An area in which the user can work with one or more databases. The Workspace object contains methods for creating and opening databases and for processing transactions.
Database	A collection of information organized into tables, along with index and relation information about the tables. The Database object contains methods for creating, modifying, and deleting the components of the database.
TableDef	A definition of the physical structure of a data table. The TableDef object contains methods for creating fields and indexes in a table.
QueryDef	A stored SQL query of information in the database.
Recordset	A collection of information records about a single topic. The Recordset object contains methods for navigating through the information in the database and for modifying that information.
Field	A column in a data table.
Index	An ordered list of records in a recordset based on a defined key field.
Relation	Stored information about the relationship between two tables.

Introducing the Data Control

To make it even easier for you to create database applications, Visual Basic gives you the *data control*. This is one of the controls in Visual Basic's standard toolbox. The data control lets you connect to a *recordset* (table or query result) in a Jet database simply by setting two properties of the control. This control, along with the bound controls, lets you quickly set up database program prototypes or full-blown applications. The data control and bound controls are covered extensively in Chapter 8, "Introduction to Classes," and Chapter 12, "Doing More with Bound Controls."

Explaining Database Integrity

One key function of a database application is to ensure, as much as possible, the accuracy of the data in the tables. Ensuring data accuracy refers not only to making sure that the individual data items are correct, but also to making sure that relationships between data tables are properly maintained. These two functions are referred to, respectively, as *data validation* and *data integrity*.

The Jet engine supports two main types of data-integrity monitoring: *primary-key integrity* and *referential integrity*. It also supports two key forms of data validation: *field-level validation* and *record-level validation*. These subjects are discussed later in this section.

In Visual Basic, the developer can invoke all these integrity and validation features using the data-access objects. The features are determined by setting the properties of the various objects at design time, when the database and tables are created. (See Chapter 11 for more information on creating data tables and fields and setting the object properties.)

▶ Creating data tables and their associated fields is discussed in the "Implementing Your Design" section of Chapter 9.

How Relations Work in a Database

When data is normalized and information is moved from one table to another, a method must exist to relate the two tables. The method for relating tables is to use *data keys*. This section discusses the two types of table relationships and how data keys are established.

Data keys are usually referred to either as *primary keys* or *foreign keys*. A primary key is the one that uniquely identifies a record in a table. For example, in the Customers table shown in Figure 9.4, each record contains information about a specific customer. The primary key then provides a unique identifier for each customer record. This primary key is used to relate customer information to data in other tables. An example of this is shown in Figure 9.5, where the customer data is tied to the data in an Orders table. As you can see in Figure 9.5, there may be multiple records in the second table relating to a single record in the primary table. In the order system, the customer key in the Orders table is a foreign key, linking the order records back to the Customers table.

One-to-Many Relationships   A *one-to-many relationship* occurs when a record in one table is related to one or more records in a second table, but each record in the second table is related to only one record in the first table. One-to-many relationships make up the majority of the table relations in a database system.

The customer/order example just given provides one look at a one-to-many relationship. In this example, a customer may make many purchases, but each purchase is made by only one customer (see Figure 9.5). Another example of a one-to-many relationship would be a membership directory. In this example (shown in Figure 9.6), each family record is related to one or more member-name records, but each member-name record is tied to only one family record.

Part
II

Ch
9

FIG. 9.4
Primary keys uniquely
identify each record in a
table.

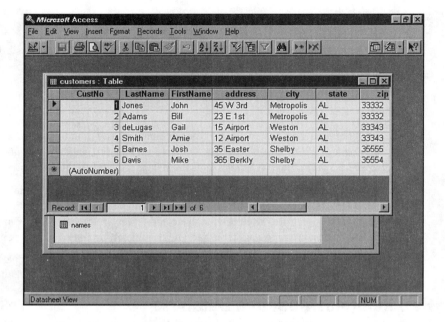

FIG. 9.5
Foreign keys point back
to related information in
another table.

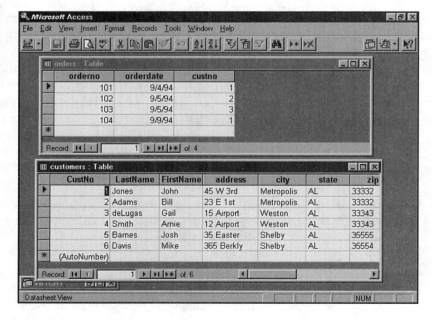

FIG. 9.6
A one-to-many relationship between tables shows the use of key fields.

The "many" side of a relationship is indicated by the infinity symbol (∞).

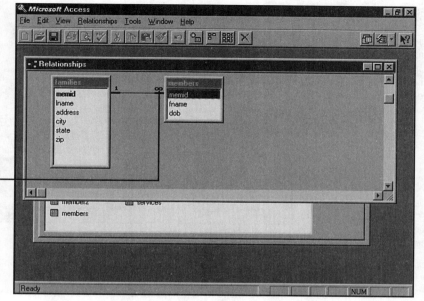

Part
II

Ch
9

Many-to-Many Relationships

Many-to-many relationships occur when each record from the first table relates to multiple records in the second table, and vice versa. When this occurs, an intermediate table is usually introduced that provides a one-to-many relationship with each of the other two tables.

An example of a many-to-many relationship is the items purchased by customers. Each customer may purchase many items, and each item can be purchased by many customers. Therefore, a many-to-many relationship exists between customers and items. Figure 9.7 shows how the data is structured with all the information in a single table. Figure 9.8 shows how the data is structured as separate Item and Customer tables with intermediate tables.

FIG. 9.7
Item and customer information in a single table is an inefficient means of handling the data.

Itemno	Description	Orderno	OrderDate	Custno	Lastname	Firstname	Phone
1001	Silver Angelfish	101	9/4/94	1	Smith	Martha	555-3344
1003	Black Lace Ang	101	9/4/94	1	Smith	Martha	555-3344
1005	Pearl Gourami	102	9/5/94	2	Jones	Frank	555-9988
1010	Sunset Gouram	102	9/5/94	2	Jones	Frank	555-9988
1001	Silver Angelfish	103	9/5/94	3	James	Sydney	555-7765
1005	Pearl Gourami	104	9/9/94	1	Smith	Martha	555-4432
0		0		0			

Record: 1 of 6

FIG. 9.8

Separate item and customer tables with intermediate tables show the resolution of the many-to-many relationship.

Intermediate tables

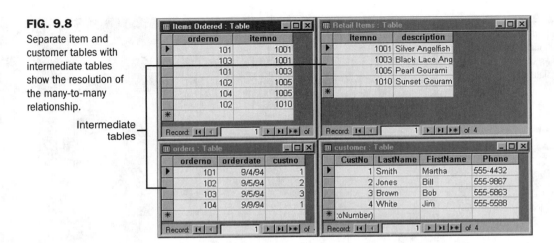

Key Fields   Tables are related to each other through *key fields*. A key field is one that uniquely identifies a record. A key field may be one that has meaningful data in it, or it may be a created field that serves the sole purpose of providing a unique identifier for the record. The main criterion for the key field is that it must be unique. Figure 9.9 shows a table with a key field added to provide a unique ID for each record. Often for dealing with customer information, an account number is created for each customer and is used as the unique identifier.

FIG. 9.9

This table shows an added key field to ensure unique record IDs.

Key field added

Unique IDs for each record

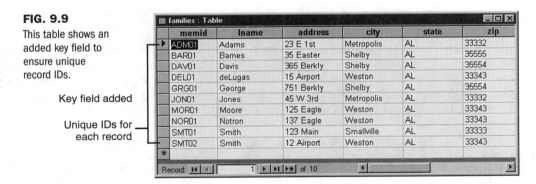

The key field is present in both databases of the relationship. For the membership directory, you can assign a unique identifier to each family record. You then include the same identifier in each of the name records to indicate the family to which the name belongs. If the key-field value is not unique, there is confusion about the family information for a member.

If you are developing an employee database, it is possible that several people have the same name. One possible unique identifier is the Social Security number. However, because this nine-digit number must be stored in every related record, it may be better to create a smaller, unique employee ID. If you know that there will never be more than 9,999 employees, for example, you can use a four-digit ID, saving five digits in every related record. Depending on the number of related records, the space savings can be significant.

T I P One way to ensure unique IDs is to use a *counter field* for the primary key. A counter field is an integer-number field that the database engine automatically increments when a new record is added. The counter field takes the responsibility of creating unique keys away from the user and places that responsibility on the database engine. One drawback in using a counter field is that the ID has no intrinsic meaning to the user.

Keeping Relations from Falling Apart

As I said in the previous section, to relate one table to another, the same value must appear in both tables. In a one-to-many relationship, the table on the one side of the relationship contains the primary key for the table (also as described in the preceding section). The table on the many side of the relationship contains a reference to this primary key in a field. This field is known as the foreign key. Figure 9.10 shows the relationship between the Family and Youth tables in a sample application, with the primary and foreign keys labeled.

FIG. 9.10
The foreign key in one table is related to the primary key in another table.

Primary key—

Foreign key—

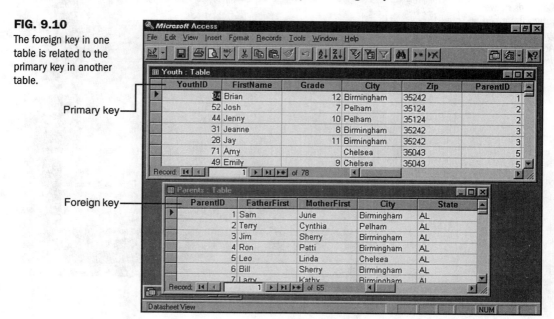

In this relationship, you can link each record in the Family table to many records in the Youth table. However, each record in the Youth table can be linked to only one record in the Family table. A one-to-many relationship is often referred to as a *parent-child relationship,* with the primary-key table being the parent table and the foreign-key table being the child table.

Referential integrity is responsible for making sure that the relationship between two tables is maintained. Jet supports the following functions of referential integrity:

- When you add or change a foreign key in a child table, the Jet engine verifies the existence of the key value in the parent table.
- When you add a new record to a child table, you must specify a foreign key.
- When you delete a parent record or change the primary key, Jet either can cascade the update or deletion through the child tables, or reject the operation if there are child records. You can set up Jet to perform either action.

With Visual Basic, you can define the relationships between tables using the data-access objects available for relations. With versions of Visual Basic before 4.0 and versions of the Jet engine before 2.0, referential integrity either was not available or you could only set it using Microsoft Access. Visual Basic now lets you set up referential integrity. However, if you have a copy of Microsoft Access, you can set up table relationships graphically (see Figure 9.11).

FIG. 9.11

Relations between tables are made graphically in Microsoft Access.

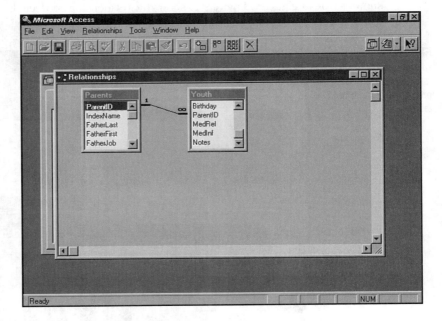

Cascading Updates and Deletions   Allowing the cascading of updates and deletions from the parent table to the child tables is one of the optional properties of a relationship. You may choose to use cascading updates, cascading deletions, or both. If you choose these options, changes to the parent table are propagated automatically through the child table. For updates, if you change the primary key of the parent table, the related foreign keys in the child table are changed to reflect the new value. For deletions, if you delete a record in the parent table, all related child records are also deleted.

Without cascading, the programmer is responsible for handling conflicts that arise from making changes to a parent record when there are dependent records in a child table. The programmer either must verify that no child records exist before making the change or deletion, or let the program make the change when a record is found or an error occurs. If you do not have the cascading options turned on, you will get an error when you try to change or delete a record with dependent records in a child table.

You set cascading options when a relation between tables is created. The options are properties of the `Relation` object. The tasks of creating a `Relation` object and setting its properties are covered in Chapter 11, "Designing and Creating Your Database."

▶ Creating Relation objects and setting their properties is discussed in the "Implementing Your Design" section of Chapter 11.

> **CAUTION**
>
> Although cascading is a very useful and powerful method for preserving referential integrity, use it with caution—especially cascading deletions. Accidentally deleting a parent record can wipe out quite a bit of data.

Handling Rejected Changes   For any type of data-integrity rule defined in the database, the Jet engine issues an error message if the rule is violated. When this happens, the program must have routines to trap the error and either handle the problem or inform the user of decisions to be made about the erroneous data. If you do not include an error-handling routine, the user sees the error message box, the attempted operation is aborted, and, in extreme cases, your program may terminate.

You handle database errors the same as other errors in your code—by using the `On Error GoTo` statement and an error-handling routine. Visual Basic's manuals and online help cover basic error handling fairly well.

Accept No Duplicates

Primary-key integrity ensures that each record in a table is uniquely identified by a field or combination of fields. Unique keys are essential for properly relating tables. For example, if you make a sale to a customer named John Smith but have no identifier other than his name, how do you determine which John Smith to send the bill to?

You can implement a primary key in either of two ways. You can define a unique field or combination of fields that is meaningful to you, or you can create a counter field. If you create a counter field, Jet automatically creates a new value for the field for each record that you add, ensuring the uniqueness of the key. If you define your own field (for example, the first three letters of a person's first and last names, such as JOHSMI), you are responsible for making sure that the values are unique and resolving any conflicts if a new value is not unique. That is, you must provide a program function that generates the key value (or gets an input value from the user) and verifies that the value is unique. If the value is not unique, you must provide a way to change the value and reverify its uniqueness.

With either method, Jet enforces primary integrity by verifying that the value of the primary key is unique before it allows the addition or updating of a record. If the value is not unique, a trappable error (typically error number 3022) is returned. Your program must be able to handle this error.

Is the Data Any Good

The other portion of ensuring the accuracy of data is data validation. Data validation is the process of verifying that the data input or changed by a user meets certain criteria. There are two ways in which data validation can be implemented in your programs: *engine-level validation* or *program validation.* Engine-level validation uses rules about data fields and tables that are stored in the database itself. When data is changed, the Jet engine checks the data against the rule prior to writing the update to the database. If the new data does not conform to the rules, an error message is returned. Program validation is made up of data rules embedded in the actual program code. These rules check the value of the data against the defined criteria when particular program events occur. A program-validation rule might be placed in the `Change` event of an object or the `Click` event code of a command button.

With either implementation method (engine-level or programmatic), data validation can take the following forms, all of which are described in the next sections:

- Field-level validation
- Record-level validation
- Required-field validation

Field-Level Validation   *Field-level validation* ensures that the information in the field is within a certain range of values. Jet supports the use of *simple expressions* in field-level validation. A simple expression can compare the value of the field to a constant. Additional types of field-level validation include the use of user-defined functions or checking for valid entries in another table. Although Jet does not support these types of validation at the engine level, you can program them into your Visual Basic code. Alternatively, if you are accessing an external database server, check to see whether your host system supports these types of validation.

For each validation rule, the Jet engine also lets you specify a custom message that is displayed if the validation rule is violated. This message is displayed in the standard message box when needed. You can set field-level validation by setting the optional `ValidationRule` and `ValidationText` properties of the data-access objects as you are creating your database. You can also use Microsoft Access or the Data Manager application that comes with Visual Basic. Figure 9.12 shows how you can set the validation rule and text with the Data Manager. In Visual Basic, field-level validation expressions are checked by the Jet engine when an update method is called by your program.

FIG. 9.12
You can set validation clauses for any field in a table.

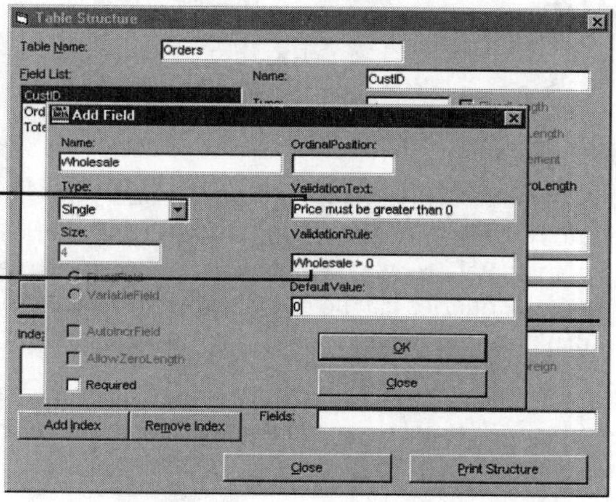

Error message for failed test

Validation expression returning *True* or *False*

> **N O T E** There is one special validation that can be performed for text fields. You can tell the database whether a text field can accept a string with no characters. The default setting of this validation check is No, which means that zero-length strings are not allowed. ■

Record-Level Validation   *Record-level validation* checks the information in a field against data in other fields of the record, or checks the results of a combination of fields against a criterion. For example, you can verify that the retail price of an item is at least 25 percent greater than the wholesale price, or that the length of the combined first- and last-name fields is less than 40 characters (for mailing labels). As with field-level validation, Jet supports the use of only simple expressions for record-level validation. In addition, you can set only one validation criterion for each table. As with field-level validation, you can enter validation text that provides a custom error message if the validation rule is violated.

As with field-level validation, you can set record-level validation with the data-access objects or Microsoft Access. When your program violates the record-level validation, a message is shown indicating the error. Any text you entered as validation text is included in the message that appears.

Required-Field Validation The Jet engine also lets you specify any field as a *required field*. If you specify a field as required, a value *must* exist for it when a record is added or changed. Jet checks each required field for a null value whenever a record is updated. If you attempt to update a record without a value in a required field, an error occurs.

> **CAUTION**
>
> If you specify required fields, make sure that you include the field on any data-entry form that adds new records to the table. Otherwise, you provide no means to input a value for the required field, and the user can't create any new records.

Posing a Query

One of the most powerful features of a DBMS is support for a *query* language. Queries let you use a single statement to retrieve or modify groups of records. Queries can also be used to change the structure of the database itself. Often, a single query can replace many lines of program code. Also, because queries can be optimized by the database engine, queries usually perform tasks faster than program code.

The Jet engine supports the use of SQL statements for defining and manipulating data. There are two main groupings of SQL statements: *data-manipulation language* statements and *data-definition language* statements.

Data-Manipulation Language (DML)

The data-manipulation language statements provide the means to insert, delete, update, and retrieve groups of records in a database. These statements work with the actual data in the database. Two basic types of queries are defined: *action queries* and *retrieval queries*.

Action Queries Action queries operate on groups of records. These types of queries let you delete records, insert new records, update fields in records, or create new tables from existing records. Jet supports all of these types of action queries. The queries are based on SQL syntax. You can run action queries with either a database Execute method or a query Execute method. The syntax of these queries and how to execute them are discussed in detail in Chapter 14, "Understanding Structured Query Language." Table 9.4 summarizes the action queries supported by the Jet engine.

▶ Executing SQL queries is discussed in the "Using SQL" section of Chapter 14.

N O T E The Execute method is one of the methods associated with the Database and QueryDef objects. By using this method, you can run an SQL query in your code. ■

Table 9.4   Action Queries Supported by the Jet Engine

Keywords	Function
DELETE...FROM	Removes records from a table based on the selection criteria.
INSERT INTO	Appends records to a table from another data source.
UPDATE...SET	Changes the values of selected fields.
SELECT INTO	Creates a new table from information in other tables.

Part

II

Ch

9

N O T E The selection criteria for deleting records is defined by a logical expression such as `Price`
`> 1.00`. Any record that meets this criteria is deleted; all other records are left alone.
The syntax of this statement is explained further in Chapter 14, "Understanding Structured Query
Language," in the section entitled "Understanding the Parts of an SQL Statement." ▪

Retrieval Queries   Retrieval queries tell the database engine to return a group of records in a dynaset- or snapshot-type recordset for viewing or processing. These queries are SQL SELECT statements that define the fields to be retrieved, the tables in which the fields are located, and the filter criteria for the fields. Jet supports standard SQL clauses such as WHERE, ORDER BY, GROUP BY, and JOIN. In addition, Jet supports the new clauses UNION, TOP *n*, and TOP *n*%. Jet also supports the use of *subqueries*, in which the results of one SELECT statement can be used as part of the WHERE clause of another statement. These capabilities of the SELECT statement give the developer a lot of flexibility in grouping and manipulating data. Table 9.5 summarizes the clauses of the SELECT statement supported by the Jet engine.

Table 9.5   Types of Retrieval Queries and Conditional Clauses Supported By the Jet Engine

Keywords	Function
UNION	Creates a recordset containing all records from the defined tables.
SELECT...FROM	Retrieves a group of fields from one or more tables subject to the conditional clauses.
WHERE *comparison*	A conditional clause that compares an expression to a single value.
WHERE...LIKE	A conditional clause that compares an expression to a pattern of values.

continues

Table 9.5   Continued

Keywords	Function
WHERE...BETWEEN	A conditional clause that compares an expression to a range of values.
WHERE...IN	A conditional clause that compares an expression to a group of values.
INNER¦LEFT¦RIGHT JOIN	A conditional clause that combines information from two tables based on identical values in a key field in each table.
ORDER BY	A conditional clause that determines the sort sequence of the output recordset.
GROUP BY	A conditional clause that combines summary information on records into groups, based on the value of one or more listed fields.

Data-Definition Language (DDL)

Data-definition language queries are another SQL feature supported by the Jet engine. Without DDL statements, you create tables and other objects in a database by defining field and index objects and then adding them to the table definition. DDL queries provide an alternative to this method, by allowing you to issue a single command to create, change, or delete a table and create or delete an index. Table 9.6 summarizes the various DDL queries.

Table 9.6   DDL Queries Used to Modify a Database Structure

Keywords	Function
CREATE TABLE	Creates a new table from a list of field definitions.
ALTER TABLE	Adds new fields to a table.
DROP TABLE	Deletes a table from the database.
CREATE INDEX	Creates a new index for a table.
DROP INDEX	Deletes an index from a table.

N O T E   If you want to set optional properties for tables or fields, such as validation rules, you will have to do this using the DAOs. DDL statements cannot handle optional properties. ■

Avoid Repeating Yourself

You often will need to write queries for use in your programs. One option for creating the queries is to generate the SQL statement in code and run the query using the `Execute` statement. This method is illustrated in the following code:

```
SQLSel = "Select * From Youth Order By LastName, FirstName"
YouthDb.Execute SqlSel
```

However, if you are going to be using a query a number of times in your program, or potentially in multiple programs, you probably want to store the query in some manner. The Jet database structure supports the storing of queries in the database itself. This way, you can create a query, store the query in the database, and then execute the query any time it is needed. To execute a query in this manner, you still use the `Execute` method, but you pass the method the name of the query stored in the database. There are several advantages to using this method of handling queries:

- You can troubleshoot the query one time and then store it to avoid making mistakes in later calls.
- Stored queries run faster than those that are created on-the-fly.
- Using stored queries makes upsizing your application to a client/server platform easier.

Queries on Non-Jet Databases

The Jet engine is not limited to running queries on only Jet databases. You can run a query on any database that the Jet engine can directly access. These databases include FoxPro, dBASE, and Paradox, as well as Excel spreadsheet files and text files. In addition, you can pass queries directly to other database engines such as SQL Server or Oracle. In the case of passing queries, you need to make sure that the query meets the syntax requirement of the database engine you are using.

Making Copies of the Database

One major new feature of version 3 of the Jet engine is *database replication*. Replication lets you make multiple copies of a database that multiple users will edit or modify (for example, by people in satellite offices). You can then synchronize these copies of the database so that the changes made to the data in any of the databases can be reflected in the master database. In addition, during synchronization, you can easily copy changes to the structure of the master database to all the replicas.

Replication is also useful if you maintain information on both a desktop and a portable system. If you replicate the desktop database before leaving on a trip and then synchronize the databases on your return, you assure that the data in both databases is current.

Part
II

Ch
9

From Here...

This chapter introduced you to the uses of databases and the features of the Jet engine. If your interest was piqued, you might also want to look at the following chapters:

- See Chapter 10, "Applications at Warp Speed," to learn how to quickly create a database application using the tools in Visual Basic.

- See Chapter 11, "Designing and Creating a Database," to learn how to set up a new database from scratch.

- See Chapter 14, "Understanding Structured Query Language," to learn more about creating SQL commands.

Applications at Warp Speed

Visual Basic is designed to enable you, the developer, to create applications for the Windows environment quickly and easily. This ease of use extends to the creation of database programs as well. If you have an existing database that you must access, Visual Basic makes it easy for you to write a complete data entry and reporting application with almost no programming. You just drop a few controls on a form and set the properties. In fact, Visual Basic makes the task so easy that you can even have Visual Basic create the data-entry forms for you.

The components that make all these capabilities possible are the data control and the bound controls for data entry forms and Crystal Reports for report generation. With just these few tools, you can create a wide variety of applications. Of course, as you progress to more complex applications, you will need to do more of the programming yourself. But even for the more complex applications, these tools provide a good first step in the programming process and enable you to create application prototypes rapidly.

To illustrate the concepts of creating data-entry screens and reports, in this chapter I walk you through the development of screens and reports based on a membership database. You can find the database and the actual forms and reports on the book's Web site. ∎

Navigating a recordset with the data control

The data control provides several buttons that allow you to move from one record to another in your recordset.

Displaying data from a recordset

We will examine how the bound controls make it easy to get information from the database to the user's screen.

Adding and deleting records

You will see how to use code to add features to your application.

Using automatic data-entry forms

If you want the easiest way to create a data-entry form, Visual Basic can create it for you. You'll see how to use a Wizard to make this happen.

Designing a report

Crystal Reports is a product that comes with Visual Basic, that allows you to graphically design reports based on the information in your database.

Running reports from your program

You'll also see how to use the Crystal Reports forms from within your program.

Understanding the Data Control

The centerpiece of easy database applications is the data control. The data control is one of the controls available in Visual Basic's toolbox, as shown in Figure 10.1. Setting up the data control requires only four simple steps:

1. Select the control from the toolbox.

2. Draw the control on your form.

3. Set the DatabaseName property of the control.

4. Set the RecordSource property of the control.

N O T E Following these four steps is the minimum required to set up the data control. If you want to access non-Jet databases or use any of the control's other capabilities, you need to set additional properties. These properties are covered in Chapter 12, "Doing More with Bound Controls." ■

▶ **See** "Exploring the Data Control In-Depth" **p. 279**

FIG. 10.1
The data control is one of the standard components of the Visual Basic toolbox.

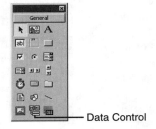

—— Data Control

What Is the Data Control

Basically, the data control is a link between the information in your database and the bound controls that you use to display the information. As you set the properties of the data control, you tell it which database and what part of the database to access. By default, the data control creates a dynaset-type recordset from one or more of the tables in your database.

The data control also provides the record navigation functions that your application needs. With these buttons, indicated on Figure 10.2, the user can move to the first or last record in the recordset, or move to a record prior to or following the current record. The design of the buttons makes their use intuitive, in that they are similar to the buttons you would find on a VCR or a CD player.

The recordset created by the data control is determined by the settings of the DatabaseName and RecordSource properties. The recordset is created as the form containing the data control loads and is activated. This recordset is active until the form is unloaded, at which time the recordset is released.

FIG. 10.2
The "VCR" buttons
on the data control
indicate their function
to the user.

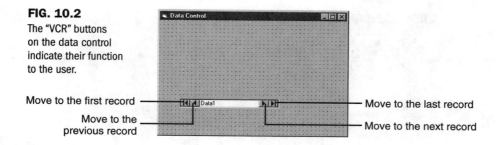

Move to the first record ———————— Move to the last record

Move to the
previous record ———————— Move to the next record

> **N O T E** A recordset is a link to the physical data in a database. Even after a recordset is released or closed, the data in the underlying tables is still in the database. ■

Adding a Data Control to Your Form

The first step in using a data control is to add the control to your application's form. Select the data control object from the Visual Basic toolbox (see Figure 10.1). Next, place and size the data control just as you do any other design object. After you set the desired size and placement of the data control on your form, you can set the Name and Caption properties of the data control.

The Name property sets the control name, which identifies the control and its associated data to the bound controls. The Name property also is the name of the recordset object that you use with any program commands that your application needs. The default name for the first data control added to a form is Data1. Additional data controls added to a form are sequentially numbered as Data2, Data3, and so on. To change the name of the data control, select the Name property from the Properties dialog box and type the name you want.

 To access the Properties dialog box quickly, press F4 or click the Properties icon on the toolbar.

The Caption property specifies the text that appears on the data control. You usually want the caption to be descriptive of the data the control accesses. The default for the Caption property is the initial setting of the Name property (for example, Data1 for the first data control). You can change the Caption property the same way you change the Name property.

For the example you're creating in this chapter, add a data control with the name datYouth and the caption Youth. Figure 10.3 shows the form with this control added.

 You also can add code to your program to change the caption of the data control to reflect the information in the current record, such as a person's name.

FIG. 10.3

Draw the data control on your form, and set its caption to an expression meaningful to your application.

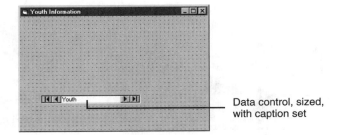

Data control, sized, with caption set

Two Properties are All You Need to Set

After you place the data control on your form, you need to make the connection between the data control and the database information. You do so by setting the properties of the data control. Although several properties can affect the way a data control interacts with the database, only two properties are required to establish the link to a Jet database: the DatabaseName and RecordSource properties. Specifying these two properties tells the data control what information to retrieve from the database and causes the data control to create a recordset that allows nonexclusive, read/write access to the data.

NOTE The DatabaseName property is not the same as the Name property mentioned earlier. The Name property specifies the name of the data control object. This name references the object in code. The DatabaseName property specifies the name of the database file that the data control is accessing. ■

What's in a Name For Jet databases, the DatabaseName property is the name of the database file, including the full path name. To enter the name, select the DatabaseName property from the Properties dialog box, and either type the database name or select the database from a list. Figure 10.4 shows the Properties dialog box with the DatabaseName property selected.

FIG. 10.4

Use the Properties dialog box to set the database name for the control.

To select the database name from the dialog box, click the ellipsis button (...) at the right of the property input line. This action displays a DatabaseName dialog box, as shown in Figure 10.5. Select the file name you want and click OK. The selected file name then appears next to the `DatabaseName` property of the data control.

FIG. 10.5
You can enter a database name or choose it from the DatabaseName dialog box.

Straight from the Source   After you designate the database to use with the `DatabaseName` property, specify the information you want from the database with the `RecordSource` property. If you are working with a single table as your recordset, you can enter the table name or select it from the list of tables, as shown in Figure 10.6.

FIG. 10.6
You can select the `RecordSource` property from a list of tables available in the database.

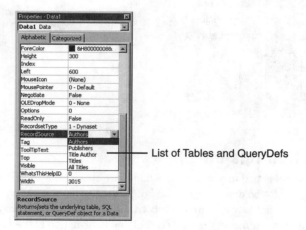

List of Tables and QueryDefs

You can access only selected information from a table or use information from multiple tables by using an SQL statement. To use an SQL statement to define the recordset, you set the `RecordSource` property to the name of a `QueryDef` (which contains the SQL statement) in the database or enter a valid SQL statement in the property definition. You can use any SQL statement that creates a dynaset. (You can also include functions in your SQL statement.) If you're using a `QueryDef`, it must be a `QueryDef` that has already been defined and stored in the database.

TIP   To make sure that your SQL statements are correct, test them in the Data Manager. Then cut and paste to place the statements in the `RecordSource` property.

Part
II

Ch
10

Getting Acquainted with Bound Control Basics

Bound controls in Visual Basic are those controls set up to work with a data control to create database applications. Most of the bound controls in Visual Basic are simply standard controls that have additional properties allowing them to perform data access functions. A few custom controls are designed specifically to work with the data controls. These controls are covered in Chapter 12, "Doing More with Bound Controls."

▶ **See** "Other Bound Controls" **p. 291**

The controls you use in this chapter are ones with which you are already familiar:

- Text Box
- Label
- Check Box
- Picture Box
- Image

These controls are shown in Figure 10.7.

FIG. 10.7
Several familiar controls also have properties that let them access data.

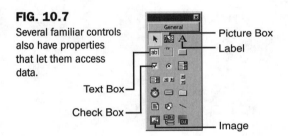

What Do These Controls Do

Each bound control is tied to a data control and more specifically to a particular field in the recordset attached to the data control. The bound control automatically displays the information in the specified field for the current record. As the user moves from one record to another using the navigation buttons of the data control, the information in the bound controls is updated to reflect the current record.

The bound controls are not limited, however, to just displaying the information in the record. They also can be used to edit the information. To change the information, the user just needs to edit the contents of the control. Then, when the current record is changed or the form is closed, the information in the database is automatically updated to reflect the changed values.

N O T E Because the Label control has no editable portion, the data displayed in the Label cannot be changed. Also, if a control is locked, or editing is otherwise prevented, the user cannot change the value of the information. ■

You use each of the basic bound controls to edit and display different types of data. With the bound controls, you can handle strings, numbers, dates, logical values, and even pictures and memos. Table 10.1 lists the five basic bound controls and the types of database fields that they can handle. The table also lists the property of the control that contains the data.

Table 10.1 Different Controls Used to Handle Different Types of Data

Control Name	Data Type	Control Property
Label	Text, Numeric, Date	Caption
TextBox	Text, Memo, Numeric, Date	Text
CheckBox	Logical, True/False	Value
PictureBox	Long Binary	Picture
Image	Long Binary	Picture

Adding Controls to Your Forms

To add one of the bound controls to your form, select the control from the toolbox, and position and size the control on the form. Figure 10.8 shows a text box added to the form with the data control on it.

FIG. 10.8
You draw bound controls on your form just as you draw any other control.

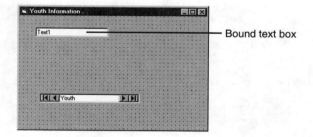

Bound text box

 TIP Hold down the Ctrl key when you click a control in the toolbar, and you can add multiple controls of that type to your form. This way, you don't have to click the control icon repeatedly.

The Name property of the bound control defines the object by which the control is referenced in any program statements. If you're using only the data control to create your program (that is, you have no program code that references the bound control), you may want to leave the Name property with its default value. If you're going to use program statements, you may want to change the name to one that has some meaning to you. The Name property does not effect how the bound control performs.

N O T E   Naming all controls with unique names is good programming practice. Also, most
programmers use a three-letter prefix to indicate the type of control, such as txt for a
TextBox, lbl for a Label, and so on. ▣

Data Display in Two Easy Properties

For a bound control to work with the data from a recordset, you must first tie the bound control
to the data control representing the recordset. You do so by setting the DataSource property of
the bound control. Depending on the specific control used, you may have to set other properties. By working on the sample Retail Items data-entry screen throughout the remainder of this
chapter, you will learn many of the bound controls, which properties you must set, and how to
set them.

Setting the *DataSource* Property   To set the DataSource property, select the property from
the Properties dialog box for your control. Click the arrow to the right of the input area to see a
list of all the data controls on the current form. To set the DataSource property, select one of
the controls from the list. Figure 10.9 shows this procedure.

T I P   Double-click the DataSource property to scroll through the list of available data controls.

FIG. 10.9

Select the DataSource
property for the bound
control from the form's
list of data controls.

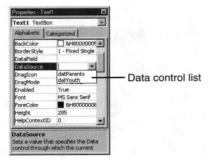

Data control list

Setting the *DataField* Property   Although the DataSource property tells the bound control
from which data control to retrieve data, you still need to tell the bound control what specific
data to retrieve. You do so by setting the DataField property. This property tells the control
which field of the recordset will be handled by this bound control.

To set the DataField property of the control, select the DataField property from the Properties dialog box, click the arrow to the right of the input area, and select one of the fields from
the displayed list. The list includes all available fields from the recordset defined in the specified DataSource (see Figure 10.10).

FIG. 10.10
Select the
`DataField` property
for the bound control
from the list of fields
in the selected data
control.

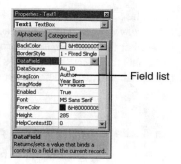

— Field list

 TIP   Double-click the `DataField` property to scroll through a list of available fields.

CAUTION
You cannot select fields from a list until the `DataSource` property has been set.

Creating a Simple Application

To help further illustrate the concepts of creating a data access application, I step you through
the process of creating a data-entry form for a membership program. You can find the database, along with the completed form, on the book's Web site, **http://www.quecorp.
com/seubs**.

Setting Up the Form

The first step in setting up the data-access form is to add a data control to your form. Select the
data control from the toolbox, and place it on the form. Change the `Name` property of the data
control to `datYouth` and the `Caption` property to `Youth Information`. Next, you need to set the
`DatabaseName` and `RecordSource` properties of the data control. First, set the `DatabaseName`
property to `C:\Youth\Youthtrk.mdb`. After you set the database name, you can set the
`RecordSource` property. From the property's selection list, select the Youth table. The data
control is now ready for use.

NOTE   You can find the sample database, Youthtrk.mdb, on the book's Web site. You might need to
change the path to the database file from the one listed in the preceding paragraph. ■

The next step in creating the data-access form is to add the bound controls. To make the example easy, just use text boxes for each of the fields. Also, for each field, place a label control
on the form to identify the information in the text box. For the sample case, you need seven

text boxes and seven corresponding labels. The DataSource property of all the text boxes is datYouth, which is the name of the data control you just created. For each text box, you also need to specify a DataField property. Remember that the DataField property ties the control to a specific field in the database. Table 10.2 lists the DataField settings for each text box and the suggested captions for the corresponding label controls. The table uses the default names for the text boxes.

Table 10.2   DataField and Caption Settings for the Data-Access Form

TextBox Name	DataField	Caption for Corresponding Label
Text1	FirstName	First Name:
Text2	LastName	Last Name:
Text3	Addr1	Address:
Text4	City	City:
Text5	State	State:
Text6	Zip	Zip Code:
Text7	HomePhone	Phone Number:

After you add the bound controls and set their properties, your form should look like the one shown in Figure 10.11.

FIG. 10.11
You can create a simple data-entry form by using just the data control and bound text boxes.

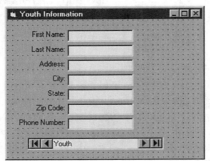

Navigating the Database

Now that you have created the data-entry form, try it out by running the program. As the program first starts, you should see the form load, and the information for the first record should appear in the text boxes. Now you can see how the data control is used to navigate through the records of the database. You can move to the first record, the previous record, the next record, or the last record by clicking the appropriate button on the data control.

TROUBLESHOOTING

You have not created an error or done anything wrong in setting up the form. You are seeing the records presented in the physical order of the table, the order in which the records were entered. If you want to see the records in alphabetical order, place the following string in the `RecordSource` property of the data control:

`Select * From Youth Order By LastName,FirstName`

Then run the program again.

Essential Functions the Data Control Forgot

As you can see, the data control is quite flexible, but it lacks a few functions that are necessary for most data-entry applications, specifically, adding and deleting records. To overcome these shortcomings, you can add the functions to the data-entry screen using program commands assigned to a command button.

To add these functions to the sample application, add two command buttons named `Add` and `Delete` to the form. To make the buttons functional, add the code segments shown in Listing 10.1 to the `Click` event of the appropriate button.

> **Listing 10.1 Program Statements Placed in the *Click* Event of Command Buttons to Add Capabilities to the Data-Entry Screen**
>
> ```
> '*********************************************************************
> 'Command to add a new record,
> 'place in click event of Add button
> '*********************************************************************
> datYouth.Recordset.AddNew
> '*********************************************************************
> 'Commands to delete a record,
> 'placed in click event of Delete button
> '*********************************************************************
> datYouth.Recordset.Delete
> If Not datYouth.EOF Then
>     datYouth.Recordset.MoveNext
> Else
>     datYouth.Recordset.MoveLast
> End If
> ```

As you can see, this listing does not enter a command to invoke the `Update` method. (Updates are done automatically by the data control whenever you move to a new record or close the form.)

> **N O T E** You add the Move command to the Delete button to force a move to a new record. After a record is deleted, it is no longer accessible but still shows on-screen until a move is executed. If you do not force a move and try to access the deleted record, an error occurs. ■

Part
II

Ch
10

Your data-entry form should now look like the one shown in Figure 10.12.

FIG. 10.12
You can add new capabilities to the data-entry screen by assigning program commands to command buttons.

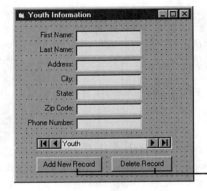

— Add and delete command buttons

Creating Forms Automatically

The bound controls make it easy for you to create data-entry forms with a minimum of effort. You just draw the controls on your form, set a few properties, and you're done. What could be easier?

Well, actually you can create data-entry forms in an even easier way: by using the Data Form Wizard (DFW). The DFW is one of the add-ins that comes with Visual Basic. Using this add-in, you can select a database and a record source; then it creates your data-entry form automatically. Of course, the form may not be exactly like you want it, but you can easily change the default design and then save the changes. Using the DFW is a great way to create a series of data-entry forms rapidly for a prototype or for a simple application.

Setting Up the Data Form Wizard

As I mentioned in the preceding section, the DFW is one of the add-ins that comes with Visual Basic. If, however, you choose the Add-Ins menu in Visual Basic, you don't see this option initially. You have to first tell Visual Basic that you want access to the form designer. You do so by choosing the Add-In Manager item from the Add-Ins menu. The dialog box shown in Figure 10.13 then appears.

FIG. 10.13
Using the Add-In Manager, you can add capabilities to your Visual Basic design environment.

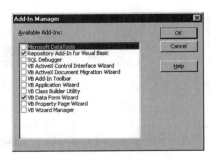

To access the DFW, click the box next to the text in the Add-In Manager. A check then appears in the box. Next, click the OK button and you're set. Now, when you select the Add-Ins menu, you see the DFW as one of the items. Selecting the DFW opens the first dialog box of the Wizard, which you can see in Figure 10.14. This screen tells you a little about the Data Form Wizard. You can choose not to have this form presented on subsequent uses of the Data Form Wizard.

FIG. 10.14
The Data Form Wizard automatically creates data-entry forms for you.

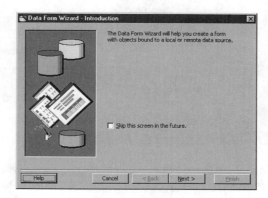

Clicking the Next button on the initial form takes you to the second screen of the DFW. This screen, shown in Figure 10.15, enables you to choose the type of database which your form will be accessing. To choose a database type, simply click the type name in the list, then click the Next button to continue creating your form.

FIG. 10.15
You can choose to create a form from many common desktop databases.

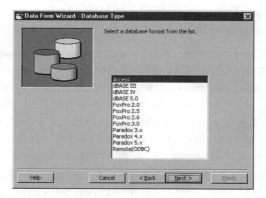

Getting to the Source of Your Data

After you have chosen the type of database to use, you will next need to choose the actual database and record source with which you will be working. The screen shown in Figure 10.16 allows you to either enter the name of the database or select the database from a dialog. Clicking the Browse button on the dialog will present you with a database dialog that allows you to choose the database to open. After selecting the database, you are returned to the Database screen of the DFW. You will notice at this point that the file name of the selected database, including the full path, has been entered in the text box on the form.

FIG. 10.16
The Database screen
allows you to specify
the database and the
types of record sources
to use.

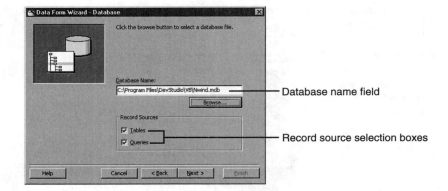

Database name field

Record source selection boxes

In addition to specifying the database name, you can also specify the types of record sources that will be displayed for selection in a later screen. You can choose to have tables, queries, or both displayed. You make your selection by clicking the appropriate check boxes. When you have finished, you need to click the Next button to proceed.

N O T E   At any time you are using the Wizard, you can click the Previous button to return to an earlier screen. ■

The next screen allows you to select the type of data-entry form that you want the DFW to create. There are three types of data-entry forms that can be created:

- Single record - This allows you to edit the information in the recordset one record at a time. This is the classic data entry type of form.

- Grid - This type of screen allows you to edit multiple records at a time. This screen would be similar to the recordset view in Access or the Browse window in FoxPro.

- Master/Detail - This type of screen allows you to edit the information of a single parent record along with its associated child records. This type of form might be used to show information about an order along with all the items ordered.

Choosing the type of form to create not only effects the appearance of the form, but determines what recordset(s) must be selected for the form. For a single record or grid form, you will only need to select a single record source. For the Master/Detail form, you will need to select two record sources. You really don't have to worry too much about this since the Wizard will guide you through it. That's what wizards are for, right?

> **CAUTION**
>
> If you are creating a Master/Detail form, you will need to have established a relation between the tables you select. The relation information is what is used to keep the information synchronized.

A Few Good fields

After you have selected the database and the type of form, you will need to select the table or query to use for the form, and the actual fields that you want to have included on the form. This is done on the Record Source screen of the Wizard, as shown in Figure 10.17.

FIG. 10.17
You choose the record source and fields using simple combo boxes and lists.

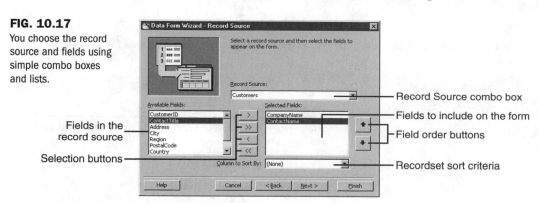

To set up the fields for the form, you will need to follow these steps:

1. Select a record source from the combo box.
2. Select the fields to include by clicking on the field names in the Available Fields list. You can double-click a field to select it, or highlight the field and click the selection button (>).
3. Place the fields in the desired order by moving them in the Selected fields list. You move a field by highlighting it, then clicking the up or down buttons. (This step is optional.)
4. Select the column on which to sort the recordset by choosing it from the Column to Sort By combo box. (This step is optional.)
5. Click the Next button to move to the next screen.

What Does This Button Do

After selecting all the fields you want on the form, you have one final set of choices to make, the buttons that you want to appear on your form. This selection is made in the Control Selection screen of the DFW, shown in Figure 10.18.

FIG. 10.18

You can choose an number of command buttons to appear on your form.

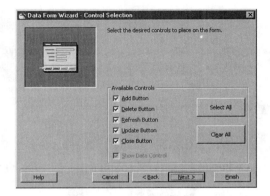

Table 10.3 lists the buttons that you can elect to have appear on your data form.

Table 10.3 Buttons You Can Elect to Have on Your Data Form

Available Controls	Function
Add	Adds a new record to the recordset and clears the data entry fields.
Delete	Deletes the current record.
Refresh	Causes the data control to reexecute the query used to create it. This process is necessary only in a multi-user environment.
Update	Stores any changes made to the data-entry fields to the database for the current record.
Close	Closes and unloads the data-entry form.

You are now ready for the final step of the DFW, actually creating your form. In the last screen of the DFW, you will specify the name of the form (the DFW gives you a default name), then click the Finish button. This will start the creation process. At this point, you sit back and relax for a minute while the DFW does the work. When it is finished, your program has a new data form, and all you did was answer a few questions and make a few selections. Figures 10.19 through 10.21 show you the various types of data forms that can be created with the DFW.

FIG. 10.19
A single record data form created by the Data Form Wizard.

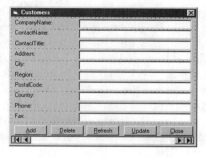

FIG. 10.20
A Grid data form created by the Data Form Wizard.

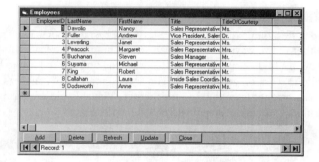

FIG. 10.21
A Master/Detail data form created by the Data Form Wizard.

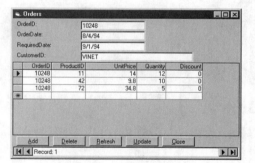

Designing Reports

Although the data control and bound controls do a great job of enabling you to create forms to enter and display data, they don't have any reporting capabilities. As a result, if you want to display reports on the screen or print them out, you need some additional capabilities. Visual Basic does have a Printer object with which you can send information to the printer. However, trying to set up a custom database report with the Printer object requires a lot of programming and a lot of trial and error.

Fortunately, you can accomplish database reporting in an easier way. Visual Basic comes with a reporting product: Crystal Reports. Crystal Reports is a stand-alone program that enables you to produce custom reports quickly and easily from the information in your database. If Crystal Reports worked only by itself, it would be a good product. But what makes it especially useful for the Visual Basic programmer is that it works in conjunction with Visual Basic. First, you can access the report designer directly from the Visual Basic design environment. Then, when the report design is completed, you can access the reports directly from your Visual Basic program. Using Crystal Reports, you have the option of previewing reports on the screen or sending them directly to the printer. All in all, Crystal Reports is a versatile report generator and print engine.

Starting Crystal Reports

The first step in designing your reports is starting Crystal Reports itself. You can run Crystal Reports in either of two ways. First, you can select the program from the Visual Basic folder on the Start menu of Windows 95. Working this way, you don't even have to have Visual Basic loaded in order to work on your reports. The second method of starting Crystal Reports is to choose Report Designer from the Add-Ins menu of Visual Basic. Either method starts Crystal Reports and places you in the startup screen shown in Figure 10.22.

FIG. 10.22
Using Crystal Reports, you can visually design database reports.

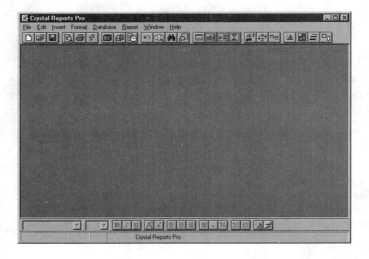

After you start Crystal Reports, you can create a new report by choosing the New item from the File menu or by clicking the new report button on the toolbar. Either of these methods presents you with the New Report dialog box. In this dialog box, shown in Figure 10.23, you can specify the type of report that you want to produce.

N O T E Crystal Reports uses Experts to help you create your reports. These Experts are similar to the Wizards used in Microsoft programs. ■

FIG. 10.23
In the New Report dialog box, you can select options for your report.

Crystal Reports supports the creation of the following basic report types:

- **Standard:** This type of report is a standard report format of rows and columns. It often has summary information at the bottom of the columns. In the report, you also can group information according to certain criteria.

- **Listing:** This type of report creates a simple listing of the information in a recordset. Each data field is represented by a column and each row represents a data record.

- **Cross Tab:** A cross-tab report basically inverts the order of a standard columnar report. The columns of a cross-tab report are the records of a particular recordset. These reports are often used to obtain a quick summary view of a more complex set of data.

- **Mail Label:** You use these reports to create items such as mailing labels or name tags from the information in your database.

- **Summary:** This report presents summary information about the data, such as total and average sales or the number of attendees.

- **Graph:** Shows the information in a graphical form.

- **Top N:** Shows only a specified number of the top records in the recordset. This can be used to show the top five salespeople in the company.

- **Drill Down:** This type of report shows the supporting information, or detail information for each record.

Selecting the type of report to create automatically start the Report Expert. For the Standard report shown in our example, the Expert has seven steps for creating the report. Each of these steps is represented on a tab in the Expert dialog, shown in Figure 10.24.

FIG. 10.24
The Report Expert guides you through the steps of creating a report.

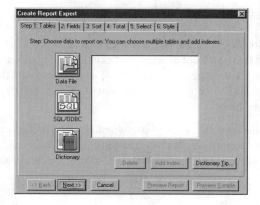

The first step to creating the report is selecting the type of data source to use for the report. Crystal Reports supports the following three different data sources for the reports:

- Data File: This is a table or query in a database. It is the most common source of your report information.

- SQL Table: With this data source, you can retrieve data from an SQL server database.

- Data Dictionary: With this data source, you can get the data from a data dictionary. A data dictionary is used with several types of database management systems to specify the type and layout of the data in the files.

For most reports, you will choose a data file as your data source. Choosing this button presents you with a dialog that allows you to select the data file. Once the data file is selected, the tables and queries of the data file will be listed in the Report Expert dialog.

The second step of the Expert allows you to add relation information to that which is already present in the data file. Typically, you will not need to add relation information.

Selecting the Data Fields

Step three of the Report Expert is to select the individual fields that you want to have appear on the report. You can access this step by clicking on the Step 3 tab of the dialog. This page of the dialog is shown in Figure 10.25.

FIG. 10.25

You select the data fields to include from a list of available fields.

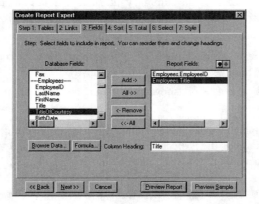

You can add fields by double-clicking the individual fields in the Database Fields list. You can also highlight the fields that you want to select and click the Add button. The list does support multiple selections. The Fields page of the dialog also allows you to set the order of the fields in the report. For each field in the Report Fields list, you can also specify a custom column heading in the text box below the list.

There are also times when you may want to combine fields or use them in a calculation. The Fields page also has a button which allows you to enter formulas for calculated fields. If you need to specify a formula, you click this button, then specify the formula name. After this, you will be presented with the Edit Formula dialog shown in Figure 10.26. After you have entered the formula, you will be returned to the Fields page.

FIG. 10.26
The formula editor allows you to combine fields and perform calculations for your report.

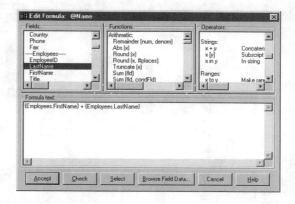

After you have specified the fields for the report, you can preview the report or go on to set other options. Previewing the report will be covered in the next section. Before we get to that, let's quickly cover what other options are available on the other pages of the Expert. These options are summarized in the following list:

- Sort - You can specify an order by which the lines of the report will be sorted.
- Total - This determines if subtotals and grand totals of numerical data will be included on the report.
- Select - Allows you to specify a selection criteria for the report. This is used to produce only a subset of the recordset that is the source of the data. Using subset can greatly increase the speed of your report.
- Style - Allows you to specify a specific style of the report, such as placing lines after each record or making the entire report appear as a table. This option also allows you to add pictures to the report.

Previewing the Report

After you set up the report fields and the other information for the report, you can preview the report to see how the actual data will look. To run the preview, click the Preview Report button on the Expert.

The preview window actually consists of two tabs – a Preview tab and a Design tab. The Preview tab shows you the way the report will actually look, with the data in the report. The Design tab will show you the sections of the report and allow you to modify the basic design that was created by the Report Expert. Figures 10.27 and 10.28 show these two views of the report.

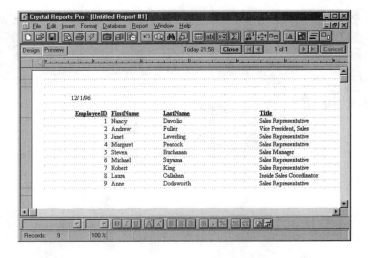

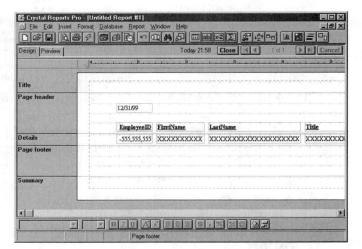

Saving the Report

After you complete the design of the report, you need to save the report file. You save the file
so that you can recall the report for further editing but also so that you can access the report
from your Visual Basic program. Saving the report can be done by either clicking the Save
button on the toolbar or by choosing the Save or Save As items from the File menu.

Running a Report

Although you can run the reports you create from within Crystal Reports, what you really want
to be able to do is access these reports from within your Visual Basic program. Using Crystal

Reports, you can do so with the Crystal Reports control. It is one of the custom controls that comes with Visual Basic. The Crystal Reports control provides a link between the Crystal Reports engine and the reports you create with the report designer.

Crystal Reports Control

The first step in accessing Crystal Reports is to make the control available to your program. First, you need to add the Crystal Reports control to your Visual Basic toolbox. To do so, choose Components from the Project menu of Visual Basic. The Components dialog box, shown in Figure 10.29, then appears. In this dialog box, you can specify which custom controls are available in your project.

FIG. 10.29
You must make the Crystal Reports control available to your project by selecting it in the Components dialog box.

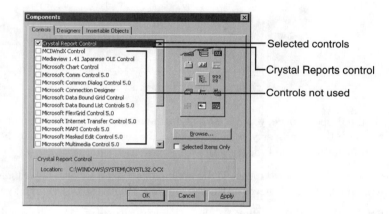

— Selected controls

— Crystal Reports control

— Controls not used

> **TIP**
> You also can access the Components dialog box by clicking the right mouse button on the toolbox and choosing Components from the pop-up menu, or by pressing Ctrl+T.

◆ **TROUBLESHOOTING**

The Crystal Reports control does not show up in the Custom Controls dialog box. If you elected to perform a custom setup of Visual Basic, you may have left Crystal Reports out of the setup process. You need to rerun the Visual Basic setup program and add Crystal Reports.

Setting Up the Control

After the Crystal Reports control is available in your toolbox, you can use it in your program. To gain access to the control, simply select it from the toolbox, and place it on the form from which you plan to access reports. Because the Crystal Reports control is not visible at runtime, it appears only as an icon on your form. Once the control is on the form, you can set the properties that access the reports you create with the report designer.

Specifying the Report to Run   The key property that you need to specify is the `ReportFileName` property. This property specifies the actual report that you will run from your program. You can easily set this property by clicking the ellipsis button that appears to the right of the property in the Properties dialog box. The Crystal Reports Property page, shown in Figure 10.30, then appears. From this page, you can specify the name of the report and whether the report should go to the printer, a preview window, a file, or to a message through the MAPI interface.

FIG. 10.30

Select the report name and destination from the Property page of Crystal Reports.

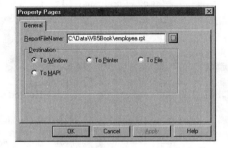

On the Property page, you can either type the name of the report into the field for the `ReportFileName` property, or you can select the report from a file dialog box by clicking the ellipsis button on the Property page.

Selecting the `ReportFileName` is the minimum setup for Crystal Reports. At this point, you can write the line of code necessary to run the report and test it by running your program.

Setting Optional Properties   Although only the `ReportFileName` is required for a report, you may want to use several optional properties with the report. The first of these properties is the `SelectionFormula` property. This property enables you to limit the number of records that will be included in the report. The `SelectionFormula` property is similar to the `Where` clause of an SQL statement but uses its own particular format to enter the information. To specify the `SelectionFormula`, you must specify the name of the recordset and the field to be compared. You must express this recordset/field combination in dot notation and enclose it in curly brackets. After specifying the recordset and field, you must specify the comparison operator and the value to be compared. The final result is an expression like the following:

```
{MemberShipList.OrgCode}=1
```

You also can use multiple expressions by including the `And` or `Or` operators.

> **CAUTION**
>
> If you enter a `SelectionFormula` when you're designing your report, any formula you enter in the `SelectionFormula` property of the Crystal Reports control provides an additional filter on the records.

Another optional property is the `CopiesToPrinter` property. This property enables you to print multiple copies of your report easily at one time. You can set this property to any integer value.

Taking Action

After you add the Crystal Reports control to your form and set its properties, you are ready to start printing, right? Well, not quite. You still have to tell Crystal Reports when to print the report. To do so, you write a line of code to initiate the report. The line of code sets the `Action` property of the Crystal Reports control to 1. The report then prints using the report file and other properties that you set. If you have your report set up to preview on the screen, it looks like the one shown in Figure 10.31. The following is the code to run this report (`rptMember` is the name of the Crystal Reports control):

```
rptMember.action = 1
```

FIG. 10.31
Printing the desired report to the screen.

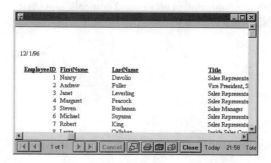

Setting Properties at Runtime

Because you will probably have a number of reports that you need to print, you need to be able to change the Crystal Reports control's properties at runtime; otherwise, you would need a separate report control for each of your reports. All the major properties of the Crystal Reports control, such as `ReportFileName` and `SelectionFormula`, are available at runtime. You set these properties, like any other properties, to new values using an assignment statement. The following code sets up the Crystal Reports control for a new report and specifies a selection criteria based on user input:

```
rptMember.ReportFileName = "CntyMbr.rpt"
rptMember.SelectionFormula = "{MemberShipList.OrgCode}=" & OrgID
rptMember.action = 1
```

The other property that you may need to set at runtime is the `DataFiles` property. This property is not available at design time. The property specifies the name of the database file to be used with the report. Now you may be thinking, "I told the report what file to use when I created it." That is true, but when you created the report, the database file was stored with a path based on your directory structure. And your path may not be the same as the directory structure of your users.

The `DataFiles` property is actually an array with the first element number of 0. If you're using more than one database in your report, you need to set the value of each `DataFiles` array element. For most of your reports, however, you will be using only a single database. The following line of code shows you how to set the value of the DataFiles property for the database. This line assumes that the database file is in the same folder as your application.

```
rptMember.DataFiles(0) = App.Path & "\Members.mdb"
```

From Here...

In this chapter, you learned how to set up a database application quickly for an existing database. If you would like to learn more about

- Creating your own database, see Chapter 11, "Designing and Creating a Database."
- Doing more with the data control and bound controls, see Chapter 12, "Doing More with Bound Controls."

Designing and Creating a Database

In Chapter 10, "Applications at Warp Speed," you learned how to use the data controls and bound controls to create a database application quickly to edit the information in an existing database. You also learned how you can use Crystal Reports to generate on-screen and printed reports of the data. Now that you have had some exposure to creating an application, you are probably ready to create your own database to handle your specific needs.

Creating a database requires you to learn about two separate tasks. First, you must learn a little about how to design a database. In the design, you decide what data goes in the database and how it will be organized. Second, you must learn how to translate the design into the actual database. You can do so in a variety of ways. In this chapter, you will walk through the process of designing and creating a sample database. This database will contain information about parents and their children. The database you create will be a portion of the database used in one of the commercial applications that tracks the members of youth groups. ■

How do you determine the data required for a database

You will see how to find out the information that needs to be stored in the database.

How do you organize the data in the database

Data in a database needs to be stored in a way that makes the information easy to retrieve and easy to maintain.

How can you create a database with a program

The methods of the Data Access Objects allow you to write programs to create or modify a database.

What can the Visual Data Manager do

The Visual Data Manager provides an easy way to create and modify databases for your programs.

Can you use Microsoft Access

If you have Access, you have the best tool for working with database structures.

How are queries used in creating databases

You can even create, delete, and modify tables in a database with SQL queries.

Designing a Database

Like most tasks, building a database starts with a design. After all, you wouldn't try to build a house without a blueprint, and most people wouldn't attempt to prepare a new dish without a recipe. Like these other tasks, having a good design for your database is a major first step to a successful project.

In designing a database application, you must not only set up the program's routines for maximum performance, but you must also pay attention to the physical and logical layout of the data storage. A good database design does the following:

- Provides minimum search times when locating specific records
- Stores data in the most efficient manner possible to keep the database from growing too large
- Makes data updates as easy as possible
- Is flexible enough to allow inclusion of new functions required of the program

Design Objectives

When you're creating the design for your database, you must keep several objectives in mind. Although meeting all these design objectives is desirable, sometimes they are mutually exclusive. The primary design objectives are as follow:

- Eliminate redundant data
- Be able to locate individual records quickly
- Make enhancements to the database easy to implement
- Keep the database easy to maintain

Key Activities in Designing Your Database

Creating a good database design involves the following seven key activities:

- Modeling the application
- Determining the data required for the application
- Organizing the data into tables
- Establishing the relationships between tables
- Setting index and validation requirements for the data
- Creating and storing any necessary queries for the application
- Reviewing the design

Now look briefly at the initial two activities in the list. First, take a look at modeling the application. When you model an application, you first should determine the tasks that the application must be able to perform. For example, if you're maintaining a membership list, you know that you will want to create phone directories and mailing lists of the members. As you're determining the tasks to be performed by the application, you are creating what is called the *functional specification*. For a project that you are creating, you probably know all the tasks that you want to perform, but writing down these tasks in a specification document is a good idea. This document can help you keep focused on what you want your program to do. If you're creating the program for another person, a functional specification becomes an agreement of what the application will contain. This specification can also show milestones that need to be achieved on a set schedule.

When you're creating the program for other people, the best way to learn what task must be performed is to talk to the people requesting the work. As a first step, you can determine if they already have a system that they are looking to replace, or if they have reports that they want to produce. Then ask a lot of questions until you understand the users' objectives for the program.

After you determine the functional specifications for the program, you can start determining what data the program needs. In the case of a membership application, knowing that you have to produce directories and mailing lists tells you that the database needs to contain the address and phone number of each of the members. Taking this a little situation further, you know that by presorting mail by ZIP code you can take advantage of reduced rate postage. Therefore, you need an index or query that places the mailing list information in ZIP code order. So you can see that the model not only tells you the data needed but also defines other components of the database as well.

Organizing the Data

One of the key aspects of a good database design is determining how the data will be organized in the database. To have a good design, you should organize the data in a way that makes the information easy to retrieve and makes maintenance of the database easy. Within a database, data is stored in one or more tables. For most database applications, you can accomplish efficient data management by storing data in multiple tables and by establishing relationships between these tables. In the following sections, I describe how you can determine what data belongs in each table of your database.

Tables as Topics   A *table* is a collection of information related to a particular topic. By thinking of a key topic for the table, you can determine whether a particular piece of data fits into the table. For example, if a country club wants to track information about members and employees, the club management may be tempted to put both in the same table (because both groups refer to people). However, look at the data required for each group. Although both groups require information about a person's name, address, and phone number, the employee group also requires information about the person's Social Security number, job category, payroll, and tax status. If you were to create just one table, many of the entries would be blank for the members. You would also have to add a field to distinguish between a member and an employee. Clearly, this technique would result in a lot of wasted space. It could also result in slower processing of employee transactions or member transactions because the program would have to skip a number of records in the table. Figure 11.1 shows a database table with the two groups combined. Figure 11.2 shows the reduction in the number of fields in a member-only database table.

FIG. 11.1

Combining the employee and member tables creates wasted space.

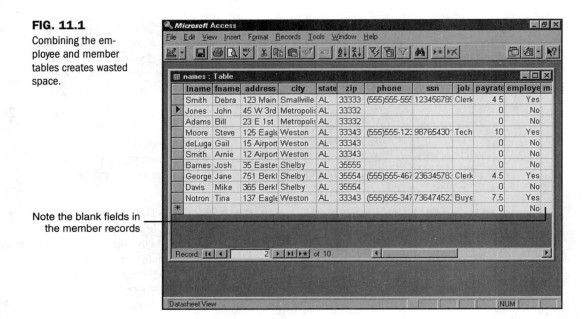

Note the blank fields in the member records

FIG. 11.2

A separate database table for members has only the required fields and is more efficient.

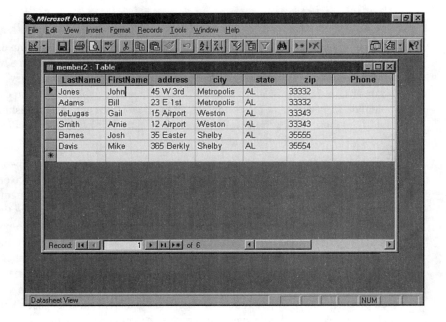

By thinking of the topic to which a table relates, you can more easily determine whether a particular piece of information belongs in the table. If the information results in wasted space for many records, the data belongs in a different table.

Data Normalization   *Data normalization* is the process of eliminating redundant data within the database. Taking data normalization to its fullest extent results in each piece of information in a database appearing only once.

Consider the example of order processing. For each item a person orders, you need the item number, description, price, order number, order date, and customer name, address, and phone number. If you place all this information in one table, the result looks like the table shown in Figure 11.3.

FIG. 11.3
Non-normalized data produces a large, inefficient data table.

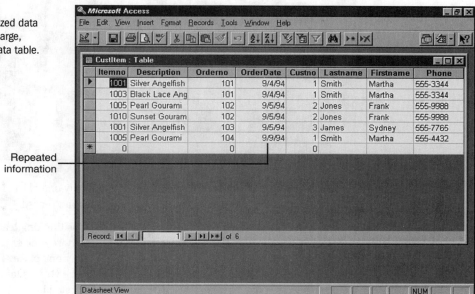

Repeated information

As you can see, much of the data in the table is repeated. This repetition introduces two problems. The first problem is wasted space because you repeat information. The second problem is one of data accuracy or currency. If, for example, a customer changes his or her phone number, you have to change it for all the records that apply to that customer—with the possibility that you will miss one of the entries. In the table in Figure 11.3, notice that Martha Smith's phone number was changed in the latest entry but not in the two earlier entries. If an employee looks up Martha Smith and uses an earlier entry, that employee would not find Martha's updated phone number.

A better solution for handling the data is to put the customer information in one table and the sales order information in another table. You can assign each customer a unique ID and include that ID in the sales order table to identify the customer. This arrangement yields two tables with the data structure shown in Figure 11.4.

Part
II

Ch
11

FIG. 11.4
Normalized custo-
mer and order tables
eliminate data
redundancy.

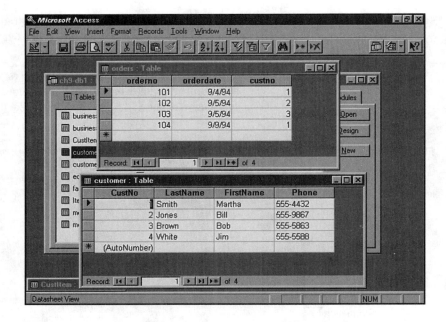

With this type of arrangement, the customer information appears in only one place. Now if a customer changes his or her phone number, you have to change only one record.

You can do the same thing to the items sold and order information. This thinking leads to the development of four tables, but the organization of the tables is much more efficient. You can be sure that when information must be changed, it has to change in only one place. This arrangement is shown in Figure 11.5. With the four-table arrangement, the Orders table and the Items Ordered table provide the links between the customers and the retail items they purchased. The Items Ordered table contains one record for each item of a given order. The Orders table relates the items to the date of purchase and the customer making the purchase.

When information is moved out of one table and into another, you must have a way of keeping track of the relationships between the tables. You can do so through the use of data keys. The topic of maintaining relations between tables is covered in Chapter 9, "Introduction to Databases and the Jet Engine."

Child and Lookup Tables   Another way to handle data normalization is to create what is known as a child table. A *child table* is a table in which all the entries share common information that is stored in another table. A simple example is a membership directory: the family shares a common last name, address, and phone number, but each family member has a different first name. The table containing the common information is called the *parent table,* and the table containing the member's first names is the *child table*. You use this data structure in the Youth system that is created later in the chapter. Figure 11.6 shows a parent table and its related child table.

FIG. 11.5
Complete normalization
of the tables provides
the greatest efficiency.

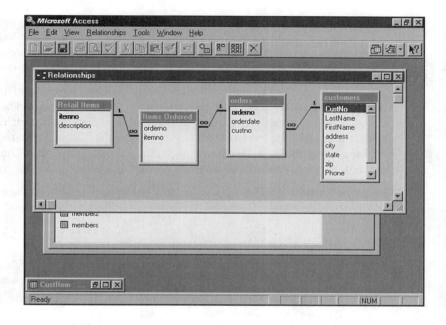

FIG. 11.6
Parent and child
tables are a form
of data normal-
ization.

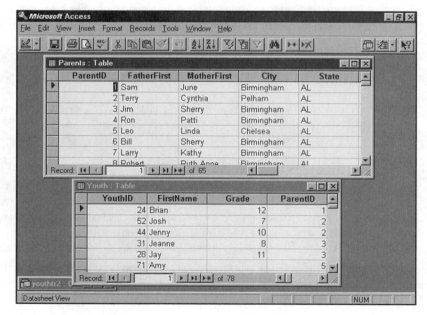

Part
II

Ch

11

A *lookup table* is another way to store information to prevent data redundancy and to increase the accuracy of data entry functions. Typically, a lookup table is used to store valid data entries (for example, a state abbreviations table). When a person enters the state code in an application, the program looks in the abbreviations table to make sure that the code exists.

You also can use a lookup table in data normalization. If you have a large mailing list, many of the entries use the same city and state information. In this case, you can use a ZIP code table as a related table to store the city and state by ZIP code (remember that each ZIP code corresponds to a single city and state combination). Using the ZIP code table requires that the mailing list use only the ZIP code of the address, and not the city and state. During data entry, you can have the program check an entered ZIP code against the valid entries.

Rules for Organizing Tables   Although no absolute rules exist for defining what data goes into which tables, here are some general guidelines to follow for efficient database design:

- Determine a topic for each table, and make sure that all data in the table relates to the topic.

- If a number of the records in a table have fields intentionally left blank, split the table into two similar tables. (Remember the example of the employee and member tables.)

- If information is repeated in a number of records, move that information to another table and set up a relationship between the tables.

- Repeated fields indicate the need for a child table. For example, if you have Item1, Item2, Item3, and so on in a table, move the items to a child table that relates back to the parent table.

- Use lookup tables to reduce data volume and to increase the accuracy of data entry.

- Do not store information in a table if it can be calculated from data in other tables.

N O T E   As stated previously, the guidelines for defining tables are not hard-and-fast rules. Sometimes it makes sense for you to deviate from the guidelines. ■

Performance Considerations

One of the most frequent reasons for deviating from the guidelines just given is to improve performance. If obtaining a total sales figure for a given salesperson requires summing several thousand records, for example, you may find it worthwhile to include a Total Sales field in the salesperson table that is updated each time a sale is made. This way, when reports are generated, the application doesn't have to do large numbers of calculations, and the report process is dramatically faster.

Another reason to deviate from the guidelines is to avoid opening a large number of tables at the same time. Because each open table uses a file handle and takes up memory, having too many open tables can slow down your application.

Deviating from the guidelines results in two major consequences. The first is increasing the size of the database because of redundant data. The second is the possibility of having incorrect data in some of the records because a piece of data was changed and not all the affected records were updated.

There are trade-offs between application performance and data storage efficiency. For each design, you must look at the tradeoffs and decide on the optimum design.

Using Indexes

When information is entered into a table, records are stored in the order in which they are entered. This is the physical order of the data. However, you usually want to view or process data in an order different from the order of entry. You also frequently have to find a specific record in a table. Doing so by scanning the table in its physical order could be quite time-consuming.

An index provides a method of showing a table in a specific order. An *index* is a special table that contains a key value (usually derived from the values of one or more fields) for each record in the data table stored in an order requested by the user. The index also contains pointers that tell the database engine where the actual record is located. This type of index is similar to the index in the back of this book. By using the book's index, you can easily look up key words or topics because it contains pointers (page numbers) to tell you where to find the information.

Why Use an Index   The structure of an index allows for rapid searches of the data. If you have a table of names indexed alphabetically, you can rapidly retrieve the record for John Smith by searching the index. To get an idea of the value of such an index, imagine a phone book that lists the customer names in the order in which they signed up for phone service. If you live in a large city, finding a person's number could take forever because you have to look at each line until you find the one you want.

A table can have a number of different indexes associated with it to give you several different organizations of the data. An employee table may have indexes on last name, date of birth, date of hire, and pay scale. Each index shows the same data in a different order, for a different purpose.

> **CAUTION**
>
> Although having many different views of the data may be desirable, keeping multiple indexes can take a toll on performance. Once again, you must consider the tradeoffs in the database design.

N O T E   You also can create different views of the information in a table by sorting the records or by specifying an order using a Structured Query Language (SQL) statement. ■

Single-Key Expressions   The most common type of index is the *single-key index,* which is based on the value of a single field in a table. Examples of this type of index are Social Security number, ZIP code, employee ID, and last name. If multiple records exist with the same index key, those records are shown in physical order within the sort order imposed by the single-key index. Figure 11.7 shows the physical order of a names table and how the table appears after being indexed on the last name field.

FIG. 11.7
The physical and logical
order of a table may be
different. Logical order
depends on indexes.

Physical order —

Logical order with
single-key index

First names
out of order

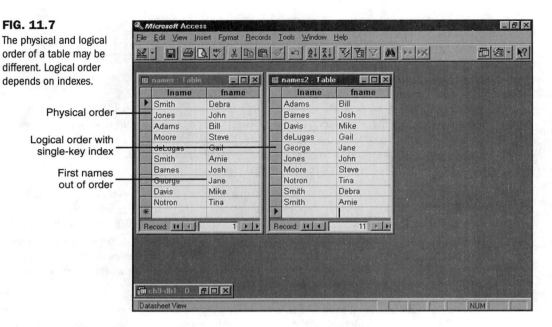

Multiple-Key Expressions   Although single-key expressions are valuable in presenting data in a specific order, imposing an even more detailed order on the table is often necessary. You can do so by using multiple-key indexes. As you can infer from the name, a *multiple-key index* is based on the values of two or more fields in a table. A prime example is to use last name and first name when indexing a membership list. Figure 11.8 updates the view of the table shown in Figure 11.7 to show how using the first name field to help sort the records changes the order of the table. As with single-key indexes, if the key values of several records are the same, the records are presented in physical order within the index order.

FIG. 11.8
Multiple-key
indexes further
refine the logical
order of a table.

First names
now in order

CAUTION

Although this point may be obvious, I must stress that the order of the fields in the index expression has a dramatic impact on the order of the records in the table. Indexing on first name and then last name produces different results than indexing on last name and then first name. Figure 11.9 shows the undesirable results of using a first name/last name index on the table used in Figure 11.7.

FIG. 11.9
An improper index field order yields undesirable results.

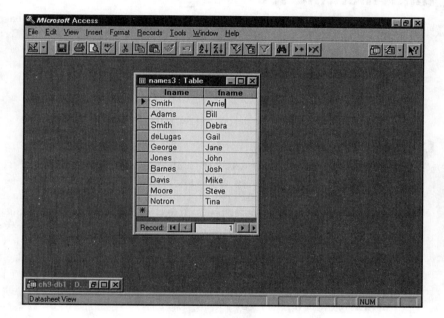

Part III

Using Queries

When you normalize data, you are typically placing related information in multiple tables. However, when you need to access the data, you want to see the information from all the tables in one place. To do so, you need to create recordsets that pull the related information from the multiple tables. You create a recordset from multiple tables using an SQL statement that specifies the desired fields, the location of the fields, and the relation between the tables. One way of using the SQL statement is to place it in the OpenRecordset method, which you use to create the recordset. However, you also can store the SQL statement as a query in the database.

Using stored queries presents several advantages:

- Using stored queries, you can more easily use the SQL statement in multiple locations in your program or in multiple programs.
- Making changes to the SQL statement in a single location is easier.

Part
II

Ch
11

- Stored queries run faster than those that are handled by parsing the statement from code.
- Using stored queries makes moving your application up to a client/server environment easier.

Implementing Your Design

The first step in implementing the database design is to create the database itself. There are three main methods of creating an Access database for use with Visual Basic. You can use the following:

- The data-access objects with a program
- The Data Manager application provided with Visual Basic
- Microsoft Access

Creating the Database

You can use Visual Basic's database commands to write a program that creates a database for use in your design work or to write a program that creates a new database while the program is running. Using the database creation commands is the only way you can make a new database at program runtime. Using the program to create the database is particularly useful in creating and distributing commercial applications because you don't have to worry about including and installing the database files with the application. If the code is included in your program, the database can be created the first time the user runs your application. Also, if future releases of the program require modifications of the database structure, you can use program commands to update the database on-the-fly, without requiring the user to handle conversions from the old format to the new.

Creating files at runtime is also useful if the user is expected to create different database files with the same structure but different user-defined names. Each time the user wants to create a new file, the program asks for the file name and then creates the database accordingly. As an example, a user might create a different database to hold data for each calendar year.

N O T E In order to do any work with databases in your program, you must add a reference to the appropriate DAO object library (typically DAO 3.5). This is done in the References dialog accessible by choosing the References item in the Project menu. ▮

To create a new database, follow these eight steps:

1. Create a new database object variable with the `Dim` statement.
2. Use the `CreateDatabase` method to create the new database.
3. Create `TableDef` objects with the `Dim` statement and `CreateTableDef` method.
4. Set the properties for the new tables.
5. Create `Field` and `Index` objects with the `Dim` statement and `CreateField` and `CreateIndex` methods.

6. Set the properties for the fields and indexes.

7. Use the Append method to add fields and indexes to the tables.

8. Use the Append method to add the table to the database.

Visual Basic contains the DBEngine and Workspace objects as data access objects. The CreateDatabase method is part of the Workspace object. A default workspace is always created for you whenever you access the Jet database engine. You can create other workspaces if necessary. If you do not include the ID of a workspace when using the functions, the default workspace is assumed.

Listing 11.1 shows the statements you use to define a database object and create the database (steps 1 and 2 defined in the preceding section) using the CreateDatabase method of the workspace.

Listing 11.1 Defining a Database Object and Creating a Database

```
'***********************************
'Full syntax of CreateDatabase method
'***********************************
Dim NewDb As Database, NewWs As Workspace
Set NewWs = DBEngine.Workspaces(0)
Set NewDb = NewWs.CreateDatabase("C:\YOUTH\YOUTHTRK.MDB",dbLangGeneral)
```

You can define any valid variable name as a database object by using the Dim statement. Although a database ("C:\YOUTH\YOUTHTRK.MDB") is specified in the argument of the CreateDatabase method, you can use a string variable to hold the name of the database to be created. This arrangement gives the user the flexibility of specifying a database name meaningful to him or her, or enables you to create multiple databases with the same structure.

TIP If you are allowing the user to create a database, you may want to use the File Open dialog box of the common dialog boxes to retrieve the filename and path for the new database.

The constant dbLangGeneral is a required argument of the CreateDatabase method. It specifies the language and code page information for the database. The dbLangGeneral constant specifies English as the language and the code page for U.S. computers. Table 11.1 lists other constants that you can use for different languages and code pages.

Table 11.1 Language Constants Specifying the Collating Order for Databases

Constant	Language
dbLangGeneral	English, German, French, Portuguese, Italian, Spanish
dbLangArabic	Arabic

Part **II**

Ch **11**

continues

Constant	Language
dbLangCzech	Czech
dbLangCyrillic	Russian
dbLangDutch	Dutch
dbLangGreek	Greek
dbLangHebrew	Hebrew
dbLangHungarian	Hungarian
dbLangIcelandic	Icelandic
dbLangNorwdan	Norwegian and Danish
dbLangPolish	Polish
dbLangSwedfin	Swedish and Finnish
dbLangTurkish	Turkish

Table 11.1   Continued

Another argument is available for the `CreateDatabase` method (this argument is optional): The options argument enables you to create a Jet 1.0, 1.1, 2.5, 3.0, or 3.5 database (the default is Jet 2.5 for Windows 3.1 and 3.5 for Windows 95 and Windows NT) and to encrypt your database. To invoke these options, you sum the constants for each option to a long integer and include the variable as the last argument of the function. The following code shows how you can change the code in Listing 11.1 to create an Access 2.5 database and encrypt it:

```
Dim NewDb As Database, NewWs As Workspace
Dim DbOpts As Long, DbName As String
Set NewWs = DBEngine.Workspaces(0)
DbName = "C:\YOUTH\YOUTHTRK.MDB"
DbOpts = dbVersion25 + dbEncrypt
Set NewDb = NewWs.CreateDatabase(DbName, dbLangGeneral, DbOpts)
```

CAUTION

When you use the `CreateDatabase` method, a trappable error occurs if the file to be created already exists. Include a trap for this error in your error-handling routine or, better yet, check for the existence of the filename before invoking the function.

Creating a Table

Creating a database using the code in Listing 11.1 creates only a file on a disk. You can't do anything with that file until you create the tables and add them to the database (refer to steps 3 through 8 in "Creating the Database," earlier in this chapter). You can think of the

`CreateDatabase` method as simply building the shell of a warehouse. To store items, you still have to lay out the aisles and build the shelves. You do just that when you create the tables.

Defining the *TableDef* Object   The first step in creating a new table is to create a new `TableDef` object. `TableDef` is the acronym for Table Definition. When you create a `TableDef`, you define to the database what type of information will be stored in the table and some optional properties of the table. Using the `TableDef` object, you can set the properties for the new table. The following lines of code show how to create a `TableDef` object and give your table a name:

```
Dim NewTbl As TableDef
Set NewTbl = NewDb.CreateTableDef("Youth")
```

The `Name` property of the table is only one of several properties for the `TableDef` object, but it is typically the only one required for the creation of an Access database. You can use some of the other properties (`Attributes`, `Connect`, and `SourceTableName`) when attaching an external table to the database. You can set the `Attributes`, `Connect`, and `SourceTableName` properties in successive arguments of the `CreateTableDef` method. You can also specify other properties by setting them equal to a value, as you do if you want to set the validation rule and validation error message for a table (as shown next). These statements follow the `CreateTableDef` method:

```
NewTbl.ValidationRule = "Age > 0"
NewTbl.ValidationText = _
    "You cannot enter an age of 0 or less."
```

Defining the Fields   After defining the `TableDef` object for the new table, you must define the field objects. A table can contain one field or a number of fields. For each field, you must define its name and type. Depending on the type of field, you may be required to define other properties, or you may want to set some optional properties.

For text fields, you must set the `Size` property to specify how long a string the field can contain. The valid entries for the `Size` property of the text field are 1 to 255. If you want to allow longer strings, set the field type to `memo`.

Listing 11.2 shows how field objects are created and field properties set for the Youth table of the sample application. You can specify the field name, type, and size as optional arguments of the `CreateField` method. You can also use the `CreateField` method without any arguments and then set all the field properties with assignment statements. Listing 11.2 shows both methods. You must use an assignment statement to set any other properties. As an example of an assignment statement, the listing sets a validation rule for the age field.

Listing 11.2   Creating Field Objects and Setting Properties

```
Dim F1 As Field, F2 As Field, F3 As Field, F4 As Field
Dim F5 As Field, F6 As Field, F7 As Field
'***************************************************************
```

continues

•

Listing 11.2 Continued

```
'Specify field name, type, and size as CreateField arguments
'****************************************************************
Set F1 = NewTbl.CreateField("LastName", dbText, 20)
Set F2 = NewTbl.CreateField("FirstName", dbText, 20)
Set F3 = NewTbl.CreateField()
'********************************
'Explicitly set field properties
'********************************
F3.Name = "Address"
F3.Type = dbText
F3.Size = 30
Set F4 = NewTbl.CreateField("Age", dbInteger)
'**************************************
'Set validation properties for a field
'**************************************
F4.ValidationRule = "Age > 0"
F4.ValidationText = "A person's age must be greater than 0."
Set F5 = NewTbl.CreateField("City", dbText, 20)
Set F6 = NewTbl.CreateField("State", dbText, 2)
Set F7 = NewTbl.CreateField()
F7.Name = "Birthdate"
F7.Type = dbDate
```

After you define each of the fields to include in the table, use the Append method of the
TableDef object to add the fields to the table definition, as shown in Listing 11.3.

Listing 11.3 Adding Fields to the Table Definition

```
NewTbl.Fields.Append F1
NewTbl.Fields.Append F2
NewTbl.Fields.Append F3
NewTbl.Fields.Append F4
NewTbl.Fields.Append F5
NewTbl.Fields.Append F6
NewTbl.Fields.Append F7
```

N O T E If you have a large number of fields, or if you want to create a generic routine for adding
fields to a table, consider using an *array* to define your fields. By using arrays, you can write
a simple FOR loop to add all the fields to the table (as shown in the following code statements).
Depending on the structure of the table, you may be able to use a loop to set the type properties of
several fields, although you must still define each field you intend to add to the table. ■

```
ReDim Fld(1 To 7) As Field
'************************************************
'Field definition statements go here for each
'array element.
'************************************************
```

```
FOR I = 1 To 7
  NewTbl.Fields.Append Fld(I)
NEXT I
```

Setting Optional Field Properties   In the preceding section, you learned how to specify the name of a field, the type of data it can store, and for some fields, the size of the field. These elements are the minimum requirements for defining a field. However, you can set several other properties of a field to further define its behavior.

The first of these properties is the Attributes property. Two key settings of this property are applicable to creating fields in a table. The first is the auto-increment setting, which tells the database to increment the value of the field each time a new record is added. This setting can provide a record counter; you can use it to ensure a unique value in that field for each record. You can then use the auto-increment field as a primary key field. The auto-increment setting is valid only for fields with the long data type. Another optional setting is the updatable setting, which enables you to specify whether a field can be changed. This setting is not typically used in initial table creation but can be useful in limiting access to information, particularly in a multiuser environment.

You set the Attributes property by assigning it a value in a code statement. For example, the following code segment creates a field and then specifies that it be used as a counter field by setting the Attributes property to auto-increment:

```
Set F1 = NewTbl.CreateField("YouthID", dbLong)
F1.Attributes = dbAutoIncrField
```

The other constants that you can use in the Attributes property are listed in Table 11.2. You can apply multiple settings to the Attributes property by combining the values of the constants and then setting the property to the sum of the values.

Part
II
Ch
11

Table 11.2   The Attributes Settings to Control the Behavior of a Field

Constant	Function
dbFixedField	The length of the field is fixed.
dbVariableField	The field size can change (Text fields only).
dbAutoIncrField	The value of the field is automatically incremented by the database engine.
dbUpdatableField	The value of the field can be changed.

In addition to the Attributes property, you can set several other optional properties for individual fields. As with the Attributes property, these optional properties are set using assignment statements; they cannot be set as part of the CreateField method. Table 11.3 lists the optional properties, their functions, and their default settings, if applicable.

Table 11.3 Optional Properties that Provide You Further Control over the Behavior of a Field

Property	Function
AllowZeroLength	Determines whether the value of a Text or Memo field can be a zero-length string. This is set to True to allow zero-length strings.
DefaultValue	Allows you to specify a default value for the field.
Required	Determines whether a value for the field must be entered.
ValidationRule	Specifies a criterion that must be met for the field before the record can be updated.
ValidationText	Specifies the error message that is displayed when the validation rule is not met.

CAUTION

If you are using Access to create a table, the default setting for the AllowZeroLength property is False. A zero-length string therefore cannot be used in the field. You may want to change this value for many of the fields you create, as your program may not need values for these fields. For example, you might have a field for a work phone but need to allow a zero-length string for people who don't work or don't provide the information.

Adding the Table to the Database   The final step in creating a database is adding the table or tables to the database. Use the Append method of the Database object to accomplish this (see the following code). The code also shows the Close method, which closes the database file and releases the system resources associated with the database object.

```
NewDb.TableDefs.Append NewTbl
NewDb.Close
```

Using a Query to Create a Table   In the preceding sections, you learned how to use the data access objects to create a table in a database. However, for many tables, you can use a query to accomplish the same purpose. The query to use is the Create Table query. In this query, you specify the table name, followed by the names, types, and optionally, sizes of the fields to include in the table. The list of fields is enclosed in parentheses. The query is run using the Execute method of the database object. The following code shows how to create the Youth table containing the LastName, FirstName, Age, and Birthdate fields using a query:

```
Dim SQLSel As String
SQLSel = "Create Table Youth (LastName TEXT(20),FirstName TEXT(20),"
SQLSel = SQLSel & "Age INTEGER,Birthdate DATETIME);"
NewDb.Execute SQLSel
```

The main drawback of the Create Table query is that you cannot use it to set optional properties of the fields. You can set these properties only with the data access objects and the CreateField method.

Creating Indexes

Defining indexes for a table is another key aspect of developing your database. The method for creating an index is closely related to the method for creating the table itself. For each index, you must assign a name, define the fields to include in the index, and determine whether the index is a primary index and whether duplicate values are allowed in the fields that comprise the index key.

To create an index, follow these six steps:

1. Use the `CreateIndex` method of the `TableDef` object to create the `Index` object.
2. Set any optional properties of the index (such as primary or unique).
3. Use the `CreateField` method of the `Index` object to create the field objects.
4. Set any optional properties of the field objects.
5. Append the fields to the `Index` object.
6. Append the index to the `TableDef` object.

Two commonly used optional properties of the `Index` object are the `Primary` property and the `Unique` property. A *primary index* is one that is typically used for finding a specific record in a table. To make an index primary, set the `Primary` property to `True`. Making an index primary ensures that the value of the index key for each record is unique and that no null values exist.

Part

II

Ch

11

CAUTION

If you create a primary index, you must include methods in your program to ensure that any records added have unique, non-null values for the fields in the primary index. If you attempt to add a record with a non-unique or null value, an error is generated.

Use the `Unique` property on a non-primary index to make sure that the values of fields other than the primary field are unique (for example, to make sure that you enter a unique Social Security number for each employee in a table).

NOTE You can specify only one primary index per table. ■

For the field objects, the only property of concern for creating indexes is the `Attributes` property. This property determines whether the sort order of the field is ascending (from A to Z) or descending (from Z to A). The default value is ascending. If you want to sort the field in descending order, set the `Attributes` property to the value of the constant `dbDescending`.

You can create a multiple-field index (for example, an index on the first and last names of a customer). To create such an index, simply set up multiple fields using the `CreateField` method. Remember that the order of the fields can have a dramatic impact on the order of your records. The order of the fields in an index is determined by the order in which the fields are appended to the index, not the order in which the field objects are created.

As I described in the preceding section, after you create the fields and set the properties of the fields and index, use the Append method to add the fields to the index and the index to the table definition.

N O T E You can create a maximum of 32 indexes per table. ▨

For the sample case, create a primary index on the YouthID field and an index on the LastName and FirstName fields. You might also want to create an index on the Birthdate field in descending order. Listing 11.4 shows how you accomplish this task.

Listing 11.4 Creating Index Objects, Assigning Properties, and Adding Indexes to the Table

```
'********************************
'Dimension the data access objects
'********************************
Dim Idx1, Idx2, Idx3 As Index
Dim Fld1, Fld2, Fld3 As Field
'********************************
'Create the primary YouthID index
'********************************
Set Idx1 = NewTbl.CreateIndex("YouthID")
Idx1.Primary = True
Set Fld1 = Idx1.CreateField("YouthID")
Idx1.Fields.Append Fld1
NewTbl.Indexes.Append Idx1
'*********************
'Create the name index
'*********************
Set Idx2 = NewTbl.CreateIndex("Name")
Idx2.Unique = False
Set Fld1 = Idx2.CreateField("LastName")
Set Fld2 = Idx2.CreateField("FirstName")
Idx2.Fields.Append Fld1
Idx2.Fields.Append Fld2
NewTbl.Indexes.Append Idx2
'*********************************************
'Create the birthdate index in descending order
'*********************************************
Set Idx3 = NewTbl.CreateIndex("Born")
Set Fld1 = Idx2.CreateField("Birthdate")
Fld1.Attributes = dbDescending
Idx3.Fields.Append Fld1
NewTbl.Indexes.Append Idx3
```

N O T E Although spaces are acceptable in field names, they are not allowed in index names. If you want a multiple-word index name, separate the words with an underscore. ▨

Creating Relations

Earlier in this chapter, I described normalizing data and the need to relate normalized tables. Tables are related with the Jet engine through the use of a `Relation` object stored in the database. The `Relation` object tells the database which two tables are related, which table is the parent and which is the child, and the key fields used to specify the relationship.

Follow these seven steps to create a relationship between two tables:

1. Use the `Dim` statement to define a `Relation` object variable.
2. Create the `Relation` object using the `CreateRelation` method of the `Database` object.
3. Set the primary table and the foreign table properties of the relationship.
4. Create the relation field for the primary table using the `CreateField` method of the `Relation` object.
5. Set the foreign field property of the `Field` object.
6. Append the field to the `Relation` object.
7. Append the `Relation` object to the database.

Listing 11.5 demonstrates the creation of a relationship, showing how to create a relation between the Family (primary) table and the Youth (foreign) table of the sample database.

Listing 11.5 Specifying a Relationship Between Two Tables Using the *Relation* Object

```
Dim NewRel As Relation
Dim Fld1 As Field
'***************************
'Create the Relation object
'***************************
Set NewRel = NewDb.CreateRelation("Parents")
'**********************************
'Set the properties of the relation
'**********************************
NewRel.Table = "Family"
NewRel.ForeignTable = "Youth"
'****************************************************
'Create the relating field and set the properties
'****************************************************
Set Fld1 = NewRel.CreateField("ParentID")
Fld1.ForeignName = "ParentID"
'************************************************************************
'Append the field to the relation and the relation to the database
'************************************************************************
NewRel.Fields.Append Fld1
NewDb.Relations.Append NewRel
```

TROUBLESHOOTING

When I try to create a relation in the database, I get the error message "Parents is not an index in this table." You get this message if you do not have a primary index on the key field in the primary table. In the preceding case, the primary index must be on the ParentID field in the Family table. Although the documentation does make this point, you must have a primary key field in your primary table. This field identifies the records to the relationship.

Creating Queries

Using queries is a powerful method of gathering information from more than one table or of selecting information from a table that matches specific criteria (for example, customer records for people who live in Alabama). As you will learn in Chapter 13, "Writing Programs with the Data-Access Objects," an object called a *recordset* can store this type of information for use in your programs. In fact, using a query is one method of creating a dynaset- or snapshot-type recordset. The advantage of creating a query is that the information about it is saved in the database itself, making it convenient to test and store information needed to create recordsets that are used often.

Setting Up the Query   To create a query, you define a QueryDef object and then use the CreateQueryDef method of the database. When calling the function, you must specify the name of the query. You can specify the SQL syntax of the query, or you can define the SQL statement in a separate program line. The following code shows two methods of creating a query:

```
Dim OldDb As Database, NewQry As QueryDef
Set OldDb = OldWs.OpenDatabase("C:\YOUTH\YOUTHTRK.MDB")
Set NewQry = OldDb.CreateQueryDef("Local")
NewQry.SQL = "SELECT * FROM Youth Where State = 'AL';"
'**************************************************
'Alternative form of query creation statement.
'**************************************************
Set NewQry = OldDb.CreateQueryDef("Local", "SELECT * FROM _
     Youth Where State = 'AL';")
```

The heart of defining queries is the SQL statement. This statement defines the fields to be included, the source of the fields, record filters, and the sort order of the resulting recordset. SQL statements are covered in Chapter 14, "Understanding Structured Query Language."

N O T E   The Jet engine can store queries only for Access (Jet) databases. It can, however, use queries to retrieve the data in many database types, such as FoxPro, Paradox, dBase, SQL Server, and others. ▦

Deleting a Query   As with most other objects in the database, if you create a query, you may, at some time, need to delete it. If you have a query that you no longer need in your database, you can remove it using the following command:

```
OldDb.DeleteQueryDef "Local"
```

> **CAUTION**
>
> When you use a query, you open the query by creating a data access object. Therefore, before deleting a query, you must close a query variable. This way, you can ensure that the query is not in use and that no error occurs during deletion. The syntax for closing a query is `NewQry.Close`.

Creating a Database with Other Tools

Although the data access objects provide you with a way to create a database using program code, this approach is not the only way to create a database. Several other methods are available to you:

- The Data Manager: Using this Visual Basic add-in, you can create databases or create, modify, and delete tables, indexes, and relations within a database.
- Microsoft Access: Using this application, you can create Jet databases. It provides the added advantage of enabling you to create relations using a visual drag-and-drop method.
- Third-party programs.

Using the Visual Data Manager

The Visual Data Manager application that comes with Visual Basic provides you with an interactive way of creating and modifying databases. You start the application by selecting the Visual Data Manager item from the Add-Ins menu in Visual Basic.

> **N O T E** The Visual Data Manager is capable of working with Access (Jet), dBase, FoxPro, Paradox, and ODBC databases as well as text files. Typically, in Visual Basic applications, you will use it to manipulate Access databases. ■

> ▶ The Visual Data Manager is also one of the sample applications that can be found in the Visual Basic folder when you installed VB. Examining this project can provide a tremendous education into creating database applications in Visual Basic.

The first step in creating a new database is to create the database file itself. This provides a physical location for the rest of your work. To do this in the Visual Data Manager, you must first choose the New item from the File menu. This brings up a sub-menu which allows you to specify the type of database to create. For the purpose of this discussion, we will create an Access database by choosing the Microsoft Access item. This brings up another sub-menu from which you can choose the version of Access database to create. If you will be sharing data with users on a Windows 3.1 system, you should choose the 2.0 version, otherwise, choose the 3.0 version. Figure 11.10 shows the different menu levels for creating a database. After you have chosen the type of database, you will be presented with a dialog box entitled "Select Microsoft Access Database to Create." This dialog allows you to choose a name and folder for your database. After entering a name, click the Save button on the dialog. This will take you to the design mode shown in Figure 11.11.

FIG. 11.10

The menus allow you to choose the type and version of database to create.

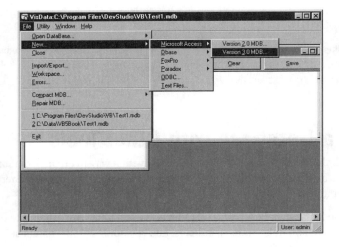

FIG. 11.11

The Visual Data Manager Database window provides access to the design functions for tables, fields, and indexes.

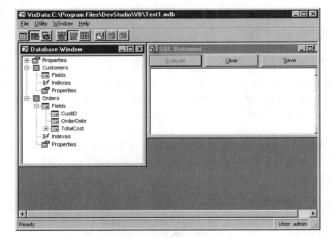

The Visual Data Manager presents the database information in a tree-like view. This type of view allows you to quickly see the tables and queries in the database. It also allows you to open the view further to see the fields and indexes of a table as well as its properties. Finally, you can open the view all the way up to see the properties of the individual fields.

Adding a New Table After creating the database, the next thing you will want to do is to create tables. The create a new table, you will need to click the right mouse button in the Database Window of the application. This will bring up a pop-up menu. From this menu, you will need to select the New Table item. This brings up the Table Structure dialog box as shown in Figure 11.12. This dialog shows you information about the table itself, as well as a list of fields and indexes in the table. There are also buttons in the dialog to add and remove fields and indexes.

To add fields to the table, click the <u>A</u>dd Field button to bring up the Add Field dialog shown in Figure 11.13.

FIG. 11.12
In the Add Table dialog box, you can specify a table name.

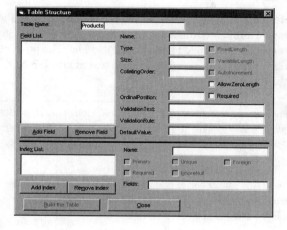

FIG. 11.13
In the Add Field dialog box, you can specify the properties of the fields for a table.

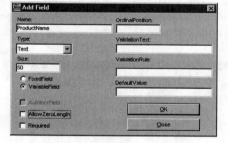

Part
II

Ch
11

Once in the Add Field dialog, you will need to follow these steps for each field you wish to add:

1. Enter the name of the field.
2. Select the field type from the Type drop-down list.
3. Enter the size of the field (if necessary).
4. Enter any optional parameters such as validation rules.
5. Click the OK button to add the field to the table.

After you have entered all the fields for your table, click the Close button in the Add Field dialog. This will return you to the Table Structure dialog.

If you want to remove a field from the table, select the field name in the field list of the dialog, then click the Remove Field button. When you are satisfied with the fields in the table, click the Build the Table button to create the table.

Making Changes to the Fields in Your Table   After you have created the fields in the table, you can set or change a number of the field properties from the Table Structure dialog. To modify the properties, select the field name in the Field List. The properties of the field that can be modified will appear in the dialog as enabled text or check boxes. All other properties will appear as disabled controls.

TIP   You can also edit the properties of a field from the Database Window of the Visual Data Manager. Simply expand the database view to show field properties, then right-click the property to be edited. You can then select Edit from the pop-up menu to change the property.

N O T E   In Visual Basic, you cannot edit or delete any field that is part of an index expression or a relation. If you need to delete such a field, you must delete the index or relation containing the field and then make the changes to the field. ■

Adding an Index to the Table   The Table Structure dialog also allows you to add, modify, or remove indexes in the table. Any indexes currently in the table will appear in the Index List at the bottom of the dialog as shown in Figure 11.14.

FIG. 11.14
You can add, edit, or delete indexes for a table from the Table Structure dialog box.

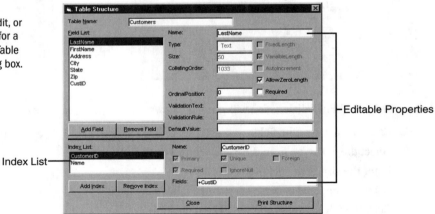

To add a new index, click the Add Index button; the Add Index dialog box then appears, as shown in Figure 11.15. In this dialog box, first enter an index name. Next, select the fields to be included in the index by clicking on the fields in the Available Fields list. As you select each field, it will be added to the Indexed Fields list in the order in which it was selected. By default, all fields are indexed in ascending order. To change the order to descending, precede the field name in the Indexed Fields list with a minus sign (-).

FIG. 11.15
The Add Index dialog box provides a visual means of creating the indexes for a table.

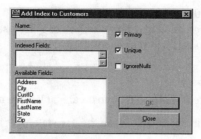

After you define the fields for the index, you can choose to require the index to be unique or to be a primary index by selecting the appropriate check box in the window. When the index is completed to your liking, save it by clicking OK. The index you have just created is added to the index list on the Table Structure dialog box. To delete an index, simply select it in the list box and click Remove Index.

Returning to the Visual Basic Design Window Closing the Visual Data Manager window or opening the File menu and choosing Exit takes you back to the Visual Basic main design window. (You can, of course, switch back and forth between the Data Manager and the Visual Basic design environment.) To manipulate databases without having to start Visual Basic every time, make the Data Manager application a program item in your Visual Basic group.

Using Microsoft Access

The other option for creating an Access database for use with a Visual Basic application is to use Microsoft Access. Access has a good visual design interface for setting up tables, indexes, queries, and table relationships. Obviously, this option is available only if you have a copy of Access.

Third-Party Database Designers

In addition to the Visual Data Manager and Access, a number of third-party programs enable you to create and maintain Jet databases. Some of them provide you with advanced data modeling capabilities. These modeling capabilities make it easy for you to determine what information goes in which table and to set up the relations easily between the tables. Then, after your data model is complete, the program can automatically generate the database for you. One such product is ERWin for Visual Basic, which is produced by Logic Works, Inc.

Modifying the Database Structure

Even if you create the perfect database for an application, sooner or later someone will come along and say, "Well, I really need this program to handle other data, too." At this point, you must modify the structure of your database and tables. Modifications can take the form of new tables, new fields or indexes in tables, or changes in the properties of tables, fields, or indexes. On occasion, you may also have to delete a table, field, or index.

In the following sections, I cover the modification of a database through the use of Visual Basic program commands. As with the creation of a database, you can also use the Data Manager application or Microsoft Access to perform the modifications.

Adding and Deleting Tables

To add a table, follow the same steps that you took to create tables in a new database:

1. Define the table, field, and index objects using the `Dim` statement and appropriate create methods.
2. Define the properties of the table, fields, and indexes.
3. Append the fields and indexes to the table.
4. Append the table to the database.

To delete a table from a database, you can use the `Delete` method of a database object, as shown in this statement:

```
OldDb.TableDefs.Delete "Members"
```

> **CAUTION**
>
> Use the `Delete` method with extreme caution. When you delete a table, all fields, indexes, and—most importantly—data is deleted with it. And when it's gone, it's gone. The only way to get the data back is to create the table again from scratch and reload all your data.

Adding, Deleting, and Editing Indexes

Adding a new index involves the same steps as creating an index for a new table. You must define an index object, set the properties of the index, and append the new index to the table. An example of these steps was shown earlier in Listing 11.4.

To delete an index, simply use the `Delete` method shown in this statement. This code deletes the Born index from the Youth table:

```
OldDb.TableDefs("Youth").Indexes.Delete "Born"
```

You cannot edit the properties of an index in a table. Therefore, if a change to an index is required, you must delete the old index from the table and create a new index with the new properties. You do so by using the methods shown in the section "Creating Indexes," earlier in this chapter.

> **NOTE** You cannot delete an index that is required by a relation. To delete such an index, you must first delete the relation. ▦

Adding, Deleting, and Editing Fields

As you learned when creating a new database, you add a field to a table by defining the field object, setting its properties, and appending it to the table. These commands are presented in Listings 11.2 and 11.3.

To delete a field, use the `Delete` method shown here. This example deletes the Address field from the Youth table:

```
NewDb.TableDefs("Youth").Fields.Delete "Address"
```

Unfortunately, you cannot change a field's properties directly. You can, however, accomplish this task in two indirect ways. If you have a new table that contains no data, or if you don't care about losing the data in the field, you can delete the field from the table and then re-create it with the new properties. If you have a table that contains data, and you want to preserve the data, you must create a whole new table (making the appropriate changes), move the data to the new table, and then delete the old table. The difficulty of this process of making changes to fields dramatically underscores the importance of a good initial design.

To move data from one table to another existing table, follow these steps:

1. Open both tables.
2. Set up a loop to process each record in the table currently containing the data.

   Then, for each record in the old table, follow these steps:

   a. Retrieve the value of each field to be transferred from the old table.
   b. Add a record to the new table.
   c. Set the values of the field in the new table.
   d. Update the new table.

NOTE If you have Microsoft Access, you can change the properties of a table's fields while preserving the fields' contents. ■

Remember that you cannot delete a field that is part of an index or relation.

Deleting a Relation

If you need to delete a relation, you can use the `Delete` method of the database object. The following statement shows how to delete the relation created in Listing 11.5:

```
NewDb.Relations.Delete "Parents"
```

Using SQL to Modify the Database

Just as you can create a table with SQL statements, you can also modify or even delete a table using SQL. To modify a table, you use the `Alter Table` query. Using this query, you can add a new field to the table or delete a field from the table. The following code segment shows how you can use the `Alter Table` query to add an Address field and delete the Birthdate field from the Youth table created earlier:

```
'*********************************
'Add an address field to the table
'*********************************
NewDb.Execute "ALTER TABLE Youth ADD COLUMN Address TEXT(30);"
'********************************************
'Delete the birthdate field from the table
'********************************************
NewDb.Execute "ALTER TABLE Youth DROP COLUMN Birthdate;"
```

If you want, you can also delete an entire table using the `Drop Table` query. The following statement deletes the entire Youth table:

```
NewDb.Execute "DROP TABLE Youth;"
```

Why Use a Program Instead of Visual Data Manager

In this chapter, you have learned that the Visual Data Manager application and Microsoft Access can create, modify, and load data into a database. So the question you may be asking is: "Why do I ever need to bother with the Visual Basic program commands for these functions?" The answer is that, in many cases, you don't. If you have direct control over the database (that is, you are the only user or you can access the database at any time), you may never need to use program commands to create or change a database.

If, however, you have an application with many customers—either throughout your company or across the country—using a program offers several benefits. One benefit is in initial installation. If the database creation routines are in the program itself, you don't have to include empty database files on your setup disks. This may reduce the number of disks required, and it certainly reduces the possibility that a key file is left out. Another benefit occurs when you distribute updates to the program. With changes embedded in a program, your user can merely run the update program to change the file structure. He or she doesn't need to reload data into a new, blank file. Also, by modifying the file in place, you can preserve most structure changes in the database made by the end user.

Another reason for putting database creation and maintenance commands in a program is for performance considerations. Sometimes it is desirable, from a performance standpoint, to create a temporary table to speed up a program or to store intermediate results and then delete the table at the completion of the program. You might also want to create a temporary index that creates a specific order or speeds up a search.

From Here...

In this chapter, you learned how to design and create a database for use in an application. To use the database, however, you must write a database access application. This topic is covered in other chapters of the book. For further information about

- Quickly creating a database application, see Chapter 10, "Applications at Warp Speed."
- Creating an application with the data access objects, see Chapter 13, "Writing Programs with the Data-Access Objects."
- Creating and using SQL statements, see Chapter 14, "Understanding Structured Query Language."

Part
II

Ch
11

CHAPTER 12

Doing More with Bound Controls

In Chapter 10, "Applications at Warp Speed," you got a first look at the data control and the bound controls that are available in Visual Basic. You saw how the controls worked together to create a data access application. What you may not have realized is that the data control and bound controls have a wider range of functionality than that presented in Chapter 10. ■

Working with other databases using the data control

While Access is the database format of choice, the data control can work with several other types of databases.

Programming the data control to do more

Some properties of the data control allow it to perform additional tasks in specific situations.

Changing the recordset of the data control with code

You are not limited to the recordset that was created in when you set that DatabaseName and RecordSource properties in design mode.

Bound lists and combo boxes

Yes, you can bind list and combo boxes to the data control. There are also versions of these controls that can populate the lists from a dataset.

Windows 95 bound controls

Several of the Windows 95 controls can also be bound to a data control.

Working with multiple data controls on a form

In many situations, you will need more than one data control on your form.

Exploring the Data Control In-Depth

One of the data control's additional capabilities is the ability to access a number of other database types besides the Jet database. It can also work with all types of recordsets, not just dynaset-type recordsets. In addition to this flexibility, you can work with program code to change the properties of the data control and enhance its capabilities. You got a brief look at this when program code was used to enable you to add and delete records in the data entry application.

What Are Its Advantages and Limitations?

While the data control does have a lot of capabilities, there are also some things that can only be done with program code. As Chapter 13, "Writing Programs with the Data-Access Objects," shows you, you can create a database application without using the data control at all. In order to help you determine whether to create your program with the data control, with just the data access objects, or with a combination of the two, you need to have an understanding of the advantages and limitations of the data control.

Advantages of the Data Control   The key advantage to using the data control is that you don't have to do much, if any, programming to develop a data access application. You don't have to provide program code to open or create a database or recordset, to move through the records, or to edit the existing records in the recordset. The data control makes the initial application development quicker and makes code maintenance easier.

When using the data control, you also have the advantage of specifying your data objects (database and recordset) at design time, and you can select these options from dialog boxes and lists. Selecting options from lists cuts down on typographical errors that you can introduce into the application.

Another advantage of the data control is that it provides a direct link to the data. You don't have to specifically invoke the Edit and Update methods to modify the data in the database. Consequently, your changes show up in the database as soon as you enter them.

In addition to these advantages of using the data control, there are several bound controls, which provide an easy way to accomplish tasks that are difficult to duplicate with just the data access objects and program commands. These bound controls are the data bound list box, data bound combo box, and data bound grid.

Limitations of the Data Control   As useful as the data control is, it also has a few limitations. These limitations are:

- No add or delete functions are built into the data control.
- Because the Edit and Update functions are automatic, implementing transaction processing in the data control is more difficult.

Later in this chapter, you see how to overcome these limitations when you learn how to combine the data control with program code.

Using Other Databases

The data control is designed to work best with Jet (Access) databases, but you can just as easily work with other database formats. These formats include some traditional database formats like FoxPro and Paradox, as well as data that is not typically thought of as a database, for example, Excel spreadsheets or text files.

For any of the database formats, you still need to set the DatabaseName and RecordSource properties of the data control. You also need to set the Connect property of the data control to identify the type of database being used. In addition, the DatabaseName property is treated differently for some database formats than for Jet databases. For example, with dBase files, the DatabaseName property refers to a directory instead of a single file.

Setting the Connect Property   The Connect property tells the Jet engine what kind of database you are using. Table 12.1 summarizes the values of the Connect property for several common database types.

Table 12.1   Connect Property Settings for Various Database Types

Database Type	Value of Connect Property
Access	Access
FoxPro 2.0	FoxPro 2.0
FoxPro 2.5	FoxPro 2.5
FoxPro 2.6	FoxPro 2.6
Visual FoxPro 3.0	FoxPro 3.0
dBASE III	dBASE III
dBASE IV	dBASE IV
dBASE V	dBASE 5.0
Excel 3	Excel 3.0
Excel 4	Excel 4.0
Excel 5	Excel 5.0
Excel 7	Excel 7.0
Lotus 1 or 2	Lotus WK1
Lotus 3	Lotus WK3

continues

Part
II

Ch
12

Table 12.1 Continued

Database Type	Value of Connect Property
Lotus 4	Lotus WK4
Paradox 3.x	paradox 3.x;pwd=password
Paradox 4.x	paradox 4.x;pwd=password
Paradox 5.x	paradox 5.x;pwd=password
ASCII Text	Text

The data control makes it easy for you to set the Connect property. To change its value, you select the desired database format from a drop-down list in the Properties window as shown in Figure 12.1.

FIG. 12.1
The Connect property lets you use the data control with other databases.

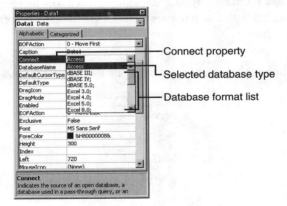

— Connect property

— Selected database type

— Database format list

Considerations for the *DatabaseName* Property   Some database formats, like Jet, store all the tables of the database along with other database information in the database file itself. Other database formats, like FoxPro 2.6 or dBase, store each table in a separate file. Depending on the database format you select, the information you specify in the DatabaseName property will be different. For Jet databases, you just specify the name of the database file. For dBase databases, the DatabaseName property must be set to the name of the folder containing the table files. Table 12.2 lists the proper settings of the DatabaseName property for each of the formats previously listed.

Table 12.2 *DatabaseName* **Property Requirements for Various Database Types**

Database Type	Database Name Value
Access	Name of database including path (d:\sub\name.MDB)
FoxPro	path (d:\sub\) for database files
dBASE	path (d:\sub\) for database files
Paradox	path (d:\sub\) for database files
Excel	path (d:\sub\) for database files
Text Files	path (d:\sub\) for database files

Working Directly with Tables and Snapshots

The data control, by default, creates a dynaset-type recordset when you specify the RecordSource property. However, you can have the data control create a snapshot or access a table directly. To handle this, you just need to change the setting of the RecordsetType property. You do this by selecting the desired type from a drop-down list in the Properties dialog box (see Figure 12.2).

FIG. 12.2
Use the RecordsetType property to determine whether the data control uses a table, dynaset, or snapshot.

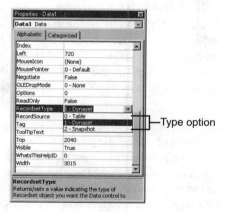

One reason you might want to change the RecordsetType is for performance. For example, if you do not need to be able to edit the contents of the recordset, you might want to use a snapshot because it provides faster access than a dynaset. In another case, you might want to use a table so that you can change the presentation order of the recordset by changing the controlling index of the table.

CAUTION

If you specify a `RecordsetType` that cannot be created, you will get an error when you try to run your program. This is most likely to occur when you set the `RecordsetType` to Table and use an SQL statement or query in the `RecordSource` property.

TROUBLESHOOTING

I tried to set an index for my recordset using the Index property of the data control, but was unable to do so. The Index property does not refer to a database index, but to the index position in an array. A data control, like any other Visual Basic control object, can be part of a control array. If you have such an array, the Index property specifies the position of the current control in that array. Remember that a data control, by default, creates a dynaset, and you cannot apply an index to a dynaset. You can use an index if you specify that the data control should use a table, but the index can be set only with a program command such as this one:

```
datYouth.Recordset.Index = "Name"
```

Also, you can only set an index for the recordset if you have set the `RecordsetType` property to Table.

In the End (BOF And EOF Properties)

You probably think of the beginning and end of a file as the first and last record, respectively, of a recordset. However, this is not actually the case. When the recordset reaches the beginning of file (BOF), the record pointer is actually set prior to the first record in the file. Similarly, the record pointer is set past the last record when the end of file (EOF) is reached. This can create problems in some data access programs because there is no current record when you are at the beginning or the end of the file.

By default, the data control avoids this problem by setting the record pointer to the first record when the beginning of file is reached and setting the pointer to the last record when the end of file is reached. This assures that there is always a current record for viewing or editing. However, there may be times when you want to know when you have actually reached the BOF or EOF positions even while using the data control. You can control what the data control does at the end of the file by setting the BOFAction and EOFAction properties of the data control.

The BOFAction property, which tells the data control what to do when the beginning of file is reached, has two possible settings:

- Execute the `MoveFirst` method to set the record pointer at the first record and the BOF flag to False (property value of 0). This is the default setting.
- Set the BOF flag to True (property value of 1).

The EOFAction property, which tells the data control what to do when the end of file is reached, has three possible settings:

- Execute the MoveLast method to set the record pointer at the last record and the EOF flag to False (property value of 0). This is the default setting.
- Set the EOF flag to True (property value of 1).
- Execute the AddNew method to set up the recordset for the addition of a new record (property value of 2).

You can choose the values of each of these properties from a drop-down list in the Properties dialog box. The AddNew setting of the EOFAction property can be useful if you have an application that adds a number of new records. As with most other properties of the data control, you can reset these properties at runtime.

N O T E   These BOF and EOF actions are triggered only when the beginning or end of file is reached using the data control (in other words, pressing the Next button). They have no effect if the beginning or end of file is reached using the data access methods in code (as in MoveNext). ▪

Other Optional Properties

In addition to the properties already covered, there are three other key properties for the data control that you can set:

Exclusive	Determines whether others can access the database while your application is using it. You can set the property to True (your application is the only one that can access the database) or False (others may access the database). The default value is False.
Readonly	Determines whether your application can modify the data in your defined recordset. You can set the property to True (your application can't modify data) or False (your application can modify data). The default value is False. Setting this property to read-only is not the same as using a snapshot. Since a snapshot-type recordset is a copy of the data in memory, it is faster than a read-only dynaset.
Options	Allows you to specify other properties for the recordset created by the data control. Chapter 13, "Writing Programs with the Data-Access Objects," summarizes these properties (refer to Tables 13.1, 13.2, and 13.3).

▶ **See** "Opening an Existing Database," **p. 303**

Part

II

Ch

12

Programming the Data Control

There are several ways that you can use program code to work with the data control and the bound controls. By using program code, you can make your program more flexible than with the data control alone. The following list gives you a few of the ways that you can have code work with the data control:

■ Change the properties of the data control and bound controls in code

■ Place code in the Validate event of the data control to handle user actions

■ Use the methods of the Recordset to provide capabilities that the data control does not have on its own

Changing Properties On-The-Fly

Like any other control that you have on your form, you can change the properties of the data control and bound controls at runtime. You change the properties by using an assignment statement to give a new value to the property. Most of the properties of the data control and the bound controls are changeable. Only a few, like the Name property are read-only at runtime.

Properties of the Data Control   You can choose to set (or reset) the DatabaseName, RecordSource, and RecordsetType properties of the data control at runtime. The following list outlines the reasons why you would want to set the properties at runtime:

■ To enable the user to select a specific database file from a group of related files. For example, a central office application keeps a separate database for each store of a chain; your application must enable the user to select the store with which he or she wants to work.

■ To enable users to set specific conditions on the data they want to see. These conditions may take the form of filters or sort orders (for example, show only salespeople with over $10,000 in sales in order of total sales). Alternatively, your application may have to set the filters as part of an access control scheme, such as allowing a department manager to see data about only the people in his or her department. If the application sets the filters, it incorporates the information into code at runtime instead of at design time. Remember that the initial values of the data control properties are set at design time.

■ You can enable the user to specify the directory in a configuration file (or have your setup program do it for them), then use the information from the configuration file to set your data control properties. If you're developing a commercial application, there is no guarantee that the user has the same directory structure as you. Many users are annoyed if you impose a specific directory structure or drive designation as a requirement for your program.

 TIP   If you distribute your application, you will often need to change the DatabaseName property of the data control to handle differences between your directory structure and that of the user.

If you need to set the parameters at runtime, simply set the properties with the code statements shown in Listing 12.1. Note that you must specify the name of your data control, the property name, and the desired property value.

After you set the properties, use the Refresh method of the data control to implement the changes. The Refresh method is shown in the last line of Listing 12.1. The changes to the data control (that is, the creation of the new recordset) take effect *after* the Refresh method is run.

Listing 12.1   Setting or Changing the *DatabaseName* and *RecordSource* Properties of a Data Control at Runtime

```
'*********************************************
'Set the value of the DatabaseName property
'*********************************************
datMembers.DatabaseName = "C:\YOUTH\YOUTHTRK.MDB"
'*********************************************
'Set the value of the RecordSource property
'*********************************************
datMembers.RecordSource = "Family"
'*****************************************************************
'Set the value of the RecordsetType property to table (0)
'*****************************************************************
datMembers.RecordsetType = vbRsTypeTable
'*************************************************
'Use the Refresh method to implement the changes
'*************************************************
datMembers.Refresh
```

Properties of the Bound Control   In a similar manner, you can set the properties of the bound controls. You can change the DataSource of a bound control to access a different data control on the form. You can also change the setting of the DataField property to have the control display the contents of a different field in the recordset.

> **CAUTION**
>
> Be careful when you change the DataSource or DataField properties in code. If you enter an invalid data control name or field name, an error will occur.

Recordsets and the Data Control (Set Command)

One particularly useful feature of the data control is the ability to create a recordset with the data access objects, then assign the recordset to the data control. This gives you increased flexibility in the recordsets that can be used. Because you can also assign the recordset of the data control to a recordset object, this means you can pass the recordset to other procedures or to class modules for processing. This feature is something that was not available in Visual Basic prior to version 4.

Part
II

Ch
12

The Set statement is the key statement to use when you want to allow recordsets to be moved back and forth between a recordset object and the data control. Use the Set statement any time you wish to assign a value to an object. You will also see the Set statement used in Chapter 13, "Writing Programs with the Data-Access Objects" when you open databases and recordsets with the data access objects.

The following code shows you how to create a recordset, then assign it to a data control:

```
'Create the recordset
SQLSel = "Select LastName, FirstName From Members "
SQLSel = SQLSel & "Where Member Order By LastName, FirstName"
Set datRec = OldDb.OpenRecordset(SQLSel, dbOpenDynaset)
'Assign the recordset to the data control
Set datNames.Recordset = datRec
```

You can use this capability to enable your users to specify sort or filter criteria for a recordset. Then with the user-defined criteria, you can create a recordset using an SQL statement. This recordset can then be assigned to an existing data control to display the results of the query in a grid or a series of bound controls.

Being able to pass the contents of a data control to a recordset object enables you to do things like write a generic routine for handling deletions. This way, you can write one procedure or class to query the user for verification of the deletion, then perform the deletion if the user agrees. The code in Listing 12.2 shows you how such a procedure works:

Listing 12.2   Procedures Let You Reuse Code Easily

```
'Define the procedure
Sub DelRecord(Navset As Recordset)
Dim MsgStr As String
'Delete the current record
MsgStr = "Are you sure you want to delete this record"
RetCode = MsgBox(MsgStr, vbYesNo, "Deletion Confirmation")
If RetCode = vbYes Then
      Navset.Delete
End If
End Sub
'********************************************************
'Call the procedure with the recordset of a data control
'********************************************************
DelRecord datNames.Recordset
```

CAUTION

A recordset object and the data control recordset are identical immediately after the Set statement, and at this time, they both point to the same record. However, once a record movement function is performed on either recordset, they are out of synchronization. Therefore, be careful when you are using both a recordset object and a data control to manipulate the same data.

Programming the Data Control's Events

The data control has two key events for which you can write program code: the Validate event and the Error event. While most of the actions of the data control are handled automatically, programming for these two events can help you add capabilities to your program and help you handle errors.

Using the Validate Event   When you create a database, you can specify validation rules to be checked before each record is saved. However, you may have situations where the validation rules for your program are more complex than those the Jet engine can handle. In this case, you need to perform the data validation in program code. How can you do this when the data control saves data automatically?

The data control has an event, the Validation event, that is triggered whenever the record pointer is about to be moved. This event occurs when the user presses one of the navigation buttons on the data control or when the form containing the data control is unloaded.

When the Validation event is triggered, the data control examines all controls that are bound to it to determine if any data in any of the controls has changed. Two parameters are then set for the Validation event: the Save parameter, which tells you whether any data has been changed, and the Action parameter, which tells you what caused the Validation event to fire. The Save parameter can be either True or False. The Action parameter can have one of twelve values as defined in Table 12.3.

Table 12.3   The Value of the Action Parameter Tells You Why the Validate Event Fired

Value	Description
0	Cancels any data control actions
1	MoveFirst
2	MovePrevious
3	MoveNext
4	MoveLast
5	AddNew
6	Update
7	Delete
8	Find
9	A bookmark was set
10	The Close method of the data control was used.
11	The form was unloaded

The following listing shows how you can use the Validation event to perform data checking:

Listing 12.3   Data Checking in the Validate Event

```
Dim CompStr As String
If Save Then
   CompStr = Trim(txtYouth(0).Text)
   If Len(CompStr) = 0 Then
      MsgBox "First Name cannot be blank"
      Action = 0
   End If
End If
```

This code checks to see if any of the data in the bound controls has been changed. If it has, the code proceeds to perform the data checking. In this case, the code is checking for a non-null string in one of the text boxes. If the string is zero length, a message displays to the user, and the action that was being processed is canceled. The program handles the cancellation by setting the Action parameter to 0.

N O T E   This particular data verification can be handled by the database engine when you set a validation rule or set the `AllowZeroLength` property of the field to True. ■

Handling Errors with the Error Event   The other event of note for the data control is the Error event. The Error event also has two parameters associated with it: the Dataerr and the Response parameters. The Error event is triggered when a data access error occurs, such as when the data control is loaded and the database specified in the `DatabaseName` property cannot be found. When the event is triggered, the error number is placed in the Dataerr parameter. You can then write code in the event to handle the different data access errors.

The Response parameter determines the action to be taken by your program. If the parameter is set to 0, your program attempts to continue with the next line of code. If the parameter is set to 1, the default value, an error message displays. When you write your error handling for the Error event, you can set the Response parameter to 0 for those errors that are corrected, and set it to 1 for all other errors.

Data Control Methods

In addition to being able to respond to events, the data control also has three methods that you need to use in your programming. These methods are presented in the following list:

- Refresh
- UpdateControls
- UpdateRecord

The Refresh method causes the data control to rerun the query that created the recordset and access all data that is currently in the recordset. There are three occasions when you need to use the Refresh method:

■ When you change the RecordSource property of the data control.

■ When you assign a recordset created with the data access objects to the data control.

■ When other users have been simultaneously accessing the same database and tables. Refreshing the data control shows any additions or deletions made by the other users.

The UpdateRecord method enables you to force the data control to save the information in the bound controls to the recordset. Typically, you will want to place a Save or Update button on any data entry form you create. (This is done automatically if you use the data form designer.) The reason for this is to enable the user to save the changes to the current record without having to move to another record. The data control only saves changes when the record pointer is moved or when the data control is closed. The following line of code shows how you can force a data control to update the current record:

```
datYouth.UpdateRecord
```

The companion method to the UpdateRecord method is the UpdateControls method. This method retrieves information from the current record and displays it in the bound controls. This has the effect of canceling any changes made by the user. By placing the following line of code in the Click event of a command button, you can implement a cancellation feature:

```
datYouth.UpdateControls
```

Other Bound Controls

In Chapter 10, "Writing Applications at Warp Speed," you were introduced to five bound controls: the TextBox, Label, CheckBox, PictureBox, and Image controls. Visual Basic actually has fifteen bound controls that you can use in your programs:

■ TextBox

■ Label

■ CheckBox

■ PictureBox

■ Image

■ ListBox

■ ComboBox

■ Data bound ListBox

■ Data bound ComboBox

■ Data bound Grid

Part

II

Ch

12

- RichTextBox
- OLE control
- MaskedEdit
- 3-D CheckBox
- 3-D Panel

Lists and Combo Boxes

The list box and combo box controls enable the user to choose one item from a list of items; in addition, the combo box lets the user enter a different item. With these controls you can bind the control to a data field to store the user's choices in a field. You do this by setting the DataSource and DataField properties of the control. To give your user a list of items from which to select, use the AddItem method of the control. For the sample case, use a combo box to enable users to select the title for the member they are editing (see Figure 12.3). Listing 12.4 shows how to populate the list of choices.

FIG. 12.3

Use a list or combo box to present your user with a list of choices.

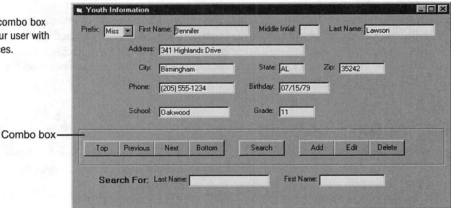

Combo box—

Listing 12.4   Populating the List with the AddItem Method

```
Combo1.AddItem "Mr."
Combo1.AddItem "Mrs."
Combo1.AddItem "Ms."
Combo1.AddItem "Miss"
Combo1.AddItem "Dr."
```

 T I P You can also enter the list items at design time using the List Property.

Data Bound Lists and Combos

The data bound list box and combo box are similar in function to their standard counterparts. They are designed to present the user with a list of choices. The key difference is that the data bound list and combo box controls get their list information from a recordset rather than from a series of AddItem statements.

Consider an example from the sample case. As your users enter data about a member, you want the user to be able to easily enter the county and state names of the member . One of the tables in the database contains county information. You can use the data bound list box to let your users select a county from those contained in the county table. The data bound list takes the county ID selected from the County table and stores it in the appropriate field of the Members table. You may think it would be hard to select the appropriate county if all you can see is the ID. However, the data bound list and combo boxes let you select a second field from the source table to serve as the display in the list. This means that you can display the name of the county in the list box but store only the county ID in the Members table. Figure 12.4 shows this concept graphically.

FIG. 12.4
The data bound list and combo boxes let you pick an item from one table for inclusion in another table.

DataSource table

DataField

BoundColumn

RowSource table

Name shown in list box

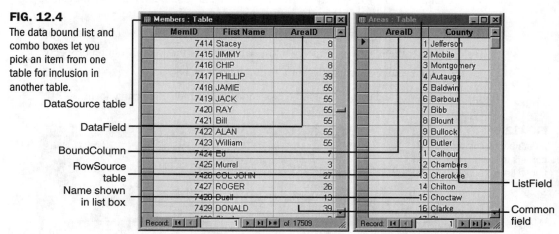

Part
II

Ch
12

ListField

Common field

You set up the data bound list or combo box by specifying five properties. Table 12.4 describes these properties.

Table 12.4   Properties for Data Bound List Box or Combo Box

Property	Sample Case Setting	Description
RowSource	datCounty	The name of the data control containing the information used to populate the list.

continues

Table 12.4   Continued

Property	Sample Case Setting	Description
BoundColumn	CountyID	The name of the field containing the value to be copied to the other table.
ListField	CountyName	The name of the field to be displayed in the list.
DataSource	datYouth	The name of the data control containing the recordset that is the destination of the information.
DataField	CountyID	The name of the destination field.

You can set each of these properties by selecting the property from the Properties dialog box and choosing the setting from a drop-down list. When setting the properties of the data bound list and combo boxes, keep in mind these points:

■ The data controls you specify for the RowSource and DataSource properties can be the same control or they can be different controls.

■ The fields for the BoundColumn and DataField properties must be of the same type.

■ You can set the ListField property to the same field as the BoundColumn property.

■ You must set all five properties, or a runtime error will occur.

Figure 12.5 shows the data bound combo box added to a sample data entry form.

FIG. 12.5
A data bound combo box lets the user select from a list of counties.

Data bound combo box

Data control for RowSource

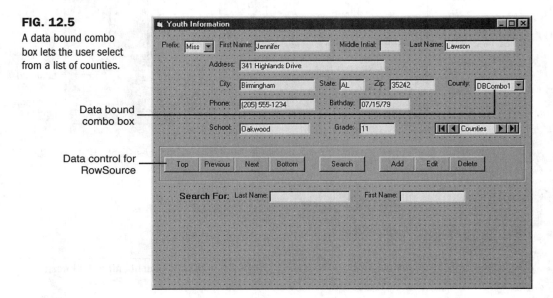

Data Bound Grids

The data bound grid provides a means to view the fields of multiple records at the same time. The data bound grid is similar to the table view used in Access or the Browse command used in FoxPro. The data bound grid displays information in a spreadsheet style of rows and columns. You can use it to display any alphanumeric information.

To set up the data bound grid, you only need to specify the DataSource property to identify the data control containing the data. The grid then displays all fields of all records in the recordset. If the information is larger than the area of the grid you defined, scroll bars are presented to let you view the remaining data.

 T I P To conserve application resources, use a QueryDef or SQL statement in the grid data control's RecordSource property. This way you can keep the number of records and fields the grid handles to a minimum.

Your user can select a grid cell to edit by clicking the cell with the mouse. To add a new record, the user positions the pointer in the last row of the grid indicated by an asterisk (*) and enters the desired data. You must specifically allow editing and record addition in the grid by setting the AllowAddNew and AllowUpdate properties of the grid to True.

For the sample case, use the data bound grid to display the Members information in a browse mode. Allow the user to switch between the browse mode and single-record mode by using the command button at the bottom right corner of the screen. This saves screen real estate. Figure 12.6 shows the data bound grid for the sample case.

FIG. 12.6
You can use the data bound grid to display information from several records at once.

Data bound grid —

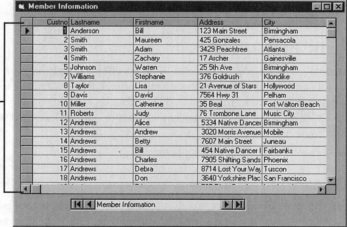

Other Visual Basic Controls

The other ound controls are set up the same way you would set up a text box or check box. Specifically, you set the DataSource property to the name of the data control containing the data to be displayed, then set the DataField property to the specific field in the recordset. Table 12.5 contains the names of the other bound controls and a brief description of their function.

Table 12.5 Other Bound Controls Can Be Used to Perform Specific Functions	
Control Name	**Description**
RichTextBox	Enables you to display and edit formatted text
MaskedEdit	Enables you to specify input masks for particular types of information like phone numbers or dates
3-D CheckBox	Handles true or false values like the standard check box
3-D Panel	Handles text display in a 3-D area of the form
OLE control	Enables you to display and edit OLE objects stored in the database

Third-Party Controls

One of the greatest features about Visual Basic is the ability to extend its functionality through the use of third-party controls. This functionality also extends to bound controls. Many third party vendors have controls that can be bound to a data control, and some vendors even market enhanced data controls. These controls enable you to perform add and delete functions without having to write any code.

Further Enhancements

In Chapter 10, "Writing Applications at Warp Speed" you saw how you needed to use code to implement some features that were not available with the data control alone. Specifically, an add and delete function were added to the capabilities of the data entry form with some simple coding. There are a few other enhancements that can be implemented with just a little bit of code and some ingenuity.

▶ **See** "Essential Functions the Data Control Forgot," **p. 231**

Find and Seek Operations

Another enhancement to the capabilities provided by the data control is the capability to search for a specific record. To add this feature, you must use either the Find method or the Seek method of the data control recordset, depending on the recordset type. For a table, use the Seek method; for a dynaset or snapshot, use the Find method. To implement the search, add a command button to the form. This command button invokes a dialog box that requests the ID to be found and then uses the appropriate method to perform the search (see Listing 12.5).

Listing 12.5   Use the Seek or Find Method to Search for a Specific Record

```
'*******************************************************************
'The variable SrchCond contains the value of the search criteria
'*******************************************************************
If dayYouth.RecordsetType = 0 Then
    datYouth.Recordset.Seek ">=", SrchCond
Else
    datYouth.Recordset.FindFirst "datYouth.Recordset([LastName]) >= " _
            & SrchCond
End If
```

What About Options (Option Buttons)

Another very useful control is the option button. Unfortunately, it is not a bound control that can be used directly with the Data control. However, this does not have to stop you from using the control. Option buttons come in handy for letting the user select between a small number of choices. A typical use would be for selecting gender in a membership application, as shown in Figure 12.7.

FIG. 12.7

Option buttons can be used to present the user with choices.

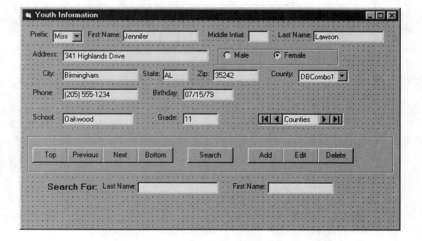

In code, you determine which option button was chosen by checking the Value property of each one. If the value of a button is True, then this was the selected button. Only one option button of a group can be selected. Option buttons can be grouped on a form, in a picture box, or in a frame. It is a good practice to set up each group of option buttons in a picture box or frame to avoid conflicts with other groups.

Once you have determined which option button was selected, you can assign the desired value for your data field based on the selection. For the membership case, either an M (male) or F (female) is stored, depending on the option button selected.

If you have more than two option buttons, you might want to put them in a control array. Then you can use a loop to look for the selected option, as shown in this code listing.

```
isel = 0
'Loop through five option buttons
For I = 0 To 4
   If Option(I).Value Then
       isel = I
       'Exit the loop when the selection is found
       Exit For
   End If
Next I
```

The option buttons are not bound controls, but you can still use them in an application with the Data control. You can place code in the Validate event of the Data control to store the desired value from the option buttons. However, there is a method that I find easier to use. (It's a sneaky way to trick the Data control.) For the field that you are modifying, create a text box and bind it to the field. Then set the Visible property of the text box to False. This keeps the box from being seen by the user. Then, in the Click event of each option button, place a line of code that changes the contents of the text box to the value represented by the option button. Then, when the Data control is invoked to move the record pointer, the field bound to the hidden box is updated along with all other bound fields. For the membership case, the following code would be used:

```
Sub Male_Click()
   Gender.Text = 'M'
End Sub
Sub Female_Click()
   Gender.Text = 'F'
End Sub
```

Using this hidden box method has an additional benefit. You can use the Change event of the box to mark the proper option box for each record that is accessed. The code for this follows:

```
If Gender.Text = 'M' Then
   Male.Value = True
Else
   Female.Value = True
End If
```

While this discussion has focused on how to use the option buttons with the Data control, you can also use them when you program with just the data access objects. In this case, you use an assignment statement to set the value of your field just like you do any other field. For the membership case (assuming the field is named Gender), you would use the following code:

```
OldTbl.Edit
If Male.Value Then
   OldTbl("Gender") = 'M'
Else
   OldTbl("Gender") = 'F'
End If
OldTbl.Update
```

From Here ...

This chapter has shown you how to use some additional features of the data control, what other bound controls are available to you, and how you can add features to enhance your data entry forms. There are other chapters which address other aspects of database applications:

- To learn how to quickly set up a data entry form, see Chapter 10, "Applications at Warp Speed."
- To see how to create a database, see Chapter 11, "Designing and Creating a Database."
- To learn how to create a database application without the data control, see Chapter 13, "Writing Programs with the Data-Access Objects."

Part
II

Ch
12

Writing Programs with the Data-Access Objects

In Chapter 10, "Applications at Warp Speed," and Chapter 12, "Doing More with Bound Controls," you saw how you can write a database application very quickly using the data control and bound controls that come with Visual Basic. These chapters showed you that with the setting of a few properties, you could create a nearly complete data entry screen. I say nearly complete, because in Chapter 10, you also saw that you needed to write some program code to handle some additional functions of a database application, for example adding or deleting records or finding a specific record. ■

Use different recordset types

Depending on your application, you may have different data access needs. There are several different recordset types to support these needs.

Move from one record to another in a recordset

Recordset navigation is one of the key functions of any database application.

Find a specific record

Most applications also need to be able to find a specific record. The method you use depends on the type of recordset you open.

Add, edit, and delete records in a database

What database application would be complete without the capability to add new records and modify old ones. You will learn about the methods that make this possible.

These additional functions introduced you to some of the programming that you can do in a database application. However, you can write an entire database application with just program commands, not using the data control at all. When you use just the program commands, you work with the data access objects of Visual Basic.

Using the data access objects and their associated program commands is more complex than using the data control and bound controls, but does offer greater programming flexibility for some applications. The data access objects and programming commands also provide the basis for the actions of the data control and the bound controls. Therefore, they help you understand the concepts behind the controls. As you saw in Chapter 10, "Applications at Warp Speed," even if you use the data control, you also need some of the programming commands to augment the capabilities of the data control.

▶ **See** "Essential Functions the Data Control Forgot," **p. 231**

To demonstrate the similarities and differences between data access objects and the data control, this chapter instructs you how to build a data entry screen similar to the ones you created in the previous chapters. This will allow you to compare how the programming commands work to how the data control implements the commands. Figure 13.1 shows the data entry screen that you build in this chapter.

FIG. 13.1

You can create this data entry screen by following this chapter's instructions.

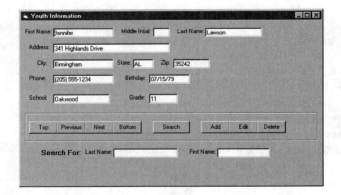

A key reason for using program commands is the flexibility they give you beyond what is available with the data control. You can perform more detailed input validation than is possible with just data engine rules because program commands do not directly access the database. You also can cancel changes to your edited data without using transactions. The use of program commands also provides an efficient way to handle data input and searches that do not require user interaction. Examples of this are receiving data from lab equipment or across a modem, or looking up the price of an item in a table. Program commands enable you to do transaction processing as well.

Opening an Existing Database

The first step in writing most data access programs is to set up a link to the database with which you want to work. When you create a new database (as described in Chapter 11, "Designing and Creating a Database"), that database is available for you to work with in your program until you exit the program or explicitly close the database. If you have an existing database, you must open it before your program can work with it. You can open a database with the OpenDatabase method of the Workspace object. To use the OpenDatabase method, create a database object and call the method, as shown in this bit of code:

▶ **See** "Implementing Your Design," **p. 258**

```
Dim OldDb As Database, OldWs As Workspace
Set OldWs = DBEngine.Workspaces(0)
Set OldDb = OldWs.OpenDatabase("C:\YOUTH\YOUTHTRK.MDB")
```

TROUBLESHOOTING

When I try to run the previous commands, I get the error "User-defined type not defined." What happened? In order to be able to use any database capabilities in your program, you must have one of the Data Access Object libraries specified in your program references. To set the program references, select the References item from the Project menu and select one of the DAO libraries from the dialog.

N O T E There are two basic DAO libraries available in Visual Basic 5. These are the 3.5 library and the 2.5/3.5 Compatibility library. If you will be programming for 32-bit clients only, and using the Access 95 format databases, you should select the 3.5 library. If you have a need to exchange data with 16-bit systems or Access 2.0 applications, you will have to use the 2.5/3.5 Compatibility library. ▓

These commands open an Access database with the default options of read/write data access and shared access. The full syntax of the OpenDatabase method lets you specify that the database should be opened exclusively (no other users or programs can access it at the same time), that it be opened in read-only mode (no updates are allowed), or, if you are connecting to a non-Access database, you can specify the database type. The use of exclusive access and read-only access are usually only required for multi-user applications (as discussed in Chapter 15, "Multi-User Programming"). Chapter 16, "Accessing Other PC Databases" covers the use of non-Access databases.

▶ **See** "Denying Table Access to Others," **p. 371**
▶ **See** "Using the Data-Access Objects with Other Databases," **p. 389**

Part
II

Ch
13

However, you may want to use the read-only mode even in a single-user application for a lookup database (for example, a ZIP Code database or a state abbreviations database you include with your application but do not want the user to be able to modify). To open the database as read-only, change the Set statement to the form shown in the following listing. The first parameter after the database name indicates whether the database is opened for exclusive access; the second parameter indicates whether read-only mode is to be used.

```
Set OldDb = OldWs.OpenDatabase("C:\ZIPCODE.MDB",False,True)
```

After you open the database, you have only created a link from your program to the database file itself. You still do not have access to the information in the database. In order to gain access to the information, you must open a recordset that specifies the tables and fields that you want to access. When you open a recordset, you can access any entire table, specific fields and records from the table, or a combination of records and fields from multiple tables.

There are four types of recordsets available in Visual Basic:

Recordset	Definition
Tables	The physical structures in a database that contain the actual data.
Dynasets	Sets of pointers that provide access to fields and records in one or more tables of a database.
Snapshots	Read-only copies of data from one or more tables. They are stored in memory.
Forward Only	This is a read-only recordset, similar to a snapshot. However, the user can only scroll forward in the recordset.

N O T E This chapter does refer to tables, dynasets, and snapshots, but it is important to remember that they are all recordsets and can only be accessed using the recordset object. ▪

The following sections describe each type of recordset, point out some of the advantages and disadvantages of each, and demonstrate the commands used to access the recordset.

Using Tables

A *table* is the physical representation of the database design. Because all data in a database is stored in tables, accessing tables provides the most direct link to the data. Tables are also the only form of recordset that supports indexes; therefore, searching a table for a specific record is quicker than searching a dynaset or snapshot.

When using tables, data is addressed or modified one table at a time, one record at a time. This arrangement provides very fine control over the manipulation of data. However, it does not give you the convenience of changing records in multiple tables with a single command, such as an action query.

Advantages of Using Tables   Using tables in your programs gives you several advantages:

- You can use or create indexes to change the presentation order of the data in the table during program execution.
- You can perform rapid searches for an individual record using an appropriate index and the Seek command.
- Changes made to the table by other concurrent users or programs are immediately available. It is not necessary to "refresh" the table to gain access to these records.

Disadvantages of Using Tables   Of course, using tables in your programs also has disadvantages:

- You can't set filters on a table to limit the records being processed to those that meet a certain criteria.
- You can't use Find commands on a table; the Seek command finds only the first record that meets its criteria. This implies that, to process a series of records in a range, you, the programmer, must provide the methods to find the additional records.

You can usually overcome these disadvantages with programming, but the solutions are often less than elegant. This chapter discusses some of the workarounds in its coverage of the various methods for moving through a recordset and for finding specific records. These topics are covered in the section "Positioning the Record Pointer."

Opening a Table for Use   To open a table for the program to use, define a recordset object and then use the OpenRecordset method to access the table. To identify the type of recordset to create, specify the dbOpenTable constant in the parameters of the method, as shown in the following segment of code. This listing assumes that you have already opened the database using the OldDb object and that the database contains a table called "Youth."

```
Dim OldTbl As Recordset
Set OldTbl = OldDb.OpenRecordset("Youth",dbOpenTable)
```

These commands open an Access table with the default parameters of shared use and read/write mode. You can include optional parameters in the OpenRecordset method to open the table for exclusive use or to open the table in read-only mode. These options are summarized in Table 13.1.

Part
II

Ch
13

Table 13.1   Some Options Used to Modify the Access Mode of Tables

Option	Action
dbDenyWrite	Prevents others in a multi-user environment from writing to the table while you have it open.
dbDenyRead	Prevents others in a multi-user environment from reading the table while you have it open.
dbReadOnly	Prevents you from making changes to the table.

Using Dynasets

A *dynaset* is a grouping of information from one or more tables in a database. This information is comprised of selected fields from the tables, often presented in a specific order and filtered by a specific condition. Dynasets address the records present in the base tables at the time the dynaset was created. Dynasets are an updatable recordset, so any changes made by the user are stored in the database. However, dynasets do not reflect additions or deletions of records made by other users or programs after the dynaset was created. This makes dynasets less useful for some types of multi-user applications.

A dynaset is actually a set of record pointers that point to the specified data that existed when the dynaset was created. Changes made to information in the dynaset are reflected in the base tables from which the information was derived as well as in the dynaset itself. These changes include additions, edits, and deletions of records.

Advantages of Using Dynasets   Some of the advantages provided by dynasets are as follows:

- Dynasets give you the ability to join information from multiple tables.
- You can use Find methods to locate or process every record meeting specified criteria.
- Dynasets enable you to limit the number of fields or records that you retrieve into the recordset.
- Dynasets make use of filters and sort order properties to change the view of data.

Disadvantages of Using Dynasets   Dynasets do have some limitations:

- You cannot create an index for a dynaset. This prevents you from changing the presentation order of a dynaset by changing the index or by creating a new one.
- A dynaset does not reflect additions or deletions made to the data by other users or other programs. A dynaset must be explicitly refreshed or re-created to show the changes.

Setting Up a Dynaset   To set up a dynaset for use within a program, you must define the recordset object with the Dim statement and then generate the dynaset using the OpenRecordset method. For creating a dynaset, the key part of the OpenRecordset method is the SQL statement that defines the records to be included, the filter condition, the sort condition, and any join conditions for linking data from multiple tables. The code shown in Listing 13.1 shows the simplest form of creating a dynaset, in which all records and fields are selected from a single table with no sort or filter conditions specified. This is the type of dynaset created by default when using a data control (though you can use a table or snapshot with the data control). The statements in Listing 13.1 provide you access to the same information as you had by accessing the table directly with the previous code. The only difference is the type of recordset that was created.

Listing 13.1   How to Create a Simple Dynaset

```
Dim OldDb As Database, NewDyn As Recordset,OldWs As Workspace
Set OldWs = DBEngine.Workspaces(0)
Set OldDb = OldWs.OpenDatabase("C:\YOUTH\YOUTHTRK.MDB")
```

```
Set NewDyn = OldDb.OpenRecordset("SELECT * FROM Youth", _
    dbOpenDynaset)
```

N O T E When creating a dynaset from a single table, you can simply specify the table name instead of using an SQL statement. ▪

When you create a dynaset, you can use any valid SQL statement. You can also specify options that affect the dynaset's behavior. Table 13.1 lists these options. (Chapter 14, "Understanding Structured Query Language" provides in-depth coverage of the use of SQL statements.)

Table 13.2   Some Options Used to Modify the Access Mode of a Dynaset

Option	Action
dbDenyWrite	Prevents others in a multi-user environment from writing to the dynaset while you have it open.
dbReadOnly	Prevents you from making changes to the dynaset.
dbAppendOnly	Enables you to add new records, but prevents you from reading or modifying existing records.
dbSQLPassThrough	Passes the SQL statement used to create the dynaset to an ODBC database server to be processed.

The following code shows how to create a dynaset-type recordset that only allows the user to read the information in the database:

```
Set NewDyn = OldDb.OpenRecordset("Youth", dbOpenDynaset, dbReadOnly)
```

N O T E An *ODBC server* is a database engine, such as Microsoft SQL Server or Oracle, that conforms to the Open Database Connectivity (ODBC) standards. The purpose of a server is to handle query processing at the server level and return to the client machine only the results of the query. ODBC drivers, which are usually written by the vendor of the database engine, handle the connection between Visual Basic and the database server. An advantage of using ODBC is that you can connect to the information on the database servers without having to know the inner workings of the engine. ▪

You can also create a dynaset from another dynaset or from a `QueryDef` object (Listing 13.2 shows the creation from another dynaset). The reason for creating a second dynaset from an initial dynaset is that you can use the filter and sort properties of the first dynaset to specify the scope of records and the presentation order of the second dynaset. Creating a second dynaset enables you to create a subset of your initial data. The second dynaset is usually much smaller than the first, which allows faster processing of the desired records. In Listing 13.2, a dynaset was created from the customer table to result in a national mailing list. A second dynaset was then created, which includes only the customers living in Alabama and sorts them by city name for further processing. Figures 13.2 and 13.3 show the results of these two dynasets.

Listing 13.2 How To Set the *filter* and *sort* Properties of a Dynaset and Create a Second Dynaset from the First

```
Dim OldDb As Database, NewDyn As Recordset, ScnDyn As Dynaset
Dim OldWs As Workspace
Set OldWs = DBEngine.Workspaces(0)
Set OldDb = OldWs.OpenDatabase("C:\YOUTH\YOUTHTRK.MDB")
Set NewDyn = OldDb.OpenRecordset("SELECT * FROM Youth", _
    dbOpenDynaset)
NewDyn.Filter = "State = 'AL'"
NewDyn.Sort = "City"
Set ScnDyn = NewDyn.OpenRecordset(dbOpenDynaset)
```

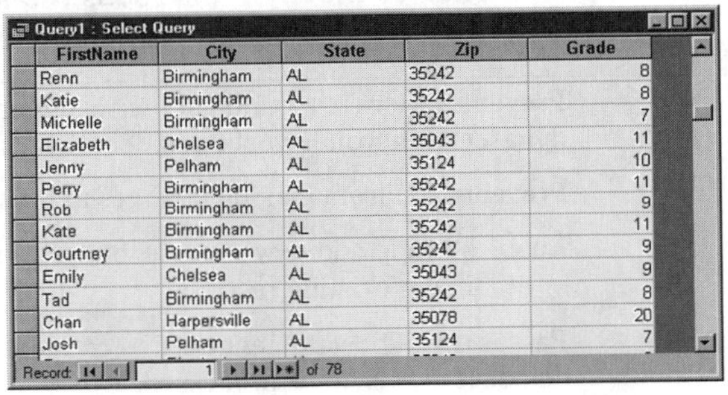

FIG. 13.2

The results of the creation of a dynaset from base tables.

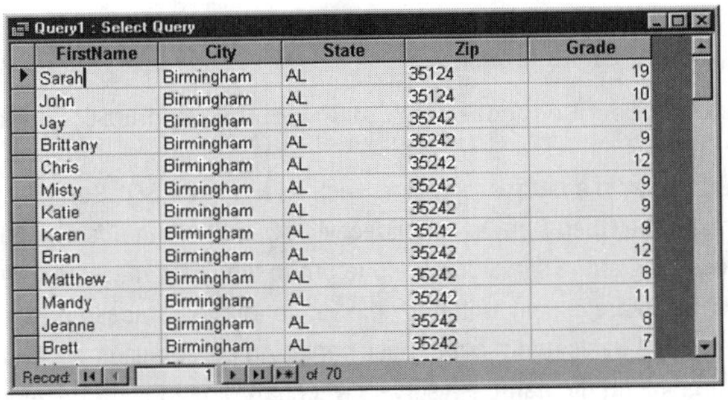

FIG. 13.3

The results of creating one dynaset from another dynaset after filter and sort conditions have been set.

You may wonder why, if you need the results in the second dynaset, you can't just create it from the base tables in the first place. The answer is that you can do so if your application needs *only* the second table. However, consider a member tracking system in which you want access to all your members (the creation of the first dynaset), and one of the functions of the system is to generate a mailing list for a particular region (the creation of the second dynaset). Because the pointers to all the required information are already present in the first dynaset, the creation of the second dynaset is faster than if it were created from scratch.

Using Snapshots

A *snapshot,* as the name implies, is a picture, or copy, of the data in a recordset at a particular point in time. A snapshot is very similar to a dynaset in that it is created from base tables, using an SQL statement, or from a QueryDef, dynaset, or another snapshot. A snapshot differs from a dynaset in that it is not updatable. The most frequent use of snapshots in a program is to generate reports or informational screens in which the data is static.

Advantages of Using Snapshots   Snapshots provide you with the following advantages:

- You can join information from multiple tables.
- You can use the Find methods to locate records.
- Record navigation and recordset creation can be faster for a snapshot than for a read-only dynaset because a snapshot is a copy of the data, not a set of pointers to the data.

Disadvantages of Using Snapshots   The primary disadvantage of using a snapshot is that it is not an updatable recordset. In addition, you can't create an index on a snapshot to help set the order of the data or locate specific records.

CAUTION

To avoid memory constraints, make sure that a snapshot returns only a small set of data.

Setting Up a Snapshot   You can create a snapshot by defining a recordset object with the Dim statement and then using the OpenRecordset method to assign the records to the object (as shown in Listing 13.3). As with a dynaset, you can specify optional parameters in the OpenRecordset method. Table 13.3 summarizes these parameters.

Listing 13.3   Create a Snapshot in Much the Same Way You Create a Dynaset

```
Dim OldDb As Database, NewSnap As Recordset, OldWs As Workspace
Set OldWs = DBEngine.Workspaces(0)
Set OldDb = OldWs.OpenDatabase("C:\YOUTH\YOUTHTRK.MDB")
Set NewSnap = OldDb.OpenRecordset("Youth",dbOpenSnapshot)
```

Table 13.3   Some Options Used to Modify the Access Mode of a Snapshot

Option	Action
dbDenyWrite	Prevents others in a multi-user environment from writing to the snapshot while you have it open
dbForwardOnly	Enables only forward scrolling through the snapshot
dbSQLPassThrough	Passes the SQL statement used to create the snapshot to an ODBC database to be processed

Part

II

Ch

13

Using a Forward-Only Recordset

The final type of recordset is the forward-only recordset. This type is new to Jet 3.5 and Visual Basic 5. The forward-only recordset is identical to the snapshot-type recordset, except that you can only move forward through the recordset. This means that the MoveFirst, MovePrevious, and Find methods will not work on the recordset. The advantage of using this type of recordset is that it is faster than a snapshot. However, the forward-only recordset should only be used in situations where a single pass through the recordset is needed.

To set up a forward-only recordset, you use the OpenRecordset method and specify the dbOpenForwardOnly constant as shown in the following line of code.

```
Set NewRSet= OldDb.OpenRecordset("Youth",dbOpenForwardOnly)
```

Placing Information On-Screen

Suppose that you have written a data-entry screen using the data and bound controls. To get information on-screen, you simply draw the bound control and then set the appropriate data field for the control. The display of the information is automatic. Using the data access objects, the process is only slightly more involved. You still use control objects (text boxes, labels, check boxes, and so on) to display the information, but you have to assign the data fields to the correct control properties with each record displayed. When used in this manner, the control objects are typically referred to as *unbound controls*. One advantage of using unbound controls is that you can use any control in the toolbox to display data, not just the controls specifically designated for use with the data control.

For the sample case in this chapter, you create a member data entry screen based on the Youth table of the sample database. To begin building this screen, start a new project in Visual Basic. Then on the default form, add the data labels and text boxes to hold the data from the table. Figure 13.4 shows the form with these controls added.

FIG. 13.4

Use unbound controls to display data from the data-access objects.

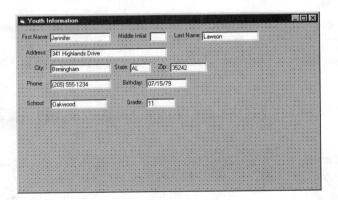

To set up the table for use, you must open the table using the OpenRecordset method. For this case, place the Dim statement that defines the data access objects in the Declarations section of the form so that the objects are available throughout all the code in the form. You then open the database and table in the Form_Load event (see Listing 13.4). At this point, the table is open and you are positioned at the first record in the table.

Listing 13.4   Placing the *OpenDatabase* and *OpenRecordset* in the *Form_Load* Event

```
Set OldWs = DBEngine.Workspaces(0)
'********************************
'Open database and Customer table
'********************************
Set OldDb = OldWs.OpenDatabase("C:\YOUTH\YOUTHTRK.MDB")
Set RcSet = OldDb.OpenRecordset("Youth",dbOpenTable)
'**********************************************
'Move to first record and display information
'**********************************************
RcSet.MoveFirst
Call ShowFields
```

To display the data, assign the value of the desired data fields to the display properties of the controls (captions for labels, text for text boxes, and so on) that contain the data. Listing 13.5 shows this process. Notice that the listing defines the text boxes as a control array; you can use a loop to quickly modify certain properties of the controls such as foreground color or visibility. Also notice that the assignments are placed in a subroutine; you can call the same routine from a number of command button events rather than repeat the code in each event. This arrangement makes the code more efficient and easier to maintain.

Listing 13.5   Assigning Data Fields to the Display Properties of the Form's Controls

```
Private Sub ShowFields()
Text1(0).Text = RcSet("Lastname")
Text1(1).Text = RcSet("Firstname")
Text1(2).Text = RcSet("Address")
Text1(3).Text = RcSet("City")
Text1(4).Text = RcSet("State")
Text1(5).Text = RcSet("Zip")
Text1(6).Text = RcSet("Phone")
End Sub
```

Part
II

Ch
13

N O T E   Since the Text property is the default, or value, property of a text box, you do not have to include the property name in the assignment statement. My personal preference is to include the name for readability. ■

You can find the commands from these listings, and the other listings used to build the data entry screen, in the YOUTHTRK.VBP file at the book's Web site (**http://www.quecorp. com/sevb5**).

Positioning the Record Pointer

Because a database with only one record is fairly useless, a database engine must provide methods for moving from one record to another within recordsets. Visual Basic provides six classes of such methods:

Class	Description
Move method	Changes the position of the record pointer from the current record to another record.
Find method	Locates the next record that meets the find condition. Find methods work on dynasets and snapshots.
Seek method	Finds the first record in a table that meets the requested condition.
Bookmark property	Identifies the location of a specific record.
AbsolutePosition	Moves the record pointer to a specific property position in the recordset.
PercentPosition	Moves the record pointer to the record property nearest the indicated percentage position in the recordset.

Each of these methods has benefits and limitations, as described in the following sections.

Using the *Move* Methods

You can use the Move methods on any recordsets available in Visual Basic. There are five different Move methods:

Move Method	Action
MoveFirst	Moves the record pointer from the current record to the first record in the opened recordset.
MoveNext	Moves the record pointer from the current record to the next record (the record following the current record) in the opened recordset. If there is no next record (that is, if you are already at the last record), the end-of-file (EOF) flag will be set.
MovePrevious	Moves the record pointer from the current record to the preceding record in the opened recordset. If there is no previous record (that is, if you are at the first record), the beginning-of-file (BOF) flag will be set.

Move Method	Action
MoveLast	Moves the record pointer from the current record to the last record in the opened recordset.
Move *n*	Moves the record pointer from the current record *n* records down (if *n* is positive) or up (if *n* is negative) in the opened recordset. If the move would place the record pointer beyond the end of the recordset (either BOF or EOF), an error will occur.

These commands move the record pointer to the record indicated based on the current order of the recordset. The current order of the recordset is the physical order, unless an index was set for a table or a dynaset or snapshot was created with the order specified. To show the use of the MoveFirst, MovePrevious, MoveNext, and MoveLast methods, add command buttons to the data entry screen so that the user can move through the recordset (see Figure 13.5). To activate these buttons, add the code shown in Listing 13.6. The code for each button is preceded by an identifying comment line.

FIG. 13.5
Add command buttons to enable the user to navigate through the recordset.

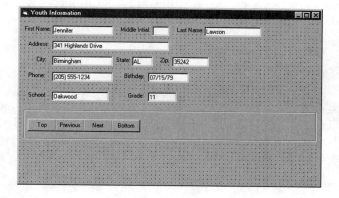

Part
II

Ch
13

Listing 13.6   Assigning *Move* Methods to Navigation Command Buttons to Make Them Work

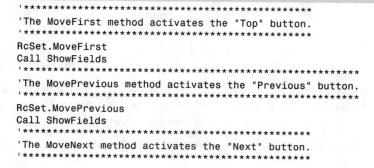

```
'**************************************************
'The MoveFirst method activates the "Top" button.
'**************************************************
RcSet.MoveFirst
Call ShowFields
'****************************************************
'The MovePrevious method activates the "Previous" button.
'****************************************************
RcSet.MovePrevious
Call ShowFields
'**************************************************
'The MoveNext method activates the "Next" button.
'**************************************************
```

continues

Listing 13.6   Continued

```
RcSet.MoveNext
Call ShowFields
'*****************************************************
'The MoveLast method activates the "Bottom" button.
'*****************************************************
RcSet.MoveLast
Call ShowFields
```

The Move *n* method lets you move more than one record from the current position. The value of *n* is the number of records to move in the recordset. This value can be either positive or negative to indicate movement either forward or backward in the recordset. The following piece of code shows the use of this method to move two records forward from the current record.

```
RcSet.Move 2
```

The Move *n* method also has an optional parameter that enables you to move a specified number of records from a bookmark. You must set the bookmark prior to using this form of the Move method. The following line of code shows how this method is used:

```
RcSet.Move 2, bkmrk
```

Using the *Find* Methods

You can use the Find methods on dynasets and snapshots only. You can't use Find methods on table objects. (Because the data entry screen was created with a table, you can't use the Find methods in the example.) The Find methods are used to locate records that meet specified criteria. You express the criteria in the same way that you specify the Where clause of an SQL command—except without the Where keyword. There are four Find methods:

Find Method	Action
FindFirst	Starting at the top of the database, finds the first record in the recordset with the specified criteria
FindNext	Starting at the current location in the recordset, finds the next record down with the specified criteria
FindPrevious	Starting at the current location in the recordset, finds the next record up with the specified criteria
FindLast	Starting at the bottom of the recordset, finds the last record in the database with the specified criteria

After the Find method is run, check the status of the NoMatch property of the recordset. If NoMatch is true, the method failed to find a record that matched the requested criteria. If NoMatch is false, the record pointer is positioned at the found record.

Listing 13.7 shows the use of the Find methods to move through a dynaset.

Listing 13.7   How to Move Through Selected Records in a Dynaset Using Find Methods

```
'****************************************
'Set up the database and Dynaset objects
'****************************************
Dim OldDb As Database, NewDyn As Recordset, FindCrit As String
Dim OldWs As Workspace
Set OldWs = DBEngine.Workspaces(0)
Set OldDb = OldWs.OpenDatabase("C:\YOUTH\YOUTHTRK.MDB")
Set NewDyn = OldDb.OpenRecordset("SELECT * FROM Youth", _
    dbOpenDynaset)
'***********************************************
'Set the search criteria for the find methods
'***********************************************
FindCrit = "State = 'AL'"
'***********************************************
'Find the first record matching the criteria
'***********************************************
NewDyn.FindFirst FindCrit
Do While Not NewDyn.NoMatch
'********************************************************
'Loop forward through all records matching the criteria
'********************************************************
    NewDyn.FindNext FindCrit
Loop
'*********************************************
'Find the last record matching the criteria
'*********************************************
NewDyn.FindLast FindCrit
Do While Not NewDyn.NoMatch
'*********************************************************
'Loop backward through all records matching the criteria
'*********************************************************
    NewDyn.FindPrevious FindCrit
Loop
```

TIP You may want to set a bookmark prior to invoking one of the Find methods. Then if a matching record is not found, you can return to the record that was current before the Find was attempted.

The Find methods work by scanning each record, starting with the current record, to locate the appropriate record that matches the specified criteria. Depending on the size of the recordset and the criteria specified, this search operation can be somewhat lengthy. The Jet engine can optimize searches if an index is available for the search field. If you are going to do many searches, consider creating an index for the field in its base table.

N O T E In many cases, it is faster to re-create the dynaset using the search criteria than it is to use the Find methods to process all matching records. You can also create a second filtered dynaset from the first dynaset by using the search criteria as the filter condition. Listing 13.8 shows the comparison of these two methods. ■

Listing 13.8   Creating a Dynaset with a *Filter* Condition in the SQL Statement or Creating a Second Dynaset After Setting the *Filter* Property of the First Dynaset

```
'*********************
'Create Initial Dynaset
'*********************
Dim OldDb As Database, NewDyn As Recordset, ScnDyn As Recordset
Dim OldWs As WorkSpace
Set OldWs = DBEngine.Workspaces(0)
Set OldDb = OpenDatabase("C:\YOUTH\YOUTHTRK.MDB")
Set NewDyn = OldDb.OpenRecordset("SELECT * FROM Youth", _
    dbOpenDynaset)
'*******************************
'Use Find method to search records
'*******************************
NewDyn.FindFirst "State = 'FL'"
Do Until NewDyn.NoMatch
   NewDyn.FindNext "State = 'FL'"
Loop
'****************************************************************
'Create second dynaset and use Move methods to process records
'****************************************************************
NewDyn.Filter = "State = 'FL'"
Set ScnDyn = NewDyn.OpenRecordset()
ScnDyn.MoveFirst
Do Until ScnDyn.EOF
   ScnDyn.MoveNext
Loop
'*********************************************************
'Create initial dynaset with "Where" clause and use Move
'*********************************************************
Set NewDyn = OldDb.OpenRecordset _
    ("SELECT * FROM Youth WHERE State = 'FL'", dbOpenDynaset)
NewDyn.MoveFirst
Do Until NewDyn.EOF
   NewDyn.MoveNext
Loop
```

TROUBLESHOOTING

When you use variables as the value to be compared to, you may encounter the error `Cannot bind name item` **when you run the program.** When the field and the variable you are comparing are string (or text) variables, surround the variable name by single quotes ('), as shown in the following sample code. For the sake of readability, you can also assign the single quote to a constant and use that constant in your code.

```
Dim FindCrit As String, FindStr As String
FindStr = "Smith"
FindCrit = "Lastname = '" & FindStr & "'"
NewDyn.FindFirst FindCrit
```

In the same manner, surround a date variable with the pound symbol (#) to compare it to a date field. You don't need to include any additional symbols when comparing numbers.

When a `Find` method is successful, the record pointer moves to the new record. If a `Find` method is not successful, the recordset's `NoMatch` property is set to `True` and the record pointer does not move. One way to use the `NoMatch` property is to write an `If` condition that checks the value, as shown in the following code:

```
If NewDyn.NoMatch Then
    'Notify user of event
    MsgBox "Record not found"
Else
    'Process found record.
    command
End If
```

Using the *Seek* Method

The `Seek` method is the fastest way to locate an individual record in a table—however, it is also the most limiting of the record-positioning methods. The following list outlines the limitations of the `Seek` method:

- Can be performed only on a table; you can't use it with a dynaset or snapshot
- Can be used only with an active index; the parameters of the `Seek` method must match the fields of the index in use
- Finds only the first record that matches the specified index values; subsequent uses do not find additional matching records

The `Seek` method, as shown in Listing 13.9, consists of the method call, the comparison operator, and the values of the key fields. The comparison operator can be <, <=, =, >=, >, or <>. The key values being compared must be of the same data type as the fields in the controlling index. Although you are not required to include the same number of key values as there are fields in the index, you *do* have to include a key value for each field you want to search. These values must appear in the same order as the fields in the index and be separated by commas, as shown in the second part of Listing 13.9.

Listing 13.9 Using the Seek Method to Find a Specific Record in a Table

```
Dim OldDb As Database, OldTbl As Recordset
Dim OldWs As WorkSpace
Set OldWs = DBEngine.Workspaces(0)
Set OldDb = OldWs.OpenDatabase("C:\YOUTH\YOUTHTRK.MDB")
Set OldTbl = OldDb.OpenRecordset("Youth",dbOpenTable)
'*******************************************
'Set the index property for the table
'*******************************************
OldTbl.Index = "Name"
'*******************************************
```

continues

Listing 13.9   Continued

```
'Execute the seek for the desired condition
'*********************************
OldTbl.Seek ">", "Smith"
'*************************************************
'Display information or "Not Found" message as appropriate
'*************************************************
If OldTbl.NoMatch Then
   MsgBox "Not Found"
Else
   MsgBox OldTbl("Lastname") & ", " & OldTbl("Firstname")
End If
'*************************************************
'Seek method with first and last name information supplied
'*************************************************
OldTbl.Seek ">=", "Smith", "M"
```

You must carefully plan for one behavior of the Seek method. When the Seek method uses the comparison operators =, >=, >, or <>, Seek starts with the first record for the current index and scans forward through the index to find the first matching occurrence. If the comparison operator is < or <=, Seek starts with the last record in the table and scans backward through the table. If the index has unique values for each record, this presents no problem. However, if there are duplicate index values for the key fields being specified, the record found depends on the comparison operator and the sort order of the index. Figure 13.6 shows a table of first and last names indexed on last name and then first name. The table on the top is indexed in ascending order; the table on the bottom is indexed in descending order. Listing 13.10 shows four possible combinations of a controlling index and comparison operator for finding a record for the last name of *Smith*. Each of these combinations is labeled in the comments of the code. Table 13.4 shows the results of each of these Seek operations.

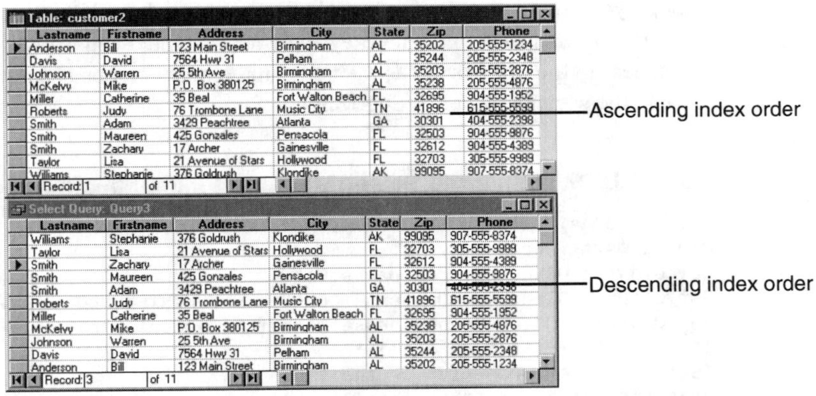

FIG. 13.6

These tables show the difference between using ascending and descending order in an index.

Listing 13.10 Varying Results Are Obtained Using Different *Seek* Operators and Index Orders on a Table

```
Dim OldDb As Database, OldTbl As Recordset
Dim OldWs As WorkSpace
Set OldWs = DBEngine.Workspaces(0)
Set OldDb = OldWs.OpenDatabase("C:\YOUTH\YOUTHTRK.MDB")
Set OldTbl = OldDb.OpenTable("Youth", dbOpenTable)
'************************
'Set ascending order index
'************************
OldTbl.Index = "Name"
OldTbl.Seek ">=", "Smith", "A"
printer.Print OldTbl("Lastname") & ", " & OldTbl("Firstname")
OldTbl.Seek "<=", "Smith", "Z"
printer.Print OldTbl("Lastname") & ", " & OldTbl("Firstname")
'************************
'Set descending order index
'************************
OldTbl.Index = "Name2"
OldTbl.Seek ">=", "Smith", "A"
printer.Print OldTbl("Lastname") & ", " & OldTbl("Firstname")
OldTbl.Seek "<=", "Smith", "Z"
printer.Print OldTbl("Lastname") & ", " & OldTbl("Firstname")
```

Table 13.4 Different *Seek* Comparison Operators and Index Sort Orders Yield Different Results

Comparison Operator	Index Order	Resulting Record
>= Smith,A	Ascending	Smith, Adam
<= Smith,Z	Ascending	Smith, Maureen
>= Smith,A	Descending	Roberts, Judy
<= Smith,Z	Descending	Smith, Zachary

Notice that you must also be careful when using the > ,< , >=,or <= operator on a descending index. The > (and >=)operator is interpreted as finding the record that occurs later in the index than the specified key value. That is why the >= "Smith" search on a descending index returns the record Roberts, Judy. Similar behavior is exhibited by the < and <= operators. As you can see from the preceding example, you must use care when choosing both the index sort order and the comparison operator with the Seek method to ensure that the desired results are achieved.

Part
II

Ch
13

As with the find methods, if a Seek is successful, the record pointer moves. Otherwise, the recordset's NoMatch property is set to True and the record pointer does not change. Figure 13.7 shows the Seek Name button and dialog box added to the sample case.

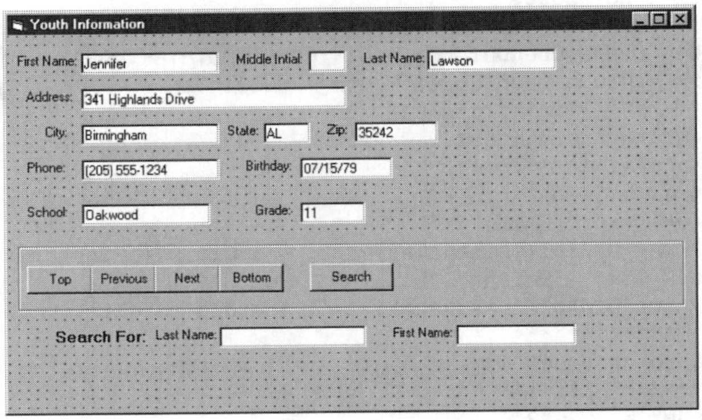

FIG. 13.7

Using a dialog box to obtain the Seek condition desired by the user.

Using the *Bookmark* Property

It is often desirable to be able to return to a specific record, after the record pointer moves or new records are added. You can do so by using the Bookmark property of the recordset. The bookmark is a system-assigned variable that is correlated to the record and is unique for each record in a recordset. Listing 13.11 shows how to obtain the value of the bookmark for the current record, move to another record, and then return to the original record using the bookmark previously obtained.

Listing 13.11   Using a *Bookmark* to Return to a Specific Record in a Recordset

```
Dim OldDb As Database, NewDyn As Recordset
Dim OldWs As WorkSpace
Set OldWs = DBEngine.Workspaces(0)
Set OldDb = OldWs.OpenDatabase("C:\YOUTH\YOUTHTRK.MDB")
Set NewDyn = OldDb.OpenRecordset _
    ("SELECT * FROM Youth", dbOpenDynaset)
'*****************************************************
'Set a variable to the bookmark of the current record
'*****************************************************
CrntRec = NewDyn.Bookmark
'*********************
'Move to another record
'*********************
NewDyn.MoveNext
'*********************************************************
'Return to the desired record by setting the bookmark property
'   to the previously defined value.
'*********************************************************
NewDyn.Bookmark = CrntRec
```

If you must store multiple bookmark values, consider storing them in an array for faster processing. Listing 13.12 shows code that, while processing a mailing list, uses a bookmark array to identify customers whose birthdays are coming up.

Listing 13.12 Storing Multiple *Bookmarks* in an Array

```
ReDim BkMrk(1)
nmbkmk = 0
NewDyn.MoveFirst
Do Until NewDyn.EOF
'***************************
'Check for birthday in month
'***************************
   If birthday Then
'********************
'Add bookmark to array
'********************
      nmbkmk = nmbkmk + 1
      If nmbkmk > 1 Then
         ReDim Preserve BkMrk(1 To nmbkmk)
      End If
      BkMrk(nmbkmk) = NewDyn.Bookmark
   End If
   NewDyn.MoveNext
Loop
'****************
'Process bookmarks
'****************
For I = 1 To nmbkmk
   NewDyn.Bookmark = BkMrk(I)
   Debug.Print Lastname, Birthday
Next I
```

Using the *PercentPosition* and *AbsolutePosition* Properties

In addition to the `Bookmark` property, the recordset object has two other properties that you can set to establish the position of the record pointer. These properties are `AbsolutePosition` and `PercentPosition`.

The `PercentPosition` property specifies the approximate position in a recordset where a record is located. By setting this property to a value between 0 and 100, you cause the pointer to move to the record closest to that location. Setting the property to a value outside the range causes an error to occur. You can use the `PercentPosition` property with all three types of recordsets.

The `AbsolutePosition` property enables you to tell the recordset to move to a specific record. The value of the property can range from 0 for the first record in the recordset to 1 less than the number of records. Setting a value greater than the number of records in the recordset causes an error. Therefore, it is a good idea to include error checking in the code used to set the `AbsolutePosition` property. The `AbsolutePosition` property can only be used with dynasets and snapshots. The following code in Listing 13.13 shows how you can use the `AbsolutePosition` and `PercentPosition` properties. Note the validation of the requested position; this is used to prevent errors.

Listing 13.13 *Absolute* and *Percent Position* Are Other Ways to Move in a Recordset

```
'Move to the percent position specified
If rcpct > 100 Then rcpct = 100
If rcpct < 0 Then rcpct = 0
NewDyn.PercentPosition = rcpct
 'Move to the absolute position specified
If rcabs > NewDyn.RecordCount Then rcabs = NewDyn.RecordCount
If rcabs < 0 Then rcabs = 0
NewDyn.AbsolutePosition = rcabs
```

Using *Filters*, *Indexes*, and *Sorts*

`Filters`, `sorts`, and `indexes` are properties of the recordset object. You can set these properties using an assignment statement such as

```
NewDyn.Filter = "Lastname = 'Smith'"
```

`Filters`, `indexes`, and `sorts` enable you to control the scope of records being processed and the order in which records are processed. *Filters* (which are available only for dynasets and snapshots) limit the scope of records by specifying that they meet certain criteria, such as "last name starts with *M*." `Indexes` (available only for tables) and *sorts* (available only for dynasets and snapshots) specify the order of a recordset based on the value of one or more fields in the recordset. For `sorts` and `indexes`, you can also specify ascending or descending sort order.

Setting the *Filter* Property

The `filter` property is available only for dynasets and snapshots. Although the following discussion refers only to dynasets, the same statements hold true for snapshots. When set, the `filter` property does not affect the current dynaset, but filters records that are copied to a second dynaset or snapshot created from the first.

You can specify the `filter` property of a dynaset the same way you specify the `Where` clause of an SQL statement, but without the `Where` keyword. The `filter` can be a simple statement, such as `State = 'AL'`, or one that uses multiple conditions, such as `State = 'FL' AND Lastname = 'Smith'`. You can also use an expression, such as `Lastname LIKE 'M*'`, to find people whose last names begin with *M*. The following sample code shows how these `filter` properties are set for a dynaset created from the Youth Information table.

```
Dim NewDyn As Recordset, ScnDyn As Recordset
Set NewDyn = OldDb.OpenRecordset("Youth",dbOpenDynaset)
NewDyn.Filter = "State = 'FL' AND Lastname = 'Smith'"
'Second recordset contains only "filtered" records.
Set ScnDyn = OldDb.OpenRecordset(dbOpenDynaset)
```

You can include added flexibility in your `filter` conditions by using functions in the condition. For example, if you want to filter a dynaset of all states with the second letter of the state code equal to L, use the `Mid` function, as shown here:

```
NewDyn.Filter = "Mid(State,2,1) = 'L'"
```

Using functions does work, but it is an inefficient way to filter a dynaset. A better approach is to include the condition in the query used to create the dynaset.

More About Filters

The `filter` condition of the dynaset has no effect on the current dynaset—only on secondary dynasets created from the current one. The only way to filter the existing recordset is to move through the recordset with the `Find` methods. By setting the `find` condition to your `filter` condition, you only process the desired records.

If you work with only the filtered dynaset, it is more efficient to create the required dynaset using the appropriate SQL clause in the `OpenRecordset` method. This method is shown here:

```
Fltr = "State = 'FL' AND Lastname = 'Smith'"
Set NewDyn = OldDb.OpenRecordset("SELECT * FROM Youth WHERE" & Fltr)
```

Setting the *Sort* Property

As with the `filter` property, the `sort` property is available only for dynasets and snapshots. Although the following discussion refers only to dynasets, the same statements apply to snapshots. You can specify the `sort` property by providing the field names and order (ascending or descending) for the fields on which the dynaset is to be sorted. You can specify any field or combination of fields in the current dynaset. The `Sort` condition is similar to the `Order By` clause of an SQL statement. Listing 13.14 shows the syntax for setting the `sort` property.

Part
II

Ch
13

Listing 13.14 Two Methods for Creating a Filtered Dynaset

```
Dim OldDb As Database, NewDyn As Recordset, ScnDyn As Recordset
Dim OldWs As WorkSpace
Set OldWs = DBEngine.Workspaces(0)
Set OldDb = OldWs.OpenDatabase("C:\YOUTH\YOUTHTRK.MDB")
'*************************************************************
'The first method sets the sort property of one dynaset then
'    creates a second dynaset from the first.
'*************************************************************
Set NewDyn = OldDb.OpenRecordset("SELECT * FROM Youth")
```

continues

Listing 13.14 Continued

```
NewDyn.Sort = "Lastname,Firstname"
Set ScnDyn = NewDyn.OpenRecordset()
'*********************************************************
'The second method creates the sorted Dynaset directly
'*********************************************************
Set ScnDyn = OldDb.OpenRecordset _
    ("SELECT * FROM Youth ORDER BY Lastname,Firstname")
```

> **CAUTION**
>
> When specifying a multiple field sort, the order of the fields is important. A sort on first name and then last name yields different results than a sort on last name and then first name.

As was the case for the `filter` property, the `sort` property has no effect on the current dynaset; it specifies the order of any dynaset created from the current one. You can also achieve the same results of a sorted dynaset by specifying the `Order By` clause of the SQL statement used to create the dynaset. This alternate technique is shown in Listing 13.14.

Setting the Current Index in a Table

You can use an index with a table to establish a specific order for the records or to work with the `Seek` method to find specific records quickly. For an `index` to be in effect, the index property of the table must be set to the name of an existing index for the table. If you want to use an index that does not already exist, you must create it using the methods described in Chapter 11, "Designing and Creating a Database," then set the index property of the recordset to the new index name. An example of how to use a program command to set the current index follows:

```
OldTbl.Index = "Name"
```

The index specified for the table must be one that has already been created and is part of the indexes collection for the given table. If the index does not exist, an error occurs. The index is not created for you!

▶ **See** "Creating Indexes," **p. 265**

Creating an Index for a New Situation

If the index you want does not exist, create it as described in Chapter 11, "Designing and Creating a Database," and then set the index property of the table to the newly created index. The example shown in Listing 13.15 creates a ZIP code index for the Youth Information table.

Listing 13.15 Creating a New Index and Setting the *Index* Property

```
Dim Idx1 As Index, Fld1 As Field
Set Idx1 = NewTbl.CreateIndex("Zip_Code")
Set Fld1 = Idx1.CreateField("Zip")
Idx1.Fields.Append Fld1
NewTbl.Indexes.Append Idx1
NewTbl.Index = "Zip_Code"
```

If your program needs an index, why not just create it at design time so you don't have to worry about creating it at runtime? There are several reasons for not doing this:

- It takes time for the data engine to update indexes after records are added, deleted, or changed. If there are a large number of indexes, this process can be quite time consuming. It may be better to create the index only when it is needed. Also, indexes take up additional disk resources; so many indexes on a large table can cause your application to exceed available resources.

- You are limited to 32 indexes for a table. Although this is a fairly large number, if you need more than 32, you must create some indexes as they are needed and then delete them.

- You may not be able to anticipate all the ways a user of your application wants to view data. By providing a method for creating indexes, specified by the user at runtime, you add flexibility to your application.

Of these reasons, the performance issue of updating multiple indexes is the one most often considered. To determine whether it is better to add the index at design time or to create it only when you need it, set up the application both ways and test the performance of each.

N O T E Although it is desirable to limit the number of indexes your table has to keep current, it is advisable to have an index for each field that is commonly used in SQL queries. This is because the Jet engine (starting with version 2.0) employs query optimization that uses any available indexes to speed up queries. ■

Considering Programs that Modify Multiple Records

Some programs, or program functions, are meant to find one specific piece of information in a database. However, the vast majority of programs and functions work with multiple records from the database. There are two basic methods of working with multiple records:

Method	Definition
Program loops	Groups of commands contained inside a DO...WHILE, DO...UNTIL, or FOR...NEXT programming structure. The commands are repeated until the exit condition of the loop is met.

continues

continued

Method	Definition
SQL statements	Commands written in the Structured Query Language that tell the database engine to process records. SQL is covered in detail in Chapter 14, "Understanding Structured Query Language."

Using Loops

Most programmers are familiar with the use of DO...WHILE and FOR...NEXT loops. In working with recordsets, all the programming principles for loops still apply. That is, you can perform a loop *while* a specific condition exists or *for* a specific number of records. Loops of this type were shown earlier in this chapter (refer to Listings 13.4 and 13.5).

Another way of working with multiple records forms an *implied loop*. Most data entry or data viewing programs include command buttons on the form to move to the next record or previous record. When a user repeatedly presses these buttons, he or she executes a type of program loop by repeating the move events. A special consideration for this type of loop is what to do when you are at the first record, the last record, or if you have an empty recordset. The problem is that if you move backward from the first record, forward from the last record, or try to move anywhere in an empty recordset, an error occurs. Fortunately, the Jet database engine provides some help in this area. There are properties of the recordset that can tell you when these conditions exist, as described in the following section.

Using the *BOF*, *EOF*, *RecordCount*, and *NoMatch* Properties   You can use four main recordset properties to control the processing of multiple records in a recordset. Table 13.5 gives the definitions of these properties.

Table 13.5   Properties Used to Control Loop Processing

Property	Indicates
BOF	Beginning of File flag, indicates whether the record pointer is positioned before the first record (BOF = True) or not (BOF = False).
EOF	End of File flag, indicates whether the record pointer is positioned past the last record (EOF = True) or not (EOF = False).
RecordCount	Indicates the number of records in the recordset that have been accessed. This gives a count of the total records in the recordset only after the last record has been accessed (for example, by using MoveLast).
NoMatch	Indicates that the last Find method or Seek method was unsuccessful in locating a record that matched the desired criteria.

You can use these properties to terminate loops or prevent errors. Consider the data entry form in Figure 13.5. To prevent an error from occurring when the user presses the Next button, use code that allows the move only if the recordset is not at the end of the file. (The following code takes this possibility into account.) Alternatively, you can disable the Next button when you reach the end of file. You can apply the same principal to the Previous button and the BOF condition. You may also want to check the RecordCount property of a recordset and enable only the Add Record button if the count is zero.

```
If NOT OldDyn.EOF Then
   OldDyn.MoveNext
   If OldDyn.EOF Then DolDyn.MoveLast
End If
```

N O T E After the MoveNext method has been executed, it is possible that the pointer is now at the end-of-file. This would mean that there is no current record. Therefore, if the end-of-file is encountered, a MoveLast method is used to make sure the record pointer is positioned at the last record in the recordset. ■

Using SQL Statements

In addition to processing records with a program loop, you can use SQL statements to handle a number of functions that apply to multiple records. The following sections discuss two main types of functions:

■ Calculation queries provide cumulative information about the requested group of records.

■ Action queries insert, delete, or modify groups of records in a recordset.

Calculation Queries   *Calculation queries* allow you to determine cumulative information about a group of records such as the total; average, minimum, and maximum values; and the number of records. Calculation queries also enable you to specify the filter criteria for the records. For example, you can extract total sales for all salesmen in the Southeast region or the maximum price of a stock on a given day (assuming, of course, that the base data is in your tables). Figure 13.8 shows a table of purchasing data for the fish inventory in an example database. The code in Listing 13.16 shows how to determine the total purchase costs for one type of fish and the minimum, maximum, and average unit cost of all the fish. Figure 13.9 shows the results table from the SQL query.

Part
II

Ch
13

Listing 13.16   Using Calculation Queries to Determine Information About Data in the Recordset

```
Dim OldDb As Database, NewDyn As Recordset, _
     NewDyn2 As Recordset, SQL As String
Dim OldWs As WorkSpace
Set OldWs = dbEngine.Workspaces(0)
Set OldDb = OldWs.OpenDatabase("C:\FISH\TRITON.MDB")
'*********************************************
```

continues

Listing 13.16 Continued

```
'Use the SUM function to get the total cost.
'*******************************************
SQL = "SELECT SUM([Total Cost]) As Grand FROM Fishbuys _
       WHERE Fishcode = 1001"
Set NewDyn = OldDb.OpenRecordset(SQL)
Print NewDyn("Grand")
NewDyn.Close
'************************************************************
'Use the MIN, AVG, and MAX functions to get unit price statistics.
'************************************************************
SQL = "SELECT MIN([Unit Price]) As Mincst, _
       AVG([Unit Price]) As Avgcst, "
SQL = SQL + _
   " MAX([Unit Price]) As Maxcst FROM Fishbuys WHERE Fishcode > 0"
Set NewDyn2 = OldDb.OpenRecordset(SQL)
Print NewDyn2("Mincst"), NewDyn2("Avgcst"), NewDyn2("Maxcst")
NewDyn2.Close
OldDb.Close
```

item code	quantity	unit price	total cost
1028	2	2.6	5.19
1077	1	3.5	3.5
1076	5	1.6	8
1041	5	2.35	11.75
1096	5	1.55	7.75
1005	5	1.6	8
1076	1	1.6	1.6
1059	3	1.2	3.6
1029	4	2.65	10.6
1027	5	1.6	8
1082	3	2.4	7.2
1022	4	2.3	9.19
1098	2	1.45	2.9
1053	1	1.85	1.85
1099	4	3.65	14.6
1001	3	1.25	3.75
1079	2	2.6	5.19
1038	2	2.8	5.59
1094	5	1.8	9
1016	1	1.85	1.85

FIG. 13.8 You can process purchasing data shown here with calculation queries or action queries.

Mincst	avgcst	Maxcst
0.75	2.2	3.7

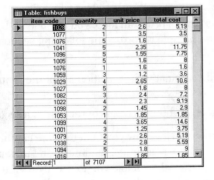

FIG. 13.9 The calculation query produces a dynaset with a single record containing the results.

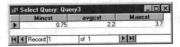

Using a calculation query can replace many lines of program code that would be required to produce the same results. In addition, a query is usually faster than the equivalent program code.

The query and the equivalent program code are contained in the project SQLCALC.VBP on the companion disc. The database, Triton.mdb, is also found on the book's Web site at **http://www.quecorp.com/sevb5**.

Action Queries   *Action queries* operate directly on a recordset to insert, delete, or modify groups of records based on specific criteria. As with calculation queries, action queries perform the same work that would require many lines of program code. Listing 13.17 shows examples of several action queries.

Listing 13.17   Using Action Queries to Perform Operations on Multiple Records

```
Dim OldDb As Database, NewDyn As Recordset, NewQry As QueryDef
Dim OldWs As WorkSpace
Set OldWs = DBEngine.Workspaces(0)
Set OldDb = OldWs.OpenDatabase("C:\FISH\TRITON.MDB")
'********************************************
'Calculate the total cost of each purchase.
'********************************************
SQL = _
    "Update Fishbuys Set [Total Cost] = [Quantity] * [Unit Price]"
Set NewQry = OldDb.CreateQueryDef("Calc Total", SQL)
NewQry.Execute
NewQry.Close
'*************************************
'Delete all records for Fishcode = 1003
'*************************************
SQL = "Delete From Fishbuys WHERE Fishcode = 1003"
Set NewQry = OldDb.CreateQueryDef("Del Fish", SQL)
NewQry.Execute
NewQry.Close
OldDb.DeleteQueryDef ("Calc Total")
OldDb.DeleteQueryDef ("Del Fish")
OldDb.Close
```

CAUTION

When using action queries to modify groups of records, be very careful while specifying the Where clause of the query that defines the records to be modified. Improperly setting this clause can produce disastrous results, such as the deletion of all records in a recordset.

Understanding Other Programming Commands

In this chapter, you have learned how to find specific records and how to move through a group of records. However, in most programs, you also must add, modify, and delete records. The commands covered in the following sections apply only to tables and dynasets (remember that snapshots are not updatable).

Adding Records

To add a new record to a recordset, use the AddNew method. AddNew does not actually add the record to the recordset; it clears the copy buffer to allow information for the new record to be input. To physically add the record, use the Update method. Listing 13.18 shows how to add a new record to the recordset.

Listing 13.18   Using *AddNew* and *Update* to Add a Record to the Recordset

```
'********************************
'Use AddNew to set up a new record
'********************************
NewDyn.AddNew
'****************************************************************
'Place the necessary information in the recordset fields
'****************************************************************
NewDyn("Lastname") = "McKelvy"
NewDyn("Firstname") = "Mike"
NewDyn("Address") = "6995 Bay Road"
NewDyn("City") = "Pensacola"
NewDyn("State") = "FL"
NewDyn("Zip") = "32561"
'****************************************************************
'Use the update method to add the new record to the recordset
'****************************************************************
NewDyn.Update
```

CAUTION

Because AddNew places information only in the copy buffer, reusing the AddNew method or moving the record pointer with any Move or Find method (before using the update method) clears the copy buffer. Any information entered in the record is therefore lost.

Editing Records

In a manner similar to adding a record, you use the Edit method to make changes to a record. The Edit method places a copy of the current record's contents into the copy buffer so that information can be changed. As with AddNew, the changes take effect only when the Update method is executed. Listing 13.19 shows the use of the Edit method.

Listing 13.19   Using *Edit* and *Update* to Change the Data in a Record

```
'****************************************************************
'Use the find method to locate the record to be changed.
'****************************************************************
NewDyn.FindFirst "Lastname = 'McKelvy'"
'********************************************
'Check the NoMatch Property to avoid an error
```

```
'**********************************************
If NewDyn.NoMatch Then
    MsgBox "Not Found"
Else
'*****************************************************
'Use the edit method to set up the record for changes
'*****************************************************
    NewDyn.Edit
'*****************************************************
'Change the necessary information in the copy buffer
'*****************************************************
    NewDyn("Address") = "P. O. Box 380125"
    NewDyn("City") = "Birmingham"
    NewDyn("State") = "AL"
    NewDyn("Zip") = "35238"
'********************************************************
'Use the update method to write the changes to the recordset
'********************************************************
    NewDyn.Update
End If
```

> **CAUTION**
>
> Because `Edit` only places information in the copy buffer, reusing the `Edit` method or moving the record pointer with any `Move` or `Find` method (before using the `Update` method) clears the copy buffer. Any information entered in the record is therefore lost.

Updating Records

The `Update` method is used in conjunction with the `AddNew` and `Edit` methods to make changes to the recordsets. The `Update` method writes the information from the copy buffer to the recordset. In the case of `AddNew`, `Update` also creates a blank record in the recordset to which the information is written. In a multi-User environment, the `Update` method also clears the record locks associated with the pending `Add` or `Edit` method. (Listings 13.17 and 13.18 show the use of the Update method.)

N O T E If you use data controls to work with recordsets, the use of the `Update` method is not required. An update is automatically performed when a move is executed by the data control. ■

Deleting Records

Deleting a record requires the use of the `Delete` method, as shown in Listing 13.20. This method removes the record from the recordset and sets the record pointer to a null value.

Part

II

Ch

13

Listing 13.20   Using *Delete* to Remove a Record from the Recordset

```
'*********************************************************
'Use the find method to locate the record to be deleted
'*********************************************************
NewDyn.FindFirst "Lastname = 'McKelvy'"
'***********************************************
'Check the NoMatch property to avoid an error
'***********************************************
If NewDyn.NoMatch Then
    MsgBox "Not Found"
Else
'*******************************************
'Use the delete method to remove the record
'*******************************************
    NewDyn.Delete
End If
```

CAUTION

Once you delete a record, it is gone. You can recover the record only if you issued a `BeginTrans` command before you deleted the record, in which case you can `RollBack` the transaction. Otherwise, the only way to get the information back into the database is to re-create the record with the `AddNew` method.

Incorporating Add, Edit, and Delete Functions in the Sample Case

Figure 13.10 shows some command buttons added to the data-entry screen for the sample case. These buttons make use of the add, edit, and delete capabilities described in the preceding sections. The Delete Record button deletes the current record. The Add New Record button blanks out the text boxes to prepare them for new input. The Edit Record button prepares the recordset for editing. As a visual indication of editing, the foreground color of the text boxes also changes. Both the Edit Record and Add New Record buttons cause the normal command buttons (the Top, Previous, Next, Bottom, and Seek Name buttons) to be hidden and two new buttons to be displayed. The new buttons are Save and Cancel. The Save button stores the values displayed in the text boxes to the appropriate fields in the recordset and issues the `Update` method. The Cancel button terminates the Edit or Add process and restores the original information for the current record. After either Save or Cancel is selected, both buttons disappear and the eight main buttons are again shown.

N O T E We stated previously that deletions and changes to the database are made without confirmation by the user. If you want your program to have confirmation built in, you have to provide it in your code. The easiest way to do this is through the `MsgBox` function. With this function, you can provide a warning to the user and ask for confirmation. ∎

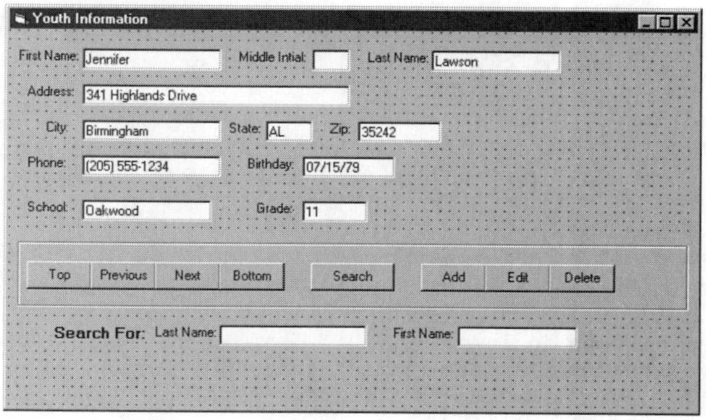

FIG. 13.10
Add, edit, and delete
functions are added to
the data entry screen
with new command
buttons.

Introducing Transaction Processing

Transaction processing enables you to treat a group of changes, additions, or deletions to a database as a single entity. This is useful when one change to a database depends on another change, and you want to make sure that all changes are made before any of the changes become permanent. For example, you have a point-of-sale application that updates inventory levels as sales are made. As each item is entered for the sales transaction, a change is made to the inventory database. However, you only want to keep the inventory changes if the sale is completed. If the sale is aborted, you want to return the inventory database to its initial state before the sale was started. Transaction processing is a function of the Workspace object and, therefore, affects all databases open in a particular workspace.

Visual Basic provides three methods for transaction processing. These methods perform the following functions:

Transaction Method	Function
BeginTrans	Starts a transaction and sets the initial state of the database.
RollBack	Returns the database to its initial state before the BeginTrans statement was issued. When RollBack is executed, all changes made after the last BeginTrans statement are discarded.
CommitTrans	Permanently saves all changes to the database made since the last BeginTrans statement. Once the CommitTrans statement has been issued, the transactions cannot be undone.

Listing 13.21 shows the BeginTrans, RollBack, and CommitTrans methods as they are used in an order entry application. The transactions are used in case the customer cancels the order prior to the completion of the order processing.

Listing 13.21 Using Transaction Processing to Handle Multiple Changes to a Database as One Group

```
OldWs.BeginTrans
'************************************************
'Perform loop until user ends sales transaction
'************************************************
Do While Sales
'************************************************
'Get item number and sales quantity from form
' Input Itemno,SalesQty
' Find item number in inventory
'************************************************
    Inv.FindFirst "ItemNum = " & Itemno
'*************************
'Update inventory quantity
'*************************
    Inv.Edit
    Inv("Quantity") = Inv("Quantity") - SalesQty
    Inv.Update
Loop
'*****************************************
'User either completes or cancels the sale
'*****************************************
If SaleComp Then
    OldWs.CommitTrans
Else
    OldWs.Rollback
End If
```

From Here...

Some of the topics mentioned in this chapter are covered in greater detail in other portions of the book. Please refer to these chapters:

- Chapter 10, "Applications at Warp Speed," explains how to quickly write data access programs using the data control.
- Chapter 12, "Doing More with Bound Controls," shows you how to make applications using the data control do more.
- Chapter 14, "Understanding Structured Query Language," explains more about the SQL statements used in creating dynasets, snapshots, and queries.

Understanding Structured Query Language

In several of the previous chapters on working with databases, you saw how SQL statements were used to determine what information would be available in a recordset. This chapter explains how to create those SQL statements and how to do much more with SQL. The examples in this chapter all use an Access database, but the techniques of using SQL are applicable to many database formats. In fact, SQL statements are the cornerstone of working with many database servers such as Oracle or SQL Server.

There are two basic types of SQL statements that are covered in this chapter: *data-manipulation language* (DML) and *data-definition language* (DDL). Most of the chapter deals with DML statements, and unless a statement is identified otherwise, you should assume that it is a DML statement. ■

Explaining SQL

SQL allows you to quickly retrieve or modify groups of records in your database.

Retrieving selected records

By setting the appropriate clauses, you can work with only a portion of a table instead of having to work with the entire table.

Getting information from multiple tables

Using SQL statements allows you to easily combine information from two or more tables.

Calculating Summary information

You can find out how many records are in a recordset, or determine the total or average values of specific fields.

Using SQL to modify the information in tables

With a single SQL statement, you can change the values of multiple records in a database. To do the same thing with a program would require a number of statements.

Using SQL to change the structure of the database

SQL statements can even be set up to create tables, modify the structure of a table, or delete a table.

Defining SQL

Structured Query Language (SQL) is a specialized set of programming commands that enable the developer (or end user) to do the following kinds of tasks:

- Retrieve data from one or more tables in one or more databases
- Manipulate data in tables by inserting, deleting, or updating records
- Obtain summary information about the data in tables, such as totals; record counts; and minimum, maximum, and average values
- Create, modify, or delete tables in a database (Access databases only)
- Create or delete indexes for a table (Access databases only)

SQL statements enable the developer to perform functions in one line or a few lines of code that would take 50 or 100 lines of standard BASIC code to perform.

As the name implies, Structured Query Language statements create a query that is processed by the database engine. The query defines the fields to be processed, the tables containing the fields, the range of records to be included, and, for record retrieval, the order in which the returned records are to be presented.

When retrieving records, a SQL statement usually returns the requested records in a *dynaset*. Recall that a dynaset is an updatable recordset that actually contains a collection of pointers to the base data. Dynasets are temporary and are no longer accessible once they are closed. SQL does have a provision for the times when permanent storage of retrieved records is required.

N O T E The Microsoft SQL syntax used in this chapter is designed to work with the Jet database engine and is compatible with ANSI SQL (there are, however, some minor differences between Microsoft SQL and ANSI SQL). In addition, if you use SQL commands to query an external database server such as SQL Server or Oracle, read the documentation that comes with the server to verify that the SQL features you want to use are supported and that the syntax of the statements is the same. ■

Understanding the Parts of the SQL Statement

A SQL statement consists of three parts:

- **Parameter declarations**   These are optional parameters that are passed to the SQL statement by the program.
- **The manipulative statement**   This part of the statement tells the Query engine what kind of action to take, such as SELECT or DELETE.
- **Options declarations**   These declarations tell the Query engine about any filter conditions, data groupings, or sorts that apply to the data being processed. These include the WHERE, GROUP BY, and ORDER BY clauses.

These parts are arranged as follows:

```
[Parameters declarations] Manipulative statement [options]
```

Most of this chapter uses only the manipulative statement and the options declarations. Using these two parts of the SQL statement, you can create queries to perform a wide variety of tasks. Table 14.1 lists the five manipulative clauses and their purposes.

Table 14.1   Parts of the Manipulative Statement

Statement	Function
DELETE FROM	Removes records from a table
INSERT INTO	Adds a group of records to a table
SELECT	Retrieves a group of records and places the records in a dynaset or table
TRANSFORM	Creates a summary table using the contents of a field as the column headers
UPDATE	Sets the values of fields in a table

Although manipulative statements tell the database engine what to do, the options declarations tell it what fields and records to process. The discussion of the optional parameters makes up the bulk of this chapter. In this chapter, I first give you a look at how the parameters are used with the SELECT statement and then let you apply the parameters to the other manipulative statements. Many of the examples in this chapter are based on the sales-transaction table of a sample database that might be used to manage an aquarium business.

The following discussions of the different SQL statements show just the SQL statement syntax. Be aware that these statements can't be used alone in Visual Basic. The SQL statement is always used to create a QueryDef, to create a dynaset or snapshot using the Execute method, or as the RecordSource property of a data control. This section explains the part of an SQL statement. Later in the chapter, the section entitled "Using SQL" will explain how these statements are actually used in code. For other examples of using SQL statements, look back through Chapters 10, 12, and 13.

N O T E   A QueryDef is a part of the database that stores the query definition. This definition is the SQL statement that you create. ■

Using *SELECT* Statements

The SELECT statement retrieves records (or specified fields from records) and places the information in a dynaset or table for further processing by a program. The SELECT statement follows this general form:

```
SELECT [predicate] fieldlist FROM tablelist [table relations]
     [range options] [sort options] [group options]
```

NOTE In my demonstrations of code statements, words in all-caps are SQL keywords, and italicized words or phrases are used to indicate terms that a programmer would replace in an actual statement. For example, *`fieldlist`* would be replaced with `Lastname, Firstname`. Phrases or words inside square brackets are optional terms.

The various components of the preceding statement are explained in this chapter. Although a SQL statement can be greatly complex, it also can be fairly simple. The simplest form of the `SELECT` statement is shown here:

```
SELECT * FROM Sales
```

Defining the Desired Fields The `fieldlist` part of the `SELECT` statement is used to define the fields to be included in the output recordset. You can include all fields in a table, selected fields from the table, or even calculated fields based on other fields in the table. You can also choose the fields to be included from a single table or from multiple tables.

The fieldlist portion of the `SELECT` statement takes the following form:

```
[tablename.]field1 [AS alt1][,[tablename.]field2 [AS alt2]]
```

Selecting All Fields from a Table The `*`, or wild-card parameter, is used to indicate that you want to select all the fields in the specified table. The wild card is used in the `fieldlist` portion of the statement. The statement `SELECT * FROM Sales`, when used with the sample database you are developing, produces the output recordset shown in Figure 14.1.

FIG. 14.1
Using * in the *fieldlist* parameter selects all fields from the source table.

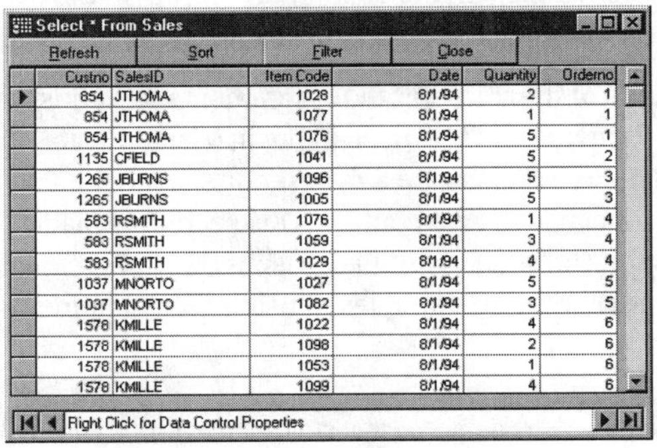

Custno	SalesID	Item Code	Date	Quantity	Orderno
854	JTHOMA	1028	8/1/94	2	1
854	JTHOMA	1077	8/1/94	1	1
854	JTHOMA	1076	8/1/94	5	1
1135	CFIELD	1041	8/1/94	5	2
1265	JBURNS	1096	8/1/94	5	3
1265	JBURNS	1005	8/1/94	5	3
583	RSMITH	1076	8/1/94	1	4
583	RSMITH	1059	8/1/94	3	4
583	RSMITH	1029	8/1/94	4	4
1037	MNORTO	1027	8/1/94	5	5
1037	MNORTO	1082	8/1/94	3	5
1578	KMILLE	1022	8/1/94	4	6
1578	KMILLE	1098	8/1/94	2	6
1578	KMILLE	1053	8/1/94	1	6
1578	KMILLE	1099	8/1/94	4	6

Selecting Individual Fields from a Table Frequently, you need only a few fields from a table. You can specify the desired fields by including a field list in the `SELECT` statement. Within the field list, the individual fields are separated by commas. In addition, if the desired field has a space in the name, such as in `Order Quantity`, the field name must be enclosed within square brackets, []. The recordset that results from the following `SELECT` statement is shown in

Figure 14.2. A recordset created with fields specified is more efficient than one created with the wild card (*), both in terms of the size of the recordset and speed of creation. As a general rule, you should limit your queries to the smallest number of fields that can accomplish your purpose.

```
SELECT [Item Code], Quantity FROM Sales
```

FIG. 14.2

This recordset results from specifying individual fields in the SELECT statement.

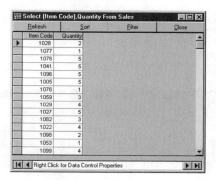

Selecting Fields from Multiple Tables   As you should remember from the discussions on database design in the "Designing the Database" section of Chapter 11, "Designing and Creating a Database," you normalize data by placing it in different tables to eliminate data redundancy. When you retrieve this data for viewing or modification, you want to see all the information from the related tables. SQL lets you combine information from various tables into a single recordset.

To select data from multiple tables, you specify three things:

- The table from which each field is selected
- The fields from which you are selecting the data
- The relationship between the tables

Specify the table for each field by placing the table name and a period in front of the field name (for example, Sales.[Item Code] or Sales.Quantity). (Remember, square brackets must enclose a field name that has a space in it.) You also can use the wildcard identifier (*) after the table name to indicate that you want all the fields from that table.

To specify the tables you're using, place multiple table names (separated by commas) in the FROM clause of the SELECT statement.

The relationship between the tables is specified either by a WHERE clause or by a JOIN condition. These elements are discussed later in this chapter.

The statement in Listing 14.1 is used to retrieve all fields from the Sales table and the Item Description and Retail fields from the Retail Items table. These tables are related by the Item Code field. Figure 14.3 shows the results of the statement.

Part
II

Ch
14

N O T E The listing shows an underscore character at the end of each of the first three lines. This is used to break the lines for the purpose of page-width in the book. When you enter the expressions, they need to be on a single line. ■

Listing 14.1 Selecting Fields from Multiple Tables in a SQL Statement

```
SELECT Sales.*, [Retail Items].[Item Description], _
    [Retail Items].Retail
    FROM Sales, [Retail Items] _
    WHERE Sales.[Item Code]=[Retail Items].[Item Code]   _
```

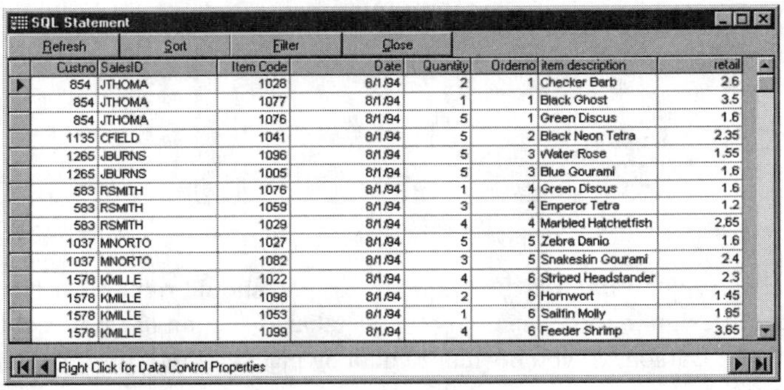

FIG. 14.3

Selecting fields from multiple tables produces a combined recordset.

Custno	SalesID	Item Code	Date	Quantity	Ordemo	item description	retail
854	JTHOMA	1028	8/1/94	2	1	Checker Barb	2.6
854	JTHOMA	1077	8/1/94	1	1	Black Ghost	3.5
854	JTHOMA	1076	8/1/94	5	1	Green Discus	1.8
1135	CFIELD	1041	8/1/94	5	2	Black Neon Tetra	2.35
1265	JBURNS	1096	8/1/94	5	3	Water Rose	1.55
1265	JBURNS	1005	8/1/94	5	3	Blue Gourami	1.8
583	RSMITH	1076	8/1/94	1	4	Green Discus	1.6
583	RSMITH	1059	8/1/94	3	4	Emperor Tetra	1.2
583	RSMITH	1029	8/1/94	4	4	Marbled Hatchetfish	2.65
1037	MNORTO	1027	8/1/94	5	5	Zebra Danio	1.6
1037	MNORTO	1082	8/1/94	3	5	Snakeskin Gourami	2.4
1578	KMILLE	1022	8/1/94	4	6	Striped Headstander	2.3
1578	KMILLE	1098	8/1/94	2	6	Hornwort	1.45
1578	KMILLE	1053	8/1/94	1	6	Sailfin Molly	1.85
1578	KMILLE	1099	8/1/94	4	6	Feeder Shrimp	3.65

Right Click for Data Control Properties

N O T E You can leave out the table name when specifying fields as long as the requested field is present only in one table in the list. However, it is very good programming practice to include the table name, both for reducing the potential for errors and for readability of your code. ■

Creating Calculated Fields   The example in Listing 14.1 has customer-order information consisting of the item ordered, quantity of the item, and the retail price. Suppose that you also want to access the total cost of the items. You can achieve this by using a *calculated field* in the SELECT statement. A calculated field can be the result of an arithmetic operation on numeric fields (for example, Price * Quantity) or the result of string operations on text fields (for example, Lastname & Firstname). For numeric fields, you can use any standard arithmetic operation (+, -, *, /, ^). For strings, you can use the concatenation operator (&). In addition, you can use Visual Basic functions to perform operations on the data in the fields (for example, you can use the MID$ function to extract a substring from a text field, the UCASE$ function to place text in uppercase letters, or the SQR function to calculate the square root of a number). Listing 14.2 shows how some of these functions can be used in the SELECT statement.

Listing 14.2 Creating a Variety of Calculated Fields with the *SELECT* Statement

```
'****************************************
'Calculate the total price for the items
'****************************************
SELECT [Retail Items].Retail * Sales.Quantity FROM _
       [Retail Items],Sales _
       WHERE Sales.[Item Code]=[Retail Items].[Item Code]
'*******************************************************************
'Create a name field by concatenating the Lastname and
'Firstname fields
'*******************************************************************
SELECT Lastname & ', ' & Firstname FROM Customers
'*******************************************************************
'Create a customer ID using the first 3 letters of the Lastname
' and Firstname fields and make all letters uppercase.
'*******************************************************************
SELECT UCASE$(MID$(Lastname,1,3)) & UCASE$(MID$(Firstname,1,3)) _
    FROM Customers
'*******************************************************************
'Determine the square root of a number for use in a data report.
'*******************************************************************
SELECT Datapoint, SQR(Datapoint) FROM Labdata
```

In the listing, no field name is specified for the calculated field. The query engine automatically assigns a name such as Expr1001 for the first calculated field. The next section, "Specifying Alternative Field Names," describes how you can specify a name for the field.

Calculated fields are placed in the recordset as read-only fields—they can't be updated. In addition, if you update the base data used to create the field, the changes are not reflected in the calculated field.

NOTE If you use a calculated field with a data control, it is best to use a label control to show the contents of the field. This prevents the user from attempting to update the field and causing an error. You also could use a text box with the locked property set to True. (You can learn more about the data control and bound controls by reviewing Chapters 10 and 12.) If you use a text box, you might want to change the background color to indicate to the user that the data cannot be edited. ■

Specifying Alternative Field Names Listing 14.2 created calculated fields to include in a recordset. For many applications, you will want to use a name for the field other than the one automatically created by the query engine.

You can change the syntax of the SELECT statement to give the calculated field a name. You assign a name by including the AS clause and the desired name after the definition of the field (refer to the second part of Listing 14.3). If you want, you can also use this technique to assign a different name to a standard field.

Listing 14.3 Naming the Field

```
'***********************************************
'Set up the SELECT statement without the name
'***********************************************
Dim NewDyn As RecordSet
SQL = "SELECT Lastname & ', ' & Firstname FROM Customers"
'********************************************
'Create a dynaset from the SQL statement
'********************************************
NewDyn = OldDb.OpenRecordset(SQL)
'*********************************
'Get the value of the created field
'*********************************
Person = NewDyn.Recordset(0)
'**************************************************************
'Set up the SELECT statement and assign a name to the field
'**************************************************************
SQL = "SELECT Lastname & ', ' & Firstname As Name FROM Customers"
'********************************************
'Create a dynaset from the SQL statement
'********************************************
NewDyn = OldDb.OpenRecordset(SQL)
'*********************************
'Get the value of the created field
'*********************************
Person = NewDyn.Recordset("Name")
```

Specifying the Data Sources   In addition to telling the database engine what information you want, you must tell it in which table to find the information. This is done with the FROM clause of the SELECT statement. Here is the general form of the FROM clause:

```
FROM table1 [IN data1] [AS alias1][,table2 [IN data2] [AS alias2]]
```

Various options of the FROM clause are discussed in the following sections.

Specifying the Table Names   The simplest form of the FROM clause is used to specify a single table. This is the form of the clause used in this statement:

```
SELECT * FROM Sales
```

The FROM clause can also be used to specify multiple tables (refer back to Listing 14.1). When specifying multiple tables, separate the table names with commas. Also, if a table name has an embedded space, the table name must be enclosed in square brackets, [] (refer to Listing 14.1).

Using Tables in Other Databases   As you develop more applications, you might have to pull data together from tables in different databases. For example, you might have a ZIP Code database that contains the city, state, and ZIP Code for every postal code in the United States. You do not want to have to duplicate this information in a table for each of your database applications that requires it. The SELECT statement lets you store that information once in its own database and then pull it in as needed. To retrieve the information from a database other than the current one, you use the IN portion of the FROM clause. The SELECT statement for retrieving the ZIP Code information along with the customer data is shown in Listing 14.4.

Listing 14.4   Retrieving Information from More than One Database

```
'*****************************************************************
'We are working from the TRITON database which is already open.
'*****************************************************************
SELECT Customers.Lastname, Customers.Firstname, Zipcode.City, _
    Zipcode.State  FROM Customers, Zipcode IN USZIPS  _
    WHERE Customers.Zip = Zipcode.Zip
```

Assigning an Alias Name to a Table   Notice the way the table name for each of the desired fields was listed in Listing 14.4. Because these table names are long and there are a number of fields, the SELECT statement is fairly long. The statement gets much more complex with each field and table you add. In addition, typing long names each time increases the chances of making a typo.

To alleviate this problem, you can assign the table an alias by using the AS portion of the FROM clause. Using AS, you can assign a unique, shorter name to each table. This alias can be used in all the other clauses in which the table name is needed. Listing 14.5 is a rewrite of the code from Listing 14.4, using the alias CS for the Customers table and ZP for the Zipcode table.

Listing 14.5   Using a Table Alias to Cut Down on Typing

```
'*********************************************************
'We use aliases to make the statement easier to enter.
'*********************************************************
SELECT CS.Lastname, CS.Firstname, ZP.City, ZP.State  _
    FROM Customers AS CS, Zipcode IN USZIPS AS ZP  _
    WHERE CS.Zip = ZP.Zip
```

Using ALL, DISTINCT, or DISTINCTROW Predicates   In most applications, you select all records that meet specified criteria. You can do this by specifying the ALL predicate in front of your field names or by leaving out any predicate specification (ALL is the default behavior). Therefore, the following two statements are equivalent:

```
SELECT * FROM Customers
SELECT ALL * FROM Customers
```

There might be times, however, when you want to determine the unique values of fields. For these times, use the DISTINCT or DISTINCTROW predicate. The DISTINCT predicate causes the database engine to retrieve only one record with a specific set of field values—no matter how many duplicates exist. For a record to be rejected by the DISTINCT predicate, its values for all the selected fields must match those of another record. For example, if you are selecting first and last names, you can retrieve several people with the last name Smith, but you can't retrieve multiple occurrences of Adam Smith.

If you want to eliminate records that are completely duplicated, use the DISTINCTROW predicate. DISTINCTROW compares the values of all fields in the table, whether or not they are among the selected fields. For the sample database, you can use DISTINCTROW to determine which products have been ordered at least once. DISTINCTROW has no effect if the query is on only a single table.

Listing 14.6 shows the uses of DISTINCT and DISTINCTROW.

Listing 14.6   Obtaining Unique Records with the *DISTINCT* or *DISTINCTROW* Predicates

```
'******************************
'Use of the DISTINCT predicate
'******************************
SELECT DISTINCT [Item Code] FROM Sales
'******************************
'Use of the DISTINCTROW predicate
'******************************
SELECT DISTINCTROW [Item Code] FROM [Retail Items], Sales  _
    [Retail Items] INNER JOIN Sales  _
    ON [Retail Items].[Item Code]=Sales.[Item Code]
```

Setting Table Relationships   When you design a database structure, you use key fields so that you can relate the tables in the database. For example, you use a salesperson ID in the Customers table to relate to the salesperson in the Salesperson table. You do this so that you don't have to include all the salesperson data with every customer record. You use these same key fields in the SELECT statement, to set the table relationships so that you can display and manipulate the related data. That is, when you view customer information, you want to see the salesperson's name, not his or her ID.

You can use two clauses to specify the relationships between tables:

- ■ **JOIN**   This combines two tables, based on the contents of specified fields in each table and the type of JOIN.
- ■ **WHERE**   This usually is used to filter the records returned by a query, but it can be used to emulate an INNER JOIN.

N O T E Using the WHERE clause to join tables creates a read-only recordset. To create a modifiable
recordset, you must use the JOIN clause. ■

Using a* JOIN *Clause   The basic format of the JOIN clause is as follows:

```
table1 {INNER¦LEFT¦RIGHT} JOIN table2 ON table1.key1 = table2.key2
```

The query engine used by Visual Basic (also used by Access, Excel, and other Microsoft
products) supports three JOIN clauses: INNER, LEFT, and RIGHT. Each of these clauses returns
records that meet the JOIN condition, but each behaves differently in returning records that do
not meet that condition. Table 14.2 shows the records returned from each table for the three
JOIN conditions. For this discussion, *table1* is the "left" table and *table2* is the "right" table. In
general, the left table is the first one specified (on the left side of the JOIN keyword) and the
right table is the second table specified (on the right side of the JOIN keyword).

N O T E You can use any comparison operator (<, <=, =, >=, >, or <>) in the JOIN clause to relate
the two tables. ■

Table 14.2   Records Returned Based on the Type of *JOIN* Used

JOIN Type Table	Records from Left Table	Records from Right Table
INNER	Only records with corresponding record in right table	Only records with corresponding record in left table
LEFT	All records	Only records with corresponding record in left table
RIGHT	Only records with corresponding record in right table	All records

To further understand these concepts, consider the sample database with its Customers and
Salesperson tables. In that database, you created a small information set in the tables consisting of ten customers and four salespeople. Two of the customers have no salesperson listed,
and one of the salespeople has no customers (he's a new guy!). You select the same fields with
each JOIN but specify an INNER JOIN, LEFT JOIN, and RIGHT JOIN (refer to Listing 14.7). Figure
14.4 shows the two base-data tables from which this listing is working. Figure 14.5 shows the
resulting recordsets for each of the JOIN operations.

Listing 14.7   Examples of the Three *JOIN* Types

```
'****************************
'Select using an INNER JOIN
'****************************
SELECT CS.Lastname, CS.Firstname, SL.Saleslast, SL.Salesfirst _
    FROM Customers AS CS, Salesmen AS SL,
    CS INNER JOIN SL ON CS.SalesID=SL.SalesID
'****************************
'Select using an LEFT JOIN
'****************************
SELECT CS.Lastname, CS.Firstname, SL.Saleslast, SL.Salesfirst _
    FROM Customers AS CS, Salesmen AS SL, _
    CS LEFT JOIN SL ON CS.SalesID=SL.SalesID
'****************************
'Select using an RIGHT JOIN
'****************************
SELECT CS.Lastname, CS.Firstname, SL.Saleslast, SL.Salesfirst _
    FROM Customers AS CS, Salesmen AS SL, _
    CS RIGHT JOIN SL ON CS.SalesID=SL.SalesID
```

FIG. 14.4

The base tables used
for the JOIN example.

Customer table

Salesperson table

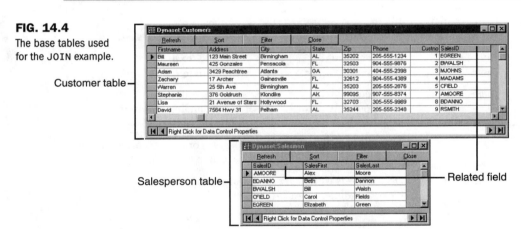

Related field

Note that in addition to returning the salesperson with no customers, the RIGHT JOIN returned all customer records for each of the other salespeople, not just a single record. This is because a RIGHT JOIN is designed to return all the records from the right table, even if they have no corresponding record in the left table.

Using the* WHERE *Clause   You can use the WHERE clause to relate two tables. The WHEREclause has the same effect as an INNER JOIN. Listing 14.8 shows the same INNER JOIN as Listing 14.7, this time using the WHERE clause instead of the INNER JOIN.

FIG. 14.5

Different records are returned with the different *JOIN* types.

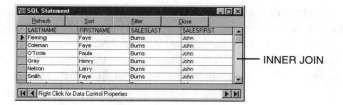

INNER JOIN

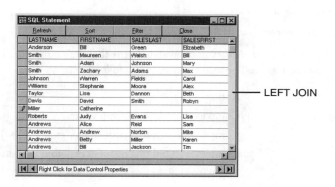

LEFT JOIN

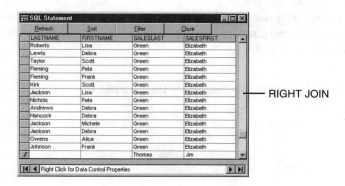

RIGHT JOIN

Listing 14.8 A *WHERE* Clause Performing the Same Function as an *INNER* JOIN

```
'****************************************
'Select using WHERE to relate two tables
'****************************************
SELECT CS.Lastname, CS.Firstname, SL.Saleslast, SL.Salesfirst _
    FROM Customers AS CS, Salesmen AS SL, _
    WHERE CS.SalesID=SL.SalesID
```

Part

II

Ch

14

Setting the Filter Criteria   One of the most powerful features of SQL commands is that you can control the range of records to be processed by specifying a filter condition. You can use many types of filters, such as Lastname = "Smith", Price < 1, or birthday between 5/1/94 and 5/31/94. Although the current discussion is specific to the use of filters in the SELECT command, the principles shown here also work with other SQL commands, such as DELETE and UPDATE.

Filter conditions in a SQL command are specified using the WHERE clause. The general format of the WHERE clause is as follows:

```
WHERE logical-expression
```

There are four types of *predicates* (logical statements that define the condition) that you can use with the WHERE clause. These are shown in the following table.

Predicate	Action
Comparison	Compares a field to a given value.
LIKE	Compares a field to a pattern (for example, A*).
IN	Compares a field to a list of acceptable values.
BETWEEN	Compares a field to a range of values.

Using the Comparison Predicate   As its name suggests, the *comparison predicate* is used to compare the values of two expressions. There are six comparison operators (the symbols that describe the comparison type) that you can use; the operators and their definitions are summarized in Table 14.3.

Table 14.3   Comparison Operators Used in the *WHERE* Clause

Operator	Definition
<	Less than
<=	Less than or equal to
=	Equal to
>=	Greater than or equal to
>	Greater than
<>	Not equal to

Here is the generic format of the comparison predicate:

```
expression1 comparison-operator expression2
```

For all comparisons, both expressions must be of the same type (for example, both must be numbers or both must be text strings). Several comparisons of different types are shown in Listing 14.9. The comparison values for strings and dates require special formatting.

Any strings used in a comparison must be enclosed in single quotes (for example, `'Smith'` or `'AL'`). Likewise, dates must be enclosed between pound signs (for example, #5/15/94#). The quotes and the pound signs tell the query engine the type of data that is being passed. Note that numbers do not need to be enclosed within special characters.

Listing 14.9   Comparison Operators Used with Many Types of Data

```
'*******************************************************
'Comparison of text data using customer table as source
'*******************************************************
SELECT * FROM Customers WHERE Lastname='Smith'
'*******************************************************
'Comparison of numeric data using Retail Items table
'*******************************************************
SELECT * FROM [Retail Items] WHERE Retail<2
'*******************************************
'Comparison of date data using Sales table
'*******************************************
SELECT * FROM Sales WHERE Date>#8/15/94#
```

Using the LIKE Predicate   With the LIKE predicate, you can compare an *expression* (that is, a field value) to a pattern. The LIKE predicate lets you make comparisons such as last names starting with *S*, titles containing *SQL*, or five-letter words starting with *M* and ending with *H*. You use the wild cards * and ? to create the patterns. The actual predicates for these comparisons would be `Lastname LIKE 'S*'`, `Titles LIKE '*SQL*'`, and `Word LIKE 'M???H'`, respectively.

The LIKE predicate is used exclusively for string comparisons. The format of the LIKE predicate is as follows:

```
expression LIKE pattern
```

The patterns defined for the LIKE predicate make use of wild-card matching and character-range lists. When you create a pattern, you can combine some of the wild cards and character lists to allow greater flexibility in the pattern definition. When used, character lists must meet three criteria:

- The list must be enclosed within square brackets.
- The first and last characters must be separated by a hyphen.
- The range of the characters must be defined in ascending order (for example, a–z, and not z–a).

In addition to using a character list to match a character in the list, you can precede the list with an exclamation point to indicate that you want to exclude the characters in the list. Table 14.4 shows the type of pattern matching you can perform with the LIKE predicate. Listing 14.10 shows the use of the LIKE predicate in several SELECT statements.

Part
II

Ch
14

Table 14.4   The *LIKE* Predicate Using a Variety of Pattern Matching

Wild Card	Used to Match	Example Pattern	Example Results
*	Multiple characters	S*	Smith, Sims, sheep
?	Single character	an?	and, ant, any
#	Single digit	3524#	35242, 35243
[list]	Single character in list	[c-f]	d, e, f
[!list]	Single character not in list	[!c-f]	a, b, g, h
combination	Specific to pattern	a?t*	art, antique, artist

Listing 14.10   Use the *LIKE* Predicate for Pattern-Matching

```
'***************************
'Multiple character wild card
'***************************
SELECT * FROM Customers WHERE Lastname LIKE 'S*'
'**************************
'Single character wild card
'**************************
SELECT * FROM Customers WHERE State LIKE '?L'
'**********************
'Character list matching
'**********************
SELECT * FROM Customers WHERE MID$(Lastname,1,1) LIKE '[a-f]'
```

Using the IN Predicate   The IN predicate lets you determine whether the expression is one of several values. Using the IN predicate, you can check state codes for customers to determine whether the customer's state matches a sales region. This example is shown in the following sample code:

```
SELECT * FROM Customers WHERE State IN ('AL', 'FL', 'GA')
```

Using the BETWEEN Predicate   The BETWEEN predicate lets you search for expressions with values within a range of values. You can use the BETWEEN predicate for string, numeric, or date expressions. The BETWEEN predicate performs an *inclusive search*, meaning that if the value is equal to one of the endpoints of the range, the record is included. You also can use the NOT operator to return records outside the range. The form of the BETWEEN predicate is as follows:

expression [NOT] BETWEEN *value1* AND *value2*

Listing 14.11 shows the use of the BETWEEN predicate in several scenarios.

Listing 14.11   Using the *BETWEEN* Predicate to Check an Expression Against a Range of Values

```
'*****************
'String comparison
'*****************
SELECT * FROM Customers WHERE Lastname BETWEEN 'M' AND 'W'
'******************
'Numeric comparison
'******************
SELECT * FROM [Retail Items] WHERE Retail BETWEEN 1 AND 2.5
'***************
'Date comparison
'***************
SELECT * FROM Sales WHERE Date BETWEEN #8/01/94# AND #8/10/94#
'**********************
'Use of the NOT operator
'**********************
SELECT * FROM Customers WHERE Lastname NOT BETWEEN 'M' AND 'W'
```

Combining Multiple Conditions   The WHERE clause can also accept multiple conditions so that you can specify filtering criteria on more than one field. Each individual condition of the multiple conditions is in the form of the conditions described in the preceding sections on using predicates. These individual conditions are then combined using the logical operators AND and OR. By using multiple-condition statements, you can find all the Smiths in the southeast, or you can find anyone whose first or last name is Scott. Listing 14.12 shows the statements for these examples. Figure 14.6 shows the recordset resulting from a query search for Scott.

Listing 14.12   Combining Multiple *WHERE* Conditions with *AND* or *OR*

```
'********************************
'Find all Smiths in the Southeast
'********************************
SELECT * FROM Customers WHERE Lastname = 'Smith' AND  _
    State IN ('AL', 'FL', 'GA')
'****************************************************
'Find all occurrences of Scott in first or last name
'****************************************************
SELECT * FROM Customers WHERE Lastname = 'Scott' _
    OR Firstname = 'Scott'
```

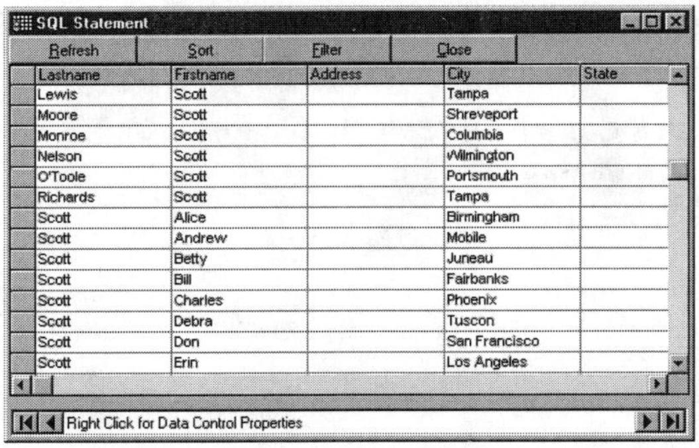

FIG. 14.6

You can use multiple conditions to enhance a WHERE clause.

Setting the Sort Conditions In addition to specifying the range of records to process, you also can use the SELECT statement to specify the order in which you want the records to appear in the output dynaset. The SELECT statement controls the order in which the records are processed or viewed. Sorting the records is done by using the ORDER BY clause of the SELECT statement.

You can specify the sort order with a single field or with multiple fields. If you use multiple fields, the individual fields must be separated by commas.

The default sort order for all fields is ascending (that is, A–Z, 0–9). You can change the sort order for any individual field by specifying the DESC keyword after the field name (the DESC keyword affects only the one field, not any other fields in the ORDER BY clause). Listing 14.13 shows several uses of the ORDER BY clause. Figure 14.7 shows the results of these SELECT statements.

N O T E When you're sorting records, the presence of an index for the sort field can significantly speed up the SQL query. ▪

Listing 14.13   Specifying the Sort Order of the Output Dynaset

```
'*****************
'Single field sort
'*****************
SELECT * FROM Customers ORDER BY Lastname
'********************
'Multiple field sort
'********************
SELECT * FROM Customers ORDER BY Lastname, Firstname
'*********************
'Descending order sort
'*********************
SELECT * FROM Customers ORDER BY Lastname DESC, Firstname
```

FIG. 14.7
The ORDER BY clause specifies the sort order of the dynaset.

Note that first names are out of order.

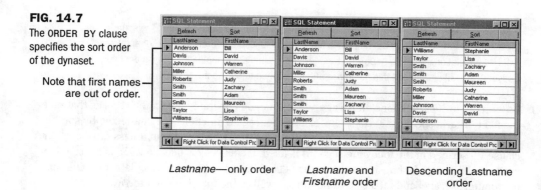

Lastname—only order   Lastname and   Descending Lastname
                Firstname order   order

Using Aggregate Functions   You can use the SELECT statement to perform calculations on the information in your tables by using the SQL *aggregate functions*. To perform the calculations, define them as a field in your SELECT statement, using the following syntax:

`function(expression)`

The expression can be a single field or a calculation based on one or more fields, such as Quantity * Price, or SQR(Datapoint). The Count function can also use the wild card * as the expression, because Count returns only the number of records. Table 14.5 shows the 11 aggregate functions available in Microsoft SQL.

Table 14.5   Aggregate Functions Provide Summary Information About Data in the Database

Function	Returns
Avg	The arithmetic average of the field for the records that meet the WHERE clause.
Count	The number of records that meet the WHERE clause.
Min	The minimum value of the field for the records that meet the WHERE clause.
Max	The maximum value of the field for the records that meet the WHERE clause.
Sum	The total value of the field for the records that meet the WHERE clause.
First	The value of the field for the first record in the recordset.
Last	The value of the field for the last record in the recordset.
StDev	The standard deviation of the values of the field for the records that meet the WHERE clause.
StDevP	The standard deviation of the values of the field for the records that meet the WHERE clause.
Var	The variance of the values of the field for the records that meet the WHERE clause.

Part

II

Ch

14

N O T E In Table 14.5, StDev and StDevP seem to perform the same function. The same is true of Var and VarP. The difference between the functions is that the StDevP and VarP evaluate populations whereas StDev and Var evaluate samples of populations. If you are into statistics, you will understand this difference and know when to use each. ◼

As with other SQL functions, these aggregate functions operate only on the records that meet the filter criteria specified in the WHERE clause. Aggregate functions are unaffected by sort order. Aggregate functions return a single value for the entire recordset unless the GROUP BY clause (described in the following section) is used. If GROUP BY is used, a value is returned for each record group. Listing 14.14 shows the SELECT statement used to calculate the minimum, maximum, average, and total sales amounts, as well as the total item volume from the Sales table in the sample case. Figure 14.8 shows the output from this query.

Listing 14.14 Using Aggregate Functions to Provide Summary Information

```
SELECT Min(SL.Quantity * RT.Retail) AS Minsls, _
    Max(SL.Quantity * RT.Retail) AS Maxsls, _
    Avg(SL.Quantity * RT.Retail) AS Avgsls, _
    Sum(SL.Quantity * RT.Retail) AS Totsls, _
    Sum(SL.Quantity) AS Totvol _
    FROM Sales AS SL, [Retail Items] AS RT _
    WHERE SL.[Item Code]=RT.[Item Code]
```

FIG. 14.8

The table shows the summary information from aggregate functions.

Creating Record Groups   Creating record groups lets you create a recordset that has only one record for each occurrence of the specified field. For example, if you group the Customers table by state, you have one output record for each state. This arrangement is especially useful when combined with the calculation functions described in the preceding sections. When groups are used in conjunction with aggregate functions, you can easily obtain summary data by state, salesperson, item code, or any other desired field.

Most of the time, you want to create groups based on a single field. You can, however, specify multiple fields in the GROUP BY clause. If you do, a record is returned for each unique combination of field values. You can use this technique to get sales data by salesperson and item code. Separate multiple fields in a GROUP BY clause with commas. Listing 14.15 shows an update of Listing 14.14, adding groups based on the salesperson ID. Figure 14.9 shows the results of the query.

Listing 14.15 Using the *GROUP BY* Clause to Obtain Summary Information for Record Groups

```
SELECT SL.SalesID, Min(SL.Quantity * RT.Retail) AS Minsls,  _
     Max(SL.Quantity * RT.Retail) AS Maxsls,  _
     Avg(SL.Quantity * RT.Retail) AS Avgsls,  _
     Sum(SL.Quantity * RT.Retail) AS Totsls,  _
     Sum(SL.Quantity) AS Totvol _
     FROM Sales AS SL, [Retail Items] AS RT _
     WHERE SL.[Item Code]=RT.[Item Code]  _
     GROUP BY SL.SalesID
```

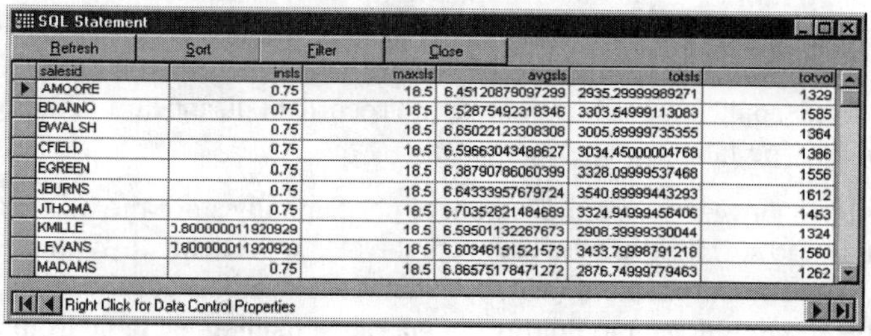
SQL Statement
Refresh
Sort
Filter
Close
salesid | insls | maxsls | avgsls | totsls | totvol
AMOORE | 0.75 | 18.5 | 6.45120879097299 | 2935.29999989271 | 1329
BDANNO | 0.75 | 18.5 | 6.52875492318346 | 3303.54999113083 | 1585
BWALSH | 0.75 | 18.5 | 6.65022123308308 | 3005.89999735355 | 1364
CFIELD | 0.75 | 18.5 | 6.59663043488627 | 3034.45000004768 | 1386
EGREEN | 0.75 | 18.5 | 6.38790786060399 | 3328.09999537468 | 1556
JBURNS | 0.75 | 18.5 | 6.64333957679724 | 3540.89999443293 | 1612
JTHOMA | 0.75 | 18.5 | 6.70352821484689 | 3324.94999456406 | 1453
KMILLE |).800000011920929 | 18.5 | 6.59501132267673 | 2908.39999330044 | 1324
LEVANS |).800000011920929 | 18.5 | 6.60346151521573 | 3433.79998791218 | 1560
MADAMS | 0.75 | 18.5 | 6.86575178471272 | 2876.74999779463 | 1262
Right Click for Data Control Properties

FIG. 14.9
Using GROUP BY creates a summary record for each defined group.

The GROUP BY clause also can include an optional HAVING clause. The HAVING clause works similarly to a WHERE clause but examines only the field values of the returned records. The HAVING clause determines which of the selected records to display; the WHERE clause determines which records to select from the base tables. You can use the HAVING clause to display only those salespeople with total sales exceeding $3,000 for the month. Listing 14.16 shows this example; Figure 14.10 shows the output from this listing.

Listing 14.16 The *HAVING* Clause Filters the Display of the Selected Group Records

```
SELECT SL.SalesID, Min(SL.Quantity * RT.Retail) AS Minsls,  _
     Max(SL.Quantity * RT.Retail) AS Maxsls,  _
     Avg(SL.Quantity * RT.Retail) AS Avgsls,  _
     Sum(SL.Quantity * RT.Retail) AS Totsls,  _
     Sum(SL.Quantity) AS Totvol _
     FROM Sales AS SL, [Retail Items] AS RT  _
     SL INNER JOIN RT ON SL.[Item Code]=RT.[Item Code]  _
     GROUP BY SL.SalesID _
     HAVING Sum(SL.Quantity * RT.Retail) > 3000
```

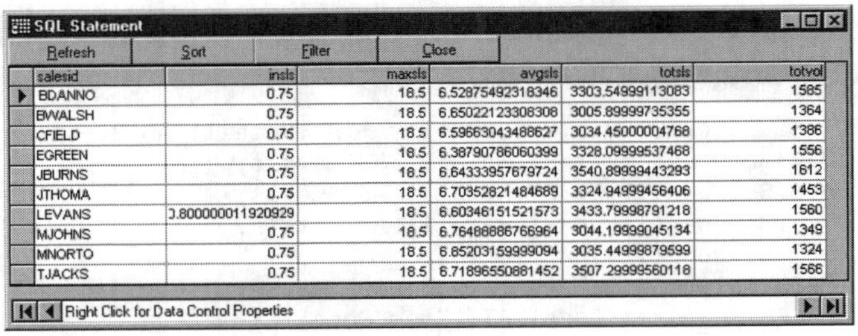
SQL Statement
Refresh
Sort
Filter
Close
salesid | insls | maxsls | avgsls | totsls | totvol
BDANNO | 0.75 | 18.5 | 6.52875492318346 | 3303.54999113083 | 1585
BWALSH | 0.75 | 18.5 | 6.65022123308308 | 3005.89999735355 | 1364
CFIELD | 0.75 | 18.5 | 6.59663043488627 | 3034.45000004768 | 1386
EGREEN | 0.75 | 18.5 | 6.38790786060399 | 3328.09999537468 | 1556
JBURNS | 0.75 | 18.5 | 6.64333957679724 | 3540.89999443293 | 1612
JTHOMA | 0.75 | 18.5 | 6.70352821484689 | 3324.94999456406 | 1453
LEVANS | 0.800000011920929 | 18.5 | 6.60346151521573 | 3433.79998791218 | 1560
MJOHNS | 0.75 | 18.5 | 6.76488886766964 | 3044.19999045134 | 1349
MNORTO | 0.75 | 18.5 | 6.85203159999094 | 3035.44999879599 | 1324
TJACKS | 0.75 | 18.5 | 6.71896550881452 | 3507.29999560118 | 1566
Right Click for Data Control Properties

FIG. 14.10
The HAVING clause limits the display of group records.

Creating a Table In all the examples of the SELECT statement used earlier in this chapter, the results of the query were output to a dynaset or a snapshot. Because these recordsets are only temporary, their contents exist only as long as the recordset is open. After a close method is used or the application is terminated, the recordset disappears (although any changes made to the underlying tables are permanent).

Sometimes, however, you might want to permanently store the information in the recordset for later use. Do so with the INTO clause of the SELECT statement. With the INTO clause, you specify the name of an output table (and, optionally, the database for the table) in which to store the results. You might want to do this to generate a mailing-list table from your customer list. This mailing-list table can then be accessed by your word processor to perform a mail-merge function or to print mailing labels. Listing 14.4, earlier in this chapter, generated such a list in a dynaset. Listing 14.17 shows the same basic SELECT statement as was used in Listing 14.4, but the new listing uses the INTO clause to store the information in a table.

Listing 14.17 Using the *INTO* Clause to Save Information to a New Table

```
SELECT CS.Firstname & ' ' & CS.Lastname, CS.Address, ZP.City, _
    ZP.State, CS.ZIP INTO Mailings FROM Customers AS CS, _
    Zipcode IN USZIPS AS ZP WHERE CS.Zip = ZP.Zip
```

CAUTION

The table name you specify should be that of a new table. If you specify the name of a table that already exists, that table is overwritten with the output of the SELECT statement.

Using Parameters So far in all of the clauses, you have seen specific values specified. For example, we specified "AL" for a state of 1.25 for a price. But what if you don't know in advance what value you want to use in comparison. Well, this is precisely what parameters are used for in a SQL statement. The parameter is to the SQL statement what a variable is to a program statement. The parameter is a placeholder whose value is assigned by your program before the SQL statement is executed.

To use a parameter in your SQL statement, you first have to specify the parameter in the PARAMETERS declaration part of the statement. The PARAMETERS declaration comes before the SELECT or other manipulative clause in the SQL statement. The declaration specifies both the name of the parameter and its data type. The PARAMETERS clause is separated from the rest of the SQL statement by a semicolon.

After you have declared the parameters, you simply place them in the manipulative part of the statement where you want to be able to substitute a value. The following code line shows how a parameter would be used in place of a state ID in a SQL statement.

```
PARAMETERS StateName String; SELECT * FROM Customers
    WHERE State = StateName
```

When you go to run the SQL statement in your program, each parameter is treated like a property of the QueryDef. Therefore, you need to assign a value to each parameter before you use the Execute method. The following code shows you how to set the property value for the SQL statement shown above and open a recordset.

```
Dim OldDb As Database, Qry As QueryDef, Rset As Recordset
Set OldDb = DBEngine.Workspaces(0).OpenDatabase("C:\Triton.Mdb")
Set Qry = OldDb.QueryDefs("StateSelect")
Qry!StateName = "AL"
Set Rset = Qry.OpenRecordset()
```

As you can see, using parameters makes it easy to store your queries in the database and still maintain the flexibility of being able to specify comparison values at runtime.

Using the *DELETE* Statement

The DELETE statement is used to create an *action query*. The DELETE statement's purpose is to delete specific records from a table. An action query does not return a group of records into a dynaset as SELECT queries do. Instead, action queries work like program *subroutines*. That is, an action query performs its functions and returns to the next statement in the calling program.

The syntax of the DELETE statement is as follows:

```
DELETE FROM tablename [WHERE clause]
```

The WHERE clause is an optional parameter. If it is omitted, all the records in the target table are deleted. You can use the WHERE clause to limit the deletions to only those records that meet specified criteria. In the WHERE clause, you can use any of the comparison predicates defined in the earlier section "Using the Comparison Predicate." Following is an example of the DELETE statement used to eliminate all customers who live in Florida:

```
DELETE FROM Customers WHERE State='FL'
```

> **CAUTION**
>
> After the DELETE statement is executed, the records are gone and can't be recovered. The only exception is if transaction processing is used. If you're using transaction processing, you can use a ROLLBACK statement to recover any deletions made since the last BEGINTRANS statement was issued.

Using the *INSERT* Statement

Like the DELETE statement, the INSERT statement is another action query. The INSERT statement is used in conjunction with the SELECT statement to add a group of records to a table. The syntax of the statement is as follows:

```
INSERT INTO tablename SELECT rest-of-select-statement
```

You build the SELECT portion of the statement exactly as explained in the first part of this chapter, in the section "Using *SELECT* Statements." The purpose of the SELECT portion of the statement is to define the records to be added to the table. The INSERT statement defines the action of adding the records and specifies the table that is to receive the records.

One use of the INSERT statement is to update tables created with the SELECT INTO statement. Suppose that you're keeping a church directory. When you first create the directory, you create a mailing list for the current member list. Each month, as new members are added, you either can rerun the SELECT INTO query and re-create the table, or you can run the INSERT INTO query and add only the new members to the existing mailing list. Listing 14.18 shows the creation of the original mailing list and the use of the INSERT INTO query to update the list.

Listing 14.18   Using the *INSERT INTO* Statement to Add a Group of Records to a Table

```
'*******************************
'Create a new mailing list table
'*******************************
SELECT CS.Firstname & ' ' & CS.Lastname, CS.Address, ZP.City, _
    ZP.State, CS.ZIP INTO Mailings FROM Members AS CS, _
    Zipcode IN USZIPS AS ZP WHERE CS.Zip = ZP.Zip
'*********************************
'Update the mailing list each month
'*********************************
INSERT INTO Mailings SELECT CS.Firstname & ' ' & CS.Lastname, _
    CS.Address, ZP.City, ZP.State, CS.ZIP _
    FROM Customers AS CS, Zipcode IN USZIPS AS ZP    _
    WHERE CS.Zip = ZP.Zip AND CS.Memdate>Lastmonth
```

Using the *UPDATE* Statement

The UPDATE statement is another action query. It is used to change the values of specific fields in a table. The syntax of the UPDATE statement is as follows:

```
UPDATE tablename SET field = newvalue [WHERE clause]
```

You can update multiple fields in a table at one time by listing multiple field = newvalue clauses, separated by commas. The inclusion of the WHERE clause is optional. If it is excluded, all records in the table are changed.

Listing 14.19 shows two examples of the UPDATE statement. The first example changes the salesperson ID for a group of customers, as happens when a salesperson leaves the company and his or her accounts are transferred to someone else. The second example changes the retail price of all retail sales items, as can be necessary to cover increased operating costs.

Listing 14.19   Using the *UPDATE* Statement to Change Field Values for Many Records at Once

```
'***********************************************
'Change the SalesID for a group of customers
'***********************************************
UPDATE Customers SET SalesID = 'EGREEN' WHERE SalesID='JBURNS'
'*****************************************************
'Increase the retail price of all items by five percent
'*****************************************************
UPDATE [Retail Items] SET Retail = Retail * 1.05
```

Using Data-Definition-Language Statements

Data-Definition-Language Statements (DDLs) let you create, modify, and delete tables and indexes in a database with a single statement. For many situations, these statements take the place of the Data-Access-Object methods described in Chapter 11, "Designing and Creating a Database." However, there are some limitations to using the DDL statements. The main limitation is that these statements are supported only for Jet databases (remember that Data-Access-Objects can be used for any database accessed with the Jet engine). The other limitation of DDL statements is that they support only a small subset of the properties of the table, field, and index objects. If you need to specify properties outside of this subset, you must use the methods described in Chapter 11.

Defining Tables with DDL Statements

Three DDL statements are used to define tables in a database:

- ■ **CREATE TABLE**   Defines a new table in a database
- ■ **ALTER TABLE**   Changes the structure of the table
- ■ **DROP TABLE**   Deletes a table from the database

Creating a Table with DDL statements   To create a table with the DDL statements, you create a SQL statement containing the name of the table and the names, types, and sizes of each field in the table. The following code shows how to create the Orders table of the sample case.

```
CREATE TABLE Orders (Orderno LONG, Custno LONG, SalesID TEXT (6), _
    OrderDate DATE, Totcost SINGLE)
```

Notice that when you specify the table name and field names, you do not have to enclose the names in quotation marks. However, if you want to specify a name with a space in it, you must enclose the name in square brackets (for example, [Last name]).

When you create a table, you can specify only the field names, types, and sizes. You can't specify optional parameters such as default values, validation rules, or validation error messages. Even with this limitation, the DDL CREATE TABLE statement is a powerful tool that you can use to create many of the tables in a database.

Modifying a Table   By using the ALTER TABLE statement, you can add a field to an existing table or delete a field from the table. When adding a field, you must specify the name, type, and (when applicable) the size of the field. You add a field using the ADD COLUMN clause of the ALTER TABLE statement. To delete a field, you only need to specify the field name and use the DROP COLUMN clause of the statement. As with other database-modification methods, you can't delete a field used in an index or a relation. Listing 14.20 shows how to add and then delete a field from the Orders table, created in the preceding section.

Listing 14.20   Using the *ALTER TABLE* Statement to Add or Delete a Field from a Table

```
'*************************************************
'Add a shipping charges field to the "Orders" table
'*************************************************
ALTER TABLE Orders ADD COLUMN Shipping SINGLE
'********************************
'Delete the shipping charges field
'********************************
ALTER TABLE Orders DROP COLUMN Shipping
```

Deleting a Table   You can delete a table from a database using the DROP TABLE statement. The following simple piece of code shows how to get rid of the Orders table. Use caution when deleting a table; the table and all its data are gone forever once the command has been executed.

```
DROP TABLE Orders
```

Defining Indexes with DDL Statements

You can use two DDL statements with indexes:

- **CREATE INDEX**   Defines a new index for a table
- **DROP INDEX**   Deletes an index from a table

Creating an Index   You can create a single-field or multi-field index with the CREATE INDEX statement. To create the index, you must give the name of the index, the name of the table for the index, and at least one field to be included in the index. You can specify ascending or descending order for each field. You also can specify that the index is a primary index for the table. Listing 14.21 shows how to create a primary index on customer number and a two-field index with the sort orders specified. These indexes are set up for the Customers table of the sample case.

Listing 14.21   Create Several Types of Indexes with the *CREATE INDEX* Statement

```
'*******************************************
'Create a primary index on customer number
'*******************************************
CREATE INDEX Custno ON Customers (Custno) WITH PRIMARY
'****************************************************************
'Create a two field index with ascending order on Lastname and
'    descending order on Firstname.
'****************************************************************
CREATE INDEX Name2 ON Customers (Lastname ASC, Firstname DESC)
```

Deleting an Index   Getting rid of an index is just as easy as creating one. To delete an index from a table, use the DROP INDEX statement as shown in the following example. These statements delete the two indexes created in Listing 14.21. Notice that you must specify the table name for the index that you want to delete.

```
DROP INDEX Custno ON Customers
DROP INDEX Name2 ON Customers
```

Using SQL

As stated at the beginning of the chapter, you can't place a SQL statement by itself in a program. It must be part of another function. This part of the chapter describes the various methods used to implement the SQL statements you can create.

Executing an Action Query

The Jet engine provides an execute method as part of the database object. The execute method tells the engine to process the SQL query against the database. An action query can be executed by specifying the SQL statement as part of the execute method for a database. An action query can also be used to create a QueryDef. Then the query can be executed on its own. Listing 14.22 shows how both of these methods are used to execute the same SQL statement.

Part
II

Ch

14

Listing 14.22   Run SQL Statements with the Database*Execute* or Query*Execute* Method

```
Dim OldDb AS Database, NewQry AS QueryDef
'*******************************************************
'Define the SQL statement and assign it to a variable
'*******************************************************
SQLstate = "UPDATE Customers SET SalesID = 'EGREEN'"
SQLstate = SQLstate + " WHERE SalesID='JBURNS'"
'*******************************************
'Use the database execute to run the query
'*******************************************
OldDb.Execute SQLstate
'*******************************************
'Create a QueryDef from the SQL statement
'*******************************************
Set NewQry = OldDb.CreateQueryDef("Change Sales", SQLstate)
'*******************************************
'Use the query execute to run the query
'*******************************************
NewQry.Execute
'*******************************************************
'Run the named query with the database execute method
'*******************************************************
OldDb.Execute "Change Sales"
```

Creating a *QueryDef*

Creating a QueryDef lets you name your query and store it in the database with your tables. You can create either an action query or a *retrieval query* (one that uses the SELECT statement). After the query is created, you can call it by name for execution (shown in a listing in the previous section, "Executing an Action Query") or for creation of a dynaset (as described in the following section). Listing 14.22 showed how to create a QueryDef called Change Sales that is used to update the salesperson ID for a group of customers.

Creating Dynasets and Snapshots

To use the SELECT statement to retrieve records and store them in a dynaset or snapshot, you must use the SELECT statement in conjunction with the OpenRecordset method. Using the OpenRecordset method, you specify the type of recordset with the options parameter. With this method, you either can use the SELECT statement directly or use the name of a retrieval query that you have previously defined. Listing 14.23 shows these two methods of retrieving records.

Listing 14.23   Using the Create Methods to Retrieve the Records Defined by a *SELECT* Statement

```
Dim OldDb As Database, NewQry As QueryDef, NewDyn As Recordset
Dim NewSnap As Recordset
'*********************************************************
```

```
'Define the SELECT statement and store it to a variable
'*********************************************************
SQLstate = "SELECT RI.[Item Description], SL.Quantity,"
SQLstate = SQLstate & " RI.Retail, _
     SL.Quantity * RI.Retail AS Subtot"
SQLstate = SQLstate & "FROM [Retail Items] AS RI, Sales AS SL"
SQLstate = SQLstate & "WHERE SL.[Item Code]=RI.[Item Code]"
'************************
'Create dynaset directly
'************************
Set NewDyn = OldDb.OpenRecordset(SQLstate, dbOpenDynaset)
'***************
'Create QueryDef
'***************
Set NewQry = OldDb.CreateQueryDef("Get Subtotals", SQLstate)
NewQry.Close
'****************************
'Create snapshot from querydef
'****************************
Set NewSnap = OldDb.OpenRecordset("Get Subtotals", dbOpenSnapshot)
```

You have seen how SELECT statements are used to create dynasets and snapshots. But, the comparison part of a WHERE clause and the sort list of an ORDER BY clause also can be used to set dynaset properties. The filter property of a dynaset is a WHERE statement without the WHERE keyword. When setting the filter property, you can use all the predicates described in the section, "Using the WHERE Clause," earlier in this chapter. In a like manner, the sort property of a dynaset is an ORDER BY clause without the ORDER BY keywords.

Using SQL Statements with the Data Control

The data control uses the RecordSource property to create a recordset when the control is loaded. The RecordSource may be a table, a SELECT statement, or a predefined query. Therefore, the entire discussion on the SELECT statement (in the section "Using SELECT statements") applies to the creation of the recordset used with a data control.

N O T E   When you specify a table name for the RecordSource property, Visual Basic uses the name to create a SELECT statement such as this:

SELECT * FROM *table* ■

Creating SQL Statements

When you create and test your SQL statements, you can program them directly into your code and run the code to see whether they work. This process can be very time-consuming and frustrating, especially for complex statements. There are, however, three easier ways of developing SQL statements that might be available to you:

■ The Visual Data Manager Add-in that comes with Visual Basic

■ Microsoft Access (if you have a copy)

N O T E Users of Microsoft Excel or Microsoft Office also have access to Microsoft Query, the tool in Access. ■

The Visual Data Manager and Access both have query builders that can help you create SQL queries. They provide dialog boxes for selecting the fields to include, and they help you with the various clauses. When you have finished testing a query with either application, you can store the query as a QueryDef in the database. This query can then be executed by name from your program. As an alternative, you can copy the code from the query builder into your program, using standard cut-and-paste operations.

Using the Visual Data Manager

The Visual Data Manager is a Visual Basic Add-in that allows you to create and modify databases for your Visual Basic programs. The Visual Data Manager also has a window which allows you to enter and debug SQL queries. And if you don't want to try to create the query yourself, VDM has a query builder that makes it easy for you to create queries by making choices in the builder.

N O T E If you want to learn about the inner workings of the Visual Data Manager, it is one of the sample projects installed with Visual Basic. The project file is VISDATA.VBP and is found in the VISDATA folder of the Samples folder. ■

To start the Visual Data Manager, simply select the Visual Data Manager item from the Add-Ins menu of Visual Basic. After starting the program, open the File menu and select the Open Database item, then select the type of database to open from the submenu. You will be presented with a dialog that allows you to open a database. After the database is opened, a list of the tables and queries in the database will appear in the left-hand window of the application. The Visual Data Manager with the Triton.Mdb database open is shown in Figure 14.11.

To develop and test SQL statements, first enter the statement in the text box of the SQL dialog box (the one on the right of Figure 14.11). When you're ready to test the statement, click the Execute SQL button. If you're developing a retrieval query, a dynaset is created and the results are displayed in a data entry form (or a grid) if the statement has no errors. If you're developing an action query, a message box appears, telling you that the execution of the query is complete (again, assuming that the statement is correct). If you have an error in your statement, a message box appears informing you of the error.

FIG. 14.11

You can use the Visual Data Manager Add-In to develop SQL queries.

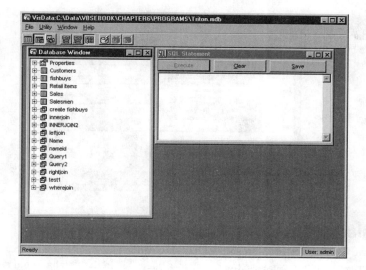

The Visual Data Manager Add-In also includes a Query Builder. You can access the Query Builder (see Figure 14.12) by choosing Query Builder from the Utilities menu of the Visual Data Manager. To create a query with the Query Builder, follow these steps:

1. Select the tables to include from the Tables list.
2. Select the fields to include from the Fields to Show list.
3. Set the WHERE clause (if any) using the Field Name, Operator, and Value drop-down lists at the top of the dialog box.
4. Set the table JOIN conditions (if any) by clicking the Set Table Joins command button.
5. Set a single-field ORDER BY clause (if any) by selecting the field from the Order By Field drop-down box and selecting either the Asc or Desc option.
6. Set a single GROUP BY field (if any) by selecting the field from the Group By Field drop-down box.

After you have set the Query Builder parameters, you can run the query, display the SQL statement, or copy the query to the SQL statement window. The Query Builder provides an easy way to become familiar with constructing SELECT queries.

When you have developed the query to your satisfaction (either with the Query Builder or by typing the statement directly), you can save the query as a QueryDef in your database. In your Visual Basic code, you then can reference the name of the query you created. Alternatively, you can copy the query from Visual Data Manager and paste it into your application code.

Part

II

Ch

14

FIG. 14.12
The Query Builder
makes it easy to build
SQL statements.

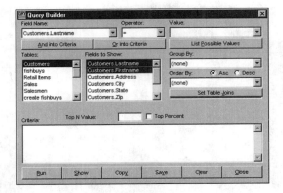

Using Microsoft Access

If you have a copy of Microsoft Access, you can use its query builder to graphically construct queries. You then can save the query as a `QueryDef` in the database and reference the query name in your Visual Basic code.

Optimizing SQL Performance

Developers always want to get the best possible performance from every aspect of their applications. Wanting high performance out of SQL queries is no exception. Fortunately, there are several methods you can use to optimize the performance of your SQL queries.

Using Indexes

The Microsoft Jet database engine uses an optimization technology called Rushmore. Under certain conditions, Rushmore uses available indexes to try to speed up queries. To take maximum advantage of this arrangement, you can create an index on each of the fields you typically use in a `WHERE` clause or a `JOIN` condition. This is particularly true of key fields used to relate tables (for example, the `Custno` and `SalesID` fields in the sample database). An index also works better with comparison operators than with the other types of `WHERE` conditions, such as `LIKE` or `IN`.

> **N O T E**   Only certain types of queries are optimizable by Rushmore. For a query to use Rushmore
> optimization, the `WHERE` condition must use an indexed field. In addition, if you use the
> `LIKE` operator, the expression should begin with a character, not a wild card. Rushmore works with Jet
> databases and FoxPro and dBASE tables. Rushmore does not work with ODBC databases. ▪

Compiling Queries

Compiling a query refers to creating a `QueryDef` and storing it in the database. If the query already exists in the database, the command parser does not have to generate the query each time it is run, and this increases execution speed. If you have a query that is frequently used, create a `QueryDef` for it.

Keeping Queries Simple

When you're working with a lot of data from a large number of tables, the SQL statements can become quite complex. Complex statements are much slower to execute than simple ones. Also, if you have a number of conditions in `WHERE` clauses, this increases complexity and slows execution time.

Keep statements as simple as possible. If you have a complex statement, consider breaking it into multiple smaller operations. For example, if you have a complex `JOIN` of three tables, you may be able to use the `SELECT INTO` statement to create a temporary table from two of the three and then use a second `SELECT` statement to perform the final `JOIN`. There are no hard-and-fast rules for how many tables are too many or how many conditions make a statement too complex. If you're having performance problems, try some different ideas and find the one that works best.

Another way to keep things simple is to try to avoid pattern-matching in a `WHERE` clause. Because pattern-matching does not deal with discrete values, pattern-matching is hard to optimize. In addition, patterns that use wild cards for the first character are much slower than those that specifically define that character. For example, if you're looking for books about SQL, finding ones with *SQL* anywhere in the title (`pattern = "*SQL*"`) requires looking at every title in the table. On the other hand, looking for titles that start with *SQL* (`pattern = "SQL*"`) lets you skip over most records. If you had a Title index, the search would go directly to the first book on SQL.

Passing SQL Statements to Other Database Engines

Visual Basic has the capability of passing a SQL statement through to an ODBC database server such as SQL Server. When you pass a statement through, the Jet engine does not try to do any processing of the query, but it sends the query to the server to be processed. Remember, however, that the SQL statement must conform to the SQL syntax of the host database.

To use the pass-through capability, set the options parameter in the `OpenRecordset` or the execute methods to the value of the `dbSQLPassThrough` constant.

 N O T E The project file, SQLDEMO.VBP, on the book's Web site contains many of the listings used in this chapter. Each listing is assigned to a command button. Choosing the command button creates a dynaset using the SQL statement in the listing and displays the results in a data-bound grid. The form containing the grid also has a text box that shows the SQL statement. ■

Part

II

Ch

14

From Here...

This chapter has taught you the basics of using SQL in your database program. You have seen how to select records and how to limit the selection using the WHERE clause. You also have seen how SQL statements can be used to modify the structure of a database and how to use aggregate functions to obtain summary information.

To see how SQL statements are used in programs and with the data control, refer to the following chapters:

- Chapter 11, " Designing and Creating a Database," explains how to write data-access programs.
- Chapter 10, "Applications at Warp Speed," and Chapter 12, " Doing More with Bound Controls," explain how to use the data control.

CHAPTER 15

Multi-User Programming

In preceding chapters, you learned several aspects of database programming, particularly how to develop an application that would be used by a single user on a stand-alone PC. However, many of today's database applications must be written for a network environment, where multiple users will be reading, modifying, deleting, and adding to the data in the database. This type of application presents an additional set of challenges for you as the database developer.

Because the database replication features added in Jet 3.0 are also a form of multi-user database access, this chapter looks at the special considerations involved in database replication. The main considerations involved in multi-user program development are database access, database security, data currency, record-locking to prevent simultaneous update attempts, and application performance.

Controlling the access of users to the database

For many programs, you want users to only be able to access certain parts.

Using Jet engine security features to keep users from accessing certain data

Jet has built-in security features.

Making sure that the data is current

Make sure that all users are accessing current information.

Using locking to keep one user from changing a record while another user is using it

Record locking schemes keep multiple users from changing the same record at the same time.

Maintaining application performance with multiple users

Many applications slow down when they are distributed across a network.

Dealing with database errors

Since database errors can occur, you need to know what they are so you can deal with them.

Replicating database and synchronizing multiple database copies

Using replication places the burden of keeping multiple copies of the data on the database engine.

Even if you don't develop applications for a network environment, you still need to be aware of some multi-user considerations. In Windows or any other multitasking environment, two programs on the same machine can try to access the same data. As an example, consider a PC monitoring a manufacturing process. One program can receive the process data from instruments and store the data in a database. Another program can then generate reports on the data or modify erroneous or abnormal data points. Although the same user may run both programs on the same machine, the two programs appear to the database to be multiple users of the data.

Determining the multiuser needs of the application is part of the design process. And, as with other aspects of programming, a good design helps tremendously in producing a good and efficient application. ■

Controlling Data Access

Controlling data access involves placing restrictions on part or all of a database. Data access restrictions can be put in place as either user restrictions or function restrictions.

You need user restrictions when you want to prevent certain people (or, as a corollary, to allow only certain people) from looking at sensitive information. An example is a payroll system, in which most people can view the names of employees, but only a select few can see or modify the actual pay information. These restrictions are usually handled through user IDs and passwords, and are the basis of data security.

Function restrictions, on the other hand, place limits on specific parts of a program, regardless of who the user is. An example is opening a price table in read-only mode in an order-entry system. You add function restrictions so that a user cannot inadvertently change the price of an item while processing an order.

You can handle the restrictions in an application in two ways: using programmatic controls or using database engine controls. A programmatic control is one that you put into the application itself. Engine-level controls restrict any program trying to access the information in the database.

Using a Database Exclusively

The most restrictive limit that you can place on a database is to open it exclusively. This limit prevents any other user or program from gaining access to any information in the database while it is in use. Because this method is so restrictive, you should use it only for operations that affect the entire database. These operations include the following:

- Compacting a database
- Updating entire tables (for example, using the UPDATE query)
- Changing the structure of the database by adding or deleting tables, fields, or indexes
- Handling special user needs, such as posting accounting information

Within a program, you can open a database exclusively using the options portion of the OpenDatabase functions, as shown in the following code:

```
Dim OldDb As Database, OldWs As Workspace
Set OldDb = OldWs.OpenDatabase("C:\Members.Mdb,True,False")
```

If the database is not in use, the database is opened, and no one else can access it until it is closed. If the database is in use, an error is returned. (Handling errors is discussed later in this chapter in the section, "Handling Errors and Conflicts.")

Denying Table Access to Others

A less restrictive form of locking part of a database is to deny other users or programs access to the table being used by your program function. You can do so by using the options of the OpenRecordset method to deny read or write access to the information with which you will be working. Similarly, you can deny write access to the information in a dynaset by using the options of the OpenRecordset method.

> **CAUTION**
>
> When you use the Deny options on a recordset, it locks out other users from the base tables used to create the dynaset.

You should use these options, as with exclusive access, only for administrative functions, when you don't want others viewing or updating any of the table's information during the process.

Using the Deny Read Option (*dbDenyRead*)   The dbDenyRead option for the OpenRecordset method prevents other users from looking at the data in the affected table until you close the table. You use this option if you need to update information in the entire table, such as a global price increase. The following code shows the use of this option:

```
Dim OldTbl As Recordset
lopt = dbDenyRead
Set OldTbl = OldDb.OpenRecordset("Retail Items", _
dbOpenTable, lopt)
```

> **N O T E**   The dbDenyRead option is available only for table type recordsets. You cannot use it with dynasets or snapshots. ■

Using the Deny Write Option (*dbDenyWrite*)   The dbDenyWrite option used in the OpenRecordset method also restricts other users' access to information. In this case, however, the users can view but not update information in the affected table or tables. Again, other users' access is restricted only until you close the table or dynaset. You might use the dbDenyWrite option if you're inserting new records into a table but not making changes to existing records. The dbDenyWrite option is available for both table and dynaset type recordsets. Listing 15.1 shows the use of the dbDenyWrite option for the two functions.

Listing 15.1   Use *dbDenyWrite* to Prevent Others from Updating Tables While You Are Working with Them

```
Dim OldTbl As Recordset, NewDyn As Recordset
lopt = dbDenyWrite
'*****************************************
' Open a table with the dbDenyWrite option.
'*****************************************
Set OldTbl = OldDb.OpenRecordset("Retail Items",dbOpenTable,lopt)
'*****************************************
' Create a dynaset with the dbDenyWrite option.
'*****************************************

lopt = dbDenyWrite
SQLSel = "Select * From Sales"
Set NewDyn = OldDb.OpenRecordset(SQLSel, dbOpenDynaset, lopt)
```

Using Read-Only Tables

Using the Deny options does restrict other users' access to information in the database, but only if they open a table while you are using it with one of the options in effect. Often you may have functions in your applications that have data you don't want the users to be able to modify. You may also have some tables that you want only certain people to modify. In these cases, you can open a table or dynaset as a read-only recordset, or you can use a snapshot.

Using Lookup Tables   One example of a read-only table is a lookup table. A *lookup table* contains reference information that is necessary for the users to see but that the users do not need to change. For instance, your application might use a ZIP code table for a mailing list application or a price table for an order-entry system. In either of these cases, you open the table in read-only mode using the options shown in Listing 15.2. Unlike the Deny options, the read-only option does not restrict other users' access to the information.

Listing 15.2   Use the Read-Only Option to Prevent Users from Modifying Data

```
Dim OldTbl As Recordset
lopt = dbReadOnly
Set OldTbl = OldDb.OpenRecordset("Zip Code", dbOpenTable, lopt)
```

Using Snapshots   Another way to restrict a program function to read-only is to use a snapshot for the recordset. Snapshots are always read-only. You can use a snapshot when data in the base tables is not being changed frequently by others or when a point-in-time look at the data is sufficient. Snapshots are usually used for reporting functions. An advantage to using snapshots is that they are stored in memory. Therefore, some operations using snapshots are faster than the same operations using tables or dynasets. However, because of the memory requirements for a snapshot and the time that it takes to load the data into memory, snapshots are best used for queries that return fewer than 200 records.

Restricting Specific Users   Finally, you may have occasion to want to restrict certain users to read-only access, no matter what program functions they are performing. You can do so only through the Jet security system. These security features are described later in this chapter in the section "Jet Security Features."

Understanding Record-Locking Schemes

The features described in the preceding section place restrictions on an entire table or even the entire database. These features are useful in multi-user programming but are often too restrictive for some aspects of an application. One of the biggest considerations in multi-user programming is assuring that a record is not in use by another user at the same time that you are trying to update it. You do so through the use of record locks. A *record lock* temporarily limits the access of other users to a specific record or group of records.

In a typical application, a record lock is set while a user updates the data in the record and then is released after the update is completed. As the developer, you must take into account the following considerations in the use of record locks:

- What to do if the record cannot be locked (for example, if another user is accessing the record)
- How to prevent a user from keeping a record locked for too long
- Whether to lock the record when the user first accesses it or only when the changes are being written to the database

How you handle these considerations has an impact on many aspects of the application development. Therefore, you should address these issues as much as possible in the design phase of the application.

Page-Locking Versus Record-Locking

The Jet engine does not support true record-locking. In record-locking, only the individual record currently being accessed by the user is locked. Instead, Jet uses a page-locking scheme. Jet reads data in pages of 2K (2,048 bytes). When it places a lock on a record, it locks the entire page containing the record.

In this locking scheme, multiple records are locked each time a lock is issued. The number of records locked depends on the size of each record. For example, each record in the customer table of the sample database is 230 bytes long. Nine records, therefore, are locked each time. On the other hand, the sales table has records that are only 30 bytes long, so each record lock affects 68 records.

When a page is locked by one user, another user cannot modify any records on that page (although the second user can read the records), although the first user is working with only one of the records. This aspect of page-locking requires you to be even more careful in the application of record locks because it increases the chances of a conflict between users.

Visual Basic has no commands to specifically request a record lock. Instead, the record locks are automatically created and released when the Add, Edit, and Update methods are used. Visual Basic supports two locking methods: pessimistic and optimistic.

Pessimistic Locking

Pessimistic locking locks the page containing a record as soon as the Edit method is used on that record. The lock on the page is released when the Update method is used and the data is written to the file. The advantage of this method is that it prevents other users from changing the data in a record while one user is editing it. The disadvantage is that it keeps the record locked for a longer period of time. In the worst case, a user could open a record for editing, place a lock on it, and then head out to lunch. This lock could keep other users from editing that record, or any others on the same page, for a long time.

N O T E To prevent locks from being held too long, you can put a timer in your code that releases the record after a specified period of inactivity. You would do this by placing code in the Timer event of the Timer control. This code would use the Idle method of the database engine as shown in the following line of code: DBEngine.Idle dbFreeLocks. ■

Optimistic Locking

Optimistic locking locks the page containing a record only when the Update method is invoked. The lock on the page is immediately released when the update operation is completed. The advantage of optimistic locking is that the lock is on the page for only a short period of time, reducing the chance that another user may try to access the same data page while the lock is in place. The disadvantage is that another user can change the data in the record between the time the Edit and Update methods are used. If the data has changed in that time period, VB issues an error message.

Which Locking Method to Use and When

For most database applications, optimistic locking is the better choice of the two methods. The probability that someone else will change or delete the record you are working on is less than the probability that someone will try to access a record on the page that you have locked. If, however, you have an application in which many users are accessing and editing records simultaneously, you may want to use pessimistic locking to ensure that the record is not changed while you are performing your edits. In this case, you should put some method in place to limit the time that the record is locked.

Pessimistic locking is the default method used by Visual Basic. To set the method of record-locking, you must set the LockEdits property of the table or dynaset with which you are working. Setting the property to True gives you pessimistic locking. Setting the property to False yields optimistic locking. Listing 15.3 shows how to set the LockEdits property for pessimistic and optimistic locking, respectively.

Listing 15.3   Set the Recordset's *LockEdits* Property to Choose the Record Locking Method

```
Dim OldTbl As Recordset
'****************************************
'Set the locking method to pessimistic
'****************************************
OldTbl.LockEdits = True
'****************************************
'Set the locking method to optimistic
'****************************************
OldTbl.LockEdits = False
```

Releasing Locks

As I stated previously, the record locks are released automatically when the Update method has completed. However, releasing record locks is a background process, and sometimes other activities are occurring so rapidly that the database does not have time to catch up. If you are developing a data-entry-intensive program, you may need to pause the processing in the application momentarily. You can do so by using the Idle method of the database engine.

The Idle method pauses the application and allows the database engine to catch up on its housekeeping work. The following line shows the syntax of the Idle method:

```
DBEngine.Idle dbFreeLocks
```

Using the Data Control

Because the data control uses tables and/or dynasets (the default) as its record source, the same locking schemes mentioned previously are used with the data control. Pessimistic locking is the default; therefore, as each record is accessed, the data control automatically performs the Edit method, which in turn automatically locks the record's page. When you move from one record to another, the lock on the current record is released by the Update method, and a lock is placed on the next record by the Edit method. In a multi-user system in which you want to use optimistic locking, you need to change the locking scheme of the data control. You do so by adding a LockEdits statement, as shown in Listing 15.3, to the Activate event of the form containing the data control.

N O T E   You must be careful when using transactions in a multi-user environment. Any record locks that are set by the Edit or Update method are not released until the transaction is committed or rolled back. Therefore, keeping transactions as short as possible is best so that you can avoid having a large number of records locked for a long period of time. In addition, you should be careful when using cascaded updates or deletes because they create more transactions and therefore more locks. ■

Exploring Jet Security Features

Another consideration of multi-user database programming is database security. Because a network environment may allow other people access to your database file, you may want to use methods to prevent them from viewing specific information in your database, or possibly prevent them from viewing any of the information.

The Jet engine provides a database security model based on user IDs and passwords. In this model, you can assign to individual users or groups of users permissions to the entire database or any parts of the database. As each user is added to the security file, you must assign him or her to one or more user groups. That user then inherits the permissions of that group. In addition, you can assign other permissions to the user.

If you're working with a secured database, you must perform the following three steps to gain access to the database from your VB program:

■ Create an INI file for your program that tells the program the name of the system database.

■ Run the IniPath method of the database engine to tell the program where the INI file is located. (Note that, for 32-bit operating systems, the information is in the Registry, not an INI file.)

■ Use the CreateWorkspace method with the workspace name, user ID, and user password specified to create a workspace to contain the database.

The syntax for each of these statements is shown in Listing 15.4.

Listing 15.4   To Gain Access to a Secured Database, You Must Specify the Location of the System Database and Include the User ID and Password in Your *CreateWorkspace* Method

```
'*********************************************
'Statements to be included in the INI file.
'*********************************************
[Options]
SystemDB=C:\VB4\test1.mda
'*********************************************
'Set the location of the application INI file
'*********************************************
DBEngine.IniPath = "C:\VB4\TEST1.INI"
'****************************
'Set the user ID and password
'****************************
DBEngine.CreateWorkspace ("WORKNAME", "MIKEMCKE", "BESTGUESS")
```

Database Permissions

Within the Jet security system, you can set two database-level permissions: Run/Open and Open Exclusive. The Run/Open permission is required for anyone who needs access to the database. Without this permission, a user cannot open a database for any function. With the Open Exclusive permission, a user can open the database exclusively. You should give this permission only to administrative users. Otherwise, another user of an application may inadvertently lock the entire database.

Table Permissions

Although database permissions affect the entire database (and every table in it), you often need finer control over the access of users to individual tables. Using the Jet engine, you can set table-level permissions for any table in a database. As with the database permissions, the table permissions can be assigned to individual users or groups of users. The following seven table-level permissions are available with the Jet engine:

- Read design: Enables the user to view the structure of the table.
- Modify design: Enables the user to change the structure of the table.
- Administer: Gives the user full control over the table.
- Read data: Enables the user to read information from the table but not to make any changes.
- Modify data: Enables the user to modify existing data but not to add or delete data.
- Insert data: Enables the user to add new data to the table.
- Delete data: Enables the user to remove data from the table.

With the Read and Modify Design permissions, the user can work with the structure of the table. The Administer permission gives a user full access to a table, including table-deletion capabilities. The four data permissions control the type of access a user has to the actual data in the table. You can assign these permissions by table, and you can grant different users different access rights to each table.

Setting Up the Security System

Visual Basic has no means of creating the system database file (usually SYSTEM.MDA) that is needed for the security system. You can create this file using Microsoft Access only. Access also provides the easiest means of establishing and modifying user IDs and setting database and table permissions. However, from Visual Basic, you can create new user IDs, assign users to existing groups, and delete users as described in the following list:

■ To add a new user, you create the user object by specifying the user name, user ID, and password. You then append the new user to the workspace. This procedure adds the new user to the system database that was in use when the workspace was created.

■ To add a user to an existing user group, you create the user object and then add the user to the Groups collection.

■ To delete a user, you use the delete method for the Users collection of the workspace.

Each of these activities is shown in Listing 15.5.

Listing 15.5   You Can Perform Security System Maintenance Using Commands from Visual Basic

```
'**************************************
'Add a new user to the system database
'**************************************
Dim OldWs As Workspace, NewUser As User, NewGrp As Group
DBEngine.IniPath = "C:\VB4\TEST1.INI"
Set OldWs = DBEngine.Workspaces(0)
Set NewUser = OldWs.CreateUser("BJONES", "44587", "HOOPS")
OldWs.Users.Append NewUser
'**************************
'Add a user to a user group
'**************************
Dim OldWs As Workspace, NewUser As User, NewGrp As Group
DBEngine.IniPath = "C:\VB4\TEST1.INI"
Set OldWs = DBEngine.Workspaces(0)
Set NewUser = OldWs.CreateUser("BJONES", "44587", "HOOPS")
OldWs.Groups("Users").Users.Append NewUser
'**************************************
'Delete a user from the system database
'**************************************
Dim OldWs As Workspace, NewUser As User, NewGrp As Group
DBEngine.IniPath = "C:\VB4\TEST1.INI"
Set OldWs = DBEngine.Workspaces(0)
OldWs.Users.Delete "BJONES"
```

Encryption

In addition to the security system, the Jet engine provides a means of encrypting a database that you create. *Encryption* is a method of disguising the data in a database so that someone using a disk-editing program cannot view the contents of the database. You can specify encryption when first creating the database by using the options portion of the CreateDatabase function. After a database has been created, you can add or remove encryption by using the CompactDatabase function. The use of these functions for encrypting data is shown in Listing 15.6.

> **Listing 15.6   You Can Add Encryption to Your Database Using the**
> ***CreateDatabase* or *CompactDatabase* Statement**

```
Dim NewDb As Database, OldDb As Database, OldWs As Workspace
'****************************
'Create an encrypted database
'****************************
Set NewDb = OldWs.CreateDatabase("A:\TRITON2.MDB", _
    dbLangGeneral,dbEncrypt)
'****************************
'Encrypt an existing database
'****************************
DBEngine.CompactDatabase "A:\TRITON.MDB", _
    "A:\TRITON3.MDB",,dbEncrypt
'*******************************
'Remove encryption from a database
'*******************************
DBEngine.CompactDatabase "A:\TRITON.MDB", _
    "A:\TRITON3.MDB",,dbDecrypt
```

The encryption method used by the Jet engine encrypts the entire database, including table definitions and queries. Also, the encryption results in a performance degradation of about 10 to 15 percent.

For some applications, you may want to encrypt only a portion of the data. For instance, in a payroll system, you may need to encrypt only the actual pay rates, not the entire database. Although no built-in method is available for this type of encryption, you can create your own encryption schemes for these situations.

As an example, a simple encryption scheme for numeric data is to convert each digit (including leading and trailing zeros) to a character, invert the character string, and then store the data as text. In this way, the number 2534.75 can be stored as EGDCEB. Although this type of encryption is by no means foolproof, it does provide some data security from casual lookers.

Application Passwords

In addition to, or in place of, the security built into the database, you also can choose to put a user ID and password system into your application. With an application-level system, you control the type of access people have to the functions of your application. The drawback to this approach is that someone could access your database using another program.

Using Network Security

Finally, most network operating systems have their own security system built in. Many of these systems are quite good and can prevent unauthorized users from even knowing that the database exists. To determine the capabilities of your network's security system, refer to your network program manuals or contact your network administrator.

Maintaining Data Currency

Currency of the data is a big issue in multi-user applications, especially those that handle a high volume of data entry and modification. Maintaining currency refers to making sure that the data at which you are looking is the most up-to-date information available. The data you're working with becomes noncurrent if another user changes or deletes the records since you retrieved them. Additionally, your recordset may be noncurrent if other users have added records since you retrieved data.

Using Only Tables

The only way to be sure that your data is always the most current is to work exclusively with tables. Only a table immediately reflects changes, additions, or deletions made by other users. If your application or function works with only one table, using the table instead of a dynaset is probably the best way to go. If your application must work with multiple tables, the drawback to using just the tables is that you have to maintain the table relationships instead of using a dynaset to do it. To decide whether to use tables or dynasets, you must determine the probability that your data will not be current, the consequences of having noncurrent data, and the effort involved in maintaining the table relationships. Weighing these three factors will help you decide which access method is best.

Requerying a Dynaset

If you need to work with a dynaset in a multi-user application, you can use the Requery method to make the dynaset current with the database. The Requery method, shown here, basically re-executes the SQL query used to create the dynaset:

```
NewDyn.Requery
```

You can requery a dynaset only a limited number of times. Therefore, after several requeries, you should close the dynaset and re-create it completely.

N O T E   You should check the Restartable property of the recordset to verify that it supports the Requery operation. ▪

Probing Performance Considerations

The performance of your multi-user application is dependent on, among other things, the type of network, the number of users, and the size of the databases with which you're working. At best, with you as the only user attached to a server, the data-transfer rates across a network are twice as slow as from your local hard drive. This means that you have to work harder in a network environment to keep the performance of your application crisp. In the following sections, I list some ideas for helping the performance of your application.

Keep Dynasets Small

The trick to keeping your dynasets small is to make your queries as specific as possible. This way, you can avoid repeatedly reading data across the network as you move through the dynaset.

Copy a Database or Table to a Local Drive

If you have a database that does not change, such as a ZIP code database, you can make a copy of the database on your local drive. This approach improves the speed of access during searches and queries. For other databases that might change only occasionally (such as a price database), you might consider making the changes at a time when no one else is using the database. That way, the data is always static to the users of the system. In other words, do your data maintenance at night.

Use Snapshots Where Possible

Because snapshots are read-only copies of the data stored in memory, they access the network only when the snapshots are created. Therefore, if you don't need to make changes to the data, use a snapshot, but only if the recordset is small.

Use Transactions for Processing Updates

Each time an update is issued, data is written to the database, requiring a disk write—that is, unless transaction processing is used. All the updates between a `BeginTrans` and a `CommitTrans` are stored in memory until the transaction is committed. At that time, all the updates are processed at once. This approach cuts down on the amount of writes being performed across the network. However, you should be careful not to allow too many updates to stack up at one time because of the record-locking concerns described earlier.

Using Database Replication to Handle Multiple Users

Although database replication may not be "multi-user" in the strictest sense of the concept (multiple users accessing the same database at the same time), you can use this process to handle a number of situations in which multiple users need to work with a database. The most easily visualized of these situations is one in which a sales force in different locations works with a common database and then sends information back to a central site where summary reports are developed.

With database replication, each person can work with a copy of the data in a database. Then, at certain times, the individual databases are recombined with the master database. At the same time that the data from the replica databases is passed back to the master database, any structure changes made to the master can be passed to the replicas.

You also can use database replication to create a read-only copy of a database for a user. You do so to make a complete copy of a network database on a user's local machine. You can use this approach to speed up processing of large reports or queries when the user has no need to modify the base information.

Managing database replication involves four basic steps:

1. Making a database replicable (that is, capable of being replicated)
2. Making copies (replicas) of the database
3. Periodically synchronizing the copies of the database
4. Handling synchronization conflicts

N O T E   Database replication features are available only for Jet version 3.5 databases. ▪

Making a Replicable Database

To create a database that can be replicated, you must use a user-defined property of the database. User-defined properties were first introduced in Visual Basic 4. Using these properties, you can add properties to a database, Querydef, table, index, or field object of your database. User-defined objects are described in detail in the Visual Basic help files.

Making a database replicable requires only a few lines of code and a single user-defined property, as shown in the following code example. This property is a text property with the name Replicable and a value of T.

```
Dim RepProp As Property
Set OldDb = OldWs.OpenDatabase(DataName, True)
Set RepProp = OldDb.CreateProperty()
RepProp.Name = "Replicable"
RepProp.Type = dbText
RepProp.Value = "T"
OldDb.Properties.Append RepProp
OldDb.Close
```

N O T E   A database must be opened exclusively in order to make it replicable. ▪

Making Copies of the Database

After you change your database so that it can be replicated, you should make copies of the database to give to the various users. You do so by using the MakeReplica method of the database object, which is shown in the following code:

```
Set OldDb = OldWs.OpenDatabase(DataName)
OldDb.MakeReplica "E:\REPLTEST\REPLICA2.MDB", 0
OldDb.Close
```

With the `MakeReplica` method, you supply a name for the database copy and a value to indicate whether the copy should be read-only. If you want the copy to be read-only, use the constant `dbRepMakeReadOnly` in place of the `0` shown in the preceding code.

Putting the Database Back Together

Finally, after making changes to the master database or one or more of the replicas, you should make the data and structure consistent between all the databases by using the `Synchronize` method. This method synchronizes the data between two databases. You define one of the databases as the database object, which is running the `Synchronize` method. You specify the other database (defined by its path and file name) as an argument of the method. The data exchange between the files can be one of the following three types as defined by the constants shown in parentheses:

- Export: Changes are passed from the current database object to the target file. (`dbRepExportChanges`)
- Import: Changes are received by the current database object from the target database. (`dbRepImportChanges`)
- Bidirectional: Changes are made in both directions. (`dbRepImExpChanges`)

The `Synchronize` method is shown in the following code:

```
Set OldDb = OldWs.OpenDatabase(DataName)
OldDb.Synchronize "E:\REPLTEST\REPLICA2.MDB", dbRepImportChanges
OldDb.Close
```

Handling Errors and Conflicts

In a multi-user application, errors are triggered when you attempt to open a table or update a record that is locked by another user. These errors can be trapped by your code, and appropriate steps can be taken to either retry the operation or exit the application gracefully. In the following sections, you look at these errors in three major groups:

- Database/Table locking errors
- Record-locking errors
- Permission errors
- Synchronization conflicts

The way to handle most errors that occur when trying to lock a table, database, or record is to wait for a few seconds and then try the operation again. Unless the other user who has the record locked maintains the lock for a long time, this method will work. In an interactive environment, I usually give the user the choice of retrying or aborting the operation.

Database/Table Locking Errors   Database or table locking errors occur when you try to access information that is currently locked or in use by another user. These errors occur either when you try to open the database or table, or when you try to lock them. When the errors occur, you need to wait until the other user has released the lock or quit using the recordset. Table 15.1 lists the error numbers and when they occur.

Table 15.1 Locking Errors that Apply to Tables and Databases

Error Number	Error Occurs When
3008	You attempt to open a table that is exclusively opened by another user.
3009	You attempt to lock a table that is in use by another user.
3211	Same as 3009.
3212	Same as 3009, except that this error provides information about the user and machine using the table.

Each of these errors can be handled as described previously, with a choice by the user to abort or retry the operation.

Record-Locking Errors   Record-locking errors occur when you try to add, update, or delete records on a page locked by another user. Depending on the type of locking you use, the error may occur either when you use the `Edit` method (pessimistic locking) or when you use the `Update` method (optimistic locking). To determine which locking method is in effect when the error occurs, you can check the `LockEdits` property of the recordset you are attempting to lock by using the routine shown in Listing 15.7. Then, if you choose to retry the operation, you can re-execute the correct method.

Listing 15.7   Determine Which Locking Method Is in Effect When an Error Occurs

```
'****************************************
'Determine the type of locking being used
'****************************************
If NewDyn.LockEdits Then
'*********************************
'If pessimistic locking, retry Edit
'*********************************
    NewDyn.Edit
Else
'*********************************
'If optimistic locking, retry Update
'*********************************
    NewDyn.Update
End If
```

Most of the record errors pertain to problems encountered while locking the record. However, one error requires special handling. This error (3197) occurs when a user attempts to update a record that has already been changed by another user. This error occurs only when optimistic locking is in effect. When it occurs, you need to present your user with the choices of "Make the new changes anyway" or "Keep the changes made by the other user." Showing the other user's changes would also be beneficial. If the user decides to make the changes anyway, he or she can execute the Update method a second time to make the changes.

Several other errors might occur when you attempt to lock a record. Table 15.2 lists the error numbers for these errors and when they occur.

Table 15.2   Other Record-Locking Errors

Error Number	Cause
3046	You attempt to save a record locked by another user.
3158	You attempt to save a record locked by another user.
3186	You attempt to save a record locked by another user. The message gives the name of the user who placed the lock.
3187	You attempt to read a record locked by another user.
3188	You attempt to update a record that another program on your machine already has locked.
3189	You attempt to access a table that another user has exclusively locked.
3218	You attempt to update a locked record.
3260	You attempt to save a record locked by another user. The message gives the name of the user who placed the lock.

Permission Errors   The other major group of errors is permission errors. These errors occur when the Jet security is in operation and the current user does not have the appropriate permission to perform the operation. The only way to handle these errors is to inform the user of the error and abort the operation. Table 15.3 summarizes the permission errors.

Table 15.3   Permission Errors that Occur When a User Does Not Have the Appropriate Rights for an Operation

Error Number	Permission Required
3107	Insert
3108	Update
3109	Delete
3110	Read definitions
3111	Create
3112	Read

From Here...

As you can see, many more design considerations are involved in creating a multi-user application than in a single-user application. This process is made even more difficult by the fact that each multi-user situation is different, in terms of hardware and network software used, the number of users of the system, and the functional requirements of the individual application. The intent of this chapter was not to provide specific solutions but to make you aware of the challenges involved in multi-user programming and some of the tools available in Visual Basic to help you meet the challenges. Refer to the following chapter for more information:

- See Chapter 11, "Designing and Creating a Database," to learn about general database design considerations.

CHAPTER 16

Accessing Other PC Databases

While the Jet database is the native database format for Visual Basic applications, there are many other types of databases in use today. These databases include other PC-based database systems, such as FoxPro or Paradox, and server-based database systems, such as SQL Server and Oracle. Odds are that you will at some time have to deal with one or more other database systems.

Types of databases Visual Basic can use

Visual Basic can use data from a wide variety of databases, spreadsheets, and even text files.

How other databases are accessed with Visual Basic

You can access other databases directly with the data control or data access object, or attach the tables to a Jet database.

Importing the data

You can import data using a program or using Microsoft Access.

The differences between importing and attaching tables

Importing the data makes a copy of the data in the external database, so future changes to the external data are not reflected.

NOTE   The Jet database is often referred to as an Access database since the Jet engine was first introduced in the Access product. Therefore, these terms are somewhat interchangeable in referring to the database format. ▪

You may be wondering, "Why should I have to work with other databases?" There are a number of circumstances where this might be necessary, including the following:

- When converting data from an older system to a new program
- When interfacing with existing programs through database files
- When retrieving corporate data from mainframe or server systems
- When meeting a client's desire for a particular format

You know why you may have to deal with other databases; now your next questions may be, "How do I access the databases?" and "Is it hard to do?"

I'll answer the second question first. No, accessing other databases does not have to be hard. For the most part, you can use the basic knowledge of the data access objects and the data control that you gained by reading some of the previous chapters on working with databases.

▶ You should refer to Chapters 10 and 12 to learn about the data control and Chapter 13 to learn about programming with the data access objects.

As for the question about accessing other databases, you have a few choices:

- Work directly with the external tables.
- Import the data into a Jet database.
- Attach the external tables to a Jet database.

Each method has strengths and weaknesses. The rest of this chapter explores the three ways to access databases and explains when it is appropriate to use each. ▪

Accessing Data Directly

Visual Basic gives you the capability to directly access other databases using either the *data-access objects (DAO)* or the *data control*. Accessing the databases directly lets you retrieve and possibly edit information without affecting the structure of the databases or creating problems for other applications that use the databases.

You might also need to access other database formats to create files for exchange with other programs or to import data from a legacy system. In one application I recently wrote, it was necessary to create a FoxPro file from the application so that some information could be sent to a billing company for processing of account payments. After I set up the initial file using FoxPro, accessing the file and exporting the data was a fairly straightforward task.

When directly accessing an external database, you will use methods that you learned in Chapter 13, "Writing Programs with the Data-Access Objects." With a few modifications in the setup of the data control or a few extra parameters in the OpenDatabase statement, you can link to the external databases and then use the standard DAO methods to work with the data. With the DAO methods, you can retrieve information, edit information, and for many database formats, you can add or delete records.

> **N O T E**　While you can delete records in some database formats, not all databases handle deletions the same way. In a Jet database, a deleted record is immediately removed from the database. However, a FoxPro database, for example, only flags the record for deletion. The record is not physically removed until the database is packed. This operation can be performed only from a FoxPro application. ■

About the only thing that you cannot do with external databases is modify their structure.

Using the Data-Access Objects with Other Databases

When you access an external database with the data-access objects, you'll use the same `OpenDatabase` and `OpenRecordset` methods that you use to access Jet databases. The only differences are that now you have to specify a value for the optional `Connect` property in the method and you may have to specify a different value for the `DatabaseName` property. Once the recordset is opened, you use the same methods for retrieving the data and modifying the data that you use for Access databases.

Setting the *Connect* Property　The `Connect` property of the `OpenDatabase` method specifies the type of data that you will access. Visual Basic lets you access all types of databases, including FoxPro, Paradox, and dBase. You can even access, as databases, Excel worksheets and certain types of text files. The following statement shows how the `Connect` property is used:

```
extDb = OldWs.OpenDatabase("C:\FoxPro\Data",False,False,"FoxPro 2.5;")
```

Notice that because the `Connect` property is the fourth argument of the `OpenDatabase` method, you also must specify a value for the exclusive and read-only arguments. These arguments both are set to `False` in the preceding statement. Table 16.1 shows the `Connect` property's values for a number of common database formats.

Table 16.1　*Connect* Property Settings for Various Database Types

Database Type	Value of *Connect* Property
Access	Access
FoxPro 2.0	FoxPro 2.0
FoxPro 2.5	FoxPro 2.5
FoxPro 2.6	FoxPro 2.6
Visual FoxPro 3.0	FoxPro 3.0
dBASE III	dBASE III
dBASE IV	dBASE IV

continues

Table 16.1 Continued

Database Type	Value of *Connect* Property
dBASE 5.	dBASE 5.0
Excel 3.0	Excel 3.0
Excel 4.0	Excel 4.0
Excel 5.0	Excel 5.0
Excel 95	Excel 5.0
Excel 97	Excel 8.0
Lotus 1 or 2	Lotus WK1
Lotus 3	Lotus WK3
Lotus 4	Lotus WK4
Paradox 3.x	paradox 3.x;pwd=password
Paradox 4.x	paradox 4.x;pwd=password
Paradox 5.x	paradox 5.x;pwd=password
ASCII text	Text

There are a couple of additional things to note about the Connect property. First, for some databases—Paradox, in particular—you must specify additional information, such as the password for the database. This information is specified as part of the Connect property and is separated from the format identifier by a semicolon. Second, while Access can be specified as the Connect property, it is not necessary to do so. If you omit the Connect property, an Access (or Jet) database is assumed.

Setting the Database Name   The DatabaseName property set in the OpenDatabase method may be different for external databases than for Access databases. For some database formats, you will specify the actual name of a file. For other database formats—FoxPro and dBase, for example—you will specify not the database name but the path to the folder that contains the table files.

The reason for these differences is the way that different database systems store information. FoxPro, for example, stores each table in a separate file. Thus, the "database" that contains the tables is a folder, not an actual file. If the database format stores all the tables in a single file, similar to the way Access does, the database name is used. Table 16.2 shows the various settings of the DatabaseName property for some common database types.

Table 16.2 *DatabaseName* **Property Requirements for Various DatabaseTypes**

Database Type	*DatabaseName* Value
Access	Name of database, including path (d:\sub\name.MDB)
FoxPro	Path (d:\sub\) for database files
dBASE	Path (d:\sub\) for database files
Paradox	Path (d:\sub\) for database files
Excel	Path (d:\sub\) for database files
Text files	Path (d:\sub\) for database files

Using the Other Data-Access Methods   Once you have opened the database, you can use the `OpenRecordset` method to access an individual table. With some databases, you can even use SQL queries to access information from multiple tables. Then, after the recordset is open, you use the standard data-access methods to access the actual information. Listing 16.1 shows an example of accessing a FoxPro file to export information for use by a service bureau.

Listing 16.1   ClubXprt.Txt—Data-Access Methods Also Handle External Database Files

```
'Set up databases for data transfer
Dim Club1 As Database
Dim ClubTbl, ClubDyn As Recordset
Dim bkdate As Double, bkcurdate As Double, bkdate2 As Double
Dim clbID As String
clbfile1 = app.Path & "\Clubsys.dbf"
clbfile2 = app.Path & "\valid.dbf"
'Create monthly table from base table
FileCopy clbfile1, clbfile2
'Open output table
Set Club1 = OldWS.OpenDatabase(app.Path, False, False, "FoxPro 2.5;")
Set ClubTbl = Club1.OpenRecordset("valid.dbf",dbOpenTable)
'Open dynaset for automatic payment information
SQLSel = "Select clients.clientnum as memo, clients.*, payments.* "
SQLSel = SQLSel & "from clients inner join payments on "
SQLSel = SQLSel & "clients.clientnum=payments.clientnum Where "
SQLSel = SQLSel & "clients.member"
SQLSel = SQLSel & " And clients.paytype > 0"
SQLSel = SQLSel & " Order By clients.clientnum"
Set ClubDyn = OldDb.OpenRecordset(SQLSel,dbOpenDynaset)
'Print bill me information
If ClubDyn.RecordCount > 0 Then
    ClubDyn.MoveFirst
    OldWS.BeginTrans
    Do Until ClubDyn.EOF
        clntname = Trim(ClubDyn("LastName")) & ", " & ClubDyn("FirstName")
        'Write information to output file
```

continues

Part

II

Ch

16

Listing 16.1   Continued

```
        ClubTbl.AddNew
        ClubTbl("Surname") = ClubDyn("LastName")
        ClubTbl("Fst_Name") = ClubDyn("FirstName")
        ClubTbl("Mem_No") = clbID & "-" & Str(ClubDyn("memno"))
        ClubTbl("Rate") = "1"
        ClubTbl("StrtDate") = Format(ClubDyn("Phase2Start"), "General Date")
        ClubTbl("Amt1") = ClubDyn("Phase2Amnt")
        ClubTbl("EffDate2") = Format(ClubDyn("Phase3Start"), "General Date")
        ClubTbl("Amt2") = ClubDyn("Phase3Amnt")
        'Input bank or Credit Card Information
        If ClubDyn("PayType") < 3 Then
            'Bank information
            ClubTbl("Type_Pay") = "M"
            ClubTbl("Bnk_Name") = ClubDyn("BankName")
            ClubTbl("B_Addr") = ClubDyn("BankAddr")
            ClubTbl("B_City") = ClubDyn("BankCity")
            ClubTbl("B_State") = ClubDyn("BankState")
            ClubTbl("B_Zip") = ClubDyn("BankZip")
            ClubTbl("Acct_No") = ClubDyn("BankAccount")
            ClubTbl("Transit") = ClubDyn("BankTransit")
        Else
            'Credit card information
            ClubTbl("Type_Pay") = "C"
            Select Case ClubDyn("PayType")
                Case 3
                    ClubTbl("Bnk_Name") = "VS"
                Case 4
                    ClubTbl("Bnk_Name") = "MC"
                Case 5
                    ClubTbl("Bnk_Name") = "AX"
                Case 6
                    ClubTbl("Bnk_Name") = "DV"
            End Select
            ClubTbl("B_Addr") = ClubDyn("BankAccount")
            ClubTbl("B_City") = ctystr
        End If
        ClubTbl.Update
        ClubDyn.MoveNext
    Loop
    OldWs.CommitTrans
End If
'Close all files
ClubDyn.Close
ClubTbl.Close
Club1.Close
```

Using the Data Control with Other Databases

If the main purpose of accessing the information in other databases is to import or export data, the data-access objects used in a program are the best way to access the data. On the other hand, if you want to display the information and possibly let a user update the information through a data-entry form, you may want to use the data control. Like the data access objects, the data control is also capable of connecting to external databases.

The basic setup of the data control for accessing external databases is the same as for accessing Jet databases. The key difference is that now you have to set the Connect property of the data control. The acceptable values of the Connect property are those that were listed in Table 16.1. However, with the data control, you don't have to type in the information. Instead, you can select the proper setting from the drop-down list for the Connect property in the Properties window. This is illustrated in Figure 16.1.

Part

II

Ch

16

FIG. 16.1
The Connect property lets you use the data control with other databases.

Connect property

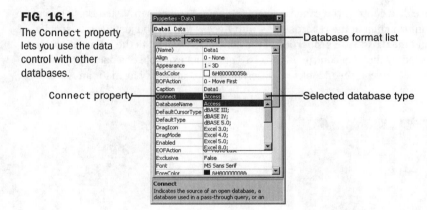

Database format list

Selected database type

After setting the Connect property, you need to set the DatabaseName property. The setting for the data control follows the same conventions as those listed in Table 16.2 for the data-access objects. Finally, after setting the DatabaseName property, you can set the RecordSource property to specify the actual information that you want to access. As with Jet databases, you can select a table from a list of available tables or, for some database formats, you can enter an SQL statement to retrieve information from multiple tables. Figure 16.2 shows a data control set up to access a FoxPro table.

FIG. 16.2
The data control can
access information in
external databases.

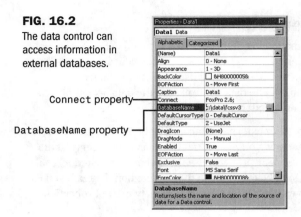

Connect property⎯⎯⎯

DatabaseName property ⎯⎯

After setting up the data control, you can use any of the bound controls in Visual Basic to display and edit the information in the recordset. As with Access tables, you just need to specify the `DataSource` and the `DataField` properties of the control to connect to the information in the recordset created by the data control. Figure 16.3 shows an example of a data–entry screen for a FoxPro table. As you can see, it looks no different than a data-entry form for an Access table.

FIG. 16.3
A data-entry form can
be used with external
databases.

Importing Data from External Databases

Another alternative for dealing with external databases is to import the data into an Access table. This gives you the advantage of having to deal with the external data only one time. After it is imported, you can manipulate the information just like any table that was initially created in Access format.

Knowing When to Import Data

There are occasions when it makes sense to import the data and others when it does not. How do you decide whether importing is the best choice? The following list gives you some things to consider when determining whether to import a database:

- Will your application be the only one to access and manipulate the data?
- Will importing the data cause any important data to be lost?
- If other applications update the database, will your application depend on the updated information?

The question referring to losing data must be considered because the Jet engine may not support all of the data types that are supported by other databases formats. For example, many databases support Binary Large Objects, or BLOBs. These are not supported by the Jet engine. Therefore, any information in a BLOB would be lost when you imported the data from the external database. If this information is not important to your application, this may be acceptable.

If you are converting an older system to one that uses Visual Basic and the Jet engine, importing the data is the logical choice. Otherwise, you will have to weigh the considerations just listed.

Using a Program to Import the Data

There are two basic ways to import the information from an external database: using a program or using Microsoft Access. To use a program, you use the data-access objects to open the database and necessary tables and then retrieve the information in each record. You then place this information in a record in an Access table, using the data-access methods. (Opening an external table was covered in the section "Using the Data-Access Objects with Other Databases.") Listing 16.2 shows a sample program that imports data from an older system for use in a new Visual Basic program.

Listing 16.2 ClubImpr.Txt—Importing External Data Using the Data-Access Objects

```
'Set up databases for data transfer
'Open input table
Set Club1 = OldWs.OpenDatabase(clbpath, False, False, "FoxPro 2.5;")
Set ClubTbl = Club1.OpenRecordSet(clbfil,dbOpenTable)
'Open recordsets
Set ClubDyn = OldDb.OpenRecordset("Clients",dbOpenDynaset)
Set ClubDyn2 = OldDb. OpenRecordset("Payments",dbOpenDynaset)
'Process import records
If ClubTbl.RecordCount > 0 Then
    ClubTbl.MoveFirst
    Do Until ClubTbl.EOF
        ClubDyn.AddNew
        ClubDyn("LastName") = ClubTbl("SurName")
        ClubDyn("FirstName") = ClubTbl("Fst_Name")
        ClubDyn("Address") = ClubTbl("Address")
        ClubDyn("City") = ClubTbl("City")
        ClubDyn("State") = ClubTbl("State")
        ClubDyn("Zip") = Left(ClubTbl("Zip"), 5)
        phnstr = ClubTbl("H_Phone")
        ClubDyn("HomePhone") = Mid(phnstr, 2, 3) & _
```

continues

Listing 16.2   Continued

```
        Mid(phnstr, 6, 3) & Mid(phnstr, 10, 4)
    phnstr = ClubTbl("B_Phone")
    ClubDyn("WorkPhone") = Mid(phnstr, 2, 3) & _
        Mid(phnstr, 6, 3) & Mid(phnstr, 10, 4)
    ClubDyn("Member") = True
    If ClubTbl("J_Date") = "1/1/01" Then
        ClubDyn("SignupDate") = Date
    Else
        ClubDyn("SignupDate") = CVDate(ClubTbl("J_Date"))
    End If
    clntid = ClubDyn("ClientNum")
    ClubDyn.Update

    ClubTbl.MoveNext
Loop
End If
'Close DAOs
ClubDyn.Close
ClubDyn2.Close
ClubTbl.Close
Club1.Close
```

Using Microsoft Access

The second way to import data into your Access database is with Microsoft Access itself. Using Access gives you an easy, menu-driven way to get data into your database. If you don't have a copy of Access, of course you can skip this section.

To start the import process, you first need to open the database file where you want to store the imported data. Once the file is open, you can select the Get External Data item from the File menu and then select the Import item from the associated submenu. This presents you with an import dialog box that lets you select the database from which to import the data. After selecting the file, click the Import button on the dialog box. Access imports the table and adds it to the database. Figure 16.4 shows the Import dialog box for bringing in a FoxPro file.

Attaching External Tables

The remaining alternative for working with external tables is to attach the table to your Access database. This gives you the ability to work directly with the information, just as if the table were an Access table. However, the information remains in its original format, leaving the data readily available to other applications that must use it.

As with importing a table, there are several considerations in determining whether you should attach the table. You should attach a table rather than import it if any of the following conditions exist:

FIG. 16.4
You can easily import a table with Access.

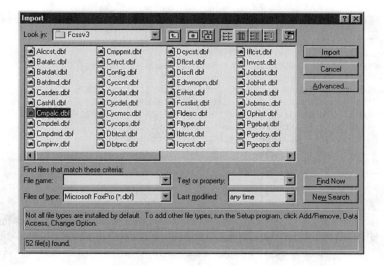

- Other applications must have access to the information that you add or modify in the table.
- Other applications make changes to the data that may be important to your application.
- Information in the external table that cannot be imported needs to be maintained for other purposes.

There are three ways that you can attach an external table to an Access database: using the data access objects, using the Data Manager application that comes with Visual Basic, or using Microsoft Access. Of these, the only way that you can attach and detach tables on-the-fly is by using the data access objects. The other two methods create more permanent attachments.

Attaching a Table with the Data-Access Objects

To attach a table to your Access database using the data-access objects, you actually will create a table definition in the database. This is similar to the process by which you create Access tables.

When attaching an external table, you need to specify the Connect property of the TableDef object and set the SourceTableName property. The Connect property specifies the type of database that you will attach and the name of the actual database file. (The type definitions and database names follow the conventions outlined in Tables 16.1 and 16.2.) After setting the properties of the TableDef object, you complete the attachment by adding the object to the TableDefs collection of the database. Listing 16.3 shows how you would attach a FoxPro table to an Access database.

Listing 16.3   Attach.txt—Easily Attach External Tables with Code

```
Dim FuelDb As Database, AtchTable As TableDef
'Open the database
Set FuelDb = DBEngine.WorkSpaces(0).OpenDatabase("C:\Fuel\Test1.MDB")
'Create the TableDef Object
Set AtchTable = FuelDB.CreateTableDef("CostBasis")
'Set the TableDef properties for the attached table
AtchTable.Connect = "FoxPro 2.6;DATABASE=C:\Fuel\FoxPro"
AtchTable.SourceTableName = "Basecost.dbf"
'Append the TableDef object to the collection
FuelDb.TableDefs.Append AtchTable
```

CAUTION

If the attached table is already defined, you will receive an error if you try to attach the table again. Therefore, you either need to make sure that the table does not already exist before running the code or detach the table when you are finished with it.

If you find it necessary to detach an external table from your Access database, you can do this as well with the data-access objects. To detach the table, use the `Delete` method of the `TableDefs` collection to remove the table definition from the database, as shown in the following code:

```
FuelDb.TableDefs.Delete "CostBasis"
```

Using the Visual Data Manager to Attach a Table

If you want to avoid having to attach tables using code, you can use the Visual Data Manager Add-In that comes with Visual Basic. The Visual Data Manager lets you examine an Access database and modify its information and its data structure.

To refresh your memory, you can run the Visual Data Manager by selecting the Visual Data Manager item from Visual Basic's Add-Ins menu. Once in the Visual Data Manager, you need to open the database file to which you want to attach an external table. Figure 16.5 shows how the Visual Data Manager looks with a database open.

FIG. 16.5

The Data Manager lets
you modify databases.

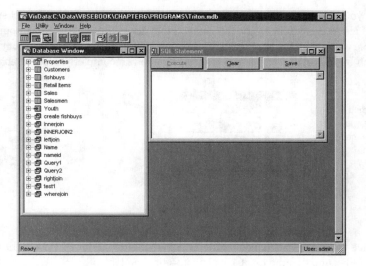

Part

II

Ch

16

To attach a table to your database, you first select the Attachments item from the Utilities
menu. You are presented with a window displaying all the tables that are attached to your database. This window displays the name used by your database to reference the table, the actual
name of the source table, and the connection information that identifies the type of database
format used by the table. The Attachments window is shown in Figure 16.6.

FIG. 16.6

The Attachments
window displays
information about all
the tables attached to
your database.

To attach a new table to the database, click the New button in the Attachments window. This
displays the New Attached Table dialog box, where you enter the information about the table
that you want to attach. In this dialog box, enter the following information:

- The name that you want to use to reference the table
- The name of the database where the table resides
- The type of database format used by the table (the connect string)
- The actual name of the table

As you identify the database name of the external table and the connect string, refer back to Tables 16.1 and 16.2 for the information to enter in these items for various databases. After you have entered all the necessary information, you complete the attachment by clicking the At-tach button on the dialog box. Figure 16.7 shows a completed New Attached Table dialog box.

FIG. 16.7
The New Attached Table dialog box lets you enter the information necessary to attach a file.

Once the table is attached and the Attached Tables window is closed, the Data Manager gives no indication that the database contains attached tables.

If you want to detach the table from the database, you simply select the table name in the Data Manager and then press the Delete key. After you confirm the action, the table is detached from the database.

Using Access to Attach a Table

The final method for attaching a table to an Access database is to use Microsoft Access. This process is similar to using Microsoft Access to import data, as described in the earlier section "Using Microsoft Access." To attach an external table, you need to follow these steps:

1. Open the database that you want to contain the attached file.
2. Select the Link item from the Get External Data submenu of the File menu.
3. Using the Link dialog box, select the file that you want to attach to your database.
4. To establish the link, click the Link button on the dialog box.
5. Close the Link dialog box.

After you link the table, the table name appears in the Access database window. The table name has an arrow to its left, indicating that the table is attached and is not an actual table in the current database. Also to the left of the table name is an icon indicating the database type of the attached table. Figure 16.8 shows the database window with several attached files.

FIG. 16.8
Attached tables are
indicated by an arrow
and an icon.

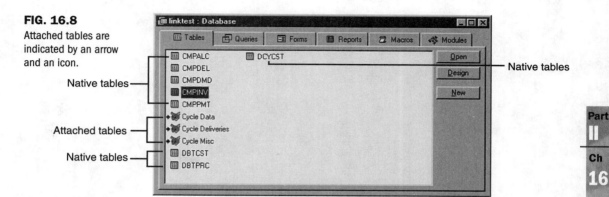

Native tables

Native tables

Attached tables

Native tables

Access also makes it easy for you to detach a table from your database. To do this, simply select the table in the database window and then press the Delete key. Access asks for confirmation of the action and then removes the link between your database and the external table.

Using an Attached Table

After attaching a table using one of the methods described in this chapter, you can use the table the same way as you would any other Access table. When referring to the table, use the name that you assigned when you attached the table, not the table's original name. The following code shows how you would open an attached table:

```
Set CostTable = FuelDb.OpenRecordset("CostBasis",dbOpenTable)
```

From Here...

This chapter has shown you how you can access data that resides in a database other than a Jet format database. You have seen how the methods of access are similar to those used for a Jet database.

- To learn more about using the data access objects to write programs, see Chapter 13, "Writing Programs with the Data-Access Objects."

- To learn more about using the data control and bound controls, see Chapter 10, "Applications at Warp Speed," and Chapter 12, "Doing More with Bound Controls."

CHAPTER 17

Using the Remote Data Objects

So far in the discussions of accessing databases, I have focused on using PC-based databases. These databases include Access, FoxPro, dBase, and Paradox. However, Visual Basic is also a great tool for creating front ends for client/server applications. These types of applications are used to access data stored in database servers such as SQL Server and Oracle. Most of your front-end work—such as designing forms and writing code to process information—will be the same whether you are writing an application for a PC database or a client/server database. The key difference is in how you make the connection to the data.

Before I delve further into actually setting up applications that access client/server databases, I'll give you a look at the difference in the philosophy of the two types of database access. In the PC-database world, the information is accessed through the database engine, which is part of the application. For Visual Basic, the Jet engine is a part of your database applications. As you issue commands to retrieve information from the database, the commands are interpreted by the Jet engine, and the processing of the commands is done locally on your PC. This is the case whether the database actually resides on your PC or is located on a file server to which you are connected.

What is client/server computing

Client/Server computing uses a database server to handle many of the data processing tasks. The client only works with a small amount of data returned by the server.

What does ODBC do

ODBC is a specification that allows your program to communicate with a variety of databases, whether on your local PC or on a mainframe server.

Is there an easy way to work with ODBC databases

The Remote Data Objects and Remote Data Control provide a rich object model that makes working with ODBC databases relatively easy.

How does RDO compare with DAO

The object model of the Remote Data Objects is very similar to that of the Data Access Objects.

In the client/server world, this is not the case. Your application issues a request for information, usually in the form of a SQL statement. This request is passed to the database server, which processes the request and returns a recordset containing the results of the request. In this way, the actual processing of the recordsets is done by the server machine, not by your PC. ■

Introducing ODBC

The method used by Visual Basic to communicate with client/server databases is called Open Database Connectivity, or ODBC. ODBC is a component of Microsoft's Windows Open System Architecture (WOSA). ODBC provides a set of *application program interface* (API) functions, which makes it easier for a developer to connect to a wide range of database formats. Because of the use of ODBC standards, you can use the same set of functions and commands to access information in SQL Server, Oracle, or Interbase, even though the actual data-storage systems are quite different. You can even access a number of PC databases using ODBC functions.

Understanding ODBC Drivers

ODBC drivers are the DLLs that contain the functions that let you connect to various databases. There are separate drivers for each database type. For many standard formats, such as PC databases and SQL Server, these drivers are provided with Visual Basic. For other databases, the ODBC driver is provided by the server manufacturer.

ODBC drivers can be one of two types: *single-tier* or *multiple-tier.* A single-tier driver is used to connect to PC-based database systems that may reside on either the local machine or a file server. Multiple-tier drivers are used to connect to client/server databases where the SQL statement is processed by the server, not the local machine.

Each ODBC driver that you encounter must contain a basic set of functions, known as the *core-level capabilities.* Here are these basic functions:

- Provide database connections
- Prepare and execute SQL statements
- Process transactions
- Return result sets
- Inform the application of errors

Setting Up an ODBC Data Source

Before you can use ODBC to connect to a database, you must have the ODBC drivers available on your system, and you must set up the ODBC data source. Both of these functions can be accomplished by using the ODBC Manager application. Also, once you have added the drivers to your system, you can set up an ODBC data source using the data-access objects.

N O T E On Windows 95 systems, you will find the ODBC manager in the Control Panel, under the Settings item on the Start menu. The ODBC manager is part of the operating system. ■

N O T E To ensure that all readers can use the information presented here, the Access ODBC driver
is used in all examples. While this is a PC database, the methods used also can be applied
to server databases. ■

Gaining Access to ODBC Drivers To set up the ODBC drivers on your system, you need to
use Windows 95's ODBC Manager application. You will find this in the Control Panel, which is
accessible by choosing the <u>C</u>ontrol Panel item from the <u>S</u>ettings submenu on the Startup
menu. The Control Panel is illustrated in Figure 17.1.

FIG. 17.1
The ODBC Manager is
located in the Control
Panel of Windows 95.

ODBC Manager

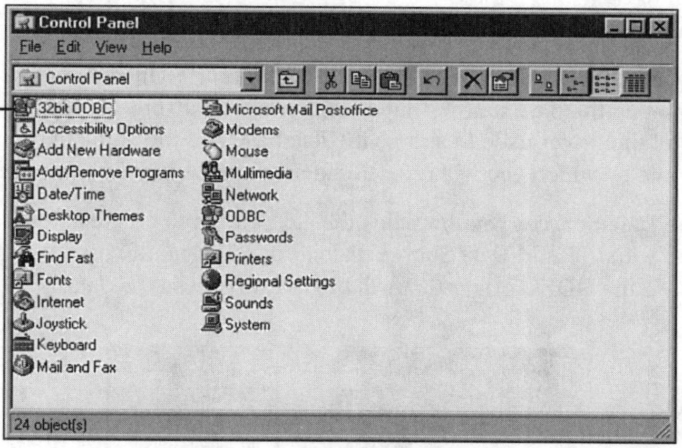

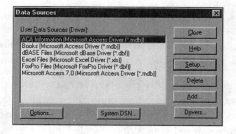

When you open the ODBC Manager, you see the Data Sources window, as shown in Figure
17.2. This window lists all the available ODBC data sources. If there are no items listed in the
window, no ODBC data sources have been set up for your system. Typically, you will see a
data-source item for each ODBC driver that is available to you.

FIG. 17.2
The Data Sources
window gives you
information about
ODBC data sources
on your machine.

To add ODBC drivers to your system, click the Drivers button at the bottom right of the window. This presents you with the Drivers dialog box, shown in Figure 17.3. The Drivers dialog
box lists the ODBC currently available on your system and lets you add or delete drivers. From
this dialog box, click the Add button to display the Add Drivers dialog box. In the Add Drivers
dialog box, you specify the source (disk or CD, typically) of the ODBC driver that you want to
install. After installation, the driver appears in the Drivers list.

FIG. 17.3

The Drivers dialog box tells you which drivers are installed on your system.

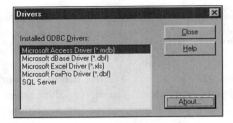

After you have installed the drivers that you need, click the Close button on the Drivers dialog box to return to the Data Sources window.

Creating an ODBC Source with the ODBC Manager   Once you have ODBC drivers available, you can set up the data sources needed for your applications. The information for a data source consists of the driver used to access the database and the name of the database. You also provide a name by which you will refer to the data source in your programs.

From the Data Sources window, click the Add button to create a new data source. This presents you with the Add Data Source dialog box, shown in Figure 17.4. In this first dialog box, you choose the ODBC driver that will be used to access the data.

FIG. 17.4

Selecting the ODBC driver is the first step to setting up a data source.

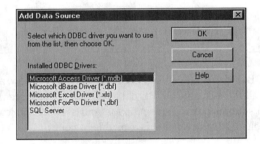

After choosing the driver and clicking the OK button, you are presented with the setup dialog box for the particular database type associated with the driver that you selected. An example of this dialog box—in this case, for a Microsoft Access database—is shown in Figure 17.5.

In this dialog box, you provide a name in the Data Source Name box. This is the name that you will use in your applications to refer to the data source. You may also choose to include a description of the data source. After setting the name, you need to choose the actual database that you want to access with your program. This is done by clicking the Select button of the dialog box. You are then presented with a Select Database dialog box (which is basically an open-file dialog box). After selecting your database and specifying a name, you can click the OK button to add the data source to the available list.

FIG. 17.5
A setup dialog box lets you specify the information necessary to connect to an ODBC data source.

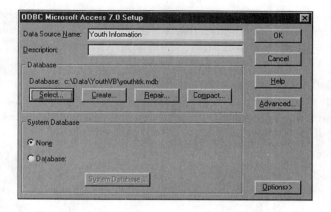

The dialog boxes for other database formats are different from the one just described. However, in each case, you specify both a data-source name to be used by your programs and the source of the data that you will access. Figures 17.6 and 17.7 show the dialog boxes for FoxPro files and SQL Server, respectively.

FIG. 17.6
The FoxPro dialog box requires you to specify the data directory and lets you optionally specify indexes.

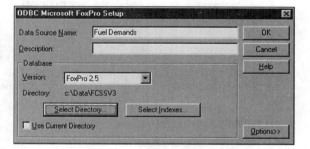

FIG. 17.7
The SQL Server Dialog box requires you to specify the server where the information is located.

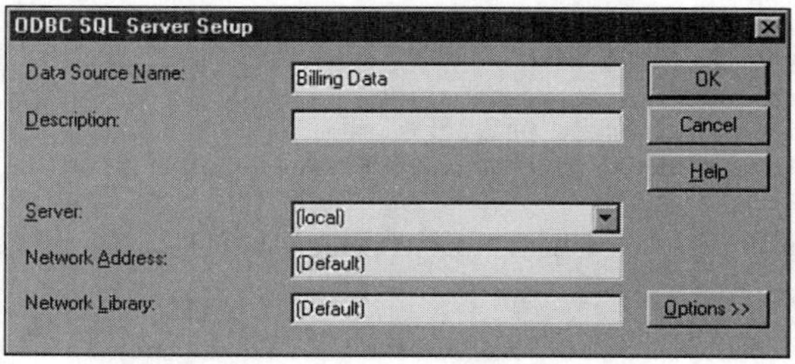

Part
II

Ch
17

The Data Sources window also gives you the capability to modify or delete ODBC sources. To modify a data source, select the data source and then click the Setup button. This presents you with the same dialog box that you used initially to set up the data source. To delete a data source, select it and then click the Delete button.

Using the DAOs to Create an ODBC Source   The ODBC Manager is not the only way for you to set up data sources. You can also use the DBEngine object in Visual Basic. This object contains the RegisterDatabase method, which lets you specify the information needed to create a data source. Here is the syntax of the RegisterDatabase method:

```
DBEngine.RegisterDatabase dbname, driver, silent, attributes
```

Table 17.1 defines the parameters used in the RegisterDatabase method.

Table 17.1   Parameters of the *RegisterDatabase* Method

Parameter	Definition
dbName	A user-definable string expression that specifies the data source's name (for example, MyDatabase).
driver	A string expression that indicates the installed driver's name (for example, ORACLE) as listed in ODBCINST.INI. Note that this expression is the name of the driver section in ODBCINST.INI, not the driver's DLL name.
silent	True specifies that the next parameter (attributes) indicates all connection information. False specifies to display the Driver Setup dialog box and ignore the contents of the attributes parameter.
attributes	All connection information for using the ODBC driver. This parameter is ignored if silent is set to False.

The following listing illustrates how the RegisterDatabase method is used to create a link to an access database.

```
Dim Attrib, DBDriver As String
Attrib = "DBQ=c:\data\forte\members.mdb"
DBDriver = "Microsoft Access Driver (*.mdb)"
DBEngine.RegisterDatabase "Forte1", DBDriver, True, Attrib
```

N O T E   You can also use the rdoRegisterDataSource method of the rdoEngine to perform the registration task. ■

N O T E   To determine all the settings required for a particular ODBC database, you should create a connection with the ODBC Manager and then examine the settings in the Registry. You will find these under HKEY_USERS\Default\Software\ODBC\ODBC.INI. To take a look at the registry, you can run the Regedit application in Windows or a third-party Registry editor. ■

Using the Remote Data Objects

Before the advent of *remote data objects* in Visual Basic, it was much more difficult to use ODBC databases in your programs. In order to use ODBC, you had to declare functions in your program and make calls directly to the ODBC API. Remote data objects changed this by providing an interface to the ODBC API that uses the familiar operations of setting properties and calling methods. Because properties and methods are used in all Visual Basic programs, this made the access of ODBC databases much easier for developers to understand and accomplish.

Comparison of RDO to DAO

The remote data objects, or RDO, are very similar to the data-access objects (DAO), which were covered in Chapter 13. This similarity not only makes RDO easier to understand, but it also makes the conversion of programs from PC databases to client/server databases much easier. In fact, once the connection to the data source is made, the same code statements can be used to access the data using RDO as were used for DAO.

To give you a feel for the similarities between the RDO and DAO models, Table 17.2 lists a number of RDO objects and their corresponding DAO objects.

Part

II

Ch

17

Table 17.2   Some RDO Objects and Their DAO Counterparts

RDO Object	DAO Object
rdoEngine	DBEngine
rdoEnvironment	Workspace
rdoConnection	Database
rdoTable	TableDef
rdoResultset	Recordset
rdoColumn	Field
rdoQuery	QueryDef
rdoParameter	Parameter

In addition, the rdoResultset object supports several types of returned sets of records, similar to the recordset types of the Recordset object. Table 17.3 summarizes these similarities.

Table 17.3 *rdoResultset* **Types and the corresponding** *Recordset* **Types**

rdoResultset Types	Recordset Types	Definition
Keyset	Dynaset	Updatable set of records in which movement is unrestricted.
Static	Snapshot	Nonupdatable set of records that were present when the set was created. Updates by other users are not reflected.
Dynamic	N/A	Similar to a keyset.
Forward-only	Forward-only	Similar to a static resultset or snapshot, but you can move forward only through the set of records. This is the default resultset type.

Notice that the remote data objects do not support any resultset that can return a table. This is because the remote data objects are geared to using SQL statements to retrieve subsets of information from one or more tables. Also, because there is no table equivalent, RDO does not support indexes. This means that you must set the order of the resultset with the Order By clause of the SQL statement used to create the set.

As you might expect with the similarity of the access objects, there are methods of the RDO that are similar to the methods of the DAO. These methods and their respective objects are summarized in Table 17.4.

Table 17.4 **RDO Objects Methods and related DAO methods**

RDO Method	RDO Object	DAO Method	DAO Object
rdoCreateEnvironment	rdoEngine	CreateWorkspace	DBEngine
BeginTrans	rdoConnection	BeginTrans	Workspace
CommitTrans	rdoConnection	CommitTrans	Workspace
OpenConnection	rdoEnvironment	OpenDatabase	Workspace
RollbackTrans	rdoConnection	Rollback	Workspace
CreateQuery	rdoConnection	CreateQueryDef	Database
Execute	rdoConnection	Execute	Database
OpenResultset	rdoConnection	OpenRecordset	Database

And finally, the rdoResultset object and the Recordset object have the following methods in common:

- **AddNew**   Adds a new row (record) to the set.
- **Delete**   Removes the current row (record) from the set.
- **Edit**   Prepares the current row for changing the information in the row.
- **MoveFirst**   Moves to the first row of the set.
- **MoveLast**   Moves to the last row in the set.
- **MoveNext**   Moves to the next row in the set.
- **MovePrevious**   Moves to the previous row in the set.
- **Update**   Commits the changes made to the copy buffer to the actual record. The copy buffer is a memory location that contains the values of the record with which the user is working.

Accessing a Database with RDO

To further illustrate the similarities between the RDO and DAO models, the code in Listings 17.1 and 17.2 perform the same function with the same Access database. The difference between the two listings is simply the objects and methods used to create the set of records to be manipulated. Once the recordset or resultset is established, all other statements are the same. The ODBC data source was created previously with the ODBC Manager.

Part

II

Ch

17

Listing 17.1   *RDOSampl.txt*—Access Information in an ODBC Data Source Using the RDO Methods

```
Dim WS As rdoEnvironment
Dim DB As rdoConnection
Dim RS As rdoResultset
Dim SQLSel As String
SQLSel = "Select * From Users"
Set WS = rdoEngine.rdoEnvironments(0)
Set DB = WS.OpenConnection("ACA Information")
Set RS = DB.OpenResultset(SQLSel,rdOpenKeyset)
RS.MoveFirst
txtName.Text = RS("FirstName")
RS.Close
DB.Close
```

Listing 17.2   *DAOSampl.txt*—Accessing the Same Information Using the DAO Methods

```
Dim WS As WorkSpace
Dim DB As Database
Dim RS As Recordset
Dim SQLSel As String
SQLSel = "Select * From Users"
Set WS = DBEngine.Workspaces(0)
Set DB = WS.OpenDatabase("C:\Data\Forte\Members.Mdb")
Set RS = DB.OpenRecordset(SQLSel,rdOpenDynaset)
```

continues

Listing 17.2   Continued

```
RS.MoveFirst
txtName.Text = RS("FirstName")
RS.Close
DB.Close
```

Using the Remote Data Control

If you want a faster way to create applications using ODBC data sources, you can use the *remote data control* (RDC). The RDC lets you set a few properties of the control, and then the RDC handles all the tasks of making the connections to the ODBC data source for you. In this way, the RDC automates the methods of the remote data objects in the same way that the data control automates the methods of the data-access objects.

After setting up the remote data control, you can use the bound controls to display and edit information that is in the resultset created by the data control. The bound controls are set up the same way they would be for use with the data control, except that now, the `DataSource` property of the bound controls points to a remote data control. Once set up, the bound controls are updated with new information each time a new row is accessed by the remote data control.

Comparing the RDC and the Data Control

The remote data objects were compared to the data-access objects in a the section "Using the Remote Data Objects;" now take a look at the similarities of the data control and the RDC. As you might expect, many of the properties of the RDC have counterparts in the data control. These properties and their functions are summarized in Table 17.5.

Table 17.5   Remote Data Control Properties Compared to Data Control Properties

RDC Property	Data Control Property	Purpose
BOFAction	BOFAction	Determines whether the beginning of file flag is set when the user invokes the `MovePrevious` method while on the first record.
DataSourceName	DatabaseName	Specifies the database containing the desired information.
EOFAction	EOFAction	Determines whether the end of file flag is set or if a new row (record) is added when the user invokes the `MoveNext` method while on the last record.
ResultsetType	RecordsetType	Determines the type of dataset created by the control.
SQL	RecordSource	The SQL statement that identifies the specific information to be retrieved.

Setting Up the RDC

Setting up the RDC for use in your program is also very similar to setting up the data control. Before you can use the RDC, you must first add it to your project. You do this by using the Components dialog box, which you access by choosing the <u>C</u>omponents item from the <u>P</u>roject menu. After you close the dialog box, the remote data control is added to your toolbox.

TROUBLESHOOTING

The remote data control does not appear as one of the available controls in the Custom Controls dialog box. You may have chosen not to install the remote data control when you first set up Visual Basic. You need to reinstall that portion of Visual Basic. Also, if you do not have the Enterprise Edition of Visual Basic, the remote data control is not available to you at all.

To set up the remote data control, follow these steps:

1. Draw the remote data control on your form.

2. Set the Name and Caption properties of the RDC to values that have meaning to you.

3. Set the DataSourceName property. You either may enter a value or choose one from the drop-down list.

4. Set the SQL property to a valid SQL statement that specifies the information you need.

As stated in the list, you can choose the DataSourceName from a drop-down list. This list contains every registered ODBC data source on your system. An example of this list is shown in Figure 17.8.

FIG. 17.8
You can choose from a list of available ODBC data sources when setting the DataSourceName.

After you have set up the remote data control, you then can attach bound controls to it by setting the DataSource property. As shown in Figure 17.9, the list in the DataSource property contains the names of any remote data controls or data controls on the current form. After the DataSource property has been set, you can select the DataField property from a list, just as you did for the controls bound to a data control.

FIG. 17.9

The `DataSource` property list contains all available data controls, remote or not.

From Here...

This chapter has given you a basic understanding of client/server applications. The chapter has also shown you how the Remote Data Objects and Remote Data Control make it easier to access the ODBC databases that are part of many client/server programs.

- To learn more about working with the data control, see Chapter 10, "Applications at Warp Speed," and Chapter 12, "Doing More with Bound Controls."

- To learn more about the data-access objects, see Chapter 13, "Writing Programs with the Data-Access Objects."

- To learn more about creating SQL statements, see Chapter 14, "Understanding Structured Query Language."

Using OLE

18 Controlling OLE Objects 417

19 Programming OLE Containers 441

20 Using Classes to Create Re-usable Objects 469

21 Creating Remote Automation Servers 497

22 Creating OCX Controls 571

23 Debugging ActiveX Components 531

24 Building and Distributing ActiveX Components 547

CHAPTER 18

Controlling OLE Objects

You control OLE objects by using the OLE control's properties and methods. All OLE objects share these properties and methods, whether they were created with the OLE control or with an insertable object. This chapter tells you how to control OLE objects in code. ∎

Create linked and embedded objects

Dynamically create OLE objects while your application is running.

Control the display of OLE objects

Resize, scroll, and scale OLE objects for their best appearance.

Take snapshots of OLE objects

Capture the image of an OLE object and display it in a picture box or image control.

Update linked objects

Use OLE methods to control when and how OLE objects are refreshed.

Activate and deactivate linked and embedded objects

Control in-place editing and application editing features of OLE.

Store OLE objects

Save and load changes to embedded objects.

Control an object's application

Use OLE Automation to get at the methods and properties provided by an object's application.

Creating OLE Objects at Runtime

To create OLE objects at runtime, you use the OLE control. It provides the methods listed in Table 18.1 to create objects.

Table 18.1 OLE Control Methods for Creating Objects	
OLE Control Method	**Use**
`oleobject.InsertObjDlg`	Displays the standard OLE Insert Object dialog box to enable the user to select an OLE object to create.
`oleobject.CreateEmbed file[, type]`	Creates an embedded object in code without displaying the OLE Insert Object dialog box.
`oleobject.CreateLink file`	Creates a linked object from a file without displaying the OLE Insert Object dialog box.

Follow these steps to create an OLE object at runtime:

1. Draw an OLE control on a form. Visual Basic displays the standard Insert Object dialog box (see Figure 18.1).

FIG. 18.1
To create a linked or embedded object at runtime, click the Insert Object dialog box's Cancel button.

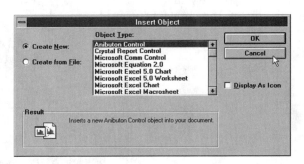

2. Click Cancel to close the Insert Object dialog box without selecting an OLE object to create.

3. In an event procedure, use the `InsertObjDlg`, `CreateEmbed`, or `CreateLink` methods to create an object for the control, as in the following example:

```
Private Sub OLE1_DblClick()
    OLE1.InsertObjDlg      ' Let the user choose an object to create.
End Sub
```

These lines display the Insert Object dialog box (see Figure 18.1) when the user double-clicks the OLE object control.

Creating an Embedded Object

To create an embedded object without displaying the Insert Object dialog box, follow the procedure in the preceding section but substitute the following code in step 3:

```
Private Sub OLE1_DblClick()
    OLE1.CreateEmbed "", "excel.sheet"
        ' Create a new embedded Excel worksheet.
End Sub
```

The preceding lines of code embed a new, empty worksheet in the OLE control OLE1. To base the embedded object on a file, specify the file name in the first argument, as in the following example:

```
Private Sub OLE1_DblClick()
    OLE1.CreateEmbed "c:\excel\stock.xls" ' Embed STOCK.XLS.
End Sub
```

If you specify a file name for CreateEmbed, Visual Basic ignores the second argument. If a file contains more than one type of object, Visual Basic simply uses the first object in the file. You cannot specify an object within a file by using CreateEmbed.

Using Class Types

The CreateEmbed method uses the class type of the OLE object to create new embedded objects (the type argument). Table 18.2 lists the class types for some commonly available OLE objects.

Table 18.2   Class Types for Common OLE Objects

Application	Class Type
Microsoft Equation Editor	Equation
Microsoft Equation Draw	MSDraw
Microsoft Word document (any version)	WordDocument
Microsoft Word document (any version)	Word.Document
Microsoft Word document (version 7.0)	Word.Document.7
Microsoft Word picture (version 7.0)	Word.Picture.7
Microsoft Note-It	Note-It
Microsoft WordArt	WordArt
A package (a file of any format)	Package
Microsoft Paint (bitmap image)	Paint.Picture
Microsoft Quick Recorder	SoundRec
Microsoft Excel chart	Excel.Chart

Part
III

Ch
18

Table 18.2 Continued

Application	Class Type
Microsoft Excel worksheet	Excel.Sheet
Microsoft Excel worksheet (version 7.0)	Excel.Sheet.7
Microsoft Excel worksheet (version 7.0)	Excel.Chart.7

The OLE class type differs from the OLE programmatic ID that CreateObject and GetObject methods use.

Creating a Linked Object

To create a linked object without displaying the Insert Object dialog box, follow the steps given earlier in "Creating OLE Objects at Runtime," but substitute this code in step 3:

```
Private Sub OLE1_DblClick()
    OLE1.CreateEmbed "c:\excel\stock.xls"
            ' Create a new link to an Excel worksheet.
End Sub
```

Obviously, this procedure causes an error if C:\EXCEL\STOCK.XLS does not exist. To prompt a file name from the user, add a Common Dialog control to the form and use the code in Listing 18.1.

Listing 18.1 OLELink.FRM—Getting a File Name to Create a Linked Object

```
Private Sub OLE1_DblClick()
    ' Show FileOpen dialog to get a file to open.
    CommonDialog1.FileName = "*.*"
    CommonDialog1.ShowOpen
    ' Check if file exists before creating link
    ' (see Function below).
    If FileExists(CommonDialog1.FileName) Then
        ' Attempt to create an embedded object.
        OLE1.CreateLink CommonDialog1.FileName
    End If
End Sub

' Checks if a file exists (uses full path and file name).
Function FileExists(strFileName) As Boolean
    ' Turn on error checking.
    On Error Resume Next
    ' FileLen causes error if file doesn't exist.
    FileLen (strFileName)
    If Err Then
        FileExists = False
        Err = 0
    Else
        FileExists = True
    End If
```

```
      ' Turn off error checking.
      On Error GoTo 0
End Function
```

The function `FileExists` verifies that the user entered a valid file name in the Open File dialog box. Using `FileLen` and error checking is one of the fastest ways of checking for a file, although it certainly is not the only way.

Controlling the Display of OLE Objects

One of biggest problems with creating OLE objects at runtime is getting them to display correctly on-screen. When you create objects at design time, you draw the object and can adjust its appearance manually. When you create OLE objects at runtime, you must write code to handle the object's display. To handle the display of OLE objects at runtime, you can use several techniques:

- Resize the control to fit the object
- Scroll the object on the form
- Scale the object to fit in the control
- Scale the object *and* size the control to create the best fit for both the object and the control

The following sections describe how to use the OLE control's `SizeMode` property and `Resize` event to perform these programming tasks.

How the *SizeMode* Property and *Resize* Event Interact

The OLE control's `SizeMode` property controls how the OLE control displays an OLE object. Table 18.3 lists the possible settings for the `SizeMode` property.

Table 18.3 *SizeMode* Property Settings

SizeMode Constant	Value	Use
vbOLESizeClip (default)	0	Clips the object to fit in the control.
vbOLESizeStretch	1	Stretches or shrinks the object's height and width to match the control without retaining the object's original proportions.
vbOLESizeAutoSize	2	Resizes the control to match the object's height and width.
vbOLESizeZoom	3	Stretches or shrinks the object's height and width to match the control while retaining the object's original proportions.

Part
III

Ch
18

If the OLE control does not match the size of the OLE object that it contains, Visual Basic triggers a `Resize` event for the object. The `Resize` event has the following form for the OLE control:

```
Private Sub OLE1_Resize(HeightNew As Single, WidthNew As Single)
    ' ... your code here.
End Sub
```

The `HeightNew` and `WidthNew` arguments indicate a recommended size for the object. This size is that of the OLE object in its original form. You can use these arguments with the `SizeMode` property to control the scaling of an OLE object. To learn more about this technique, see the section "Scaling the Object to Fit the Control," later in this chapter.

The `Resize` event occurs when the displayed size of an OLE object changes, as in the situations described in Table 18.4.

Table 18.4   Situations that Result in a *Resize* Event

A *Resize* Event Occurs When	If the Current *SizeMode* Setting Is
A new object is inserted in the control.	Any setting
The size of an object changes because it was updated.	Any setting but `vbOLESizeClip`
The OLE control's `Height` and `Width` properties are used to change the object's size.	Any setting but `vbOLESizeClip`
The `SizeMode` property changes to a new setting.	`vbOLESizeClip`
The `SizeMode` property changes to `vbOLESizeAutosize`.	`vbOLESizeStretch` or `vbOLESizeZoom`

The `Resize` event does *not* occur when `SizeMode` changes from any setting to `vbOLESizeClip` or `vbOLESizeAutoSize` to any setting. In the latter situation, the control size matches the object size, so no visual change occurs, either.

Displaying Objects in a Sizable Window (Form)

A simple way to size an OLE object is to display it on a separate form that matches the size of the OLE control, and then enable the user to resize the form. Use the `ScaleMode` settings `vbOLESizeClip` or `vbOLESizeAutoSize` when creating OLE objects to display in a sizable window.

To see how this scheme works, follow these steps to create the project OLESize.VBP:

1. Create a new project.

2. Add an OLE control to Form1 and move the control so that its upper-left corner is in the form's upper-left corner.

3. Add the following lines of code to the Form1_Load event procedure:

```
Private Sub Form_Load()
' Automatically adjust the control to fit the object.
OLE1.SizeMode = vbOLESizeAutosize
' Display the Insert Object dialog
' to get an object to display.
OLE1.InsertObjDlg
End Sub
```

4. Add these lines of code to the Form1_Resize event procedure:

```
Private Sub Form_Resize()
If WindowState = vbMaximized Then
' Cancel maximize.
WindowsState = vbNormal
ElseIf WindowsState = vbMinimized Then
' Ignore change.
Else
' Prevent the form from exceeding
' the size of the OLE object.
If OLE1.Width < Form1.Width Then Form1.Width = OLE1.Width
If OLE1.Height < Form1.Height Then Form1.Height = OLE1.Height
End If
End Sub
```

5. Run the project and select an OLE object to display. The object appears on the form as shown in Figure 18.2.

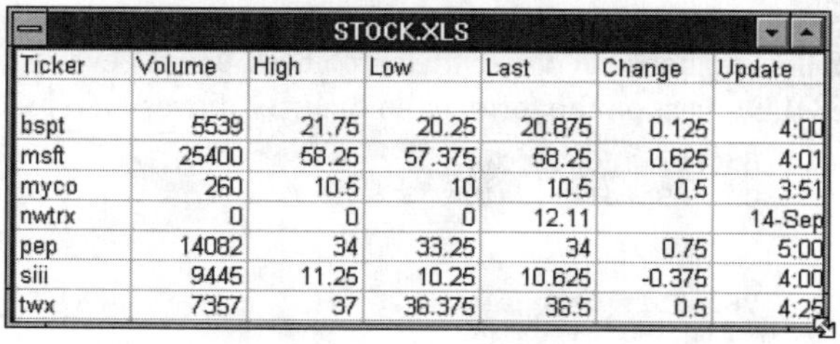

FIG. 18.2
When you resize a form, you can see more of the object. This "object in a window" approach is good for multiple-document interface (MDI) applications.

Ticker	Volume	High	Low	Last	Change	Update
bspt	5539	21.75	20.25	20.875	0.125	4:00
msft	25400	58.25	57.375	58.25	0.625	4:01
myco	260	10.5	10	10.5	0.5	3:51
nwtrx	0	0	0	12.11		14-Sep
pep	14082	34	33.25	34	0.75	5:00
siii	9445	11.25	10.25	10.625	-0.375	4:00
twx	7357	37	36.375	36.5	0.5	4:25

STOCK.XLS

Scrolling the Control for Large Objects

Another way to size objects is to enable the user to scroll large objects up, down, right, or left. To create scrollable OLE objects, you use the ScaleMode setting vbOLESizeAutoSize, as described in these steps which create the OLEScroll.VBP sample:

1. Create a new project.

2. Draw horizontal and vertical scroll bars on the form and an OLE control (see Figure 18.3).

FIG. 18.3

The OLE control starts at the form's origin (0,0) and covers the entire form. The scroll bars appear on top of the OLE control, so they are obscured when you activate the object for editing.

Scroll bars on top —

(0,0) —

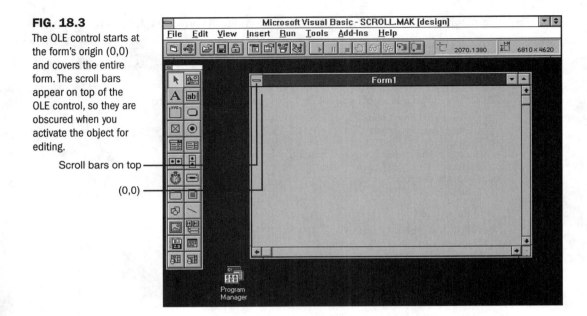

3. Add the following lines of code to the form's Load event procedure:

```
Private Sub Form_Load()
' Use the default SizeMode, OLE control
' automatically resize to match the object's size.
OLE1.SizeMode = vbOLESizeAutoSize
' Display the InsertObject dialog box to
' let the user choose anobject to embed or link.
OLE1.InsertObjDlg
End Sub
```

4. Add the following lines of code to the scroll bars' Scroll event procedures. These lines scroll the OLE object on the form when the user moves either scroll bar.

```
Private Sub HScroll1_Change()
OLE1.Left = 0 - HScroll1.Value
End Sub

Private Sub VScroll1_Change()
OLE1.Top = 0 - VScroll1.Value
End Sub
```

5. Add the following lines of code to the OLE control's Resize event procedure. These lines control the scroll bars' display and determine the scroll bars' scale and maximum values based on the OLE object's size.

```
Private Sub OLE1_Resize(HeightNew As Single,
WidthNew As Single)
If HeightNew > Form1.Height Then
VScroll1.Visible = True
VScroll1.Max = HeightNew
```

```
VScroll1.LargeChange = _
HeightNew / (HeightNew / OLE1.Height)
VScroll1.SmallChange = VScroll1.LargeChange / 10
Else
VScroll1.Visible = False
End If
If WidthNew > Form1.Width Then
HScroll1.Visible = True
HScroll1.Max = WidthNew
HScroll1.LargeChange = WidthNew / _
(WidthNew / OLE1.Width)
HScroll1.SmallChange = HScroll1.LargeChange / 10
Else
HScroll1.Visible = False
End If
End Sub
```

6. Add the following lines of code to the form's Resize event procedure. These lines trigger the OLE control's Resize event to elicit the correct behavior when the user resizes the form.

```
Private Sub Form_Resize()
' Skip first Resize on Load.
Static bFlag As Boolean
If bFlag Then
' If form resizes, trigger OLE control
'   resize behavior.
OLE1_Resize OLE1.Height, OLE1.Width
Else
bFlag = True
End If
' Call support procedure to adjust the placement
' and size of scroll bars on the form.
AdjustScrollBars Me
End Sub
```

Part

III

Ch

18

7. Run the project. When displaying on the form, the OLE object appears with scroll bars if it is larger than the current form, as shown in Figure 18.4.

FIG. 18.4
After creating the sample in this section, you can resize the form or scroll it to see more of the object.

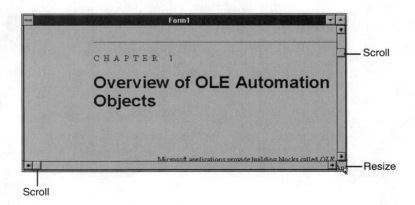

Scroll

Resize

Scroll

In step 6, you use the support procedure in Listing 18.2 to adjust the scroll bars' positions on the form. This procedure is useful in a variety of contexts, so the book's Web site presents it as a separate procedure instead of building it into the form's Resize event.

Listing 18.2   GenForm.BAS—A Procedure for Adjusting Scroll Bars When a Form Is Resized

```
' AdjustScrollBars procedure
'
' Keeps scroll bars on the outer edges of a form
' after resizing. Assumes that the horizontal
' and scroll bars in the form's controls
' collect apply to the form.
Sub AdjustScrollBars(frmTarget As Form)
    ' Declare size and object variables.
    Dim sHeight As Single, sWidth As Single
    Dim objCount As Object
    Dim scrHScroll As Control, scrVScroll As Control
    ' Search through the form's controls collection...
    For Each objCount In frmTarget.Controls
        ' Find the horizontal scroll bar.
        If TypeName(objCount) = "HScrollBar" Then
            ' Initialize object variable.
            Set scrHScroll = objCount
            ' If visible, then record height to help position
            ' vertical scroll bar later.
            If scrHScroll.Visible = True Then
                sHeight = scrHScroll.Height
            End If
        ' Find the vertical scroll bar.
        ElseIf TypeName(objCount) = "VScrollBar" Then
            ' Initialize object variable.
            Set scrVScroll = objCount
            ' If visible, then record width to help position
            ' horizontal scroll bar later.
            If scrVScroll.Visible = True Then
                sWidth = scrVScroll.Width
            End If
        End If
    Next objCount
    ' Set position of horizontal scroll bar (if one exists).
    If Not IsEmpty(scrHScroll) Then
        scrHScroll.Top = frmTarget.ScaleHeight - sHeight
        scrHScroll.Width = frmTarget.ScaleWidth - sWidth
    End If
    ' Set position of vertical scroll bar (if one exists).
    If Not IsEmpty(scrVScroll) Then
        scrVScroll.Left = frmTarget.ScaleWidth - sWidth
        scrVScroll.Height = frmTarget.ScaleHeight - sHeight
    End If
End Sub
```

Scaling the Object to Fit the Control

OLE objects are often (but not always) much larger than the OLE control drawn on a form. Therefore, scaling the object to fit in the control often results in an object that's hard to read on-screen.

This type of display is useful when legibility is not an issue or when you are displaying small objects, such as small graphics. Use the ScaleMode settings vbOLESizeZoom or vbOLESizeStretch when scaling objects to fit the OLE control.

 TIP Usually, vbOLESizeZoom is more useful than vbOLESizeStretch, because vbOLESizeZoom maintains the object's original proportions.

Zooming an Object for the Best Fit

Scaling enables you to fit more on-screen than other display methods. However, to create legible objects, you must combine scaling with sizing the OLE control. To create a best fit, use the SizeMode setting vbOLESizeZoom, the Resize event, and the Height and Width properties together.

To see how to create the best fit for OLE objects inserted at runtime, follow these steps to create the OLEZoom.VBP sample:

1. Create a new project.

2. Add an OLE control to the form and move the control so that its upper-left corner is in the form's upper-left corner. Then add to the form a vertical scroll bar to control zooming. Figure 18.5 shows the desired form.

3. Add the following lines of code to the form's Load event procedure. When run, these lines display the Insert Object dialog box that enables the user to select an OLE object to insert in the control.

```
' Declare module-level variables used.
Dim msHeightRatio As Single, msWidthRatio As Single
Dim msIdealHeight As Single, msIdealWidth As Single
Dim msActualHeight As Single, msActualWidth As Single
Dim mResized As Boolean

Private Sub Form_Load()
' Scale the object to fit the control.
OLE1.SizeMode = vbOLESizeZoom
' Display the Insert Object dialog to get
' an object to display.
 OLE1.InsertObjDlg
End Sub
```

FIG. 18.5

The scroll bar controls the zoom ratio of the OLE control.

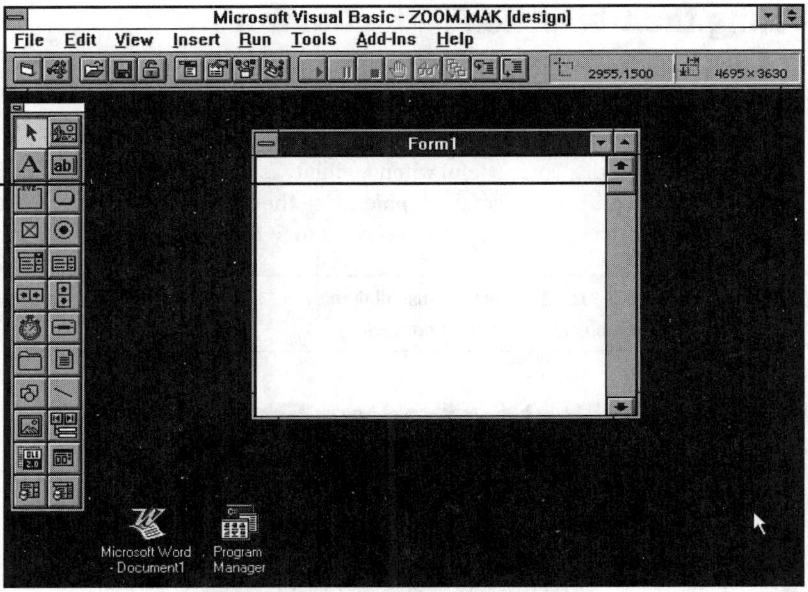

Scroll to zoom ──

4. Add the following lines of code to the OLE object's Resize event procedure. This event procedure calculates the ratio of the object's actual size (HeightNew and WidthNew) to the size of the control. It also determines the display and Max value of the scroll bar used to control zooming.

```
Private Sub OLE1_Resize(HeightNew As Single, WidthNew As Single)
' Get the actual height and width of the object
' from the application.
If Not mResized Then
' Get the control size.
msActualHeight = OLE1.Height
msActualWidth = OLE1.Width
' Temporarily switch SizeMode to get
' the actual size.
OLE1.SizeMode = vbOLESizeAutoSize
' Get the actual height and width of the object.
msIdealHeight = OLE1.Height
msIdealWidth = OLE1.Width
' Reset size mode and height/width
OLE1.SizeMode = vbOLESizeZoom
OLE1.Height = msActualHeight
OLE1.Width = msActualWidth
' Choose which ratio is greater.
msHeightRatio = OLE1.Height / msIdealHeight
msWidthRatio = OLE1.Width / msIdealWidth
' Use the greater ratio for the scroll bar zoom.
If msHeightRatio >= msHeightRatio Then
' Set the maxium value (400%)
```

```
VScroll1.Max = msWidthRatio * 4
Else
' Set the maxium value (400%)
VScroll1.Max = msWidthRatio * 4
End If
' Set the initial scrollbar position.
VScroll1.Min = 1
VScroll1.Value = 1
' Set module-level variable.
mResized = True
End If
End Sub
```

5. Add the following lines of code to the scroll bar's `Change` event procedure. This code scales the size of the OLE control up or down and also automatically scales the object displayed in the control to match the control's size.

```
' Zoom OLE control.
Private Sub VScroll1_Change()
' Scale Height and Width.
OLE1.Height = msActualHeight * VScroll1.Value
OLE1.Width = msActualWidth * VScroll1.Value
End Sub
```

6. Run the project. When the OLE object displays on the form, drag the scroll bar slider to scale the object up or down (see Figure 18.6).

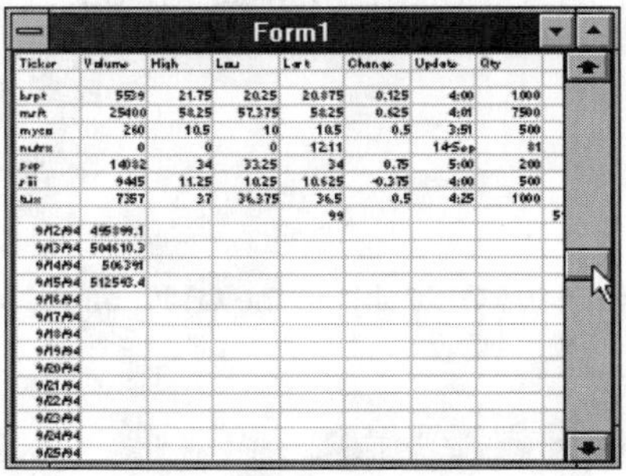

FIG. 18.6
After creating the sample in this section, you can zoom the size of the object by using the scroll bar.

Part
III

Ch
18

Unfortunately, relying on the `ScaleMode` property settings `vbOLESizeZoom` and `vbOLESizeStretch` does not work well for all applications. In particular, Microsoft Word updates scaled objects in a peculiar way. You can work around these display problems by capturing the image of the OLE control with its `Picture` property. To learn how to do so, see the section "Capturing the Object's Picture," later in this chapter.

Moving and Sizing Embedded Objects During In-Place Editing

By default, Visual Basic prevents you from moving embedded objects while they are being edited in place (see Figure 18.7).

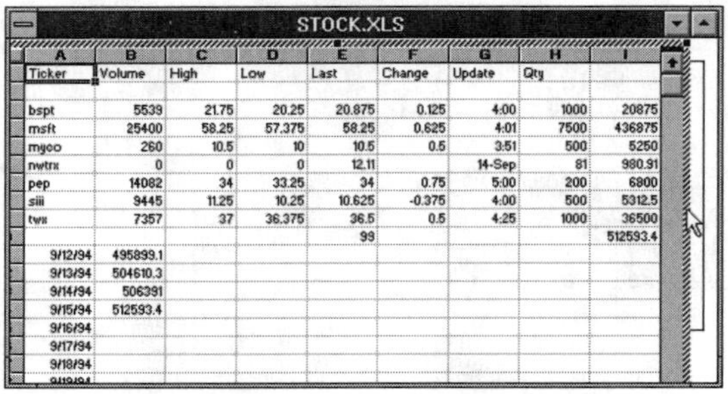

FIG. 18.7

When you try to move or resize an embedded object, it "snaps back" to its original position.

To enable users to move or size OLE objects at runtime, use the ObjectMove event procedure. ObjectMove has the following form:

```
Private Sub OLE1_ObjectMove(Left As Single, Top As Single, _
     Width As Single, Height As Single)
     '...your code here
End Sub
```

The arguments to the ObjectMove event procedure are the position and dimensions to which the user dragged the object. To make the object respond to the user's action, simply assign the ObjectMove arguments to the OLE control's Left, Top, Width, and Height properties, as follows:

```
Private Sub OLE1_ObjectMove(Left As Single, Top As Single, _
     Width As Single, Height As Single)
     OLE1.Left = Left
     OLE1.Top = Top
     OLE1.Width = Width
     OLE1.Height = Height
End Sub
```

Now when the user moves or resizes the OLE object, the OLE control adjusts to the new size and location, as shown in Figure 18.8.

FIG. 18.8

The ObjectMove event procedure enables the OLE control to respond when the user moves or resizes an embedded object.

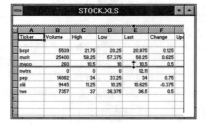

Capturing the Object's Picture

The OLE control's `Picture` property enables you to capture the image on the control. This is useful for performance tricks and for low-level control of the object's appearance. You need to use the `Picture` property when the object's application doesn't update the display correctly or when you want to display the object quickly, without loading the object's application.

To see how to capture the OLE object's picture, follow these steps to create the sample OLEPic.VBP:

1. Create a project.

2. Add an OLE control and picture box to Form1.

3. Add the following lines of code to the form's `Load` event procedure. When run, these lines display the Insert Object dialog box to enable the user to select an OLE object to insert in the control. Then the code captures the OLE control's image and displays it in the picture box. The code automatically scales the image to fit in the picture box.

```
Private Sub Form_Load()
' Use the automatic size mode to get a picture
' of the whole object.
OLE1.SizeMode = vbOLESizeAutoSize
OLE1.InsertObjDlg
' Capture the image of the control.
Picture1.Picture = OLE1.Picture
End Sub
```

Part

III

Ch

18

4. Add the following lines of code to the form's `Resize` event procedure. These lines resize the picture control to match the size of the form.

```
Private Sub Form_Resize()
Picture1.Height = Form1.Height
Picture1.Width = Form1.Width
End Sub
```

5. Run the project. The OLE object's image displays in a picture box (see Figure 18.9). Notice that when you resize the form, the image in the picture box scales up or down.

You can also save an OLE object's image as a Windows metafile by using the `SavePicture` statement, as in the following example:

```
SavePicture OLE1.Picture "OLE1.WMF"
```

By saving the images of objects to disk before exiting, you can make your OLE container applications appear to start up instantaneously—without waiting for other applications to load.

FIG. 18.9
Displaying the image of an OLE object in a picture box or image control can fix display problems with scaling. It also can speed up applications and save memory.

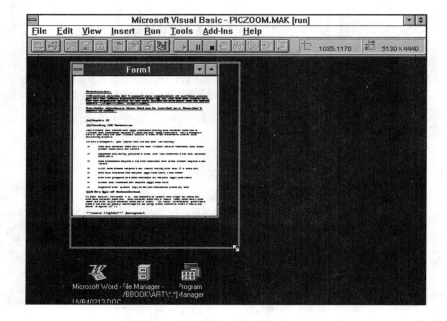

Updating Linked Data

By default, Visual Basic updates linked objects whenever the user saves the source data while editing the linked object. However, Visual Basic currently does not automatically handle changes that other users make to the source file (such as storing a file on a network), nor do such changes currently trigger events in Visual Basic.

To control updating in code, use the OLE control's UpdateOptions property, the Updated event, and the Update method.

Table 18.5 describes the UpdateOptions property's three settings.

Table 18.5   The *UpdateOptions* Property Settings

UpdateOptions Setting	Value	Description
vbOLEAutomatic (default)	0	Updates the OLE control when the user changes or saves the data in the linked object. Not all applications update the OLE control on every edit, however.
vbOLEFrozen	1	The user can edit the object, but the displayed object does not reflect the edits. Calling the Update method does *not* update the object from its source.
vbOLEManual	2	The user can edit the object, but the displayed object doesn't reflect the edits. You can use the Update method to update the object from its source.

The Updated event occurs when the user edits, closes, or renames the source file while editing the object from within the OLE control. The Updated event also can occur when the OLE control first loads (as at startup) if the source file for the link has changed since the last time that the control loaded.

These events occur regardless of the UpdateOptions property setting. However, not all applications notify the OLE control as they are updated. For instance, Microsoft Word does not trigger the Updated event until the user saves or closes the file. Microsoft Excel, however, triggers the Updated event each time a cell of data on a worksheet changes.

The Updated event procedure has this form:

```
Private Sub OLE1_Updated(Code As Integer)
    '... your code here.
End Sub
```

The Code argument corresponds to the type of update that occurred. Table 18.6 describes the possible values.

Table 18.6   Possible Values of the *Code* Argument

Code Constant	Value	Meaning
vbOLEChanged	0	The object's data has changed.
vbOLESaved	1	The application that created the object has saved the object's data.
vbOLEClosed	2	The application that created the linked object has closed the file that contains the object's data.
vbOLERenamed	3	The application that created the linked object has renamed the file that contains the linked object's data.

Part
III

Ch
18

Some actions might cause more than one event to occur. For example, if the user closes a file and saves changes, the OLE control receives three Updated successive events: vbOLEChanged, vbOLESaved, and vbOLEClosed.

Use the Update method to update linked objects from their source files. In Visual Basic 4.0, Microsoft has changed this method, which in Visual Basic 3.0 used the Action property setting OLE_UPDATE to update links. In Visual Basic 4.0, the Action property still works, but using the Update method makes code clearer and easier to understand.

Controlling Object Activation

By default, the OLE control activates its linked or embedded object as specified by the application that provides the object (usually by double-clicking) or when the user chooses Edit or Open from the object's pop-up menu. To control activation in code, use the AutoActivate property and the DoVerb method.

Table 18.7 describes the AutoActivate property's settings.

Table 18.7   The *AutoActivate* Property Settings

AutoActivate Constant	Value	Description
vbOLEActivateManual	0	Activates the object when you call the DoVerb method.
vbOLEActivateGetFocus	1	Activates the object when the OLE control receives focus.
vbOLEActivateDoubleClick (default)	2	Activates the object when the user double-clicks the OLE control.
vbOLEActivateAuto	3	Activates the object when the application-specified event occurs; usually this is the same as vbOLEActivateDoubleClick.

The DoVerb method has this form:

```
olecontrol.DoVerb [verbnumber]
```

The verbnumber argument corresponds to the index of the verb on the object's pop-up menu. If you omit this argument, the method performs the default verb (usually Edit).

Activating an Object for Editing

To activate an object for editing, use the DoVerb method with no arguments. This triggers the default response from the object's application. The default response of most applications is to edit the object.

To ensure that the action taken is Edit, check the OLE control's ObjectVerbs property. The following code checks the OLE object's list of verbs. If it finds an Edit verb, it performs it.

Listing 18.3   Use This Code to Activate an OLE Object for In-Place Editing

```
Private Sub Command1_Click()
    Dim iVerbCount As Integer
    ' Check each verb in the object's verb list.
    For iVerbCount = 0 To oleObject.ObjectVerbsCount - 1
        ' If the object contains an Edit verb, perform that verb.
        If oleObject.ObjectVerbs(iVerbCount) = "&Edit" Then
            oleObject.DoVerb iVerbCount
            Exit Sub
        End If
    Next iVerbCount
End Sub
```

Opening an Object Within Its Application

When you activate a linked object, it opens in its application. Embedded objects can activate in place. To ensure that an object opens in its application, use the object's Open verb.

The following code checks the OLE object's list of verbs. If the code finds an Open verb, it performs that verb.

Listing 18.4   Use This Code to Open an Object Within Its Application

```
Private Sub Command1_Click()
    Dim iVerbCount As Integer
    ' Check each verb in the object's verb list.
    For iVerbCount = 0 To oleObject.ObjectVerbsCount - 1
        ' If the object contains an Edit verb, perform that verb.
        If oleObject.ObjectVerbs(iVerbCount) = "&Open" Then
            oleObject.DoVerb iVerbCount
            Exit Sub
        End If
    Next iVerbCount
End Sub
```

Deactivating an Object

To deactivate an object, switch focus to another object on the form. Switching focus does not close any objects that are open in another application window.

When you open objects in another application window, you also must close those objects from within that application. If the application supports OLE Automation, you can close the objects programmatically through the OLE control's Object property.

The following lines of code activate an Excel object for editing. These lines open the object in the Excel application. Then the code uses the Excel Close method to close the workbook in Excel.

Listing 18.5   Use Excel's Close Method to Deactivate an OLE Workbook Object that Is Open Within the Excel Application

```
Private Sub cmdOpenClose_Click ()
    ' Open an Excel worksheet in the application window.
    shtExcel.DoVerb 2
    ' Close the sheet's workbook in Excel.
    oleExcel.Object.Parent.Close SaveChanges:=True
End Sub
```

To use the Object property, you need special knowledge of the objects, properties, and methods that the application exposes. For instance, the following code shows how to close a Microsoft Word document. Note that this example differs significantly from the previous Excel example.

> **Listing 18.6   Use Word's DocClose Method to Deactivate an OLE Workbook Object that Is Open Within the Word Application**
>
> ```
> Private Sub cmdOpenClose_Click ()
>     ' Open a Word document in the application window.
>     docWord.DoVerb 2
>     ' Close the document in Word.
>     docWord.Object.Application.WordBasic.DocClose Save:=1
> End Sub
> ```

For more information on using OLE Automation methods and properties with an OLE object, see the section "Getting the OLE Automation Object from Linked or Embedded Objects," later in this chapter.

Storing and Retrieving OLE Objects

As mentioned, you store linked objects in separate files on disk and store embedded objects with their container. When you embed an object on a form, you store the embedded object's data with the form in your Visual Basic application.

The application that provides an OLE object supplies ways to save linked or embedded objects through the application's user interface. If your application saves its objects, you can load them into an OLE control by using the CreateEmbed or CreateLink methods. For information on using CreateEmbed and CreateLink, see the section "Creating OLE Objects at Runtime," earlier in this chapter.

To save a linked or embedded object from within code, use the OLE control's SaveToFile method. If you save OLE objects this way, their original application cannot open them directly; instead, you must open them by using the OLE control's ReadFromFile method. SaveToFile and ReadFromFile enable you to store and retrieve individual OLE objects in code.

Saving OLE Objects to Files

Use the OLE object's SaveToFile method to save a linked or embedded object directly to a file, by following these steps:

1. Open a file for binary access. The following code opens the file FOO.OLE:

   ```
   Open "foo.ole" For Binary As #1
   ```

2. Call the SaveToFile method on the OLE control that contains the object that you want to save. The following code saves the object in the oleObject control:

   ```
   oleObject.SaveToFile 1
   ```

3. Close the file. The following code line closes the file opened in step 1:

   ```
   Close 1
   ```

When you use SaveToFile, you cannot save more than one object to a particular file. The method always overwrites the entire file.

Reading OLE Objects from Files

Use the OLE object's ReadFromFile method to load a linked or embedded object directly from a file. To read an OLE object from a file, follow these steps:

1. Open the file to read for binary access. The following code opens the file FOO.OLE:

   ```
   Open "foo.ole" For Binary As #1
   ```

2. Call the ReadFromFile method on the OLE control that should display the object. The following code loads the object into the control oleObject:

   ```
   oleObject.ReadFromFile 1
   ```

3. Close the file. The following code line closes the file opened in step 1:

   ```
   Close 1
   ```

 TIP   Reading a linked object that SaveToFile saved restores the link to the original file.

Getting the OLE Automation Object from Linked or Embedded Objects

Use the OLE control's Object property to get the OLE Automation object from a linked or embedded object on a form. Not all applications provide OLE Automation objects. If an object does not support OLE Automation, the Object property returns Nothing.

When working with OLE Automation objects, you should create an object variable to contain the OLE Automation object. For example, the following lines of code shown in Listing 18.7 declare an object variable and establish a reference to an embedded worksheet when the form loads.

> **Listing 18.7   Use a Module-Level Object Variable to a Contain Reference to an OLE Automation Object**

```
Option Explicit
Dim mobjExcelSheet

Private Sub Form_Load()
    ' Embed a worksheet in the OLE control named oleExcel.
    oleExcel.CreateEmbed "c:\excel\stock.xls"
    ' Establish a reference to the OLE Automation object for the
    ' embedded worksheet.
    Set mobjExcelSheet = oleExcel.Object
End Sub
```

In Listing 18.7, the variable mobjExcelSheet has *module-level scope*; that is, other procedures in the module have access to the variable. For instance, the following Click event procedure uses the OLE Automation object mobjExcelSheet to print the embedded worksheet:

```
Private Sub cmdPrintSheet()
    mobjExcelSheet.PrintOut
End Sub
```

Unlike other applications that support OLE Automation, Microsoft Word requires the following special syntax to get its OLE Automation object:

```
Set objVar = olecontrol.Object.Application.WordBasic
```

You must use this special syntax because Word exposes only the WordBasic language for OLE Automation. When working with the Word OLE Automation object, remember that methods and properties apply to the current document, which might not be the one that the OLE control is currently displaying.

Listing 18.8 establish a reference to the WordBasic OLE Automation object.

Listing 18.8   Use the Object.Application.Word Method to get the OLE Automation Object from a Word OLE Object

```
Option Explicit
Dim mobjWordBasic

Private Sub Form_Load()
    ' Embed a Word document in the OLE control named oleWord.
    oleWord.CreateEmbed "c:\docs\products.doc"
    ' Establish a reference to the OLE Automation object for the
    ' embedded worksheet.
    Set mobjWordBasic = oleWord.Object.Application.Word
End Sub
```

Listing 18.7 demonstrates how the WordBasic methods apply to the current document. If cmdOpenNew runs before cmdPrintDocument, Word prints the newly opened document rather than the one that the OLE control is currently displaying.

Listing 18.9   Use WordBasic Methods to Control the Word OLE Automation Object

```
' Open a new file in Word (changes the current document).
Private Sub cmdOpenNew()
    mobjWordBasic.FileOpen
End Sub
' Print the current document in Word.
Private Sub cmdPrintDocument()
    mobjWordBasic.Print
End Sub
```

TROUBLESHOOTING

My OLE controls do not always update the display correctly. If the control appears grayed after you edit an object, try closing the object's application. If that does not help, reload the object on the form. In extreme cases, you might have to capture the OLE object's image and display it within a picture box or image control. For information on how to do so, see the section "Capturing the Object's Picture," earlier in this chapter.

When I edit linked or embedded objects, my application crashes. Be careful when opening linked or embedded objects for editing. Having more than one object open in the same application might cause that application to crash.

When using an OLE object's OLE Automation object, I frequently encounter `Method or property does not exist` **errors.** Usually, this error indicates that you are using the wrong syntax. Check the application's documentation for the method. Often the problem involves the number of arguments or their data types.

My application doesn't recognize an object that it created. Even if your application creates an object, it doesn't recognize that object after the `SaveToFile` method saves it. You can load such objects only by using the `ReadFromFile` method.

From Here...

For more information on the following topics, see the following chapters:

- Chapter 19, "Programming with OLE Containers," describes how to save multiple OLE objects to a single file and register your application with the Registry.

- Chapter 23, "Debugging ActiveX Components," explains how to locate and fix problems unique to these applications.

Programming OLE Containers

Design for Windows 95

Plan your application to take advantage of the Windows 95 interface. Visual Basic 5.0 makes it much easier to create Windows 95 certified applications.

Drag-drop operations

Visual Basic 5.0 adds new OLE capabilities to all intrinsic controls that make it easier to implement drag-drop between applications.

In previous versions of Visual Basic, it was extremely hard to create an application that was consistent with the OLE features of other Windows applications. Visual Basic 5.0 solves many of these problems by adding OLE features to just about every control in the Toolbox.

This means that you can now create applications that make full use of OLE drag-drop for moving data across applications. You also have greater control of OLE errors and timeouts that can occur when working across applications.

This chapter describes how to use the standard Visual Basic controls along with the OLE container control to create full-featured OLE applications. ■

File associations

You use the Registry to associate file types with your application. Then the user can start your application by double-clicking on data files in Windows Explorer.

OLE storage

You must save embedded objects to files to preserve changes. You can create a storage system for saving multiple objects to one file.

Handle OLE errors and timeouts

OLE objects present their own set of unique problems that require special error-handling techniques.

Understanding OLE and ActiveX Terminology

Microsoft has added a new term to our lexicon; *ActiveX* replaces the phrase *OLE Automation* in most sentences. The term OLE is still around, but now it refers to only the visual aspects of linking and embedding data.

In other words, OLE objects appear on-screen and represent data linked from a source document or embedded in the current document. Some OLE objects can be controlled by Visual Basic through ActiveX (formerly called OLE Automation). An Excel worksheet is an example of an OLE object that provides properties and methods through ActiveX.

Applications that don't provide linked or embedded objects can still be ActiveX components. For example, DLLs and custom controls created in Visual Basic are ActiveX components. Table 19.1 compares old and new terms.

Table 19.1 VB5 OLE/ActiveX Terminology Changes

Old Term	New Term	Meaning in VB5
OLE Object	No change	A linked or embedded object included in an OLE container control
OLE Automation Object	ActiveX object	A programmable object that provides properties and methods
OLE Server (visual)	No change	An application that provides linked or embedded objects
OLE Server (programmable)	ActiveX .EXE	An application that provides programmable objects
OLE DLL	ActiveX DLL	A dynamic link library that provides programmable objects
Custom Control	ActiveX Control	Add-on controls that can be included in applications
None	ActiveX Document .EXE	An application that can appear as a Web page displayed by Microsoft Internet Explorer
None	ActiveX Document .DLL	A component that can appear as part of a Web page displayed by Microsoft Internet Explorer

Designing Applications for Windows 95

Most Windows 95 and NT applications are *document-centric*, which means the user uses the document to load the application—for example, by double-clicking the document's desktop icon.

Document-centric applications let the user think about *content* rather than the *process* of using a computer. Though this makes life easier for computer users, it complicates things for us programmers. To create an application that is document-centric, you must consider the following programming tasks:

- Enable drag-drop to and from your application.
- Create a system for saving and loading the OLE objects used in your documents.
- Create a file to register your program documents with the Registry.
- Register your application when it starts. This ensures that the registration database doesn't become out-of-date if your application's executable file is moved to another directory.
- Handle OLE errors and timeouts from applications that provide objects.

The following sections explain each of these tasks in greater detail.

Enabling OLE Drag-Drop

With Visual Basic 5.0, some controls now provide OLEDragMode and OLEDropMode properties that enable OLE drag-drop. By default, these properties are set to 0 - None because previous versions of the controls didn't provide drag-drop. To enable drag-drop, simply reset these properties to Automatic where possible.

Part
III

Ch
19

To see how this works, create a new project and add a Text Box control to Form1. Set the control's OLEDragMode property to 1 - Automatic and its OLEDropMode property to 2 - Automatic. Run the project, then start WordPad and drag-drop text between the text box and the WordPad application as shown in Figure 19.1.

The Automatic setting tells Visual Basic to determine whether or not the data from the drag source is appropriate for the drop target. If the data's not valid—for instance, a bitmap is dragged to a text box—Visual Basic displays the vbNoDrop cursor and prevents the drop. Otherwise, the drop occurs normally.

Of course, not all controls are automatically draggable. For instance, it's not clear what dragging a label should do, so the Label control doesn't have an OLEDragMode property. Similarly, not all objects allow an Automatic setting for OLEDropMode; Visual Basic can't determine what type of data is valid to drop in a frame or on a command button. In these cases, you have to use the new OLE drag-drop events to manually manage OLE drag-drop.

The following sections tell you how to add OLE drag-drop to objects that don't provide Automatic settings for OLEDragMode or OLEDropMode properties.

FIG. 19.1

Set OLEDragMode and OLEDropMode to *Automatic* to enable OLE drag-drop.

Drag text to other applications

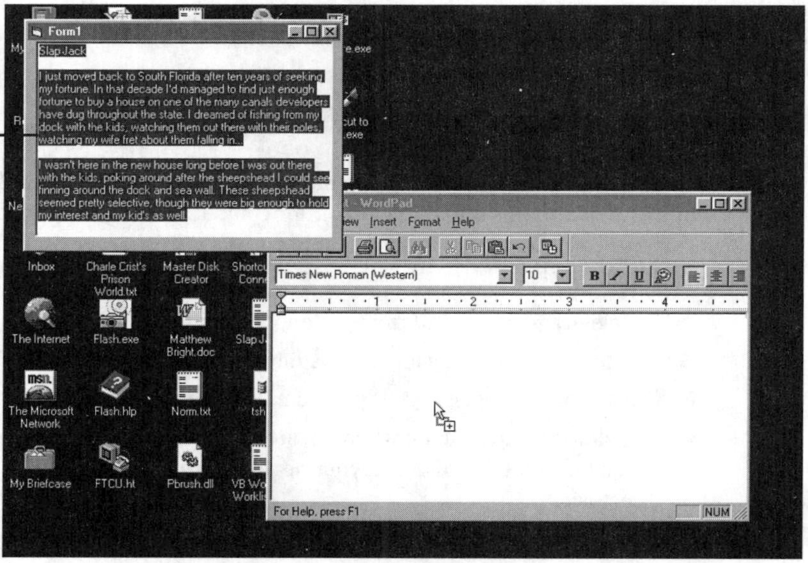

Handling Drop Events

The following objects do not provide automatic drop operations: Form, Label, Command Button, Frame, Check Box, Option Button, Combo Box, List Box, Drive List, Dir List, File List, and Bound Data control. To allow users to drop OLE data on any of these objects, or to modify the drop behavior of other objects, set the OLEDropMode property to Manual and use the events described in Table 19.2 to respond to drop operations.

Table 19.2   Events to Use When Performing Manual Drop Operations

Event	Occurs When	Use to
OLEDragOver	A source object is dragged over a control	Test for valid data
OLEDragDrop	A source object is dropped onto a control	Perform drop action

Use the OLEDragOver event to provide visual feedback during a drop operation. Use the Data parameter to check if the type of data is valid for the target object, and use the Effect parameter to change the mouse pointer to let the user know whether or not the data is valid for the target. For instance, the code in Listing 19.1 lets the user drag text data onto a form; if any other data is dragged onto the form, the vbNoDrop mouse pointer is displayed and the drop is prevented.

Listing 19.1 Using OLEDragOver to Drop Text on a Form

```
' Form properties:
'    OLEDropMode = Manual

Private Sub Form_OLEDragOver(Data As DataObject, _
   Effect As Long, Button As Integer, Shift As Integer, _
   X As Single, Y As Single, State As Integer)
      ' If the data is text, allow drop.
      If Data.GetFormat(vbCFText) Then
         Effect = vbDropEffectCopy
      ' Otherwise, prohibit drop (displays vbNoDrop
      ' mouse pointer).
      Else
         Effect = vbDropEffectNone
      End If
End Sub
```

Use the OLEDragDrop event to perform the action of the drop operation. For instance, the preceding code allows text to be dropped on a form. Listing 19.2 prints the dragged text data on the form after the drop operation.

Listing 19.2 Using the *OLEDragDrop* Event to Display Text Dropped on a Form

```
Dim mstrBackground As String

Private Sub Form_OLEDragDrop(Data As DataObject, _
   Effect As Long, Button As Integer, Shift As Integer, _
   X As Single, Y As Single)
      ' Save the text for later drag operation.
      mstrBackground = Data.GetData(vbCFText)
      ' Print the text on the form background.
      Print mstrBackground
End Sub
```

Handling Drag Events

The following objects do not provide an OLEDragMode property: Form, Label, Command Button, Frame, Check Box, Option Button, and Bound Data control. To allow users to drag OLE data from any of these objects, call the OLEDrag method on the object, as shown in Listing 19.3. You usually call OLEDrag from the MouseDown event procedure of the object.

Listing 19.3 Starting a Manual Drag with the *OLEDrag* Method

```
Private Sub Form_MouseDown(Button As Integer, Shift As Integer, _
   X As Single, Y As Single)
      ' Start drag operation.
      Form1.OLEDrag
End Sub
```

Part
III

Ch

19

The OLEDrag method triggers the OLE drag events described in Table 19.3. Use these events to enable OLE drag operations for objects that don't provide an OLEDragMode property, or to control the drag behavior when OLEDragMode is set to Manual.

Table 19.3　Events to Use When Performing Manual Drag Operations

Event	Occurs When	Use to
OLEStartDrag	The OLEDrag method is called from code —usually in a MouseDown event.	Set the data and formatof the data being dragged.
OLEGiveFeedback	The source object is dragged over a target object.	Change the mouse pointer as the object is dragged over different targets.
OLESetData	The target object requests data from the source object after the user releases the mouse button, dropping the source object.	Retrieve the source data to drop on the target. This isn't needed if the data was set in OLEStartDrag.
OLECompleteDrag	The drag operation is completed successfully.	Update the source object to reflect moved or deleted data.

The OLE drag events give you some flexibility in structuring what happens when. If you want, you can load all your tasks into the first event, OLEStartDrag, as shown in Listing 19.4.

Listing 19.4　Using the *OLEStartDrag* Event to Drag Text Off a Form

```
Private Sub Form_OLEStartDrag(Data As DataObject, _
   AllowedEffects As Long)
     ' Set OLE data and format (mstrBackground variable
     ' is set by earlier OLEDragDrop event).
     Data.SetData mstrBackground, vbCFText
     ' Display the move mouse pointer..
     AllowedEffects = vbDropEffectCopy
End Sub
```

OLEStartDrag alone works fine for copy operations, but when you want to move data you need to write code in the OLECompleteDrag event to update the source object. For instance, the two events in Listing 19.5 move the text from the form background, clearing the form and the variable mstrBackground when the drag operation is complete.

Listing 19.5   Using *OLECompleteDrag* to Delete Moved Text When the Drag Completes

```
Private Sub Form_OLEStartDrag(Data As DataObject, _
   AllowedEffects As Long)
     ' Set data and format.
     Data.SetData mstrBackground, vbCFText
     ' Display the move mouse pointer..
     AllowedEffects = vbDropEffectMove
End Sub

Private Sub Form_OLECompleteDrag(Effect As Long)
     ' Check if move is successful
     If Effect And vbDropEffectMove Then
         ' Reset the text variable.
         mstrBackground = ""
         ' Clear the form.
         Cls
     End If
End Sub
```

It's important to wait for `OLECompleteDrag` before deleting moved items from their source. This ensures that the data is not lost if the drag operation is canceled. Alternatively, you can do this in the `OLESetData` event. `OLESetData` occurs when the target object requests data from the drag source—just before `OLECompleteDrag` occurs. `OLESetData` is generally used to retrieve large items or items that require extra processing. This avoids delays when starting a drag operation and doing unnecessary processing if the drag operation is canceled. You might want to use `OLESetData` when retrieving items from a database, opening and reading files, connecting to servers or Web pages, or any other time-intensive operation.

When using the `OLESetData` event, be sure to set the data format and allowed effects in the `OLEStartDrag` event. Listing 19.6 sets the OLE data format in `OLEStartDrag`, but waits to create the data (a bitmap file) until the OLE drop target requests the data in `OLESetData`.

Part
III

Ch

19

Listing 19.6   Defer Time-Intensive Operations to *OLESetData*

```
Private Sub Form_OLEStartDrag(Data As DataObject, _
   AllowedEffects As Long)
     ' Set data format to file.
     Data.SetData , vbCFFiles
     ' Display the move mouse pointer..
     AllowedEffects = vbDropEffectCopy
End Sub

Private Sub Form_OLESetData(Data As DataObject, _
   DataFormat As Integer)
     ' Save the form background as a bitmap file.
     SavePicture Form1.Picture, "temp.bmp"
     ' Add the file to the data object files list.
     Data.Files.Add CurDir & "\" & "temp.bmp"
End Sub
```

The preceding code drags a file (temp.bmp) rather than bitmap data because applications like Microsoft Paint let you drag in files, but not other data. If you try to use the vbCFBitmap format, Windows displays the vbNoDrop mouse pointer when you try to drag the form's image into Microsoft Paint. When working with OLE applications, you'll often need to try out different data formats to see which they accept.

You use the OLEGiveFeedback event primarily to change the default mouse pointers displayed by Windows during an OLE drag. If you set the DefaultCursors parameter to False, you can override the standard OLE mouse pointers with the code in Listing 19.7.

Listing 19.7   Using *OLEGiveFeedback* to Change the Mouse Pointer

```
Private Sub Form_OLEGiveFeedback(Effect As Long, _
   DefaultCursors As Boolean)
      ' Turn off default mouse pointers.
      DefaultCursors = False
      ' Change mouse pointer based on Effect parameter.
      Select Case Effect
          ' Use the normal pointer for no drop.
          Case vbDropEffectNone
              Screen.MousePointer = vbNoDrop
          ' Use custom mouse pointers for copy and move.
          Case vbDropEffectCopy
              Screen.MousePointer = vbCustom
              Screen.MouseIcon = LoadPicture("drop1pg.ico")
          Case vbDropEffectMove
              Screen.MousePointer = vbCustom
              Screen.MouseIcon = LoadPicture("drag2pg.ico")
      End Select
End Sub

Private Sub Form_OLECompleteDrag(Effect As Long)
      ' Reset mouse pointer when drag is through.
      Screen.MousePointer = vbDefault
End Sub
```

Be sure to reset the mouse pointer in OLECompleteDrag; otherwise, the custom mouse pointer remains after the drag is finished.

Dragging and Dropping Files

When you drag objects off the Windows Desktop or out of the Windows Explorer, you are actually dragging files. In these cases, the format of the OLE DataObject is vbCFFiles and the object's Files collection, which contains the file names being dragged.

Listing 19.8 shows a simple file viewer. Drag a desktop icon onto the form, and the file's contents are displayed on the form background.

Listing 19.8   Using the *DataObject's* *Files* Collection

```
' Form property settings:
'    OLEDropMode = Manual

Private Sub Form_OLEDragOver(Data As DataObject, _
  Effect As Long, Button As Integer, Shift As Integer, _
  X As Single, Y As Single, State As Integer)
    ' Allow files to be dragged onto this form.
    If Data.GetFormat(vbCFFiles) Then
        Effect = vbDropEffectCopy
    ' Exclude other types of data.
    Else
        Effect = vbDropEffectNone
    End If
End Sub

Private Sub Form_OLEDragDrop(Data As DataObject, _
  Effect As Long, Button As Integer, Shift As Integer, _
  X As Single, Y As Single)
    Dim strTemp As String
    Dim filData
    ' Clear any text on the form.
    Cls
    ' Clear any background graphics on the form.
    Picture = LoadPicture("")
    ' Get the first file from the Files collection
    ' (ignore multiple selections).
    filData = Data.Files(1)
    ' Turn on error trapping.
    On Error Resume Next
    ' Try to load file as graphic...
    Picture = LoadPicture(filData)
    ' If error load as text.
    If Err Then
        ' Blast the file into a string variable.
        Open filData For Binary As #1 Len = FileLen(filData)
        strTemp = Space(FileLen(filData))
        Get #1, , strTemp
        ' Print the string on the form.
        Print strTemp
        Close #1
    End If
    ' Reset and turn off error handling.
    Err = 0
    On Error GoTo 0
End Sub
```

The preceding code only deals with one file at a time. Also, it simply ignores directories; you can drag them onto the form, but nothing happens. To deal with multiple files, add a For...Each loop. For instance, Listing 19.9 creates a new form instance for each file selected.

Listing 19.9   Modifications to Listing 19.8 to Handle Multiple File Selections

```
Private Sub Form_OLEDragDrop(Data As DataObject, _
  Effect As Long, Button As Integer, _
  Shift As Integer, x As Single, Y As Single)
    Dim strTemp As String
    Dim filData, frmNew
    For Each filData In Data.Files
        Set frmNew = New Form1
        frmNew.Show
        ' Display the file name.
        frmNew.Caption = filData
        ' Turn on error trapping.
        On Error Resume Next
        ' Try to load file as graphic...
        frmNew.Picture = LoadPicture(filData)
        ' If error load as text.
        If Err Then
            ' Blast the file into a string variable.
            Open filData For Binary As #1 Len = FileLen(filData)
            strTemp = Space(FileLen(filData))
            Get #1, , strTemp
            ' Print the string on the form.
            frmNew.Print strTemp
            Close #1
        End If
    Next filData
    ' Reset and turn off error handling.
    Err = 0
    On Error GoTo 0
    ' Remove this instance of the form.
    Unload Me
End Sub
```

To exclude directories from the file list, use a For...Next loop in the OLEDragOver event. You need to use For...Next so you can keep track of the item number in the Files collection. You also need to count backwards (Step -1) so you don't get a Subscript out of range error when you remove items from the list. This is because collections automatically renumber their indexes as items are deleted. Listing 19.10 shows the modifications to Listing 19.8 that exclude directories from the file list.

Listing 19.10   Using GetAtter to Prevent Directories from Being Dragged

```
Private Sub Form_OLEDragOver(Data As DataObject, _
  Effect As Long, Button As Integer, Shift As Integer, _
  x As Single, Y As Single, State As Integer)
    Dim i As Integer
    Dim filData
    ' Allow files to be dragged onto this form.
    If Data.GetFormat(vbCFFiles) Then
        ' For each file in the collection, counting
```

```
            ' backwards...
            For i = Data.Files.Count To 1 Step -1
                filData = Data.Files(i)
                ' Check if it's a directory, if it is
                ' remove it from the collection.
                If GetAttr(filData) And vbDirectory Then
                    Data.Files.Remove (i)
                End If
            Next i
            ' If there are any files left in the collection,
            ' let the user drop them, otherwise prohibit the drop.
            If Data.Files.Count Then
                Effect = vbDropEffectCopy
            Else
                Effect = vbDropEffectNone
            End If
        Else
            Effect = vbDropEffectNone
        End If
End Sub
```

Creating an OLE Storage System

By default, Visual Basic stores OLE objects in the form that contains them. For linked objects, Visual Basic stores the image of the object and the location of its source document. For embedded objects, Visual Basic stores the image of the object and the object's data.

When you compile a Visual Basic form, the object's image is written into your application's executable file. This has the effect of "freezing" the initial state of the object. Changes you make to embedded objects at run-time are lost when the application closes. Changes to linked objects are preserved, but the start-up image of the object doesn't reflect those.

As mentioned in Chapter 18, "Controlling OLE Objects," you save OLE objects to files using the SaveToFile method and read OLE files using the ReadFromFile method. Listing 19.11 shows using a form's Load event procedure to update an OLE object when the form is displayed.

Listing 19.11   Using the ReadFromFile Method

```
Option Explicit
Const OLE_FILE = "c:\foo.ole"
Dim miOLE_File As Integer

Private Sub Form_Load()
    miOLE_File = FreeFile
    Open OLE_FILE For Binary As miOLE_File
    oleObject.ReadFromFile miOLE_File
End Sub
```

Listing 19.12 shows using the Unload event to save changes to the OLE object in a file.

Listing 9.12   Using the SaveToFile Method

```
Private Sub Form_Unload(Cancel As Integer)
        oleObject.SaveToFile miOLE_File
        Close miOLE_File
End Sub
```

Because the file you use with ReadFromFile and SaveToFile is open for Binary access, you don't have to close the file between loading and saving the OLE object. Binary access files support read/write access.

Storing Multiple Objects in a Single File

The Load and Unload event procedures in Listing 19.11 and Listing 19.12 only support access to one OLE object per file. To store more than one object in a single file, you must keep track of the byte position in the file where each object begins. One way to do this is to write header information to the file that tracks the positions of objects in the file (see Figure 19.2).

FIG. 19.2

Write the byte positions of OLE objects at the beginning of a file to be able to store multiple objects to a single file.

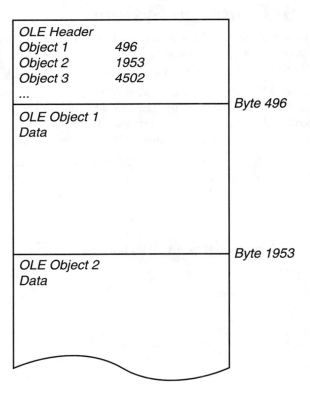

OLE Header	
Object 1	496
Object 2	1953
Object 3	4502
...	

Byte 496

OLE Object 1
Data

Byte 1953

OLE Object 2
Data

Because you don't know an object's size in bytes until you save it, you must create a new file every time you save OLE objects in Visual Basic. To save multiple objects to a single file, follow these steps:

1. Create a temporary disk file to receive the OLE objects.
2. Write a header at the beginning of the file containing the number of OLE objects, their names, and their start positions in the file.
3. Write the first OLE object to the file.
4. Update the file header with the name and start position of the object that was just saved.
5. Repeat steps 3 and 4 for each object to save to the file.
6. Copy the temporary file to its permanent file name and location.
7. Delete the temporary file created in step 1.

The following sections discuss each of these steps in greater detail using the OLESTORE example.

Creating a Temporary File   It is a good idea to write all OLE objects to a temporary file before overwriting permanent storage. Saving multiple objects in multiple applications can be prone to interruptions, and it is important to have a safe recovery mechanism if something goes wrong. When using a temporary file, you avoid corrupting the last saved state if the user's system fails in the middle of a save operation.

To get the name of a temporary file to create, use the Windows API functions `GetTempFileName` and `GetTempDrive`. The `GetOLETempFileName` procedure in Listing 19.13 uses these two functions to return a unique temporary file name. Because the file name is guaranteed to be unique, you create the file simply by opening it for `Random` access.

Part
III

Ch
19

Listing 19.13   Getting a Temporary File Name

```
Declare Function GetTempDrive Lib "Kernel32" (ByVal cDriveLetter As Integer) As
Integer
Declare Function GetTempFileName Lib "Kernel32" (ByVal cDriveLetter As Integer,
_
    ByVal lpPrefixString As String, ByVal wUnique As Integer, _
    ByVal lpTempFileName As String) As Integer

Function GetOLETempFileName() As String
    Dim iWorked As Integer, iTempDrive As Integer
    Dim strTempFileName As String, strPrefix As String * 3
    ' Provide a three-character prefix for the temporary file.
    strPrefix = "ole"
    ' Create a buffer full of spaces for GetTempFileName function.
    ' 144 is the maximum length of path/filenames in Windows 3.1.
    strTempFileName = String(144, 32)
    iWorked = GetTempDrive(iTempDrive)
    If iWorked = 0 Then GoTo errGetOLETempFileName
    iWorked = GetTempFileName(iTempDrive, strPrefix, 0, strTempFileName)
    If iWorked = 0 Then GoTo errGetOLETempFileName
```

continues

Listing 19.13   Continued

```
    GetOLETempFileName = Trim(strTempFileName)
    Exit Function
errGetOLETempFileName:
    MsgBox "Temporary file could not be created. Check your TEMP environment " _
        & "variable in your AUTOEXEC.BAT file."
    GetOLETempFileName = ""
End Function
```

Creating an OLE File Header   The header information in an OLE storage file is structured information. The easiest way to write structured information to a file is to use the Random access mode and a user-defined type that defines the information's structure. With OLE storage there are three key pieces of information you need to know:

- How many objects are in the file
- The identity of each object
- Where each object starts—the byte position to start reading from

Because you know the location of the first record in any file (1), you can use the first record to list the number of objects in the file. This means you only need to declare one type, as shown in the following:

```
Type OLEHeader
    strName As String
    lStartPos As Long
End Type
```

The CreateHeader procedure in Listing 19.14 uses OLEHeader structure to record the number of objects in the first record's lStartPos field and then reserves space for each of the OLE objects to save.

Listing 19.14   Creating a File Header for OLE Storage

```
Sub CreateHeader(strFileName As String, iObjectCount As Integer)
    Dim usrObjectRecord As OLEHeader
    Dim iFileNum As Integer
    iFileNum = OpenForRandom(strFileName)
    ' Write first record to show size of header.
    usrObjectRecord.ObjectName = "Objects in this file"
    usrObjectRecord.StartPos = iObjectCount
    Put iFileNum, 1, usrObjectRecord
    ' Initialize record for new entries.
    usrObjectRecord.ObjectName = String(80, 32)
    usrObjectRecord.StartPos = 0
    ' Write blank records to reserve space for each object location.
    For Index = 2 To iObjectCount + 1
        Put iFileNum, Index, usrObjectRecord
    Next Index
    Close iFileNum
End Sub
```

Writing an Object to the OLE File   To write an OLE object to a file, follow these steps:

1. Open the file for Binary access. OLE objects can only be written to files that are open for Binary access.

2. Reposition the file pointer to the end of the file. If you don't reposition the file pointer, the object overwrites the header information in your file.

3. Write the OLE object to the file using the SaveToFile method.

4. Close the file.

The StoreOLEObject procedure in Listing 19.15 writes an OLE object to a file. At the end, StoreOLEObject calls the UpdateHeader procedure, which is discussed in the next section, "Updating the File Header."

Listing 19.15   Writing an OLE Object to a File

```
Sub StoreOLEObject(strFileName As String, oleObject As Object, Optional
vStartPos As Variant)
    Dim iFileNum As Integer
    Dim lStartPos As Long
    iFileNum = OpenForBinary(strFileName)
    ' If a start position is not provided, append the
    ' object to the end of the file.
    If IsMissing(vStartPos) Then
        ' If arg was ommitted, start at end of file.
        lStartPos = LOF(iFileNum) + 1
    Else
        ' Otherwise convert to a long integer.
        lStartPos = CLng(vStartPos)
    End If
    ' Write object to file.
    Seek iFileNum, lStartPos
    ' Save object to file.
    'oleObject.SaveToFile iFileNum
    ' Update the header file information.
    UpdateHeader strFileName, oleObject, lStartPos
    Close iFileNum
End Sub
```

Part

III

Ch

19

Updating the File Header   To update the header information for an OLE object you've just saved, follow these steps:

1. Open the file for Random access.

2. Search through the list of objects in the file's header to retrieve the record that contains the name of the object being saved.

3. Update the start position information for the OLE object.

4. Close the file.

The UpdateHeader procedure in Listing 19.16 locates the record for the OLE object in the file's header and updates the object's position. If UpdateHeader finds a blank ObjectName field, it adds the object name to the file header at that record location. This initializes the object's header information the first time the file is saved.

Listing 19.16   Updating the File Header

```
Sub UpdateHeader(strFileName As String, objOLEObject As Object, lStart As Long)
    Dim usrFirstRecord As OLEHeader
    Dim usrObject As OLEHeader
    Dim bContinue As Boolean
    Dim iFileNum As Integer
    Dim Index As Integer
    iFileNum = OpenForRandom(strFileName)
    Get iFileNum, 1, usrFirstRecord
    For Index = 2 To usrFirstRecord.lStartPos
        Get iFileNum, Index, usrObject
        ' Record exists, so use the current index and name.
        If InStr(usrObject.ObjectName, objOLEObject.Name) Then
            ' Record was found, so set flag to continue.
            bContinue = True
            Exit For
        ' Record is new, so set the index.
        ElseIf usrObject.ObjectName = String(80, 32) Then
            ' Record is new, so set flag to continue.
            bContinue = True
            usrObject.ObjectName = objOLEObject.Name
            Exit For
        End If
    Next
    ' Reached the end of the header before finding
    ' the object or a space to add the object to.
    If bContinue = False Then GoTo errWriteHeader
    ' Write first record to show size of header.
    usrObject.lStartPos = lStart
    Put iFileNum, 1, usrObject
    Close iFileNum
    Exit Sub
errWriteHeader:
    MsgBox objOLEObject.Name & " does not belong to the file. Not saved."
    Close iFileNum
End Sub
```

Repeating for All Objects to Save   To store subsequent objects in the OLE file, repeat writing the object and updating the header for each object to save. The Click event procedure in Listing 19.17 shows how to use the GetOLETempFileName, CreateHeader, and StoreOLEObject procedures together. The code calls StoreOLEObject for each OLE control on the current form. At the end, it uses MoveFile to copy the temporary file to its permanent location. The MoveFile procedure is described in the following section.

Listing 19.17 Saving All OLE Objects to a File

```
' Module-level file name variable for OLE storage.
Dim mstrFileName As String

Private Sub cmdSave_Click()
    Dim objControl  As Object
    Dim iObjectCount As Integer
    Dim strTempFileName As String
    ' Get temporary file name.
    strTempFileName = GetOLETempFileName()
    ' Set permanent file name (usually, you'd prompt user for this information).
    mstrFileName = "c:\oledemo\objects.ole"
    ' Count OLE controls on a form.
    For Each objControl In Me.Controls
        If TypeName(objControl) = "OLE" Then
            iObjectCount = iObjectCount + 1
        End If
    Next objControl
    ' Saving the OLE objects!
    ' Create the OLE file header.
    CreateHeader mstrFileName, iObjectCount
    ' For each OLE object on the form, save to file.
    For Each objControl In Me.Controls
        If TypeName(objControl) = "OLE" Then
            iObjectCount = iObjectCount + 1
            ' Save the object to the file.
            StoreOLEObject strTempFileName, oleObject
        End If
    Next objControl
    MoveFile strTempFileName, mstrFileName
End Sub
```

Moving the Temporary File to Its Permanent Location   Saving OLE objects to a temporary file protects you from corrupting your permanent storage if a system failure occurs while you are writing the OLE objects to disk. After you've successfully written the temporary file, you can commit the changes by copying the file using a single statement. To move a temporary file to its permanent storage location, follow these steps:

1. Use the `FileCopy` statement to copy the file to its permanent location and file name.

2. Use the `Kill` statement to delete the temporary file.

Both `FileCopy` and `Kill` are fast operations. They don't add a lot of time to the save process for OLE objects, but they do temporarily double the required free disk space, because the OLE file exists briefly at two locations. The `MoveFile` procedure in Listing 19.18 shows how to move a temporary file to its permanent location.

Listing 19.18   Moving the File to Its Permanent Location

```
' Move the temporary file to the permanent file location.
Sub MoveFile(strTempFileName As String, mstrFileName As String)
    FileCopy strTempFileName, mstrFileName
    Kill strTempFileName
End Sub
```

The OpenForBinary and OpenForRandom Support Procedures   The task of saving multiple OLE objects to a single file uses two types of file access: Random for writing the file header and Binary for writing the object. The OpenForBinary and OpenForRandom procedures streamline the process of using two file modes. The OpenForRandom and OpenForBinary procedures are shown in Listing 19.19.

Listing 19.19   *OpenForBinary* and *OpenForRandom* Support Procedures

```
Function OpenForRandom(strFileName As String) As Integer
    Dim iFileNum As Integer
    iFileNum = FreeFile()
    Open strFileName For Random As iFileNum Len = 84
    OpenForRandom = iFileNum
End Function

Function OpenForBinary(strFileName As String) As Integer
    Dim iFileNum As Integer
    iFileNum = FreeFile()
    Open strFileName For Binary As iFileNum
    OpenForBinary = iFileNum
End Function
```

Retrieving Multiple Objects from a Single File

Retrieving OLE objects from a file that contains multiple objects is a reversal of the save procedure. To retrieve the OLE objects from a file, follow these steps:

1. Read the file's header information for the first OLE object to load.

2. Move the file pointer to the location of the first object and use the ReadFromFile method to load the object.

3. Repeat steps 1 and 2 for each object in the file.

The following sections discuss each of these steps in greater detail using the OLESTORE example.

Reading OLE File Header Information   To read the header information from an OLE storage file, follow these steps:

1. Open the file for Random access.

2. Read each record in the file header until you find the name of the object to load in the ObjectName field.

3. Return the lStartPos field in the corresponding record.

4. Close the file.

The ReadHeader procedure in Listing 19.20 reads through the header information in an OLE storage file to get the location in the file where the OLE object is stored.

Listing 19.20   Reading an OLE File Header

```
Sub ReadHeader(strFileName As String, objOLEObject As Object, lStart As Long)
    Dim usrFirstRecord As OLEHeader
    Dim usrObject As OLEHeader
    Dim bContinue As Boolean
    Dim iFileNum As Integer
    Dim Index As Integer
    iFileNum = OpenForRandom(strFileName)
    Get iFileNum, 1, usrFirstRecord
    For Index = 2 To usrFirstRecord.lStartPos
        Get iFileNum, Index, usrObject
        ' Record found, so use the current index and name.
        If InStr(usrObject.ObjectName, objOLEObject.Name) Then
            ' Record was found, so set flag to continue.
            bContinue = True
            Exit For
        End If
    Next
    ' Reached the end of the header before finding
    ' the object or a space to add the object to.
    If bContinue = False Then GoTo errReadHeader
    ' Write first record to show size of header.
    lStart = usrObject.StartPos
    Close iFileNum
    Exit Sub
errReadHeader:
    MsgBox objOLEObject.Name & " not found in file."
    Close iFileNum
End Sub
```

Reading the Object from the OLE File   To read an object from an OLE storage file, follow these steps:

1. Open the file for Binary access.

2. Move the file pointer to the location recorded in the lStartPos field of the object's OLEHeader record.

3. Use the ReadFromFile method to read the OLE object from the file.

4. Close the file.

The RetrieveOLEObject procedure in Listing 19.21 loads the OLE object at a specified byte position in a file.

Part

III

Ch

19

Listing 19.21   Retrieving an Object from the File

```
Sub RetrieveOLEObject(strFileName As String, objOLEObject As Object, lStartPos)
    Dim iFileNum As Integer
    iFileNum = OpenForBinary(strFileName)
    ' Move file pointer to beginning of object.
    Seek iFileNum, lStartPos
    ' Load object from file.
    oleObject.ReadFromFile iFileNum
    Close iFileNum
End Sub
```

Repeating for All Objects to Load   To load the remaining OLE objects from a file, repeat reading the header record and loading the object for each OLE control. The Click event procedure in Listing 19.22 uses the ReadHeader and RetrieveOLEObject procedures to load the data for each object on a form.

Listing 19.22   Loading All Objects

```
Private Sub cmdLoad_Click()
    Dim objControl  As Object
    Dim iObjectCount As Integer
    Dim lStartPos As Long
    mstrFileName = "c:\perm.ole"
    ' Loading the OLE objects!
    '
    ' For each OLE object on the form...
    For Each objControl In Me.Controls
        If TypeName(objControl) = "OLE" Then
            iObjectCount = iObjectCount + 1
            ' Get the start position for the object.
            ReadHeader strFileName, oleObject, lStart
            ' Load the object from the file
            RetrieveOLEObject mstrFileName, oleObject, lStartPos
        End If
    Next objControl
End Sub
```

Registering Your Application

Document-centric applications can be run by double-clicking an icon for a specific document in Windows or the file name in the Windows Explorer (see Figure 19.3).

You should register your application in the Registry if you want your users to be able to open application documents directly through the Windows Desktop or Explorer.

FIG. 19.3
Most applications require users to start the application, then load the document. Document-centric applications can start directly from the documents they create.

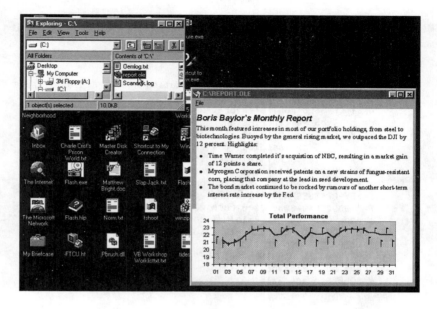

Two system registration tasks are of vital interest to Visual Basic programmers:

- Associating a file type with your application
- Identifying the icon to display for application-specific documents in the Program Manager

The following sections describe these tasks.

The Registry is a powerful tool for Windows programmers. The following sections merely scratch the surface of the subject. To really understand the Registry, see *Inside the Registry for Windows 95* by Gunter Born, Microsoft Press 1997.

Associating a File Type with Your Application

The Registry contains *File Type* keys that identify specific file extensions as belonging to specific applications. These keys allow the Windows shell functions to start an application for loading the file when the user double-clicks the file name in the Explorer or a shortcut for the file on the Windows desktop.

To associate a file type with your application, follow these steps:

1. Create a registration file for your application. The Listing 19.23 shows how to register OLESTORE.EXE and create associations for loading and printing the file.

Listing 19.23   Registering the OLE File Type

```
; Comments: OLESTORE.REG
REGEDIT
; Register OLESTORE.EXE.
HKEY_CLASSES_ROOT\olestore.application = OLE Samples Storage View Utility
; Provide open and edit command lines for the Explorer
HKEY_CLASSES_ROOT\olestore.application\shell\open\command
@= c:\\vb5 se\\samples\chapter 17\\olestore.exe %1
HKEY_CLASSES_ROOT\olestore.application \shell\print\command
@= c:\\vb5 se\\samples\\chapter 17\\olestore.exe %1
; Associate .OLE file extension with the progID.
HKEY_CLASSES_ROOT\.ole = olestore.application
; Enables drag-drop to program icon (starts application)
[HKEY_CLASSES_ROOT\olestore.application\shellex\d0phandler]
@="{99920810-0000-0000-C000-000000000046}"
: Adds OLEStore to File/New context menu from desktop
[HKEY_LOCAL_MACHINE\SOFTWARE\Classes\.ole]
@="olestore.application"
 [HKEY_LOCAL_MACHINE\SOFTWARE\Classes\.ole\ShellNew]
"Command"="c:\\vb5 se\\samples\\olestore.exe /n\""
@="OLE Storage File"
```

2. Merge the registration file. The following command line merges the file
   OLESTORE.REG with the Registry. The /s switch merges the changes silently—no
   confirmation dialog box is shown.

   ```
   regedit /s olestore.reg
   ```

3. After merging the file, you can view the changes using the Registration Info Editor (see
   Figure 19.4).

FIG. 19.4
The Registry entries for
OLESTORE.REG.

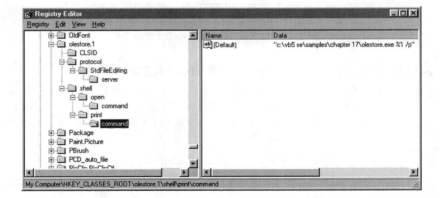

Registering Program Manager Icons

Associating a file type with your application causes the Program Manager to use your
application's default icon for program items created from files with the specified type (see
Figure 19.5).

FIG. 19.5

When you add a program item with the file type .OLE, it is displayed with the icon from OLESTORE.EXE.

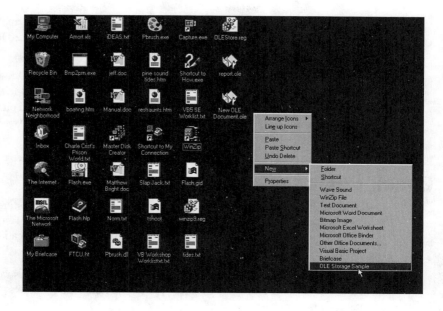

To use an icon other than the one displayed by default for the application, specify a DefaultIcon key in the application's registration entry file. To do this, follow these steps:

1. Add a class module to your application. Name the class module after the last portion of the programmatic ID for your application. For example, if your programmatic ID is OleStore.Application, set the Name property of the class module to Application.

2. Compile the application into an .EXE file.

3. Run the .EXE file. When the application runs, it registers a class ID in the Registry for the class module you created in step 2. The following entries are added for the OLESTORE application:

```
REGEDIT
HKEY_CLASSES_ROOT\olestore.application\CLSID = {A4C17767-BB44-101B-BADD-
4C696E65044C}
HKEY_CLASSES_ROOT\CLSID\{A4C17767-BB44-101B-BADD-4C696E65044C}\TypeLib
@= {A4C17761-BB44-101B-BADD-4C696E65044C}
HKEY_CLASSES_ROOT\CLSID\{A4C17767-BB44-101B-BADD-4C696E65044C}\InprocHandler
= OLE2.DLL
HKEY_CLASSES_ROOT\CLSID\{A4C17767-BB44-101B-BADD-4C696E65044C}\LocalServer @
= c:\\vb5 se\\samples\\chapter 17\\olestore.exe
HKEY_CLASSES_ROOT\CLSID\{A4C17767-BB44-101B-BADD-4C696E65044C}\ProgID =
olestore.application
```

4. Add a DefaultIcon key to the class ID key in the Registry. For example, the following key indicates that OLESTORE should use the second icon stored in the application OLESTORE.EXE:

```
HKEY_CLASSES_ROOT\CLSID\{A4C17767-BB44-101B-BADD-4C696E65044C}\DefaultIcon
@= c:\\vb5 se\\samples\\chapter 17\\olestore.exe, 2
```

Part
III

Ch
19

To register this line, you can either add it to the .REG file for the application and merge the registration file again, or you can add the key directly using the Registration Info Editor.

You should only use Visual Basic or an OLE utility called GUIDGEN.EXE to create class IDs. GUIDGEN.EXE is included in the \Tools\Idgen directory of the VB CD-ROM. Class IDs are very large numbers that are unique among all the applications installed on your system. If two applications use the same class ID, OLE can't distinguish between the two applications, and errors occur.

Check Registration Entries at Start-Up

If your application has an entry in the Registry, it should check its registered entries at start-up to verify that the .EXE's file path has not changed since the application last ran. If the .EXE's current file path does not match the registered file path, then the application should update its registration.

Visual Basic does not provide built-in support for checking system registration entries, so you must use Windows API functions. Table 19.4 lists the functions Windows provides to help you maintain Registry entries.

Table 19.4   Windows Registry Functions

Function	Use to
RegCloseKey	Close a key after opening it with RegOpenKey
RegCreateKey	Create a new key
RegDeleteKey	Delete an existing key
RegEnumKey	Get the next subkey of a specified key
RegOpenKey	Open a key
RegQueryValue	Retrieve the value setting of a key as a text string
RegSetValue	Set the value of a key

To check a registered key in the Registry, follow these steps:

1. Use RegOpenKey to open the registration key that contains path and file name information. For example, `"olestore.application\shell\open."`
2. Use RegQueryValue to return the value of the subentry containing path and file name information.
3. Compare the returned value to the application's current path and file name. If the two values don't match, use RegSetValue to change the registered value of the subentry.
4. Use RegCloseKey to close the registration key opened in step 1.

The CheckRegistrationEntry procedure in Listing 19.24 shows the declarations for the system registration Windows API functions, and demonstrates how to check the registration entry for the OLESTORE application.

Listing 19.24 Checking Registration Entries on Start-Up

```
Declare Function RegOpenKey Lib "Shell32" _
    (ByVal HKeyIn As Long, ByVal LPCSTR As String, HKeyOut As Long) As Long
Declare Function RegCloseKey Lib "Shell32" _
    (ByVal HKeyIn As Long) As Long
Declare Function RegEnumKey Lib "Shell32" _
    (ByVal HKeyIn As Long, ByVal SubKeyIn As Long, _
    ByVal KeyName As String, ByVal KeyNameLen As Long) As Long
Declare Function RegQueryValue Lib "Shell32" _
    (ByVal HKeyIn As Long, ByVal SubKey As String, _
    ByVal KeyValue As String, KeyValueLen As Long) As Long
Declare Function RegSetValue Lib "Shell32" _
    (ByVal HKeyIn As Long, ByVal SubKey As String, _
    ByVal lType As Long, ByVal strNewValue As String, _
    ByVal lIngnored As Long) As Long
Declare Function RegDeleteKey Lib "Shell32" _
    (ByVal HKeyIn As Long, ByVal SubKeyName As String)

Const HKEY_CLASSES_ROOT = 1

Sub CheckRegistrationEntry()
    Dim hkroot As Long, x As Long, lLen As Long
    Dim strKeyID As String, strKeyDesc As String
    Dim strSearchKey As String
    Dim strAppName As String
    ' Get current application path and file name.
    strAppName = App.Path & "\" & App.EXEName & ".EXE"
    lLen = 80
    ' Specify registration key to check.
    strSearchKey = "olestore.1\shell\open"
    ' Specify subentry value to check.
    strKeyID = "command"
    ' Initalize key description (value returned by RegQueryValue).
    strKeyDesc = String(lLen, 0)
    ' Open the registration key.
    x = RegOpenKey(HKEY_CLASSES_ROOT, strSearchKey, hkroot)
    ' Get the value of the "command" subentry.
    x = RegQueryValue(hkroot, strKeyID, strKeyDesc, lLen)
    ' Check the value against the current installation.
    If strKeyDesc <> strAppName Then
            ' If it doesn't match, change the registered value.
            x = RegSetValue(hkroot, strKeyID, 1, strAppName, 0)
    End If
    ' Close the registration key.
    x = RegCloseKey(hkroot)
End Sub
```

Part **III**

Ch **19**

Handling OLE Errors and Timeouts

Applications that use OLE objects need to anticipate that errors and delays can occur in the applications that provide the objects. Because these events occur outside of the application that contains the OLE object, Visual Basic needs a special mechanism for communicating these errors and timeouts. Fortunately, version 5.0 adds a set of App object properties that lets you control how OLE objects deal with problems as described in Table 19.5.

Table 19.5   *App* Object Properties that Control VB's Response to OLE Timeouts

App Object Property	Determines
OleRequestPendingMsgText	The error message displayed to users when an OLE server times out while processing a request
OleRequestPendingMsgTitle	The title on the pending request timeout dialog box
OleRequestPendingTimeout	The number of milliseconds to wait before the pending message is displayed
OleServerBusyMsgText	The error message displayed to users when an OLE server fails to respond to a request
OleServerBusyMsgTitle	The title on the server busy dialog box
OleServerBusyRaiseError	Whether or not a trappable error is generated after a busy error occurs
OleServerBusyTimeout	The number of milliseconds to wait before the busy message is displayed

The difference between a pending error and a busy error is how far the OLE request got before encountering a problem.

With pending errors, the OLE server has received and acknowledged the request—it's just taking longer than you might expect. Perhaps the server is in an infinite loop or merely retrieving a very large chunk of data.

With busy errors, the OLE server has rejected the request— usually because the server is doing some modal task for another user. In Excel, you get a busy error any time you request OLE data while Excel is displaying a dialog box.

In either case, the default timeout interval is 5 seconds. You might want to change the default OleServerPendingTimeout property before performing tasks you know will take a long time for the server to handle. Because busy errors generally occur because of user actions with the OLE server, the standard OleServerBusyTimeout value is generally okay.

Turning off busy errors by setting OleServerBusyRaiseError to False is often useful because Visual Basic will still display the server busy dialog box. Turning the busy error off prevents

OLE from halting your application unexpectedly—the user can still correct the problem using the OLE dialog box to switch to the application or cancel the request.

Handling Trappable Errors from OLE Servers

When programming with OLE objects, you can receive trappable errors from three sources:

- Visual Basic. The Visual Basic OLE trappable error codes range from 430-450. Most of these errors deal with OLE Automation objects.

- The OLE .DLLs. These errors come across as user-defined error codes in the range 31000-32000. These are the error codes you usually see when dealing with linked and embedded objects.

- The OLE object's application. Each application has its own defined range of error codes it returns. Word error messages range from 1000-1600. Excel's error codes range from 1000-1006. These errors only occur when working with each application's objects through OLE Automation.

There are two programming strategies for trapping these errors, as follows:

- Polling using `On Error Resume Next`
- Error handlers using `On Error Goto`

Polling is essential when programming with OLE objects. Errors from an OLE object's applications tend to be vague—Excel defines seven errors to cover about 1400 methods and properties. You usually need to know exactly what line of code failed to handle the situation effectively.

Polling for Errors

This method is called *polling* because you check for errors after each statement. The advantage of this is that you know exactly what line of code caused the error. Listing 19.25 shows how to poll for errors.

Listing 19.25   Polling for OLE Errors

```
Sub PollingDemo()
    ' (1) Start polling for errors.
    On Error Resume Next
    ' (2) This line returns error 1004 if an outline can't be created.
    oleSheet.Object.Selection.AutoOutline
    ' (3) If there was an error...
    If Err.Number Then
        ' (4) Alert user of the error.
        MsgBox "Can't create outline on this selection."
        Beep
        ' (5) Important! Reset error back to 0.
        Err.Clear
    End If
    '(6) Turn off error trapping.
    On Error GoTo 0
End Sub
```

The following numbered list corresponds to the comment numbers shown in Listing 19.24.

1. Turn on polling. `On Error Resume Next` prevents errors from halting the program; instead, Visual Basic simply assigns the error value to `Err` and continues to the next line of code.

2. The Excel `Worksheet` object's `AutoOutline` method does not work on all selections, and it is impossible to test the selection to see if it will work *before* you call `AutoOutline`. Your only choice is to test *after*—possibly causing an error.

3. If there was an error, `Err.Number` is set to a non-zero value (in this case 1004). This tells you that the method failed, but unless you parse the string returned by `Err.Description`, you can't tell *what* method failed. Parsing error strings is a bad idea, because they can change from version to version of Visual Basic. Your only real solution is to poll for errors after each method you think might fail.

4. Alerting the user is a good idea. Here it is done through the status bar. Using the status bar rather than a message box is less intrusive and doesn't interrupt the user's work. Be sure to clear the status bar on the next user action so the message doesn't stay up forever.

5. Clear `Err`. Otherwise, subsequent polling will reflect the current error value (1004) even if no error occurs.

6. Turn off polling before exiting the procedure.

From Here...

In this chapter, you learned how to create OLE container applications that support drag-drop, register their own file types, and effectively handle errors from their objects. For more information on related topics, see the following chapters:

■ Chapter 20, "Using Classes to Create Re-usable Objects," describes how to create ActiveX DLLs and .EXEs in Visual Basic.

■ Chapter 22, "Creating OCX Controls," explains how to create ActiveX controls in Visual Basic.

■ Chapter 31, "Integrating Visual Basic with Internet Explorer and IIS," explains how to create Visual Basic applications that display in Microsoft Internet Explorer.

Using Classes to Create Re-usable Objects

You create ActiveX components using classes. Classes are the definitions of the ActiveX components you can reuse from Visual Basic, Visual C++, Hypertext Markup Language (HTML), and all Microsoft Office 97 applications. ■

Choose a project type

Reusable components can take many forms.

Create and use a simple class

Start out by creating a simple Math class to learn the basics.

Use the Class Builder

Add to your Math class using the Class Builder Wizard.

Specify a default property

Set a property that represents the value of your object to be the default.

Create read/write, read-only, and object properties

Control how users access properties.

Add enumerations

Use enumerations to make static values available to other applications.

Create collections

Use collections to group actions and to organize your classes.

Make existing applications ActiveX components

Turn ordinary applications into programmable ActiveX components that can be used from other applications.

Document your new components

Add descriptive information and help contexts to components .

Choosing a Project Type

Any project that you create in Visual Basic can contain reusable classes. The project type determines how the classes are used. Before you create a class, think about the type of project in which it belongs.

There are seven types of projects you can create in Visual Basic. Table 20.1 lists these types and when to use them.

Table 20.1	**Types of Projects and Their Uses**	
Project Type	**Public**	**Use to Create**
Standard .EXE	No	A general application that does not share components
ActiveX .EXE	Yes	A shared component that runs in a separate process
ActiveX DLL	Yes	A shared component that runs within the caller's process
ActiveX control	Yes	A visual component for use within Visual Basic, Visual C++, and other OCX-compliant applications
Add-In	Yes	A tool that can be loaded in the Visual Basic development environment
ActiveX document .EXE	Yes	An application that runs in Internet Explorer or other hosting environments
ActiveX document DLL	Yes	A shared component that runs within Internet Explorer

Of the project types listed in Table 20.1, only the Standard .EXE is completely private; that is, it does not provide classes for reuse in other applications. All other types of projects can contain both private and public classes.

This creates a special case for Standard .EXEs. With other project types, classes have an Instancing property that controls how new objects are created; with Standard .EXE projects, the Instancing property is not available—all classes are private. Table 20.2 shows what Instancing settings are available from different project types.

Table 20.2 Available *Instancing* Property Settings by Project Type

Instancing	Standard Document	ActiveX Document			ActiveX	ActiveX *Add-In*
Setting	**.EXE**	**.EXE**	**DLL**	**Control**	**.EXE**	**DLL**
1—Private	X	X	X	X	X	X
2—PublicNotCreatable		X	X	X	X	X
3—SingleUse		X	X	X		
4—GlobalSingleUse		X	X	X		
5—MultiUse		X	X	X	X	X
6—GlobalMultiUse		X	X	X	X	X

Be sure to choose a project type that allows the type of classes you want to create. You can change project type at any time, but sometimes doing so means that other settings will change as well. The terms used in the Instancing settings list have special meanings:

- SingleUse classes create a new instance each time another application calls New or CreateObject to create an object.

- MultiUse classes create only one instance, regardless of how many times New or CreateObject are called.

- Global classes make their properties and methods available to other applications without a qualifying object name. Methods and properties defined for global objects look just like Visual Basic statements from within code. For example, mthTest.Average(1, 3, 5) can be written Average(1, 3, 5) if the class is global.

Creating Your First Class

When you begin programming with classes, it is easy to confuse a class with an object. Repeat this to yourself: A class is a definition, an object is an instance. Listing 20.1 shows the code for a simple class module:

Listing 20.1 *Math.cls*—A Simple Class

```
' Math.Cls
Function Average(ParamArray Values()) As Variant
    Dim Item, Count, TempValue
    ' For each number in the Values array.
    For Each Item In Values
        ' Keep track of the number of items.
```

Part
III

Ch

20

continues

Listing 20.1 Continued

```
        Count = Count + 1
        ' Total the items.
        TempValue = TempValue + Item
    Next Item
    ' Return the average.
    Average = TempValue / Count
End Function
```

By itself, `Math.Cls` can't do any work. To use it, you need to create an instance of the class from a code or form module. You create an instance using the `New` keyword. Listing 20.2 demonstrates how to use `Math.Cls`:

Listing 20.2 Using the Math Class

```
' TestObject.Bas -- Start-up code.
Sub Main()
    ' Declare an object variable and create an instance.
    Dim mthTest As New Math
    ' Use the Average method.
    MsgBox mthTest.Average(1, 2, 3, 4, 5, 6, 7, 8, 9)
End Sub
```

In Listing 20.2, the variable `mthTest` contains an object based on the class `Math`. As a variable, `mthTest` follows the Visual Basic rules of scope. When the procedure ends, `mthTest` passes out of scope and is destroyed. If you want `mthTest` to persist, declare the variable at the module level, as shown in Listing 20.3.

Listing 20.3 *Math.BAS*—Objects Follow the Same Scoping Rules Used By All Variables

```
' Declare the object variable.
Dim mthTest As Math

Sub Main()
    ' Create the object instance.
    Set mthTest = New Math
    ' Call some other procedure.
    ShowAverage
End Sub

Sub ShowAverage()
    ' Use the Average method.
    MsgBox mthTest.Average(1, 2, 3, 4, 5, 6, 7, 8, 9)
End Sub
```

Listing 20.3 divides the tasks of declaring the variable and creating the instance. Set is an executable statement; it triggers the Class_Initialize event in Math.Cls. You can see how this works if you add some code to the event in Math.Cls:

```
' Math.Cls
Private Sub Class_Initialize()
    Debug.Print "Math class initialized."
End Sub
```

Similarly, when mthTest is destroyed, the Class_Terminate event occurs:

```
Private Sub Class_Terminate()
    Debug.Print "Math class is dismissed."
End Sub
```

If you step through Math.BAS, you see that the class is initialized at the Set statement and destroyed just before the program ends. If you use Dim As New rather than Set, the class is initialized on first reference—much the same way forms are loaded implicitly on first reference.

Using a Class from Another Project

To use the Math class in the preceding section from another project, follow these steps:

1. With the Math class project loaded in Visual Basic, set the project type to ActiveX .EXE. From the Project menu, choose project Properties. Visual Basic displays the Project Properties dialog box (Figure 20.1).

FIG. 20.1
Choose the project type from the Project Properties dialog box.

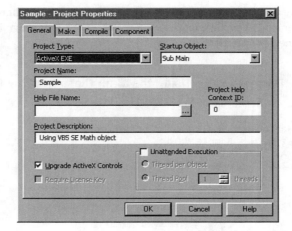

2. In the Project Type list box, choose ActiveX .EXE.
3. In the Startup Object list box, choose (None).
4. Click the Component tab and select ActiveX Component in the Start Mode frame.

5. Start another instance of Visual Basic and create a new project that uses the component.

6. From the Project menu, choose References. Visual Basic displays the References dialog box (Figure 20.2).

FIG. 20.2
Visual Basic displays the References dialog box.

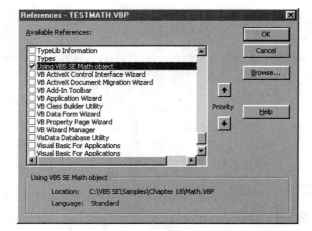

7. Select the check box next to the name identifying the Math class and then click OK. The References list is sorted alphabetically, and the names shown are either the project name or the project description if one is entered for the project.

8. Run the project.

Listing 20.4 shows a project that uses the Math class. Notice that it is almost the same code used in the former startup module for the Math project. The only change is the addition of the project name to the Dim statement.

Listing 20.4   *TestMath.BAS*—Using the Math Class from Another Project

```
' TestMath.Bas -- Start-up code.
Sub Main()
    ' Declare an object variable and create an instance.
    Dim mthTest As New Sample.Math
    ' Use the Average method.
    MsgBox mthTest.Average(1, 2, 3, 4, 5, 6, 7, 8, 9)
End Sub
```

Using the Class Builder

When you create a new class, Visual Basic presents the option of creating an empty class or starting the Class Builder (Figure 20.3).

FIG. 20.3
Clicking Class Builder
starts a tool to help you
organize classes in your
application.

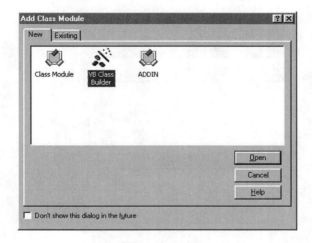

The Class Builder can be used to generate outlines for new classes or modify and reorganize existing classes. Figure 20.4 shows the Class Builder with the Math class loaded.

To add an item to your project, click one of the toolbar buttons; the Class Builder displays a dialog box where you can enter all the attributes of the new item. Figure 20.5 shows the dialog box presented for a new method.

When you close the Class Builder, it updates your project with any changes or additions that you entered. You still have to fill in the working code, but the Class Builder generates the appropriate declarations and supporting code.

FIG. 20.4
The Class Builder
provides a graphic
interface to the classes,
properties, methods,
constants, and events in
your application.

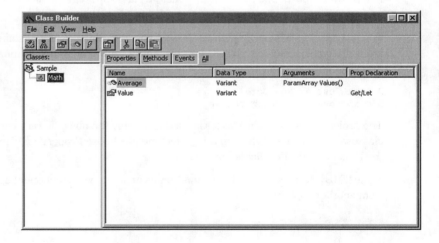

Part
III

Ch
20

FIG. 20.5

The Method Builder dialog box presents all options available for a method.

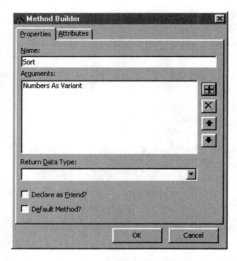

Naming Classes, Objects, and Projects

Classes are identified by their module name. By default, Visual Basic names class modules Class1, Class2, and so on. Instead of relying on these default names, you should take care to choose descriptive names for your classes—just as you would for procedures, variables, and other symbols in your project.

The class names that you choose should be as obvious as possible. For example, an application that provides one public class might name the class Application. Instances of that class would use a prefix, app, to identify that the type of object is Application.

Many folks add a cls prefix to their class names. We think this is a mistake, because classes really are types, just like Integer, Variant, Array, and so on. It makes more sense to us to save prefixes for the variables you create. For example:

```
Dim mthTest As New Math
Dim xlsLoan As Excel.Worksheet
```

The project name of public classes is used to identify the object library containing those classes. To name a project from the Project menu, choose Properties. Visual Basic displays the Project Properties dialog box.

Table 20.3 describes where the various names in an ActiveX component appear when viewed from another application.

Table 20.3   These Names Appear to Other Applications That Use the ActiveX Component

Item	Appears as
Project name	The first part of the programmatic ID in the system registration database and as the library name in the Object Browser
Project description	The library description in the References dialog box
Class module name for	The second part of the programmatic ID creatable objects in the system registration database
Public class name	The name in the Classes list of the Object Browser.
Public `Sub`, `Function`,	The name in the Members list of the `Property`, `Enum`, and `Event` Object Browser names

Creating Methods and Properties

You use special `Property` procedures to create properties for an object. Table 20.4 describes the types of procedures you use in classes.

Table 20.4   Types of Procedures Used by Classes

Procedure Type	Used to
`Sub`	Define methods that don't return a value
`Function`	Define methods that return a value
`Property Get`	Return the value of a property
`Property Let`	Assign the value of a property
`Property Set`	Set the property to a reference to an object

Assigning the Default Method or Property

You can set one of the properties or methods of a class to be the default. The default method or property is the one used when you use the object name by itself. For example, the following code sets the `mthTest` object's default property to 42:

```
mthTest = 42
```

It's common for the `Value` property to be the default. `Value` usually represents some static data maintained by the object. For text boxes, this is the text entered on the control; for scroll bars, it is the position of the slider. For the sample `Math` class, it's a numeric value as shown in Listing 20.5.

Part
III

Ch
20

Listing 20.5   CompMath.CLS—Adding a Default Property to the *Math* Class

```
' Math.Cls
' Private storage.
Dim mValue

' Default property.
Property Let Value(Setting)
    mValue = Setting
End Property

Property Get Value()
    Value = mValue
End Property
```

To make a property or method the default, follow these steps:

1. In the code window, select the name of the property or method that you want to make the default.

2. From the Tools menu, select Procedure Attributes. Visual Basic displays the Procedure Attributes dialog box. Click Advanced, and Visual Basic displays the full dialog box (Figure 20.6).

FIG. 20.6
Use the Procedure Attributes dialog box to make a property or method the default for the class.

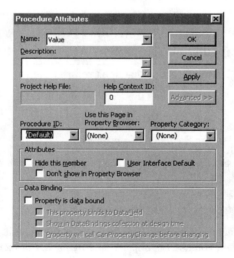

3. From the Procedure ID drop-down list, select (Default) and then click OK. Visual Basic makes the selected property or method the default for the class.

Making Friends

As mentioned, the visibility of a class is determined by its `Instancing` property. Within a class, the visibility of properties and methods is determined by their declarations. Properties and methods can be declared as `Public`, `Private`, or `Friend`.

`Friend` properties and methods are visible to other modules in the project but not to other applications, even if the class is public. This lets you share a class's properties and methods within an application without making them generally available.

`Friend` can be used in any module, but primarily it is useful in public classes. In form and code modules, `Friend` is equivalent to `Public`. To declare a property or method as a friend, add the `Friend` keyword to the declaration as shown here:

```
Friend Sub MyMethod()
```

Creating Read/Write Properties

Properties can have one or all three types of property procedures. Usually, they have both a `Property Get` and `Property Let` procedure. The property procedures in Listing 20.6 define the NumLock property.

Listing 20.6   *Keyboard.CLS*—The Keyboard NumLock Property is Read/Write

```
' Keyboard.CLS
'
' Declare Windows API calls used to get and set keyboard states.
Declare Sub GetKeyboardState Lib "USER32" (lpKeyState As Any)
Declare Sub SetKeyboardState Lib "USER32" (lpKeyState As Any)
' The index for the NumLock key in the 256-byte lpKeyState array.
Const VK_NUMLOCK = &h90

' Returns the state of the NumLock key: True = on, False = Off
Property Get NumLock() As Boolean
    ' Create an array to hold key states (256 bytes = 128 integers)
    Dim lpbKeyState(128) As Integer
    ' Get key state settings.
    GetKeyboardState lpbKeyState(0)
    ' Check the VK_NUMLOCK element of the array.
    If (lpbKeyState(VK_NUMLOCK / 2)) Then
        NumLock = True
    Else
        NumLock = False
    End If
End Property

' Changes the state of the NumLock key: True = on, False = off
Property Let NumLock(bState As Boolean)
    ' Create an array to hold key states (256 bytes = 128 integers)
    Dim lpbKeyState(128) As Integer
    ' Get key state settings.
    GetKeyboardState lpbKeyState(0)
    ' If the current state is the same as the bState, then no change needed.
    If lpbKeyState(VK_NUMLOCK / 2) And bState Then Exit Property
    ' Otherwise, set the correct value in the array.
    If bState Then
        lpbKeyState(VK_NUMLOCK / 2) = 1
```

continues

Part III

Ch 20

Listing 20.6   Continued

```
    Else
            lpbKeyState(VK_NUMLOCK / 2) = 0
    End If
    ' Set the keyboard state.
    SetKeyboardState lpbKeyState(0)
End Property
```

Use a property procedure the same way you use any object property. Listing 20.7 displays the NumLock key state and then turn the NumLock key on:

Listing 20.7   Using the NumLock Property

```
Sub UseNumLock()
    ' Get property
    MsgBox Keyboard.NumLock
    ' Set property.
    Keyboard.NumLock = True
End Sub
```

Creating a Read-Only or Write-Only Property

To create a read-only property, create the Property Get procedure for the property. Omit the Property Let procedure. Listing 20.8 shows a read-only SystemDirectory property that returns the Windows system directory:

Listing 20.8   *System.CLS*—SystemDirectory is a Read-Only Property

```
' Environmental Windows functions
Declare Function GetSystemDirectory Lib "KERNEL32" (ByVal lpBuffer As String, _
    ByVal nSize As Integer) As Integer

Property Get SystemDirectory() As String
    Dim lpBuffer As String * 256
    iLen = GetSystemDirectory(lpBuffer, 256)
    If iLen Then
        SystemDirectory = Mid$(lpBuffer, 1, iLen)
    Else
        SystemDirectory = ""
    End If
End Property
```

You can read the new SystemDirectory property, but you can't set it. The assignment statement in Listing 20.9 causes a procedure type mismatch error.

> **Listing 20.9   Assigning to a Read-Only Property Causes an Error**

```
Sub TestSystemDirectory()
    ' Display SystemDirectory
    MsgBox SystemDirectory
    ' Set SystemDirectory (causes procedure type mismatch error)
    SystemDirectory = "c:\win\system"
End Sub
```

`Procedure type mismatch` is not a trappable error. That is, you can't handle such an error in code. To be a little kinder to your users, define a `Property Let` procedure that triggers an error, as shown here:

```
Property Let SystemDirectory(s As String)
    ' Error 383 is the same error that VB displays when you try to set a read-
only property.
    Error 383
End Property
```

You can trigger any error value with the `Error` statement. We've chosen `Error 383` because this is the error code that Excel returns when you try to assign a value to one of its read-only properties.

To create a write-only property, define a `Property Let` procedure and omit (or return an error for) the `Property Get` procedure. Write-only properties are far less common than read-write and read-only properties.

Creating Object Properties

Properties that contain objects have `Property Get` and `Property Set` procedures. As you might expect, working with objects is more complicated than setting or returning simple values. Listing 20.10 demonstrates four common operations:

- `Create()` shows how to create an embedded Word document. It calls the `Basic()` `Property Set` procedure to initialize the `Basic` property.

- `Property Set SetBasic()` sets the `mobjBasic` object variable. Both the variable and the `Property Set` procedure are private—they are not available to other modules. If you want to let users set the object variable themselves, remove the `Private` keyword.

- `Property Get Basic()` returns the `mobjBasic` object variable. It is common to use `Property Get` functions to provide access to private variables like `mobjBasic`. This provides a level of control over the variable.

- `Property Let Basic()` allows users to set the object variable using assignment syntax rather than `Set`. This procedure delegates to the private `SetBasic()` procedure and may be omitted.

Part

III

Ch

20

Listing 20.10   *Document.FRM*—**The Document Class Demonstrates a Read/Write Object Property**

```
' Document.FRM
'   This is the code for a form named "Document" containing an
'   OLE container control named oleWord.
'
' Internal variable for WordBasic object.
Private mobjBasic As Object

Public Function Create() As Object
    ' Add a Word object to an OLE container object on a form.
    With Me.oleWord
        ' Create the embedded object
        .CreateEmbed "", "Word.Document"
        ' Set the position and size.
        .Top = 0
        .Left = 0
        .Width = Width
        .Height = Height
        ' Set the Basic property of the Word object
        Set SetBasic = .Object.Application.WordBasic
        ' Return the object that was created.
        Set Create = Me
    End With
End Function

Private Property Set SetBasic(obj As Object)
    ' Check if this is a WordBasic object.
    If TypeName(obj) = "wordbasic" Then
        Set mobjBasic = obj
    Else
        Error 1005
    End If
End Property

Public Property Get Basic() As Object
    ' If there is an object in mobjBasic.
    If IsEmpty(mobjBasic) = False Then
        ' Return the WordBasic object.
        Set Basic = mobjBasic
    Else
        ' No current object, trigger "Unable to get property" error (same as
➥Excel uses).
        Error 1006
    End If
End Property

' Optional, allow users to assign an object to the object variable.
Public Property Let Basic(objSetting As Object)
    ' Delegates to SetBasic().
    Set SetBasic = objSetting
End Property
```

```
Public Sub Activate()
    ' Activate the document.
    oleWord.DoVerb 0
End Sub

Public Sub Deactivate()
    ' Deactivate the object.
    oleWord.Close
End Sub
```

Listing 20.11 demonstrates how to use the `Property Get Basic` procedure.

Listing 20.11   *Document.BAS— Main()* Creates a Document Object and Adds Some Text

```
Sub Main()
    ' Create an embedded document.
    With Document.Create
        ' Show the form.
        .Show
        ' Activate the object.
        .Activate
        ' Get the Basic property and call Word's Insert method.
        .Basic.Insert "Some text"
        ' Close the object.
        .Deactivate
    End With
End Sub
```

The `SetObject()` procedure demonstrates how to use the `Property Let Basic` procedure to set an object reference with assignment rather than using the `Set` statement:

```
Sub AssignObject()
    ' Set an object reference using property assignment.
    Basic = Me.oleWord.Object.Application.WordBasic
End Sub
```

You may or may not want to let users create object references using assignment. This really is a matter of whether or not you feel it is clearer to allow assignment, require the `Set` statement, or prohibit setting a reference altogether.

Creating Public Constants as Enumerations

You can't declare public constants in a public class module, so how do you make constants available to other applications through a class? You use an *enumeration,* or, in Visual Basic, `Enum`.

Public enumerations in a public class are available to other applications and viewable through the Object Browser. Listing 20.12 shows the definition for an enumeration. Figure 20.7 shows how `Enum` looks in the Object Browser from another application.

Listing 20.12   A Simple Enumeration (Enum)

```
Public Enum Numbers
      One = 1
      Two
      Three
      Four
      Five
End Enum
```

FIG. 20.7

The Enum name appears in the Classes list, and the items appear in the Members list of the Object Browser.

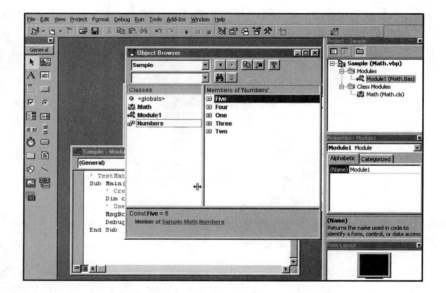

Creating Classes that Contain Collections

A *collection* is a group of objects that is itself a type of object. Visual Basic has two built-in collections: the Forms collection and the Controls collection. You can use these collections with the For Each...Next statement to perform actions on all the objects they contain. The MinimizeAll procedure, Listing 20.13, minimizes each loaded form in an application:

Listing 20.13   Forms Is One of Visual Basic's Built-In Collections

```
' Minimizes all loaded forms.
Sub MinimizeAll()
    Dim frmElement As Form
    ' For each loaded form.
    For Each frmElement In Forms
        ' Minimize the form.
        frmElement.WindowState = vbMinimized
    Next frmElement
End Sub
```

By doing the following, collections solve the three problems faced by most programmers when working with objects:

- They provide a standardized way to create and track multiple instances of an object.
- They group similar objects for fixed tasks, such as changing color properties or dragging to a new location.
- They organize large systems of objects into a hierarchy.

The following sections describe each of these aspects of using collections when creating object-oriented applications in Visual Basic.

Standard Collection Properties and Methods

Collections share a common set of properties and methods. Some collections may have additional properties and methods, but all collections have at least the set described in Table 20.5.

Table 20.5 Properties and Methods Common to All Collections

Item	Use to
Count property	Find the number of objects in a collection
Item method	Get a single object from a collection

In addition to the items in Table 20.5, collections usually provide two more methods. The methods in Table 20.6 are common to *most* collections.

Table 20.6 Methods Common to Most Collections

Item	Use to
Add method	Add an object to a collection
Remove method	Delete an object from a collection

The Add and Remove methods provide programmers a standard way to create and delete items in a collection. The Visual Basic Forms and Controls collections are maintained by Visual Basic, so they don't support these methods. Add and Remove are very common in object libraries, such as those provided by Microsoft Excel and Microsoft Project.

Creating a New Collection for Grouped Actions

You can create new collections to contain forms, controls, and ActiveX objects. Use the Collection object data type when creating a new collection. The following declaration creates a new collection named colSelected:

```
Dim colSelected As New Collection
```

Declaring a variable as a Collection object gives you four built-in properties and methods, as shown in Table 20.7.

Table 20.7 *Collection* **Object Built-In Properties and Methods**

Item	Task
Count property	Returns the number of objects in the collection
Add method	Adds an object to the collection
Item method	Gets a single object from the collection
Remove method	Deletes an object from the collection

Listing 20.14 creates a new collection named colTextBoxes and adds all the text boxes on a form to the new collection.

Listing 20.14   Create a Collection of Text Boxes to Group Actions

```
Option Explicit

' Create a new collection to contain all the
' text boxes on a form
Dim colTextBoxes As New Collection

Private Sub Form_Initialize()
    ' Variable used in For Each to get controls.
    Dim cntrlItem As Control
    ' Loop through the controls on the form.
    For Each cntrlItem In Me.Controls
        ' If the control is a text box, add it to the
        ' collection of text boxes.
        If TypeName(cntrlItem) = "TextBox" Then
            colTextBoxes.Add cntrlItem
        End If
    Next cntrlItem
End Sub
```

Listing 20.15 uses the collection colTextBoxes to clear all the text entered on the form.

Listing 20.15   The *cmdClear* Procedures Clears All the Text Boxes in the Collection

```
Sub cmdClear_Click()
    ' Variable used in For Each to get controls.
    Dim cntrlItem As Control
    ' Clear each of the text boxes in the collection.
    For Each cntrlItem In colTextBoxes
        cntrlItem.Text = ""
    Next cntrlItem
End Sub
```

Using Collections to Organize Objects

Object hierarchies are necessary when an application defines a large number of classes that relate to each other. The hierarchy defines an understandable way for users to choose from among the many objects. You use collections to create a hierarchical organization of classes. The Excel object library is a good example of a large class hierarchy, part of which is shown in Figure 20.8.

FIG. 20.8
Excel uses collections to form a hierarchy of objects.

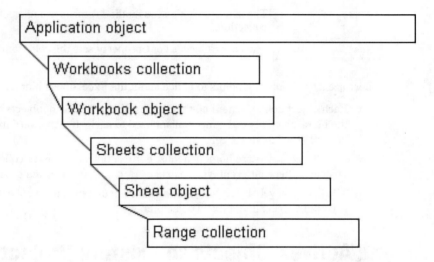

In Figure 20.8, you can use Excel collections to find individual objects. For example, the following line makes a cell in a worksheet boldfaced:

```
Application.Workbooks("stock.xls").Sheets("Portfolio).Range(1,1).Font = xlBold
```

The following table describes the action taken by each method or property in the preceding line of code:

Table 20.8   Collections in the Excel Object Hierarchy

Item	Action
Application	This object returns the top-level object in Excel.
Workbooks	The Application object's Workbooks method returns the collection of all loaded workbooks in Excel.
("stock.xls")	The default method for the Workbooks collection is the Item method, so "stock.xls" returns the STOCK.XLS Workbook object within the Workbooks collection.
Sheets	The Workbook object's Sheets method returns a collection of all the sheets in a workbook. This includes worksheets, dialog sheets, chart sheets, and so on.

continues

Part
III

Ch
20

Table 20.8   Continued

Item	Action
("Portfolio")	Again, the implicit Item method returns a single Sheet object from within the Sheets collection.
Range	The Worksheet object's Range method returns the collection of cells on a worksheet.
(1,1)	The Range object's Item method returns a single cell from the Range collection.
Font = xlBold	The Range object's Font property sets the cell's font to appear bold.

There are a few important points to notice about the Excel object hierarchy:

- Each object defines a method that returns the collection of objects the next level down in the hierarchy. This is the mechanism used to navigate downward from the top-level object to the individual cell.

- Not all collections are homogeneous. For example, the Sheets collection can contain objects of these different types: Worksheet, Chart, Module, and DialogSheet.

- The bottom-level object (Range) is a collection of items, not a collection of objects. There is no Cell object in the Excel object library.

Adding ActiveX Objects to Existing Projects

One of the fastest ways to get up and running with ActiveX is to add a class module to an existing application. Here's how to do this:

1. Change the application type to ActiveX .EXE.
2. Change the declarations of selected event procedures in an application to Public.
3. Create a set of methods and properties in a class module that call the newly Public event procedures.
4. Compile the application and run the .EXE to register it in the system registration database.

The following sections describe each of these steps in greater detail using the VB Terminal (VBTERM.VPJ) sample application included on the Visual Basic distribution disks.

Changing the Project Type

The first thing you need to do to convert a Standard .EXE project to an ActiveX .EXE project is to change the project type. To do this, follow these steps:

1. Open the project in Visual Basic.
2. From the Project menu, choose project Properties. Visual Basic displays the Project Properties dialog box.

3. From the Project Type drop-down list, choose ActiveX .EXE and then click OK.

After you've changed the project type, you can add public classes to the project. Standard .EXE projects do not allow classes to be public or display an `Instancing` property for classes.

Making Form Event Procedures Public

To make the VB Terminal sample application an ActiveX object that you can use from other applications, you must change event procedures' declarations in VBTERM.FRM from `Private` to `Public`. This lets you call the event procedures from the class module that provides the ActiveX object used by other applications.

To change the VB Terminal event procedure declarations to `Public`, follow these steps:

1. Load the project VBTERM.VPJ in Visual Basic.

2. In the Project window, select the form file VBTERM.FRM and then click View Code.

3. Change each of the `Private` declarations to `Public`, as shown in the following code. You need to change only the following declarations at this time. Other event procedures may remain `Private` for now.

   ```
   Public Sub MDial_Click()

   Public Sub MHangup_Click()
   ```

4. Save the project.

You use these `Public` `Mdial` and `Mhangup` event procedures in the next section.

Calling Form Events from a Class Module

After you've made it possible to call the crucial event procedures from outside a form, you can create a class module to repackage those procedures as methods. To create a class module for VB Terminal (`VBTerm.CLS`), follow these steps:

1. From the Project menu, choose Add Class Module.

2. Change the `Name` property of the new class module to `Application` and the `Instancing` property to `5-MultiUse`.

3. Select the code window for the class module and then enter the following lines:

   ```
   ' Dial method -- same as clicking the Dial Phone Number
   ' menu item in the user interface.
   Sub Dial()
   Form1.MDial_Click
   End Sub

   ' Hangup method -- same as clicking the Hangup Phone menu
   ' item in the user interface.
   Sub HangUp()
   Form1.MHangup_Click
   End Sub
   ```

4. Save the project.

Running and Using the New ActiveX Object

After making event procedures `Public` and creating a class module to call those event procedures, you can run and test VB Terminal as an ActiveX object. To run VB Terminal as an ActiveX object, follow these steps to create the `TestTerm.VBP` project:

1. From the Project menu, choose project Properties. Visual Basic displays the Project Properties dialog box.

2. On the General tab of the dialog, change the Project Name to VBTerminal. The project name is used to identify the application through ActiveX.

3. Click the Component dialog page and then select ActiveX component from the Start Mode frame. The start mode tells Visual Basic to watch for ActiveX requests from another instance of Visual Basic. Now click OK.

4. Save the project.

5. Run the project.

6. Start another instance of Visual Basic. You need to have two instances of Visual Basic running at the same time, so you can step through code in both the ActiveX object application and the container application that uses the object.

7. In the new instance of Visual Basic, write some code to test the VB Terminal ActiveX object. The following code is a sample of a simple test:

```
' Declare a module-level variable for the ActiveX
' object being tested.
Dim objVBTerm As Object

Private Sub Command1_Click()
' Get a reference to the VB Terminal application
Set objVBTerm = CreateObject("VBTerm.Application")
' Call the Dial method.
objVBTerm.Dial
End Sub
```

8. Run the test code. You may want to step through the test procedure and use the Immediate window to test the other methods.

N O T E The start mode options have an affect only while you are running the application within Visual Basic. They have no affect on the final, built .EXE file.

After you're satisfied with the VB Terminal ActiveX object, you can build it as an .EXE file and test it outside the Visual Basic environment. To build and test the VB Terminal application as an .EXE file, follow these steps:

1. Stop the test application and the VB Terminal application in both instances of Visual Basic.

2. In the instance of Visual Basic containing VB Terminal, choose Make from the File menu. Visual Basic compiles the application.

3. Close the VB Terminal application.

4. Change your test code, used previously, to make sure that the VB Terminal application is registered. The following code runs VB Terminal from the .EXE file:

```
' Declare a module-level variable for the ActiveX
' object being tested.
Dim objVBTerm As Object

Private Sub Command1_Click()
' Start the VB Terminal application and get a reference.
Set objVBTerm = CreateObject("VBTerm.Application")
' Call the Dial method.
objVBTerm.Dial
End Sub
```

5. Run the test code. The CreateObject method starts the VB Terminal application if it is not running already (this is different from the previous example, which used CreateObject to get the VB Terminal application running in another instance of Visual Basic).

Running the .EXE file reregisters the application in the system registration database. This maintains the registration entry if the file moves or is renamed. In some cases, you need to rerun the application outside Visual Basic to get CreateObject to work after changes are made to the ActiveX object.

Refining the ActiveX Object

The methods defined so far for VB Terminal are simple—they merely repackage existing event procedures with no additional logic. The limitation of doing this is that the interface is not as programmable as you might want it to be. For example, the Dial method displays an input box to get the phone number, but letting Dial accept a phone number argument would more useful.

The next sections show you how to refine the VB Terminal ActiveX object in the following ways:

- Modify the Dial method to receive a phone number argument.
- Add a PortOpen property that can open and close the COM port.
- Add a SendLine method to send command lines and text to the VB Terminal window.
- Add TrapText and Text properties to detect COM port events and get the text displayed in the VB Terminal window.

With these features, VB Terminal becomes useful to other applications.

Adding a Phone Number Argument to the *Dial* Method   The Dial method calls the MDial_Click event procedure in VBTERM.FRM, which displays an input box. This isn't necessary if Dial has a phone number argument. To add a phone number argument to Dial, you need to make changes in the VBTERM.FRM and the VBTERM.CLS files.

The first change is to break the MDial_Click event procedure into two procedures, as shown in Listing 20.16.

**Listing 20.16   *VTERM.CLS*—Adding a Phone Number Argument to the
Dial Method in VB Term**

```
Public Sub MDial_Click()
    On Local Error Resume Next
    Static Num$

    ' Get a number from the user.
    Num$ = InputBox$("Enter Phone Number:", "Dial Number", Num$)
    If Num$ = "" Then Exit Sub

    ' Call new DialNumber procedure.
    DialNumber Num$

    ' Move to new DialNumber procedure.    comment out here.
    ' Open the port if it isn't already open.
    'If Not MSComm1.PortOpen Then
    '    MOpen_Click
    '    If Err Then Exit Sub
    'End If

    ' Dial the number.
    'MSComm1.Output = "ATDT" + Num$ + Chr$(13) + Chr$(10)
End Sub

' New procedure bypasses user input for Dial method.
Public Sub DialNumber(Num$)
    On Local Error Resume Next
    ' Open the port if it isn't already open.
    If Not MSComm1.PortOpen Then
        MOpen_Click
        If Err Then Exit Sub
    End If

    ' Dial the number.
    MSComm1.Output = "ATDT" + Num$ + Chr$(13) + Chr$(10)
End Sub
```

Next, change the Dial method in VBTERM.CLS to take an optional argument. If the argument
is omitted, call MDial_Click as before; if it is included, call the new DialNumber procedure.
Listing 20.17 shows the final Dial method.

Listing 20.17   *VTERM.CLS*—Making the Phone Number Argument Optional

```
Sub Dial(Optional PhoneNumber As String)
    If IsMissing(PhoneNumber) Then
        Form1.MDial_Click
    Else
        Form1.DialNumber Cstr(PhoneNumber)
    End If
End Sub
```

Adding a *PortOpen* Property   Knowing whether or not the COM port is open is important to any application that wants to send a command string directly to VB Terminal. It also is useful if other applications can open or close the port at will. To provide these features, you should add a read/write PortOpen property to the VB Terminal ActiveX object.

> **N O T E**   Sometimes, it's difficult to tell if an item should be provided as a property or as a method. In general, properties represent the *state* of an object, and methods represent an *action* that the object takes. ■

The PortOpen property, shown in Listing 20.18, lets other applications get and set the PortOpen property for the MSComm control on the VB Terminal form.

Listing 20.18   *VTERM.CLS*—Adding a *PortOpen* Property to VB Term

```
' PortOpen property
' Read/Write, Boolean
'    True if Comm port is open.
'    False if Comm port is closed.
Property Get PortOpen() As Boolean
    PortOpen = Form1.MSComm1.PortOpen
End Property

Property Let PortOpen(bSetting As Boolean)
    Form1.MSComm1.PortOpen = bSetting
End Property
```

Adding a *SendLine* Method   Another useful feature to provide is a way to send command strings directly to the VB Terminal application. This would let another application configure the modem using standard modem commands, and to send strings for logging on to services, exchanging data, and so on.

The SendLine method sends a string of characters to the COM port. If the VB Terminal Echo flag is on, the characters are echoed in the terminal window; otherwise, they are not displayed. Listing 20.19 shows the SendLine method.

Listing 20.19   *VTERM.CLS*—Adding a *SendLine* Method to VB Term

```
' SendLine method.
' Sends a command string to the VB Terminal window.
Sub SendLine(strText As String)
    If Form1.MSComm1.PortOpen Then
        ' Send the line to the comm port.
        Form1.MSComm1.Output = strText & Chr$(13)
        ' If Echo is on, send the string to the
        ' textbox on the VB Terminal form.
        If Echo Then
            Form1.Term.Text = Form1.Term.Text _
```

continues

Part

III

Ch

20

Listing 20.19   Continued

```
                    & strText & Chr(13)
        End If
    End If
End Sub
```

Adding *TrapText* and *Text* Properties   If you want to send commands to VB Terminal, you probably also want to get information back. For these purposes, you need to define two related properties: TrapText and Text.

Normally, data received from the COM port triggers the OnComm event procedure in VBTERM.FRM; the data is retrieved and the buffer is cleared. In order to retrieve this data from another application, you need to delay the OnComm event by raising the threshold value that triggers the event. Setting the TrapText property, shown in Listing 20.20, to True changes the MSComm control's threshold value to its maximum setting. This lets you retrieve the data in the buffer from another application using the Text property, shown in Listing 20.21.

Listing 20.20   *VTERM.CLS*—Create a *TrapText* Property to Buffer Text Received from VB Term

```
' TrapText property
' Read/write
'    True turns on trapping -- Text property
'    returns the text from the comm port.
'    False turns off trapping -- data received
'    from the comm port is passed through to the
'    terminal window via the OnComm event.
Property Let TrapText(bSetting As Boolean)
    ' If True, set to the current buffer size.
    If bSetting Then
        Form1.MSComm1.RThreshold = Form1.MSComm1.InBufferSize
    Else
        Form1.MSComm1.RThreshold = 0
    End If
End Property

Property Get TrapText() As Boolean
    If Form1.MSComm1.RThreshold <> 0 Then
        TrapText = True
    Else
        TrapText = False
    End If
End Property
```

The Text property returns the text that was in the COM port's input buffer. It also echos the received text in the VB Terminal window if Echo is on, as shown in Listing 20.21.

> **Listing 20.21   *VTERM.CLS* — Create a *Text* Property So Other Applications Can Retrieve Data from VB Term**
>
> ```
> ' Text property
> ' Read only.
> '   Returns the text waiting in the comm port
> '   input buffer. Display the text in the VB
> '   Terminal window if Echo is on.
> Property Get Text() As String
>     ' Set InputLen to 0 so all data is retrieved.
>     Form1.MSComm1.InputLen = 0
>     ' Get the data.
>     Text = Form1.MSComm1.Input
>     ' If Echo is on, display the data in the
>     ' Terminal window.
>     Form1.Term.Text = Form1.Term.Text _
>                 & Text
> End Property
> ```

Documenting Objects, Properties, and Methods

You can document your objects, properties, and methods at two levels:

- In the Description line of the Object Browser.
- In a help file that accompanies your application.

To document the object's properties and methods in a project, follow these steps:

1. From the Project menu, choose project Properties. Visual Basic displays the Project Properties dialog box.

2. Enter the name of the project's help file in the Help File Name text box. The user interface items in your project share the same help file with the application's more technical aspects, such as programming with objects, properties, and methods.

3. From the Tools menu, choose Procedure Attributes. Visual Basic displays the Procedure Attributes dialog box.

4. Select the method or property that you want to document. Type the description that you want to appear in the Object Browser in the Description text box. Type the help context ID for the method or property in the Help Context ID text box.

5. Repeat Step 4 for each item that you want to document.

Help for a project's objects, properties, and methods resides in the same help file as for the rest of the project. When designing your help file, be careful not to confuse users by including highly technical programming topics in the same table of contents used by people seeking help on your application's user interface.

TROUBLESHOOTING

If you have the Professional Edition of Visual Basic but get an error message when you try to create a Public class module, your installation may be corrupt. Try reinstalling the Visual Basic development environment.

If your ActiveX object doesn't recognize methods and properties that you've just defined, check to make sure that you are running the correct version of the object. When debugging, it is easy to accidentally load the .EXE version rather than the new version that hasn't yet been compiled. To avoid this, be sure to start the ActiveX application in the other instance of Visual Basic before calling it from the container application.

If you encounter a "Duplicate Definition" error when trying to add an object to a collection, make sure that the key argument is unique within the collection.

From Here...

This chapter provided a substantial introduction to using classes to create components. You learned how to choose a project type, create and use a class, create and use a collection, and how to convert an existing application into an ActiveX component.

Later chapters tell you how to create ActiveX controls (.OCX), debug and test components, and distribute components to others. For more information on these topics, see the indicated chapters:

- Chapter 22, "Creating OCX Controls," describes how to create ActiveX control components and explains how to add events to a class or user control.
- Chapter 23, "Debugging ActiveX Components," explains how to locate and fix problems unique to applications that provide components.
- Chapter 24, "Building and Distributing ActiveX Components," explains how to compile and install components on users' machines.

CHAPTER 21

Creating Remote Automation Servers

ActiveX applications running on server machines can make their objects available to client machines across the network. This is done through part of ActiveX called *remote automation*. Remote automation makes it possible to distribute processing tasks among machines making efficient use of resources and reducing the amount of time it takes to accomplish tasks.

You can use remote automation to perform database transactions, administer servers remotely, monitor user activity, or do just about any task that can be separated from the user interface on a client machine. Remote automation is the application of a fundamental programming concept called *distributed computing*—this concept has been explored in computer science labs for some time, but is only coming to the desktop now.

Remote applications are just like any other ActiveX application, but they have special design, setup, and configuration requirements which will be discussed in this chapter. ■

Install DCOM 95

Windows 95 requires DCOM 95 before remote automation will run.

Compile a Remote Application

Remote applications have .VBR and .TLB files.

Use Remote Applications

Remote applications must be registered before they will run.

Debug Remote Applications

Remote applications should be debugged locally.

Optimize Performance

You optimize remote applications by pre-loading instances of the application on the server.

Different approaches for developing with SQL Server

You have several options for the specifics of how you'll communicate with SQL Server.

Cross-platform development capabilities

All of the major development platforms from Microsoft and Borland are SQL-ready.

Exposed object model for SQL administration

You can create administrative modules for your SQL Server using new object-oriented techniques.

N O T E   To create remote applications, you need the Enterprise Edition of Visual Basic and Windows
NT or Windows 95 with DCOM 95 installed.   ■

Installing DCOM 95

Windows NT includes built-in support for remote automation. If you are running Windows 95,
however, you need to install DCOM 95 to enable the distributed component object model
(DCOM) used by remote automation. The Visual Basic CD includes DCOM 95 in the
\Tools\DCOM95 directory.

To install DCOM 95, follow these steps:

1. Run the executable DCOM95.EXE from the Visual Basic CD. This file is a self-extracting
   installation file that runs DCOM 95 setup.

2. Restart your computer to enable the changes made by setup.

Windows NT provides complete security profiles for all users, however, Windows 95 has more
limited capabilities. This results in some differences in using remote automation on Windows
95. Under Windows 95, you need to be aware of the following things:

■ You must have user-level security in your Windows 95 networking settings. Share-level
  security, which is common under Windows 95, is not supported for remote automation.

■ DCOM 95 supports only the TCP/IP protocol at the time of this writing. Future releases
  should support the NetBeui and IPX protocols as well.

■ Windows 95 servers do not allow clients to start remote applications. Remote applications must be started manually on the server before they are available to clients. This
  restriction might change in the future.

■ Windows 95 does not support access control lists (ACLs) for remote applications.
  DCOM 95 is supposed to provide a work-around for this, but it is not available at the time
  of this writing.

Remote automation under Windows 95 is very new. Expect to see changes and improvements
in the technology as we approach the release of Windows 97. You can find out the latest information about DCOM 95, by checking Microsoft's developer's Web site at **http://www.
microsoft.com/oledev/**.

Compiling Remote Applications

A remote application is simply an ActiveX .EXE project that has been compiled with the Remote
Server Files option checked. To enable remote server files for a project, follow these steps:

1. From the Project menu, choose project Properties. Visual Basic displays the project
   Properties dialog box.

2. Click the Component tab. Visual Basic displays the component properties, as shown in
   Figure 21.1.

FIG. 21.1
Selecting the Remote Server Files check box causes Visual Basic to generate a type library and registration file for the application.

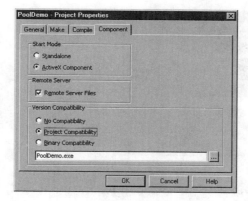

3. Select Remote Server Files in the Remote Server options. Click OK.

4. From the File menu, choose Make to compile the application.

When Visual Basic compiles a remote application, it creates two special files for use on the client machines: a registry file (.VBR) and a type library (.TLB). The registry file is used with the CLIREG32.EXE utility to register the application. The type library is used when establishing a reference to the remote application from a client machine. Both of these files are discussed further in the following sections.

Registering a Remote Application

Remote applications need to be registered on the server and the client machines that will be accessing the application. The registry procedures for the server and client machines are different.

To register a remote application on a server, simply run the application once. Visual Basic applications are self-registering at start-up. Running the application registers the application on the current (server) machine for use locally or remotely across the network.

To register the application on a client machine, follow these steps:

1. Run the CLIREG32.EXE utility on the remote application's .VBR file. The utility displays a dialog box as shown in Figure 21.2.

2. Select the Distributed COM option if your client machine is running Windows 95; otherwise, select Remote Automation. Type the Network Address of the server machine and select the network Protocol (if available). Then click OK.

CLIREG32.EXE can also be run silently, without displaying a dialog box. The utility uses the command-line switches described in Table 21.1.

FIG. 21.2

The Client Registration utility provides a front-end to the client machine's System Registry entries for a remote application.

Table 21.1 CLIREG32.EXE Command-Line Parameters and Switches

Switch	Use to
VBRfilename	Specify the remote application's .VBR file to register on the client machine.
-s servername	Specify the server that contains the remote application. Note that servername is the network name of the server machine, without backslashes (\\) or share name.
-t typelibrary	Specify the local copy of the type library to use when referencing the remote application.
-d	Register the application for use with DCOM 95 (on Windows 95). Omitting this switch registers the application for use under Windows NT.
-p protocol	Specify the protocol search sequence. Not currently supported for Windows 95.
-a level	Specify security authentication level 0-6. Not currently supported for Windows 95.
-u	Remove the application's Registry entries.
-l	Record error information in a log file: CLIREG.LOG.
-nologo	Bypass copyright screen.
-q	Run silently, without dialog boxes.
-h	Display help.

The following sample command line registers a client machine to use RemoteApp from the Wombat2 server using the NetBeui protocol. The -q switch tells CLISVR32.EXE to run silently without displaying a dialog box:

```
CLISVR32 RemoteApp.VBR -t RemoteApp.TLB -s Wombat2 -p ncacn_nb_nb -q
```

NOTE The -p and -a switches are not currently available under Windows 95 and DCOM 95. This might change in future releases of DCOM 95. ■

Using Remote Applications

To use a remote application from a client machine, follow these steps:

1. Start the Remote Automation Manager (AUTMGR32.EXE) on the server containing the remote application. You might want to add this application to the server's Start menu's Startup group so the application loads automatically when the machine starts Windows.

2. If the server is running Windows 95, start the remote application. Windows 95 does not allow clients to start remote applications. You can skip this step if the server is running Windows NT.

3. Connect to the network from the client machine. This happens automatically when you start Windows if your computer is part of a network. If you are using dial-up networking, you need to connect to the network using the Windows Dial-Up Networking software.

4. Run the client application that uses objects from the remote application.

You can access a remote application while developing client applications in the Visual Basic environment. To do this, perform the preceding steps one through three to set up the remote application, then follow these steps from the Visual Basic environment:

1. Load the client application that uses objects from the remote application or start a new project. Client applications can be any type—.EXE, .DLL, standard, or ActiveX.

2. Establish a reference to the local copy of the remote application's type library. This provides Visual Basic with information about the remote application's objects, properties, methods, and events. To establish a reference to a type library, choose References from the Project menu.

3. In the Available References list, select the check box next to the project description of the remote application. Then click OK. If the remote application doesn't appear in the list, you forgot to register the remote application on the client machine. See the earlier section "Registering a Remote Application" for instructions on how to do this.

4. Create an instance of an object from the remote application in code. You can use CreateObject or the New keyword in a Dim or Set statement to do this.

5. Run the code.

When you first start working with remote automation, you might want to use the Windows Task Manager to make sure the remote application is running on the server and *not* on the client machine. This can happen if the remote application's .EXE file is accidentally registered to run locally on the client machine.

Part
III

Ch
21

To view the Task Manager, press Ctrl+Alt+Del. If the remote application is running on the client machine, close the application and re-register the remote application on the client using the procedure described earlier in the section "Registering a Remote Application."

Debugging Problems with Remote Applications

Be sure to debug the behavior of your remote application locally before installing it on a server and attempting remote access. Any time you recompile the application, it must be re-registered on the server and client machines, so you save a lot of time if you're sure the remote application is working correctly before you proceed to testing it for remote access.

 While you are debugging an application that uses another ActiveX .EXE or .DLL, you might want to use late binding to connect to the component rather than early binding. *Late binding* establishes a reference to the component at runtime using the `CreateObject` statement. *Early binding* establishes the reference at design time through the References dialog box and uses the New keyword to create an instance of the object.

 Early binding is faster, but the reference needs to be reestablished every time you recompile the referenced component. After you've debugged the application, you can switch to early binding to receive the performance benefits that it provides.

After you've verified that your remote application runs correctly and can provide objects to other applications locally, install it on the server and register the application on the server and client machines.

Next, run the client application that uses the object from the remote application. If you've done everything correctly, the two applications will run smoothly. If there are problems with the network connection, software installation, or application registration you will receive a remote automation error. Here are some of the common errors and a description of the possible causes:

Number	Error Message	Possible Cause(s)
&H800706ba	The RPC server is unavailable.	The server name is wrong in the client machine's System Registry entry for the remote application. The remote application has shut down on the server. The remote application's .EXE file was not found on the server.
&H800706be	The remote procedure call failed.	Network connection to server was dropped or timed out waiting for a response.

800706d1	The procedure number is out of range.	The client referred to an item that doesn't exist in the remote application, but is mysteriously registered on the client machine.
&H800706d9	There are no more endpoints from the endpoint mapper.	The Remote Automation Manager (AUTMGR32.EXE) is not running on the server machine.
&H8007801d	Library not registered.	The remote application is not registered properly on the server machine.

Remote application can leave instances running on the server even after there are no more references from client applications. Be sure to check the Task Manager on the server to make sure the remote application ends when it should.

These "phantom" instances can cause problems installing new versions of the remote application on the server, consume memory, and cause incorrect data to be returned to clients in some cases.

If you notice that your remote application leaves instances running after all client applications have finished using it, check that the application is correctly de-referencing its own internal objects. The most common problem occurs when an application creates an instance of a hidden form, but doesn't destroy that instance when it is done. Listing 21.1 shows `Class_Initialize` and `Class_Terminate` event procedures that start an instance of a form and correctly destroy that instance before the object is destroyed—preventing a phantom instance.

Listing 21.1 Initializing and Terminating an Object that Displays a Form

```
Private Sub Class_Initialize()
    ' Start an invisible instance of the form.
    frmLaunch.Hide
End Sub

Private Sub Class_Terminate()
    ' Be sure to close the form when you're done.
    Unload frmLaunch
End Sub
```

Improving Remote Automation Performance

There are two types of objects that a remote application can provide to clients: multi-use objects and single-use objects.

As the name suggests, multi-use objects can be used by multiple clients. One instance of the remote application is loaded into memory, but it can provide objects to any number of clients.

Part
III

Ch
21

In contrast, single-use objects load a new instance of the application each time a client requests a new object.

Client applications respond fastest during object creation if the remote object they request is multi-use and the remote application is already running on the server. Single-use objects take longer to create, because a new instance of the remote application is loaded on the server for each new object that gets created.

FIG. 21.3

Multi-use objects start faster, but single-use objects avoid conflicts between clients.

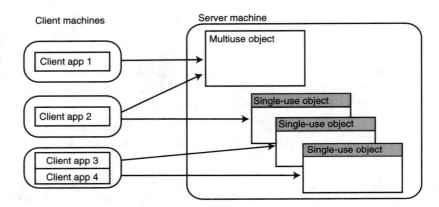

Multi-use objects in remote applications can cause problems for clients, however. For instance, if multiple clients are using a remote application and one of the clients triggers an internal error causing the remote application to quit, the objects in use by the other clients are destroyed as well.

Similarly, operations that tie up the application can cause problems for clients of multi-use objects. All clients must wait for each operation to complete as shown in Figure 21.3. This isn't a problem if the remote application is performing small tasks for a limited number of clients, but it can seriously degrade the performance of all clients as demands increase.

N O T E Whether an object is multi-use or single-use is determined by the `Instancing` property of the object's class module. ■

Optimizing Multi-Use Object Applications

You can optimize performance of multi-use objects by using multiple execution threads. With multiple threads, each new multi-use object runs independently—one client can't tie up the remote application for other clients. Figures 21.4 and 21.5 illustrate how multiple threads avoid conflicts between clients.

FIG. 21.4
Multi-use objects running in a single thread force clients to wait as objects compete for the execution thread.

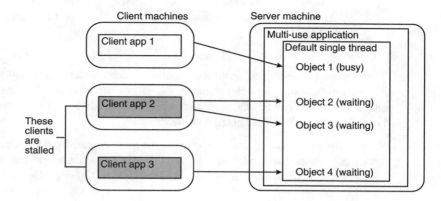

FIG. 21.5
Run multi-use objects in separate threads to prevent one client from tying up the remote application for other clients.

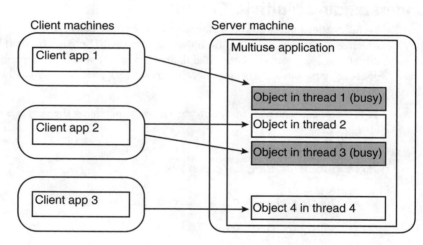

To make an application multithreaded, follow these steps:

1. From the Project menu, choose project Properties, as shown in Figure 21.6.

FIG. 21.6
The Unattended Execution check box is grayed if your project contains forms. Only applications without forms can be multithreaded.

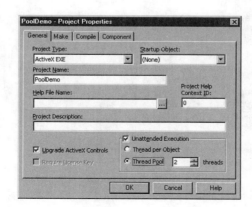

2. Select the Unattended Execution check box on the Project Properties dialog box and click OK.

3. Compile your project.

There is one big restriction on creating multithreaded, multi-use objects—the application can't include forms. If your project includes one or more form modules, the Unattended Execution check box will be grayed, and you can't select it. If you add a form to a project with the check box selected, it will be deselected automatically.

You can work around this problem by using the multithreaded application to dole out running instances of single-use application objects. This type of multi-use application is called a *pool manager* and it is discussed in the later section "Optimizing Single-Use Object Applications."

Understanding Multiple Threads

Multithreaded applications can allocate one thread per object or a fixed number of threads, which are used in rotation as new objects are created. There is a tradeoff here: Allocating one thread per object can consume an unlimited amount of system resources, but using a thread pool can cause the same performance problems that occur with single-threaded multi-use applications.

To see how a thread pool works, create a project containing the simple class module shown in Listing 21.2.

Listing 21.2   A Simple Thread Pool

```
' PoolApp.Cls
' Application class - Global Multiuse, 2 threads
Dim mValue
Private Declare Function GetTickCount _
  Lib "kernel32" () As Long

Property Get Value()
    Value = mValue
End Property

Property Let Value(Setting)
    mValue = Setting
End Property

' Pause the object.
Sub Pause()
    Dim lTicks As Long
    lTicks = GetTickCount() + 30000
    Do While lTicks > GetTickCount
    Loop
End Sub
```

Set the project properties as follows: set the project name to PoolDemo, select Unattended Execution, 2 threads, and select Remote Server files on the Components tab of the Project Properties dialog box.

Compile PoolDemo and install it as a remote application on a server and a client machine.

Next, create a client application that uses PoolDemo. Listing 21.3 uses `CreateObject` for a late-bound reference to PoolDemo. This prevents you from having to reestablish a reference to the remote application if you recompile it to test different thread settings.

Listing 21.3   Using a Thread Pool

```
' TestPool.Frm
Dim x As Object

Private Sub Form_Load()
    ' Create and instance of
    ' the demo application.
    Set x = CreateObject("PoolDemo.Application")
    x.Value = InputBox("Enter a value to identify the " & _
        "remote application's instance.")
End Sub

Private Sub Form_Click()
    Caption = x.Value & " Paused."
    x.Pause
    Caption = x.Value & " Not Paused."
End Sub
```

Compile the test application, then run three instances of it on a client machine. When each instance of the client application starts, it asks for a value to identify the instance of the remote application. This value helps show that each remote object has its own unique storage for variables. Click the client application you started last to pause the remote application for 30 seconds. This also pauses one of the other two instances of the client, as shown in Figure 21.7.

Because the remote application allocated only two threads, the third instance of your client shares an execution thread with one of the first two clients. Pausing the shared thread pauses the two clients that share the thread. If you close the client that does not share a thread, the remote application frees that thread for use by a new client.

Optimizing Single-Use Object Applications

You can combine applications that provide multi-use objects with applications that provide single-use objects to fully optimize remote applications.

For example, a remote application might provide a multi-use Application object that uses five execution threads. On startup, the multi-use application creates an array of five instances of another application that contains a single-use object.

Part
III

Ch
21

FIG. 21.7

Instance one does not respond to user events while Instance three is paused because they share an execution thread within the remote application. Instance two does respond, however.

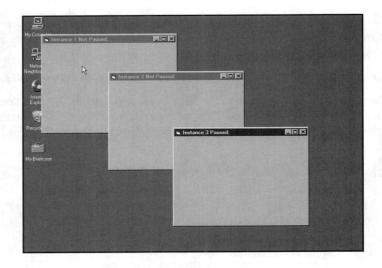

Each time a client creates an object from the remote multi-use application, that application returns an instance from the array of running single-use objects.

If a sixth object is requested, the remote multi-use application can either deny the request and return an error to the client, or it can start a new instance of the single-use application and provide that object after a slight delay.

When a client is done using an object from the remote application, the multi-use object can reset the running single-use object and recycle it for use by another client.

In this scenario, the multi-use object manages access to a pool of running instances of single-use applications, which is why this type of application is called a pool manager.

A complete example of this type of arrangement is included on the VB CD in the \VB\CliSvr directory. The Application Performance Explorer (AEMANAGR.EXE) shown in Figure 21.8 demonstrates all the different client/server configurations you can use for remote applications.

FIG. 21.8

Choose different client/ server models, then test their performance using the Application Performance Explorer.

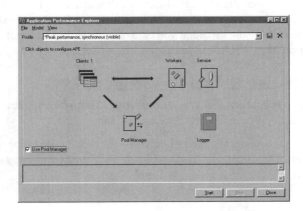

From Here . . .

In this chapter you learned how to create, debug, and optimize remote applications. Remote applications are a type of ActiveX component that make object available over the network. Other chapters in this book cover creating components using classes and making information available over the Internet. For more information about these related topics, see the following chapters:

- Chapter 20, "Using Classes to Create Re-usable Components," introduces you to using object-oriented programming techniques to create ActiveX components.

- Chapter 31,"Integrating Visual Basic with Internet Explorer and IIS," include information on how to create Active Server Pages that run tasks on Internet or intranet servers while making information available to client machines.

CHAPTER 22

Creating OCX Controls

Visual Basic, version 5.0, can create custom controls to use in Visual Basic, Visual C++, Visual FoxPro, and Microsoft Office 97 applications. This chapter shows you the specifics of how to create these components. ■

Create a control

Visual Basic includes a Control Wizard to help you get started, but before you plunge in you should understand the parts of a control by creating one manually.

Create properties, methods, and events

For the most part properties, methods, and events are the same for controls as they are for other classes. However, design-time properties require special coding.

Debug and test a control

Controls can't run by themselves in the programming environment. You need to create a project group to debug and test a control.

Use a custom control

Controls are available in Visual Basic, Visual C++, FoxPro, Access, and all Office 97 applications.

Use the ActiveX Control Interface Wizard

The Wizard lets you base your control's properties, methods, and events on those of its constituent controls.

Understand property pages

Use the Property Page Wizard add-in to create a rough draft of a property page, then refine the property page to include enumerated property settings.

Creating Your First Control

Visual Basic now calls custom controls *ActiveX* controls. This does not change the underlying facts about these components—they still reside in .OCX files and are used by .OCX hosting environments. Currently, these development environments can use .OCX controls: Visual Basic, Visual C++, Visual FoxPro, and Microsoft Office 97.

Custom controls can be as simple or complex as you want them to be. One of the really neat features of Visual Basic, version 5.0 is the ActiveX Control Interface Wizard, which lets you base new custom controls on existing controls. The code generated by the Control Wizard can be a bit overwhelming, however. For now we'll stick to doing things by hand; later sections discuss using the Control Wizard.

To create a custom control in Visual Basic, follow these steps:

1. Start a new project of the type ActiveX control.
2. Draw the interface of the control using other controls from the Toolbox, just as you would for a form.
3. Add code to implement the behavior of your control.
4. Add code to provide the properties, methods, and events that your control will provide to applications using it.
5. Add a new Standard .EXE project within the Visual Basic environment to provide a way to test and debug the control.
6. Compile the control as an .OCX file.

The following sections discuss these steps in detail using an .OCX control that controls .WAV file playback volume as a sample.

Starting a New .OCX Project

To start a new project for an .OCX control, follow these steps:

1. From the File menu, choose New Project. Visual Basic displays the New Project dialog box.
2. Click the ActiveX Control icon. Visual Basic creates a new project with the default settings for creating a custom control. An ActiveX Control project contains a blank User Control window as shown in Figure 22.1.
3. From the Project menu, choose Project Properties to set the Project Name and Project Description. These settings determine the control's file name and description that appears in the Visual Basic Components dialog box.
4. In the Properties window, set the Name property of the User Control. The Name property determines the default name used when creating the custom control on a form and is

displayed as ToolTip text in the Toolbox. Figure 22.2 shows how a control's names are used in the development environment.

5. Save the project (.VBP) and user control file (.CTL).

FIG. 22.1
You draw a control on a User Control window, rather than a blank form.

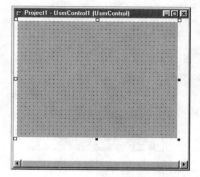

An .OCX file can contain more than one control so you usually want to use different names for the project and user control. This will help you avoid confusion if you add controls to future versions of the .OCX file. Remember that components such as custom controls can have long lives. You need to think about maintenance from the very start.

The settings shown in Figure 22.2 are for the sample Volume control described in the following sections. If you want to follow along as a tutorial, create a project as described previously with the project and property settings shown in Table 22.1.

Table 22.1   Project and Property Settings for the Volume Custom Control

Item	Setting
Project Type	ActiveX Control
Project Name	SoundControls
Project Description	Sample Sound controls for VB5 Special Edition
User control Name property	Volume
User control Public property	True

N O T E   The Public property is True by default. It is shown to draw your attention to it. Private controls can only be used within the project where they are defined. They provide a way to share features among other public controls in a ActiveX Control project. ■

FIG. 22.2

Project Name defines the .OCX file name, Description appears in the Components dialog box, and the user control Name property identifies the control in the Toolbox.

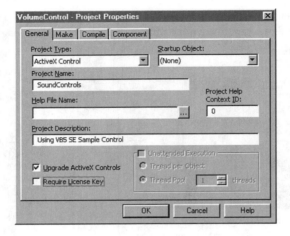

Drawing a Control's Interface

The interface for a custom control is created the same way as you create the interface for a form. Simply select the control you want to add from the Toolbox, then click and drag the User Control window.

To draw the Volume sample control, follow these steps:

1. From the Project menu, choose Components. Visual Basic displays the Components dialog box.

2. Click the check box beside the Microsoft Windows Common Controls 5.0 custom control and click OK.

3. In the Toolbox, click the Slider control.

4. Draw the Slider control on the User Control window starting at the coordinates (0,0) (see Figure 22.3).

5. Set the Slider control properties as shown in Table 22.2.

Table 22.2   Slider Control Property Settings for the Volume Sample

Property	Setting
Name	sldVolume
Max	&HFFFF
Min	0 (Default)
TickFrequency	&HFFF

FIG. 22.3

The Slider control should be positioned at the coordinates (0,0) to make resizing the control easier in code.

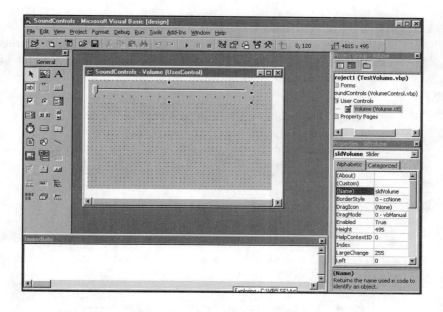

Most custom controls created in Visual Basic are based on other controls. It is possible to create the custom control's interface completely from scratch using the background `Picture` property, `Line`, and `Circle` methods, but this is not the most common practice.

Custom controls that are based on other custom controls need to install runtime versions of those controls when they are distributed. This means that the Volume control is dependent on the Microsoft Windows Common Controls file (COMCTL32.OCX). If you want to avoid this, use a scroll bar instead. Intrinsic controls, such as the scroll bar, are part of the Visual Basic runtime.

Writing Code for Resizing the Control

The Volume control's appearance is determined by the Slider control it contains. When a user draws the Volume control on a form, you need to make sure the Slider control fills the space created. To do this, add the following code to the control's `Resize` event:

```
Private Sub UserControl_Resize()
    sldVolume.Height = Height
    sldVolume.Width = Width
End Sub
```

Because the Slider control begins at the coordinates (0,0) on the user control window, this `Resize` event keeps the user control and the Slider control exactly in sync.

Writing Code to Initialize the Control

Next, you need to write code to set the initial position of the Slider control. The Slider position should match the current system sound volume setting. You can get this value using the waveOutGetVolume API function, as shown in Listing 22.1.

Listing 22.1 Volume.CTL—Initializing the Control

```
' Types for handling Long/Integer conversions.
Private Type ulLong
    HiWord As Integer
    LoWord As Integer
End Type

Private Type uvLong
    n As Long
End Type

' Variables for handling Long/Integer conversions.
Private ulVol As ulLong
Private uvVol As uvLong

' MM API functions for getting/setting sound level.
Private Declare Function waveOutGetVolume _
    Lib "winmm.dll" (ByVal uDeviceID As Long, _
    lpdwVolume As Long) As Long
Private Declare Function waveOutSetVolume _
    Lib "winmm.dll" _
    (ByVal uDeviceID As Long, _
    ByVal dwVolume As Long) As Long

Private Sub UserControl_Initialize()
    lmmErr = waveOutGetVolume(0, uvVol.n)
    LSet ulVol = uvVol
    If lmmErr Then
        Err.Raise vlmErrCantGetDevice, "Volume control", _
            "Couldn't get sound device."
    End If
    sldVolume = ulVol.LoWord And &HFFFF&
End Sub
```

The preceding code includes two user-defined types to handle conversion between the value returned by waveOutGetVolume and the volume settings for the right and left speakers, which are the high and low words of the returned value. The range for these settings is 0 to &hFFFF, which correspond to the Min and Max property settings of the Slider control you set earlier.

The Initialize event occurs any time the control is created. This includes when you draw a new control on a form at design time. In the case of the Volume control, the design time position of the slider reflects the current system volume setting. This is OK for the Volume control (actually, it's kind of good), but in some cases you'll want to initialize a control only during runtime.

To initialize a control only at runtime, add a code module to the control's project and write your initialization code in `Sub Main`. Then, set `Sub Main` as the startup object in the Project Properties dialog box. `Sub Main` runs only when the hosting application starts the control.

Writing Code to Respond to Changes

So far, you've created a control that can be drawn on a form that reflects the system settings at runtime. To be able to control the volume setting at runtime, you need to add the code shown in Listing 22.2.

Listing 22.2   Volume.CTL—Changing the Sound Volume

```
' Volume.Ctl
Private Sub sldVolume_Change()
    ulVol.HiWord = (sldVolume And &H7FFF&) - (sldVolume And &H8000&)
    ulVol.LoWord = (sldVolume And &H7FFF&) - (sldVolume And &H8000&)
    LSet uvVol = ulVol
    Dim lmmErr As Long
    lmmErr = waveOutSetVolume(0, uvVol.n)
    If lmmErr Then
    Err.Raise vlmErrCantGetDevice, "Volume control", _
            "Couldn't get sound device."
    End If
End Sub
```

This code updates the system .WAV volume setting when the user moves the slider in the Volume control. You can even skip ahead at this point and try the control out.

Adding Public Properties, Methods, and Events

If you skipped ahead and tried the Volume control, you might have noticed two things:

■ You can't get or set the volume setting from within code.

■ You can't detect changes to the volume setting.

That's because, as it stands now, the Volume control doesn't define any public properties, methods, or events. To fix this, add the property definition shown in Listing 22.3 to the Volume control's User Control module:

Listing 22.3   Volume.CTL—Creating a Value Property

```
Public Property Get Value() As Long
    ' Return the left speaker setting.
    Value = ulVol.LoWord And &HFFFF&
End Property
```

continues

Listing 22.3   Continued

```
Public Property Let Value(Setting As Long)
    If 0 > Setting > &HFFFF& Then
        Err.Raise vlmErrInvalidSetting, "Volume control", _
          "Volume must be between 0 and &HFFFF&."
        Exit Property
    End If
    ' Update the slider (triggers Change event).
    sldVolume = Setting
End Property
```

The `Value` property in Listing 22.3 and earlier code uses some constants I haven't defined yet. I waited until now, because I wanted to show all the public members together. Visual Basic uses *enumerations* to provide public constants in a class or user control module. Listing 22.4 defines the error codes used by the Volume control.

Listing 22.4   Volume.CTL—Error Code Definitions

```
' Volume.Ctl - public constants.
Public Enum VolumeControlConstants
    vlmErrCantGetDevice = 8601
    vlmErrInvalidSetting = 8602
End Enum
```

The preceding code will group these error constants under the class `VolumeControlConstants` in the Object Browser. `Enums` provide a way to group constants by category.

Finally, changes to the slider control should also trigger a `Change` event that is available to the user. To do this, you need to declare a public event, then trigger the event at the end of the Slider control's `Change` event. Listing 22.5 shows the definition and modification to `sldVolume_Change` in **bold**.

Listing 22.5   Volume.CTL—Raising an Event

```
' Public events.
Public Event Change()

Private Sub sldVolume_Change()
    ulVol.HiWord = (sldVolume And &H7FFF&) - (sldVolume And &H8000&)
    ulVol.LoWord = (sldVolume And &H7FFF&) - (sldVolume And &H8000&)
    LSet uvVol = ulVol
    Dim lmmErr As Long
    lmmErr = waveOutSetVolume(0, uvVol.n)
    If lmmErr Then
        Err.Raise vlmErrCantGetDevice, "Volume control", _
          "Couldn't get sound device."
```

```
        End If
        ' Trigger the user control's Change event.
        RaiseEvent Change
    End Sub
```

Adding Design-Time Properties

The Value property in the preceding section is a runtime property. You can't get or set it from the development environment. To add a design-time property to a control, create the property, then add code to the control's ReadProperties and WriteProperties events as shown in Listing 22.6.

> **Listing 22.6   Volume.CTL—Adding a Design-Time Property**
>
> ```
> Public Enum VolumeSpeakerConstants
>     vlmBoth
>     vlmRight
>     vlmLeft
> End Enum
>
> Dim mSpeaker As VolumeSpeakerConstants
>
> Property Get Speaker() As VolumeSpeakerConstants
>     Speaker = mSpeaker
> End Property
>
> Property Let Speaker(Setting As VolumeSpeakerConstants)
>     mSpeaker = Setting
>     PropertyChanged "Speaker"
> End Property
>
> Private Sub UserControl_ReadProperties(PropBag As PropertyBag)
>     mSpeaker = PropBag.ReadProperty("Speaker", vlmBoth)
> End Sub
>
> Private Sub UserControl_WriteProperties(PropBag As PropertyBag)
>     PropBag.WriteProperty "Speaker", mSpeaker, vlmBoth
> End Sub
> ```

The ReadProperties event occurs when the user selects the control in the design environment. The WriteProperties event occurs when the user changes the settings in the Properties window. The PropertyBag object provides static storage for the control's design-time properties. The PropertyBag ReadProperty method adds properties to the list displayed in the Properties window; and the WriteProperty method retrieves the setting from the Property window and stores it in a variable for use within the control.

Notice that you need to add a PropertyChanged statement to the Property Let procedure. This updates the PropertyBag when the user changes the property's setting.

The Speaker property affects the Volume control's Initialize event, Change event, and Value property. It determines which speaker the Volume control refers to—right, left, or both (default). Listing 22.7 shows the changes to the Initialize event and Value property in **bold**.

Listing 22.7   Volume.CTL—Adding a Speaker Property

```
Private Sub UserControl_Initialize()
    lmmErr = waveOutGetVolume(0, uvVol.n)
    LSet ulVol = uvVol
    If lmmErr Then
        Err.Raise vlmErrCantGetDevice, "Volume control", _
            "Couldn't get sound device."
    End If
    Select Case mSpeaker
    ' Average two settings.
    Case vlmBoth
        sldVolume = (ulVol.LoWord And &HFFFF&) _
            + (ulVol.HiWord And &HFFFF&) \ 2
    ' Return left setting.
    Case vlmLeft
        sldVolume = ulVol.LoWord And &HFFFF&
    ' Return right setting.
    Case vlmRight
        sldVolume = ulVol.HiWord And &HFFFF&
    End Select
End Sub

Private Sub sldVolume_Change()
    Select Case mSpeaker
    ' Set both speakers.
    Case vlmBoth
        ulVol.HiWord = (sldVolume And &H7FFF&) - (sldVolume And &H8000&)
        ulVol.LoWord = (sldVolume And &H7FFF&) - (sldVolume And &H8000&)
    ' Set left speaker.
    Case vlmLeft
        ulVol.LoWord = (sldVolume And &H7FFF&) - (sldVolume And &H8000&)
    ' SSet right speaker.
    Case vlmRight
        ulVol.HiWord = (sldVolume And &H7FFF&) - (sldVolume And &H8000&)
    End Select
    LSet uvVol = ulVol
    Dim lmmErr As Long
    lmmErr = waveOutSetVolume(0, uvVol.n)
    If lmmErr Then
        Err.Raise vlmErrCantGetDevice, "Volume control", _
            "Couldn't get sound device."
    End If
    RaiseEvent Change
End Sub

Public Property Get Value() As Long
    Select Case mSpeaker
        ' Average two settings.
        Case vlmBoth
```

```
                        Value = (ulVol.LoWord And &HFFFF&) _
                              + (ulVol.HiWord And &HFFFF&) \ 2
                  ' Return left setting.
                  Case vlmLeft
                        Value = ulVol.LoWord And &HFFFF&
                  ' Return right setting.
                  Case vlmRight
                        Value = ulVol.HiWord And &HFFFF&
                  End Select
            End Property
```

Running the Control Under Development

You can't just run a control in the Visual Basic development environment. By their nature, controls need a form to exist on. To run a control that's under development, add a standard .EXE project to the current Visual Basic session to create a *project group* containing both the ActiveX Control project and a Standard .EXE project.

To create a project group and run the custom control, follow these steps:

1. With the ActiveX Control project loaded in Visual Basic, choose <u>A</u>dd Project from the File menu. Visual Basic displays the New Project dialog box.

2. Click the Standard .EXE project icon. Visual Basic creates a default Standard .EXE project containing one form.

3. Close the User Control window in the development environment and click the form window in the Standard .EXE project (see Figure 22.4).

FIG. 22.4

Visual Basic won't let you draw your new control on the form if the control's design window is open.

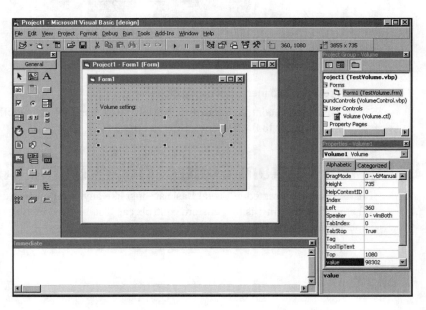

4. Click the user control in the Toolbox and draw the control on the form.

5. Write code in the form's event procedures to test the properties, methods, and events in the control.

6. Run the Standard .EXE project.

When you run the Standard .EXE project you can step into the control's code, set breakpoints, add watches, and so on just as you would when debugging any executable.

Compiling the Finished Control

Once you're satisfied with your control, you can compile it into an .OCX executable file.

1. Set the control's version number and description. From the Project menu, choose Properties. On the Project Properties dialog box, click the Make tab (see Figure 22.5).

FIG. 22.5
Increment the minor version number until you are ready to release the control. Version information fields provide information you can view from the Windows file system.

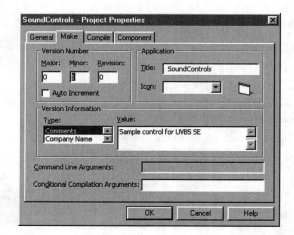

2. From the File menu, choose Make.

3. To make the control automatically available to Visual Basic and other applications, copy the .OCX file to the Windows System directory.

Using the Custom Control from VB and VBA

Custom controls created in Visual Basic are just like any other custom control you've used. What is truly amazing, is that custom controls can also be used in the Microsoft Office 97 applications as well.

The Office 97 applications include the Visual Basic for Applications (VBA) environment. To add a custom control to a form in any of the Office 97 applications, follow these steps:

1. Within the application, start the VBA environment.

2. From the Insert menu, choose User Form. VBA displays a form and the control Toolbox (see Figure 22.6).

FIG. 22.6
Right-click the VBA Toolbox to add a custom control.

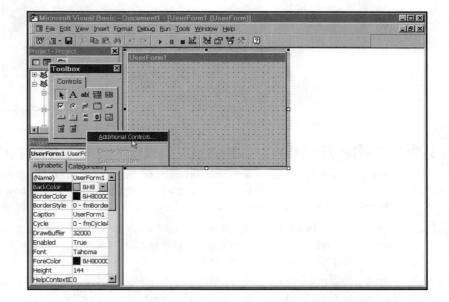

3. Right-click the Toolbox and select Additional Controls. VBA displays the Additional Controls dialog box (see Figure 22.7).

4. Select the check box next to the custom control you want to use, then click OK. VBA adds the control to the Toolbox.

Microsoft Access provides a slightly different VBA forms interface than the other Office applications. In Access, custom controls are part of a scrolling list off of the Toolbox, but the same basic steps apply.

One important thing—the VBA will only display controls that are in the System Registry. To register a control, run the REGOCX32.EXE application found in the Tools/RegistrationUtilities directory of the Visual Basic CD-ROM. The following example shows the command line to use:

```
REGOCX32.EXE SoundControls.OCX
```

FIG. 22.7
VBA only displays the
.OCX controls that are in
the System Registry.

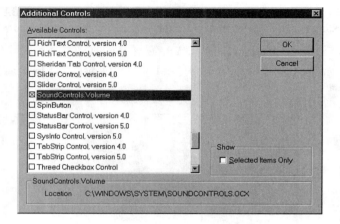

Using the ActiveX Control Interface Wizard

The preceding sections walked you through creating a custom control from scratch. Controls are pretty complicated, and this is an important step in understanding how they work. Once you've got that down you can leap ahead by using the ActiveX Control Interface Wizard add-in.

This add-in generates code to allow your custom control to use the properties, methods, and events of contained controls as its own. This is called *delegating* tasks from the custom control to the items the custom control contains.

To see how this works, open the Volume control project created earlier in this chapter. The following steps implement an Orientation property for the Volume control based on the Slider control's Orientation property:

1. From the Add-Ins menu, choose Add-In Manager. Visual Basic displays the Add-In Manager dialog box.

2. Select the check box next to the VB ActiveX Control Interface Wizard and click OK. Visual Basic adds an item for the wizard to the Add-In menu.

3. From the Add-Ins menu, choose ActiveX Control Interface Wizard. Visual Basic starts the wizard and displays the opening dialog box (see Figure 22.8).

4. Click the Next button. The wizard displays the Select Interface Members dialog box (see Figure 22.9).

5. Click the << button to remove the default properties displayed in the Select Names list. Then, select Orientation in the Available names list and click the > button to add it to the Selected Names list. Repeat for the Value and Change items. Click Next. The wizard displays the Create Custom Interface Members step (see Figure 22.10).

FIG. 22.8

The ActiveX Control Interface Wizard generates code based on controls already drawn on the custom control.

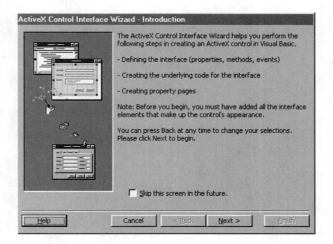

FIG. 22.9

Select items to include in your control from a list of standard names.

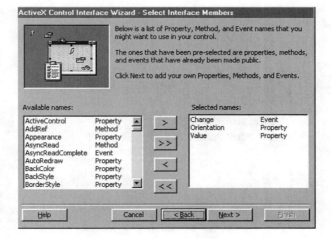

6. Click Next. The wizard displays the Set Mapping step (see Figure 22.11).

7. Click the Orientation property, then select the sldVolume control in the Control list and Orientation in the Member list. Click Next. The wizard displays the Set Attributes step (see Figure 22.12).

8. Click Next. The wizard displays the Finished step (see Figure 22.13).

It's imperative to start with a custom control containing no code, so you can get a clear view of the code generated by the Control Wizard. The preceding steps generate the code in Listing 22.8.

FIG. 22.10
Add unique property, method, and event names here to generate empty template code for those items.

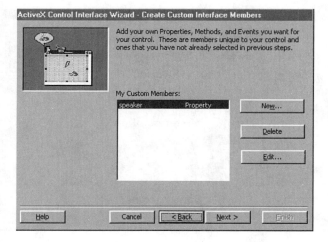

FIG. 22.11
Set mapping delegates items in your custom control to items in the controls it contains.

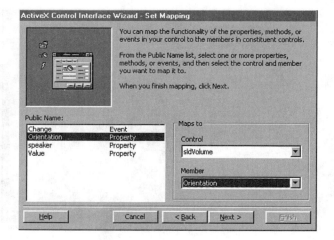

FIG. 22.12
Set attributes determine the attributes of existing items in your custom control that are not delegated to another control's member.

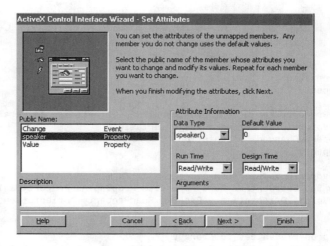

FIG. 22.13
Select View Summary Report to see a description of how to save and test the generated code.

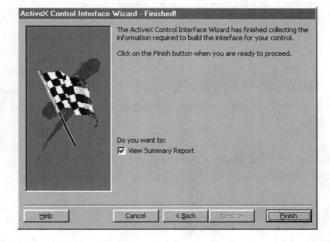

Listing 22.8   Volume.CTL—Code Generated by the ActiveX Control Interface Wizard

```
Public Property Get Orientation() As DataBinding
    Orientation = sldVolume.Orientation
End Property

Public Property Let Orientation(ByVal New_Orientation As DataBinding)
    sldVolume.Orientation = New_Orientation
    PropertyChanged "Orientation"
End Property

'Load property values from storage
Private Sub UserControl_ReadProperties(PropBag As PropertyBag)
    sldVolume.Orientation = PropBag.ReadProperty("Orientation", 0)
End Sub

'Write property values to storage
Private Sub UserControl_WriteProperties(PropBag As PropertyBag)
    Call PropBag.WriteProperty("Orientation", sldVolume.Orientation, 0)
End Sub
```

The `DataBinding` data type in Listing 22.8 ensures the settings for Orientation are transferred from the Slider control to the custom control.

You can use the Control Wizard to explore how to implement various aspects of a control. Be aware that it will comment out code for existing members if you remove them in one of the wizard's steps.

Sometimes, it's handy to run the Control Wizard on a version of your control containing no code, then copy the generated control into the complete version of your control. This gives you more control and understanding of the changes being made.

Understanding Property Pages

Property pages provide an alternative interface to a custom control's properties at design time. Rather than using the Properties window, you right-click the control and select Properties. Visual Basic displays the design-time properties for the control as shown in Figure 22.14.

To add a property page for a control, follow these steps:

1. From the Project menu, choose Add Property Page. Visual Basic adds a new property page to the project.

2. Set the Name property of the property page. This is the name used to link the page to the control.

3. Select the custom control's design window and set its PropertyPage property to the name entered in step 2.

4. Select the property page and add text boxes, labels, and code to reflect the design-time properties you want to modify from the control's property page.

FIG. 22.14

Property pages display design-time settings for a custom control.

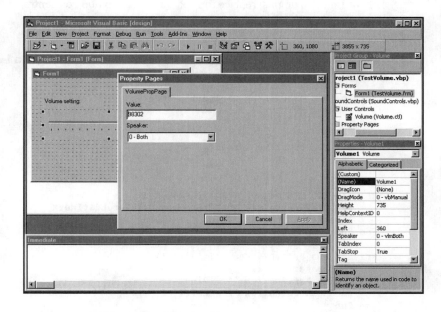

The Property Page Wizard add-in provides a quick way to generate property pages based on an existing custom control. Listing 22.9 was generated by running the wizard on the Volume control.

Listing 22.9   Volume.PAG—Code Generated by the Property Page Wizard

```
Private Sub txtSpeaker_Change()
    Changed = True
End Sub

Private Sub txtValue_Change()
    Changed = True
End Sub

Private Sub PropertyPage_ApplyChanges()
    SelectedControls(0).Speaker = txtSpeaker.Text
    SelectedControls(0).value = txtValue.Text
End Sub

Private Sub PropertyPage_SelectionChanged()
    txtSpeaker.Text = SelectedControls(0).Speaker
    txtValue.Text = SelectedControls(0).value
End Sub
```

This code provides a good starting point for the property page. One change you might want to make is to change the txtSpeaker control to a combo box reflecting the valid settings Right, Left, or Both. To do this, replace the text box with a combo box control and make the modifications in Listing 22.10 shown in **bold**.

Listing 22.10   Volume.PAG—Changing the Property Page to List Enumerated Values

```
Private Sub cmbSpeaker_Change()
    Changed = True
End Sub

Private Sub cmbValue_Change()
    Changed = True
End Sub

Private Sub PropertyPage_ApplyChanges()
    SelectedControls(0).Speaker = cmbSpeaker.ListIndex
    SelectedControls(0).value = txtValue.Text
End Sub

Private Sub PropertyPage_Initialize()
    cmbSpeaker.AddItem "0 - Both", 0
    cmbSpeaker.AddItem "1 - Right", 1
    cmbSpeaker.AddItem "2 - Left", 2
End Sub

Private Sub PropertyPage_SelectionChanged()
    cmbSpeaker.ListIndex = SelectedControls(0).Speaker
    txtValue.Text = SelectedControls(0).value
End Sub
```

From Here. . .

In this chapter, you created a simple control and learned how to implement design-time properties and property pages. You also learned about using your control from applications other than Visual Basic.

Controls are a type of class. More information about programming with classes can be found in the following chapters:

- Chapter 20, "Using Classes to Create Re-usable Objects," explains the fundamentals of object-oriented programming, including how to create properties with different attributes such as default properties.

- Chapter 24, "Building and Distributing ActiveX Components," explains how to compile and install components on users' machines.

CHAPTER 23

Debugging ActiveX Components

Designing and writing code is only a portion of the process of creating an application. Debugging prior to release can take more time and effort than most programmers are willing to admit—or schedule. Applications that provide objects can be especially problematic, because they expose a whole new, programmatic interface with a whole new set of problems. This chapter discusses those problems and supplies approaches for solving them. ■

Anticipate problems

When developing an application that provides objects, you need to consider a whole new set of problems that can occur.

Determine the instance of an object

Visual Basic's Watch window can now view object variables and their members. This makes it much easier to determine what instance of an object is being referred to in code.

Prevent lost references

Applications that don't terminate after their last reference consume resources and can cause errors.

Avoid conflicts

When two applications share an object, you need to be sure that one application doesn't inadvertently affect the other through global data in the shared object.

Debug applications that provide objects

You should test applications in-process, cross-process, and as compiled executables before final release.

Maintain released objects

Subsequent versions of an application must maintain the original programmable interface in order to avoid breaking compatibility.

Solving Problems Unique to Objects

Debugging an application that uses objects internally or provides objects to other applications presents these new problems:

- It can be hard to tell if an object variable refers to the correct instance of an object.
- Objects might leave unused instances in memory.
- If an application that provides objects is already running, the application's objects might be improperly reinitialized.
- Applications that use objects from the same object application can affect each other through the object application's global variables or procedures.
- Multiple applications can access the same object, causing problems with concurrency.
- Problems in the application's registration database entries can cause the wrong version of an object's executable file to run.

The following sections discuss these problems in detail and explain how you solve them.

Watching Object Instances During Debugging

VB5 lets you watch object variables, as shown in Figure 23.1. This is a huge improvement over VB4, which displayed the value "Object doesn't support this action" whenever you tried to watch an object variable.

FIG. 23.1
Visual Basic now can watch object variables directly.

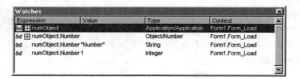

Members of the object can be viewed in the Watch Window simply by clicking them. When debugging objects, it helps if you've defined two standard properties:

- The Name property uniquely identifies the instance of the object.
- The Parent property identifies the object that created the current object.

Placing a watch expression on Object.Name tells you whether you're looking at the correct object. Checking Object.Parent helps you look backward in code to discover how the object was created.

The Name and Parent properties aren't automatic for all objects. Programmers must define the properties in code. Although defining these properties for *all* objects might seem like extra work, the properties can save you much trouble when tracing through complex object interactions.

Single-Use versus Multiuse Objects

Multiple instances of an application can be loaded in memory at the same time, but how Visual Basic deals with instances depends on the object's `Instancing` property. All objects created in VB have one of the `Instancing` settings shown in Table 23.1.

N O T E   The `Instancing` property is new in VB5. VB4 used the `Creatable` and `Public` properties to control instancing in a more limited way. Also changed in VB5 is the `GetObject` function—this function no longer works with VB-created objects. ◼

Table 23.1   The New *Instancing* Property and VB4 Equivalents

Instancing setting	Value	Description	VB4 Equivalent
Private	1	Object is only visible and available within its project.	Creatable = False, Public = False
PublicNotCreatable	2	Object is visible to other projects, but can only be created within its project.	Creatable = False, Public = True
SingleUse	3	Object is visible to and can be created by other projects. Each new CreateObject or Dim As New creates a new instance of the object.	None
GlobalSingleUse	4	Same as SingleUse, but all methods and properties of the object can omit the object name (for example, Reset instead of objCD.Reset).	None
MultiUse	5	Object is visible to and can be created by other projects, but only one instance of the object is created and all references share that instance.	Creatable = True, Public = True
GlobalMultiUse	6	Same as MultiUse, but all methods and properties of the object can omit the object name (for example, Reset instead of objCD.Reset).	None

Single-use objects create a new instance for every new object created with `CreateObject` or `Dim As New` statements. Multiuse objects use only one instance, regardless of how many times you call `CreateObject` or `Dim As New`. These two types of applications pose different problems, as shown in Figure 23.2.

FIG. 23.2

Single-use and multiuse objects pose different sets of problems for programmers.

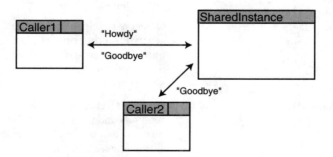

```
'Single Use can lose references
For I= 1 to 3
    Set x = CreateObject("Number.Application")
Next I
```

These references are lost

Only Instance3 can be used.

```
'Multiuse objects can cause calling applications to
'affect each other inadvertently.

'Caller1.Frm
Set x= CreateObject("Simpletext.Application")
x.Text = "Howdy"

'Caller2.Frm
Set x= CreateObject("Simpletext.Application")
'Resets text for Caller1 as well.
x.Text = "Goodbye"
```

Single-Use Applications and Lost References

Single-use applications can create *lost references*. A lost reference is an instance of the application that is loaded in memory with no object variable associated with it. Listing 23.1 creates three instances of the Number application, but only the last one has an object variable associated with it.

Listing 23.1   Creating a Lost ReferenceDim mobjNumber

```
Private Sub Form_DblClick()
    For i = 1 To 3
        ' Start an instance of Number (created in VB).
        Set mobjNumber = CreateObject("Number.Application")
    Next I
End Sub
```

There is no way to control or shut down the lost instances of the Number application from within the controlling application, because GetObject doesn't work with VB-created object applications. You have to close the application manually from Windows (for applications that don't display forms, you must use the Windows Task List to do this; press Ctrl+Alt+Del).

To avoid this problem, use module-level object variables and don't set the object variable to Nothing unless you've already closed the application. Most applications should provide a Quit method that lets you close them programmatically.

For object applications created in languages other than VB, such as Microsoft Excel, you can use GetObject to retrieve lost references. This is especially important, since invisible instances of Excel don't show up in the Windows Task List.

GetObject retrieves the earliest created instance of an application. Listing 23.2 creates lost references to Excel and then retrieves each lost reference and displays the instance in turn.

Listing 23.2   Showing Lost References to Excel

```
Private Sub Form_DblClick()
    For i = 1 To 3
        ' Start Excel invisibly.
        Set xlInstance = CreateObject("Excel.Application")
        ' Set caption to identify instance.
        xlInstance.Caption = "Instance " & i
    Next i
    For i = 1 To 3
        ' Get a lost reference to Excel.
        Set xlInstance = GetObject(, "Excel.Application")
        ' Display the instance.
        xlInstance.Visible = True
    Next i
End Sub
```

You can substitute xlInstance.Quit for xlInstance.Visible = True to close each instance programmatically. Since you can get a running instance of Excel with GetObject, Excel is really both single-use and multiuse. This may change in future versions, so be sure to test for this behavior.

Multiuse Objects and Initialization

With multiuse objects, the `CreateObject` function does not start a new instance if the application is already running. Instead, `CreateObject` reinitializes the existing object. This can cause problems if the application initializes global object variables at startup. Figure 23.3 illustrates how this problem can occur.

FIG. 23.3

If the object's application is already running, *CreateObject* does not run the *Sub Main* procedure, but it does run *Class_Initaliz*.

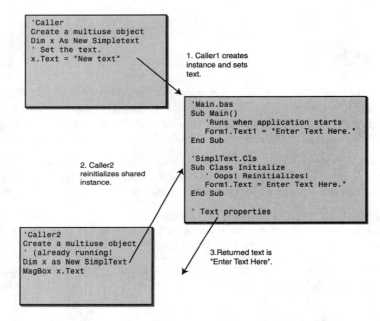

```
'Caller
Create a multiuse object
Dim x As New Simpletext
' Set the text.
x.Text = "New text"
```

1. Caller1 creates instance and sets text.

```
'Main.bas
Sub Main()
    'Runs when application starts
    Form1.Text1 = "Enter Text Here."
End Sub

'SimplText.Cls
Sub Class Initialize
    ' Oops! Reinitializes!
    Form1.Text = Enter Text Here."
End Sub

' Text properties
```

2. Caller2 reinitializes shared instance.

```
'Caller2
Create a multiuse object
' (already running!
Dim x as New SimplText
MagBox x.Text
```

3.Returned text is "Enter Text Here".

To avoid problems with initializing multiuse objects, use the object's startup procedure (`Sub Main`) to initialize application-wide data and entirely avoid `Class_Initialize`.

Listing 23.3 shows the `Text` property of a simple, multiuse `Editor` object. The `Class_Initialize` event inadvertently resets the `Text` property every time a new reference is created.

Listing 23.3   Incorrect Initialization

```
' Editor.cls - Multiuse object

Private Sub Class_Initialize()
    ' ERROR!!! Resets Text property for each
    ' new reference!
    Form1.Text1.Text = "Enter Text Here."
End Sub

Public Property Get Text() As String
    Text = Form1.Text1.Text
End Property
```

```
Public Property Let Text(Setting As String)
    Form1.Text1.Text = Setting
End Property
```

To correct this, move the initialization code to the object application's startup procedure and delete `Class_Initialize`, as shown in Listing 23.4.

Listing 23.4   One-Time Initialization

```
' Main.Bas - Start-up code for Editor.Exe
Sub Main()
    ' Initialize Text property once.
    Form1.Text1.Text = "Enter Text Here."
End Sub
```

Multiuse Objects and Global Data

In Figure 23.4, both multiuse `Application` objects share the same address space. This can lead to other bugs, because both objects have access to the same global variables and functions. You can't see from the other applications the global data in the object's application, but you can affect the data through the object's methods and properties, as shown in Figure 23.5.

FIG. 23.4

All the objects that an application provides share global variables.

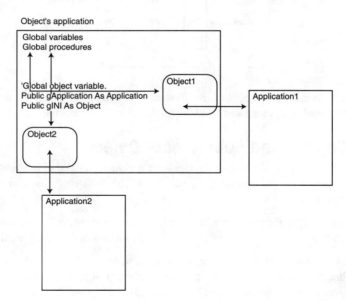

By causing `Object1` to change a global variable that `Object2` uses, Application1 can inadvertently affect Application2. This problem underscores the importance of not using global variables or procedures in applications that provide objects. Objects that must share data with their subordinate objects should do so through instances of a `Private` object. Figure 23.5 illustrates how you use a `Private` object to share data among subordinate objects.

FIG. 23.5
Create a *Private* data object instead of using global variables.

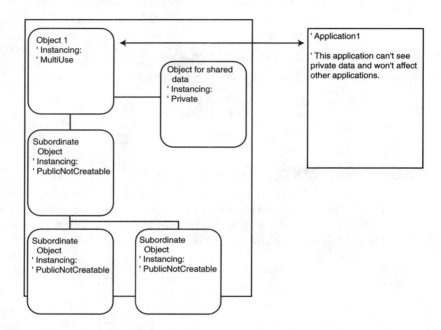

Using a `Private` data object ensures that each new top-level object has its own, private data that other top-level objects created by other applications will not affect.

Multiuse Objects and Subordinate Objects

If you use `CreateObject` or `Dim As New` for a multiuse object that is already running, VB returns a reference to the running object. The object can't detect that more than one application has access to it.

Therefore, one application can affect another through a shared object. Sometimes you want this is to happen. However, in other instances, it causes unexpected results.

Because an object has no built-in knowledge of which application will use it, you either need to trust that other programmers will be careful when getting running instances of objects, or you must limit access to subordinate objects through some sort of password mechanism. Listing 23.5 shows a method that returns a subordinate object only when the appropriate `KeyValue` argument is provided.

Listing 23.5 Creating a Secure Method

```
Const ACCESS_KEY = &h1234
Public Function Secure(KeyValue As Integer) As Object
    If KeyValue = ACCESS_KEY Then
        Dim SubordinateObject As New clsSubObj
        Set Secure = SubordinateObject
    End If
End Function
```

Problems with the Registration Database

When creating OLE Automation objects during debugging, Visual Basic seems to prefer compiled versions of the object over the object's project loaded in another instance of Visual Basic. During debugging, an application might actually have two entries in the Registry, as shown in Figure 23.6.

FIG. 23.6
The compiled version of the object exists at the root level; the debug version exists under the *VBKeySave* entry.

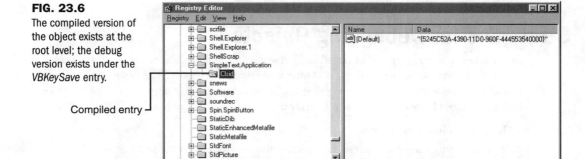

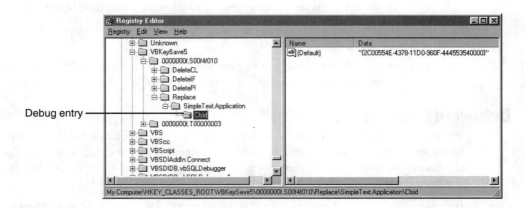

When attempting to create the object, another application searches for the object in this order:

1. In memory. If the object is already running, Visual Basic creates a new instance of the running object.

2. At the root level of the registration database. Visual Basic uses the object's programmatic ID to find the object's class ID and then finds the path to the executable file from the class ID's entry.

3. In the VBKeySave entry of the registration database.

To ensure that you are using the correct object when debugging, close all instances of the object's application. Check the Windows Task List to ensure that no hidden instances of the application are running. Then start the correct version of the object's application in another instance of Visual Basic.

As an added precaution, avoid creating an executable file for an object until you have completely debugged it. This saves you much work in maintaining correct System Registry entries on your system.

Strategies for Debugging Objects

Approaches to debugging are as varied and personal as driving habits. Some programmers debug their applications defensively, and others are more aggressive. The following list constitutes the "rules of the road" for debugging applications that provide objects, but like the rules of the paved road, they are subject to interpretation:

1. Debug objects in-process.

2. Debug objects cross-process. Use each of the following start modes:
   - The object is not running.
   - The object is already running; create a new object.
   - The object is already running; get an existing object (multiuse objects only).

3. Debug multiple access cross-process, using each of the preceding start modes (multiuse object only).

4. Test the application before release by running through the preceding three steps, using the compiled executable on systems that simulate each of your target platforms.

Debugging In-Process (.EXE)

When designing an application that provides objects, consider starting it from a Sub Main procedure rather than from a form. In addition to helping you think clearly about how the application starts up, this technique gives the application a place to add some conditional code that tests the application in-process, whether it has a visual interface or not.

 Because applications that provide objects shouldn't use global variables or procedures or initialize dependent objects outside of a class's Initialize event procedure, you should dedicate

most of the code in your Sub Main procedures to debugging the application in-process, as
shown in Listing 23.6, which is on the book's Web site located at **http://www.quecorp.com/
sevb5** from the OUTLINE.VBP sample.

Listing 23.6 Use a *Main* Procedure for In-Process Testing

```
#Const DebugBuild = -1
Option Explicit
' Module-level variable.
Dim Outline As New Topic

Sub Main()
    #If DebugBuild Then
    Dim strLine As String, strName As String
    Dim Topic As Topic
    Open "org.txt" For Input As #1
    Do Until EOF(1)
        Line Input #1, strLine
        AddLevel strLine, Outline
    Loop
    Close 1
    strName = InputBox("Enter your name")
    Set Topic = SearchTree(strName, Outline)
    MsgBox "Your boss is " & Topic.Parent.Value
    Set Outline = Nothing
    #End If
End Sub


#If DebugBuild Then
Sub AddLevel(strLine As String, objTopic As Topic)
    ' If the line starts with a tab...
    If Mid(strLine, 1, 1) = Chr$(9) Then
        ' Trim off the character and call again.
        AddLevel Right(strLine, Len(strLine) - 1), _
            objTopic.Topics.Item(objTopic.Topics.Count)
    Else
        objTopic.AddSubtopic.Value = strLine
    End If
End Sub
#End If


#If DebugBuild Then
Function SearchTree(strName As String, objTopic As Topic) As Topic
    Dim Item As Topic
    If objTopic.Topics.Count > 0 Then
        For Each Item In objTopic.Topics
            If Item.Value = strName Then
                Set SearchTree = Item
            Else
                Set SearchTree = SearchTree(strName, Item)
            End If
        Next Item
    End If
End Function
#End If
```

Part
III

Ch
23

The `#Const DebugBuild = -1` setting at the beginning of the module includes all the subsequent debugging code. The code in `Sub Main` and the `AddLevel` and `SearchTree` procedures are designed to go through all the possible code paths for the `Topic` object. Placing this code in `Sub Main` rather than doing ad hoc testing builds a consistent debugging path that you can use cross-process and for platform testing later.

When you compile the release version of the executable file, change the `DebugBuild` option to 0. This prevents the debug code from being built into the executable file, and thus saves code space.

Debugging In-Process (DLL)

Dynamic-link libraries (DLLs) can't be run stand-alone as shown in the preceding section. Instead, you need to call them from another project loaded in the VB development environment. Here's how to debug a DLL project:

1. Load the DLL project in Visual Basic.
2. Load the project that calls the DLL in the same instance of Visual Basic.
3. In the calling project, establish a reference to the DLL project. From the Project menu, choose References and then select the DLL project name from the references list.
4. Run the calling project.

Debugging Cross-Process (.EXE)

To debug an object for cross-process access, follow these steps:

1. Check the Windows Task List and end any running instances of the object's application.
2. Load the object's application project (.VBP) in Visual Basic.
3. Start the application.
4. Start another instance of Visual Basic and load the project that tests cross-process access to the previous application.
5. Run the application loaded in Step 4. Visual Basic lets you step into the object application whenever the current application calls the object application.

As you debug an object's application, test the logic of your objects under different access paths. One of the most critical areas for objects is their initialization. Therefore, it is important to test starting an instance of the application with no previous instances loaded, then test starting an instance with one or more previous instances loaded.

In addition to runtime errors, you must watch for unexpected results that can result from uninitialized data or from multiple initialization of the same object. Comparing expected results to actual results is important.

Creating New Objects from a Running Application   If you created debug code in `Sub Main` while debugging in-process, you can use very similar code to debug cross-process access. Listing 23.7 contains procedures that show the modifications made to the in-process debug code for OUTLINE.VBP.

Listing 23.7 Debugging OUTLINE.VBP Cross-Process

```
Option Explicit

Sub Main()
Dim strLine As String, strName As String
    Dim Outline As Object, Topic As Object
                   ' << changed to generic Object type
    Set Outline = CreateObject("outline.topic")
                   ' << added CreateObject
    Open "org.txt" For Input As #1
    Do Until EOF(1)
        Line Input #1, strLine
        AddLevel strLine, Outline
    Loop
    Close 1
    strName = InputBox("Enter your name")
    Set Topic = SearchTree(strName, Outline)
    MsgBox "Your boss is " & Topic.Parent.Value
    Set Outline = Nothing
End Sub

Sub AddLevel(strLine As String, objTopic As Object)
                   ' << Changed to Object type
' If the line starts with a tab...
    If Mid(strLine, 1, 1) = Chr$(9) Then
        ' Trim off the character and call again.
        AddLevel Right(strLine, Len(strLine) - 1), _
            objTopic.Topics.Item(objTopic.Topics.Count)
    Else
        objTopic.AddSubtopic.Value = strLine
    End If
End Sub

Function SearchTree(strName As String, objTopic As Object) _
    As Object           ' << Changed to Object type
    Dim Item As Object  ' << Changed to Object type
    If objTopic.Topics.Count > 0 Then
        For Each Item In objTopic.Topics
            If Item.Value = strName Then
                Set SearchTree = Item
            Else
                Set SearchTree = SearchTree(strName, Item)
            End If
        Next Item
    End If
End Function
```

The test code in Listing 23.7 uses the generic Object data type and CreateObject to avoid having to establish a reference to the object's application. References to the object's application type library aren't available until the application is compiled. You should not compile object applications before debugging them for cross-process access, because creating an executable file results in registering with your system two versions of the applications.

Getting Existing Objects from a Running Application   To ensure that the way that you get an existing object from a running application works correctly, add a new procedure call before the end of your cross-process-debug Sub Main. The new procedure, GetRunningObject (see Listing 23.8), should use CreateObject to manipulate the object that you created earlier.

Listing 23.8   The *GetRunningObject* Procedure

```
Sub Main()
    ' Code omitted here...
    ' Call procedure that debugs multiuse access
    GetRunningObject
    Set Outline = Nothing
End Sub

Sub GetRunningObject()
    Dim RunningObject As Object
    ' Get a reference to the Outline object created earlier.
    Set RunningObject = CreateObject("outline.topic")
    ' Add a new topic to the outline.
    RunningObject.AddSubtopic.Value = "New Name"
    ' Search the outline for the topic.
    Set RunningObject = SearchTree("New Name", RunningObject)
    ' Display the result
    MsgBox "New name's boss is " & RunningObject.Name
End Sub
```

The GetRunningObject procedure uses the CreateObject function, rather than a passed-in variable, to get an existing object reference. This tests the code path for returning and modifying an existing object.

Starting the Object's Application   You should test starting the application by using CreateObject, with the object application not running. By doing so, you run the object application's Sub Main procedure. Using CreateObject with a multiuse object already running doesn't test this path for cross-process access.

You must use a compiled version of the object's application to test whether CreateObject correctly starts the object's application. Be sure to register the object's application by running it once stand-alone before testing with the compiled application.

Testing on Target Platforms

After completing the steps described in the preceding sections, you can build your debug executable file to start testing for errors on target platforms. You should not rely on debugging performed on developers' machines as a final test, because developers tend to have more available memory and faster processors than many of the users for whom they develop.

Try to get a couple of unused machines that are representative of those used by the users for whom you develop. You might be surprised at the diversity of problems that can reveal themselves when you are running the same code on computers from different manufacturers. Some manufacturers are more fastidious than others at following standards and doing quality checks. You'll soon learn which types of machines, video cards, and disk drives are "tolerant" and which aren't.

If you've followed the steps in this chapter to this point, you should have a good code base for creating some automated testing on your target platforms. If not, return to the earlier section "Strategies for Debugging Objects" and start over. When testing on target platforms, you should use compiled objects and test code. If a problem develops on a particular machine, you can install Visual Basic and step through the code to find the error.

Testing on target platforms also gives you a good chance to test your setup procedure. Object applications must be properly registered in the Registry. If your application isn't registered properly, its objects won't be available to other applications.

Maintaining Compatibility with Released Versions

After releasing an application that provides objects, you have a whole new problem: maintenance. Some applications just keep chugging away like old Volvos. Others seem more like MGs. Whichever type of application you're responsible for, you don't want to kill the driver every time you make a few changes under the hood.

Visual Basic gives you a handy feature for maintaining compatibility with released object libraries: the Compatible Object Application text box on the Options properties pages.

Entering a name in the Compatible OLE Server text box compares the loaded application to the existing executable file's object library when you run or compile your application. If you've broken compatibility with the released version, you get a warning message.

The following types of changes cause a warning to occur, because they break compatibility with released object libraries:

- Changing the name of a released project, class, method, or property
- Changing a `Public` class, method, or property to `Private`
- Changing a property from read/write to read-only or write-only
- Removing arguments or changing the order of arguments in a method
- Changing an optional argument to a required one in a method

These aren't the only types of changes that can break compatibility with released object libraries. Changes in behavior, memory requirements, or software requirements can be just as deadly.

From Here...

In this chapter you learned the special tasks associated with debugging applications that provide objects. You saw how to set watches on object variables, trace execution in-process and cross-process, and analyze your object's initialization for potential problems. For information on creating objects and distributing them after they are debugged, see the following chapters:

- Chapter 20, "Using Classes to Create Re-usable Objects," explains the fundamentals of object-oriented programming.
- Chapter 24, "Building and Dist

ributing ActiveX Components," tells you how to compile and build installation programs for applications that provide objects to other applications. It also discusses how to maintain applications so that future versions don't break compatibility with previous versions.

Building and Distributing ActiveX Components

ActiveX components are designed specifically for reuse by other applications. You must take special precautions when installing ActiveX components or you can break the applications that depend on them.

This chapter covers the steps you must take to correctly build and distribute ActiveX components. It does not cover using the Setup Wizard which is a very good way of creating installation programs for use on a variety of media—including the Internet. The Setup Wizard is fairly self-explanatory, plus it also includes good documentation. The tasks in this chapter supplement and expand on the tasks performed by the installation programs generated by the Setup Wizard. ■

Manage versions and editions

ActiveX components provide compatibility information in the form of version and edition numbers. New versions of a component are compatible with earlier versions. New editions may break compatibility with earlier versions.

Install and register components

The Setup Wizard generates a setup program capable of installing and registering components. In some cases, you need to perform these registration tasks yourself in code.

De-register objects

When you remove a component, you need to remove its Registry entries as well. Doing this in code is often easier than relying on the setup program generated by the Setup Wizard.

Adding Version Information to Objects

Applications that provide objects have two levels of versioning:

- File version
- File edition

The *file version* differentiates between files with the same name. For example, you might distribute an updated version of an object library that contains bug fixes. In this case, the new file would have a later file version and simply replace the earlier file when installed.

The file name itself includes the *file edition*. You must issue a new edition of an application if it breaks compatibility with the previous edition. New editions of an application must not overwrite prior editions or they may break applications that use their objects.

Creating New Versions

If you are distributing an application that replaces a previous version, the new version must be *code-compatible* with the previous version. That is, other programs written using objects in the previous version should not break when users install the new version. There are many ways that you can break compatibility with previous versions of an application, but the ones that OLE defines as critical are all related to the syntax of the objects, properties, and methods that your application provides. Any of the following changes breaks compatibility with previous versions:

- Changing the name of a public project, class, method, or property
- Changing the declaration of a public class, method, or property to private
- Changing the `Instancing` property of a class
- Changing `Public` property access from read/write to read-only or write-only
- Removing arguments or order of arguments in a `Public` method
- Changing data types of arguments or values returned by `Public` methods or properties
- Changing an optional argument to a required one in a `Public` method

To have Visual Basic check for compatibility, you can enter the name of the previous version of your released application in the Version Compatibility text box on the Project Properties dialog Component page.

If you do not make any of the changes in the preceding list, you can safely overwrite the previous version of your application according to the ActiveX rules. The setup program created by the Setup Wizard automatically determines whether a file should be overwritten, by checking the file's version information. To add version information to a Visual Basic application, follow these steps from the programming environment:

1. Choose <u>P</u>roject, Prope<u>r</u>ties. Visual Basic displays the Project Properties dialog box (see Figure 24.1).

FIG. 24.1

The Make tab on the Project Properties dialog box sets version information.

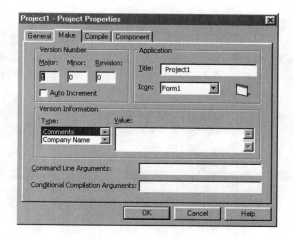

2. Click the Make tab.
3. Enter new version numbers in the Version Number frame and then click OK.

In the Version Number text boxes, you can choose from three version-number fields (see Table 24.1).

Table 24.1   Version-Number Fields

Field	Increment If
Major	You are releasing a new edition of your application with significant new features.
Minor	You are releasing an updated version of your application with new features and bug fixes.
Revision	You are revising an existing Minor version with bug fixes. You can also use the Revision field to track builds of your application prior to release.

Each time you update a field, you should reset the less significant fields to 00. The accepted convention for prerelease software is to keep Major revision set to 00 until the initial release; this limits you to only 99,999,999 iterations before you have to ship it.

Creating New Editions

If an application that provides objects is not compatible with the previous version, you must release it as a new edition. Application editions have unique file names, such as OUT0100.DLL. The new edition must not overwrite the previous edition, or you risk breaking other, dependent applications on the user's system.

Applications that use editions must include edition information in the Registry. You must create registration entries that append the edition number to the programmatic ID for each creatable object, as shown in Figure 24.2.

FIG. 24.2
The programmatic ID for a new edition includes the edition number.

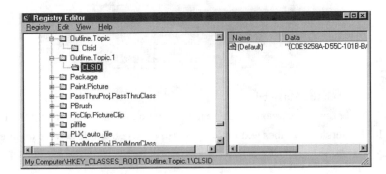

Applications can also register an entry in the registration database that indicates the most current edition. This entry does not include an edition number. Figure 24.2 shows both edition-specific and general entries for OUT0100.DLL. Both programmatic IDs (`Outline.Topic` and `Outline.Topic.1`) share the same class ID number. OLE uses the class ID to locate the executable file, so both programmatic IDs start the same application when used with `CreateObject` or `GetObject`. The following two lines have equivalent results:

```
Set Outline = CreateObject("outline.topic")
Set Outline = CreateObject("outline.topic.1")
```

The only difference between the preceding two lines is compatibility. If a new edition of the OUTLINE.VBP application is released, the first line might cause subsequent code to break. The second line, however, always starts the original edition of the application.

Installing Objects

Visual Basic writes registration information into each application that provides public, creatable objects. During installation, you can write this information to the Registry by running the application with the /REGSERVER switch. For example, the following line registers the OUTLINE.EXE application:

```
Shell "outline.exe /REGSERVER"
```

If your executable is a .DLL, you can't use the Shell function to register the executable's objects, because .DLLs cannot run by themselves. Instead, you must use the DLLSelfRegister API function included in the Setup Toolkit .DLL. Listing 24.1 shows the declarations and use of the function:

Listing 24.1   Registering a DLL at Start-Up

```
Public gstrPath = "c:\windows\system"
' Change this to get the right path at install time.
Public gstrDLLName = "OUT100.DLL"

Declare Sub DLLSelfRegister Lib _
"STKIT432.DLL" (ByVal lpDllName As String)

Sub RegisterMe()
    DLLSelfRegister(gstrPath & gstrDLLName)    ' Register the DLL.
End Sub
```

The Setup Wizard automatically registers an application file if you add the $(EXESelfRegister) flag as the sixth argument for the file's entry in the SETUP.LST file. The following line shows the .LST file line that registers OUTLINE.EXE during setup:

```
File12=2,,OUTLINE.EX_, ,$(WinSysPath),$(EXESelfRegister), _
    8/23/94,69904,1.0.0.0
```

To register .DLLs, use the $(DLLSelfRegister) flag, as in the following example:

```
File12=2,,OUTLINE.DLL, ,$(WinSysPath),$(DLLSelfRegister), _
    8/23/94,69904,1.0.0.0
```

If your application needs to register a new edition, you must create a separate .REG file that registers both the current version and the edition-specific entries for your application.

Creating a Registration File

To create a .REG file that contains edition information, follow these steps:

1. Build your application on your system.
2. Run the application to register it in your Registry.
3. Run the Registration Info Editor (see Figure 24.3) by entering **REGEDIT**.
4. Select the registration entry of the application that you just registered and choose File, Save Registration File.
5. Locate the matching entry for the class ID registered for the application that you just registered. You can locate the key by copying the value of the CLSID entry into the Find dialog box, as shown in Figure 24.3. To display the dialog box, choose Edit, Find Key.
6. Select the CLSID entry and choose File, Save Registration File. Figure 24.4 shows a key selected for the CLSID entry before being saved.

FIG. 24.3

To locate the class ID entry, copy the value of the CLSID key into the Find dialog box.

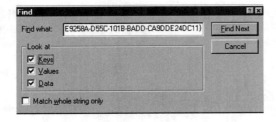

7. Repeat steps four through six for each creatable object that your application provides.

8. Merge all the saved files by using a text editor.

FIG. 24.4

The CLSID entry contains the location and name of the executable file for the object.

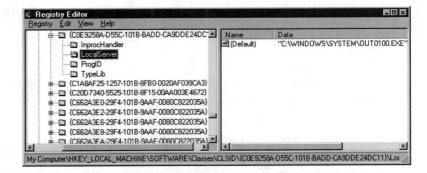

9. Add edition information to the programmatic ID for each object.

Listing 24.2 shows the .REG file entries for OUT0100.EXE. The file contains edition-specific entries and general entries indicating the current edition.

Listing 24.2   OUTLINE.REG—Registering the OUTLINE application

```
REGEDIT
; General entry -- indicates current edition.
HKEY_CLASSES_ROOT\Outline.Topic\CLSID =
    ➡{C0E9258A-D55C-101B-BADD-CA9DDE24DC11}
HKEY_CLASSES_ROOT\CLSID\{C0E9258A-D55C-101B-BADD-CA9DDE24DC11}
    ➡ \TypeLib = {C0E92535-D55C-101B-BADD-CA9DDE24DC11}
HKEY_CLASSES_ROOT\CLSID\{C0E9258A-D55C-101B-BADD-CA9DDE24DC11}
    ➡\InprocHandler = OLE2.DLL
HKEY_CLASSES_ROOT\CLSID\{C0E9258A-D55C-101B-BADD-CA9DDE24DC11}
    ➡\LocalServer = C:\WINDOWS\SYSTEM\OUT0100.EXE
HKEY_CLASSES_ROOT\CLSID\{C0E9258A-D55C-101B-BADD-CA9DDE24DC11}
    ➡\ProgID = Outline.Topic
; Edition-specific entry.
HKEY_CLASSES_ROOT\Outline.Topic.1\CLSID =
    ➡{C0E9258A-D55C-101B-BADD-CA9DDE24DC11}
HKEY_CLASSES_ROOT\CLSID\{C0E9258A-D55C-101B-BADD-CA9DDE24DC11}
    ➡\TypeLib = {C0E92535-D55C-101B-BADD-CA9DDE24DC11}
```

```
HKEY_CLASSES_ROOT\CLSID\{C0E9258A-D55C-101B-BADD-CA9DDE24DC11}
    ➥\InprocHandler = OLE2.DLL
HKEY_CLASSES_ROOT\CLSID\{C0E9258A-D55C-101B-BADD-CA9DDE24DC11}
    ➥\LocalServer = C:\WINDOWS\SYSTEM\OUT0100.EXE
HKEY_CLASSES_ROOT\CLSID\{C0E9258A-D55C-101B-BADD-CA9DDE24DC11}
    ➥\ProgID = Outline.Topic.1
```

Listing 24.2 includes the file path (\WINDOWS\SYSTEM) where the Setup program installed the application. During setup, you must modify this information to indicate the actual installed path and file name.

Registering a Registration File

To register a .REG file during setup, modify the SETUP.LST file generated by the Setup Wizard to include the application's .REG file name, as follows:

```
File12=2,,OUT0100.EX_, ,$(WinSysPath),OUT0100.REG,8/23/94,69904, _
    1.0.0.0
```

Be sure to include the .REG file in the list of files to be installed. The Setup program generated by the Setup Wizard decompresses all files before registering them, so you need not worry about the order of .REG and executable files in SETUP.LST.

To register a .REG file without using the Setup Wizard, run the Registration Info Editor with the /S switch, as follows:

```
Shell "REGEDIT /S out0100.reg"
```

The /S switch runs the Registration Info Editor silently, without displaying a confirmation message after the application is registered.

De-Registering Objects

The Setup Wizard provided with Visual Basic creates an installation program that can both install and uninstall your application. This automatically handles most issues with the Registry; however, it is sometimes useful to remove entries yourself without running the uninstall procedure provided by the setup program generated by the Setup Wizard.

Running your application with the /UNREGSERVER switch automatically removes the application's registration database entries. Do this before you remove the executable file from disk. The following lines show how you might remove the OUTLINE.VBP sample:

```
Shell "outline.exe /UNREGSERVER"
Kill "outline.exe"
```

The /UNREGSERVER switch removes only the OLE Automation entries for an application. If you created associations among file types and your application in the Registry, you must use the Windows registration APIs to delete the keys. The SYSTEM.VBP sample includes a

`Registration` object to provide methods that invoke these functions. Listing 24.3 shows how to use the `Registration` object to delete the registration entry for the OUT0100.EXE application:

Listing 24.3 Removing Registration Entries

```
Sub DeRegister()
    Dim Registration As Object
    Set Registration = CreateObject(""System.Application""). _
        Registration
    ' Delete .cdc file type from Registration database.
    Registration.DeleteKey ".cdc"
End Sub
```

To de-register DLLs, use the utility REGSVR32.EXE included in the Tools/REGISTRATION UTILITIES directory of the Visual Basic CD. To de-register custom controls (.OCX), use REGOCX32.EXE in the same directory. Both utilities use a /U switch to de-register objects.

From Here. . .

In this chapter, you learned about creating versions and editions of ActiveX components. You also learned about how to manage registration information in your own code, rather than relying on the setup program generated by the Setup Wizard.

For more information on the following topics, see the indicated chapters:

- Chapter 23, "Debugging ActiveX Components," gives you important insight into solving the many new problem areas that crop up as you program with objects.

- Chapter 30, "Creating Internet Applications with Visual Basic," includes information on using the Setup Wizard.

Integrating Visual Basic with Other Applications

25 Comparison of Visual Basic, VBA, and VBScript   557

26 Integration with Excel   573

27 Integration with Access and PowerPoint   609

28 Integrating Visual Basic with Mail, Schedule, and Exchange   645

29 Integration with Other OLE Applications   683

30 Creating Internet Applications with Visual Basic   713

31 Integrating Visual Basic with Internet Explorer and IIS   733

CHAPTER 25

Comparison of Visual Basic, VBA, and VBScript

On May 20, 1991, Microsoft announced Visual Basic at Windows World '91 in Atlanta, and since then the programming world hasn't been the same. Windows programmers finally had a powerful programming language that was simple to use and intuitive. Visual Basic was the first of a new series of RAD (Rapid Application Development) products that have let the average user develop complex Windows applications.

Visual Basic for Applications and VBScript take the success of Visual Basic one step further. In this chapter, you will learn when to use each of these products to help make your job as a programmer much easier. ■

Learn about differences and similarities of VB, VBA, and VBScript

All of the different varieties of Visual Basic can be difficult to discern, so this chapter will explain when and how to use each variety of VB.

Write a function that will work with VB, VBA, and VBScript

Because all of the varieties of Visual Basic are derived from the same origin, this chapter will show you how to write code that will work with all varieties of Visual Basic.

Program Outlook 97 and Web pages using VBScript

Learn how to programmatically add your own features to Microsoft Outlook and HTML pages using VBScript.

Use the appropriate "flavor" of VB for a specific task

By the end of this chapter you should be familiar enough with all of the varieties of Visual Basic, so that you will know which VB to use for any task.

Understanding the Differences between VB and VBA

Visual Basic for Applications (VBA) is Microsoft's attempt to create a common macro language for Windows products. VBA is based on the highly successful Visual Basic (VB) product. This second-generation version of Visual Basic is as easy to use as VB and shares most of its core features. Here are some of the shared features:

- Close integration with OLE (including enhanced OLE Automation support)
- A VBA type library with a fundamental subset of the Visual Basic language
- The ability to use ActiveX controls developed for VB 4.0 or greater
- Consistency across different implementations in the form of a common user-interface called VBE (Visual Basic Editor)

These features help make VBA a more robust language for shared code across multiple applications. However, VBA's ties to VB make it a mature language, even though it was first released in 1993.

N O T E   For the first time ever, Microsoft has made it possible for any company to purchase the rights to include VBA (and the VBE environment) in that company's own applications. This means your current VB/VBA code can be ported to other applications in addition to those developed by Microsoft. Look for upcoming ads in your favorite computer magazines for new applications that will be using VBE/A. ■

Although VB and VBA are similar, they differ in some important ways. Perhaps the most important difference is the definition of the two languages. Table 25.1 provides these definitions.

Table 25.1   Defining VB and VBA

Language	Definition
Visual Basic	Beginning with Visual Basic 5.0, VB now contains a shared version of VBA 97. The most important feature of VB is that it enables you to create a stand-alone executable or automation server that you can distribute to users who do not own a Microsoft application.
Visual Basic for Applications	Introduced in the Fall of 1993 as a replacement for Microsoft Excel's XLM macro language, VBA 97 is now included in Access, Excel, PowerPoint, and Word. Additional products will also be released with VBA. The most significant difference between VBA and VB is that VBA requires the product in which code was developed in order to run. In addition, its form and control support is significantly different from the traditional versions you'll find in Visual Basic 5.0.

All this is rather confusing, but there's a simple way to differentiate between VB and VBA: VB is a separate programming product that enables you to make executables, and VBA is a macro language for applications. As of VB 4.0, both products can share elements (type libraries) through the Object Browser.

Using Visual Basic for Applications

Starting with Visual Basic 5.0, VB has included all the features of VBA (in the form of a shared type library); code written in pure VBA can be shared across all products that use the VBA 97 type library. For example, the code in Listing 25.1 could appear in either VB or VBA.

Listing 25.1 GREETINGS.TXT—The Greetings Routine Is Compatible with Both VB and VBA

```
Sub Greetings(YourName As String)
Dim Reply As Integer

    Reply = MsgBox("Hello " & YourName & _
    ", are you ready to compute?", vbQuestion + vbYesNo)

    If Reply = vbYes Then
        MsgBox "Well then, let's get busy!", vbInformation
    Else
        MsgBox "I'm sorry to hear that, but you must.", _
               vbInformation
    End If

End Sub
```

From looking at the code in Listing 25.1 in its editor, it is difficult to determine which language was used. Figure 25.1 shows an example of VBA in Microsoft Excel, and Figure 25.2 shows an example of Visual Basic 5.0. Unlike in the past, viewing the editor doesn't tell you right away which product is being used, because both VBA and VB share the same common user-interface: VBE.

N O T E The Web site for this book (**http://www.quecorp.com/sevb5**) contains an implemented sample of Greetings that will work with Access, Excel, PowerPoint, Word, and Visual Basic 5.0. ■

Type Libraries and the Object Browser

How can one language meet all the needs of all these different products? That's where *type libraries* enter the picture. A type library is a file that each variation of Visual Basic provides to add product-specific features (for example, accessing a range of cells in Excel). In fact, all products with VBA share a common VBA type library called VBA. What's more, any variation of VBA can use type libraries from other applications to perform OLE Automation.

Part
IV

Ch

25

FIG. 25.1

Here is the VBA Code in Microsoft Excel 97.

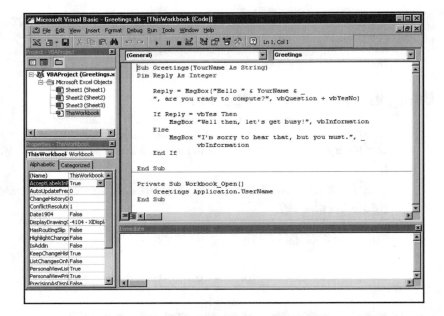

FIG. 25.2

The same code (as shown in Figure 25.1) in Visual Basic 5.0.

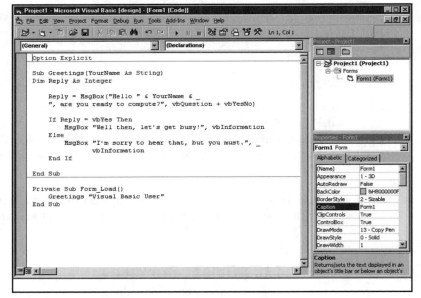

N O T E While most people use the terms *type library* and *object library* interchangeably, there is an arguable difference. A type library (.tlb) is a library that typically describes a single object. An object library (.olb) is a library that contains two or more type libraries within a single file. However, this definition is subject to criticism, because there are type libraries with olb extensions and object libraries with tlb extensions. What's worse is that there are even object and type libraries with a dll extension (such as VBA5.DLL). Ultimately, the distinction is unimportant so long as you know what these libraries are used for. For simplicity's sake, I use these terms interchangeably. ■

Type libraries can be viewed in a program called the Object Browser, which is built into VBE. Object Browser (see Figure 25.3) provides the user with a list of the available libraries and their elements.

FIG. 25.3
The Object Browser in VBE provides a view of the features of each object.

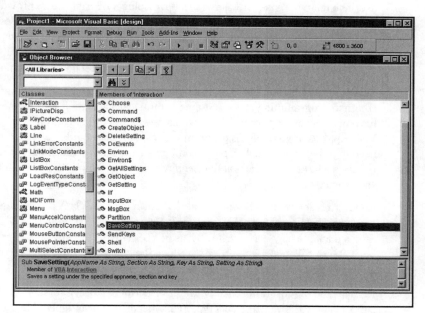

Although type libraries are a bit more than just aids to make programming easy in VB, as a VB programmer, that's all you need to know about them. More information is available on type libraries (including developing type libraries for DLLs written in C) on the Microsoft Developer's Network CD.

Introducing the Newest Visual Basic: VBScript

Currently, Microsoft has three shipping versions of BASIC for Windows: Visual Basic, Visual Basic for Applications, and VBScript. You've already seen the two Visual Basic forms, and you've probably heard of VBScript.

VBScript is a scaled-down version of Visual Basic that can be thought of as a batch language (similar to batch files in DOS) that uses fundamental VB syntax. VBScript code is typically found embedded directly in a Web page, as is JavaScript, but it doesn't have to be. For example, Outlook 97 uses VBScript as its macro language. This section provides a brief overview of VBScript, as well as comments on how it differs from the other varieties of Visual Basic.

An Overview of VBScript

VBScript uses a small subset of the features you'll find in the VBA type library. The reason why VBScript is a scaled-down version of Visual Basic is that VBScript's code is interpreted on-the-fly; there are also security reasons. This section briefly discusses each of these issues.

Prior to the introduction of VBScript, JavaScript was established as the industry standard for Web-page scripting, but JavaScript's similarity to C++ made it difficult for most programmers to use. The main purpose for Microsoft's developing VBScript was to provide a Web scripting language compatible with Microsoft's industry standard for Windows development, Visual Basic. However, this new language was going to be embedded into Web pages, so it needed to be scaled-down enough so that it could be interpreted as quickly as JavaScript. To accomplish this, rarely used features of the Visual Basic language needed to be removed.

Since the introduction of VB 1.0, many features have been added to Visual Basic to simplify common programming tasks, but many of the tasks accomplished by these new features could have been accomplished in VB 1.0 with a few extra lines of code. Therefore, the goal of VBScript was to give the VB programmer a small set of fundamental features that could be used together to accomplish more complex tasks. This means that programming in VBScript requires a little more effort and ingenuity than required by VB, but the end result can be just as powerful.

Another reason why VBScript was scaled down from its VB/VBA siblings was for security concerns. If Microsoft let VBScript programmers call the Windows API or perform file I/O, then a hacker easily could write a virus in VBScript to crash every system that executed his or her VBScript Web page. In order to reduce the chances of someone's writing malicious scripts, all the features of VB that potentially could be abused were removed.

Perhaps the biggest difference between VBScript and other versions of VB is that VBScript supports only the `Variant` data type. This means that a statement like `Dim x As Integer` would trigger an error in VBScript, because the Integer data type is not supported. This change was made because it simplifies the code for the interpreter, thus making execution much faster. However, this change really isn't a limitation for VB programmers, because the `Variant` data type is flexible enough to support all the data types used by VB.

Another major omission from VBScript is the many predefined constants found in the VBA type library. For example, the Greetings routine shown in Listing 25.1 demonstrates how the code looks in VB or VBA; Listing 25.2 shows how the Greetings routine would look in VBScript.

Listing 25.2   GREETINGS.VBS—VB Code Works in VBScript, but Not Without Minor Modifications

```
Sub Greetings(YourName)
    Dim Reply

    Reply = MsgBox("Hello " & YourName & _
    ", are you ready to compute?", 32 + 4)
```

```
    If Reply = 6 Then
        MsgBox "Well then, let's get busy!", 64
    Else
        MsgBox "I'm sorry to hear that, but you must.", _
                64
    End If

End Sub
```

Notice how in Listing 25.2 all the constants now appear as their numeric values. Also notice that we no longer use specific data types. Instead, we just declare a variable and use it. While this may be a little different from what you are used to, you can see that your knowledge of VB goes a long way in creating great VBScript code.

The omission of predefined constants in VBScript is something you can actually get around, in order to make porting your code as easy as possible. Although VBScript does not support defining constants, you can simply define variables that use the same name and leave your original VB code virtually unchanged. The code in Listing 25.3 demonstrates this technique.

Listing 25.3   GREETINGS2.VBS—Defining Variables for Missing Constants Makes Porting Easier

Part

IV

Ch

25

```
Sub Greetings(YourName)
    Dim Reply
    Dim vbQuestion, vbYesNo, vbYes, vbInformation

    vbQuestion = 32
    vbYesNo = 4
    vbYes = 6
    vbInformation = 64

    Reply = MsgBox("Hello " & YourName & _
    ", are you ready to compute?", vbQuestion + vbYesNo)

    If Reply = vbYes Then
        MsgBox "Well then, let's get busy!", vbInformation
    Else
        MsgBox "I'm sorry to hear that, but you must.", _
                vbInformation
    End If

End Sub
```

By declaring the constants in your VB programs, porting becomes even easier. The only changes made in Listing 25.3 from the original code in Listing 25.1 were the "constants" list and removing any references to data types (such as strings and integers).

Table 25.2 shows a complete listing of all VBA language elements missing from VBScript. This information was taken directly from the VBScript documentation available at **http://www.microsoft.com/vbscript/us/vbslang/vsgrpnonfeatures.htm**.

Table 25.2 VBA Features Not in VBScript

Category	Omitted Feature/Keyword

Array Handling	`Array` function
	`Option Base`
	`Private, Public`
	Declaring arrays with lower-bound <> 0

Collection	`Add, Count, Item, Remove` Access to collections using ! character (for example, MyCollection!Foo)
Conditional Compilation	`#Const` `#If...Then...#Else`
Constants/Literals	`Const` All intrinsic constants Type-declaration characters (for example, 256&)

Control Flow	`DoEvents`
	`For Each...Next`
	`GoSub...Return, GoTo`
	`On Error GoTo`
	`On...GoSub, On...GoTo`
	line numbers, line labels
	`With...End With`

Conversion	`CCur, CVar, CVDate`
	`Format`
	`Str, Val`

Data Types	All intrinsic data types except `Variant` `Type...End Type`
Date/Time	`Date` statement, `Time` statement `Timer`
DDE	`LinkExecute, LinkPoke, LinkRequest, LinkSend`
Debugging	`Debug.Print` `End, Stop`

Declaration	`Declare` (for declaring DLLs)
	`Property Get, Property Let, Property Set`
	`Public, Private, Static`
	`ParamArray, Optional`
	`New`

Error Handling	`Erl`
	`Error`
	`On Error...Resume`
	`Resume, Resume Next`

Category	Omitted Feature/Keyword
File Input/Output	All
Financial	All financial functions

Object Manipulation	`CreateObject`
	`GetObject`
	`TypeOf`

Objects	`Clipboard` `Collection`
Operators	`Like`

Options	Def*type*
	`Option Base`
	`Option Compare`
	`Option Private Module`

Strings	Fixed-length strings
	`LSet, RSet`
	`Mid` statement
	`StrConv`

Using Objects	`TypeName` Collection access using !

At first, this long list of omissions may be intimidating, but don't give up. The most important features of VB are included in VBScript, so you still can write powerful scripts. The only difference is that now you'll have to be more creative, which requires you to think in a new way. You may find that some of the tricks you invent to overcome these limitations are so good that you want to port them back to your VB applications. VBScript is a new challenge, but it can be a lot of fun.

Using VBScript on a Web Page

The information in the previous section focused on using the VBScript language. The code samples in that section could be used in any host that supports VBScript, but using VBScript in a Web page is a little more complex. To use VBScript in your Web page, you must add some HTML code that tells the browser that your Web page supports VBScript. In addition, VBScript doesn't support the forms that you are used to using in VB or VBA. This means that your code also must include information about which controls to use and where to place them. This section discusses how to use VBScript in a Web page and how to simplify the processing of VBScript development.

To begin using VBScript in your Web page, you must first tell your Web browser which scripting language you plan to use. This is easily accomplished by adding a line that reads `<SCRIPT LANGUAGE="VBScript">` in the `HEAD` section of your Web page. Most programmers usually put their code after the `SCRIPT` statement, so this is what we do in this discussion.

Immediately after the SCRIPT statement, write your VBScript code in an HTML comment block. Your code must appear inside a comment block, so browsers that do not support VBScript do not display your code in the Web page. At the end of your comment block, inform your browser that there is no more code by closing the script block using the </SCRIPT> tag. Listing 25.4 demonstrates a minimal Web page that displays a message box every time the page is accessed.

Listing 25.4   SIMPLE.HTM—Simple.htm Demonstrates a Minimal VBScript Web Page

```
<HTML>
<HEAD>
<SCRIPT LANGUAGE="VBScript">
<!--
    MsgBox "Hello World!"
-->
</SCRIPT>
</HEAD>
</HTML>
```

There are some cases where you want your code executed as soon as the page is loaded, but typically you'll want to execute your code in response to an event (as you do in VB). To do this, you need both a control on the page that the user can interact with and an event handler for that control. In VB, this is done for you when you place a command button on a form; for example, the Click event is created when you double-click the control. In VBScript, you must do this yourself, but it isn't too difficult. For example, Listing 25.5 shows how to create a command button on the form and display a message box in response to the Click event.

Listing 25.5   VBSCRIPT.HTM—VBScript.htm Demonstrates How to Interact with the User

```
<HTML>
<HEAD>
<SCRIPT LANGUAGE="VBScript">
<!--
Sub Command1_OnClick()
    MsgBox "Hello World!"
End Sub
-->
</SCRIPT>
<FORM>
    <INPUT NAME="Command1" TYPE="BUTTON" VALUE="Click Me">
</FORM>
</HEAD>
</HTML>
```

Now that you've seen how to work with simple VBScript Web pages, take another look at the Greetings sample. As you learned from Listing 25.4, the Greetings routine will appear in the comment block in the HEAD section. In Listing 25.5, you learned how to interact with the user by using a command button. Now you can apply these techniques to create a program where the user enters his or her name into a text box, clicks a button, and is greeted with the Greetings routine.

Listing 25.6   GREETINGS.HTM—Greetings.htm Is a Complete VBScript Application in a Web Page

```
<HTML>
<HEAD>
<TITLE>VBScript Demonstration Page</TITLE>
<SCRIPT LANGUAGE="VBScript">
<!--
'*************************************************************************
' VBScript.htm - Demonstrates a simple VBScript application in a web
'     page
'*************************************************************************
Option Explicit
'*************************************************************************
' Our Greetings sub ported from VBA
'*************************************************************************
Sub Greetings(YourName)
    Dim Reply
    Dim vbQuestion, vbYesNo, vbYes, vbInformation

    vbQuestion = 32
    vbYesNo = 4
    vbYes = 6
    vbInformation = 64

    Reply = MsgBox("Hello " & YourName & _
    ", are you ready to compute?", vbQuestion + vbYesNo)

    If Reply = vbYes Then
        MsgBox "Well then, let's get busy!", vbInformation
    Else
        MsgBox "I'm sorry to hear that, but you must.", _
               vbInformation
    End If

End Sub
'*************************************************************************
' The click event for our command button calls Greetings with the
' text from the Text1 text box
'*************************************************************************
Sub Command1_OnClick()
    Greetings Form1.Text1.Value
End Sub
-->
</SCRIPT>
<!--*******************************************************************-->
<!-- Display some HTML text to tell the user what to do            -->
<!--*******************************************************************-->
```

continues

Listing 25.6 Continued

```
<H3>Enter your name:</H3>
<P>
<!--************************************************************-->
<!-- Create a form called Form1 with a text box and command button -->
<!--************************************************************-->
<FORM NAME="Form1">
    <INPUT NAME="Text1" TYPE="TEXT" VALUE="">
    <INPUT NAME="Command1" TYPE="BUTTON" VALUE="Click Me">
</FORM>
</HEAD>
<BODY>
</BODY>
</HTML>
```

The only major difference between the sample in Listing 25.6 and previous samples is that we included a text box on the form and used its contents as the argument for Greetings. At this point, you have a VBScript application similar to one created in VB. The source code looks a little different, and it was a little more difficult to write, but the same result was achieved. This is an important concept to remember when planning VBScript projects. These projects will require a little more thought and time than you may be used to, so allow yourself that extra time when setting your client's expectations.

A Quick Look at VBScript Programming in Outlook

Although Internet Explorer is technically the first application to use VBScript as its macro language, Outlook is the first non-Web-based application to use VBScript. This means that you can write simple VBScript code to add interesting features to Outlook (as shown in Figure 25.4). While a complete discussion of programming Outlook using VBScript is beyond the scope of this book, this section walks you through a simple demonstration upon which you can build.

Programs written in Outlook using VBScript are designed to be executed in response to an event, such as opening an e-mail message. The way you assign code to these events is a little tricky, but the following steps make it easy:

1. From the File menu, choose New. Select any type of Outlook form (for example, a Mail Message).
2. From the Tools menu on the form, choose Design Outlook Form. Your form should now be in design mode, as shown in Figure 25.5.
3. From the Form menu, choose View Code. You should now see the Script Editor (shown in Figure 25.4).

FIG. 25.4

The Script Editor in Outlook isn't quite as advanced as VBE.

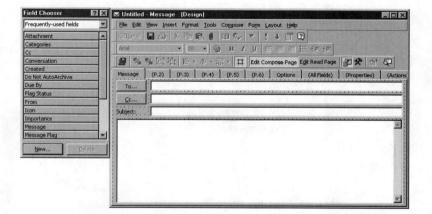

```
Sub Greetings(YourName)
    Dim Reply
    Dim vbQuestion, vbYesNo, vbYes, vbInformation

    vbQuestion = 32
    vbYesNo = 4
    vbYes = 6
    vbInformation = 64

    Reply = MsgBox("Hello " & YourName & _
    ", are you ready to compute?", vbQuestion + vbYesNo)

    If Reply = vbYes Then
        MsgBox "Well then, let's get busy!", vbInformation
    Else
        MsgBox "I'm sorry to hear that, but you must.", _
                vbInformation
    End If

End Sub

Function Item_Open()
    Greetings Item.Recipients(1).Name
End Function
```

FIG. 25.5

Using design mode in Outlook is similar to editing forms in VBE.

Part
IV

Ch
25

4. From the Script menu, choose Event. Select an event (for example, Open).

5. Type in some VBScript code (for example, `MsgBox "Hello World!"`) and then close the Script Editor. (You will not be prompted to save your changes, but that's okay.)

6. Return to the form that you put into design mode in step 2 and then choose File, Publish Form As.

7. Enter a name and click Publish. Close the form and, when prompted, save the changes.

8. To test your new form, choose File, New, Choose Form. Select your form and click OK. (If you chose the Open event in step 4, your code is executed now.)

9. Execute your form. For example, if you chose Mail Message in step 1, send an e-mail message to yourself using the custom form that you opened in step 8.

10. If you followed our examples, when you try to open your e-mail message you will get a message box that displays "Hello World!" Don't be alarmed if you see the macro virus protection warning message.

Now return to the familiar Greetings example. Using the ten steps just listed, replace the code in step 5 with the code in Listing 25.7. This code is the same VBScript code that we put in our Web page, plus a new line in the Item_Open event.

Listing 25.7   OUTLOOK.VBS—The VBScript Version of Greetings Can Be Ported with No Modifications

```
Sub Greetings(YourName)
    Dim Reply
    Dim vbQuestion, vbYesNo, vbYes, vbInformation

    vbQuestion = 32
    vbYesNo = 4
    vbYes = 6
    vbInformation = 64

    Reply = MsgBox("Hello " & YourName & _
    ", are you ready to compute?", vbQuestion + vbYesNo)

    If Reply = vbYes Then
        MsgBox "Well then, let's get busy!", vbInformation
    Else
        MsgBox "I'm sorry to hear that, but you must.", _
                vbInformation
    End If

End Sub

Function Item_Open()
    Greetings Item.Recipients(1).Name
End Function
```

The code in the Item_Open event calls Greetings using the name of the first recipient in your e-mail message as the name passed to Greetings. Easy, right?

Well, you're probably wondering how I knew about the Recipients collection and the Name property. After all, that's the only real Outlook programming in this example. The answer is easy; Outlook uses an object library, the same as VBA. The problem is that VBScript editors have no way of displaying this object library, so it doesn't do you much good if you can't use it.

To view the Outlook object library, launch your favorite version of VBE (such as VB5) and then add a reference to the "Microsoft Outlook 8.0 Object Library." From there, you can view all of the objects (such as the `Recipients` collection or the `MailItem` object) in the Object Browser. While we wish we could say there is a great reference book on programming Outlook, we can't. You have to trudge through the object library and learn by trial and error. However, if you stick to the ten steps listed previously, half of your battle is complete.

Knowing When to Use Which Variety of Visual Basic

Many programmers often complain that they are confused by all the "Basics" found in Microsoft products. In this section, I will try to clear up this confusion for you. Each of the different flavors of VB has a specific purpose, so choosing the correct one is important.

When should you use any one of these versions of Visual Basic? The answer depends on your needs. Use Table 25.3 as a guide to help decide which version is best for you.

Table 25.3 Choosing the Right Language

Language	Usage
Visual Basic	If your application requires the maximum amount of flexibility, or if you need to create a stand-alone execut- able or shared component, then Visual Basic is right for you.
Visual Basic for Applications	If your application depends on an application that uses VBA as its macro language (for example, Excel or Word), then use VBA. Unless your users do not have one of these products, VBA is probably the right choice for your application. Remember that VBA includes support for OLE Automation, so your possibilities are virtually endless. (For more advice, see the Note that follows this table.)
VBScript	If you're programming a Web page or programming in Outlook, then you'll have to use VBScript. Although VBScript isn't as feature-rich as VB or VBA, it still can be used to write sophisticated applications.

NOTE If you're developing a custom application and your customer doesn't have Microsoft Office 97, consider buying that customer a copy. Even the smallest customized solution can cost several thousand dollars, so including Office (typically, you can purchase a competitive upgrade copy for about $199) can save weeks or months of development time. ■

Part
IV
Ch
25

While the choice between VBA and VBScript is clear, knowing when to use VB instead of VBA is a little more complex. The best way to think of VB is as an object factory. VB is best suited for creating objects (for example, custom controls, shared OLE objects, and so on). VB is also the better choice for advanced custom solutions that need to be both fast and stand-alone. VBA, on the other hand, is most useful for automating or adding features to powerful products such as Microsoft Excel or even your Web pages in Internet Explorer.

From Here...

Now that you know a bit about the varieties of Visual Basic, we spend the next chapters discussing Visual Basic 5.0. Although the focus will be on VB 5.0, many of the techniques discussed are applicable to VBA. On the other hand, VBScript won't apply to the integrating with Office concepts in upcoming chapters, so the discussion on VBScript is now complete. To learn more about the different versions of Visual Basic, consult the following resources:

- For more information about VBA programming, consult the Microsoft Developers Network CD or visit the MSDN World Wide Web site at **http://www.microsoft.com/msdn**.

- For more information on VBScript, visit the Visual Basic Scripting Edition Web site at **http://www.microsoft.com/vbscript**.

- Additional information on VB programming with Microsoft Office is available in the upcoming chapters of this book.

CHAPTER 26

Integration with Excel

No discussion of custom applications or Visual Basic for Applications (VBA) is complete without discussing Microsoft Excel. This product is arguably the most powerful single application ever written for Windows, so you'll certainly want to take advantage of it. In this chapter, you will see how to exploit the power of Excel so that you can develop world-class custom applications. ■

Leverage the power of Excel in your application using OLE automation

You will learn how to include some of the most powerful features of Excel in your Visual Basic applications to create "world class" applications.

Link and embed Excel into your application using the OLE container control

Using linking and embedding, you will learn how to leverage the power of Excel's user-interface in your own applications.

Create an OLE automation server in VB that can be used in your Excel applications

You will learn how to write a OLE Automation server that contains a set of useful methods that can be used in VBA hosts such as Excel.

Using OLE Automation with Excel

In late 1993, Excel for Windows 5.0 became the first Microsoft product to be released with VBA. It introduced new features to the Visual Basic languages, as well as the concept of shareable OLE type libraries. This release introduced a whole new way to integrate applications with Visual Basic, and this section describes how you can benefit from this powerful enhancement.

Using Excel's Macro Recorder to Write OLE Automation Code

Because both Excel and Visual Basic (VB) use VBA, you can paste most of your Excel code directly into VB without encountering errors. What's more, you can take advantage of Excel's macro recorder to get a rough script of what you need to do through OLE Automation, without writing a single line of code. For example, the code in Listing 26.1 was recorded in Excel and pasted directly into VB to perform an OLE Automation task.

Listing 26.1   MACRO.FRM—Code Can Be Recorded in Excel and Pasted into VB with Little Modification

```
Option Explicit
Private Excel As Object

Private Sub RecordedForVB()
'********************************************************
' This code was unmodified from Excel's recorder,
' except the With Excel...End With statement. This
' statement is required because VB needs to know which
' object it should reference.
'********************************************************
    With Excel
        .Workbooks.Add
        .Range("A2").Select
        .ActiveCell.FormulaR1C1 = "North"
        .Range("A3").Select
        .ActiveCell.FormulaR1C1 = "South"
        .Range("A4").Select
        .ActiveCell.FormulaR1C1 = "East"
        .Range("A5").Select
        .ActiveCell.FormulaR1C1 = "West"
        .Range("B1").Select
        .ActiveCell.FormulaR1C1 = "Spring"
        .Range("C1").Select
        .ActiveCell.FormulaR1C1 = "Summer"
        .Range("D1").Select
        .ActiveCell.FormulaR1C1 = "Fall"
        .Range("E1").Select
        .ActiveCell.FormulaR1C1 = "Winter"
        .Range("B2").Select
        .ActiveCell.FormulaR1C1 = "100"
        .Range("C2").Select
        .ActiveCell.FormulaR1C1 = "125"
        .Range("D2").Select
        .ActiveCell.FormulaR1C1 = "108"
```

```
                    .Range("E2").Select
                    .ActiveCell.FormulaR1C1 = "97"
                    .Range("E3").Select
                    .ActiveCell.FormulaR1C1 = "118"
                    .Range("D3").Select
                    .ActiveCell.FormulaR1C1 = "110"
                    .Range("C3").Select
                    .ActiveCell.FormulaR1C1 = "109"
                    .Range("B3").Select
                    .ActiveCell.FormulaR1C1 = "110"
                    .Range("B2:E3").Select
                    .Selection.AutoFill Destination:=.Range("B2:E5") _

                    .Range("B2:E5").Select
                    .Range("A1:E5").Select
                    .Calculate
                    .Charts.Add
          End With
    End Sub

    Private Sub Command1_Click()
    '*********************************************************
    ' Create the object, make Excel visible, run the macro,
    ' then free the object.
    '*********************************************************
          Set Excel = CreateObject("Excel.Application")
          Excel.Visible = True
          RecordedForVB
          Excel.ActiveWorkbook.Saved = True 'Ignore changes
          Show 'Bring the form to the top
          MsgBox "Macro Complete!"
          Excel.Quit
          Set Excel = Nothing
          Unload Me
    End Sub
```

Part
IV

Ch

26

T I P Notice that in the Command1_Click event of Listing 26.1, we set the .Saved property equal to True to discard all changes that were made to the worksheet. We also could have set the SaveChanges parameter of the Quit method to False to accomplish this, but that would discard the changes to *all* of the open workbooks. Did we really want to do that? In this case yes, but in scenarios where users could have their own open documents, you would discard their data. The sample demonstrates the pessimistic approach to closing an application.

The macro recorder in Excel is incredibly powerful, because it's like having an OLE Automation recorder built into VB. No matter how complex your task might be, you can just turn on Excel's recorder and let Excel write your code for you.

N O T E Macro recorder code requires some editing because it records your every keystroke. Therefore, you should examine the recorded code to remove unnecessary elements. You also must surround your recorded code within a With block and prefix each line with a period. ■

Tips for OLE Automation with Excel

When you use OLE Automation with Excel, you should remember the following:

- Creating an OLE Automation object variable with Excel automatically launches Excel but does *not* make the object visible to your user. Therefore, you must explicitly enter a Visible = True statement so that your users can see Excel.

- If creating your object variable (for example, Excel in the RecordedForVB() example) starts Excel, Excel does *not* close when that variable loses scope. Therefore, you must explicitly close Excel by using its Quit method.

- Excel notes any changes that you make to it through OLE Automation. Therefore, Excel prompts the user to save changes when a workbook is closed. This could cause your application to hang until the user responds, unless you either save the workbooks you have modified yourself or set their Saved property equal to True.

- Excel supports GetObject properly, so you should determine whether Excel is already started before creating a new object. If you neglect to do this while Excel is running, you might get an "Out of Memory" error message. This happens because Excel tries to launch a new instance of itself, and there might not be enough system resources available to complete this task.

- If OLE Automation starts Excel, no workbooks are open on startup. Therefore, your application always must use the .Workbooks.Add or .Workbooks.Open method before performing any actions.

- Listing 26.1 defines Excel As Object when establishing an OLE Automation connection with Excel. Although this works, it is not efficient, because each OLE Automation call must be looked up as it is executed (this is called *late binding*). A major performance improvement to this code can easily be achieved by adding a reference to the Excel type library and defining the Excel object As New Excel.Application. By using this method (called *early binding*), OLE COM no longer has to look up internal information such as the argument list for each OLE Automation call.

NOTE Because Excel includes VBA and support for custom forms, you easily can create powerful custom applications using Excel alone. In some cases, you might want to choose Excel as your primary application environment and expose your VB application's classes as an OLE object. This enables your Excel application to use some of the powerful features you already developed in VB without the application's being written entirely in VB. ■

TIP As a general rule, make sure you are using the latest updates of any applications that you are using with OLE Automation.

Using the OLE Container Control with Excel

The first time we used the OLE container Control with Excel, we were amazed to see all the cool things we could include in our program. We found ourselves doing things that we never dreamed one person could do. What's more, we saw VB and Excel handle these incredibly difficult tasks with the greatest of ease. After seeing this section's code example at work, you will appreciate the power these two objects possess.

The sample program in this section is an MDI application that presents information from Excel in chart and table form. By using tabs, the user can switch between the two views shown in Figure 26.1 and Figure 26.2.

FIG. 26.1
Using the OLE Container control, you can view data in a chart.

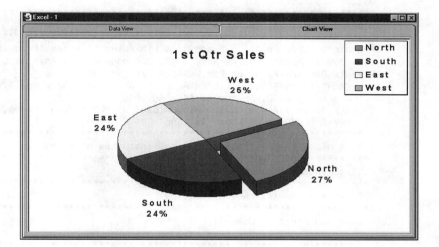

FIG. 26.2
By adding tabs, you can switch from the chart to the data.

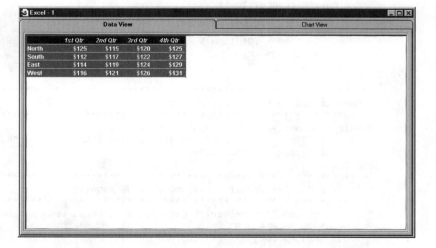

It is a good programming practice to build a set of "helper functions" for use with large-scale applications. Listing 26.2 contains code that must be accessible to two or more modules in the project at runtime. Placing this code in a separate module prevents your having to maintain the identical code in several modules.

Listing 26.2 PUBLIC.BAS—Shared Procedures and Declarations Should Be Stored in Modules

```
'**********************************************************************
'  PUBLIC.BAS - Global constants, functions, and variables
'**********************************************************************
Option Explicit
'**********************************************************************
'  API Declarations for this module
'**********************************************************************
Private Declare Function FindWindow Lib "user32" Alias "FindWindowA" _
    (ByVal lpClassName As Any, ByVal lpWindowName As Any) As Long
Private Declare Function PostMessage Lib "user32" Alias _
    "PostMessageA" (ByVal hWnd As Long, ByVal wMsg As Long, ByVal _
    wParam As Long, lParam As Any) As Long
Private Declare Function ShowWindow Lib "user32" (ByVal hWnd&, _
    ByVal nCmdShow As Long) As Long
'**********************************************************************
'  This global keeps track of the new instances of frmExcel
'**********************************************************************
Public gintXLInstances As Integer
'**********************************************************************
'  Creates a new instance of frmExcel
'**********************************************************************
Public Sub CreateNewWindow()
    Dim objExcel As New frmExcel
    '**********************************************************************
    '  Avoid showing your newly created form until you are finished
    '  making changes to it
    '**********************************************************************
    With objExcel
        .Caption = .Caption & " - " & CStr(Forms.Count - 1)
        .Visible = True
    End With
End Sub
'**********************************************************************
'  Generic update status bar routine.
'**********************************************************************
Public Sub UpdateStatus(lblStatusBar As Label, _
                        Optional strStatusText As String = "Ready")
    lblStatusBar = strStatusText
End Sub
'**********************************************************************
'  Start a OLE Server, if it is not already running
'**********************************************************************
Public Function StartServer(strClassName$, strProgram$) As Long
    Const SW_SHOWNA = 8
    Dim hWnd As Long
```

```
'*****************************************************************
' Prevent any error messages from interrupting the program
'*****************************************************************
On Error Resume Next
'*****************************************************************
' Check to see if its already running. If so, then activate it
'*****************************************************************
hWnd = FindWindow(strClassName, 0&)

If hWnd Then
    ShowWindow hWnd, SW_SHOWNA
    '*********************************************************
    ' Return False to indicate that it was already running
    '*********************************************************
    StartServer = False
Else
    '*********************************************************
    ' Otherwise, start it and return its hWnd
    '*********************************************************
    Shell strProgram, vbMinimizedNoFocus
    DoEvents
    StartServer = FindWindow(strClassName, 0&)
End If
End Function
'*****************************************************************
' Posts a WM_CLOSE message to an application
'*****************************************************************
Public Sub CloseApp(hWnd As Long)
    Const WM_CLOSE = &H10
    PostMessage hWnd, WM_CLOSE, 0, 0&
End Sub
```

Listing 26.3 contains the minimum amount of code needed to display the *splash screen*. This form (see Figure 26.3) gives the user "visual candy" during long processing times. A splash screen reassures users that their system has not locked up during heavy processing.

Listing 26.3   SPLASH.FRM—Splash Screens Help Calm Users' Fears that Your Application Has Locked Up

```
'*****************************************************************
' FRMSPLASH - This is just a splash form that is used to display
'             messages to the user during long processes.
'*****************************************************************
Option Explicit
'*****************************************************************
' Declare SetWindowPos so this window can be "AlwaysOnTop".
'*****************************************************************
Private Declare Sub SetWindowPos Lib "user32" (ByVal hWnd As Long, _
    ByVal hWndInsertAfter As Long, ByVal X As Long, ByVal Y As Long, _
    ByVal cx As Long, ByVal cy As Long, ByVal wFlags As Long)
'*****************************************************************
' Initialize the form.
'*****************************************************************
```

Part
IV

Ch
26

continues

Listing 26.3 Continued

```
Private Sub Form_Load()
    Const HWND_TOPMOST = -1
    Const SWP_NOMOVE = 2
    Const SWP_NOSIZE = 1
    Const FLAGS = SWP_NOMOVE Or SWP_NOSIZE
    '**********************************************************************
    ' Set the mouse pointer.
    '**********************************************************************
    Screen.MousePointer = vbHourglass
    '**********************************************************************
    ' Set the window to TopMost, and ignore the return value.
    '**********************************************************************
    SetWindowPos hWnd, HWND_TOPMOST, 0, 0, 0, 0, FLAGS
    '**********************************************************************
    ' Reposition the label to the center of the form.
    '**********************************************************************
    lblMessage.Move (ScaleWidth - lblMessage.Width) / 2, _
                    (ScaleHeight - lblMessage.Height) / 2
End Sub
'**********************************************************************
' Restore the mouse pointer.
'**********************************************************************
Private Sub Form_Unload(Cancel As Integer)
    Screen.MousePointer = vbDefault
End Sub
```

FIG. 26.3
Splash screens give users "visual candy" during lengthy operations.

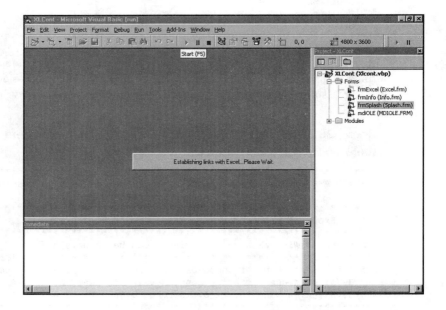

Listing 26.4 contains code to size frmSplash and its command button. This form displays information, gathered through OLE Automation, about the linked OLE object in this application (see Figure 26.4).

FIG. 26.4

The Object Information dialog box displays data gathered via OLE Automation using the control's *Object* property.

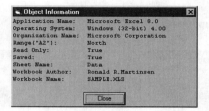

Object Information	
Application Name:	Microsoft Excel 8.0
Operating System:	Windows (32-bit) 4.00
Organization Name:	Microsoft Corporation
Range("A2"):	North
Read Only:	True
Saved:	True
Sheet Name:	Data
Workbook Author:	Ronald R.Martinsen
Workbook Name:	SAMPLE.XLS

Close

Listing 26.4   INFO.FRM—Information Dialog Boxes Should Contain Little to No Code

```
'**********************************************************************
' FRMINFO.FRM - This is essentially a "stupid" dialog used by
'               frmExcel. Its only purpose is to display information.
'**********************************************************************
Option Explicit
'**********************************************************************
' Initialize the form so that it can hold 10, 40 char lines.
'**********************************************************************
Private Sub Form_Load()
    '******************************************************************
    ' Get the height and width of a character to set the form size.
    '******************************************************************
    Width = TextWidth(String(50, "X"))
    Height = TextHeight("X") * 14
    '******************************************************************
    ' Move the command button to the bottom center of the form.
    '******************************************************************
    With cmd
        .Move (ScaleWidth - .Width) / 2, ScaleHeight - .Height - 10
    End With
End Sub
'**********************************************************************
' Always unload this form, since it loads so fast.
'**********************************************************************
Private Sub cmd_Click()
    Unload Me
End Sub
```

Part
IV

Ch
26

Listing 26.5 is the MDI parent. This form contains code that starts Excel, if necessary, and maintains the toolbar and the status bar (see Figure 26.5). You develop the toolbar and status bar, shown in Figure 26.5, entirely in Visual Basic by using picture boxes and image controls. You use no custom controls, so your application loads faster and your distribution disk is smaller. This is important when you are writing large applications, because every control in your project increases the startup time.

FIG. 26.5
The MDI form contains only a minimal menu, a toolbar, and status bar.

Listing 26.5   MDIOLE.FRM—An MDI Form Should Only Manage Itself and Load the First Child Form

```
'**********************************************************************
' MDIOLE.FRM - MDI Parent Form.
'**********************************************************************
Option Explicit
Private mlngStartedExcel As Long
'**********************************************************************
' Saves the button image in imgHold, and inserts the down picture.
'**********************************************************************
Private Sub imgTools_MouseDown(Index As Integer, Button As Integer, _
                        Shift As Integer, X As Single, Y As Single)
    imgHold.Picture = imgTools(Index).Picture
    imgTools(Index).Picture = imgTools(Index + 1).Picture
End Sub
'**********************************************************************
' Updates the status bar.
'**********************************************************************
```

```
Private Sub imgTools_MouseMove(Index As Integer, Button As Integer, _
                      Shift As Integer, X As Single, Y As Single)
    UpdateStatus lblStatus, imgTools(Index).Tag
End Sub
'**********************************************************************
' Restores the graphic, and processes toolbar clicks.
'**********************************************************************
Private Sub imgTools_MouseUp(Index As Integer, Button As Integer, _
                      Shift As Integer, X As Single, Y As Single)
    '**********************************************************************
    ' Restore the toolbar picture.
    '**********************************************************************
    imgTools(Index).Picture = imgHold.Picture
    '**********************************************************************
    ' Execute the appropriate toolbar action.
    '**********************************************************************
Select Case Index
    Case 0 ' Hand
        Unload Me
    Case 2 ' Question Mark
        '**********************************************************************
        ' Bring up the splash form again, because the first OLE
        ' Automation call will require Excel to be started. After
        ' it is started, any subsequent calls will be performed
        ' as fast as they would be in a native Excel macro.
        '**********************************************************************
        frmSplash.lblMessage = _
        "Gathering OLE Automation information from Excel...Please Wait!"
        frmSplash.Show
        frmSplash.Refresh
        '**********************************************************************
        ' Load the info dialog, and start printing to it.
        '**********************************************************************
        Load frmInfo
        '**********************************************************************
        ' NOTE: Using the OLE Container's Object property, you can
        '       execute OLE Automation statements on the object in
        '       the control.
        '**********************************************************************
        ' Cache a couple helpful object to prevent unnecessary OLE
        ' automation lookups.
        '**********************************************************************
        Dim objExcelSheet As Object, objExcelApp As Object
        Dim objExcelWorkbook As Object
        '**********************************************************************
        ' Although the Class property contains Excel.Sheet, beginning
        ' with Excel 97, all embedded Excel objects are now Workbooks.
        ' Since we will be making multiple calls to the Workbook
        ' object, we will cache this variable.
        '**********************************************************************
        Set objExcelWorkbook = ActiveForm.Excel(0).Object
        '**********************************************************************
        ' We will also be making a few calls to the worksheet object,
        ' so we should cache it to by retrieving a pointer to the
```

continues

Part

IV

Ch

26

Listing 26.5   Continued

```
                    ' active worksheet via the ActiveSheet method of the workbook
                    ' object.
                    '****************************************************************
                    Set objExcelSheet = objExcelWorkbook.ActiveSheet
                    '****************************************************************
                    ' Query Excel for the information and send the results off
                    ' to a helper function that will print the results to a
                    ' form.
                    '****************************************************************
                    With objExcelSheet.Application
                        PrintMessage "Application Name:", _
                            .Name & " " & _
                            .Version

                        PrintMessage "Operating System:", _
                            .OperatingSystem

                        PrintMessage "Organization Name:", _
                            .OrganizationName
                    End With

                    PrintMessage "Range(""A2""):", _
                        objExcelSheet.Range("A2")

                    PrintMessage "Read Only:", _
                        objExcelWorkbook.ReadOnly

                    PrintMessage "Saved:", _
                        objExcelWorkbook.Saved

                    PrintMessage "Sheet Name:", _
                        objExcelSheet.Name

                    PrintMessage "Workbook Author:", _
                        objExcelWorkbook.Author

                    PrintMessage "Workbook Name:", _
                        objExcelWorkbook.Name
                    '****************************************************************
                    ' Make sure all activity is complete, before unloading the
                    ' the splash.
                    '****************************************************************
                    DoEvents
                    Unload frmSplash
                    '****************************************************************
                    ' Display the information to the user.
                    '****************************************************************
                    frmInfo.Show vbModal
            End Select
    End Sub
    '****************************************************************
    ' Print the formatted string to frmInfo.
```

```
'***************************************************************************
Private Sub PrintMessage(strItem As String, varResult As Variant)
    Dim strLeft As String * 20, strRight As String * 30
    strLeft = strItem
    strRight = varResult
    frmInfo.Print strLeft & strRight
End Sub
'***************************************************************************
' Prepares the application for use.
'***************************************************************************
Private Sub MDIForm_Load()
    Dim strXLClassID As String, strXLPath As String
    '***********************************************************************
    ' Always use the system defined backcolor.
    '***********************************************************************
    BackColor = vb3DFace
    picStatusBar.BackColor = vb3DFace
    Toolbar.BackColor = vb3DFace
    '***********************************************************************
    ' Lookup the location of Excel in the registry by getting its
    ' class id (a GUID) and then finding that GUID in the CLSID
    ' section. Once you've found it, then just take the default
    ' value from the LocalServer (or LocalServer32) entry.
    '***********************************************************************
    strXLClassID = GetRegString(HKEY_CLASSES_ROOT, "Excel.Sheet\CLSID", "")
    strXLPath = GetRegString(HKEY_CLASSES_ROOT, _
        "CLSID\" & strXLClassID & "\LocalServer", "")
    '***********************************************************************
    ' If necessary, start Excel to prevent annoying message boxes.
    '***********************************************************************
    mlngStartedExcel = StartServer("XLMAIN", strXLPath)
    WindowState = vbMaximized
    CreateNewWindow
    Arrange vbTileHorizontal
End Sub
'***************************************************************************
' Updates the status bar with the default text.
'***************************************************************************
Private Sub MDIForm_MouseMove(Button As Integer, Shift As Integer, _
                                             X As Single, Y As Single)
    UpdateStatus lblStatus
End Sub
'***************************************************************************
' If you had to start Excel, then close it. Otherwise, leave it alone.
'***************************************************************************
Private Sub MDIForm_Unload(Cancel As Integer)
    If mlngStartedExcel Then CloseApp mlngStartedExcel
End Sub
'***************************************************************************
' Terminates the application.
'***************************************************************************
Private Sub mnuFileItems_Click(Index As Integer)
    Unload Me
End Sub
```

Part

IV

Ch

26

continues

Listing 26.5   Continued

```
'********************************************************************
' Updates the status bar with the default text.
'********************************************************************
Private Sub StatusBar_MouseMove(Button As Integer, Shift As Integer, _
                                        X As Single, Y As Single)
    UpdateStatus lblStatus
End Sub
'********************************************************************
' Adds a 3D appearance to the status bar.
'********************************************************************
Private Sub picStatusBar_Paint()
    HighlightBar picStatusBar
    Highlight picStatusBar, lblStatus
End Sub
'********************************************************************
' Updates the status bar with the default text.
'********************************************************************
Private Sub Toolbar_MouseMove(Button As Integer, Shift As Integer, _
                                        X As Single, Y As Single)
    UpdateStatus lblStatus
End Sub
'********************************************************************
' Adds a 3D appearance to the toolbar.
'********************************************************************
Private Sub Toolbar_Paint()
    HighlightBar Toolbar
End Sub
'********************************************************************
' Adds a 3D effect to a picture box.
'********************************************************************
Private Sub HighlightBar(picBar As PictureBox)
    With picBar
        picBar.Line (0, 5)-(.ScaleWidth, 5), vb3DHighlight
        picBar.Line (0, .ScaleHeight - 15)-(.ScaleWidth, _
            .ScaleHeight - 15), vb3DShadow
    End With
End Sub
'********************************************************************
' Adds a 3D border around a control.
'********************************************************************
Private Sub Highlight(ctlSurface As Control, ctlSource As Control)
    Const HORIZONTAL_OFFSET = 50
    Const VERTICAL_OFFSET = 70
    With ctlSource
        '********************************************************
        ' Top
        '********************************************************
        ctlSurface.Line (.Left - HORIZONTAL_OFFSET, .Top - _
            HORIZONTAL_OFFSET)-(.Width, .Top - HORIZONTAL_OFFSET), _
            vb3DShadow
        '********************************************************
        ' Left
```

```
'*************************************************************
ctlSurface.Line (.Left - HORIZONTAL_OFFSET, .Top - _
    HORIZONTAL_OFFSET)-(.Left - HORIZONTAL_OFFSET, .Height _
    + VERTICAL_OFFSET), vb3DShadow
'*************************************************************
' Bottom
'*************************************************************
ctlSurface.Line (.Left - HORIZONTAL_OFFSET, .Height + _
    VERTICAL_OFFSET)-(.Width, .Height + VERTICAL_OFFSET), _
    vb3DHighlight
'*************************************************************
' Right
'*************************************************************
ctlSurface.Line (.Width, .Top - HORIZONTAL_OFFSET)-(.Width, _
                .Height + VERTICAL_OFFSET + 15), vb3DHighlight
    End With
End Sub
```

Listing 26.6 is the child form. This form is the heart of the application, because it contains all the code necessary to display the data and tabs. It also keeps the status bar up to date when the user moves the mouse around the screen.

Listing 26.6 EXCEL.FRM—In an MDI Application, Most Code Should Reside in the Child Form

```
'***************************************************************************
' EXCEL.FRM - MDI Child form with a OLE container control.
'***************************************************************************
Option Explicit
'***************************************************************************
' The RECT and GetClientRect decs are required for PositionFrame.
'***************************************************************************
Private Type RECT
    rLEFT As Long
    rTOP As Long
    rWIDTH As Long
    rHEIGHT As Long
End Type
Private Declare Sub GetClientRect Lib "user32" (ByVal hWnd As Long, _
    lpRect As RECT)
'***************************************************************************
' Gets the client area of a frame, and sizes an object to it.
'***************************************************************************
Private Sub PositionFrame(fraSource As Frame, ctlChild As Control)
Dim Client As RECT, X As RECT
    GetClientRect fraSource.hWnd, Client
    With Client
        X.rLEFT = (.rLEFT * Screen.TwipsPerPixelX) + 50
        X.rTOP = (.rTOP * Screen.TwipsPerPixelY) + 150
        X.rWIDTH = (.rWIDTH * Screen.TwipsPerPixelX) - 90
        X.rHEIGHT = (.rHEIGHT * Screen.TwipsPerPixelY) - 190
    End With
```

Part
IV

Ch
26

continues

Listing 26.6   Continued

```
        ScaleMode = vbTwips
        ctlChild.Move X.rLEFT, X.rTOP, X.rWIDTH, X.rHEIGHT
        ScaleMode = vbPixels
End Sub
'************************************************************************
' Forces Excel to be the topmost window when you double-click.
'************************************************************************
Private Sub Excel_DblClick(Index As Integer)
        Excel(Index).Object.Application.Visible = True
End Sub
'************************************************************************
' Initializes this form instance. This code is also called every time
' a new form is created.
'************************************************************************
Private Sub Form_Load()
        '************************************************************************
        ' Establishing links takes a few minutes, so give the user
        ' something to look at.
        '************************************************************************
        With frmSplash
            .lblMessage = "Establishing links with Excel...Please Wait."
            .Show
            .Refresh
        End With
        '************************************************************************
        ' Always create your recreate links in case the program has been
        ' moved. In a real program, you should NEVER hard-code your links.
        '************************************************************************
        Excel(0).CreateLink App.Path & "\" & "SAMPLE.XLS!R1C1:R5C5"
        Excel(1).CreateLink App.Path & "\" & "SAMPLE.XLS!Pie"
        '************************************************************************
        ' Call DoEvents to process the links, and to prevent the splash
        ' screen from disappearing prematurely.
        '************************************************************************
        DoEvents
        Unload frmSplash
End Sub
'************************************************************************
' Updates the status bar with the default text.
'************************************************************************
Private Sub Form_MouseMove(Button As Integer, Shift As Integer, _
                                               X As Single, Y As Single)
        UpdateStatus mdiOLE.lblStatus
End Sub
'************************************************************************
' This procedure controls the tab redrawing to handle switching.
'************************************************************************
Private Sub Form_MouseUp(Button As Integer, Shift As Integer, _
                                               X As Single, Y As Single)
        Dim intRes As Integer
        intRes = Abs(DrawTabs(Me, X, Y) - 1)
        If intRes < 2 Then Tabs(intRes).ZOrder
End Sub
```

```
'*********************************************************************
' Repositon the frames and resize the tabs.
'*********************************************************************
Private Sub Form_Resize()
    Dim sngActivateTab As Single
    '*********************************************************************
    ' When the form is resized, the tabs must be rescaled to fit.
    '*********************************************************************
    SetupTabs Me, 2
    '*********************************************************************
    ' Position the OLE Containers to fit inside the frames.
    '*********************************************************************
    PositionFrame Tabs(0), Excel(0)
    PositionFrame Tabs(1), Excel(1)
    '*********************************************************************
    ' SetupTabs will make the first tab active. Determine which
    ' tab should be active, and send it a MouseUp event.
    '*********************************************************************
    sngActivateTab = IIf(gintXLInstances = 0, 10, _
                    ((ScaleWidth - 2) / 2) + 100)
    Form_MouseUp 0, 0, sngActivateTab, 20
End Sub
'*********************************************************************
' The following code demonstrates how to close a workbook without
' being prompted to save the changes.
'*********************************************************************
Private Sub Form_Unload(Cancel As Integer)
    Excel(0).Object.Saved = True
End Sub
'*********************************************************************
' Handles clicks from the File Submenu.
'*********************************************************************
Private Sub mnuFileItems_Click(Index As Integer)
    On Error Resume Next
    Select Case Index
        Case 1 'New
            CreateNewWindow
        Case 3 'Exit
            Unload mdiOLE
    End Select
End Sub
'*********************************************************************
' Handles clicks from the Object Submenu.
'*********************************************************************
Private Sub mnuObjectItems_Click(Index As Integer)
    Select Case Index
        Case 1 'Update Links
            Excel(0).Update
            Excel(1).Update
        Case 2 'Close Object
            Excel(gintXLInstances).Close
    End Select
End Sub
'*********************************************************************
' Updates the status bar.
```

Part

IV

Ch

26

continues

Listing 26.6   Continued

```
'********************************************************************
Private Sub Excel_MouseMove(Index As Integer, Button As Integer, _
                           Shift As Integer, X As Single, Y As Single)
    UpdateStatus mdiOLE.lblStatus, Excel(Index).Tag
End Sub
'********************************************************************
' Handles clicks from the Window Submenu.
'********************************************************************
Private Sub mnuWindowItems_Click(Index As Integer)
    mdiOLE.Arrange Index - 1
End Sub
'********************************************************************
' Set the gintXLInstances. This isn't foolproof, but it works for this
' demonstration. In the "real world," this wouldn't be enough.
'********************************************************************
Private Sub Tabs_MouseMove(Index As Integer, Button As Integer, _
                          Shift As Integer, X As Single, Y As Single)
    gintXLInstances = Index
End Sub
```

In addition to all the code and forms in Visual Basic, the XLCONT.VBP project also includes some code inside Excel that enables the user to return to your application. Listing 26.7 includes the essential Excel macros.

Listing 26.7   SAMPLE.XLS—Supporting Code in Excel Can Help in Two-Way Communication Between Your Applications

```
'********************************************************************
' Returns control to your VB Program, and minimizes Excel.
'********************************************************************
Sub ReturnToExample()
    On Error Resume Next
    AppActivate Title:="OLE Container Control Example"
    If Err Then MsgBox "The example program isn't open.", _
            vbInformation
    Application.WindowState = xlMinimized
End Sub
```

The ReturnToExample() procedure enables you to add a macro button to the worksheet, as shown in Figure 26.6. Such a button clearly shows users what they must do in order to return to your application. In addition, you can modify your menus (see Figure 26.7) to prevent users from closing the file or Excel. Notice how the Exit menu item has been removed.

FIG. 26.6
When using linked objects, you usually should give the user a viable way to return to your application.

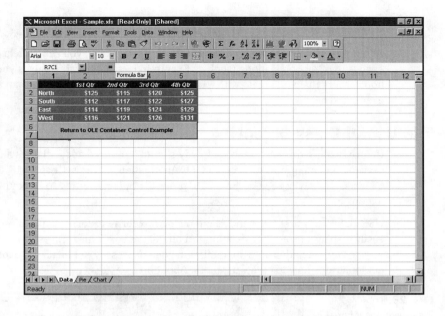

FIG. 26.7
Modifying Excel's menus can help ensure that users can't do anything they shouldn't.

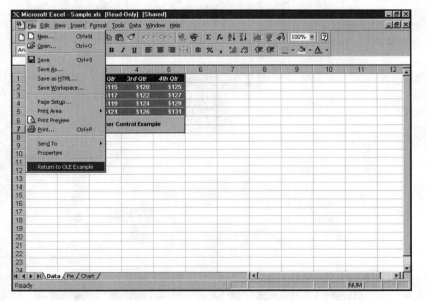

Using Your VB Application as a DLL for Excel

Although you can't write a traditional DLL in Visual Basic, you *can* write a class that you can expose to other applications (such as Excel). In fact, this section shows you how OLE Automation servers that you create with VB are more useful and easy to use than any traditional DLL ever could be.

The Useful Class Object

Before reading this section, you already should have read about classes and OLE Automation servers, including how to write an OLE Automation server in Chapter 18, "Controlling OLE Objects." However, the USEFUL.VBP project is rather lengthy, so it requires additional explanation.

USEFUL.VBP's first file is the About dialog box form. External applications use this form to easily display a professional-looking About dialog box. This form (shown at design time in Figure 26.8) includes only the minimum code necessary to initialize the form. Listing 26.8 demonstrates how to create a generic About box.

FIG. 26.8

The generic About box at design time differs significantly from its runtime counterpart.

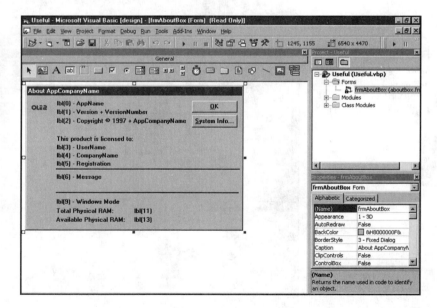

Listing 26.8   ABOUTBOX.FRM—A Generic About Box Is Useful for Giving Your Applications a Consistent Look and Feel

```
'***********************************************************************
' ABOUTBOX.FRM - This form contains a generic about dialog box which
'    is accessed by the About class.
'***********************************************************************
Option Explicit
```

```
'****************************************************************************
' Form level variables for preserving the pointer, and creating an
' About object
'****************************************************************************
Private mintOrigPointer As Integer
Private mstrMSInfo As String
'****************************************************************************
' Form Initialization
'****************************************************************************
Private Sub Form_Load()
    Dim clsMemorySnap As New clsMemorySnapshot
    '****************************************************************************
    ' Remember the current pointer, and change it to an hourglass
    '****************************************************************************
    mintOrigPointer = Screen.MousePointer
    Screen.MousePointer = vbHourglass
    '****************************************************************************
    ' If this form isn't being displayed as a splash screen
    '****************************************************************************
    If Not gblnSplashScreen Then
    '****************************************************************************
    ' Set the visible property of the button based on the existence of
    ' msinfo32.exe (from Microsoft)
    '****************************************************************************
        mstrMSInfo = GetRegString(HKEY_LOCAL_MACHINE, _
            "Software\Microsoft\Shared Tools\MSInfo", "Path")
        cmdSysInfo.Visible = FileExists(mstrMSInfo)
    '****************************************************************************
    ' NOTE: You CAN NOT distribute MSINFO.EXE, so this is the next
    '    best thing
    '****************************************************************************
    End If
    '****************************************************************************
    ' Set the label to reflect the windows version information
    '****************************************************************************
    lbl(9) = GetWindowsVersion()
    '****************************************************************************
    ' Get memory information from clsMemory
    '****************************************************************************
    With clsMemorySnap
        lbl(11) = Format(.TotalMemory \ 1024, "###,###,##0") & " KB"
        lbl(13) = Format(.FreeMemory \ 1024, "###,###,##0") & " KB"
    End With
    '****************************************************************************
    ' Center the form
    '****************************************************************************
    Move (Screen.Width - Width) \ 2, (Screen.Height - Height) \ 2
    '****************************************************************************
    ' Set the pointer to default, so the user doesn't see and
    ' hourglass on the about box
    '****************************************************************************
    Screen.MousePointer = vbDefault
End Sub
'****************************************************************************
' Restore the pointer to its previous state, and free memory
```

continues

Listing 26.8   Continued

```
'*********************************************************************
Private Sub Form_Unload(Cancel As Integer)
    Screen.MousePointer = mintOrigPointer
    Set frmAboutBox = Nothing
End Sub
'*********************************************************************
' Dismiss the dialog box, and run Form_Unload
'*********************************************************************
Private Sub cmdOk_Click()
    Unload Me
End Sub
'*********************************************************************
' If this button is visible, then this will work. Since we ignore the
' return value, you don't need parenthesis or variable =
'*********************************************************************
Private Sub cmdSysInfo_Click()
    Shell mstrMSInfo, vbNormalFocus
End Sub
```

Listing 26.9 is the private, noncreatable About class. This class contains all the code required to display the About dialog box. To prevent exposing multiple classes for a single project, you expose only the Application class and hide the About class.

Listing 26.9   ABOUT.CLS—Noncreatable Classes Are Useful for Creating an Object Hierarchy

```
'*********************************************************************
' ABOUT.CLS - This is the About class which is used to display the
'    about dialog. Its Instancing properties have been set so that it
'    is only visible to this project.
'*********************************************************************
Option Explicit
DefVar A-Z
'*********************************************************************
' Declare private variables for your properties as Variant so you can
' take advantage of IsEmpty(). Remember that Variants are very
' inefficient because they are the largest data type, so you should try
' to limit your use of them. I included variants, just to demonstrate
' a variety of techniques, but I normally avoid variants at all costs.
'*********************************************************************
Private mvntApp, mvntAppCompany, mvntVerNum, mvntUser, mvntCompany
Private mvntRegNum, mvntAboutMsg
'*********************************************************************
' You can also create a read/write property by using a public
' variable, but this goes against the basic object-oriented
' programming rule of encapsulation (or data hiding)
'*********************************************************************
Public Copyright As String
'*********************************************************************
' NOTE: For all of the following properties, if a Get is performed
' before a Let, then a default value will be returned
```

```vb
'**********************************************************************
' This is a Read/Write property which should be set with the name of
' the program that is using this object
'**********************************************************************
Public Property Let AppName(str As String)
    mvntApp = str
End Property

Public Property Get AppName() As String
    AppName = IIf(IsEmpty(mvntApp), "AppName Default", mvntApp)
End Property
'**********************************************************************
' This is a Read/Write property which should be set with the name of
' the company who wrote the application that is calling this object
'**********************************************************************
Public Property Let AppCompanyName(str As String)
Attribute AppCompanyName.VB_Description = "The software vendors name who will
➥appear in the about box. (Read/Write)"
    mvntAppCompany = str
End Property

Public Property Get AppCompanyName() As String
    AppCompanyName = IIf(IsEmpty(mvntAppCompany), _
                        "AppCompanyName Default", mvntAppCompany)
End Property
'**********************************************************************
' This is a Read/Write property which should be set with the version
' number of the application which is using this object
'**********************************************************************
Public Property Let VersionNumber(str As String)
Attribute VersionNumber.VB_Description = "The version number of the calling
➥application as you want it to appear in the about box. (Read/Write)"
    mvntVerNum = str
End Property

Public Property Get VersionNumber() As String
    VersionNumber = IIf(IsEmpty(mvntVerNum), "1.00", mvntVerNum)
End Property
'**********************************************************************
' This is a Read/Write property which should be set with the name of
' the end user who is using your application
'**********************************************************************
Public Property Let UserName(str As String)
    mvntUser = str
End Property

Public Property Get UserName() As String
    UserName = IIf(IsEmpty(mvntUser), "UserName Default", mvntUser)
End Property
'**********************************************************************
' This is a Read/Write property which should be set with the user's
' (see above) company name
'**********************************************************************
Public Property Let CompanyName(str As String)
Attribute CompanyName.VB_Description = "The end user's company name that will
```

Part

IV

Ch

26

continues

Listing 26.9 Continued

```
➡appear in the about box. (Read/Write)"
    mvntCompany = str
End Property

Public Property Get CompanyName() As String
    CompanyName = IIf(IsEmpty(mvntCompany), "CompanyName Default", _
                      mvntCompany)
End Property
'****************************************************************************
' This is a Read/Write property which should be set with a
' registration or serial number of the product that called this object
'****************************************************************************
Public Property Let Registration(str As String)
Attribute Registration.VB_Description = "The registration or serial number you
➡want to appear in the about box. (Read/Write)"
    mvntRegNum = str
End Property

Public Property Get Registration() As String
    Registration = IIf(IsEmpty(mvntRegNum), "Registration Default", _
                       mvntRegNum)
End Property
'****************************************************************************
' This is a Read/Write property which can contain up to two lines of
' text to display in the about box. The text will automatically wrap,
' so carriage returns aren't required.
'****************************************************************************
Public Property Let Message(str As String)
Attribute Message.VB_Description = "Any additional info you want to appear in
➡the about box between the black lines. (Read/Write)"
    mvntAboutMsg = str
End Property

Public Property Get Message() As String
    Message = IIf(IsEmpty(mvntAboutMsg), "Message Default", mvntAboutMsg)
End Property
'****************************************************************************
' This method determines how the dialog box should be displayed, then
' it loads it with the appropriate values and displays it
'****************************************************************************
Public Sub ShowAbout(blnAsSplash As Boolean)
    '****************************************************************************
    ' Set the global variable so the about box knows how to display
    ' itself
    '****************************************************************************
    gblnSplashScreen = blnAsSplash
    '****************************************************************************
    ' Set the common elements used by the splash screen and
    ' about box.
    '****************************************************************************
    With frmAboutBox
        .lbl(0) = AppName
        .lbl(1) = "Version " & VersionNumber
        .lbl(2) = Copyright
```

```
          .lbl(3) = UserName
          .lbl(4) = CompanyName
          .lbl(5) = Registration
          .lbl(6) = Message
      End With

      If blnAsSplash Then
          '***********************************************************
          ' Show About Box as Splash Screen by removing its caption,
          ' hiding the ok button, and displaying it as modeless
          '***********************************************************
          With frmAboutBox
              .cmdOk.Visible = False
              .Caption = ""
              .Show
              '*******************************************************
              ' NOTE: This refresh is required, because splash screens
              '    are usually show during peak processing times. If you
              '    don't refresh, then you'll just display an empty form
              '*******************************************************
              .Refresh
          End With
          '***********************************************************
          ' Set the about box on top to prevent it from disappearing
          ' during event processing
          '***********************************************************
          AlwaysOnTop frmAboutBox.hWnd, False
      Else
          With frmAboutBox
              .cmdOk.Visible = True
              .Caption = "About " & AppCompanyName
              .Show vbModal
          End With
      End If
  End Sub
  '***************************************************************
  ' Unloads the about box
  '***************************************************************
  Public Sub CloseAbout()
      Unload frmAboutBox
  End Sub
```

Listing 26.10 is the common module that contains elements that all objects in the class share. However, because this is a module, you cannot expose it.

Listing 26.10   COMMON.BAS—Modules Are Helpful When Two or More Files in a Project Need Access to the Same Procedure or Declaration

```
'*******************************************************************
' COMMON.BAS - This module contains declarations and procedures that
'    are needed by more than one form or class in this project. It also
'    includes the required starting point for the project by declaring
'    a public Sub Main().
```

continues

Listing 26.10   Continued

```
'*****************************************************************
Option Explicit
'*****************************************************************
' API calls that are only used by this module don't need to be public
'*****************************************************************
Private Declare Function SetWindowPos Lib "user32" (ByVal hWnd&, _
    ByVal hWndInsertAfter As Long, ByVal x As Long, ByVal y As Long, _
    ByVal cx As Long, ByVal cy As Long, ByVal wFlags As Long) As Long

Public Declare Function SendMessage Lib "user32" Alias _
    "SendMessageA" (ByVal hWnd As Long, ByVal wMsg As Long, ByVal _
    wParam As Long, lParam As Any) As Long

Public Declare Function PostMessage Lib "user32" Alias _
    "PostMessageA" (ByVal hWnd As Long, ByVal wMsg As Long, ByVal _
    wParam As Long, lParam As Any) As Long
'*****************************************************************
' Types, constants and declarations required to get the Win version
'*****************************************************************
Private Type OSVERSIONINFO
        dwOSVersionInfoSize As Long
        dwMajorVersion As Long
        dwMinorVersion As Long
        dwBuildNumber As Long
        dwPlatformId As Long
        szCSDVersion As String * 128 'Maintenance string for PSS usage
End Type

Private Declare Function GetVersionEx Lib "kernel32" Alias _
    "GetVersionExA" (lpVersionInformation As OSVERSIONINFO) As Long
'*****************************************************************
' Global splash screen variable
'*****************************************************************
Public gblnSplashScreen As Boolean
'*****************************************************************
' This procedure will set or restore a window to the topmost position
' above all open windows
'*****************************************************************
Public Sub AlwaysOnTop(hWnd As Long, blnResetWindow As Boolean)
Const HWND_TOPMOST = -1
Const HWND_NOTOPMOST = -2
Const SWP_NOMOVE = 2
Const SWP_NOSIZE = 1
Const FLAGS = SWP_NOMOVE Or SWP_NOSIZE

    On Error GoTo AlwaysOnTop_Err

    If blnResetWindow Then
        SetWindowPos hWnd, HWND_NOTOPMOST, 0, 0, 0, 0, FLAGS
    Else
        SetWindowPos hWnd, HWND_TOPMOST, 0, 0, 0, 0, FLAGS
    End If

    Exit Sub
```

```
AlwaysOnTop_Err:
    ErrHandler Err, "AlwaysOnTop " & CStr(blnResetWindow)
    Exit Sub
End Sub
'*********************************************************************
' This is a generic error handler which will display a message, close
' any open files, and restore the pointer and Err.
'*********************************************************************
Public Sub ErrHandler(lngErrType As Long, strFromWhere As String)
    '*********************************************************************
    ' We wouldn't be here if there wasn't an error, so be sure to turn
    ' error handling off
    '*********************************************************************
    On Error Resume Next
    '*********************************************************************
    ' lngErrType = 32755 is Cancel button was selected
    ' lngErrType = 3197 Then data has changed when 2 users accessing
    '   one record
    '*********************************************************************
    If lngErrType = 32755 Or lngErrType = 3197 Then Exit Sub
    '*********************************************************************
    ' This statement prevents a error message if this function was
    ' accidentally called
    '*********************************************************************
    If lngErrType Then
        '*********************************************************************
        ' Restore the mouse, and display a descriptive message
        '*********************************************************************
        Screen.MousePointer = vbDefault
        MsgBox "An error of type" & str(lngErrType) & " occurred in " _
            & strFromWhere & ".", vbExclamation, Error
        '*********************************************************************
        ' Restore Err, and close any open files to prevent corrupting
        ' files
        '*********************************************************************
        Err.Clear
        'Close ' You might want to consider using this line
    End If
End Sub
'*********************************************************************
' Uses the Dir command to see if a file exists. Resume Next is
' required in case strFileName contains an invalid path or drive.
'*********************************************************************
Public Function FileExists(strFileName As String) As Boolean
    On Error Resume Next
    FileExists = IIf(Len(strFileName), Len(Dir(strFileName)), False)
End Function
'*********************************************************************
' Returns a string suitable for displaying in a dialog box
'*********************************************************************
Public Function GetWindowsVersion() As String
    Dim strOS As String
    Dim osvVersion As OSVERSIONINFO
    Dim strMaintBuildInfo As String
    Const VER_PLATFORM_WIN32_NT = 2
    Const VER_PLATFORM_WIN32_WINDOWS = 1
```

Part
IV

Ch
26

continues

Listing 26.10   Continued

```
'*****************************************************************
' Many Win32 API's have a first parameter that indicates the size
' of the structure (in bytes) so these structures will be portable
' to future OS versions or different systems (such as 64 bit
' systems or OS's). It is your responsibility to set this field
' prior to making the API call, and the Len function helps you
' to do that.
'*****************************************************************
osvVersion.dwOSVersionInfoSize = Len(osvVersion)
'*****************************************************************
' Get the version (exit if the GetVersionEx failed)
'*****************************************************************
If GetVersionEx(osvVersion) = 0 Then Exit Function
'*****************************************************************
' Get a string that represents the installed Operating System
'*****************************************************************
Select Case osvVersion.dwPlatformId
    Case VER_PLATFORM_WIN32_WINDOWS
        strOS = "Windows "
    Case VER_PLATFORM_WIN32_NT
        strOS = "Windows NT "
    Case Else ' Impossible because VB doesn't run under Win32s
        strOS = "Win32s "
End Select
'*****************************************************************
' Get the major, minor, and build numbers and concatenate them
' to the OS name
'*****************************************************************
With osvVersion
    strOS = strOS & CStr(.dwMajorVersion) & "." & _
        CStr(.dwMinorVersion) & "." & _
        CStr(.dwBuildNumber And &HFFFF&)

    strMaintBuildInfo = Left(.szCSDVersion, _
        InStr(.szCSDVersion, Chr(0)))
End With
'*****************************************************************
' If this isn't a maintenance build (i.e., 4.xx.xxxx A)...
'*****************************************************************
If strMaintBuildInfo = Chr(0) Then
    GetWindowsVersion = strOS
'*****************************************************************
' Otherwise include the maintenance build info
'*****************************************************************
Else
    GetWindowsVersion = strOS & " " & _
        Left(strMaintBuildInfo, Len(strMaintBuildInfo) - 1)
End If
End Function
'*****************************************************************
' Returns the path to the Windows directory with or without a trailing
' backslash
'*****************************************************************
Public Function GetWinDir(Optional blnWithSlash As Boolean) As String
```

```
        Dim strWinDir As String
        '*******************************************************************
        ' Get the windows directory using the windir environment variable
        ' that is available in all versions of Windows
        '*******************************************************************
        strWinDir = Environ$("windir")
        '*******************************************************************
        ' Add or Remove the slash depending on what was returned,
        ' and the value of blnWithSlash.
        '*******************************************************************
        If Right$(strWinDir, 1) <> "\" And blnWithSlash Then
            GetWinDir = strWinDir & "\"
        ElseIf Right$(strWinDir, 1) = "\" And Not blnWithSlash Then
            GetWinDir = Left$(strWinDir, Len(strWinDir) - 1)
        Else
            GetWinDir = strWinDir
        End If
End Function
'*******************************************************************
' All projects must have an entry point (either a startup form
' or Sub Main()). This one just initializes our variables.
'*******************************************************************
Sub Main()
        '*******************************************************************
        ' If this program is started manually, then show the about box
        '*******************************************************************
        If App.StartMode = vbSModeStandalone Then
            Dim thisApp As New Application
            thisApp.ShowAboutBox blnAsSplash:=False, _
                strApp:=App.ProductName, _
                strAppCompany:=App.CompanyName, _
                strVerNum:=App.Major & "." & App.Minor, _
                strCopyright:=App.LegalCopyright, _
                strUser:="John Doe", _
                strCompany:="XYZ Incorporated", _
                strAboutMsg:="This OLE object was started manually.", _
                strRegNum:="Registration Number: 12345"
        End If
End Sub
```

Listing 26.11 is the Application class. This public, creatable class is USEFUL.VBP's exposed interface. It contains a routine to display the About box and includes other helpful functions that your calling application might need.

Listing 26.11   APP.CLS—An Exposed Class Provides an Interface for Your OLE Server

```
'*******************************************************************
' APP.CLS - This is the application class which is exposed to other
'   OLE Automation clients. It provides some handy routines that
'   aren't included in VB, and it is a good demonstration on how to
'   write a OLE server that can be used with other Office apps.
```

Part

IV

Ch

26

continues

Listing 26.11   Continued

```
'*************************************************************************
Option Explicit
'*************************************************************************
' Hidden API Functions for private use only
'*************************************************************************
Private Declare Function GetPrivateProfileInt Lib "kernel32" _
    Alias "GetPrivateProfileIntA" (ByVal lpApplicationName$, _
    ByVal lpKeyName As String, ByVal nDefault As Long, ByVal _
    lpFileName As String) As Long

Private Declare Function GetPrivateProfileString Lib "kernel32" _
    Alias "GetPrivateProfileStringA" (ByVal lpApplicationName$, _
    lpKeyName As Any, ByVal lpDefault As String, ByVal _
    lpReturnedString As String, ByVal nSize As Long, ByVal _
    lpFileName As String) As Long

Private Declare Function WritePrivateProfileString Lib _
    "kernel32" Alias "WritePrivateProfileStringA" (ByVal _
    lpApplicationName As String, lpKeyName As Any, lpString _
    As Any, ByVal lplFileName As String) As Long

Private Declare Function GetShortPathName Lib "kernel32" Alias _
    "GetShortPathNameA" (ByVal lpszLongPath As String, ByVal _
    lpszShortPath As String, ByVal cchBuffer As Long) As Long
'*************************************************************************
' Hidden variable for this class
'*************************************************************************
Private mclsAbout As New About
'*************************************************************************
' Description: This procedure displays an about box
'
' Arguments:
'   blnAsSplash  (Boolean)- Display as splash screen?
'   strApp       (String) - The name of your application
'   strAppCompany(String) - The name of your company
'   strVerNum    (String) - The version number of your app
'   strCopyright (String) - The copyright info for your product
'   strUser      (String) - The name of the registered user
'   strCompany   (String) - The User's company name
'   strRegNum    (String) - The User's registration number
'   strAboutMsg  (String) - Your about box message that goes
'                           between the 2 black lines
'*************************************************************************
Public Sub ShowAboutBox(blnAsSplash As Boolean, _
                        Optional strApp As String, _
                        Optional strAppCompany As String, _
                        Optional strVerNum As String, _
                        Optional strCopyright As String, _
                        Optional strUser As String, _
                        Optional strCompany As String, _
                        Optional strRegNum As String, _
                        Optional strAboutMsg As String)
```

```vb
'****************************************************************
' You should only set the properties If Len(the argument was provided.
' Otherwise, just let the default values appear.
'****************************************************************
    With mclsAbout
        If Len(strApp) Then .AppName = strApp
        If Len(strAppCompany) Then .AppCompanyName = strAppCompany
        If Len(strVerNum) Then .VersionNumber = strVerNum
        If Len(strCopyright) Then
            .Copyright = strCopyright
        Else
            .Copyright = "Copyright " & Chr(169) & _
                str(Year(Now)) & " " & .AppCompanyName
        End If
        If Len(strUser) Then .UserName = strUser
        If Len(strCompany) Then .CompanyName = strCompany
        If Len(strRegNum) Then .Registration = strRegNum
        If Len(strAboutMsg) Then .Message = strAboutMsg
        '****************************************************************
        ' Show it using the About object
        '****************************************************************
        .ShowAbout blnAsSplash
    End With
End Sub
'****************************************************************
' Returns a reference to an About object so that its properties may be
' accessed individually - HIDDEN - FOR INTERNAL USE ONLY
'****************************************************************
Public Property Get About() As Object
    Set About = mclsAbout
End Property
'****************************************************************
' Unload via the About object
'****************************************************************
Public Sub UnloadAbout()
    mclsAbout.CloseAbout
End Sub
'****************************************************************
' The following methods are just a wrappers for the public BAS module
' functions that the about object needs. This programming style
' demonstrates how you can expose non-creatable class objects to your
' external object users
'****************************************************************
Public Sub AlwaysOnTop(hWnd As Long, blnResetWindow As Boolean)
    basCommon.AlwaysOnTop hWnd, blnResetWindow
End Sub
'****************************************************************
' This method is a wrapper for basCommon.FileExists
'****************************************************************
Public Function FileExists(strFileName As String) As Boolean
    FileExists = basCommon.FileExists(strFileName)
End Function
'****************************************************************
' This method is a wrapper for basCommon.GetWinDir
```

Part

IV

Ch

26

continues

Listing 26.11   Continued

```
'*****************************************************************
Public Function GetWinDir(blnWithSlash As Boolean) As String
    GetWinDir = basCommon.GetWinDir(blnWithSlash)
End Function
'*****************************************************************
' This function converts a long file name into a DOS compatible short
' file name
'*****************************************************************
Private Function GetShortName(strLongFileName As String) As String
    Dim strFileName As String
    strLongFileName = Space(270)
    GetShortName = Left(strFileName, GetShortPathName _
        (strLongFileName, strFileName, Len(strFileName)))
End Function
'*****************************************************************
' This method extracts the filename (with extension) from a fully
' qualified path. If path = "c:\autoexec.bat", then this method
' returns "autoexec.bat"
'*****************************************************************
' NOTE: This method is not used by any modules or forms in this
' project, so its code belongs here.
'*****************************************************************
' WARNING: This function modifies Path, so ByVal is required.
'*****************************************************************
Public Function ExtractFileName(ByVal strPath As String) As String
    Dim res As Integer
    '*****************************************************************
    ' One of the few uses for GoTo is as an error handler, and this is
    ' a great example of how to use them
    '*****************************************************************
    On Error GoTo ExtractFileName_Err
    '*****************************************************************
    ' Convert LFN's to SFN's
    '*****************************************************************
    strPath = GetShortName(strPath)
    '*****************************************************************
    ' Since a filename (with extension) in DOS can only be a maximum
    ' of 13 chars (8 + 1 + 3), get rid of the rest
    '*****************************************************************
    If Len(strPath) > 13 Then strPath = Right(strPath, 13)
    res = InStr(strPath, "\")
    '*****************************************************************
    ' Get rid of the rest of the garbage by looking for slashes
    '*****************************************************************
    Do While res <> 0
        strPath = Mid$(strPath, res + 1, Len(strPath))
        res = InStr(strPath, "\")
    Loop
    '*****************************************************************
    ' Return the result, and exit the function to prevent executing
    ' the error handler
    '*****************************************************************
    ExtractFileName = strPath
    Exit Function
```

```vb
'**********************************************************************
' Our error handler calls an external module's generic error handler,
' and exits to prevent further damage.
'**********************************************************************
ExtractFileName_Err:
    ErrHandler Err, "ExtractFileName"
    Exit Function
End Function
'**********************************************************************
' Returns a string suitable for displaying in a dialog box
'**********************************************************************
Public Function GetWindowsVersion() As String
    GetWindowsVersion = basCommon.GetWindowsVersion()
End Function
'**********************************************************************
' Calls the API to read an INI file, and return the results
'**********************************************************************
' NOTE: ByVal is used, so you can pass control values such as
'       Text1.Text without surrounding it in parenthesis
'**********************************************************************
Public Function GetINI(ByVal strSection$, ByVal strKey$, ByVal _
                       strDefault$, ByVal strFileName$) As String
    Dim res As Long, strBuffer As String
    strBuffer = Space$(2048)
    res = GetPrivateProfileString(strSection, strKey, strDefault, _
                         strBuffer, Len(strBuffer), strFileName)
    GetINI = Left$(strBuffer, res)
End Function
'**********************************************************************
' Same as above, but it returns an integer
'**********************************************************************
Public Function GetINIInt(ByVal strSection$, ByVal strKey$, ByVal _
                       intDefault%, ByVal strFileName$) As Integer
    GetINIInt = GetPrivateProfileInt(strSection, strKey, _
        intDefault, strFileName)
End Function
'**********************************************************************
' This methods accepts alphanumeric settings to write to an INI file.
' In addition, you can delete a section or key by, passing the
' special "_DELETE_" string.
'**********************************************************************
Public Sub WriteINI(ByVal strSection As String, ByVal strKey As String, _
    ByVal vntSetting As Variant, ByVal strFileName As String)
    '**********************************************************************
    ' If key is set to _DELETE_, then delete the section
    '**********************************************************************
    If strKey = "_DELETE_" Then
        WritePrivateProfileString strSection, 0&, 0&, strFileName
    '**********************************************************************
    ' If setting is set to _DELETE_, then delete the key
    '**********************************************************************
    ElseIf vntSetting = "_DELETE_" Then
        WritePrivateProfileString strSection, strKey, 0&, strFileName
    '**********************************************************************
    ' Otherwise, convert the setting to a string and write it
    ' to the INI file.
```

Part

IV

Ch

26

continues

Listing 26.11   Continued

```
'****************************************************************
    Else
        WritePrivateProfileString strSection, strKey, _
            CStr(vntSetting), strFileName
    End If
End Sub
'****************************************************************
' This function is useful with SendMessage and GetVersion so you can
' get the low order word
'****************************************************************
Public Function GetLoWord(ByVal lngDWord As Long) As Integer
    If lngDWord And &H8000& Then
        GetLoWord = &H8000 Or (lngDWord And &H7FFF&)
    Else
        GetLoWord = lngDWord And &HFFFF&
    End If
End Function
'****************************************************************
' Same as above, but returns the high order word
'****************************************************************
Public Function GetHiWord(ByVal lngDWord As Long) As Integer
    GetHiWord = lngDWord \ &H10000
End Function
'****************************************************************
' This method demonstrates how you can expose API calls. Since you
' can't use As Any with functions, SendMessage requires type-safe
' versions.
'****************************************************************
Public Function SendMessageAsLong(hWnd As Long, wMsg As Long, wParam _
    As Long, lParam As Long) As Long
    SendMessageAsLong = SendMessage(hWnd, wMsg, wParam, lParam)
End Function
'****************************************************************
' See above.
'****************************************************************
Public Function SendMessageAsStr(hWnd As Long, wMsg As Long, wParam _
    As Long, lParam As String) As Long
    SendMessageAsStr = SendMessage(hWnd, wMsg, wParam, ByVal lParam)
End Function
'****************************************************************
' See above.
'****************************************************************
Public Function PostMessage(ByVal hWnd As Long, ByVal wMsg As Long, _
    ByVal wParam As Long, lParam As Long) As Long
    PostMessage = PostMessage(hWnd, wMsg, wParam, lParam)
End Function
```

The net result of this project is an exposed class that other VBA applications, such as Access, can use to display a dialog box (see Figure 26.9) and access helpful routines. It also demonstrates how you can create reusable objects that are more useful than DLLs without having to learn C.

FIG. 26.9
You can call this generic About box from Excel or any other OLE Automation server.

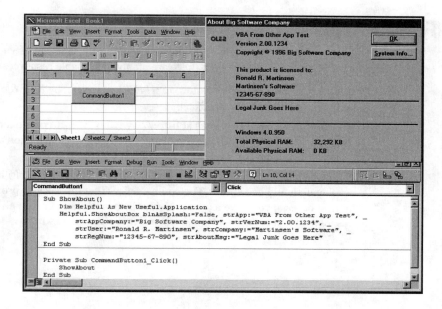

To use this handy OLE server from Excel, you need only create an object variable of our new Useful object, add the object in the References dialog box, and then access Useful's member functions. The code in Listing 26.12 demonstrates how to use the ShowAboutBox method, but the same method applies for all its member functions.

Listing 26.12   SHOWABOUT.TXT—This Code Can Be Useful in Excel or Any Other VBA Host

```
Sub ShowAbout()
    Dim Helpful As New Useful.Application
    Helpful.ShowAboutBox blnAsSplash:=False, strApp:="VBA From Other App Test", _
        strAppCompany:="Big Software Company", strVerNum:="2.00.1234", _
        strUser:="Ronald R. Martinsen", strCompany:="Martinsen's Software", _
        strRegNum:="12345-67-890", strAboutMsg:="Legal Junk Goes Here"
End Sub

Private Sub CommandButton1_Click()
    ShowAbout
End Sub
```

Part IV

Ch 26

N O T E Because Visual Basic can create OLE Automation servers, you might find that other applications (such as Excel or Word) are better source programs for your application code. By developing your code in a product that uses VBE and VBA, you can leverage its features and use shared OLE Automation objects written in VB. This allows you to choose the right product for the right task, so you can avoid writing unnecessary code. ∎

From Here...

Unfortunately, this chapter could cover only a few of the amazing things you can do when integrating VB with Excel. However, there are plenty of available resources on this topic:

- *Using Visual Basic for Applications, Excel Edition*, written by Jeff Webb, is a helpful aid for understanding VBA with Excel.

- The Excel and Office Web sites at **http://www.microsoft.com/excel** and **http://www.microsoft.com/office** are valuable resources for information about VBA programming with Excel and Office.

- *Microsoft Developers Network CD* (available directly from Microsoft) is a resource that no developer should be without. The compact discs that this service provides are priceless. In most cases, if you have a problem, this CD has the answer. You also can find much of this information online at **http://www.microsoft.com/msdn**.

CHAPTER 27

Integration with Access and PowerPoint

When you look at this chapter title, you might wonder why we've included Access and PowerPoint in the same chapter. The reason is that each of these two products has an object model that isn't quite as extensive as Excel and Word. However, Access and PowerPoint's object models still are quite extensive and warrant a discussion of their own. The purpose of this chapter is to give you a quick tour of the most helpful features of these object models, so you can start using them quickly. ■

Create and use a class object that simplifies Data Access Objects (DAO)

You will learn how to build a class object that encapsulates the most common tasks performed when programming DAO.

Control the Microsoft Access user interface from Visual Basic

By using the Microsoft Access Object Library, you will learn how to programmatically control the user-interface features of Microsoft Access.

Create and run a PowerPoint presentation

By using a custom class object (described in this chapter) that wraps the common features of the PowerPoint Object Library, you will be able to build and run a complex presentation from your Visual Basic application.

Integrating with Access

At the heart of many custom applications is a database, and Microsoft Access has quickly become one of the most popular programs for database management. This section describes how you can tap the power of Access for use in your Visual Basic (VB) applications.

Programmers often ask how their programs can control Access, but this question is rather silly due to Access's nature. If you own a copy of Visual Basic 3.0 or greater, you already have most of the power of Access. The only part of Access over which you don't have control is its user interface. However, that part of Access isn't important for custom applications, because with Visual Basic you create your own user interface. To help clarify this point, the next few sections describe some of the components of Access and how you can access them.

Jet Database Engine

The real power behind Microsoft Access (MSACCESS.EXE) is its database engine, Jet. Everything else in Access is a user interface for the Jet. This concept is important to you as a Visual Basic programmer, because you also have control of the Jet database engine (controlled via an OLE COM interface called *data access objects,* or DAO). Consider the following scenarios:

- Suppose that your application needs the titles of all books in a database file created in Microsoft Access. Because Visual Basic has access to the Jet database layer, you can directly retrieve this information using Visual Basic code, without even having Access installed.

- Suppose that your application needs to create, modify, and compact database files created in Access. Again, Visual Basic has access to the Jet database layer, so you can perform these actions directly using Visual Basic code.

- Suppose that your application needs to perform actions on SQL Server or some other foreign database format. Because the Jet supports many database formats (through Open Database Connectivity, or ODBC), you can directly access these files using Visual Basic code.

These scenarios show some of the most common uses of Access, but your copy of VB already has much of the power of MSACCESS.EXE to perform these tasks. In most cases, if you *really* need the Access interface, you shouldn't use Visual Basic, you should use Access. For more information about Jet, read Chapter 9, "Introduction to Databases and the Jet Engine."

Using Jet and DAO

Although several chapters in this book demonstrate how to use DAO, no discussion of Microsoft Office integration would be complete without a brief example. This section assumes that you have read Chapter 13, "Writing Programs with Data-Access Objects," because there is no significant overlap here. Instead, the example presented here focuses on how to make DAO even easier by wrapping it in a Visual Basic class module. Not only does this example make DAO easier to use, but it also is designed to work with any VBA (Visual Basic for Applications) host application.

EasyDAO.cls DAO Made Easy   EASYDAO.CLS (Listing 27.1) is a database class that is useful in any VBA project. Its purpose is to simplify the data access features of DAO by making them easier to use. The class begins by declaring some necessary variables and initialization and continues by performing some extensive data access functions.

N O T E   EASYDAO.CLS requires your project to have a reference to the Microsoft DAO 3.5 Object Library. If you attempt to run this example without this reference, you will get an error. ◼

Listing 27.1   EASYDAO.CLS—Preparing Our Simple Database Class

```
'**********************************************************************
' EasyDAO.CLS - A database class with a set of common routines
'**********************************************************************
Option Explicit
DefVar A-Z
'**********************************************************************
' Internal class members
'**********************************************************************
Private mwspMain As Workspace     ' Class Workspace
Private mdbMain As Database        ' Class Database
Private mrecMain As Recordset      ' Class RecordSet
Private mstrDBFile As String       ' Filename of the current database
Private mtbdMain As TableDef       ' For creating new tables
Private mfldMain As Field          ' For creating new fields
'**********************************************************************
' This event creates the default workspace
'**********************************************************************
Private Sub Class_Initialize()
    Set mwspMain = DBEngine.Workspaces(0)
End Sub
'**********************************************************************
' The Recordset, Database, and Workspace are closed when the object
' goes out of scope to prevent corrupting the database
'**********************************************************************
Private Sub Class_Terminate()
    On Error Resume Next
    mrecMain.Close
    mdbMain.Close
    mwspMain.Close
End Sub
    ...
```

Part
IV

Ch
27

EASYDAO.CLS provides four read-only properties—`GetWorkspace`, `GetDatabase`, `Filename`, and `Data`—that enable calling functions to manipulate the database directly in ways that the class itself does not provide. Listing 27.2 shows the code for these properties.

Listing 27.2   EASYDAO.CLS—EasyDAO's Properties Let You Use Its DAO Objects

```
...
'*********************************************************************
' Returns a reference to the workspace
'*********************************************************************
Public Property Get GetWorkspace() As Workspace
    Set GetWorkspace = mwspMain
End Property
'*********************************************************************
' Returns a reference to the database
'*********************************************************************
Public Property Get GetDatabase() As Database
    Set GetDatabase = mdbMain
End Property
'*********************************************************************
' Returns the filename of the database that is currently open
'*********************************************************************
Public Property Get FileName() As String
    FileName = mstrDBFile
End Property
'*********************************************************************
' Returns a reference to the currently open Recordset
'*********************************************************************
Public Property Get Data() As Recordset
    Set Data = mrecMain
End Property
```

The most common data access method is OpenDatabase, which makes data access easier and more reliable. Listing 27.3 shows EasyDAO's custom OpenDatabase method, called OpenDB. This method begins by ensuring that the file exists; if it does, OpenDatabase tries to open the file. If it cannot open the database, the error number is checked to see if the database is corrupt. If it is, the user is prompted to automatically repair it, using EasyDAO's Repair method.

Listing 27.3   EASYDAO.CLS—Opening a Database Couldn't Be Easier

```
'*********************************************************************
' Opens a database for use with this class
'*********************************************************************
Public Sub OpenDB(strFile As String, _
        Optional blnOpenExclusive As Boolean, _
        Optional blnOpenReadOnly As Boolean)
    Dim intRes As Integer
    '*************************************************************
    ' Don't stop for errors
    '*************************************************************
    On Error Resume Next
    '*************************************************************
    ' Open the database
    '*************************************************************
```

```
        mstrDBFile = strFile
        Set mdbMain = mwspMain.OpenDatabase(mstrDBFile, _
            blnOpenExclusive, blnOpenReadOnly)
        '*****************************************************************
        ' If the database is corrupted, then prompt to repair it
        '*****************************************************************
        If Err.Number = 3049 Then
            intRes = MsgBox(Err.Description & vbLf & vbLf & _
                    "Would you like attempt to repair this database?", _
                    vbQuestion + vbYesNo)
            '*************************************************************
            ' If no, then bug out
            '*************************************************************
            If intRes = vbNo Then Exit Sub
            '*************************************************************
            ' Otherwise repair it, clear the error flag, and try again
            '*************************************************************
            Repair mstrDBFile: Err.Clear
            Set mdbMain = mwspMain.OpenDatabase(mstrDBFile, _
                blnOpenExclusive, blnOpenReadOnly)
            '*************************************************************
            ' If there is another error, then give up
            '*************************************************************
            If Err.Number Then
              MsgBox "An attempt to open the database failed!", vbCritical
            End If
        '*****************************************************************
        ' If some other error, then just report it
        '*****************************************************************
        ElseIf Err.Number And Err.Number <> 3049 Then
            MsgBox Err.Description, vbExclamation
        End If
    End Sub
```

`CreateRecordset` (Listing 27.4) creates a recordset for use with the methods in this class. If you don't specify a recordset type, then `Dynaset` is assumed. Although this method is almost identical to what `OpenRecordset` already does, it is included to make using this class easier. Anyone who uses EasyDAO will have to create a recordset, and this method prevents the user from having to use the `Data` property to get a pointer to the internal database variable.

Part IV

Ch 27

Listing 27.4 EASYDAO.CLS—*CreateRecordset* Is Similar to *OpenRecordset*

```
'*********************************************************************
' Creates a Recordset for use with this class
'*********************************************************************
Public Sub CreateRecordSet(strSource As String, Optional vntType, _
        Optional vntOptions)
    '****************************************************************
    ' If any arguments are missing, add default values
    '****************************************************************
    If IsMissing(vntType) Then vntType = dbOpenDynaset
```

continues

Listing 27.4 Continued

```
    If IsMissing(vntOptions) Then
        Set mrecMain = mdbMain.OpenRecordset(strSource, vntType)
    Else
        Set mrecMain = mdbMain.OpenRecordset(strSource, vntType, _
            vntOptions)
    End If
End Sub
```

The methods in Listing 27.5—Create, CreateTable, CommitTable, CreateField, AddField, and CreateIndex—simplify the process of creating a database and appending fields and indexes to a database.

Listing 27.5 EASYDAO.CLS—Database, Table, and Field Creation Methods

```
'*****************************************************************
' Creates a new database
'*****************************************************************
Public Function Create(strFile As String) As Database
    mstrDBFile = strFile
    Set mdbMain = mwspMain.CreateDatabase(mstrDBFile, dbLangGeneral)
    Set Create = mdbMain
End Function
'*****************************************************************
' Creates a TableDef
'*****************************************************************
Public Function CreateTable(strTableName As String) As TableDef
    Set mtbdMain = mdbMain.CreateTableDef(strTableName)
    Set CreateTable = mtbdMain
End Function
'*****************************************************************
' Writes the TableDef to the table, so a new table can be created
'*****************************************************************
Public Sub CommitTable()
    mdbMain.TableDefs.Append mtbdMain
    Set mtbdMain = Nothing
End Sub
'*****************************************************************
' Creates a new field definition. Other attributes should be set by
' obtaining the NewField reference, and make the changes directly
'*****************************************************************
Public Function CreateField(strFieldName As String, vntType, _
        Optional vntFieldSize) As Field
    Set mfldMain = mtbdMain.CreateField(strFieldName, vntType)
    If Not IsMissing(vntFieldSize) Then
        mfldMain.Size = CInt(vntFieldSize)
    End If
    Set CreateField = mfldMain
End Function
'*****************************************************************
' Writes the field definition to the current TableDef
'*****************************************************************
```

```
Public Sub AddField()
    mtbdMain.Fields.Append mfldMain
    Set mfldMain = Nothing
End Sub
'********************************************************************
' Writes a index to a TableDef
'********************************************************************
Public Sub CreateIndex(strFieldName As String, _
        blnPrimaryKey As Boolean, blnUniqueKey As Boolean)
    Dim idxNew As New Index      ' For creating new indexes
    With idxNew
        .Name = "idx" & strFieldName
        .Fields = strFieldName
        .Primary = blnPrimaryKey
        .Unique = IIf(blnPrimaryKey, True, blnUniqueKey)
    End With
    mtbdMain.Indexes.Append idxNew
End Sub
```

The next three methods—`GetData`, `GetArrayData`, and `GetControlData`—provide an easy way to return all the records in a field, either as a string, an array, or loaded into a control. The key to the success of these functions is to start at the first record in the recordset and iterate to the last using a clone of the internal recordset. Listing 27.6 shows these three methods.

Listing 27.6   EASYDAO.CLS—EasyDAO Simplifies Returning All the Records from a Field

```
'********************************************************************
' Returns all (up to ~43k) of the records of a field in a delimited
' string. This is a useful feature for inserting data into a text box
'********************************************************************
Public Function GetData(strFieldName As String, _
        Optional strDelimiter As String = "¦") As String
    Dim vntRetData As Variant
    Dim strReturn As String
    Dim intDelimLen As Integer
    Dim recTemp As Recordset
    On Error Resume Next
    '********************************************************************
    ' We will be changing the cursor, so work with a copy
    '********************************************************************
    Set recTemp = mrecMain.Clone
    '********************************************************************
    ' Cache the length of the delimiter
    '********************************************************************
    intDelimLen = Len(strDelimiter)
    '********************************************************************
    ' Move to the first record
    '********************************************************************
    recTemp.MoveFirst
    '********************************************************************
    ' Build a large (<=~43k) delimited string of the records
```

Part

IV

Ch

27

continues

Listing 27.6   Continued

```
'************************************************************
Do Until recTemp.EOF
    vntRetData = recTemp(strFieldName)
    If (Len(vntRetData) + Len(strReturn) + intDelimLen) > 44000 Then
        Exit Do
    End If
    strReturn = strReturn & vntRetData & strDelimiter
    recTemp.MoveNext
Loop
'************************************************************
' Return the results
'************************************************************
GetData = strReturn
End Function
'************************************************************
' Same as GetData, but the data is stored in an array
'************************************************************
Public Sub GetArrayData(strFieldName As String, strRetArr() As String)
    Dim vntRetData As Variant
    Dim recTemp As Recordset
    Dim i As Integer
    On Error Resume Next
    '************************************************************
    ' We will be changing the cursor, so work with a copy
    '************************************************************
    Set recTemp = mrecMain.Clone
    '************************************************************
    ' Move to the end of the recordset to update the .RecordCount
    ' property
    '************************************************************
    recTemp.MoveLast
    '************************************************************
    ' Resize the array in advance. Note, this may fail if there are
    ' a large number of records.
    '************************************************************
    ReDim strRetArr(recTemp.RecordCount) As String
    '************************************************************
    ' Return the cursor to the first record
    '************************************************************
    recTemp.MoveFirst
    '************************************************************
    ' Load the array with the records returned for strFieldName
    '************************************************************
    Do Until recTemp.EOF
        vntRetData = Trim(recTemp(strFieldName))
        If Not IsNull(vntRetData) Then
            strRetArr(i) = vntRetData
            i = i + 1
        End If
        recTemp.MoveNext
    Loop
End Sub
'************************************************************
```

```
' Same as GetData, but the data is loaded into a control. The control
' MUST support the AddItem method in order for this to work.
'*********************************************************************
Public Sub GetControlData(strFieldName As String, ctlDest As Control)
    Dim vntRetData As Variant
    Dim recTemp As Recordset
    On Error Resume Next
    '*****************************************************************
    ' We will be changing the cursor, so work with a copy
    '*****************************************************************
    Set recTemp = mrecMain.Clone
    recTemp.MoveFirst
    '*****************************************************************
    ' Load the array with the records returned for strFieldName
    '*****************************************************************
    Do Until recTemp.EOF
        vntRetData = recTemp(strFieldName)
        If Not IsNull(vntRetData) Then ctlDest.AddItem vntRetData
        recTemp.MoveNext
    Loop
    '*****************************************************************
    ' Set the list index to the first item
    '*****************************************************************
    If ctlDest.ListCount Then ctlDest.ListIndex = 0
End Sub
```

AddOrEditRecord adds a new record or edits an existing one. Its first argument determines whether to add or edit the data that the vntFieldPipeValue parameter array stores. The second parameter, vntFieldPipeValue, is a parameter array that contains values delimited by the pipe character (¦) in the form vntFieldName¦Value.

This function begins by ensuring that the parameter array isn't empty and then sets the current recordset Add or Edit properties based on the action specified by the blnAdd parameter. Next, AddOrEditRecord iterates through the parameter array, determines the data type, and updates the recordset. Listing 27.7 shows the AddOrEditRecord method.

Part

IV

Ch

27

Listing 27.7   EASYDAO.CLS—AddOrEditRecord Adds or Edits Records in OneStep

```
'*********************************************************************
' Adds a new record, or edits an existing one. This method should not
' be used when adding or editing > 20 records (for performance reasons)
'*********************************************************************
Public Sub AddOrEditRecord(blnAdd As Boolean, _
        ParamArray vntFieldPipeVal() As Variant)
    Dim intItems As Integer
    Dim i As Integer
    Dim intWhere As Integer
    Dim strFieldName As String
    Dim vntVal As Variant
    On Error Resume Next
```

continues

Listing 27.7 Continued

```
'******************************************************************
' Find out how many parameters were passed. If none, then exit
'******************************************************************
If IsMissing(vntFieldPipeVal) Then Exit Sub
'******************************************************************
' Determine whether to add or edit the record
'******************************************************************
If blnAdd Then
    mrecMain.AddNew
Else
    mrecMain.Edit
    '******************************************************************
    ' If there was no current record, then notify the user
    '******************************************************************
    If Err.Number = 3021 Then
        MsgBox Err.Description, vbCritical, "AddOrEditRecord"
        Exit Sub
    End If
End If
'******************************************************************
' If loop through each parameter
'******************************************************************
For i = 0 To intItems
    '******************************************************************
    ' Separate the field name from its value
    '******************************************************************
    strFieldName = vntFieldPipeVal(i)
    intWhere = InStr(strFieldName, "¦")

    If intWhere = 0 Then
        If i > 1 Then Exit For
        If i < 1 Then Exit Sub
    End If

    vntVal = Mid(strFieldName, intWhere + 1)
    strFieldName = Left(strFieldName, intWhere - 1)
    '******************************************************************
    ' Determine the record type, and convert the value
    '******************************************************************
    Select Case mrecMain(strFieldName).Type
        Case dbBoolean
            mrecMain(strFieldName) = CBool(vntVal)
        Case dbByte, dbInteger
            mrecMain(strFieldName) = CInt(vntVal)
        Case dbLong
            mrecMain(strFieldName) = CLng(vntVal)
        Case dbCurrency
            mrecMain(strFieldName) = CCur(vntVal)
        Case dbSingle
            mrecMain(strFieldName) = CSng(vntVal)
        Case dbDouble
            mrecMain(strFieldName) = CDbl(vntVal)
        Case dbText, dbMemo
```

```
'*********************************************************
' If the record is too long, then clip it
'*********************************************************
                intWhere = mrecMain(strFieldName).Size
                If intWhere And (Len(vntVal) > intWhere) Then
                    vntVal = Left(vntVal, intWhere)
                End If
                mrecMain(strFieldName) = CStr(vntVal)
            Case Else
                MsgBox "Type not supported by AddOrEditRecord!"
        End Select
    Next i
    '*****************************************************************
    ' Complete the transaction
    '*****************************************************************
    mrecMain.Update
End Sub
```

The next four methods—MoveFirst, MoveLast, MoveNext, and MovePrev—navigate through the recordset and return the current record. The advantage of these methods over the versions in DAO is that they handle errors gracefully and return the data from a provided field in the current record. The last two methods—FindRecord and GetFieldValue—provide methods for searching for a specific record and retrieving the current record. Listing 27.8 contains all six of these methods.

Listing 27.8   EASYDAO.CLS—Record Navigation Couldn't Be Simpler

```
'***********************************************************************
' Move to the first record
'***********************************************************************
Public Function MoveFirst(Optional strFieldName As String) As Variant
    On Error Resume Next
    mrecMain.MoveFirst
    If Len(strFieldName) Then MoveFirst = mrecMain(strFieldName)
End Function
'***********************************************************************
' Move to the last record
'***********************************************************************
Public Function MoveLast(Optional strFieldName As String) As Variant
    On Error Resume Next
    mrecMain.MoveLast
    If Len(strFieldName) Then MoveLast = mrecMain(strFieldName)
End Function
'***********************************************************************
' Move to the next record
'***********************************************************************
Public Function MoveNext(Optional strFieldName As String) As Variant
    On Error Resume Next
    mrecMain.MoveNext
    If mrecMain.EOF Then mrecMain.MoveLast
    If Len(strFieldName) Then MoveNext = mrecMain(strFieldName)
End Function
```

continues

Listing 27.8   Continued

```
'*********************************************************************
' Move to the previous record
'*********************************************************************
Public Function MovePrev(Optional strFieldName As String) As Variant
    On Error Resume Next
    mrecMain.MovePrevious
    If mrecMain.BOF Then mrecMain.MoveFirst
    If Len(strFieldName) Then MovePrev = mrecMain(strFieldName)
End Function
'*********************************************************************
' Locates a record, and returns its result
'*********************************************************************
Public Function FindRecord(strField As String, vntFind, Optional _
        blnExactMatch As Boolean, _
        Optional blnMoveFirst As Boolean = True) As Variant
    On Error Resume Next
    '*****************************************************************
    ' The default is to start at the beginning, and find the record
    '*****************************************************************
    If blnMoveFirst Then mrecMain.MoveFirst
    '*****************************************************************
    ' If exact match, then use = 'vntFind'
    '*****************************************************************
    If blnExactMatch Then
        mrecMain.FindFirst strField & " = '" & vntFind & "'"
    '*****************************************************************
    ' Otherwise use LIKE
    '*****************************************************************
    Else
        mrecMain.FindFirst "[" & strField & "] LIKE '" & vntFind & "'"
    End If
    '*****************************************************************
    ' If no match, then return ""
    '*****************************************************************
    FindRecord = IIf(mrecMain.NoMatch, "", mrecMain(strField))
End Function
'*********************************************************************
' Returns the value from a specific field
'*********************************************************************
Public Function GetFieldValue(strFieldName As String) As Variant
    On Error Resume Next
    GetFieldValue = mrecMain(strFieldName)
End Function
```

Databases sometimes become damaged, so the Repair method (Listing 27.9) provides a simple way to repair a corrupted database. Not only does this method first create a backup, but it also performs a compact on the database (as suggested by the DAO documentation).

Listing 27.9 EASYDAO.CLS—*Repair* Performs a Safe Repair of a CorruptDatabase

```
'*********************************************************************
' Repairs and Compacts a damaged database
'*********************************************************************
Public Sub Repair(strFileName As String)
    Dim strBackup As String
    '*****************************************************************
    ' Make sure we don't try to repair the open database
    '*****************************************************************
    If Not (mdbMain Is Nothing) And _
        StrComp(strFileName, mstrDBFile, vbTextCompare) = 0 Then
            MsgBox "You can't repair an open database!!!"
            Exit Sub
    End If
    '*****************************************************************
    ' Make a copy of the database to work on
    '*****************************************************************
    On Error Resume Next
    strBackup = "Backup of " & strFileName
    FileCopy strFileName, strBackup
    DBEngine.RepairDatabase strBackup
    '*****************************************************************
    ' If it was successfully repaired, then kill the original
    '*****************************************************************
    If Err.Number = 0 Then
        Kill strFileName
        '*************************************************************
        ' Repaired databases should be compacted, so do it now
        '*************************************************************
        DBEngine.CompactDatabase strBackup, strFileName
        '*************************************************************
        ' If it succeeded, then ask the user if they want to delete
        ' the backup copy
        '*************************************************************
        If Err.Number = 0 Then
            If MsgBox("Would you like to delete the backup file?", _
                vbYesNo + vbQuestion) = vbYes Then Kill strBackup
        End If
    End If
End Sub
```

Part

IV

Ch

27

Now that you have a small arsenal of easy-to-use database routines in EasyDAO, it's time to put them to use in an example. The next section provides a simple example that uses several (but not all) of the methods in the EasyDAO object.

Using the EasyDAO object with BUGS.FRM FRMBUGS.FRM (shown in Figure 27.1 through Figure 27.3) is a bug-reporting wizard that uses EasyDAO to store information into an Access database. The form begins by declaring some form-level constants. Next, the SetupForm procedure initializes the form by positioning all the controls, loading the combo boxes, and playing an opening tune. Listing 27.10 also includes the LoadCombos procedure, which uses the GetControlData method from the EasyDAO object to load all the combo boxes on the form.

FIG. 27.1

The first step of the Bug Wizard contains user information.

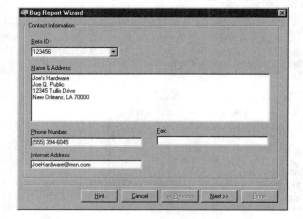

FIG. 27.2

The second step contains system-configuration information.

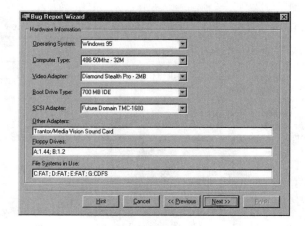

FIG. 27.3
The last step contains the bug-report information.

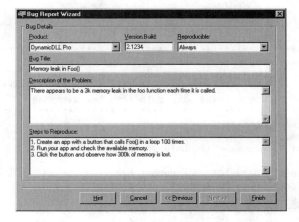

Listing 27.10   BUGS.FRM—Creating Wizards Is Cumbersome but Easy

```
'*********************************************************************
' BUGS.FRM - This is a bug reporting form that writes to a Access
'    database via direct calls to the Jet database layer
'*********************************************************************
Option Explicit
Private mdbMain As New clsEasyDAO
Private mintFrameIdx As Integer
Private mstrBetaID As String
'*********************************************************************
' Create more descriptive names for the cmd array indices
'*********************************************************************
Private Const CMD_HINT = 0
Private Const CMD_CANCEL = 1
Private Const CMD_PREV = 2
Private Const CMD_NEXT = 3
Private Const CMD_FINISH = 4
Private Const MAX_FRAMES_INDEX = 2
'*********************************************************************
' Position everything, open the database, load the combos, and play
' and opening tune
'*********************************************************************
Private Sub Form_Load()
    SetupForm
    LoadFrames
    '****************************************************************
    ' Open the database, and load the combos from its contents
    '****************************************************************
    mdbMain.OpenDB App.Path & "\bugs.mdb"
    LoadCombos
    '****************************************************************
```

continues

Part
IV

Ch

27

Listing 27.10   Continued

```
        ' Play an introductory tune
        '*************************************************************
        PlayWaveRes "Game"
    End Sub
    '*****************************************************************
    ' Load all of the combo boxes with data from the database
    '*****************************************************************
    Private Sub LoadCombos()
        With mdbMain
            .CreateRecordSet "List Defaults"

            .GetControlData "OS", cboHardware(0)
            .GetControlData "Computer", cboHardware(1)
            .GetControlData "Video", cboHardware(2)
            .GetControlData "Boot", cboHardware(3)
            .GetControlData "SCSI", cboHardware(4)

            .GetControlData "Products", cboBugs(0)
            .GetControlData "Repro", cboBugs(1)
            .Data.Close

            .CreateRecordSet fra(0)
            .GetControlData "BetaID", cboContact
        End With
    End Sub
    '*****************************************************************
    ' Position the buttons, form, and frames
    '*****************************************************************
    Private Sub SetupForm()
        Const CMD_TOP = 5350
        Const CMD_WIDTH = 1095
        Const CMD_HEIGHT = 375

        cmd(0).Move 1880, CMD_TOP, CMD_WIDTH, CMD_HEIGHT
        cmd(1).Move 3095, CMD_TOP, CMD_WIDTH, CMD_HEIGHT
        cmd(2).Move 4310, CMD_TOP, CMD_WIDTH, CMD_HEIGHT
        cmd(3).Move 5480, CMD_TOP, CMD_WIDTH, CMD_HEIGHT
        cmd(4).Move 6695, CMD_TOP, CMD_WIDTH, CMD_HEIGHT

        Width = 8125
        Height = 6300
        Move (Screen.Width - Width) / 2, (Screen.Height - Height) / 2

        LoadFrames
        Draw3DLine
    End Sub
    '*****************************************************************
    ' Draw a 3D line above the command buttons
    '*****************************************************************
    Private Sub Draw3DLine()
        Dim intStartX As Integer, intEndX As Integer
        Dim intStartY As Integer
        Dim intPixel As Integer
```

```
'*********************************************************************
' Calculate where the line should be drawn
'*********************************************************************
intPixel = Screen.TwipsPerPixelY
intEndX = cmd(CMD_FINISH).Left + cmd(CMD_FINISH).Width
intStartX = fra(0).Left + intPixel
intStartY = cmd(0).Top - (intPixel * 10)
'*********************************************************************
' Draw the grey line, then the white line underneath
'*********************************************************************
Line (intStartX, intStartY)-(intEndX, intStartY), vb3DShadow
intStartY = intStartY + intPixel
Line (intStartX, intStartY)-(intEndX, intStartY), vb3DHighlight
End Sub
'*********************************************************************
' Initializes the frames
'*********************************************************************
Private Sub LoadFrames()
Dim i As Integer
    '*****************************************************************
    ' Position the frames
    '*****************************************************************
    For i = 2 To 0 Step -1
        fra(i).Move 135, 135, 7665, 4875
        fra(i).ZOrder
    Next i
    '*****************************************************************
    ' Change the captions
    '*****************************************************************
    fra(0) = "Contact Information"
    fra(1) = "Hardware Information"
    fra(2) = "Bug Details"
End Sub
```

The NavigatePages procedure (Listing 27.11) handles the navigation between different pages in the wizard by hiding and displaying the appropriate frames. In addition, this routine is responsible for handling the enabled state of the navigation buttons at the bottom of the form.

Listing 27.11   BUGS.FRM—*NavigatePages* Handles Traversing Wizard Steps

```
'*********************************************************************
' Handles changing frames
'*********************************************************************
Private Sub NavigatePages(ByVal blnMoveNext As Boolean)
    '*****************************************************************
    ' If you can't update the data, then exit
    '*****************************************************************
    If blnMoveNext And Not UpdateData(mintFrameIdx) Then Exit Sub
    '*****************************************************************
    ' Hide the current frame, increment mintFrameIdx, then show the new
    ' frame
    '*****************************************************************
```

continues

Listing 27.11 Continued

```
        fra(mintFrameIdx).Visible = False
        mintFrameIdx = IIf(blnMoveNext, mintFrameIdx + 1, mintFrameIdx - 1)
        fra(mintFrameIdx).Visible = True
        '******************************************************************
        ' Open the table for the current page, and load the data
        '******************************************************************
        mdbMain.Data.Close
        mdbMain.CreateRecordSet fra(mintFrameIdx)
        LoadPage
        '******************************************************************
        ' Change the enabled status of the command buttons
        '******************************************************************
        If mintFrameIdx = 0 Then
            cmd(CMD_PREV).Enabled = False
        ElseIf mintFrameIdx = MAX_FRAMES_INDEX Then
            cmd(CMD_NEXT).Enabled = False
        Else
            cmd(CMD_PREV).Enabled = True
            cmd(CMD_NEXT).Enabled = True
        End If
End Sub
```

As you change each page, a call is made to UpdateData (Listing 27.12) to write the data to the database. This begins by calling the VerifyRequiredField function, to verify that required fields are filled, then the AddOrEditRecord method, to write data to the database.

Listing 27.12 BUGS.FRM—*UpdateData* Is Responsible for Writing the Wizard Contents to the Database

```
'******************************************************************
' Write the changes or additions to the database
'******************************************************************
Private Function UpdateData(intPage As Integer, _
              Optional blnAdd As Boolean = True) As Boolean
    Static sintIterations As Integer
        '******************************************************************
        ' sintIterations is used to prevent uncontrolled recursive loops
        '******************************************************************
        sintIterations = sintIterations + 1
        '******************************************************************
        ' Clear the error handler (for recursive calls only)
        '******************************************************************
        If sintIterations > 0 Then Err.Clear
        '******************************************************************
        ' Update the appropriate page
        '******************************************************************
        Select Case intPage
        '******************************************************************
        ' Contact Information
        '******************************************************************
```

```
Case 0
    '******************************************************************
    ' Verify required fields
    '******************************************************************
    If Not VerifyRequiredField(txtMultiContact(0)) Then Exit Function
    If Not VerifyRequiredField(txtContact(0)) Then Exit Function
    mdbMain.AddOrEditRecord blnAdd, _
        "NameAddress¦" & txtMultiContact(0), _
        "Phone¦" & txtContact(0), _
        "Fax¦" & txtContact(1), _
        "InternetAddress¦" & txtContact(2), _
        "BetaID¦" & cboContact
'******************************************************************
' Hardware Information
'******************************************************************
Case 1
    If Not VerifyRequiredField(cboHardware(0)) Then Exit Function
    If Not VerifyRequiredField(cboHardware(1)) Then Exit Function
    If Not VerifyRequiredField(cboHardware(2)) Then Exit Function
    If Not VerifyRequiredField(cboHardware(3)) Then Exit Function
    mdbMain.AddOrEditRecord blnAdd, _
        "OperatingSystem¦" & cboHardware(0), _
        "ComputerType¦" & cboHardware(1), _
        "VideoAdapter¦" & cboHardware(2), _
        "BootDiskType¦" & cboHardware(3), _
        "SCSI¦" & cboHardware(4), _
        "OtherDiskTypes¦" & txtHardware(0), _
        "Floppies¦" & txtHardware(1), _
        "FileSystems¦" & txtHardware(2), _
        "BetaID¦" & mstrBetaID
    '******************************************************************
    ' Bug Details
    '******************************************************************
Case 2
    If Not VerifyRequiredField(txtBugs(0)) Then Exit Function
    If Not VerifyRequiredField(txtBugs(1)) Then Exit Function
    If Not VerifyRequiredField(txtMultiBugs(0)) Then Exit Function
    If Not VerifyRequiredField(txtMultiBugs(1)) Then Exit Function
    mdbMain.AddOrEditRecord blnAdd, _
        "Product¦" & cboBugs(0), _
        "Build¦" & txtBugs(0), _
        "Reproducible¦" & cboBugs(1), _
        "Title¦" & txtBugs(1), _
        "Problem¦" & txtMultiBugs(0), _
        "Steps¦" & txtMultiBugs(1), _
        "BetaID¦" & mstrBetaID
End Select
'******************************************************************
' If intPage is 2 and duplicate key error, then notify the user
' that the title is invalid
'******************************************************************
If intPage = MAX_FRAMES_INDEX And Err = 3022 Then
    PlayWaveRes "Ring"
```

continues

Part

IV

Ch

27

Listing 27.12   Continued

```
        MsgBox "A report with the same name has already been reported.", _
                     vbExclamation
        sintIterations = 0
        UpdateData = False
    '********************************************************************
    ' If less than 2 sintIterations, then recursively call to edit
    '********************************************************************
    ElseIf sintIterations < 2 And Err Then
        UpdateData = UpdateData(intPage, False)
        sintIterations = 0
    '********************************************************************
    ' Otherwise return true and reset the sintIterations variable
    '********************************************************************
    Else
        UpdateData = True
        sintIterations = 0
    End If
End Function
```

As the cboContact drop-down combo box loses its focus, the cboContact procedure (Listing 27.13) checks whether the combo box is blank. If it is, the procedure displays a message and returns the focus to the combo box. If not, the user information (if any) in the database fills the page.

Listing 27.13   BUGS.FRM—User Validation Is Done in the *LostFocus* Event

```
'********************************************************************
' Make sure a Beta ID is listed
'********************************************************************
Private Sub cboContact_LostFocus()
    '********************************************************************
    ' Set the global variable
    '********************************************************************
    mstrBetaID = Trim(cboContact)
    '********************************************************************
    ' If one wasn't entered, then alert the user and halt
    '********************************************************************
    If mstrBetaID = "" Then
        PlayWaveRes "Ding"
        MsgBox "This field can not be blank!", vbCritical
        cboContact.SetFocus
    '********************************************************************
    ' Otherwise load the other controls with the data from that id
    '********************************************************************
    Else
        LoadPage
    End If
End Sub
```

The cmd_Click procedure handles click events from the command buttons on the wizard. The only control with any significant code is the Finish button. This button writes the bug report to the database and then asks the user if he or she wants to enter another bug. If not, the procedure dismisses the form. Otherwise, the procedure clears the page and returns the focus to the first drop-down combo box. The txtMultiBugs_Change event handles the enabled status of the Finish button to prevent users from finishing prematurely. Listing 27.14 shows these event-handling routines.

Listing 27.14   BUGS.FRM—Event-Handling Routines

```
'*********************************************************************
' Process command button clicks
'*********************************************************************
Private Sub cmd_Click(Index As Integer)
    Select Case Index
        '*********************************************************
        ' Display a hint (from the frame's .Tag) in a message box
        '*********************************************************
        Case CMD_HINT
            PlayWaveRes "Chimes"
            MsgBox fra(mintFrameIdx).Tag, vbInformation
        '*********************************************************
        ' Cancel is used to quit without filing a report
        '*********************************************************
        Case CMD_CANCEL
            If MsgBox("Are you sure you want to Quit?" _
                    , vbQuestion + vbYesNo) = vbYes Then
                PlayWaveRes "Hasta"
                Unload Me
            End If
        '*********************************************************
        ' The next two are used to navigate between frames
        '*********************************************************
        Case CMD_PREV
            NavigatePages False
        Case CMD_NEXT
            NavigatePages True
        '*********************************************************
        ' File the bug report
        '*********************************************************
        Case CMD_FINISH
            '*****************************************************
            ' If UpdateData failed, then the title must have already
            ' appeared in the database. Set the focus to the title
            ' text box, and exit.  If the user wants to quit without
            ' fixing the problem, then they'll have to use cancel.
            '*****************************************************
            If Not UpdateData(mintFrameIdx) Then
                txtBugs(1).SetFocus
                Exit Sub
            End If
            '*****************************************************
```

continues

Listing 27.14   Continued

```
            ' If the report was successfully filed, then ask the user
            ' if they want to file another.  If so, clear the page.
            '*********************************************************
            If MsgBox("Would you like to report another bug?" _
                        , vbQuestion + vbYesNo) = vbYes Then
                txtBugs(1) = ""
                txtMultiBugs(0) = ""
                txtMultiBugs(1) = ""
                txtBugs(1).SetFocus
            '*********************************************************
            ' Otherwise tell the user goodbye, and unload
            '*********************************************************
            Else
                PlayWaveRes "ItsBeen"
                MsgBox "Thank you for completing this report.", _
                                                vbInformation
                Unload Me
            End If
    End Select
End Sub
'*************************************************************************
' If the "Steps" text box is empty, then disable the finish button
'*************************************************************************
Private Sub txtMultiBugs_Change(Index As Integer)
    If Index = 1 Then cmd(CMD_FINISH).Enabled = Len(txtMultiBugs(1))
End Sub
```

The LoadPage procedure loads a page with data from the database. The next procedure, ClearAll, clears all the form's controls. Finally, the VerifyRequiredField procedure verifies that the field isn't Null. If it is, the procedure displays an error message and adds a space to the field to prevent multiple errors. Listing 27.15 shows all three of these procedures.

Listing 27.15   BUGS.FRM—Data Manipulation Routines

```
'*************************************************************************
' Loads the data from the database into the controls
'*************************************************************************
Private Sub LoadPage()
    '*********************************************************
    ' Find the record based on its BetaID value
    '*********************************************************
    If mdbMain.FindRecord("BetaID", mstrBetaID) = "" Then
        ClearAll
        Exit Sub
    End If
    '*********************************************************
    ' Use the mintFrameIdx value to determine which frame to load
    '*********************************************************
    Select Case mintFrameIdx
        Case 0
```

```
                '************************************************************
                'NOTE: & "" is appended to each line to prevent triggering
                '      an error if the return value from the record is NULL
                '************************************************************
                With mdbMain
                    txtMultiContact(0) = .GetFieldValue("NameAddress") & ""
                    txtContact(0) = .GetFieldValue("Phone") & ""
                    txtContact(1) = .GetFieldValue("Fax") & ""
                    txtContact(2) = .GetFieldValue("InternetAddress") & ""
                End With
            Case 1
                With mdbMain
                    cboHardware(0) = .GetFieldValue("OperatingSystem") & ""
                    cboHardware(1) = .GetFieldValue("ComputerType") & ""
                    cboHardware(2) = .GetFieldValue("VideoAdapter") & ""
                    cboHardware(3) = .GetFieldValue("BootDiskType") & ""
                    cboHardware(4) = .GetFieldValue("SCSI") & ""
                    txtHardware(0) = .GetFieldValue("OtherDiskTypes") & ""
                    txtHardware(1) = .GetFieldValue("Floppies") & ""
                    txtHardware(2) = .GetFieldValue("FileSystems") & ""
                End With
        End Select
    End Sub
'**************************************************************************
' Clear and reset selected controls
'**************************************************************************
Private Sub ClearAll()
    Dim ctl As Control
    For Each ctl In Controls
        If TypeOf ctl Is TextBox Then
            ctl = ""
        ElseIf ctl.Name = "cboHardware" Then
            ctl.ListIndex = 0
        End If
    Next ctl
End Sub
'**************************************************************************
' If the field is required, then make sure it isn't blank
'**************************************************************************
Private Function VerifyRequiredField(ctl As Control) As Boolean
    If ctl.Text = "" Then
        MsgBox "This is a required field!", vbExclamation
        '************************************************************
        ' Put a blank space in the control to prevent another error
        '************************************************************
        ctl.Text = " "
        ctl.SetFocus
        VerifyRequiredField = False
        Exit Function
    End If
    '************************************************************
    ' If its data is valid, then return True
    '************************************************************
    VerifyRequiredField = True
End Function
```

Bug.frm is a small example of what you can do with EasyDAO. From here, we encourage you to experiment with this class to get hands-on experience of what it has to offer. We're confident that you'll enjoy how easy EasyDAO is to use, but you also may want to expand it to include some of your own DAO wrappers.

Communicating with Access through OLE Automation

With the introduction of Access 7.0, the idea of communicating with Access via OLE Automation has become more feasible. Although you shouldn't use OLE Automation as your primary method of extracting data from a table, there are helpful features built into Access (such as its OutputTo method) that will make your life much easier. The code in Listing 27.16 demonstrates some of our favorite OLE Automation properties and methods in Access. To get the most out of this code, you should single-step rather than run through it. Each line performs some interesting task that you might want to consider doing in Access via OLE Automation.

Listing 27.16   ACCESS.FRM—Access OLE Automation Is Simple Yet Powerful

```
'********************************************************************
' ACCESS.FRM - Interacts with the Access user interface
'********************************************************************
Option Explicit
'********************************************************************
' Performs some common user-interface features using OLE Automation
'********************************************************************
Private Sub cmdCallAccess_Click()
    Const strBugs = "Bug Details"
    '********************************************************************
    ' Access is the first Microsoft application to support early
    ' binding with VB, so take advantage of it by using the New
    ' keyword instead of using CreateObject.
    '********************************************************************
    Dim MSAccess As New Access.Application
    '********************************************************************
    ' These variables will be used in conjunction with data returned
    ' from Access via OLE Automation.
    '********************************************************************
    Dim db As Database, rs As Recordset
    '********************************************************************
    ' The fewest number of <obj>.<method> calls you can make, the
    ' faster your code will be. Use With clauses like this wherever
    ' possible.
    '********************************************************************
    With MSAccess
        '********************************************************************
        ' Open a database the same as you would if you were in Access.
        '********************************************************************
```

```
.OpenCurrentDatabase App.Path & "\report.mdb"
'****************************************************************
' Use the CurrentDb property to init your db variable
'****************************************************************
Set db = .CurrentDb
'****************************************************************
' Build a recordset off of your new pointer
'****************************************************************
Set rs = db.OpenRecordset("SELECT * FROM [Bug Details]")
'****************************************************************
' Begin printing below the command button
'****************************************************************
CurrentY = cmdCallAccess.Top + cmdCallAccess.Height + 10
'****************************************************************
' Iterate through the recordset as you normally do in DAO
'****************************************************************
Do Until rs.EOF
    '****************************************************************
    ' Print the current record from the recordset variable,
    ' and use the MSAccess objects DLookup method to directly
    ' access a specific record in the table.
    '****************************************************************
    Print rs(0), _
        .DLookup("Build", "[Bug Details]", _
        "Product='" & rs(0) & "'")
    '****************************************************************
    ' This is only necessary for the rs variable.
    '****************************************************************
    rs.MoveNext
Loop
'****************************************************************
' Press F8 to continue in single step mode (don't use F5)
'****************************************************************
Stop
'****************************************************************
' Use the DoCmd to execute Access UI commands
'****************************************************************
With .DoCmd
    '****************************************************************
    ' Make a new copy of the Bug Details table called New Copy
    '****************************************************************
    .CopyObject , "New Copy", acTable, "Bug Details"
    '****************************************************************
    ' Open a datasheet of the newly created table.
    '****************************************************************
    .OpenTable "New Copy"
    '****************************************************************
    ' Print the new datasheet view of the table.
    '****************************************************************
    .PrintOut
    '****************************************************************
```

continues

Part

IV

Ch

27

Listing 27.16 Continued

```
                  ' Close the new table and delete it.
                  '************************************************************
                  .Close
                  .DeleteObject acTable, "New Copy"
                  '************************************************************
                  ' Export the Bug Details table to Excel, Word, and
                  ' Notepad without even starting them.
                  '************************************************************
                  .OutputTo acTable, strBugs, acFormatXLS, strBugs & ".xls"
                  .OutputTo acTable, strBugs, acFormatRTF, strBugs & ".rtf"
                  .OutputTo acTable, strBugs, acFormatTXT, strBugs & ".txt"
                  '************************************************************
                  ' Open the Bug Details report in the database in preview
                  ' mode. (NOTE: If you ignore the last parameter, then
                  ' your report will immediately print to the default
                  ' printer without user interaction.)
                  '************************************************************
                  .OpenReport "Bug Details", View:=acPreview
                  '************************************************************
                  ' Maximize the window and Zoom to Fit
                  '************************************************************
                  .Maximize
                  MSAccess.Reports(0).ZoomControl = 0
                  '************************************************************
                  ' Close the report and database windows
                  '************************************************************
                  .Close: .Close
              End With
          End With
      End Sub
```

Figure 27.4 shows our Access automation demo at work. In addition to the cool methods shown in this code sample, there are three methods you also might want to consider:

- TransferDatabase
- TransferSpreadsheet
- TransferText

These three DoCmd methods let you import or link data from external ODBC DataSources such as SQL Server, Excel, and text files. You definitely should explore these features to discover how they can enhance the functionality of your programs.

FIG. 27.4
Access.frm at work.

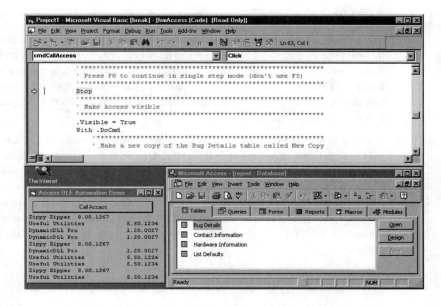

Integrating with PowerPoint

If you were unfortunate enough to use the "undocumented" PowerPoint object model in PowerPoint 95, then you probably have high expectations for PowerPoint 97. After all, Office 97 is supposed to erase the differences between the products' object models. However, somebody forgot to tell the folks in the PowerPoint group this, because its object model is a perfect example of what *not* to do when creating an object model. In fact, this object model is so bad that it isn't much of an improvement over the horrible thing that shipped with PowerPoint 95. What's worse is that this version is documented, so we're stuck with it for at least another two or three versions, so you'd better get used to it.

The purpose of this section is to try to make sense of this poorly implemented and documented object model by wrapping it into a usable class object. While this class object doesn't solve all of your problems, it does give you something to start with. We strongly encourage you to expand this object to suit your needs, so you won't waste your time floundering through PowerPoint's object model.

N O T E To control PowerPoint via OLE Automation, you will need not only the Microsoft PowerPoint 8.0 Object Library reference but also the Microsoft Office 8.0 Object Library. PowerPoint's object model has a large number of dependencies on the Office object library, so many of its methods will fail without this reference. ▦

Part
IV

Ch

27

Understanding the *clsPowerPoint* Object

The purpose of the `clsPowerPoint` object is to provide a simple interface to control PowerPoint by wrapping its complex object library in a fewer number of properties and methods. However, this object is not as complete as what you'll find in PowerPoint, because a large number of the features in PowerPoint's object library are going to be rarely used. To overcome this limitation, this object exposes its private member variables (described later) to let you directly access the PowerPoint object model as needed.

The `clsPowerPoint` object begins by creating a new `PowerPoint.Application` object in its `Initialize` event and displaying PowerPoint, as shown in Listing 27.17. In addition, a new default presentation is created. When this object goes out of scope, the default presentation has its `Saved` flag set to `TRUE` to prevent the user from being prompted to save changes, and PowerPoint is closed. This means that you are responsible for saving any changes prior to the destruction of your `clsPowerPoint` object; otherwise, all changes will be lost. This is by design, because automated projects shouldn't rely on user input from the `Initialize` and `Terminate` events.

Listing 27.17   POWERPNT.CLS—The Core of clsPowerPoint

```
'*********************************************************************
' POWERPNT.CLS - A simple wrapper for PowerPoint's object model
'*********************************************************************
Option Explicit
DefVar A-Z
'*********************************************************************
' Internal member variables
'*********************************************************************
Private mpptApp As New PowerPoint.Application
Private mprsCurPres As PowerPoint.Presentation
Private msldCurSlide As PowerPoint.Slide
Private mstrTemplatePath As String              'Default template path
'*********************************************************************
' Our PowerPoint.Application object is instantiated and displayed
' during the initialize event. In addition, we create a new presentation
' and cache the default template path.
'*********************************************************************
Private Sub Class_Initialize()
    mpptApp.Visible = msoTrue
    Set mprsCurPres = mpptApp.Presentations.Add
    mstrTemplatePath = Left(mpptApp.Path, Len(mpptApp.Path) _
        - Len("Office")) & "Templates\Presentation Designs\"
End Sub
'*********************************************************************
' This object always quits without saving changes, so it is the
' callers responsibility to make sure changes are saved before this
' object is destroyed. NOTE: This object only maintains one
' presentation, so if additional unsaved presentations are open, then
' PowerPoint will prompt the user.
'*********************************************************************
```

```
Private Sub Class_Terminate()
    mprsCurPres.Saved = msoTrue
    mpptApp.Quit
End Sub
```

As mentioned earlier, the `clsPowerPoint` object (shown in Listing 27.18) provides extensibility by exposing its private member variables so that you may interact directly with PowerPoint. This technique provides read-only access to our member variables without violating any encapsulation (also know as *data-hiding*) rules of object-oriented programming, so we encourage you to use this technique in all your "wrapped" classes.

Listing 27.18 POWERPNT.CLS—You Can Extend *clsPowerPoint* by Directly Using Its Objects

```
'*********************************************************************
' Our object can't include everything, so give the user a way to
' access our private application, presentation, and slide members
'*********************************************************************
Public Property Get Application() As PowerPoint.Application
    Set Application = mpptApp
End Property

Public Property Get CurrentPresentation() As PowerPoint.Presentation
    Set CurrentPresentation = mprsCurPres
End Property

Public Property Get CurrentSlide() As PowerPoint.Slide
    Set CurrentSlide = msldCurSlide
End Property
```

When you add a new slide in PowerPoint, three things happen. The new slide is created, you are prompted for a layout, and the new slide is activated. The `AddSlide` method in Listing 27.19 lets you do all three steps in one shot. Even better, it does this using optional arguments, so you can create a default title slide simply by calling the `AddSlide` method.

Listing 27.19 POWERPNT.CLS—Working with Slides

```
'*********************************************************************
' Adds a slide to the current presentation and activates it
'*********************************************************************
Public Sub AddSlide(Optional lngPos As Long, _
        Optional pslLayout As PpSlideLayout = ppLayoutTitle)
    '*****************************************************************
    ' Make sure lngPos is valid before proceeding
    '*****************************************************************
    If lngPos > mprsCurPres.Slides.Count Or lngPos < 1 Then
```

continues

Listing 27.19   Continued

```
        lngPos = mprsCurPres.Slides.Count + 1
    End If
    '******************************************************************
    ' Add the slide
    '******************************************************************
    Set msldCurSlide = mprsCurPres.Slides.Add(lngPos, pslLayout)
    '******************************************************************
    ' Activate it
    '******************************************************************
    mpptApp.ActiveWindow.View.GoToSlide msldCurSlide.SlideIndex
End Sub
'******************************************************************
' The caller provides a valid SlideIndex and this method activates it
'******************************************************************
Public Function GoToSlide(lngSlide As Long) As PowerPoint.Slide
    On Error Resume Next
    mpptApp.ActiveWindow.View.GoToSlide lngSlide
    '******************************************************************
    ' If GoToSlide didn't work, then bail
    '******************************************************************
    If Err.Number Then Exit Function
    '******************************************************************
    ' Update the internal slide pointer and return the slide so the
    ' caller can use Is Nothing to see if this call worked (or simply
    ' manipulate the slide directly)
    '******************************************************************
    Set msldCurSlide = mprsCurPres.Slides(lngSlide)
    Set GoToSlide = msldCurSlide
End Function
```

In addition to AddSlide, Listing 27.19 shows the wrapped version of GoToSlide, which lets you jump to another slide *and* keep your internal member variables in sync.

In PowerPoint, all the objects on a slide are part of the Shapes collection, which makes sense. However, PowerPoint makes it extraordinarily complex for you to simply set or retrieve text to or from a shape, because PowerPoint's object model is very complex. To simplify this, the ShapeText and BulletListItem properties in Listing 27.20 let you set and retrieve text in the manner to which you're accustomed in VB.

Listing 27.20   POWERPNT.CLS—Working with Text in Shapes

```
'******************************************************************
' This read/write property retrieves and sets the text of a text shape
'******************************************************************
Public Property Get ShapeText(vntShape As Variant) As String
    ShapeText = msldCurSlide.Shapes(vntShape).TextFrame.TextRange.Text
End Property

Public Property Let ShapeText(vntShape As Variant, strText As String)
    msldCurSlide.Shapes(vntShape).TextFrame.TextRange.Text = strText
```

```
End Property
'*********************************************************************
' This read/write property provides an easy way to modify a single
' bullet entry in a PowerPoint "textbox"
'*********************************************************************
Public Property Get BulletListItem(vntShape As Variant, _
        lngBullet As Long) As String
    Dim strReturn As String
    Dim intWhere As Integer
    '*****************************************************************
    ' Retrieves the single bullet item from a text shape
    '*****************************************************************
    strReturn = msldCurSlide.Shapes(vntShape).TextFrame.TextRange _
        .Paragraphs(lngBullet).Text
    '*****************************************************************
    ' Trim the trailing vbCr before returning it to the caller
    '*****************************************************************
    intWhere = InStr(strReturn, vbCr)
    BulletListItem = Left(strReturn, intWhere)
End Property

Public Property Let BulletListItem(vntShape As Variant, _
    lngBullet As Long, strText As String)
    '*****************************************************************
    ' This modifies only one bullet (actually a paragraph) in the
    ' list
    '*****************************************************************
    msldCurSlide.Shapes(vntShape).TextFrame.TextRange. _
        Paragraphs(lngBullet).Text = strText & vbCr
End Property
```

In addition to text shapes, there are a wide variety of shapes supported by PowerPoint. Shapes of any type always are created via the AddShape method, so naturally, clsPowerPoint wraps this object in a method called AddShape (as shown in Listing 27.21).

Listing 27.21   POWERPNT.CLS—Working with Shapes

```
'*********************************************************************
' Adds a shape to the current slide
'*********************************************************************
Public Function AddShape(shpType As MsoShapeType, sngLeft As Single, _
        sngTop As Single, sngWidth As Single, sngHeight As Single) _
        As PowerPoint.Shape
    Set AddShape = msldCurSlide.Shapes.AddShape(shpType, sngLeft, _
        sngTop, sngWidth, sngHeight)
End Function
'*********************************************************************
' Applies a preset texture to a shape
'*********************************************************************
Public Sub ApplyTextureFill(vntShape, texPreset As MsoPresetTexture)
    msldCurSlide.Shapes(vntShape).Fill.PresetTextured texPreset
End Sub
'*********************************************************************
```

Part
IV

Ch

27

continues

Listing 27.21   Continued

```
' Applies a preset 3D format to a shape
' ***********************************************************************
Public Sub Apply3DToShape(vntShape, thdPreset As MsoPresetThreeDFormat)
    msldCurSlide.Shapes(vntShape).ThreeD.SetThreeDFormat thdPreset
End Sub
' ***********************************************************************
' Applies an action setting to a shape
' ***********************************************************************
Public Sub ApplyClickActionSettings(vntShape As Variant, _
        macActivateType As PpMouseActivation, actAction As PpActionType)
    With msldCurSlide.Shapes(vntShape).ActionSettings(macActivateType)
        .Action = actAction
    End With
End Sub
' ***********************************************************************
' Attaches a wave file to a shape for slideshow playback
' ***********************************************************************
Public Sub ApplySoundEffect(vntShape, strFile As String)
    With msldCurSlide.Shapes(vntShape).AnimationSettings
        With .SoundEffect
            .Type = ppSoundFormatWAV
            .ImportFromFile strFile
        End With
    End With
End Sub
' ***********************************************************************
' Applies an animated entry effect to a shape
' ***********************************************************************
Public Sub ApplyAnimation(vntShape, eefEntryEffect As PpEntryEffect)
    With msldCurSlide.Shapes(vntShape).AnimationSettings
        .Animate = msoTrue
        .EntryEffect = eefEntryEffect
    End With
End Sub
```

However, shapes aren't impressive unless you can do things like apply textures, effects, actions, and sounds, so clsPowerPoint provides some thin wrappers around these methods, too.

What good would clsPowerPoint be if you couldn't use it to run a slide show? Not good at all, we'd say, so Listing 27.22 includes a RunSlideShow method. However, slide shows will require user intervention without the SlideShowTransition property being set for our slides, so this listing also includes a wrapper method called SetSlideTransition. The purpose of this method is to let you simply specify a transition time (in seconds), so your slide will be ready to run in your slide show. However, this method is flexible enough to let you change some of the default if you so choose, but in most cases, that won't be necessary.

Listing 27.22   POWERPNT.CLS—Working with Slide Shows

```
'**********************************************************************
' Sets the transition properties of the slide
'**********************************************************************
Public Sub SetSlideTransition(intAdvanceInSecs As Integer, _
    Optional eefEffect As PpEntryEffect = ppEffectAppear, _
    Optional trsTransSpeed As PpTransitionSpeed = ppTransitionSpeedMedium, _
    Optional blnAdvanceOnClick As Boolean = True)

    With msldCurSlide.SlideShowTransition
        .AdvanceTime = intAdvanceInSecs
        .EntryEffect = ppEffectAppear
        .Speed = ppTransitionSpeedMedium
        .AdvanceOnTime = msoTrue
        .AdvanceOnClick = blnAdvanceOnClick
    End With
End Sub
'**********************************************************************
' Runs a slide show synchronously using common defaults
'**********************************************************************
Public Sub RunSlideShow(Optional blnLoop As Boolean, _
        Optional blnNarration As Boolean = True, _
        Optional ssamAdvanceMode As PpSlideShowAdvanceMode _
        = ppSlideShowUseSlideTimings)

    With mprsCurPres.SlideShowSettings
        .ShowType = ppShowTypeSpeaker
        .LoopUntilStopped = blnLoop
        .ShowWithNarration = blnNarration
        .RangeType = ppShowAll
        .AdvanceMode = ssamAdvanceMode
        .PointerColor.SchemeColor = ppForeground
        .Run
    End With
    '**********************************************************************
    ' Locate the slide show window for this presentation
    '**********************************************************************
    Dim ssw As SlideShowWindow
    For Each ssw In mpptApp.SlideShowWindows
        If ssw.Presentation.Name = mprsCurPres.Name Then Exit For
    Next ssw
    '**********************************************************************
    ' Loop while the show is running
    '**********************************************************************
    On Error Resume Next
    Do While ssw.IsFullScreen
        DoEvents
        '**********************************************************************
        ' When the slide show is finished, ssw will be invalid because
        ' the slide show window has been destroyed. When this happens
        ' we need to exit the loop.
        '**********************************************************************
        If Err.Number Then Exit Do
    Loop
End Sub
```

The `RunSlideShow` method provides a simple mechanism for synchronously running a slide show (which is important, because by default slide shows are asynchronous). While PowerPoint provides a wealth of changes that you can make to customize how your show is displayed, this technique keeps it simple, which is the purpose of the `RunSlideShow` method.

Using the *clsPowerPoint* Object

Now that you know what the `clsPowerPoint` object is all about, it's time to use it. While the code in Listing 27.23 is a little lengthy, much of what appears are the comments that describe what is happening. Again, we encourage you to single-step through this form and read the comments along the way. This will help you get a good understanding of the `clsPowerPoint` object, as well as how to accomplish the basic PowerPoint tasks that `clsPowerPoint` wraps.

Listing 27.23   PPTDEMO.FRM—*clsPowerPoint* Makes Creating and Running Presentations Easy

```
'*********************************************************************
' PPTDEMO.FRM - Demonstrates how to use the clsPowerPoint object
'*********************************************************************
Option Explicit
'*********************************************************************
' Create a form-level variable so it won't go out of scope until this
' form is destroyed
'*********************************************************************
Private mpptDemo As New clsPowerPoint
'*********************************************************************
' Demonstrates how to use some of the common features of clsPowerPoint
' to create and run a simple presentation
'*********************************************************************
Private Sub cmdCreatePres_Click()
    Dim shpArrow As PowerPoint.Shape
    '*************************************************************
    ' With our form-level PowerPoint object...
    '*************************************************************
    With mpptDemo
        '*********************************************************
        ' Add a slide (to our new default presentation)
        '*********************************************************
        .AddSlide
        '*********************************************************
        ' Apply the notebook template from the default template dir
        '*********************************************************
        .SetTemplate "notebook.pot"
        '*********************************************************
        ' Set the title and subtitle text using our ShapeText property
        '*********************************************************
        .ShapeText(1) = "clsPowerPoint Demo"
        .ShapeText(2) = "Demonstrates how to use many of the "
```

```
        .ShapeText(2) = .ShapeText(2) & "clsPowerPoint object methods"
        .ShapeText(2) = .ShapeText(2) & " and properties."
        '*****************************************************************
        ' Add a default shape on the bottom corner of our slide
        '*****************************************************************
        Set shpArrow = .AddShape(msoShapeRightArrow, 540, 456, 120, 54)
        '*****************************************************************
        ' Use the apply methods to format our shape object
        '*****************************************************************
        .Apply3DToShape shpArrow.Name, msoThreeD8
        .ApplyAnimation shpArrow.Name, ppEffectFlyFromLeft
        .ApplySoundEffect shpArrow.Name, App.Path & "\driveby.wav"
        .ApplyTextureFill shpArrow.Name, msoTextureBrownMarble
        '*****************************************************************
        ' Set the transition time for the slide
        '*****************************************************************
        .SetSlideTransition 3
        '*****************************************************************
        ' Add another slide and apply a bulleted list layout
        '*****************************************************************
        .AddSlide
        .SlideLayout = ppLayoutText
        '*****************************************************************
        ' Set the title
        '*****************************************************************
        .ShapeText(1) = "Bullet List Slide Demo"
        '*****************************************************************
        ' Create the bulleted list
        '*****************************************************************
        .ShapeText(2) = "Item 1" & vbCr & "Item" & vbCr & "Item 3"
        '*****************************************************************
        ' Modify the second item in the bulleted list
        '*****************************************************************
        .BulletListItem(2, 2) = "Item 2"
        '*****************************************************************
        ' Set the transition time and display a slide show
        '*****************************************************************
        .SetSlideTransition 2
        .RunSlideShow
        '*****************************************************************
        ' Display this form when the slide show is over
        '*****************************************************************
        Show
    End With
End Sub
```

The form in Listing 27.23 demonstrates how to use clsPowerPoint, by creating a two-slide presentation with a fully featured shape and slide template (as shown in Figure 27.5). While the presentation itself isn't anything to write home about, this example does show how powerful this object really is. If you supply the content, clsPowerPoint makes it easy to turn that content into a fully featured presentation without any user-intervention.

FIG. 27.5
Creating PowerPoint presentations is a snap with `clsPowerPoint`.

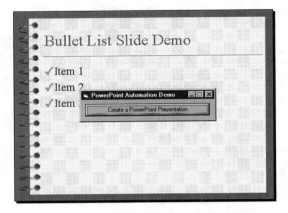

Perhaps the most interesting thing you will notice about the sample in Listing 27.23 is that when your slide show is complete, the `PPTDemo` form is displayed as the foreground window. This is accomplished by using the `RunSlideShow` method to run the show synchronously. This prevents the `Show` method (which brings the form to the foreground) from being executed until the slide show has completed.

From Here...

While there are thousands of resources available that discuss DAO, you aren't going to find much information on integration with the Access user interface. However, the samples shown in this chapter should prove a valuable resource in helping you to accomplish the most common tasks with Access and PowerPoint. With a little research and trial and error, you easily could expand the classes shown in this chapter into more robust objects that fulfill all your automation needs, and we encourage you to do just that.

In addition to the Object Browser and the product documentation for Access and PowerPoint, you can find more information about these object models from the following resources:

- The Microsoft Developer's Network (MSDN), available from Microsoft or online at **http://www.microsoft.com/msdn**, is a resource that no developer should live without.

- The Microsoft KnowledgeBase, at **http://www.microsoft.com/kb**, is by far the best free resource of information because it contains the answers to the most commonly asked technical support questions.

- The Microsoft Office Web site, at **http://www.microsoft.com/office**, contains the latest news and tips on Microsoft Office and Office related programming issues.

CHAPTER 28

Integrating Visual Basic with Mail, Schedule, and Exchange

The purpose of this chapter is to demonstrate how to use several OLE server objects to create messages. In the case of Word, the message is usually a document. In the case of Outlook and MAPI, the message is in the form of an electronic mail message. However, the net result of all three servers is to get your message across to others. This chapter shows how to accomplish that important task. ■

Leveraging the features of Microsoft Word

This chapter will show you how to improve the quality of your application while writing a minimal amount of code.

How to create local and shared items in Microsoft Outlook

You will learn how to integrate your application with Microsoft Outlook 97 to perform such tasks as sending e-mail, creating appointments, and adding items to a task list.

Send mail to any MAPI-compliant E-Mail client

Using the OLE Messaging Type Library included with Windows 95 and Windows NT 3.51 (and greater), you will learn how to add send mail using your MAPI-compliant e-mail host.

Automating Microsoft Word

At last, Microsoft Word 97 for Windows now includes Visual Basic for Applications (VBA). This means that Word finally can support OLE Automation in a manner that is consistent with the guidelines Microsoft set forth in the OLE Component Object Model (COM). This also means that Visual Basic programmers finally can depend on common properties and methods (such as `Visible` and `Quit`) being available in Word, so the steep learning curve of the past has been removed. The Speller program shown in Figure 28.1 demonstrates the power of VBA in Word.

FIG. 28.1

Speller demonstrates the power of OLE Automation with Word.

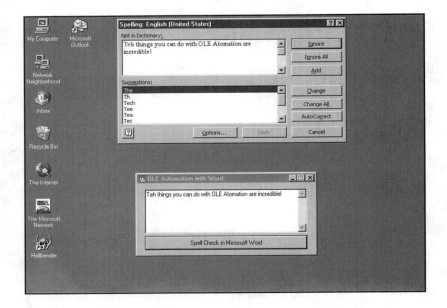

Listing 28.1 is a simple demonstration of how to use Word's powerful spelling checker in your application via OLE Automation. Although you are using Word's spelling checker, because you're keeping Word invisible, your user has no idea that you are doing this. As far as your users are concerned, this spelling checker is a part of your application.

Listing 28.1   SPELLER.FRM—OLE Automation with Word Can Save You Hours of Work

```
'****************************************************************
' Performs a spell check in Word and returns the corrected string
'****************************************************************
Public Function SpellCheck(ByVal strSourceText As String) As String
    '****************************************************************
    ' Don't stop for errors
    '****************************************************************
    On Error Resume Next
    '****************************************************************
```

```
            ' Create the object
            '***************************************************************
            Dim Word As New Application
            ' OR
            'Dim Word As Object
            'Set Word = CreateObject("Word.Application")
            '***************************************************************
            ' Change the active window to WinWord, and insert strSourceText
            ' into Word
            '***************************************************************
            With Word
                '***********************************************************
                ' If you want to see what Word is doing, then uncomment the
                ' following line
                '***********************************************************
                '.Visible = True
                '***********************************************************
                ' Since objects created via OLE Automation do not have a
                ' default blank document open, you need to create one
                ' yourself. This is done by adding a new document to the
                ' documents collection.
                '***********************************************************
                .Documents.Add
                '***********************************************************
                ' Text is inserted into the document using the TypeText
                ' method of the selection object
                '***********************************************************
                .Selection.TypeText strSourceText
                '***********************************************************
                ' Perform a spell check on the active document
                '***********************************************************
                ' NOTE: Visual Basic will not regain control and execute the
                '    next line until the spell check is complete
                '***********************************************************
                .ActiveDocument.CheckSpelling
                '***********************************************************
                ' Trim the trailing line feeds from the selected text
                '***********************************************************
                SpellCheck = RTrimCR(.ActiveDocument.StoryRanges(wdMainTextStory))
                '***********************************************************
                ' Close Word
                '***********************************************************
                .Quit wdDoNotSaveChanges ' = 0
            End With
        End Function
```

CAUTION

OLE Automation requires that your application, the server application, and the OLE dynamic link libraries (DLLs) be loaded. Consequently, OLE Automation applications consume a great deal of RAM and system resources. You should prepare your program for low-memory situations, which could prevent the program from running. Under 32-bit Windows, low-memory situations are unlikely to occur, but you still should error trap for them.

TIP In our humble opinion, we believe that *no* integrated solution should be run on anything less than a 486-66 with 16MB of RAM. In some cases, a Pentium 90 with 16MB (32MB if run under NT) or greater will be required for usable performance.

The SpellCheck function provides an easy way to spell-check text in your application with only a few lines of code, but this is only the beginning. You can find a listing of all the features Word supports in the Word type library and help file using Object Browser.

Tips for OLE Automation with Word

Here are some tips to remember when automating Word:

- Unlike previous versions of Word, Word 97 will not quit when your OLE Automation object is destroyed. This means that to terminate Word you must specifically call the Quit method of the Application object. If you do not, you will leave orphaned versions of Word (which are invisible by default) on your user's system. Although this is different from previous versions of Word, this is the correct behavior for all automation servers.

- When terminating Word via the Quit method, always provide a value for the SaveChanges parameter. If you fail to save or discard changes and terminate Word, your application will hang while Word waits for the user to answer the Save Changes dialog box. If Word is invisible, then your user won't see this dialog box, and your application will simply hang.

- If you start Word with OLE Automation, no documents are open on startup. Therefore, your application usually will need to execute the .Documents.Add or .Documents.Open methods before performing any actions.

- The Selection object and macro recorder are your friends. Virtually any task that you wish to perform via OLE Automation can be accomplished by recording a macro and examining the code. Because the recorder depends on the Selection object to emulate user actions, almost anything can be done with the Selection object.

Using the OLE Container Control with Word

Because most new applications use OLE, Visual Basic includes a powerful control for hosting embeddable OLE objects in your applications. Here are some of the features of the OLE container control:

- Events, methods, and properties, which provide an enormous amount of flexibility and control over the object

- The capability to print or modify the contents of an embedded OLE object at runtime using the Object property

- Data-binding to the data control with OLE fields in your Access database

The container control gives you the power to create the program shown in Figure 28.2, as well as more control of your inserted object. Figure 28.2 shows a sample application that adds a full-featured word processor to your application with very little code (when you exclude the comments).

FIG. 28.2

OLECONT.VBP demonstrates how to host embeddable OLE objects.

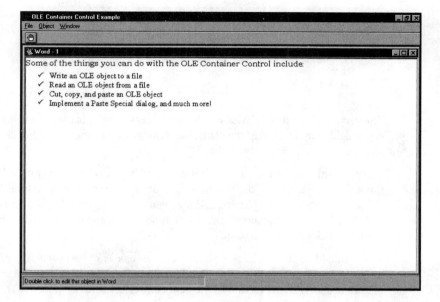

The first file in the OLECONT.VBP is PUBLIC.BAS. It keeps track of all the public constants, variables, and functions for this project. Because this application uses a multiple document interface, you have to maintain variables that keep track of the open forms in a module that all of the project's forms in the project can access. This module also contains a public function, `UpdateStatus`, which gives any procedure in the project the capability to update the status bar.

Listing 28.2   PUBLIC.BAS—Public.bas Includes the Shared Code for OLECONT.VBP

```
'**********************************************************************
' PUBLIC.BAS - Global constants, functions, and variables
'**********************************************************************
Option Explicit
'**********************************************************************
' Creates a new instance of frmWord
'**********************************************************************
Public Sub CreateNewWindow()
    Dim WinWord As frmWord
    Set WinWord = New frmWord
    With WinWord
        .Caption = .Caption & " - " & CStr(Forms.Count - 1)
        .Visible = True
    End With
```

Part

IV

Ch

28

continues

Listing 28.2   Continued

```
End Sub
'*********************************************************************
' Generic update status bar routine
'*********************************************************************
Public Sub UpdateStatus(lblStatusBar As Label, _
       Optional strStatusText As String = "Ready")
   lblStatusBar = strStatusText
   End Sub
```

The second file in the OLECONT.VBP project is the MDI parent form, mdiOLE. This form is responsible for controlling the status bar, toolbar, and its menu. Listing 28.3 begins by demonstrating how to maintain its toolbar.

The application stores the toolbar buttons in an image control array called imgTools. You set the picture property and the control's position in the array at design time. The odd controls in the array contain the up picture, and the even (odd number + 1) controls contain the down picture. The imgHold image control is a temporary location to store the toolbar picture when the user clicks a toolbar button.

When an odd-numbered image control receives a Mouse_Down event, the application stores its image in an image control called imgHold. Next, the application sets the imgTools(Index) picture property to the picture of the next control in the array (Index + 1), which should be its down picture. Finally, when the control receives a Mouse_Up event, the application restores the control's up picture by setting imgTools(Index) to the picture currently stored in imgHold. Listing 28.3 shows how to accomplish this.

Listing 28.3   MDIOLE.FRM—The MDI Parent Maintains the Code for the Toolbar

```
'*********************************************************************
' MDIOLE.FRM - MDI Parent Form
'*********************************************************************
Option Explicit
'*********************************************************************
' Saves the button image in imgHold, and inserts the down picture
'*********************************************************************
Private Sub imgTools_MouseDown(Index As Integer, _
            Button As Integer, Shift As Integer, X As Single, _
            Y As Single)
    imgHold.Picture = imgTools(Index).Picture
    imgTools(Index).Picture = imgTools(Index + 1).Picture
End Sub
'*********************************************************************
' Restores the graphic, and closes the application
'*********************************************************************
Private Sub imgTools_MouseUp(Index As Integer, _
        Button As Integer, Shift As Integer, _
```

```
        X As Single, Y As Single)
    imgTools(Index).Picture = imgHold.Picture
    Unload Me
End Sub
```

N O T E Because this toolbar has only one tool, you place its code in the Mouse_Down event. If this toolbar had more than one button, you would place the action code for the imgTools control array in a large Select Case statement in the Click event. ■

Every time the user moves the mouse over a toolbar button, you should update the status bar to reflect the action that the tool performs. The following code demonstrates how to do this.

```
'***********************************************************************
' Updates the status bar
'***********************************************************************
Private Sub imgTools_MouseMove(Index As Integer, _
                               Button As Integer, _
                               Shift As Integer, X As Single, _
                               Y As Single)
    UpdateStatus lblStatus, "Closes " & Caption
End Sub
```

As Listing 28.4 demonstrates, the MDIForm_Load procedure maximizes the window and tiles all open child windows, and the MouseMove procedures set the caption of lblStatus equal to "Ready" whenever the user moves the mouse over the MDI form.

Listing 28.4 MDIOLE.FRM—The MDI Form Contains Only Code that Applies to All the Child Windows

```
'***********************************************************************
' Prepares the application for use
'***********************************************************************
Private Sub MDIForm_Load()
    BackColor = vb3DFace
    Toolbar.BackColor = vb3DFace
    StatusBar.BackColor = vb3DFace
    WindowState = vbMaximized
    CreateNewWindow
    Arrange vbTileHorizontal
End Sub
'***********************************************************************
' Updates the status bar with the default text
'***********************************************************************
Private Sub MDIForm_MouseMove(Button As Integer, _
                              Shift As Integer, _
                              X As Single, Y As Single)
    UpdateStatus lblStatus
End Sub
'***********************************************************************
' Updates the status bar with the default text
'***********************************************************************
```

Part
IV

Ch
28

continues

Listing 28.4   Continued

```
Private Sub Toolbar_MouseMove(Button As Integer, _
                             Shift As Integer, _
                             X As Single, Y As Single)
    UpdateStatus lblStatus
End Sub
'**********************************************************************
' Updates the status bar with the default text
'**********************************************************************
Private Sub StatusBar_MouseMove(Button As Integer, _
                             Shift As Integer, _
                             X As Single, Y As Single)
    UpdateStatus lblStatus
    End Sub
```

To make the code in Listing 28.4 application-independent, you create separate procedures for Highlight and HighlightBar. You then can use these procedures in OLECONT.VBP but also can copy and paste them into another project. Listing 28.5 adds a three-dimensional appearance to the status bar and the toolbar using these procedures.

Listing 28.5   MDIOLE.FRM—The *Paint* Event Adds a Custom Three-Dimensional Affect When You Use the *Highlight* Procedures

```
'**********************************************************************
' Adds a 3-D appearance to the status bar
'**********************************************************************
Private Sub StatusBar_Paint()
    HighlightBar StatusBar
    Highlight lblStatus
End Sub
'**********************************************************************
' Adds a 3-D appearance to the toolbar
'**********************************************************************
Private Sub Toolbar_Paint()
    HighlightBar Toolbar
    End Sub
```

Listing 28.6 shows two functions that demonstrate how to use a series of line methods to create a three-dimensional effect around controls. Although most controls now come with a 3-D appearance, there still are special cases (like our toolbar and status bar) where you need to perform these 3-D effects yourself.

Listing 28.6   MDIOLE.FRM—Adding a Three-Dimensional Appearance to Controls

```
'**************************************************************************
' Adds a 3-D effect to a picture box
'**************************************************************************
Private Sub HighlightBar(picBar As PictureBox)
    With picBar
        If .ScaleMode <> vbTwips Then .ScaleMode = vbTwips
        picBar.Line (0, 5)-(.ScaleWidth, 5), vb3DHighlight
        picBar.Line (0, .ScaleHeight - 15)-(.ScaleWidth, _
            .ScaleHeight - 15), vb3DShadow
    End With
End Sub
'**************************************************************************
' Adds a 3-D border around a control
'**************************************************************************
Private Sub Highlight(ctl As Control)
    Const HORIZONTAL_OFFSET = 50
    Const VERTICAL_OFFSET = 70
    If StatusBar.ScaleMode <> vbTwips Then StatusBar.ScaleMode = vbTwips
    With ctl
        '**************************************************************
        ' Top
        '**************************************************************
        StatusBar.Line (.Left - HORIZONTAL_OFFSET, _
            .Top - HORIZONTAL_OFFSET)-(.Width, _
            .Top - HORIZONTAL_OFFSET), vb3DShadow
        '**************************************************************
        ' Left
        '**************************************************************
        StatusBar.Line (.Left - HORIZONTAL_OFFSET, _
            .Top - HORIZONTAL_OFFSET)-(.Left - HORIZONTAL_OFFSET, _
            .Height + VERTICAL_OFFSET), vb3DShadow
        '**************************************************************
        ' Bottom
        '**************************************************************
        StatusBar.Line (.Left - HORIZONTAL_OFFSET, _
            .Height + VERTICAL_OFFSET)-(.Width, _
            .Height + VERTICAL_OFFSET), vb3DHighlight
        '**************************************************************
        ' Right
        '**************************************************************
        StatusBar.Line (.Width, .Top - HORIZONTAL_OFFSET)-(.Width, _
            .Height + VERTICAL_OFFSET + 15), vb3DHighlight
    End With
End Sub
```

Listing 28.7 shows FRMWORD.FRM, an MDI child form with an OLE container control. This form is the controlling interface for your Word document. With the aid of the OLE container control, it actually *is* a Word document window. The code in this module demonstrates how to handle such basic operations as cut/copy/paste, printing, saving and reading files, and window and menu management. Although the techniques shown in this form were designed for use with Word, they can be applied easily to any object that is embedded into an OLE container control.

Listing 28.7 FRMWORD.FRM—A MDI Child Form with an OLE Container

```
'*********************************************************************
' FRMWORD.FRM - MDI Child form with a OLE container control.
'*********************************************************************
Option Explicit
'*********************************************************************
' This insures that the Word object is always the same size as the
' client area of the window.
'*********************************************************************
Private Sub Form_Resize()
    Word.Move 0, 0, ScaleWidth, ScaleHeight
End Sub
'*********************************************************************
' Handles clicks from the File Submenu
'*********************************************************************
Private Sub mnuFileItems_Click(Index As Integer)
    Dim intFile As Integer
    On Error Resume Next
    Select Case Index
        Case 1 'New
            CreateNewWindow
        Case 2 'Open...
            OLEOpenFile Word
        Case 3 'Save As...
            OLESaveFile Word
        Case 5
            OLEPrintObject Word
        Case 7 'Exit
            Unload mdiOLE
    End Select
End Sub
'*********************************************************************
' Updates the Object Submenu's enabled status
'*********************************************************************
Private Sub mnuObject_Click()
    With Word
        mnuObjectItems(1).Enabled = Not (.OLEType = vbOLENone)
        mnuObjectItems(2).Enabled = Not (.OLEType = vbOLENone)
        mnuObjectItems(3).Enabled = .PasteOK
        mnuObjectItems(4).Enabled = .PasteOK
        mnuObjectItems(5).Enabled = Not (.OLEType = vbOLENone)
    End With
End Sub
'*********************************************************************
' Handles clicks from the Object Submenu
'*********************************************************************
Private Sub mnuObjectItems_Click(Index As Integer)
    With Word
        Select Case Index
```

```vb
                    Case 1 'Cut
                        .DoVerb vbOLEShow
                        .Copy
                        .Close
                        .Delete
                    Case 2 'Copy
                        .DoVerb vbOLEShow
                        .Copy
                        .Close
                    Case 3 'Paste
                        .Paste
                    Case 4 'Paste Special...
                        .PasteSpecialDlg
                    Case 5 'Delete
                        .Delete
                    Case 7 'Close Object
                        .Close
            End Select
        End With
End Sub
'**********************************************************************
' Updates the status bar
'**********************************************************************
Private Sub Word_MouseMove(Button As Integer, Shift As Integer, X As _
                                                Single, Y As Single)
    UpdateStatus mdiOLE.lblStatus, _
        "Double click to edit this object in Word"
End Sub
'**********************************************************************
' Handles clicks from the Window Submenu
'**********************************************************************
Private Sub mnuWindowItems_Click(Index As Integer)
    mdiOLE.Arrange Index - 1
End Sub
'**********************************************************************
' Displays a Open dialog, and loads the file into a OLE Container
'**********************************************************************
Private Sub OLEOpenFile(OLEObject As OLE)
    On Error Resume Next
    Dim intFile As Integer
    With mdiOLE.cdlg
        .InitDir = App.Path
        .Flags = cdlOFNFileMustExist + cdlOFNHideReadOnly _
                    + cdlOFNNoChangeDir
        .ShowOpen
        If Err = cdlCancel Then Exit Sub
        intFile = FreeFile
        Open (.filename) For Binary As intFile
            OLEObject.ReadFromFile intFile
        Close intFile
    End With
End Sub
'**********************************************************************
' Displays a Save As dialog, and saves the contents of a OLE Container
'**********************************************************************
```

continues

Part

IV

Ch

28

Listing 28.7   Continued

```
Private Sub OLESaveFile(OLEObject As OLE)
    On Error Resume Next
    Dim intFile As Integer
    With mdiOLE.cdlg
        .Flags = cdlOFNOverwritePrompt + cdlOFNNoChangeDir
        .ShowSave
        If Err = cdlCancel Then Exit Sub
        intFile = FreeFile
        Open (.filename) For Binary As intFile
            OLEObject.SaveToFile intFile
        Close intFile
    End With
End Sub
'****************************************************************************
' Prints the contents of an OLE Container Control.
'****************************************************************************
Private Sub OLEPrintObject(OLEObject As OLE)
    On Error Resume Next
    With mdiOLE.cdlg
        .Flags = cdlPDDisablePrintToFile + cdlPDNoPageNums _
                        + cdlPDNoSelection
        .ShowPrinter
        If Err = cdlCancel Then Exit Sub
        With OLEObject
            .DoVerb vbOLEShow
            Printer.PaintPicture .Picture, 0, 0
            .Close
            Printer.EndDoc
        End With
    End With
End Sub
```

As this application demonstrates, the power of the OLE container control can yield amazing results. In addition, you can spare yourself hundreds of hours of coding by using this powerful feature.

Optimizing Performance for Complex OLE Automation Tasks

While OLE Automation is great for controlling other apps, there comes a point at which the tasks you are doing would be better done in the application you are controlling. For example, if your application has hundreds of lines of Word automation code, then it probably makes more sense to create the macro in Word and launch that macro from VB. By using this scheme, you still can get your task accomplished in Word, but the performance of your program is much better.

One example of such a task is a program that "pretty-prints" a VB code module in Word. While you could read in the file from VB, insert the text into Word, and apply formatting, it makes more sense to let Word do most of the work. The code in Listing 28.8 is a series of Word macros that appear in the PrettyPrint.dot template, which pretty-prints a VB code module.

Listing 28.8 PRETTYPRINT.BAS—PrettyPrint.bas Is a Code Module Found in PrettyPrint.dot

```
'*********************************************************************
' basPrettyPrint - Inserts and formats a code module into Word
'*********************************************************************
Option Explicit
'*********************************************************************
' Word does not support parameter passing for the Run method, so
' our public interface to the code in this module is a parameterless
' method
'*********************************************************************
Public Sub InvokePrettyPrint()
    Dim strFileName As String
    '*****************************************************************
    ' Our parameter is passed via a special CustomDocumentProperties
    ' called SourceFile which is predefined in PrettyPrint.dot
    '*****************************************************************
    strFileName = ActiveDocument.CustomDocumentProperties("SourceFile")
    '*****************************************************************
    ' If the SourceFile document property is blank,then bail
    '*****************************************************************
    If Len(Trim(strFileName)) = 0 Then
        '*************************************************************
        ' Always display Word before displaying error messages in
        ' case the caller started Word in an invisible state
        '*************************************************************
        Application.Visible = True
        MsgBox "The SourceFile document property was not set!", vbCritical
    '*****************************************************************
    ' Otherwise, run our PrettyPrint macro
    '*****************************************************************
    Else
        PrettyPrintFile strFileName
    End If
End Sub
'*********************************************************************
' This is the main method of this module. It actually PrettyPrint's
' the file in Word using the helper routines in this module.
'*********************************************************************
Private Sub PrettyPrintFile(strFileName As String)
    '*****************************************************************
    ' If this file can't be found, then bail
    '*****************************************************************
    If Len(Dir(strFileName)) = 0 Then
        Application.Visible = True
        MsgBox "File not found!", vbCritical
    End If
    '*****************************************************************
    ' Insert the title of the file on the first line using the
    ' Heading1 style
    '*****************************************************************
    InsertHeading LCase(strFileName)
    '*****************************************************************
```

Part
IV

Ch
28

continues

Listing 28.8 Continued

```
' Insert the source file
'*******************************************************************
    With Selection
        .InsertFile FileName:=strFileName, Range:="", _
        ConfirmConversions:=False, Link:=False, Attachment:=False
        .HomeKey Unit:=wdStory
    End With
'*******************************************************************
    ' Format the paragraph style of all items found in the first
    ' parameter with the paragraph style found in the second parameter
    '*******************************************************************
    ApplyFormatToParagraph "Function", "Function"
    ApplyFormatToParagraph "Sub", "Sub"
    ApplyFormatToParagraph "Const", "Const"
    ApplyFormatToParagraph "Type", "Type"
    ApplyFormatToParagraph "#If", "ConditionalComp"
    ApplyFormatToParagraph "#Else", "ConditionalComp"
    ApplyFormatToParagraph "#End", "ConditionalComp"
    ApplyFormatToParagraph "Declare", "Declare"
    ApplyFormatToParagraph "Property", "Property"
    '*******************************************************************
    ' Format from the point where the 1st parameter was found until
    ' the end of the paragraph (not including the paragraph marker)
    ' with the character style in the second parameter
    '*******************************************************************
    ApplyFormatFromCharToEnd " _^p", "ContinueChar"
    ApplyFormatFromCharToEnd "'", "Comment"
    '*******************************************************************
    ' Return to the top of the document
    '*******************************************************************
    Selection.HomeKey Unit:=wdStory
    '*******************************************************************
    ' Word is left alone (without saving) for the caller or user to
    ' do whatever else is necessary with the document
    '*******************************************************************
End Sub
'*******************************************************************
' Returns true if any of the strings passed in are found in the
' current paragraph
'*******************************************************************
Private Function IsStringInParagraph(ParamArray vntFind()) As Boolean
    Dim lngStartPos As Long
    Dim blnFound As Boolean
    Dim i As Integer
    Dim intFindItems As Integer
    '*******************************************************************
    ' Get the current cursor position (assuming no chars selected)
    '*******************************************************************
    lngStartPos = Selection.Start
    '*******************************************************************
    ' Select the current paragraph
    '*******************************************************************
    Selection.Expand wdParagraph
```

```
'*********************************************************************
' Cache the upper bounds of the ParamArray
'*********************************************************************
intFindItems = UBound(vntFind)
'*********************************************************************
' Check the selection for each of the search strings
'*********************************************************************
For i = LBound(vntFind) To intFindItems
    blnFound = InStr(Selection.Text, vntFind(i))
    '*********************************************************************
    ' If any are found, then no need to continue looping
    '*********************************************************************
    If blnFound Then Exit For
Next i
'*********************************************************************
' Restore the cursor to its previous location
'*********************************************************************
ActiveDocument.Range(lngStartPos, lngStartPos).Select
'*********************************************************************
' Return the result of our search
'*********************************************************************
IsStringInParagraph = blnFound
End Function
'*********************************************************************
' Select from the current position to the end of the paragraph
' (excluding the paragraph mark)
'*********************************************************************
Private Sub SelectFromCurToEnd()
    Dim lngCurPos As Long
    With Selection
        '*********************************************************************
        ' Get the current start pos
        '*********************************************************************
        lngCurPos = .Start
        '*********************************************************************
        ' Select the paragraph
        '*********************************************************************
        .Expand wdParagraph
        '*********************************************************************
        ' Set the start pos to the original start pos
        '*********************************************************************
        .Start = lngCurPos
        '*********************************************************************
        ' Deselect the paragraph mark
        '*********************************************************************
        .End = .End - 1
    End With
End Sub
'*********************************************************************
' Format and insert a string with the Heading 1 format
'*********************************************************************
Private Sub InsertHeading(strHeading As String)
    With Selection
        '*********************************************************************
```

continues

Listing 28.8 Continued

```
' Apply the Heading 1 style to the current paragraph
'*****************************************************************
        .Style = ActiveDocument.Styles("Heading 1")
'*****************************************************************
        ' Insert the given string
'*****************************************************************
        .TypeText Text:=strHeading
'*****************************************************************
        ' Advance to the next line
'*****************************************************************
        .TypeParagraph
    End With
End Sub
'*****************************************************************
' Locates a given string and applies the given paragraph style
'*****************************************************************
Private Sub ApplyFormatToParagraph(strFind As String, _
                                          strStyle As String)
    '*************************************************************
    ' Set the current find properties
    '*************************************************************
    With Selection.Find
        .Text = strFind
        .Forward = True              'Forward search
        .Wrap = wdFindContinue       'Search the entire document
        .MatchCase = True            'Case-sensitive
        .MatchWholeWord = True       'Whole words only
    End With
    '*************************************************************
    ' Loop while the search string is found
    '*************************************************************
    Do While Selection.Find.Execute
        '*********************************************************
        ' The Selection object will be used frequently so use With
        '*********************************************************
        With Selection
            '*****************************************************
            ' Make sure there is a space either before or after the
            ' found item (that is, make sure you haven't selected
            ' something in the middle of a word or constant)
            '*****************************************************
            If ActiveDocument.Range(.Start - 1, .Start).Text = " " Or _
               ActiveDocument.Range(.End, .End + 1).Text = " " Then
                '*************************************************
                ' Check for invalid strings
                '*************************************************
                If Not IsStringInParagraph("Exit", "'") Then
                    '*********************************************
                    ' If you got this far then it's safe to apply
                    ' the paragraph style
                    '*********************************************
                    .Style = ActiveDocument.Styles(strStyle)
                    '*********************************************
```

```
                         ' If there is a line continuation character, then
                         ' keep on applying the current style until the
                         ' next code statement is found
                         '**********************************************************
                         Do While IsStringInParagraph(" _")
                             .MoveDown wdParagraph
                             .Style = ActiveDocument.Styles(strStyle)
                         Loop
                    End If
                End If
                '**********************************************************
                ' Clear the current selection
                '**********************************************************
                .Move Unit:=wdCharacter
            End With
        Loop
End Sub
'**********************************************************************
' Locates a given string and applies the given character style
'**********************************************************************
Private Sub ApplyFormatFromCharToEnd(strFind As String, _
                                                    strStyle As String)
    '**********************************************************************
    ' Set the current find properties
    '**********************************************************************
    With Selection.Find
        .Text = strFind
        .Forward = True                  'Forward search
        .Wrap = wdFindContinue           'Search the entire document
        .MatchCase = True                'Case-sensitive
        .MatchWholeWord = True           'Whole words only
    End With
    '**********************************************************************
    ' Loop while strFind is found in the document
    '**********************************************************************
    Do While Selection.Find.Execute
        '**********************************************************
        ' Select the current paragraph, starting with the current
        ' selection and excluding the paragraph marker
        '**********************************************************
        SelectFromCurToEnd
        '**********************************************************
        ' If not within a string then apply the character style to
        ' the selection and clear the selection
        '**********************************************************
        With Selection
            If InStr(.Text, """") = 0 Then
                .Style = ActiveDocument.Styles(strStyle)
            End If
            .Start = .End
        End With
    Loop
End Sub
```

Although there is a lot of code in this listing, the actual concept is quite simple. If you were using Word and wanted to pretty-print your code, what would you do? You'd probably create a template with a set of styles that define how each type of keyword (Sub, Function, Property, and so on) should be formatted. Once you had your styles, you'd search your document (using the Find dialog box), locate each of these keywords, and then apply the appropriate style to them. Well, this is exactly what this module does. Because all of the code appears in Word, it is very fast.

Now that you have a template with the predefined styles and code, you are ready to create a VB application that lets your users pretty-print the documents of their choice. In Listing 28.9, we have a form that lets the user select a file (using the File Open dialog box) that will be pretty-printed in Word. The form is shown in Figure 28.3 with its final output.

Listing 28.9 PRETTYPR.FRM—PrettyPr.frm Demonstrates How to Call Macros and Pass Parameters to Word

```
'****************************************************************
' PrettyPr.frm - Demonstrates how to run complex macros with
'    parameters in Microsoft Word 97
'****************************************************************
Option Explicit
'****************************************************************
' Allows the user to select a module to pretty print
'****************************************************************
Private Sub cmdSelectFile_Click()
    Dim mWordApp As New Word.Application
    On Error Resume Next
    '************************************************************
    ' Display a common file open dialog
    '************************************************************
    cdlg.Flags = cdlOFNFileMustExist Or cdlOFNHideReadOnly _
                Or cdlOFNPathMustExist
    cdlg.ShowOpen
    '************************************************************
    ' Exit if the cancel button was pressed
    '************************************************************
    If Err.Number = cdlCancel Then Exit Sub
    '************************************************************
    ' Otherwise start Word
    '************************************************************
    With mWordApp
        '********************************************************
        ' Display Word maximized and activate it so the user can have
        ' something to watch during this long process
        '********************************************************
        .Visible = True
        .WindowState = wdWindowStateMaximize
        .Activate
        '********************************************************
        ' Add a new document based on the PrettyPrint template
        '********************************************************
        With .Documents.Add(App.Path & "\PrettyPrint.dot")
```

```
'**********************************************************
' You can't pass parameters to the Run method, so set the
' SourceFile document property with the filename of the
' file that will be formatted
'**********************************************************
      .CustomDocumentProperties("SourceFile") = cdlg.FileName
   End With
'**********************************************************
   ' Run the PrettyPrint macro in the Word PrettyPrint template
'**********************************************************
   .Run "InvokePrettyPrint"
  End With
End Sub
```

FIG. 28.3

PrettyPr.frm does a lot of work in Word without paying a performance price.

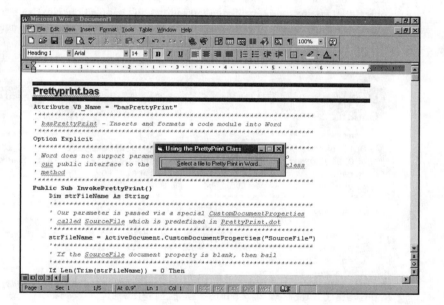

Users who have run macros from Excel may already be familiar with its Run method, which lets you specify a macro name and pass the parameters required by that macro. However, in Word, the Run method does not support parameters. Instead, you can pass only the name of the macro. Initially this seems like a major roadblock, but fortunately, there is a work-around to this serious shortcoming.

Word 97 documents support custom-document properties that may be of almost any VBA data type. Therefore, you can pass parameters to your macro by setting a predefined set of document properties and have your parameterless macro check the properties before the macro begins running its code. The CustomDocumentProperties line in Listing 28.9 shows how to set this property, and the InvokePrettyPrint macro in Listing 28.8 shows how to read this property as a parameter. Although this work-around is an ugly hack, it works. What's more, using the strategy here (even with the hack) creates a much more robust and better performance-integrated application than keeping all the code in Listing 28.8 in your VB app.

Part
IV

Ch
28

Automating Microsoft Outlook

Now that Microsoft Outlook is included with Microsoft Office, many people will be using Outlook both as their personal information manager and their e-mail client. This means that eventually you'll want to integrate some of Outlook's features (such as creating tasks and appointments and sending mail) into your VB applications. While Outlook doesn't include VBE/A (remember, it uses VBScript internally), the folks at Microsoft were kind enough to give us a great object library that provides full control of most of its features. Using the Outlook 8.0 Object Library reference in your project, your VB apps can fully tap the power of Outlook without user intervention.

To demonstrate how to program Outlook, we first decided it would be best to have a class object that created and terminated our automation connection. Next, our code needed to see if Outlook was already running when we started, so we would know if we needed to close Outlook when we were done. The code in Listing 28.10 demonstrates how to do this, as well as some methods that work with various Outlook items (e-mail, appointments, and tasks).

Listing 28.10 OUTLOOK.CLS—Sending Mail and Appointments Is Easy with Outlook.cls

```
'********************************************************************
' Outlook.cls - A simple class that encapsulates a basic set of
'   OLE automation functionality exposed by Outlook. This class
'   requires the Outlook 8.0 Object Library to be referenced in your
'   project.
'********************************************************************
Option Explicit
'********************************************************************
' The Outlook member variable is the actual pointer to our Outlook
' application interface. The mblnTerminateOutlook is a flag that is
' used in the Terminate event that allows this object to Quit the
' instances it started.
'********************************************************************
Private Outlook As New Outlook.Application
Private mblnTerminateOutlook As Boolean
'********************************************************************
' If the ActiveExplorer property is nothing, then Outlook has just
' been started by this class.
'********************************************************************
Private Sub Class_Initialize()
    mblnTerminateOutlook = Outlook.ActiveExplorer Is Nothing
End Sub
'********************************************************************
' If we started Access in the Initialize event, then we should
' terminate it in our Terminate event.
'********************************************************************
Private Sub Class_Terminate()
    If mblnTerminateOutlook Then Outlook.Quit
    Set Outlook = Nothing
End Sub
'********************************************************************
```

```
' Sends mail using Outlook
'*********************************************************************
Public Sub SendMail(strTo As String, strSubject As String, _
    strMessageText As String, Optional strCC As String, _
    Optional vntAttachmentPath As Variant)
    Dim i As Integer
    '*****************************************************************
    ' With our Outlook object...
    '*****************************************************************
    With Outlook
        '*************************************************************
        ' Create a new MailItem object...
        '*************************************************************
        With .CreateItem(olMailItem)
            '*********************************************************
            ' Set the properties of this object using the arguments
            ' provided
            '*********************************************************
            .To = strTo
            .CC = strCC
            .Subject = strSubject
            '*********************************************************
            ' Append two CRLF's to the string so attachments will
            ' appear on a separate line with a space between the last
            ' line of text
            '*********************************************************
            .Body = strMessageText & vbCrLf & vbCrLf
            '*********************************************************
            ' Attachments must be passed as an array of variants
            ' using file paths, so add the attachments to the
            ' Attachments collection of this MailItem.
            '*********************************************************
            If IsArray(vntAttachmentPath) Then
                For i = 0 To UBound(vntAttachmentPath)
                    .Attachments.Add vntAttachmentPath(i), , Len(.Body)
                Next i
            End If
            '*********************************************************
            ' Send the MailItem
            '*********************************************************
            .Send
        End With
    End With
End Sub
'*********************************************************************
' Creates an appointment in Outlook
'*********************************************************************
Public Sub SendAppointment(vntAttendees As Variant, strSubject$, _
    dtmWhen As Date, Optional lngHowLong As Long, Optional strWhere$, _
    Optional strMessage As String)
    Dim i As Integer
    '*****************************************************************
    ' With the Outlook object...
    '*****************************************************************
```

Part
IV

Ch
28

continues

Listing 28.10   Continued

```vb
With Outlook
        '****************************************************************
        ' Create an AppointmentItem object...
        '****************************************************************
        With .CreateItem(olAppointmentItem)
            '************************************************************
            ' Fill in the properties with the values provided...
            '************************************************************
            .Subject = strSubject
            .Start = dtmWhen
            .Location = strWhere
            .Body = strMessage
            '************************************************************
            ' The default duration is 30 minutes
            '************************************************************
            .Duration = IIf(lngHowLong, lngHowLong, 30)
            '************************************************************
            ' Make sure you set the ReminderSet property, otherwise
            ' the attendees won't get a reminder before the meeting
            '************************************************************
            .ReminderSet = True
            '************************************************************
            ' Create a meeting instead of an appointment (OPTIONAL)
            '************************************************************
            .MeetingStatus = olMeeting
            '************************************************************
            ' Attendees must be passed in the form of a variant array
            ' and each item must be added to the Recipients collection
            '************************************************************
            If IsArray(vntAttendees) Then
                For i = 0 To UBound(vntAttendees)
                    .Recipients.Add vntAttendees(i)
                Next i
                '********************************************************
                ' You MUST resolve all recipients before sending
                '********************************************************
                .Recipients.ResolveAll
                '********************************************************
                ' Send the appointment to the attendees
                '********************************************************
                .Send
            End If
        End With
    End With
End Sub
'********************************************************************
' Creates a task in your local personal store (PST)
'********************************************************************
Public Sub CreateLocalTask(strTask As String, _
    Optional dtmDueDate As Date)
    With Outlook
        With .CreateItem(olTaskItem)
            .Subject = strTask
```

```
'***********************************************************
' Use tomorrow as the default due date
'***********************************************************
If dtmDueDate < Now Then
    dtmDueDate = DateSerial(Year(Now), Month(Now), _
        Day(Now) + 1)
End If
.DueDate = dtmDueDate
'***********************************************************
' Save the task to your local task folder
'***********************************************************
.Save
        End With
    End With
End Sub
```

Although the SendMail, SendAppointment, and CreateLocalTask methods are included separately in Listing 28.10, the trick to each is the same. To create a new mail message, appointment, or task, you first need to call the CreateItem method of the Application object. The same method applies to other Outlook items (such as journal entries, notes, and contacts). We chose to include only these three techniques because each is unique, but their methods can be applied to the remaining items. For example, both of the Send methods send a mail message, but the CreateLocalTask method saves a task to your local folder. The only difference between saving locally and sending a message is that you use the Send method to send and the Save method to save locally.

The only significant difference between the SendMail and SendAppointment methods is the way they handle recipients. The MailItem object returned from CreateItem takes a recipient list string exactly as you would type it in the Compose Mail dialog box, whereas AppointmentItem requires you to add your recipients to a Recipients collection and resolve the names. Besides this name resolution difference (and the obvious different properties), the SendMail and SendAppointment methods do the same thing.

Creating Items in Outlook Using a VB Form

Now that your object is complete and ready to create objects, you need a user interface for creating these items. Figure 28.4 shows a crude Compose Mail dialog box. While its support for attachments is limited, it still can be used to create rather complex e-mail messages.

Outlook.frm (shown in Listing 28.11) is designed to use the Outlook class object to create a mail, appointment, and task item. This form is a dynamic form that changes its appearance depending on the option button selected for the type of item you want to create (as shown in Figure 28.5). In addition to using the Outlook class object to create these items, this form is a good example of how to reconfigure your app to do multiple tasks without using additional controls or forms. Although it requires a little extra work, the net result in performance is well worth the effort.

Part
IV

Ch
28

FIG. 28.4

Outlook.frm mimics a
Compose Mail dialog
box.

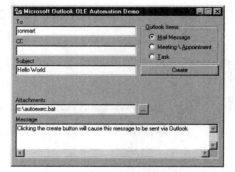

**Listing 28.11   OUTLOOK.FRM—Outlook.frm Demonstrates How to Use the
Outlook Class Object**

```
'************************************************************************
' Outlook.frm - A user-interface for testing the
'************************************************************************
Option Explicit
Option Compare Text
'************************************************************************
' Constants that map to the indices of option buttons on our form
'************************************************************************
Const MAIL_MESSAGE As Integer = 0
Const MEETING As Integer = 1
Const TASK As Integer = 2
'************************************************************************
' Constants that map to the indices of text boxes on our form
'************************************************************************
Const TEXT_TO As Integer = 0
Const TEXT_INVITE As Integer = 0
Const TEXT_TASK As Integer = 0
Const TEXT_CC As Integer = 1
Const TEXT_WHEN As Integer = 1
Const TEXT_DUE As Integer = 1
Const TEXT_SUBJECT As Integer = 2
Const TEXT_WHERE As Integer = 3
Const TEXT_ATTACHMENTS As Integer = 4
Const TEXT_HOWLONG As Integer = 4
Const TEXT_MESSAGE As Integer = 5
'************************************************************************
' Create a new clsOutlook object
'************************************************************************
Private mOutlook As New clsOutlook
'************************************************************************
' Returns the caption for a given text box based on the intOption
' passed in
'************************************************************************
Private Function GetCaption(intIndex As Integer, _
    intOption As Integer) As String
    Dim strCaption As String
```

```
        Dim intFirstPipe As Integer
        Dim intSecondPipe As Integer
        '*******************************************************************
        ' Don't stop for errors
        '*******************************************************************
        On Error Resume Next
        '*******************************************************************
        ' Get the pipe delimited caption from the label
        '*******************************************************************
        strCaption = lbl(intIndex).Tag
        '*******************************************************************
        ' Locate the first and second pipes
        '*******************************************************************
        intFirstPipe = InStr(strCaption, "¦")
        intSecondPipe = InStr(intFirstPipe + 1, strCaption, "¦")
        If intSecondPipe = 0 Then intSecondPipe = Len(strCaption)
        '*******************************************************************
        ' Return the appropriate string based on the intOption param
        '*******************************************************************
        Select Case intOption
            Case MAIL_MESSAGE
                GetCaption = Left(strCaption, intFirstPipe - 1)
            Case MEETING
                GetCaption = Mid(strCaption, intFirstPipe + 1, _
                    intSecondPipe - (intFirstPipe + 1))
            Case TASK
                GetCaption = Mid(strCaption, intSecondPipe + 1)
        End Select
End Function
'***********************************************************************
' Displays an Open dialog so attachments can be selected
'***********************************************************************
Private Sub cmdBrowse_Click()
    On Error Resume Next
        '*******************************************************************
        ' Display the open dialog
        '*******************************************************************
    With cdlg
        .DialogTitle = "Select an Attachment"
        .Filter = "All Files (*.*)¦*.*"
        .FilterIndex = 1
        .Flags = cdlOFNFileMustExist Or cdlOFNPathMustExist Or _
            cdlOFNHideReadOnly
        .ShowOpen
        '*******************************************************************
' If the user didn't choose cancel, then put the return filename
    ' into the attachments text box
        '*******************************************************************
        If Err = cdlCancel Then Exit Sub
        txt(TEXT_ATTACHMENTS) = .filename
    End With
End Sub
'***********************************************************************
```

continues

Part

IV

Ch

28

Listing 28.11   Continued

```vb
' Creates (or sends) a mail message, meeting or task
'*********************************************************************
Private Sub cmdCreate_Click()
    '*****************************************************************
    ' Examine the tag of fraOutlookItems to see what type to create
    '*****************************************************************
    Select Case Val(fraOutlookItems.Tag)
        Case MAIL_MESSAGE
            '*********************************************************
            ' Attachments must be in a variant array, so load the
            ' contents of the attachments text box into a variant
            ' array
            '*********************************************************
            Dim vntarray() As Variant
            If Len(txt(TEXT_ATTACHMENTS)) Then
                ReDim vntarray(0)
                vntarray(0) = txt(TEXT_ATTACHMENTS)
            End If
            '*********************************************************
            ' Send the message using the values from the text box
            '*********************************************************
            mOutlook.SendMail txt(TEXT_TO), txt(TEXT_SUBJECT), _
                txt(TEXT_MESSAGE), txt(TEXT_CC), vntarray
        Case MEETING
            '*********************************************************
            ' Get the recipients array using GetRecipients, then
            ' get the remaining arguments from the text boxes
            '*********************************************************
            mOutlook.SendAppointment GetRecipients(txt(TEXT_INVITE)), _
                txt(TEXT_SUBJECT), CDate(txt(TEXT_WHEN)), _
                CLng(txt(TEXT_HOWLONG)), txt(TEXT_WHERE), _
                txt(TEXT_MESSAGE)
        Case TASK
            '*********************************************************
            ' Create a task in your local task folder using today's
            ' date as the due date
            '*********************************************************
            mOutlook.CreateLocalTask txt(TEXT_TASK), _
                CDate(txt(TEXT_DUE))
    End Select
End Sub
'*********************************************************************
' Set the default option button when loading the form
'*********************************************************************
Private Sub Form_Load()
    Dim ctl As Control

    For Each ctl In Controls
        If TypeOf ctl Is Label Then ctl.Tag = ctl.Caption
    Next ctl

    optItems(0).Value = True
End Sub
```

```
'**********************************************************************
' When an option button is clicked, the index needs to be stored in
' the frame tag and the form needs to be updated
'**********************************************************************
Private Sub optItems_Click(Index As Integer)
    Dim i As Integer
    '******************************************************************
    ' Store the index of the clicked button in the tag of the
    ' container frame
    '******************************************************************
    fraOutlookItems.Tag = CStr(Index)
    '******************************************************************
    ' Set the caption for all of the labels and clear the text boxes
    '******************************************************************
    For i = 0 To 5
        lbl(i).Caption = GetCaption(i, Index)
        txt(i) = ""
        '**************************************************************
        ' Hide all text boxes under empty labels and display text
        ' boxes under filled labels
        '**************************************************************
        txt(i).Visible = Len(lbl(i))
    Next i
    '******************************************************************
    ' If the current index is MAIL_MESSAGE(0) then make the browse
    ' button visible, otherwise hide the browse button
    '******************************************************************
    cmdBrowse.Visible = (Index = MAIL_MESSAGE)
    '******************************************************************
    ' If the Index is > 0 then add the default date/time to txt(1)
    '******************************************************************
    If Index Then txt(1) = Date & " " & Time
    '******************************************************************
    ' If the current index is MEETING (1) then set some defaults
    '******************************************************************
    If Index = MEETING Then
        txt(TEXT_HOWLONG) = "30"
        txt(TEXT_WHERE) = "My Office"
    End If
    '******************************************************************
    ' If the form is visible, then set the focus to the first textbox
    '******************************************************************
    If Visible Then txt(0).SetFocus
End Sub
'**********************************************************************
' Returns a variant with an array of the recipients passed in strList
'**********************************************************************
Private Function GetRecipients(ByVal strList As String) As Variant
    Dim strArray() As String
    Dim intWhere As Integer
    Dim intIndex As Integer
    '******************************************************************
    ' Only continue if a non-empty string was provided
```

continues

Part

IV

Ch

28

Listing 28.11   Continued

```
'********************************************************************
If strList = "" Then Exit Function
'********************************************************************
' strList should be a semi-colon delimited list of valid e-mail
' names, so parse the string into the new array
'********************************************************************
Do
    intWhere = InStr(strList, ";")
    ReDim Preserve strArray(intIndex) As String
    If intWhere = 0 Then Exit Do
    strArray(intIndex) = Left(strList, intWhere - 1)
    strList = Mid(strList, intWhere + 1)
    intIndex = intIndex + 1
Loop
'********************************************************************
' Add the last (or only) item to the array
'********************************************************************
strArray(intIndex) = strList
'********************************************************************
' Return the array as a single variant
'********************************************************************
GetRecipients = strArray
End Function
```

Excluding the cmdCreate_Click event and the GetRecipients method, most of the code in this form is simply managing the user interface of the form. The cmdCreate_Click event uses the Outlook class object to create the Outlook item specified by the current option button selected on the form. The GetRecipients method is required by the SendAppointment method to parse the recipient list string into a variant array of recipients. Your own application should, at a minimum, include code similar to each of these routines. The remaining code is a demonstration of how to implement a multifunctional form.

FIG. 28.5
This dynamic form adjusts itself when a new option is selected.

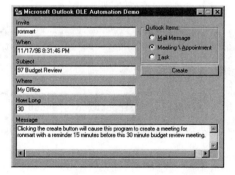

Integrating with OLE Messaging (MAPI)

Personally, we wish that we never had to program e-mail–integrated applications with anything except Outlook. However, in the real world, we know that some clients still will be using other mail clients. For these nonconformists, you will have to use MAPI to send mail. For the purpose of this section, we assume that Exchange or Microsoft Mail is your mail client, but the code here should work with any MAPI-compliant mail product.

Creating a Generic *SendMail* Method

The code in Listing 28.12 demonstrates how to use the OLE Messaging type library that comes with Windows 95 and Windows NT 3.51 (or greater). To use this type library in your project, you first must add it to the References dialog box, using the Browse button. Locate mdisp32.tlb in your system(32) directory and voila, VB automatically registers OLE Messaging for you. The documentation for this little beast can be found in the MAPI SDK (available at **http://www.quecorp.com**).

Listing 28.12 MAPI.CLS—Sending Mail to MAPI-Compliant Apps is Easy with the *MAPI Object*

```
'*********************************************************************
' MAPI.CLS - A simple wrapper class for the OLE/Messaging 1.0 type
'    library that demonstrates how to send mail
'*********************************************************************
Option Explicit
Private MapiSession As Object
'*********************************************************************
' Creates a new MAPI Session object
'*********************************************************************
Private Sub Class_Initialize()
    Set MapiSession = CreateObject("MAPI.SESSION")
End Sub
'*********************************************************************
' If LogOn succeeded, then LogOff when this object is destroyed
'*********************************************************************
Private Sub Class_Terminate()
    If Not IsNull(MapiSession.MAPIOBJECT) Then MapiSession.Logoff
End Sub
'*********************************************************************
' You MUST call this method first in order to get a handle to a
' valid MAPI session. If you are using Exchange, then you don't need
' the Password argument. You MUST provide a valid user name otherwise
' the LogOn dialog will appear.
'*********************************************************************
Public Sub LogOn(strUserName As String, Optional strPassword As String)
    If Len(strPassword) Then
        MapiSession.LogOn strUserName, strPassword
```

continues

Part
IV

Ch
28

Listing 28.12   Continued

```
        Else
            MapiSession.LogOn strUserName
        End If
End Sub
'**********************************************************************
' Sends an e-mail message
'**********************************************************************
Public Sub SendMail(vntTo As Variant, strSubject As String, _
        strMessage As String, Optional vntCC, Optional vntBCC, _
        Optional clsAttachedFiles As clsAttachments)
    Dim Message As Object
    '******************************************************************
    ' Make sure a valid MapiSession exists before proceeding
    '******************************************************************
    If IsNull(MapiSession.MAPIOBJECT) Then
        MsgBox "You must first call LogOn!", vbCritical
        Exit Sub
    End If
    '******************************************************************
    ' Add a new message to the Outbox and fill the properties
    '******************************************************************
    Set Message = MapiSession.Outbox.Messages.Add
    With Message
        .Subject = strSubject
        .Text = strMessage
        '**************************************************************
        ' Add the array of recipients to the message
        '**************************************************************
        AddRecipients Message, vntTo, mapiTo
        AddRecipients Message, vntCC, mapiCc
        AddRecipients Message, vntBCC, mapiBcc
        '**************************************************************
        ' Add the attached files to the message using the
        ' clsAttachments object's AttachToMessage method
        '**************************************************************
        If Not (clsAttachedFiles Is Nothing) Then
            clsAttachedFiles.AttachToMessage Message
        End If
        '**************************************************************
        ' Send the message. The first param saves the message to the
        ' Sent Items folder and the second param prevents the compose
        ' mail dialog from being displayed.
        '**************************************************************
        .Send True, False
    End With
End Sub
'**********************************************************************
' Adds recipients to a message object
'**********************************************************************
Private Sub AddRecipients(Message As Object, vntNames, vntType)
```

```
            Dim Recipient As Object
            Dim intMax As Integer
            Dim i As Integer
            '*****************************************************************
            ' We can only work with arrays, so bail if not an array
            '*****************************************************************
            If Not IsArray(vntNames) Then Exit Sub
            '*****************************************************************
            ' Cache the upper boundary of the array
            '*****************************************************************
            intMax = UBound(vntNames)
            '*****************************************************************
            ' Loop through the array adding each recipient to the message
            '*****************************************************************
            For i = LBound(vntNames) To intMax
                Set Recipient = Message.Recipients.Add
                With Recipient
                    .Name = vntNames(i)
                    .Type = vntType
                    '*********************************************************
                    ' You MUST resolve the names before sending. If the name
                    ' can't be resolved, then the user will be prompted to
                    ' resolve the name using a MAPI name resolution dialog.
                    '*********************************************************
                    .Resolve
                End With
                '*************************************************************
                ' Update the message to reflect the new changes
                '*************************************************************
                Message.Update
            Next i
        End Sub
```

This code simply wraps an OLE Messaging (MAPI) session for logging on and sending a mail message. Although you could use this library for doing other tasks, such as traversing the folders and messages in your mail file, we have not included this functionality in this code sample. However, we encourage you to experiment with this type of library to learn more about how to interact with your mail client.

While we tried to make this object work similarly to the Outlook SendMail method, some subtle differences exist. However, the major features of a recipient list string and support for attachments are included.

Handling Attachments

The code in Listing 28.13 performs the arduous task of maintaining a collection of attachments for a message; the code also provides the AttachToMessage method that is used internally by SendMail to add the attachments to your message.

Part

IV

Ch

28

Listing 28.13   ATTACHMENTS.CLS—The *Attachments* Class Simplifies Adding Attachments to Messages

```
'*********************************************************************
' Attachments.cls - Maintains a collection of attachment objects for
'   that will be bound to a message
'*********************************************************************
Option Explicit
'*********************************************************************
' The private collection will be maintained without requiring the
' user to pass a collection of attachments
'*********************************************************************
Private colAttachments As New Collection
'*********************************************************************
' Returns the number of attachments currently belonging to this
' object
'*********************************************************************
Public Property Get Count() As Integer
    Count = colAttachments.Count
End Property
'*********************************************************************
' The user calls this method to add files to the internal collection
'*********************************************************************
Public Sub Add(strSourceFile As String, Optional vntPosition, _
    Optional vntType)
    '*********************************************************************
    ' If the source file is blank or doesn't exist then exit
    '*********************************************************************
    If Len(strSourceFile) = 0 Or _
        Len(Dir(strSourceFile, vbHidden Or vbSystem)) = 0 Then
            MsgBox strSourceFile & " could not be found!", vbCritical
            Exit Sub
    End If
    '*********************************************************************
    ' A new clsAttachment is created each time a file is added
    '*********************************************************************
    Dim NewAttachment As New clsAttachment
    '*********************************************************************
    ' Add the source file at the position the caller requested
    '*********************************************************************
    With NewAttachment
        .Source = strSourceFile
        .Position = IIf(IsMissing(vntPosition), -1, vntPosition)
        '*********************************************************************
        ' By default files are attached, but they could be linked
        ' using the mapiFileLink type
        '*********************************************************************
        .vntType = IIf(IsMissing(vntType), mapiFileData, vntType)
    End With
    '*********************************************************************
    ' Add the new attachment to our internal collection
    '*********************************************************************
    colAttachments.Add NewAttachment
End Sub
'*********************************************************************
```

```
' When SendMail is called in clsMAPI, a check is made to see if a
' clsAttachments object was passed. If it was, then AttachToMessage
' is called
'*********************************************************************
Public Sub AttachToMessage(Message As Object)
    Dim i As Integer
    '*****************************************************************
    ' Loop through our internal attachments collection
    '*****************************************************************
    For i = 1 To colAttachments.Count
        '*************************************************************
        ' Add the attachment to the message
        '*************************************************************
        With Message.Attachments.Add
            '*********************************************************
            ' We always use the filename for the caption
            '*********************************************************
            .Name = colAttachments(i).Source
            '*********************************************************
            ' Specifies linked or attached
            '*********************************************************
            .Type = colAttachments(i).vntType
            '*********************************************************
            ' Place at the end of the file or at the specified pos
            '*********************************************************
            If colAttachments(i).Position < 0 Then
                Message.Text = Message.Text & " "
                .Position = Len(Message.Text)
            Else
                .Position = colAttachments(i).Position
            End If
            '*********************************************************
            ' Read the binary object into the message from file
            '*********************************************************
            .ReadFromFile = .Name
            '*********************************************************
            ' Commit the changes
            '*********************************************************
            Message.Update
        End With
    Next i
    '*****************************************************************
    ' After we've attached our files, then we need to reset our
    ' collection to prepare for the next set of attachments
    '*****************************************************************
    Set colAttachments = Nothing
End Sub
```

The way this object works is that you add attachments via the Add method and maintain an internal collection of Attachment objects, shown here:

```
'*********************************************************************
' Attachment.cls - An object that can be added to a collection
'*********************************************************************
Public Source As String
```

```
Public Position As String
Public vntType As Variant
```

When `SendMail` is called, it calls the `AttachToMessage` method to attach all the attachments in the collection to the outbound message. Once this process is complete, the internal collection is cleared. Although this code is tedious, it is an elegant way to mimic the underlying code of the `Attachments` collection in the Outlook type library.

Using the *MAPI* Class Object to Send Mail

Now that you have created the `MAPI` class object, you need a user interface for composing mail. Figure 28.6 shows a simplistic Compose Mail dialog box that includes support for a single attachment. While this form isn't as sophisticated as your e-mail browser, it easily could be modified to support multiple in-place attachments.

FIG. 28.6

Message.frm is a simple Compose Mail dialog box.

Listing 28.14 shows the code to create a simple Compose Mail dialog box. Like Outlook.frm (shown in Listing 28.11), it includes a File Open dialog box for attachment selection and a `GetRecipients` function to parse a recipient list string into an array.

Listing 28.14   MESSAGE.FRM—Message.frm Demonstrates How to Send Mail with Attachments Using *clsMAPI*

```
'*********************************************************************
' Message.frm - Demonstrates how to create a mail message using
'    clsMAPI
'*********************************************************************
Option Explicit
'*********************************************************************
' Constants that map to the indices of text boxes on our form
'*********************************************************************
Const TEXT_TO As Integer = 0
Const TEXT_CC As Integer = 1
Const TEXT_ATTACHMENTS As Integer = 2
Const TEXT_SUBJECT As Integer = 3
Const TEXT_MESSAGE As Integer = 4
```

```vb
'**********************************************************************
' Displays an Open dialog so attachments can be selected
'**********************************************************************
Private Sub cmdBrowse_Click()
    On Error Resume Next
    '**********************************************************************
    ' Display the open dialog
    '**********************************************************************
    With cdlg
        .DialogTitle = "Select an Attachment"
        .Filter = "All Files (*.*)¦*.*"
        .FilterIndex = 1
        .Flags = cdlOFNFileMustExist Or cdlOFNPathMustExist Or _
            cdlOFNHideReadOnly
        .ShowOpen
        '**********************************************************************
        ' If the user didn't choose cancel, then put the return filename
        ' into the attachments text box
        '**********************************************************************
        If Err = cdlCancel Then Exit Sub
        txt(TEXT_ATTACHMENTS) = .filename
    End With
End Sub
'**********************************************************************
' Returns a variant with an array of the recipients passed in strList
'**********************************************************************
Private Function GetRecipients(ByVal strList As String) As Variant
    Dim strArray() As String
    Dim intWhere As Integer
    Dim intIndex As Integer
    '**********************************************************************
    ' Only continue if a non-empty string was provided
    '**********************************************************************
    If strList = "" Then Exit Function
    '**********************************************************************
    ' strList should be a semi-colon delimited list of valid e-mail
    ' names, so parse the string into the new array
    '**********************************************************************
    Do
        intWhere = InStr(strList, ";")
        ReDim Preserve strArray(intIndex) As String
        If intWhere = 0 Then Exit Do
        strArray(intIndex) = Left(strList, intWhere - 1)
        strList = Mid(strList, intWhere + 1)
        intIndex = intIndex + 1
    Loop
    '**********************************************************************
    ' Add the last (or only) item to the array
    '**********************************************************************
    strArray(intIndex) = strList
    '**********************************************************************
    ' Return the array as a single variant
    '**********************************************************************
    GetRecipients = strArray
End Function
```

continues

Listing 28.14 Continued

```
'******************************************************************
' Establishes a MAPI connection, sends the mail and resets the form
'******************************************************************
Private Sub cmdSend_Click()
    '**************************************************************
    ' Establish a new MAPI session
    '**************************************************************
    Dim MapiSession As New clsMAPI
    MapiSession.LogOn ""
    '**************************************************************
    ' If there is an attachment, then create an attachments object
    '**************************************************************
    If Len(txt(TEXT_ATTACHMENTS)) Then
        Dim Attach As New clsAttachments
        '**********************************************************
        ' Attachments are easily added by calling the Add method of
        ' the clsAttachments object
        '**********************************************************
        Attach.Add txt(TEXT_ATTACHMENTS)
        '**********************************************************
        ' Send the message with attachments
        '**********************************************************
        MapiSession.SendMail GetRecipients(txt(TEXT_TO)), _
        txt(TEXT_SUBJECT), txt(TEXT_MESSAGE), _
        GetRecipients(txt(TEXT_CC)), , Attach
    Else
        '**********************************************************
        ' Send the message without attachments
        '**********************************************************
        MapiSession.SendMail GetRecipients(txt(TEXT_TO)), _
        txt(TEXT_SUBJECT), txt(TEXT_MESSAGE), _
        GetRecipients(txt(TEXT_CC))
    End If
    '**************************************************************
    ' Clear all of the textboxes on the form
    '**************************************************************
    Dim ctl As Control
    For Each ctl In Controls
        If TypeOf ctl Is TextBox Then ctl = ""
    Next ctl
End Sub
```

The cmdSend_Click event however, is the real workhorse. This event takes the values entered into the form and passes them to the SendMail method to mail the message. If an attachment was provided, it is added to the Attachments internal collection via its Add method. When the message has been sent, all the text boxes are cleared to prepare for a new message.

From Here...

Now that you have seen some samples of what you can do with the Word, Outlook, and OLE Messaging type libraries, we encourage you to explore them further on your own. By viewing these libraries in the Object Browser, you can gain insight on the full potential of these servers. Take the samples in this chapter, expand them to include new features, and begin to build a reusable library of helpful integration routines. In addition to this exploration, you might find the following resources helpful:

- The MAPI SDK is the only official resource for the OLE Messaging type library. This resource includes code samples of many common tasks not discussed in this chapter. The easiest place to find this SDK is on the Microsoft Developers Network CD or Web site (at **http://www.microsoft.com/msdn**).

- Keep an eye out at your local bookstore for new titles released on Word and Outlook programming. Although we can't make recommendations at this time, we are sure that by the time you read this book, several great resources will be available.

- Visit the Microsoft Office Web site at **http://www.microsoft.com/office** to get the latest information on Microsoft Office 97 and integrated programming techniques.

CHAPTER 29

Integration with Other OLE Applications

Many companies offer lots of powerful applications that you might want to integrate into your custom programs. Some of these applications will support OLE (or even DDE), others will have exposed APIs in the form of a documented DLL, and still others will not provide any mechanism for customization or integration (for example, America Online). This chapter demonstrates how to do generic integration with OLE apps, as well as how to hack your way to an integrated app. By focusing on the techniques used in this chapter, you should be better prepared to integrate with any type of application, not just Microsoft products. ■

Perform generic steps to connect to an OLE Automation Server

You will learn how to establish a connection easily with any OLE Automation server.

Take advantage of OLE Miniservers

Microsoft's products use Miniservers quite extensively, so we'll teach you how to use them in your programs.

Communicate with applications that do not support OLE

Learn how to handle low-tech applications using advanced programming tricks.

Connecting to OLE Automation Servers

You might think that once you've seen one OLE Automation server, you've seen them all. For the most part, this is true. Connecting to any OLE Automation server requires the same basic steps, but using the server and disconnecting isn't so easy. Every server has its own way of doing things, so sometimes you have to be careful. To demonstrate this point, this chapter introduces a simple text editor written in MFC (Microsoft Foundation Classes), called TextServer, that supports OLE Automation (see Figure 29.1). This chapter also introduces Talker, a sample Visual Basic (VB) program, to demonstrate the communication between a VB application and TextServer (see Figure 29.2).

FIG. 29.1

TextServer is a text editor that can serve as an OLE Automation testing tool.

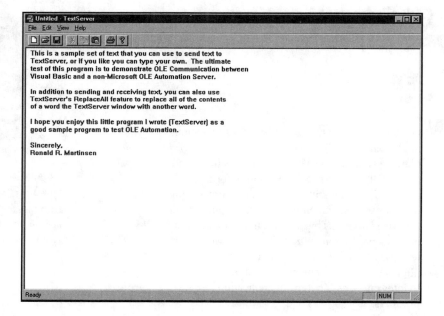

FIG. 29.2

Talker demonstrates that OLE Automation with TextServer is similar to Microsoft applications.

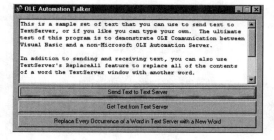

To demonstrate OLE Automation between a VB application and a typical non-Microsoft application (TextServer), this section discusses the steps required to write Talker. To begin this project, you first create an object variable that does not go out of scope. By doing so, you prevent yourself from accidentally losing your OLE Automation connection. Next, use `CreateObject` to establish a connection with TextServer. Listing 29.1 shows how you begin building Talker.

Listing 29.1   TALK.FRM—Establishing a Connection with TextServer

```
'**********************************************************************
' TALK.FRM - Demonstrates OLE Automation to a MFC server app
'**********************************************************************
Option Explicit
'**********************************************************************
' Create an object that won't go out of scope too early
'**********************************************************************
Private mobjTextServer As Object
'**********************************************************************
' Loads the form and establishes a connection with mobjTextServer
'**********************************************************************
Private Sub Form_Load()
    On Error Resume Next
    '**********************************************************************
    ' As a precaution, it is useful to always register your server first
    '**********************************************************************
    RegisterServer "Textserver.exe"
    '**********************************************************************
    ' As this line demonstrates, all objects are created the same way
    '**********************************************************************
    Set mobjTextServer = CreateObject("TextServer.Document")
    LoadText
    '**********************************************************************
    ' Show is one of TextServer's OLE Automation commands. It causes
    ' mobjTextServer to be activated and visible
    '**********************************************************************
    ' NOTE: TextServer (and most OLE Automation apps) are invisible
    '       by default, so you must make them visible by some method
    '       if you want the user to see the application. If the user
    '       doesn't need to see the application, then it isn't
    '       necessary to make it visible
    '**********************************************************************
    mobjTextServer.Visible = True
    Show ' Bring this form back to the top
End Sub
```

The first two buttons in the `cmd` control array simply send or receive text to or from TextServer. Listing 29.2 shows how we use the `Text` property of this automation server to both set and retrieve the contents of its main window (or view). Although this object uses a text property, this name could have been anything. In addition, a call is made to TextServer's `Activate` method, which causes its window to be brought to the foreground, so you can see the results of clicking `cmd(0)`.

Listing 29.2 TALK.FRM—Sending and Receiving Text to and from TextServer

```
'*********************************************************************
' Process command button clicks.
'*********************************************************************
Private Sub cmd_Click(Index As Integer)
    Dim strFindText As String
    Dim strReplaceWith As String
    Select Case Index
        Case 0 'Send Text to Text Server
            '*******************************************************
            ' SetEditText takes 1 argument (a string). TextServer
            ' uses this string to populate its text box
            '*******************************************************
            mobjTextServer.Text txtMain
            mobjTextServer.Activate
        Case 1 'Get Text from Text Server
            '*******************************************************
            ' GetEditText returns a string that contains the contents
            ' of mobjTextServer's text box.
            '*******************************************************
            txtMain = mobjTextServer.Text
        ...
```

The last button in the control array prompts the user for a word to find in TextServer's text window and replaces every occurrence of that word with another user-provided word. Next, the button calls TextServer's ReplaceAll method and brings the TextServer window to the foreground to show the user the results of ReplaceAll. Listing 29.3 shows how to use TextServer's ReplaceAll method.

Listing 29.3 FRMTALK.FRM—Using TextServer's ReplaceAll Method

```
        ...
        Case 2 'Get Text from Text Server
            '*******************************************************
            ' ReplaceAll finds every occurrence of a word, and replaces
            ' it with a new word. After the replace is complete, the
            ' TextServer text box is updated to reflect the changes
            '*******************************************************
            strFindText = InputBox("Find What?")
            If strFindText = "" Then Exit Sub
            strReplaceWith = InputBox("Replace With?")
            If strFindText = "" Then Exit Sub
            mobjTextServer.ReplaceAll strFindText, strReplaceWith
            mobjTextServer.Activate
    End Select
End Sub
```

LoadText (see Listing 29.4) simply opens SAMPLE.TXT from the directory in which the project or executable resides, loads all the file's text, and inserts the text into the text box.

Listing 29.4 FRMTALK.FRM—The *LoadText* Procedure

```
'**********************************************************************
' This procedure just loads the text box with some sample text.
'**********************************************************************
Private Sub LoadText()
    Dim intSource As Integer
    intSource = FreeFile
    Open App.Path & "\sample.txt" For Input As intSource
        txtMain = Input(LOF(intSource), intSource)
    Close intSource
End Sub
```

TIP You can store small text files in a resource file and use either LoadResString or LoadResData to extract the text files.

When writing applications that depend on OLE applications being properly registered, it is helpful to write a procedure that automatically registers those applications. Your application need only run REGEDIT.EXE (included with Windows) with the OLE servers .REG file as the command-line argument.

The RegisterTextServer procedure (see Listing 29.5) goes a step further by inserting the App.Path to the executable in the .REG file. By doing so, the exe doesn't need to be in the OS search path.

Listing 29.5 TALK.FRM—The *RegisterTextServer* Procedure

```
'**********************************************************************
' Adds strPath to the strServerExe of the .reg file in strPath
' directory, and registers it using regedit in silent mode
'**********************************************************************
Private Sub RegisterServer(strServerExe As String, _
                      Optional strPath As String)
    Dim intSource As Integer
    Dim intDest As Integer
    Dim strRead As String
    Dim intWhere As Integer
    '******************************************************************
    ' If strPath wasn't provided, then create a default value
    '******************************************************************
    If strPath = "" Then strPath = App.Path & "\"
    '******************************************************************
    ' Appends a backslash (if necessary) to strPath
    '******************************************************************
    If Right(strPath, 1) <> "\" Then strPath = strPath & "\"
    '******************************************************************
    ' Opens the first reg file in strPath for input
    '******************************************************************
    intSource = FreeFile
    Open strPath & Dir(strPath & "*.reg") For Input As intSource
```

continues

Listing 29.5   Continued

```
'**************************************************************
' Open a temp registry file (or clear an existing one)
'**************************************************************
intDest = FreeFile
Open "temp.reg" For Output As intDest
    '**********************************************************
    ' Loop through the source file
    '**********************************************************
    Do
        Line Input #intSource, strRead
        '******************************************************
        ' If the ServerExe is located, then append strPath
        ' to it (prevents your exe from being required to
        ' be in the OS search path)
        '******************************************************
        intWhere = InStr(1, strRead, strServerExe, vbTextCompare)
        If intWhere Then
            strRead = Left(strRead, intWhere - 1) & strPath _
                & Mid(strRead, intWhere)
        End If
        '******************************************************
        ' Output strRead to the temp file
        '******************************************************
        Print #intDest, strRead
    Loop Until EOF(intSource)
    Close intDest
Close intSource
'**************************************************************
' Run regedit in silent mode on the modified reg file
'**************************************************************
Shell "regedit.exe /s temp.reg", vbMinimizedNoFocus
'**************************************************************
' When registration is complete, delete the temp reg file
'**************************************************************
DoEvents
Kill "temp.reg"
End Sub
```

N O T E The `RegisterTextServer` procedure in Listing 29.5 demonstrates how you can register an OLE application on the fly. Even if the user doesn't have the .REG file, you usually can just run the application once to allow it to self-register. ■

N O T E You can access all OLE Automation servers in a manner similar to that demonstrated in the Talker example. This is important to know, because new OLE Automation servers are being released every day. ■

For a more detailed discussion on communicating with OLE Automation servers, see Chapter 18, "Controlling OLE Objects."

Using Microsoft's OLE Miniservers

You might have noticed that Microsoft has several programs in the MSAPPS subdirectory of your Windows directory. One or more Microsoft applications use these programs to provide some special feature, such as a clip art manager. However, if you ever try to run one of these programs directly, you get a message telling you that you can run the program only from within a host application. This is because these small programs are OLE *miniservers,* which run only if an OLE host application (such as Word or your Visual Basic application) calls them. This section explains how you can use these handy miniservers in your VB applications.

> **CAUTION**
>
> You cannot redistribute these miniservers. Therefore, your programs should use them only if they already are installed on the user's system. Otherwise, your application must handle this situation gracefully.

Although the exact number is always changing, Microsoft currently distributes several OLE miniservers. Table 29.1 lists some of these miniservers, along with the application with which the miniserver is bundled.

Table 5.1   Some of Microsoft's OLE Miniservers

Miniserver	Microsoft Shared Path	Application
ClipArt Gallery	..\artgalry\artgalry.exe	Office 97, Publisher, Works
Draw	..\msdraw\msdraw.exe	Publisher, Works
Equation Editor	..\equation\eqnedt32.exe	Office 97, Works
Graph	program files\microsoft office \office\graph8.exe	Office 97
Note-It	..\note-it\note-it.exe	Works
Organization Chart	..\orgchart\orgchart.exe	Office 97
WordArt	..\wordart\wrdart32.exe	Publisher, Works

N O T E Table 29.1 refers to only the 1997 and later versions of each application, so earlier versions might not include the listed miniserver. For more information on which miniserver the applications include, visit Microsoft's World Wide Web site. ▪

To demonstrate how easy it is to use these miniservers in your applications, Listing 29.6 presents a portion of the code for MINISERV.VBP, a program that uses the currently installed OLE miniservers in the OLE container control. This program contains seven OLE container controls on the form, with a miniserver embedded in each of the controls. When you run the program, it adds an item to a drop-down list box for each miniserver that exists on the system.

This drop-down list box enables you to navigate between the available miniservers so that you can view and edit an object of each type of available miniserver.

Listing 29.6   MINISERV.FRM—Determining Which Miniservers Are Available

```
'*****************************************************************
' MINISERV.FRM - Takes advantage of installed OLE mini-servers
'*****************************************************************
Option Explicit
Private Type OSVERSIONINFO
    dwOSVersionInfoSize As Long
    dwMajorVersion As Long
    dwMinorVersion As Long
    dwBuildNumber As Long
    dwPlatformId As Long
    szCSDVersion As String * 128
End Type

Private Declare Function GetVersionEx Lib "kernel32" Alias _
        "GetVersionExA" (lpVersionInformation As OSVERSIONINFO) As Long
'*****************************************************************
' Show the item in the dropdown list
'*****************************************************************
Private Sub cboServers_Click()
    Select Case cboServers.ItemData(cboServers.ListIndex)
        Case 0 'MS ClipArt
            ShowObject MSClipArt
        Case 1 'MS Draw
            ShowObject MSDraw
        Case 2 'MS Equation Editor
            ShowObject MSEquation
        Case 3 'MS Graph
            ShowObject MSGraph
        Case 4 'MS Note-It
            ShowObject MSNoteIt
        Case 5 'MS Organization Chart
            ShowObject MSOrgChart
        Case 6 'MS WordArt
            ShowObject MSWordArt
    End Select
End Sub
'*****************************************************************
' Initialize the form
'*****************************************************************
Private Sub Form_Load()
    '*****************************************************************
    ' Set the ScaleMode to pixels for drawing purposes, and load the
    ' listbox
    '*****************************************************************
    ScaleMode = vbPixels
    LoadList
    '*****************************************************************
    ' Position the form and controls then unload the splash form
    '*****************************************************************
```

```
            Move 0, 0, Screen.Width, Screen.Height
            lbl.Move 10, 10
            With cboServers
                .Move 10, 27, lbl.Width
                If .ListCount > 0 Then .ListIndex = 0
            End With
        End Sub
        '**********************************************************************
        ' Show the object in the center of the form with a 3D frame
        '**********************************************************************
        Sub ShowObject(ctlSource As Control)
            Dim ctl As Control
            '**********************************************************************
            ' Make sure all of the controls are hidden first
            '**********************************************************************
            For Each ctl In Controls
                If TypeOf ctl Is OLE Then
                    ctl.Visible = False
                End If
            Next ctl
            '**********************************************************************
            ' Clear the form, and show the object in the center
            '**********************************************************************
            Cls
            With ctlSource
                .Move (ScaleWidth - .Width) / 2, (ScaleHeight - .Height) / 2
                .Visible = True
            End With
        End Sub
        '**********************************************************************
        ' Only load mini-servers that exist
        '**********************************************************************
        Private Sub LoadList()
            Dim strSharedRoot As String
            Dim strOfficeRoot As String
            '**********************************************************************
            ' Get the root directory for the shared apps
            '**********************************************************************
            If Win95UI() Then
                strSharedRoot = GetRegString(HKEY_LOCAL_MACHINE, _
                    "Software\Microsoft\Windows\CurrentVersion", _
                    "CommonFilesDir") & "\Microsoft Shared\"
            Else
                strSharedRoot = Environ("windir") & "\msapps\"
            End If
            '**********************************************************************
            ' Graph 97 is located in the Office 97 directory, not MSFT Shared
            '**********************************************************************
            strOfficeRoot = GetRegString(HKEY_LOCAL_MACHINE, _
                "Software\Microsoft\Office\8.0", "BinDirPath") & "\"
            '**********************************************************************
            ' Load only the apps installed on the system
            '**********************************************************************
            With cboServers
                If FileExists(strSharedRoot & "artgalry\artgalry.exe") Then
```

continues

Listing 29.6   Continued

```
                                .AddItem "MS ClipArt"
                                .ItemData(.NewIndex) = 0
                        End If

                        If FileExists(strSharedRoot & "msdraw\msdraw.exe") Then
                                .AddItem "MS Draw"
                                .ItemData(.NewIndex) = 1
                        End If

                        If FileExists(strSharedRoot & "equation\eqnedt32.exe") Then
                                .AddItem "MS Equation Editor"
                                .ItemData(.NewIndex) = 2
                        End If

                        If FileExists(strOfficeRoot & "graph8.exe") Then
                                .AddItem "MS Graph 97"
                                .ItemData(.NewIndex) = 3
                        End If

                        If FileExists(strSharedRoot & "note-it\note-it.exe") Then
                                .AddItem "MS Note-It"
                                .ItemData(.NewIndex) = 4
                        End If

                        If FileExists(strSharedRoot & "orgchart\orgchart.exe") Then
                                .AddItem "MS Organization Chart"
                                .ItemData(.NewIndex) = 5
                        End If

                        If FileExists(strSharedRoot & "wordart\wrdart32.exe") Then
                                .AddItem "MS WordArt 2.0"
                                .ItemData(.NewIndex) = 6
                        End If
        End With
End Sub
'*********************************************************************
' Check to see if a file exists
'*********************************************************************
Private Function FileExists(strFileName As String) As Boolean
        On Error Resume Next
        FileExists = IIf(Len(strFileName), Len(Dir(strFileName)), False)
End Function
'*********************************************************************
' Check to see if the user is running the Windows 95 shell
'*********************************************************************
Private Function Win95UI() As Boolean
        Dim OSInfo As OSVERSIONINFO
        With OSInfo
                .szCSDVersion = Space$(128)
                .dwOSVersionInfoSize = Len(OSInfo)
                GetVersionEx OSInfo
                Win95UI = (.dwMinorVersion > 51) Or (.dwMajorVersion = 4)
        End With
End Function
```

> **CAUTION**
>
> Don't let their name fool you: miniservers are full-blown graphical applications. They consume as much memory and resources as most large-scale applications. If you do run out of system resources, you will get "Unable to Activate Object" or "Object Not Properly Registered" errors when you try to activate a miniserver.

Although Listing 29.6 contains a fair amount of code, most of it is for cosmetic purposes. The most important element of this project occurs at design time, when you load your OLE custom controls from the available miniservers installed on your system.

Using Other Microsoft Applications in Your Applications

You've seen plenty of information about integration with Access, Excel, and Word, but you may wonder about integration with other Microsoft applications. This section puts together a quick application that demonstrates how to use the OLE container control to display objects from five other Microsoft applications—Paintbrush, PowerPoint, Project, Sound Recorder, and Video for Windows (see Figure 29.3–Figure 29.7). Although this example uses Microsoft products, it can really be applied to any OLE server or ActiveX document.

FIG. 29.3

Paintbrush can be embedded in your application.

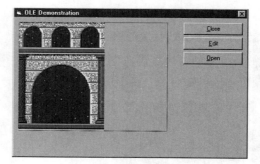

FIG. 29.4

PowerPoint can be embedded in your application.

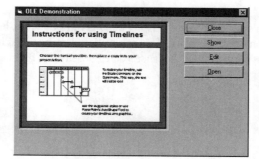

FIG. 29.5
Project can be embedded in your application.

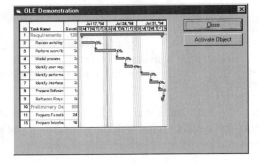

FIG. 29.6
Sound Recorder can be embedded in your application.

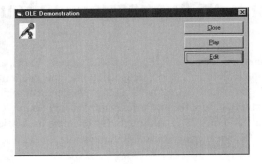

FIG. 29.7
Video for Windows can be embedded in your application.

The sample application's code (shown in Listing 29.7) is rather simple, because the OLE container control does most of the work. This application demonstrates how advantageous it is to own applications that support OLE, because you can easily use them to enhance your application's functionality.

Listing 29.7 FRMOBJECT.FRM—FRMOBJECT.FRM Takes Advantage of Some Available OLE Servers

```
'*************************************************************************
' OBJECT.FRM - Used to display an object and its verbs
'*************************************************************************
Option Explicit
Private moleObject As OLE
'*************************************************************************
' Unload the dialog
'*************************************************************************
Private Sub cmdClose_Click()
    Unload Me
End Sub
'*************************************************************************
' Execute a verb (verbs are from 1 to x, so you need to add 1)
'*************************************************************************
Private Sub cmdVerbs_Click(Index As Integer)
    On Error Resume Next
    moleObject.DoVerb (Index + 1)
    If Err Then MsgBox "Err = " & Format(Err) & ": " & Error, vbCritical
End Sub
'*************************************************************************
' This public method is used to display the form and to call necessary
' loading routines
'*************************************************************************
Public Sub Display(oleObj As OLE)
    Set moleObject = oleObj
    moleObject.Visible = True
    PrepareForm
    Show vbModal
End Sub
'*************************************************************************
' Center the form and load the command buttons for its verbs
'*************************************************************************
Public Sub PrepareForm()
    Dim i As Integer
    '*********************************************************************
    ' Create and label a command button on the form for each verb
    '*********************************************************************
    For i = 1 To moleObject.ObjectVerbsCount - 1
        '*****************************************************************
        ' cmdVerbs(0) already exists, so skip it
        '*****************************************************************
        If i > 1 Then Load cmdVerbs(i - 1)
        With cmdVerbs(i - 1)
            If i > 1 Then
                .Top = cmdVerbs(i - 2).Top _
                    + cmdVerbs(i - 2).Height + 75
            End If
            .Caption = moleObject.ObjectVerbs(i)
            .Visible = True
        End With
    Next i
End Sub
```

Listing 29.7 includes three important procedures: the `PrepareForm` procedure, the `Display` method, and the `cmdVerbs_Click` event.

The `PrepareForm` procedure uses the `ObjectVerbCount` property of the OLE container control to determine how many command buttons are to appear on the form. `PrepareForm` also uses the `ObjectVerbs` property to set the button's caption. When the user clicks one of these buttons, the application invokes the `DoVerb` method.

The `Display` method enables a function from another form to specify which OLE container control should be used when displaying the form. By knowing which control to use, the form can then prepare itself (through `PrepareForm`) for use and display itself modally.

The `cmdVerbs_Click` event invokes a verb for the object in the visible OLE container control. This invocation is important, because it enables the user to display, open, or edit the object.

Using Other Microsoft Applications that Don't Support OLE or DDE

If you want to integrate with an application that doesn't support OLE or DDE, your choices are limited to the following:

- Use "brute force" to control the application with the Windows API.
- Run the application with Shell, give control to the user, and then work on the file after the user exits the application.
- Use Visual Basic's `SendKeys` method.
- Rewrite the application in Visual Basic and do whatever you want.

The next example program, shown in Figure 29.8 and Figure 29.9, demonstrates how to accomplish the first three alternatives. (I'll leave the last as an exercise for you.)

EXCHANGEDATA.CLS (Listing 29.8) is a good exercise in using the Win32 API to extend Visual Basic. The functions in this module enable an application to send or grab text to or from any window that supports the `GETTEXT` and `SETTEXT` messages.

Listing 29.8   EXCHANGEDATA.CLS—An Object Designed to Manually Exchange Data Between Windows

```
'*********************************************************************
' EXCHANGEDATA.CLS - Used to manually exchange data with other windows
'*********************************************************************
Option Explicit
Option Compare Text
'*********************************************************************
' The API functions we are using in this module require us to define
' two new types
'*********************************************************************
```

```
Private Type PointAPI
    x As Long
    y As Long
End Type

Private Type RECT
    Left As Long
    Top As Long
    Right As Long
    Bottom As Long
End Type
'**********************************************************************
' Mouse Capture API's
'**********************************************************************
Private Declare Function SetCapture& Lib "user32" (ByVal hWnd As Long)
Private Declare Sub ReleaseCapture Lib "user32" ()
'**********************************************************************
' Window Coordinates API's
'**********************************************************************
Private Declare Function GetClassName Lib "user32" Alias "GetClassNameA" _
    (ByVal hWnd&, ByVal lpClassName$, ByVal nMaxCount As Long) As Long
'**********************************************************************
' Window Coordinates API's
'**********************************************************************
Private Declare Sub ClientToScreen Lib "user32" (ByVal hWnd As Long, _
    lpPoint As PointAPI)
Private Declare Sub GetWindowRect Lib "user32" (ByVal hWnd As Long, _
    lpRect As RECT)
Private Declare Function WindowFromPoint Lib "user32" (ByVal _
    ptScreenX As Long, ByVal ptScreenY As Long) As Long
'**********************************************************************
' Window Device Contexts API's
'**********************************************************************
Private Declare Function GetWindowDC& Lib "user32" (ByVal hWnd As Long)
Private Declare Function ReleaseDC Lib "user32" (ByVal hWnd As Long, _
    ByVal hdc As Long) As Long
'**********************************************************************
' Brushes and Painting API's
'**********************************************************************
Private Declare Function GetStockObject& Lib "gdi32" (ByVal nIndex&)
Private Declare Function CreatePen Lib "gdi32" (ByVal nPenStyle&, _
    ByVal nWidth&, ByVal crColor&) As Long
Private Declare Function SetROP2 Lib "gdi32" (ByVal hdc As Long, _
    ByVal nDrawMode As Long) As Long
Private Declare Function Rectangle Lib "gdi32" (ByVal hdc&, ByVal X1&, _
    ByVal Y1&, ByVal X2&, ByVal Y2&) As Long
Private Declare Function SelectObject Lib "gdi32" (ByVal hdc As Long, _
    ByVal hObject As Long) As Long
Private Declare Function DeleteObject& Lib "gdi32" (ByVal hObject&)
'**********************************************************************
' Misc. API Functions
'**********************************************************************
Private Declare Function SendMessage Lib "user32" Alias "SendMessageA" _
    (ByVal hWnd As Long, ByVal wMsg As Long, ByVal wParam As Long, _
    ByVal lParam As Any) As Long
```

continues

Listing 29.8 Continued

```
Private Declare Function SetFocusAPI Lib "user32" Alias "SetFocus" _
    (ByVal hWnd As Long) As Long
Private Declare Sub InvalidateRect Lib "user32" (ByVal hWnd&, _
    lpRect As Any, ByVal bErase As Long)
Private Declare Function GetSystemMetrics& Lib "user32" (ByVal nIndex&)
Private Declare Function IsZoomed Lib "user32" (ByVal hWnd&) As Long
```

FIG. 29.8

The Stubborn program highlights the client area of any window on the screen.

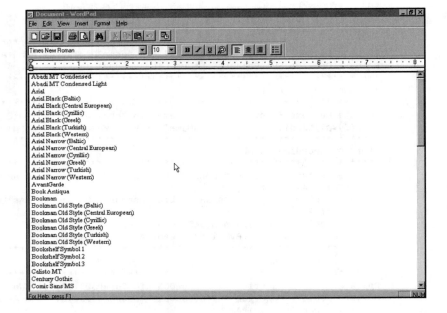

FIG. 29.9

After you release the mouse over the desired window, the text from that window is inserted into the Stubborn program.

The object in Listing 29.8 starts by declaring a number of APIs and structures required internally. Although this object is written in Visual Basic, it is mostly an SDK application that could be easily ported to any Windows programming language. Before proceeding, we encourage you to look at the APIs in Listing 29.8 and read about them in the Win32 SDK (included with VB). This will help you to get a better understanding about what these functions do and why they are included in this object.

The code in Listing 29.9 starts with the hidden member variables of the `ExchangeData` object that maintains information about the current tracking and tracked window. The tracked window is the window being pointed to, and the tracking window is the one receiving the `MouseMove` events (for example, the calling form).

Listing 29.9   EXCHANGEDATA.CLS—The *ExchangeData* object properties.

```
'*************************************************************************
' Private member variables
'*************************************************************************
Private mintPrevScaleMode As Integer     'Original ScaleMode
Private mfrmSource As Form        'The calling (or attached) form
Private mlngHandle As Long        'Handle of the window under the cursor
Private mblnPointMode As Boolean     'Maintains tracking or point mode
'*************************************************************************
' The public text property holds the result from the last
' ExchangeData call
'*************************************************************************
Public Text As String
'*************************************************************************
' PointMode allows the caller to check if the MouseMove events are
' currently being captured
'*************************************************************************
Public Property Get PointMode() As Boolean
    PointMode = mblnPointMode
End Property
```

This code also contains two public properties. The first is the read/write `Text` property, which holds the results of a `GETTEXT` message using `ExchangeData`. Although this property supports writing, there currently is no defined behavior for this action. In addition to the `Text` property, an important `PointMode` property is exposed. This method is critical for the calling form, because it helps to determine which "mode" the `ExchangeData` object is currently in. During tracking mode, `PointMode` returns `TRUE` so the caller can call the `Move` method from his or her `MouseMove` event. The `PointMode` property returns `FALSE` once `EndCapture` has been called.

Because Visual Basic doesn't support arguments in the `Initialize` event, `ExchangeData` has to create its own special constructor. This method, called `Attach` (as shown in Listing 29.10), is the first method you should call when using the ExchangeData object. The purpose of `Attach` is to maintain an internal member variable that points to the calling form, so you do not continuously have to provide this information in all the methods in this object.

Listing 29.10 EXCHANGEDATA.CLS—*Attach* Is Really a Custom *Class_Initialize* Event That Requires an Argument

```
'*********************************************************************
' To use this class, the caller needs to "attach" a form. This allows
' routines within this class to know which form is being captured,
' without requiring the user to continuously supply this information
'*********************************************************************
Public Sub Attach(frmName As Form)
    Set mfrmSource = frmName
    mintPrevScaleMode = mfrmSource.ScaleMode
End Sub
```

Although we couldn't use the default Class_Initialize event, there is nothing preventing our using the default Class_Terminate event. This event, shown in Listing 29.11, is responsible for doing cleanup on the "attached" form. In addition to being the destructor for our object, this method is called by the EndCapture event to do cleanup.

Listing 29.11 EXCHANGEDATA.CLS—The *Class_Terminate* Event Also Acts as a Helper Method to *EndCapture*

```
'*********************************************************************
' When the class is terminated, you should restore the form defaults
'*********************************************************************
Private Sub Class_Terminate()
    '*****************************************************************
    ' If the form has the capture, then release it
    '*****************************************************************
    If PointMode Then ReleaseCapture
    '*****************************************************************
    ' Restore ScaleMode and MousePointer, then redisplay the form
    '*****************************************************************
    mfrmSource.ScaleMode = mintPrevScaleMode
    Screen.MousePointer = vbDefault
    mfrmSource.Visible = True
End Sub
```

StartCapture (shown in Listing 29.12) probably is the most important method in the class. It initiates the capture mode (also referred to as PointMode) that lets the user point and capture or exchange text from windows that support GETTEXT and SETTEXT messages. The StartCapture method needs to be called in response to a MouseDown event on a window, because the SetCapture API requires the user to hold down the mouse button while tracking windows in another process space.

Listing 29.12   EXCHANGEDATA.CLS—*StartCapture* Initiates the Window-Tracking Code

```
'*********************************************************************
' This method initiates the SetCapture mode
'*********************************************************************
Public Sub StartCapture()
    '*****************************************************************
    ' Make sure that the caller has attached a form to this object
    '*****************************************************************
    If mfrmSource Is Nothing Then
        MsgBox "You must call the Attach method first!", vbExclamation
        Exit Sub
    End If
    '*****************************************************************
    ' Make sure the scalemode is pixels
    '*****************************************************************
    mfrmSource.ScaleMode = vbPixels
    '*****************************************************************
    ' Turn on the PointMode and hide the form
    '*****************************************************************
    mblnPointMode = True
    mfrmSource.Visible = False
    '*****************************************************************
    ' Set the capture mode and change the pointer to an arrow
    '*****************************************************************
    If SetCapture(mfrmSource.hWnd) Then Screen.MousePointer = vbUpArrow
End Sub
```

Move (Listing 29.13) uses the WindowFromPoint API to determine the handle of the window under the mouse pointer. If the current handle of the window differs from that of the last window, then Move draws an inverted box around the window. This lets the user get a better visual representation of the window to which he or she actually is pointing. This is especially useful for drop-down combo boxes that contain both a list and an edit box window.

Listing 29.13   EXCHANGEDATA.CLS—The *Move* Method Highlights the Current Window

```
'*********************************************************************
' Handles the MouseMove event for the calling form when in PointMode
'*********************************************************************
Public Sub Move(x As Single, y As Single)
    Dim pt As PointAPI
    Dim hWndCurrent As Long
    '*****************************************************************
    ' Don't continue unless in PointMode
    '*****************************************************************
    If Not PointMode Then
        MsgBox "Move can only be called during PointMode", vbCritical
        Exit Sub
    End If
```

continues

Listing 29.13   Continued

```
'*****************************************************************
' Store the current points into a POINTAPI struct
'*****************************************************************
pt.x = x: pt.y = y
'*****************************************************************
' Change coordinates in pt into screen coordinates
'*****************************************************************
ClientToScreen mfrmSource.hWnd, pt
'*****************************************************************
' Get the window that is under the mouse pointer
'*****************************************************************
hWndCurrent = WindowFromPoint(pt.x, pt.y)
'*****************************************************************
' Only redraw if there is a new active window
'*****************************************************************
If hWndCurrent <> mlngHandle Then
    '*****************************************************************
    ' If there is a mlngHandle, then restore it
    '*****************************************************************
    If mlngHandle Then HighlightWindow mlngHandle
    '*****************************************************************
    ' Draw an border around the current window, and remember the
    ' last hWnd
    '*****************************************************************
    HighlightWindow hWndCurrent
    mlngHandle = hWndCurrent
End If
End Sub
```

Another important method in this class is EndCapture (shown in Listing 29.14), which restores
the screen to normal and either grabs or sends text to or from the window under the cursor.

Listing 29.14   EXCHANGEDATA.CLS—*EndCapture* Stops Tracking and Exchanges the Data

```
'*****************************************************************
' Ends PointMode, exchanges the data, and restores the form
'*****************************************************************
Public Function EndCapture(Optional strSendText As String) As Boolean
    '*****************************************************************
    ' Exchange the data, and return true if the exchange worked
    '*****************************************************************
    EndCapture = ExchangeData(strSendText)
    '*****************************************************************
    ' Refresh the screen to in case there were drawing problems
    '*****************************************************************
    InvalidateRect 0, 0&, True
    '*****************************************************************
    ' Reset all variables and back out of all changes made during
    ' capture mode
```

```
'*****************************************************************
    mlngHandle = 0: mblnPointMode = False
    Class_Terminate
End Function
```

The `ExchangeData` method (shown in Listing 29.15) performs the physical data exchange between your application and another window. This method begins by declaring some API constants and determining the type (or class) of control to which the user is pointing. This helps to determine how data should be extracted from the window. For example, if the window contained a list, then you would want to extract all the items from the list. To do this, you would need to iterate through the list and individually extract each list item. `ExchangeData` accomplishes this via a helper function called `GetListStrings`, which supports both list boxes and combo boxes.

Listing 29.15   EXCHANGEDATA.CLS—*ExchangeData* Exchanges Data Differently Depending on the Class of the Window

```
'*****************************************************************
' This is the magic cookie of this module. It takes a handle and
' sends or receives text to and from standard windows controls
'*****************************************************************
Private Function ExchangeData(strSendText As String) As String
    Dim lngRetChars As Long
    Dim strCtlType As String
    '*****************************************************************
    ' API constants required by this routine
    '*****************************************************************
    Const WM_GETTEXT = &HD:      Const WM_SETTEXT = &HC
    Const LB_GETTEXT = &H189:    Const LB_GETTEXTLEN = &H18A
    Const CB_GETLBTEXT = &H148:  Const CB_GETLBTEXTLEN = &H149
    Const CB_GETCOUNT = &H146:   Const LB_GETCOUNT = &H18B
    '*****************************************************************
    ' Assume success
    '*****************************************************************
    ExchangeData = True
    '*****************************************************************
    ' Find out the class type of the control
    '*****************************************************************
    strCtlType = GetClass()
    '*****************************************************************
    ' If it is a combo box, then use combo messages to communicate
    '*****************************************************************
    If InStr(strCtlType, "Combo") Then
        Text = GetListStrings(CB_GETCOUNT, CB_GETLBTEXTLEN, CB_GETLBTEXT)
        Exit Function
    '*****************************************************************
    ' If it is a list box, then use list functions
    '*****************************************************************
    ElseIf InStr(strCtlType, "List") Then
        Text = GetListStrings(LB_GETCOUNT, LB_GETTEXTLEN, LB_GETTEXT)
        Exit Function
```

Although you extract the data from combo and list boxes in the same way, these controls use different API constants. To get around this problem, you simply call the method with the appropriate API constants and apply the same extraction algorithm for both. The key to capturing a list is to find out how many items are in the list (using GETCOUNT) and individually capture each line (using GETTEXT) by iterating through the list. The code in Listing 29.16 demonstrates how you determine this number.

Listing 29.16   EXCHANGEDATA.CLS—Returns All the Strings from a List as a Single String

```
'*********************************************************************
' Returns all of the items in a list box as a single string
'*********************************************************************
Private Function GetListStrings(lngGetCount As Long, _
        lngGetLen As Long, lngGetText As Long) As String
    Dim lngItems As String
    Dim strCurItem As String
    Dim strRet As String
    Dim lngRetChars As Long
    Dim i As Long
    '*********************************************************************
    ' Find out how many items are in the list
    '*********************************************************************
    lngItems = SendMessage(mlngHandle, lngGetCount, 0, 0&) - 1
    '*********************************************************************
    ' Iterate through the list to retrieve every item
    '*********************************************************************
    For i = 0 To lngItems
        '*********************************************************************
        ' Find out how long the current item is, and build a
        ' buffer large enough to hold it
        '*********************************************************************
        strCurItem = Space(SendMessage(mlngHandle, lngGetLen, i, 0&) _
            + 1)
        '*********************************************************************
        ' Limit the return string to 32000 bytes or less
        '*********************************************************************
        If Len(strRet) + Len(strCurItem) - 1 > 32000 Then Exit For
        '*********************************************************************
        ' Retrieve the item from the list
        '*********************************************************************
        lngRetChars = SendMessage(mlngHandle, lngGetText, i, strCurItem)
        '*********************************************************************
        ' Trim the null terminator, and append it to strRet
        '*********************************************************************
        strRet = strRet & Left(strCurItem, lngRetChars) & vbCrLf
    Next i
    '*********************************************************************
    ' Return the list as a single crlf delimited string
    '*********************************************************************
    GetListStrings = strRet
End Function
```

If the control isn't a combo or list box, then try WM_GETTEXT or WM_SETTEXT (as shown in Listing 29.17). These messages used to work on most standard Windows controls and some nonstandard controls, but an increasing number of new controls no longer are responding to these messages. In those cases, ExchangeData returns FALSE, and no data is set or returned.

Listing 29.17   EXCHANGEDATA.CLS—If All Else Fails, Try *WM_GETTEXT* and *WM_SETTEXT*

```
    '****************************************************************
    ' Otherwise, try WM_GETTEXT and WM_SETTEXT
    '****************************************************************
    Else
        '****************************************************************
        ' If strSendText, then send the text to the window
        '****************************************************************
        If Len(strSendText) Then
            '****************************************************************
            ' If the window is an edit box, then paste text to it.
            ' Otherwise don't. This prevents you from changing the
            ' captions of labels, buttons, etc...
            '****************************************************************
            If InStr(strCtlType, "Edit") _
                Or InStr(strCtlType, "Text") Then
                '****************************************************************
                ' Put the text into the window, and activate it
                '****************************************************************
                SendMessage mlngHandle, WM_SETTEXT, 0, strSendText
                SetFocusAPI mlngHandle
                Exit Function
            End If
        '****************************************************************
        ' Otherwise, get the text from the window
        '****************************************************************
        Else
            '****************************************************************
            ' Build a huge strBuffer, and retrieve the text
            '****************************************************************
            Text = Space(32000)
            lngRetChars = SendMessage(mlngHandle, WM_GETTEXT, _
                Len(Text), Text)
            '****************************************************************
            ' Keep all text to the left of the null terminator
            '****************************************************************
            Text = Left(Text, lngRetChars)
            Exit Function
        End If
    End If
    '****************************************************************
    ' If you got here, then this function was unsuccessful
    '****************************************************************
    ExchangeData = False
End Function
```

The `GetClass` method simply returns the class name of a window as shown here:

```
'*********************************************************************
' Returns the class name of a window.
'*********************************************************************
Private Function GetClass() As String
    Dim lngRetChars As Long
    Dim strClassName As String
    '*****************************************************************
    ' Get the class name of the window
    '*****************************************************************
    strClassName = Space$(256)
    lngRetChars = GetClassName(mlngHandle, strClassName, _
        Len(strClassName))
    '*****************************************************************
    ' Trim off the null terminator
    '*****************************************************************
    GetClass = Left$(strClassName, lngRetChars)
End Function
```

The `HighlightWindow` method (shown in Listing 29.18) draws an inverted box around a window to indicate visually to the user the window to which he or she currently is pointing. This method simply gets a handle to the window's device context (an `hDC`) and draws the inverted box around it.

Listing 29.18   EXCHANGEDATA.CLS—*HighlightWindow* Contains Only API Drawing Calls Written in VB

```
'*********************************************************************
' Highlights a window by drawing a box in its client area
'*********************************************************************
Private Sub HighlightWindow(hwndDest As Long)
    Dim cxBorder&, cxFrame&, cyFrame&, cxScreen&, cyScreen&
    Dim hdcDest&, hPen&, hOldPen&, hOldBrush&
    Dim rc As RECT
    '*****************************************************************
    ' API constants required by this routine
    '*****************************************************************
    Const NULL_BRUSH = 5: Const R2_NOT = 6: Const PS_INSIDEFRAME = 6
    '*****************************************************************
    ' Get some windows dimensions
    '*****************************************************************
    cxScreen = GetSystemMetrics(0): cyScreen = GetSystemMetrics(1)
    cxFrame = GetSystemMetrics(32): cyFrame = GetSystemMetrics(33)
    cxBorder = GetSystemMetrics(5)
    '*****************************************************************
    ' Get the Device Context for the window to highlight
    '*****************************************************************
    hdcDest = GetWindowDC(hwndDest)
    '*****************************************************************
    ' Get the size of the window
    '*****************************************************************
    GetWindowRect hwndDest, rc
```

```
'*****************************************************************
' Change the raster op mode to NOT to create an inverse border
'*****************************************************************
SetROP2 hdcDest, R2_NOT
'*****************************************************************
' Create a new pen and select it (and a stock brush) into the
' device context
'*****************************************************************
hPen = CreatePen(PS_INSIDEFRAME, 3 * cxBorder, RGB(0, 0, 0))
hOldPen = SelectObject(hdcDest, hPen)
hOldBrush = SelectObject(hdcDest, GetStockObject(NULL_BRUSH))
'*****************************************************************
' Draw a box around the selected window
'*****************************************************************
If IsZoomed(hwndDest) Then
    Rectangle hdcDest, cxFrame, cyFrame, cxScreen + cxFrame, _
        cyScreen + cyFrame
Else
    Rectangle hdcDest, 0, 0, rc.Right - rc.Left, rc.Bottom - rc.Top
End If
'*****************************************************************
' Restore the old brush and pen
'*****************************************************************
SelectObject hdcDest, hOldBrush
SelectObject hdcDest, hOldPen
'*****************************************************************
' Release the Device Context back to its owner
'*****************************************************************
ReleaseDC hwndDest, hdcDest
'*****************************************************************
' Delete the pen
'*****************************************************************
DeleteObject hPen
End Sub
```

STUBBORN.FRM (shown in Listing 29.19) is both the user interface for this application, and the clsExchangeData object. It begins making some necessary API declarations, declaring the clsExchangeData object, and maintains a form-level hotspot using a RECT variable.

Listing 29.19   STUBBORN.FRM—Declarations and Initialization Code

```
'*****************************************************************
' STUBBORN.FRM - This program demonstrates some alternative ways to
'    communicate with apps that do not respond via DDE or OLE
'*****************************************************************
Option Explicit
'*****************************************************************
' Win32 API's, types and constants used by this form
'*****************************************************************
Private Type RECT
    Left As Long
    Top As Long
```

continues

Listing 29.19 Continued

```
      Right As Long
      Bottom As Long
End Type

Private Declare Function PtInRect Lib "user32" (lpRect As RECT, _
    ByVal x As Long, ByVal y As Long) As Long

Private Declare Function LoadCursor Lib "user32" Alias "LoadCursorA" _
    (ByVal hInstance&, ByVal lpCursor&) As Long
Private Declare Function DrawIcon Lib "user32" (ByVal hdc As Long, _
    ByVal x As Long, ByVal y As Long, ByVal hIcon As Long) As Long

Private Declare Function OpenProcess& Lib "kernel32" (ByVal _
    dwDesiredAccess&, ByVal bInheritHandle&, ByVal dwProcessId&)
Private Declare Function GetExitCodeProcess Lib "kernel32" (ByVal _
    hProcess As Long, lpExitCode As Long) As Long

Private Const PROCESS_QUERY_INFORMATION = &H400
Private Const STILL_ACTIVE = &H103

Private Const IDC_UPARROW = 32516&
'********************************************************************
' Our one and only ExchangeData object
'********************************************************************
Private mclsExchange As New clsExchangeData
'********************************************************************
' Form-level hotspot for hit testing
'********************************************************************
Private mrctHotSpot As RECT
'********************************************************************
' Form Initialization
'********************************************************************
Private Sub Form_Load()
    txtExchange_Change
    '****************************************************************
    ' This app needs to use vbPixels ScaleMode in its Paint event
    '****************************************************************
    ScaleMode = vbPixels
    '****************************************************************
    ' This creates and attaches this form to an ExchangeData object
    '****************************************************************
    mclsExchange.Attach Me
End Sub
```

In the Form_Load event, the ScaleMode is changed to pixels, because some of the Paint event code includes an API call (DrawIcon) that requires a pixel scale mode. While we could have used the ScaleX and ScaleY methods, it was easier in this case simply to change the default ScaleMode. Next, and most important, you attach the form to the clsExchangeData object. This tells the object that stubborn.frm will be responsible for tracking windows on the screen.

To make it easier for users to drag (instead of point and click) your cursor around the screen when in `PointMode`, you paint (in the `Paint` event, as shown in Listing 29.20) a pointing cursor on the form with the instructions. This, along with your hotspot, makes it easier for users to discover that they need to click and drag the cursor around the screen to enter your capture or pointing mode.

Listing 29.20 STUBBORN.FRM—The *Paint* Event Draws a Pointer on the Form, with Instructions

```
'*********************************************************************
' Paints a cursor and instructions on the form
'*********************************************************************
Private Sub Form_Paint()
    Static sngX As Single, sngY As Single
    Static lngIconLeft As Long
    '*****************************************************************
    ' If paint coordinates haven't been set, then set them (once)
    '*****************************************************************
    If sngX = 0 Then
        '*************************************************************
        ' Build positioning variables
        '*************************************************************
        With fraChoices
            sngX = .Left + .Width
            lngIconLeft = sngX + ((ScaleWidth - sngX) / 2) + 10

            With txtExchange
                sngY = .Top + .Height
            End With
            sngY = sngY + ((ScaleHeight - (.Top + .Height)) / 2) + 5
        End With
        '*************************************************************
        ' Set the hotspot coordinates (once)
        '*************************************************************
        With mrctHotSpot
            .Left = lngIconLeft
            .Top = sngY
            .Right = .Left + 32 ' 32 = width of the cursor
            .Bottom = .Top + 32 ' 32 = height of the cursor
        End With
    End If
    '*****************************************************************
    ' Set CurrentX & CurrentY
    '*****************************************************************
    CurrentX = sngX
    CurrentY = sngY
    '*****************************************************************
    ' Draw MousePointer vbUpArrow on the form
    '*****************************************************************
    DrawIcon hdc, lngIconLeft, sngY, LoadCursor(0, IDC_UPARROW)
    '*****************************************************************
    ' Give the user some instructions about why the arrow is painted
    ' on the form
```

continues

Listing 29.20   Continued

```
'*****************************************************************
    Print "  Click & drag this arrow ->"
    CurrentX = sngX
    Print "  to exchange data."
End Sub
```

The next two procedures, MouseDown and MouseMove, execute only while the application is capturing the mouse. During this time, the application draws a box around the window to which the user is pointing. When the user chooses a window, the program calls ExchangeData. Listing 29.21 shows the code for these two procedures.

Listing 29.21   STUBBORN.FRM—The Mouse Events Simply Call
***clsExchangeData* to Do the Real Work**

```
'*****************************************************************
' SetCapture requires the left mouse button to be depressed in order
' to capture data from other processes and the MouseUp event
' automatically does a ReleaseCapture (via EndCapture)
'*****************************************************************
Private Sub Form_MouseDown(Button As Integer, Shift As Integer, x!, y!)
    '*************************************************************
    ' Only start the capture when the user clicks in the hotspot
    '*************************************************************
    If PtInRect(mrctHotSpot, x, y) Then mclsExchange.StartCapture
End Sub
'*****************************************************************
' During the PointMode, this window receives a MouseMove event for the
' entire desktop, which we pass to the Move method for further
' processing
'*****************************************************************
Private Sub Form_MouseMove(Button As Integer, Shift As Integer, x!, y!)
    If mclsExchange.PointMode Then mclsExchange.Move x, y
End Sub
'*****************************************************************
' Stop capturing and exchange the text on when the mouse is released
'*****************************************************************
Private Sub Form_MouseUp(Button As Integer, Shift As Integer, x!, y!)
    '*************************************************************
    ' If not it PointMode, then bail
    '*************************************************************
    If Not mclsExchange.PointMode Then Exit Sub
    '*************************************************************
    ' Get text from a window
    '*************************************************************
    If opt(0) Then
        If mclsExchange.EndCapture() Then
            txtExchange = mclsExchange.Text
        Else
            MsgBox "Sorry, but that window did not respond.", 48
        End If
```

```
'*****************************************************************
' Send text to a window
'*****************************************************************
    Else
        If Not mclsExchange.EndCapture(txtExchange) Then
            MsgBox "Sorry, but that window will not accept text.", 48
        End If
    End If
End Sub
```

Although this program (stubborn.vbp) mainly focuses on using the `clsExchangeData` object to communicate between windows, it also includes a small demo that shows a creative use of `SendKeys`. While we discourage you from using `SendKeys` as much as possible, it does provide a fast, easy mechanism for interprocess communication that at times can be necessary.

When the user clicks the `SendKeys` command button (called `cmd`), it fires the `Click` event shown in Listing 29.22. This code starts Notepad, enters some text, lets the user edit and save the file, and waits for Notepad to close. After Notepad stops running, the event continues by opening the edited data file and inserting its contents into `txtExchange`. Although this is an ugly, hacked way to communicate with an application, unfortunately there are some cases where it is the only alternative.

Listing 29.22   STUBBORN.FRM—Although Using *SendKeys* Is Ugly, Sometimes It Is the Only Feasible Way to Integrate with Other Applications

```
'*****************************************************************
' Demonstrates one ugly way to communicate with an app using SendKeys
'*****************************************************************
Private Sub cmd_Click()
    Dim pidNotepad As Long, hProcess As Long, lngExitCode As Long
    Dim intSource As Integer, strTempFile As String, strMsg As String
    '*****************************************************************
    ' Build a temporary strTempFile. Kill it if it already exists
    '*****************************************************************
    strTempFile = App.Path & "\~test~.txt"
    If FileExists(strTempFile) Then Kill strTempFile
    '*****************************************************************
    ' Run Notepad maximized with the new file, and store its process
    ' id (pid) into a variable for later use
    '*****************************************************************
    pidNotepad = Shell("notepad.exe " & strTempFile, vbNormalFocus)
    '*****************************************************************
    ' This statement hits enter to create the new file
    '*****************************************************************
    SendKeys "~", True
    '*****************************************************************
    ' Build an instruction screen, and insert it into Notepad
    '*****************************************************************
    strMsg = "Enter your text in here." & vbCrLf & "When you are done"
    strMsg = strMsg & ", quit Notepad and save your changes."
    SendKeys strMsg, True
```

continues

Listing 29.22   Continued

```
'*********************************************************************
' Finally, highlight the instructions so the user can easily
' delete them
'*********************************************************************
SendKeys "^+{Home}", True
'*********************************************************************
' Wait while Notepad is still open
'*********************************************************************
hProcess = OpenProcess(PROCESS_QUERY_INFORMATION, False, pidNotepad)
Do
    GetExitCodeProcess hProcess, lngExitCode
    DoEvents
Loop While lngExitCode = STILL_ACTIVE
'*********************************************************************
' Once Notepad is unloaded, open the file and insert it into
' txtExchange
'*********************************************************************
intSource = FreeFile
Open strTempFile For Input As intSource
    txtExchange = Input(LOF(intSource), intSource)
Close intSource
'*********************************************************************
' Kill the temporary file
'*********************************************************************
Kill strTempFile
End Sub
```

Stubborn is a good sample program for testing whether you can communicate with other applications. If you are not able to communicate with another application using OLE, DDE, or Stubborn, you should contact the application's vendor to see whether you can try anything else. If all else fails, consider either rewriting the application yourself or purchasing a similar product from another vendor. Although this isn't a great solution, it sometimes is the only satisfactory one.

From Here...

Unfortunately, there are few resources available that cover interapplication communications without focusing on a specific product. However, there are some helpful resources to steer you in the right direction:

- The *Microsoft Win32 SDK* (included with VB) contains important information on several key libraries, API calls, and file formats. Although these books can be difficult to understand, if you dig long enough, often you can find helpful information.

- *Visual Basic Programmer's Guide to the Win32 API* (Ziff-Davis), by Daniel Appleman, will be your bible if you decide to explore extensive API programming with Visual Basic.

CHAPTER 30

Creating Internet Applications with Visual Basic

Visual Basic applications can create documents that can be displayed in Microsoft Internet Explorer over the World Wide Web. In this chapter, you will learn how to do the following tasks. ■

- Create a simple Internet application

- Debug an Internet application locally

- Compile an Internet application

- Run your application over the Internet

- Understand the security requirement of Internet applications

- Navigate between user documents

- Respond to events that occur within your Internet application

- Exchange data between user documents

N O T E You can create applications that run over the Internet using Windows 95 or NT, but you will need Windows NT 4.0 running Peer Web Services or Windows 95 running Personal Web Server to provide access to your application over a network. ■

Creating Your First Internet Application

Creating an Internet application is simple for any programmer who's worked with Visual Basic forms—you just substitute user documents anywhere you formerly used a form.

To see how this works, follow these steps:

1. Start a new project in Visual Basic. From the File menu, choose New Project. Visual Basic displays the New Project dialog box.

2. Select the ActiveX Document DLL template icon and click OK. Visual Basic creates a new project containing one user document as shown in Figure 30.1.

FIG. 30.1

User Documents are "forms" for Internet applications.

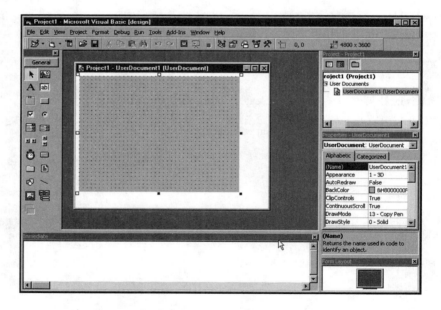

3. Draw controls on the user document and add code just as you would for a Visual Basic form. Figure 30.2 shows a mortgage calculator created on a user document.

FIG. 30.2

An Internet-based mortgage calculator.

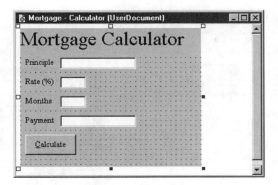

The executable code for the sample mortgage calculator resides in the command button's event procedure, just as it would on a form:

```
Option Explicit

Private Sub cmdCalculate_Click()
    txtPayment = Format(PPmt(txtRate / 1200, 1, txtMonths, -txtPrinciple, 0) + _
        Ipmt(txtRate / 1200, 1, txtMonths, -txtPrinciple, 0), "Currency")
End Sub
```

All this is just as I said: easy as pie. The obstacles start occurring as soon as you try to run the sample application. If you press F5 in the programming environment, nothing seems to happen.

The problem is this, Internet applications are hosted in a browser, namely Microsoft Internet Explorer. To see the application run, follow these steps:

1. Start the Internet application in the programming environment by pressing F5. Visual Basic starts the application as an ActiveX component.

2. Start Internet Explorer. If your computer is set up to dial out to an Internet service provider, you can cancel the dial operation. You don't need a connection to the Internet to see your application run locally.

3. From the Internet Explorer File menu, choose Open. Internet Explorer displays the Open dialog. Click on Browse to select the .VBD file for the user document as shown in Figure 30.3.

4. Once you open the user document's .VBD file from the directory where Visual Basic is installed, Internet Explorer displays the user document that is running in the Visual Basic programming environment, as shown in Figure 30.4.

FIG. 30.3
While debugging, Visual Basic creates a .VBD file for each running user document in the directory where VB5.EXE is installed.

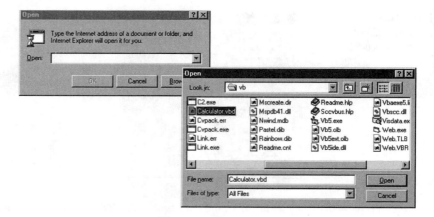

FIG. 30.4
You can set breakpoints, watch variables, and step through code in Visual Basic when you load the application's .VBD file from the directory where VB5.EXE is installed.

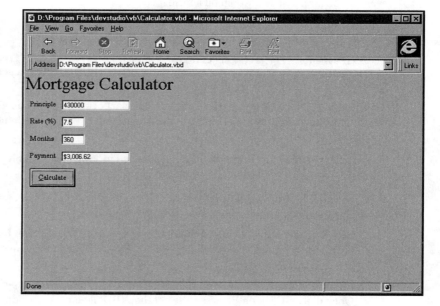

Once you've tested your Internet application in the Visual Basic programming environment, it's time to compile! To compile, follow these steps:

1. Close Internet Explorer. This optional step closes the reference to the Visual Basic application established in the earlier procedure and prevents an error when you stop running the application in the programming environment.

2. Stop the application running in the Visual Basic environment by clicking the Stop toolbar button.

3. From the Visual Basic File menu, choose Make. Visual Basic displays the Make Project dialog box.

4. Select the directory to save the executable file to and click OK. Visual Basic creates an executable file and one .VBD file for each user document in your application. All these files are saved in the directory specified for the executable.

After you have compiled an Internet application, you can run it by opening the .VBD files in the Internet Explorer to run the file locally. Running the application over the Internet or an intranet requires you to run the Setup Wizard as discussed in the following section.

Part

IV

Ch

30

Preparing Your First Application for the Internet

You can't simply open .VBD files across the Internet the way you would an .HTM file. Internet applications require special setup programs to package the executable, data, and dependent files in a way that can be safely and efficiently transmitted across the network.

FIG. 30.5

Select the Create Internet Download Setup option to build a setup program that enables people to use your Internet application from the Internet or an intranet.

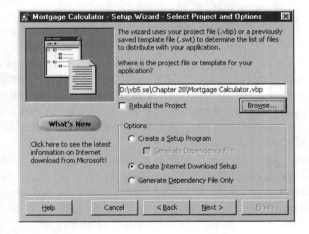

To build a setup program for your Internet application, follow these steps:

1. Run the Visual Basic Application Setup Wizard. Click Next on the Introduction dialog. The Setup Wizard displays the Select Project and Options dialog, as shown in Figure 30.5.

2. Click the Browse button and select the project file (.VBP) for your Internet application. In the Options group, select Create Internet Download Setup, then click Next. The wizard displays the Internet Distribution Location dialog, as shown in Figure 30.6.

3. Select the target directory for the setup files. You can use the default directory (/Temp/ SWSetup) then copy the files to another directory later. Click Next when you are done. The Wizard displays the Internet Package dialog (see Figure 30.7).

FIG. 30.6

Place the Internet setup files in a subdirectory of your server's Internet root directory so Internet/intranet users can get to the files.

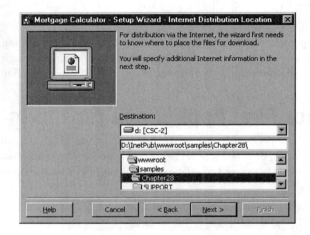

4. If you are using an intranet, you'll probably want to select the Use local copy option so the VB runtime and Microsoft .OCX files can be copied from the current server or from another location on your network. If the application is being distributed on the Internet, you'll probably want to select Download from the Microsoft web site so users always get the latest versions of these files. Click on the Safety button. The Wizard displays the Safety dialog (see Figure 30.8).

5. For the Mortgage Calculator application, check Safe for initialization and Safe for scripting. For other applications, see the section "Is It Safe?" later in this chapter for a description of these criteria. Click OK, then Next once you've completed this dialog. The Wizard displays the ActiveX Components dialog (see Figure 30.9).

6. The Wizard includes any dependencies it finds in the project file in this dialog. If there are other ActiveX components your application uses, you need to specify them here. Click Next. The Wizard displays the File Summary dialog (see Figure 30.10).

7. Click Next. The Wizard displays the Finished dialog. Click Finish to build the Internet setup files.

The Application Setup Wizard generates the types of files described in Table 30.1. Only the first three file types (shown in **bold**) are placed on the web site for downloading.

FIG. 30.7
The Runtime Components options let you use the Microsoft servers for the VB runtime and associated distribution files, rather than your own servers.

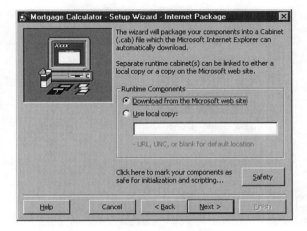

FIG. 30.8
These safety options determine whether or not other components can use your Internet application. See "Is It Safe?" for more information.

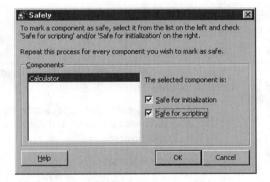

FIG. 30.9
The Wizard displays the safety dialog.

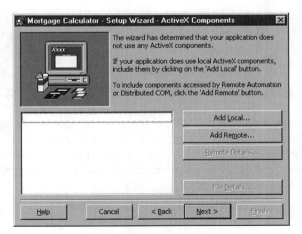

FIG. 30.10

This dialog simply reviews the files to be distributed.

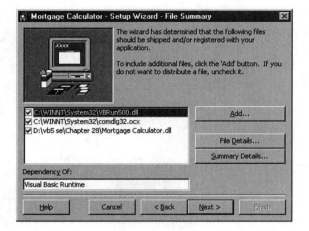

Table 30.1.   **These files are generated by the Setup Wizard for use installing applications over the Internet.**

File type	Description
.CAB	Contains compressed versions of the application's executable and dependent files.
.HTM	Generated web page that automatically installs the files from the .CAB file on the user's machine and then opens the installed .VBD files in the browser.
.VBD	Compiled user documents.
.DDF	The project file used by the Setup Wizard to create the .CAB file.
.DEP	The dependency file used by the Setup Wizard.
.INF	Setup file information file used to customize the installation of the application.
.SWT	Setup Wizard template for the application. Open this file in the Setup Wizard to make changes to the application's installation.

Copy the generated .HTM and .CAB files to one of the directories on your web site. Windows NT Peer Web Services creates the \InetPub\WWWRoot directory as a default web site. Users access files from this directory using your machine's name on an intranet. For instance, the following Internet Explorer Address line installs and runs the Mortage Calculator off the root directory of my intranet server named wombat1:

http://wombat1/Mortgage Calculator.HTM

Alternately, you can use the IP address of your web server instead of your server name. This may be necessary if you are using dial-in networking and aren't running a name service like WINS. Here is the equivalent address using the IP address of my wombat1 server:

http://9.8.7.6/Mortgage Calculator.HTM

To find the IP address of a server, follow these steps:

1. From the web server's Windows Control Panel, choose Network. Windows displays the Network dialog.

2. On the Network dialog, click the Protocols tab, select the TCP/IP Protocol and click the Properties button. Windows displays the TCP/IP properties (see Figure 30.11).

3. Write down the number shown in IP Address. Include the periods but omit spaces. The number shown in Figure 30.10 is entered 9.8.7.6 as an http: address. Click Cancel to close the properties dialog.

4. Click Cancel to close the Networking dialog.

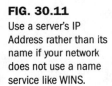

FIG. 30.11
Use a server's IP Address rather than its name if your network does not use a name service like WINS.

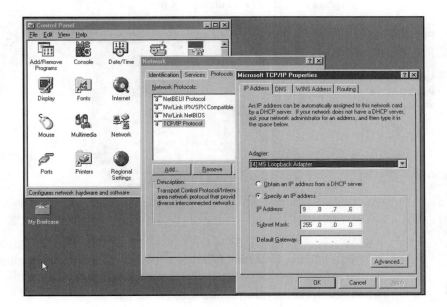

Part
IV

Ch
30

Using Your First Application over the Internet

Once you've built your Internet application, created a setup procedure for it, and copied the setup files to your Web site, you can use the application from any computer that has access to your web site. To use the application, follow these steps:

1. Establish a network connection. If your computer is part of a corporate network, this may happen automatically when you turn the computer on. For dial-in networks, you'll need to enter the phone number and password information in Internet Explorer's connection settings.

2. To set Internet Explorer's connection information, choose Options from the View menu and click the Connection tab.

3. Change the Internet Explorer's default security settings so you can view your application. From the View menu, choose Options then click the Security tab.

4. On the Security page of the Options dialog box, click Safety Level. Internet Explorer displays the Safety Level dialog box (see Figure 30.12).

FIG. 30.12
You need to set your security level to Medium to be able to use the Internet application you create.

5. Select the Medium security level option. This will display a warning every time you run your Internet application (which is a little annoying), but it will help you avoid untested or deliberately destructive applications created by others. Click OK.

6. Click OK to close the Options dialog box.

7. Enter the address of the .HTM file generated by the Setup Wizard for your Internet application. The Internet Explorer displays a warning before installing the application (see Figure 30.13).

FIG. 30.13
Warning Will Robinson!
You are about to install
some executable code.

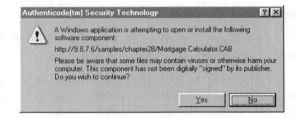

8. Click OK. Internet Explorer installs the needed files from the .CAB file, then displays the .VBD file as shown in Figure 30.14.

FIG. 30.14
After Internet Explorer
opens the .HTM file and
installs the application
components, it
immediately navigates
to the .VBD file.

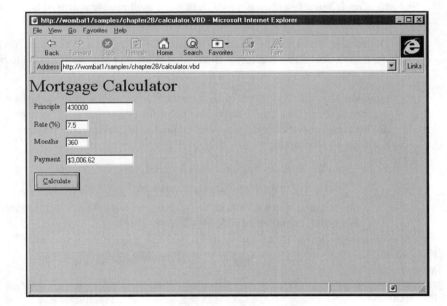

Is It Safe

As you may have guessed, there is nothing built-in to Visual Basic's Internet features that prevents you from doing really nasty stuff to a user's machine. VBScript and Java are deliberately hobbled to discourage viruses and (more likely) carelessly destructive coding. But Visual Basic is a full programming language with complete access to the Windows API and all the good and bad that implies.

To prevent mischief, Microsoft provides two levels of authentication:

- Component-level security determines if a component is safe to initialize and safe to script.
- Digital signatures identify the author of the component.

Component-level security is set by the Setup Wizard in step 5 of the procedure shown in the section "Preparing Your First Application for the Internet" earlier in this chapter. The Visual Basic documentation does a good job of describing what is meant by "Safe to initialize" and "Safe to script."

Basically, you should apply the Golden Rule. If the component does something you wouldn't want done to your machine, it's not safe. It's OK to create temporary files, add data to those files, or delete those files. It's not OK to write unlimited amounts of data to the user's hard drive, modify unrelated files, or reboot the system.

Digital signatures are the means to identify the source of a component. You receive a special ID file from a Certificate Authority, then run a utility like Microsoft Authenticode on each of your components to embed your ID in the code.

How well this will work is yet to be seen. In theory, malicious or careless component authors can be prosecuted or sued into correct behavior. More immediately useful however, is the ability to add specific vendors to your "approved list" in Internet Explorer. To see this approved list, follow these steps:

1. From the Internet Explorer's View menu, choose Options.
2. Click the Security tab on the Options dialog.
3. In the Certificates group, click Publishers. Internet Explorer displays the Authenticode Security Technology dialog (see Figure 30.15).

FIG. 30.15
Authenticode certificates are available from Microsoft.

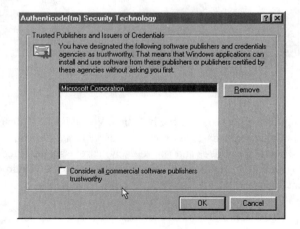

If you receive a digital signature file from Microsoft and process your component using Authenticode, you should be able to run your component on user's machines using the default Internet Explorer security settings.

Moving Between User Documents

Whew, setup and preparation are really the hardest things about Internet programming — mainly because it's all evolving and there are competing standards. Let's get back to something a bit easier . . .

The .HTM file generated by the Setup Wizard uses VBScript to navigate to the first compiled user document in your Internet application. The following HTML listing shows the .HTM file for the Mortgage Calculator application:

```
<HTML>
<OBJECT
    classid="clsid:6FF44831-5535-11D0-B92B-1E081C000000"
    id=Calculator
    codebase="Mortgage Calculator.CAB#version=1,0,0,0">
</OBJECT>

<SCRIPT LANGUAGE="VBScript">
Sub Window_OnLoad
    Navigate "Calculator.VBD"
End Sub
</SCRIPT>

</HTML>
```

Within Visual Basic, you use the Hyperlink object's NavigateTo method, as shown here:

```
#Const DebugVer = False

Private Sub mnuAmort_Click()
    #If DebugVer Then
        Hyperlink.NavigateTo CurDir & "\Amortization.VBD"
    #Else
        Hyperlink.NavigateTo "http://wombat1/samples/chapter28/Amortization.VBD"
    #End If
End Sub
```

> **N O T E** IMPORTANT: If you include paths with the NavigateTo method, you need to remember that the .VBD files are placed in the VB5.EXE directory during debugging, but are generally somewhere else once that application is compiled. ■

When an Internet application contains more than one user document, the Setup Wizard can't determine which document to display first, so it includes code in the generated .HTM file to display all of the user documents.

You need to edit the .HTM file to remove the VBScript instructions that display user documents other than your start-up document. The following .HTM file for the Mortgage Calculator sample shows the lines to delete in **bold**:

```
<HTML>
<OBJECT
     classid="clsid:6FF44831-5535-11D0-B92B-1E081C000000"
     id=Calculator
     codebase="Mortgage Calculator.CAB#version=1,0,0,0">
</OBJECT>

<SCRIPT LANGUAGE="VBScript">
Sub Window_OnLoad
     Navigate "Calculator.VBD"
End Sub
</SCRIPT>

<OBJECT
     classid="clsid:6FF44833-5535-11D0-B92B-1E081C000000"
     id=Amortization
     codebase="Mortgage Calculator.CAB#version=1,0,0,0">
</OBJECT>


' Delete these lines.
<SCRIPT LANGUAGE="VBScript">
Sub Window_OnLoad
     Navigate "Amortization.VBD"
End Sub
</SCRIPT>
</HTML>
```

Passing Data Between User Documents

Once you navigate to another user document, you'll notice something strange—you can't access data on the preceding user document! User documents aren't like forms, you can't access the controls on one user document from another.

That's because user documents live and die at the behest of the browser—there's no guarantee a user document will be there to supply the requested data. To solve this problem, store shared data in global variables or in a global object.

The following lines declare global variables used by the Mortgage Calculator sample. These lines reside in a code module (Globals.BAS) so they are available to all user documents in the application.

```
' Global.Bas
Option Explicit

' Variables for sharing data between
' documents.
Public gsPrinciple As Single
Public gsRate As Single
Public giMonths As Integer
Public gsPayment As Single
```

The Calculator user document records the data in each text box in these global variable before displaying the Amortization user document. Notice that the code for displaying the Amortization user document is in a menu event procedure—menus added to user documents appear in their container applications, in this case Internet Explorer.

```
Private Sub mnuAmort_Click()
    ' Record user document data in
    ' global variables.
    giMonths = txtMonths
    gsRate = txtRate
    gsPrinciple = txtPrinciple
    gsPayment = txtPayment
    #If DebugVer Then
        Hyperlink.NavigateTo CurDir & "\Amortization.VBD"
    #Else
        Hyperlink.NavigateTo "http://wombat1/samples/chapter28/Amortization.VBD"
    #End If
End Sub
```

The Amortization user document uses the global variables to display an amortization table in a text box. The code that creates the table resides in the UserDocument_Initialize event procedure, so it is updated when the document is displayed.

```
' Display an amortization table.
Private Sub UserDocument_Initialize()
    Dim Index As Integer
    ' Text for column headings.
    txtAmort = "Month" & vbTab & "Principle" & _
        vbTab & "Interest" & vbCrLf
    ' Write table.
    For Index = 1 To giMonths
        txtAmort = txtAmort & _
            Index & vbTab & _
            Format(PPmt(gsRate / 1200, Index, giMonths, -gsPrinciple, 0), "Cur-
➥rency") & _
            vbTab & _
            Format(IPmt(gsRate / 1200, Index, giMonths, -gsPrinciple, 0), "Cur-
➥rency") & _
            vbCrLf
    Next Index
End Sub
```

Figure 30.16 shows the Amortize user document in action.

FIG. 30.16

Amortize.VBD displays an amortization table based on the data entered in Calculator.VBD.

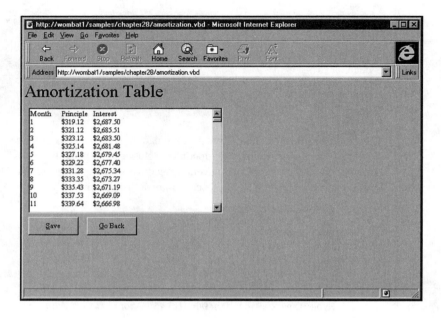

Users may want to save the table displayed on Amortize.VBD, so the Save command button includes the following event procedure.

```
Private Sub cmdSave_Click()
    Dim iFile As Integer
    Dim strFile As String
    ' Get a file number.
    iFile = FreeFile
    ' Get a file name.
    dlgSave.ShowSave
    strFile = dlgSave.filename
    ' If the user entered a name.
    If Len(strFile) Then
        ' Open the file.
        Open strFile For Binary As iFile Len = Len(txtAmort)
        ' Put the data in the file.
        Put iFile, , txtAmort.Text
        ' Close the file.
        Close iFile
    End If
End Sub
```

The code for the Go Back button is very simple:

```
Private Sub cmdGoBack_Click()
    Hyperlink.GoBack
End Sub
```

Passing Data to the Server

The preceding section showed how to save data locally on the user's machine with the File Open statement. Passing data from the user's machine back to the server is a very different matter. There are three main ways of sending data back to the server over the Internet:

- Mail the data using the Mail Application Interface (MAPI). Integrating applications with mail is covered in Chapter 28, "Integrating Visual Basic with Mail, Schedule, and Exchange."

- Exchange the data via an ODBC database. Chapter 31, "Integrating Visual Basic with Internet Explorer and IIS" discusses using databases over the Internet.

- Use a remote automation component running on the server. Creating Remote Automation applications is covered in Chapter 21, "Creating Remote Automation Servers."

Remote automation servers are the most general approach to retrieving data from users, since you have complete control on both the server and client sides of the operation. For that reason, I've included a short remote automation sample in the following sections.

Creating a Remote Logging Service

Remote Automation servers can gather information from users by writing to a log file as users access the Internet application. This is one of the simplest applications of remote automation, and therefore makes a manageable demonstration.

The WebLog sample application contains one class, User.Cls, shown below:

```
' User.Cls
Option Explicit
Dim miFile As Integer
Dim miLang As Integer
Dim mstrUser As String

Private Sub Class_Initialize()
    miFile = FreeFile
    Open "c:\calc.log" For Append As miFile
End Sub

Private Sub Class_Terminate()
    Close miFile
End Sub

Public Property Let User(Setting As String)
    mstrUser = Setting
End Property

Public Property Let Language(Setting As Integer)
    miLang = Setting
End Property

Public Sub WriteLog()
    Print miLang, mstrUser, miLang
End Sub
```

The WebLog project has the Remote Server Files check box selected on the project Properties Component dialog page. This causes Visual Basic to create the .TLB and .VBR files required for installing the application on client computers—in this case users on the Internet.

Calling the Remote Logging Service

The Mortgage Calculator application calls the Remote Logging service to track the names and language IDs of users that access the application over the Internet.

The code is placed in the the Calculator user document's UserDocument_Initialize event procedure. This ensures the log gets written when the user first opens the application over the Internet.

```
' Calculator.DOB
' Windows API functions for log information
' sent to server.
Private Declare Function GetUserName Lib "advapi32.dll" _
    Alias "GetUserNameA" (ByVal lpBuffer As String, _
    nSize As Long) As Long
Private Declare Function GetSystemDefaultLangID _
    Lib "kernel32" () As Integer

Private Sub UserDocument_Initialize()
    ' Declare variables.
    Dim strUser As String
    Dim iLang As Integer
    Dim lLength As Long

    ' Create a remote object that keeps a log
    ' of the users of this page.
    Dim UserLog As Object
    ' Use late binding. This is slower, but
    ' you don't have to recompile if WebLog.EXE changes.
    Set UserLog = CreateObject("WebLog.User")

    ' Use the Windows API to collect user info.
    GetUserName strUser, lLength
    iLang = GetSystemDefaultLangID()

    ' Set the remote object's properties.
    UserLog.User = strUser
    UserLog.Language = iLang
    ' Write the log entry.
    UserLog.WriteLog
End Sub
```

Notice that the user document uses late binding. In other words, it uses CreateObject rather than Dim As New to create the remote object variable. Late binding is slower than early binding, but it keeps you from having to recompile the client application every time the remote application changes. This is a very important issue when applications are deployed over the Internet.

Using late binding also means the Setup Wizard won't automatically detect that the Mortgage Calculator needs files from the WebLog project. You'll need to remember this when creating the Internet setup procedure, as discussed in the next section.

Installing the Remote Automation Server

To use the WebLog remote application, the Mortgage Calculator needs to install WebLog.VBR and WebLog.TLB on the user's machine. The fifth step of the Setup Wizard lets you add remote components as shown in Figure 30.17.

FIG. 30.17
Click Add Remote to add a .VBR file to the setup process for an Internet application.

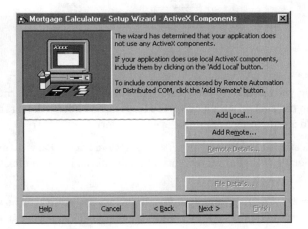

When you add a remote component to an Internet application setup procedure, you need to specify the connection details for the client. In some cases, this can be problematic since Windows NT clients support remote automation, but Windows 95 clients require DCOM 95. One solution is to create two setup procedures: one for Windows 95 clients and one for Windows NT users. Figure 30.18 shows the Remote Connection Details dialog the Setup Wizard uses to specify this information.

When the Setup Wizard finishes, it adds the .VBR file to the .CAB file for downloading over the Internet. The generated setup procedure automatically registers the remote component on the client's machine when they install the Internet application over the Internet.

FIG. 30.18

Specify the remote connection information to configure a client to use the remote component.

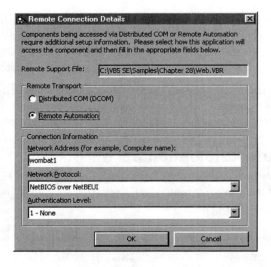

From Here...

In this chapter, you learned how to create applications that run in Internet Explorer as web pages off of an Internet or intranet site. You also learned how to debug those applications locally and build a setup program for use over the Internet.

Internet applications can also run on servers as Active Server Pages using Microsoft Internet Information Server (IIS). For more information on this and related topics, see the following chapters:

- Chapter 21, "Creating Remote Automation Servers," describes how to create ActiveX components that provide their objects to other applications over a network.

- Chapter 31, "Integrating Visual Basic with Internet Explorer and IIS," tells you how to use the Internet controls included with Visual Basic and provides examples database access over the Internet.

Integrating Visual Basic with Internet Explorer and IIS

Microsoft Internet Explorer provides client access to the Internet. Microsoft Internet Information Server (IIS) provides the content. Visual Basic negotiates between these two applications and provides a rich set of tools for exchanging information between clients and servers over the Internet.

The preceding chapter showed you how to create applications that reside on Internet servers but run on clients under Internet Explorer. This chapter shows you how to create your own browser that incorporates Internet Explorer and how to exchange data with Internet Information Server (IIS). It also covers how to perform direct communications over the network. ■

- Build an Internet browser that you can embed in your applications

- Control the Internet Explorer application with Visual Basic code

- Create a browser add-in to use when debugging Internet applications developed in Visual Basic

- Use the Inet ActiveX control for direct access to FTP and WWW files

- Use the WinSock ActiveX control for handling TCP/IP connections

- Copy databases over the Internet

- Synchronize copied databases with their source over the Internet

- Run components on a server as Active Server Pages

Creating a Browser Application

The Internet provides a great way to distribute current information to your users and to retrieve data about your installed base. You may want to build a Web browser into your application so users can retrieve current help, register their copy of the software, or browse other products available from your company.

The WebBrowser ActiveX control (SHDOCVW.DLL) encapsulates all the capabilities of Microsoft Internet Explorer for inclusion on your forms. To add a Web browser to your application:

1. Add the WebBrowser control to the Visual Basic Toolbox. From the Project menu, choose Components. Visual Basic displays the Components dialog box.

2. Select the Microsoft Internet Controls check box. Click OK. Visual Basic adds the WebBrowser control to the Toolbox.

3. Click the WebBrowser control in the Toolbox and draw the control on a form.

4. Add code to use the control's Navigate method to view specific addresses on the Internet.

Figure 31.1 shows a Web browser created in Visual Basic. The Address text box is named txtAddress and the back and next buttons are named cmdBack and cmdNext in code.

FIG. 31.1

This Web browser is easy to create and can be included in any application to make it "Internet aware."

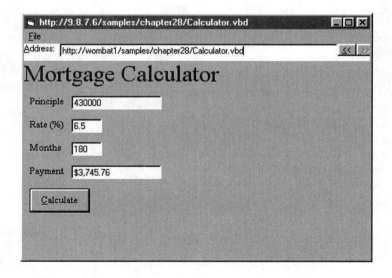

The event procedures for txtAddress, cmdBack, and cmdNext show how to use the WebBrowser control's navigation methods. The procedure txtAddress_Keypress navigates to the given address when the user presses Enter. The procedures cmdBack_Click and cmdNext_Click use the GoBack and GoForward methods.

```
Private Sub cmdBack_Click()
    webView.GoBack
End Sub

Private Sub cmdNext_Click()
    webView.GoForward
End Sub
```

Part

IV

Ch

31

Listing 31.1 WebBrowser.FRM—Navigating to URLs Using the WebBrowser Control

```
Private Sub txtAddress_KeyPress(KeyAscii As Integer)
    If KeyAscii = Asc(vbCr) Then
        ' Eat the keystroke.
        KeyAscii = 0
        ' Select the text.
        txtAddress.SelLength = Len(txtAddress)
        ' Navigate to the address.
        webView.Navigate txtAddress
    End If
End Sub
```

After the Web page is displayed, the webView_NavigateComplete event procedure updates the displayed address. Some pages automatically navigate to another page. It's important to update the displayed address so the user knows where he or she really is. Listing 31.2 demonstrates updating a Form caption navigation is complete.

Listing 31.2 WebBrowser.FRM—Updating the Caption After Navigation Completes

```
Private Sub webView_NavigateComplete(ByVal URL As String)
    ' Update the text box with the final address.
    txtAddress.Text = URL
    txtAddress.SelLength = Len(txtAddress)
    ' Display the page title in the form's caption.
    Caption = webView.LocationName
End Sub
```

The webView_CommandStateChange event occurs when the GoBack and GoForward methods are enabled. Use this event procedure to enable or disable the cmdBack and cmdNext command buttons to prevent navigation errors, as shown in Listing 31.3.

Listing 31.3   WebBrowser.FRM—Enabling/Disabling Forward and Back Commands

```
Private Sub webView_CommandStateChange(ByVal Command As Long, ByVal Enable As
Boolean)
    ' Enable or disable the Back and Next command buttons
    ' based on whether or not there is an address to go to.
    Select Case Command
        Case CSC_NAVIGATEBACK
            cmdBack.Enabled = Enable
        Case CSC_NAVIGATEFORWARD
            cmdNext.Enabled = Enable
        Case CSC_UPDATECOMMANDS
    End Select
End Sub
```

Finally, I've added some code to let you resize the form. This demonstrates that the Web-Browser control adds or removes scroll bars so you can view the entire Web page, regardless of the size of the viewport, as shown in Listing 31.4.

Listing 31.4   WebBrowser.FRM—Resizing the Browser

```
Private Sub Form_Resize()
    If Me.WindowState <> vbMinimized Then
        webView.Height = ScaleHeight - txtAddress.Height
        webView.Width = ScaleWidth
        txtAddress.Width = ScaleWidth - lblAddress.Width - cmdBack.Width -
        ➥cmdNext.Width
        cmdBack.Left = txtAddress.Left + txtAddress.Width
        cmdNext.Left = cmdBack.Left + cmdBack.Width
    End If
End Sub
```

Controlling Internet Explorer

As you may have guessed, SHDOCVW.DLL is really just a wrapper for Microsoft Internet Explorer. You can embed it on a form, as shown in the preceding section, or you can run it as a stand-alone application.

To control Internet Explorer as a stand-alone application, follow these steps:

1. Add a reference to the Microsoft Internet Controls type library. From the Project menu, choose References. Visual Basic displays the References dialog box.

2. Select the Microsoft Internet Controls check box. Click OK.

3. In code, declare an object variable of the type InternetExplorer. Declare the variable at the module level so it is available to all the procedures in the module.

4. Add code to use the object variable's Navigate method to view specific addresses on the Internet.

The Web Tool application shown in Figure 31.2 shows how to control the Internet Explorer with Visual Basic.

FIG. 31.2
The Web Tool application displays a given Internet address in the Internet Explorer.

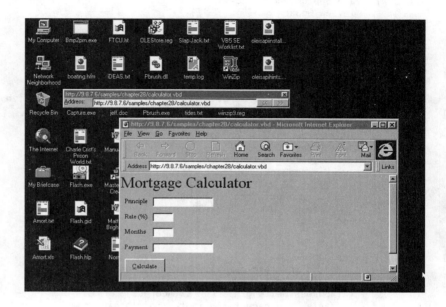

The code for the Web Tool application is nearly identical to the Web browser sample in the preceding section. The main difference is that it uses the Object variable `ieView` instead of the control `webView`. The Object variable is declared `WithEvents` to intercept the Internet Explorer events, as shown in Listing 31.5.

Listing 31.5   WebTool.FRM—Connecting to Internet Explorer Events

```
' Create an Internet Explorer object variable.
Dim WithEvents ieView As InternetExplorer

Private Sub Form_Load()
    ' Establish a reference to the application object.
    Set ieView = New InternetExplorer
End Sub

Private Sub txtAddress_KeyPress(KeyAscii As Integer)
    If KeyAscii = Asc(vbCr) Then
        ' Eat the keystroke.
        KeyAscii = 0
        ' Select the text.
        txtAddress.SelLength = Len(txtAddress)
        ' Navigate to the address.
        ieView.navigate txtAddress
        ' Make sure Internet Explorer is visible.
        ieView.Visible = True
    End If
End Sub
```

Listing 31.5   Continued

```
Private Sub cmdBack_Click()
    ieView.GoBack
End Sub

Private Sub cmdNext_Click()
    ieView.GoForward
End Sub

Private Sub ieView_CommandStateChange(ByVal Command As Long, ByVal Enable As
➥Boolean)
    ' Enable or disable the Back and Next command buttons
    ' based on whether or not there is an address to go to.
    Select Case Command
        Case CSC_NAVIGATEBACK
            cmdBack.Enabled = Enable
        Case CSC_NAVIGATEFORWARD
            cmdNext.Enabled = Enable
        Case CSC_UPDATECOMMANDS
    End Select
End Sub

Private Sub ieView_NavigateComplete(ByVal URL As String)
    ' Update the text box with the final address.
    txtAddress.Text = URL
    txtAddress.SelLength = Len(txtAddress)
    ' Display the page title in the form's caption.
    Caption = ieView.LocationName
End Sub

Private Sub ieView_Quit(Cancel As Boolean)
    ' Close this application if user closes Internet
    ' Explorer.
    End
End Sub
```

When controlling the Internet Explorer from code you need to remember two things:

■ The Internet Explorer starts invisibly. You need to set its Visible property to True in order to see results.

■ Remember to respond to the Quit event. The user may close the referenced instance of Internet Explorer, so you need to respond by closing the referencing application (as Web Tool does) or by establishing a new reference before calling Internet Explorer methods or properties.

Implementing the Browser as an Add-In

The Web browser sample is useful as an add-in for use when developing Internet applications in Visual Basic. To implement the Web browser as an add-in, follow these steps:

1. Start a new project based on the Add-In template. From the File menu, choose New Project. Visual Basic displays the New Project dialog.

2. Double click the ADDIN icon. Visual Basic creates an Add-In project template.

3. Remove the default form. In the Project window, select the form `frmAddIn` and then choose Remove from the Project menu.

4. Add the `frmWebBrowser` form. From the Project menu, choose Add Form, then select the form from a list of existing files.

5. Set the project name to `WebBrowser`. From the Project menu, choose Properties, then type the new project name.

6. Declare public `VBInstance` and Connect object variables in the form module.

7. Modify AddIn.Bas to register the object `WebBrowser.Connect`.

8. Change the form name `frmAddIn` to `frmWebBrowser` in the class module `Connect.Cls`.

Listing 31.6 shows snippets from each module with the code changes you must make.

Listing 31.6   WebAddin.VBP—Modifications for the VB WebBrowser Add-In

```
' Addin.Bas Changes
Sub AddToIni()
    Dim ErrCode As Long
    ErrCode = WritePrivateProfileString("Add-Ins32", "WebAddin.Connect", "0",
"vbaddin.ini")
End Sub

' frmWebBrowser.Frm
Public VBInstance As VBIDE.VBE
Public Connect As Connect

' Connect.Cls
Dim mfrmAddIn                    As New frmWebBrowser

    ' From Sub Show() . . .
    If mfrmAddIn Is Nothing Then
        Set mfrmAddIn = New frmWebBrowser
    End If
```

Once you've created the add-in, run `AddToIni` from the Immediate window to make the add-in available to new instances of Visual Basic.

Using the Browser Add-In

The Web browser add-in lets you view user documents while debugging them in Visual Basic. This is useful because you need to restart Internet Explorer every time you stop the loaded user document in Visual Basic.

Figure 31.3 shows the Web browser in use while debugging the Mortgage Calculator application created in Chapter 28, "Integrating Visual Basic with Mail, Schedule, and Exchange."

FIG. 31.3

If you stop the Mortgage Calculator application in VB, you'll have to restart Internet Explorer. The Web browser add-in makes that easier.

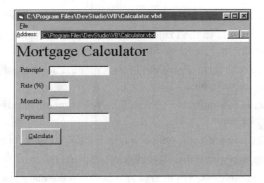

Since Visual Basic puts .VBD files in its application directory while debugging, you may want to add some code to the Web browser add-in to look in that directory by default. You may also want to add an OnTop property so you can keep the Web browser on top of the Visual Basic windows during runtime. The following code shows the additions and changes to the the Web browser that accommodate the changes shown in Listing 31.7.

Listing 31.7   WebAddin.VBP—Making the VB WebBrowser Add-In More Useful

```
' frmWebBrowser.frm - Enhancements to Web Browser Add-In.
' Change this to your "home" directory for VB5.EXE
Const VBDir = "c:\program files\devstudio\vb"

' Internal variable to track windows state.
Private mbOnTop As Boolean

' Windows API and constants for placing a window on top.
Private Declare Function SetWindowPos Lib "user32" _
  (ByVal hwnd As Long, _
  ByVal hWndInsertAfter As Long, _
  ByVal x As Long, ByVal y As Long, _
  ByVal cx As Long, ByVal cy As Long, _
  ByVal wFlags As Long) As Long
Const SWP_NOACTIVATE = &H10
Const SWP_SHOWWINDOW = &H40
Const SWP_NOSIZE = &H1
Const SWP_NOMOVE = &H2
Const HWND_TOPMOST = -1
Const HWND_NOTOPMOST = -2

' OnTop property (read/write).
Public Property Let OnTop(Setting As Boolean)
    If Setting Then
        SetWindowPos Me.hwnd, HWND_TOPMOST, _
            0, 0, 0, 0, _
            SWP_NOSIZE Or SWP_NOMOVE Or swpnoactivate
        mbOnTop = True
    Else
        SetWindowPos Me.hwnd, HWND_NOTOPMOST, _
```

```
                    0, 0, 0, 0, _
                    SWP_NOSIZE Or SWP_NOMOVE Or swpnoactivate
                    mbOnTop = False
            End If
    End Property

    Public Property Get OnTop() As Boolean
            OnTop = mbOnTop
    End Property

    ' Menu event procedures.
    Private Sub mnuOnTop_Click()
            OnTop = Not mbOnTop
            mnuOnTop.Checked = Not mnuOnTop.Checked
    End Sub

    Private Sub mnuClose_Click()
            Unload Me
    End Sub

    ' Changes to KeyPress event.
    Private Sub txtAddress_KeyPress(KeyAscii As Integer)
            If KeyAscii = Asc(vbCr) Then
                ' Eat the keystroke.
                KeyAscii = 0
                ' Select the text.
                txtAddress.SelLength = Len(txtAddress)
                ' Navigate to the address.
                ' Changes for Add-In: don't ever read
                ' from cache (always get fresh copy)
                ' and use VB directory as default.
                On Error GoTo errNotFound
                If InStr(1, txtAddress, "c:\") Then
                    webView.Navigate txtAddress, navNoReadFromCache
                Else
                    webView.Navigate "file://" & VBDir & "\" & txtAddress,
➥navNoReadFromCache
                End If
            End If
            Exit Sub
    errNotFound:
    End Sub
```

Adding the navNoReadFromCache flag in the Navigate method is a significant enhancement to the add-in. This flag ensures that the most current version of the .VBD file is used, rather than the Internet Explorer's cached copy. This lets you see changes to the .VBD file without closing the Internet Explorer each time you restart your Internet application.

Using the Internet Controls

In addition to being able to control Internet Explorer through the WebBrowser ActiveX control (SHDOCVW.DLL), Visual Basic includes two ActiveX controls for low-level interaction with the Internet:

■ The Internet Transfer control (Inet.OCX) lets you download files from the Internet using the Hypertext Transport Protocol (HTTP) or the File Transfer Protocol (FTP).

■ The Winsock control (Winsock.OCX) provides a standardized interface to the TCP and UDP network protocols. This lets you communicate directly between two or more computers using the network.

The following sections show an application for each of these controls.

Creating an FTP Browser

The Internet Transfer control (Inet.OCX) gives you direct access to files on the Internet. The advantage of this is that you don't have the overhead associated with running Internet Explorer. The disadvantage is that you have to write your own code to handle browsing and saving files—tasks that Internet Explorer handles for you.

When using the Internet Transfer control you need to consider the asynchronous nature of the Internet. Most tasks are dispatched as requests which return data through an event procedure. The FTP Browse sample shown in Figure 31.4 demonstrates how to handle asynchronous browsing in an FTP directory.

FIG. 31.4

When you choose a directory, FTP Browse displays the status as the request proceeds and, finally, the result.

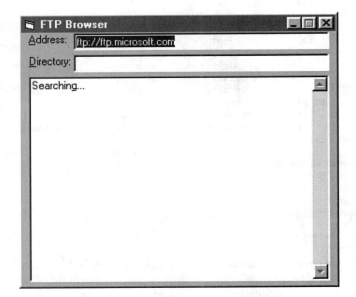

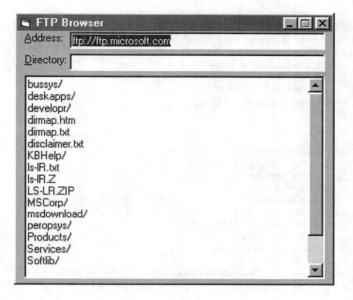

FTP Browse responds to key and mouse events. Type the name of an FTP site in Address, then press Enter. FTP Browse displays the files and directories in the FTP root. Select a directory from the displayed list and FTP Browse displays that subdirectory. Select a file and FTP Browse retrieves that file.

Listing 31.8 shows the key and mouse event procedures.

Listing 31.8   FTPBrowse.FRM—Using the Internet Transfer Control

```
Option Explicit

Private Sub txtAddress_KeyPress(KeyAscii As Integer)
    If KeyAscii = Asc(vbCr) Then
        ' Eat the keystroke.
        KeyAscii = 0
        ' Select the text.
        txtAddress.SelStart = 0
        txtAddress.SelLength = Len(txtAddress)
        ' Set the FTP address to view.
        inetBrowse.URL = txtAddress.Text
        ' Clear the txtDir to show top-level.
        txtDir = ""
        ' Call txtDir Keypress event.
        txtDir_KeyPress Asc(vbCr)
    End If
End Sub

Private Sub txtContents_MouseUp(Button As Integer, Shift As Integer, x As
➥Single, y As Single)
```

continues

Listing 31.8 Continued

```
      ' Browse the selected directory.
      If txtContents.SelLength Then
          ' Add the selected item to the directory.
          txtDir = txtDir & "/" & txtContents.SelText
          ' Call the txtDir Keypress event.
          txtDir_KeyPress Asc(vbCr)
      End If
End Sub

Private Sub txtDir_KeyPress(KeyAscii As Integer)
    If KeyAscii = Asc(vbCr) Then
        ' Eat the keystroke.
        KeyAscii = 0
        ' Select the text.
        txtDir.SelStart = 0
        txtDir.SelLength = Len(txtDir)
        ' Trap errors (important!).
        On Error GoTo errBrowse
        ' Show the directory.
        inetBrowse.Execute inetBrowse.URL, "DIR " & txtDir & "/*"
    End If
errBrowse:
    ' Display error.
    txtContents = Err & " " & Err.Description
    Err = 0
End Sub
```

The Execute method called in txtDir_KeyPress retrieves the directory listing. Execute occurs *asynchronously*, which means you need to use the StateChanged event to detect when the data is returned. Once the request is complete, you can retrieve the data using GetChunk, as shown in Listing 31.9.

Listing 31.9 FTPBrowse.FRM—Detecting Events in the Internet Transfer Control

```
Private Sub inetBrowse_StateChanged(ByVal State As Integer)
    Select Case State
        Case icError
            txtContents = inetBrowse.ResponseCode & " " & _
                inetBrowse.ResponseInfo
        Case icResolvingHost, icRequesting, icRequestSent
            txtContents = "Searching..."
        Case icHostResolved
            txtContents = "Found."
        Case icReceivingResponse, icResponseReceived
            txtContents = "Receiving data."
        Case icResponseCompleted
            Dim strBuffer As String
            ' Get the data.
            strBuffer = inetBrowse.GetChunk(1024)
```

```
                    ' If the data is a directory, display it.
                    If strBuffer <> vbCrLf Then
                        txtContents = strBuffer
                    ' If the data is a file, save it.
                    Else
                        tmrSaveFile.Enabled = True
                    End If
                Case icConnecting, icConnected
                    txtContents.Text = "Connecting."
                Case icDisconnecting
                Case icDisconnected
                Case Else
            End Select
End Sub
```

The code for Case icResponseCompleted is a bit tricky; if the item the user selected was a file name, GetChunk returns a carriage return-linefeed rather than a directory listing. In that case, FTP Browse saves the file to disk. You have to wait a bit to do this, however. If you try another Execute method from the StateChanged event, you'll get an error — the Internet Transfer control can only handle one request at a time.

The Timer event procedure in Listing 31.10 waits until the Internet Transfer control has finished before starting another request.

Listing 31.10 FTPBrowse.FRM—Using a Timer to Wait for Requests to Complete

```
Private Sub tmrSaveFile_Timer()
    If inetBrowse.StillExecuting Then
        ' Try again later
    Else
        ' Launch save.
        tmrSaveFile.Enabled = False
        SaveFile
        ' Clear contents.
        txtContents = ""
    End If
End Sub

Sub SaveFile()
    Dim iFile As Integer
    Dim strBuffer As String
    ' Get a file name.
    dlgSave.ShowSave
    If Len(dlgSave.filename) = 0 Then Exit Sub
    ' Save the data to a variable.
    strBuffer = inetBrowse.OpenURL _
        (inetBrowse.URL & txtDir)
    ' Put the data into a file.
    iFile = FreeFile()
```

continues

Listing 31.11   Chat.FRM—Using the Winsock Control

```
    Open dlgSave.filename For Binary _
      As iFile Len = Len(strBuffer)
    Put iFile, , strBuffer
    Close iFile
    dlgSave.filename = ""
End Sub
```

Notice that SaveFile in Listing 31.10 uses the OpenURL method, rather than Execute. OpenURL returns the data directly to a variable, rather than using GetChunk. The StateChanged event still occurs, though.

Debugging code written for the Internet Transfer control can be problematic. A request may time-out while you are in Break mode; it's a good idea to set the RequestTimeout property to 0 before you start debugging.

Figuring out a problem in the StateChanged event is difficult. Visual Basic seems to miss state changes if you are in Break mode when they occur—you can't always step through code to see each of the StateChange events. Instead, you need to set a single breakpoint for the state you want to detect.

Creating a Chat Application

The Winsock control (Winsock.OCX) provides the lowest level of network control you'll probably want to deal with. Basically, it packages the TCP and UDP network protocols into an understandable interface.

You use Winsock to exchange data between any two computers connected to the network, but you need to provide the application to run on either side of the connection. A good example of this is a Chat application that allows messages to be sent between two networked computers, as shown in Figure 31.5.

To see how the Chat sample works, start the application on two networked computers. On one of the computers, enter the network name of the other computer. Once the connection is completed, you can send a messages between the two computers.

The Chat sample functions as both the sender and recipient. Either side can initiate or terminate the connection. At start-up the Winsock control listens for connection information, as shown in Listing 31.11.

Listing 31.11   Chat.FRM—Using the Winsock Control

```
Option Explicit

Private Sub Form_Load()
    ' Listen for requests.
    sckChat.LocalPort = 101
  sckChat.Listen
  ShowText "Listening"
End Sub
```

FIG. 31.5
In addition to exchanging data, the Chat sample displays each Winsock event as it occurs.

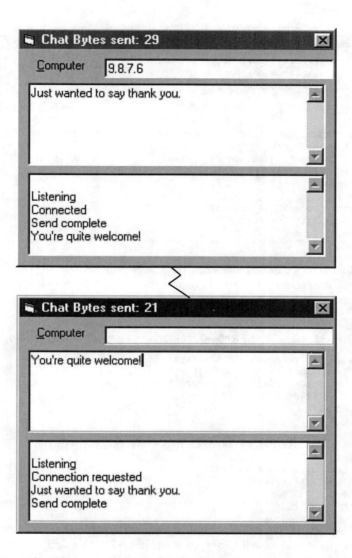

If the computer recieves a connection request, the ConnectionRequest event occurs. Once the connection is complete, the computer that requested the connection receives a Connect event. Listing 31.12 requests a connection, accepts the connection, and acknowledges the connection.

Listing 31.12   Chat.FRM—Connecting to Another Computer with Winsock

```
Private Sub txtComputer_KeyPress(KeyAscii As Integer)
    If KeyAscii = Asc(vbCr) Then
        sckChat.Close
```

continues

Listing 31.12 Continued

```
        sckChat.RemoteHost = txtComputer
        sckChat.RemotePort = 101
        sckChat.Connect
    End If
End Sub

Private Sub sckChat_ConnectionRequest(ByVal requestID As Long)
    sckChat.Close
    ShowText "Connection requested"
    sckChat.Accept requestID
End Sub

Private Sub sckChat_Connect()
    ShowText "Connected"
End Sub
```

Now that a connection is established, data can be sent between the two computers. To send data, call the SendData method. To receive data, use the GetData method in the DataArrival event as shown in Listing 31.13.

Listing 31.13 Chat.FRM—Transferring Data with the Winsock Control

```
Private Sub txtSend_KeyPress(KeyAscii As Integer)
    If KeyAscii = Asc(vbCr) Then
        sckChat.SendData txtSend.Text
        txtSend.Text = ""
    End If
End Sub

Private Sub sckChat_DataArrival(ByVal bytesTotal As Long)
    Dim strText As String
    sckChat.GetData strText
    ShowText strText
End Sub
```

If one application closes the connection, the other application receives a Close event. If this occurs, you should close the connection and begin listening again, as shown in Listing 31.14.

Listing 31.14 Chat.FRM—Reinitializing the Winsock Control

```
Private Sub sckChat_Close()
    ShowText "Close"
    ' When connection closed, go back to listening.
    sckChat.Close
    sckChat.Listen
    ShowText "Listen"
End Sub
```

The last pieces of code respond to errors and display status. Listing 31.15 isn't really necessary here, but it helps illustrate the flow of events.

Listing 31.15   Chat.FRM—Tracing Winsock Events

```
Private Sub sckChat_Error(ByVal Number As Integer, Description As String, _
   ByVal Scode As Long, ByVal Source As String, ByVal HelpFile As String, _
   ByVal HelpContext As Long, CancelDisplay As Boolean)
     ShowText Number & " " & Description
End Sub

Private Sub sckChat_SendComplete()
     ShowText "Send complete"
End Sub

Private Sub sckChat_SendProgress(ByVal bytesSent As Long, ByVal bytesRemaining
➥As Long)
     Caption = "Chat Bytes sent: " & bytesSent
End Sub

Sub ShowText(Text As String)
     txtReceive = txtReceive & vbCrLf & Text
End Sub
```

Part
IV

Ch
31

You may want to check the connection status before performing operations on the Winsock control. The State property tells you whether the control is listening, connected, in the process of connecting, or in an error state.

Accessing Databases over the Internet

You don't access databases over the Internet directly. Instead, you create a local replica and then synchronize the local copy with the remote one.

Figure 31.6 shows a simple data grid form generated using the Visual Basic Data Form Wizard. I've added Internet capabilities to the generated code by creating Form_Load and Form_Unload event procedures.

FIG. 31.6

This simple data form copies a database from the Internet upon loading and synchronizes the data upon unloading.

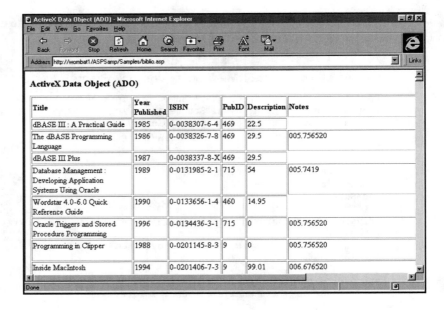

The Form_Load event procedure for the form checks to see if the database exists locally; if it doesn't, the code uses an Internet Transfer control (Inet.OCX) to retrieve the file from an FTP server, as shown in Listing 31.16.

Listing 31.16   InetBiblio.FRM—Retrieving a Database Using the Internet Transfer Control

```
' Add for Internet access.
Private Sub Form_Load()
    ' Get a copy of the database if none exists locally.
    If Len(Dir("biblio.mdb")) Then Exit Sub
    Dim bytData() As Byte, iFile As Integer
    inetCopy.RequestTimeout = 0
    bytData = inetCopy.OpenURL("ftp://wombat1/biblio.mdb", icByteArray)
    iFile = FreeFile
    Open "biblio.mdb" For Binary As iFile
    Put iFile, , bytData
    Close iFile
End Sub
```

When the form unloads, the local database is synchronized over the Internet. The Synchronize method's dbRepSyncInternet flag causes the database engine to create a special package file containing only update information. This file is sent to the server which automatically incorporates the changes and negotiates conflicts based on each transaction's time stamp. All this is done with a few lines of code shown in Listing 31.17.

Listing 31.17   InetBiblio.FRM—Synchronizing Changes to a Database Over the Internet

```
Private Sub Form_Unload()
    datPrimaryRS.Database.Synchronize _
      "ftp://wombat1/biblio.mdb", _
      dbRepSyncInternet Or dbRepImpExpChanges
    'This is only needed for multi user apps
    datPrimaryRS.Refresh
End Sub
```

The Internet synchronize process uses optimistic locking. For systems that require a more pessimistic outlook, you can create a remote automation server to handle transactions. You will probably still want a local copy of the database for browsing records, but updates may be sent to the remote object for better concurrency.

Part
IV

Ch
31

Creating Applications that Run on IIS

The Visual Basic Internet applications described in Chapter 28, "Integrating Visual Basic with Mail, Schedule, and Exchange," run on client machines accessing the Internet. To create an application that runs on a server and provides information to clients, use Microsoft Active Server Pages (ASP). ASP is available from Microsoft for free download at **http://www.microsoft.com/iis**.

Active Server Pages are written in HTML syntax and contain VBScript procedures. Unlike ordinary HTML pages, however, the scripts are processed by the server before being sent to the client. Active Server Pages have ready access to data stored on the server through the ADODB object provided with ASP.

N O T E   ASP is a huge improvement over OLEISAPI.DLL, which is used by many to access objects on servers. If you don't know about OLEISAPI.DLL, don't worry; its day has passed. If you are already using OLEISAPI.DLL, congratulations on mastering a difficult task. You'll appreciate the improvements found in ASP. ■

The following code shows an ASP page that retrieves a table of title information from the Biblio.MDB database provided with Visual Basic. Listing 31.18 is based on the ADO1.ASP sample provided with ASP.

Listing 31.18   Biblio.ASP—Retrieving a Database Using Active Server Pages

```
<HTML>
<HEAD>
<TITLE>ActiveX Data Object (ADO)</TITLE>
</HEAD>
<BODY BGCOLOR=#FFFFFF>
```

continues

Listing 31.18   Continued

```
<H3>ActiveX Data Object (ADO)</H3>
<!--#include virtual="/ASPSamp/Samples/adovbs.inc"-->
<%
Set RS = Server.CreateObject("ADODB.RecordSet")
RS.Open "SELECT * FROM Titles", _
   "DATABASE=Pubs; UID=sa;PWD=;DSN=Biblio", _
   adOpenKeySet, _
   adLockBatchOptimistic
%>
<P>
<TABLE BORDER=1>
<TR>
<% For i = 0 to RS.Fields.Count - 1 %>
    <TD><B><% = RS(i).Name %></B></TD>
<% Next %>
</TR>
<% Do While Not RS.EOF %>
    <TR>
    <% For i = 0 to RS.Fields.Count - 1 %>
        <TD VALIGN=TOP><% = RS(i) %></TD>
    <% Next %>
    </TR>
    <%
    RS.MoveNext
Loop
RS.Close
Conn.Close
%>
</TABLE>
<BR>
<BR>
<!—#include virtual="/ASPSamp/Samples/srcform.inc"—>
</BODY>
</HTML>
```

When a client accesses the page Biblio.ASP, the server machine processes the request and then returns a Web page containing a table with all the information.

ASP copies some excellent documentation and samples on your local machine when you install it. The documentation can be found in the /inetsvr/docs/ASPDocs subdirectory of your Windows System32 directory. The samples are installed in your WWW root directory under /ASPSamp/Samples. ASP establishes the aliases /IASDocs and /ASPSamp for these directories with IIS. You must access the documentation and sample files through IIS. Internet Explorer can't view these files using the absolute path. For example, on my machine Wombat1, I use this address to view the documentation roadmap:

http://Wombat1/IASDocs/ASPDocs/roadmap.asp

The rest of this section provides an overview of the objects provided with ASP and shows how to use objects created in Visual Basic from Active Server Pages. See the ASP documentation for more information about programming in VBScript.

Objects Provided with ASP

Active Server Pages can use any ActiveX object that is installed on the server. ASP includes five built-in objects listed in Table 31.1 and about a dozen more objects provided with components installed with ASP. The objects in Table 31.1 are intrinsic within scripts—you refer to them by name as shown here:

```
Application("StoredVariable") = 42
```

Table 31.1   These Objects Are Built-In to ASP and Are Described in the Type Library ASP.DLL

Object	Use to
Application	Create global variables that share information between multiple clients.
Request	Get information from a form field.
Response	Return information to the client as HTML.
Server	Create objects on the server and access other utility methods.
Session	Create session-wide variables that store information for one client.

directly.

To use the objects in Table 31.2 within an Active Server Page, use the CreateObject method with the object's programmatic ID which is shown in parentheses under each object name, as shown here:

```
Set RS = Server.CreateObject("ADODB.RecordSet")
```

Table 31.2   These Objects Are Provided as Components Installed with ASP

Component	Object (ProgID)	Use to
ADROT.DLL	AdRotator (MSWC.AdRotator)	Rotate advertisement images based on a schedule file that determines the order that ads should be displayed.
BROWSCAP.DLL	BrowserType (MSWC.BrowserType)	Determine the capabilities of the client's browser software.
ADODB.DLL	RecordSet (ADODB.RecordSet)	Get a set of data from a database. Get or set a data item from a record set. Field is subordinate to the RecordSet object and is not created directly.
	Field, Fields	
	Property, Properties	Get or set an attribute of a field. Property is subordinate to the Field object and is not created directly.

Part
IV

Ch

31

	Connection (ADODB.Connection)	Open a data source.
	Command	Create a record set and perform batch operations. Command is subordinate to the Connection object and is not created directly.
	Error, Errors	Get the error state of a command. Error is subordinate to the Connection object and is not created directly.
	Parameter, Parameters	Get or set a parameter from a command. Parameter is subordinate to the Command object and is not created directly.
NEXTLINK.DLL (MSWC.NextLink)	NextLink	Determine the order of pages for viewing at a Web site.
SCRRUN.DLL	FileSystemObject (Scripting.FileSystem Object)	Create, open, and close data to files on the server.
	TextStream	Write data to and read data from files on the server. TextStream is subordinate to the FileSystemObject and is not created directly.

Using VB-Created Objects from ASP

You can also use ActiveX objects written in Visual Basic or other languages with an Active Server Page. The Active Server Page Mortgage.ASP uses a modified version of the Mortgage object created in Chapter 28.

Notice that the Mortgage Internet application featured in Chapter 28 runs on the client machine, while Mortgage.ASP does all its processing on the server.

Listing 31.19 shows how to use the CreateObject method to access the Mortgage object from an Active Server Page.

Listing 31.19   Biblio.ASP—Using ActiveX Components from ASP

```
<HTML>
<HEAD><TITLE>VB SE Active Server Page Sample</TITLE></HEAD>
<BODY BGCOLOR=#FFFFFF>
<H3>Calling a VB-Created Object</H3>
<HR>
```

```
<%
On Error Resume Next
%>
    <P>This sample shows how to use the Request collection to get information
    ➥from a posted form.
    <FORM METHOD=POST ACTION="Mortgage.asp">
    <P>Principle: <INPUT TYPE=TEXT SIZE=10 MAXLENGTH=10 NAME="sPrinciple"><BR>
    <P>Rate: <INPUT TYPE=TEXT SIZE=4 MAXLENGTH=4 NAME="sRate"><BR>
    <P>Months: <INPUT TYPE=TEXT SIZE=4 MAXLENGTH=4 NAME="iMonths"><BR>
    </FORM>
<%
    Set objMort = CreateObject("Mortgage.Info")
    temp = objMort.Payment(Request.Form("sPrinciple"), _
        Request.Form("sRate"), _
        Request.Form("iMonths"))
%>

<P>Your payment is: <%=temp%>
<% AmortTable = objMort.AmortTable() %>
<P>Your amortization is as follows:
<%=AmortTable%>
<BR>
<BR>
<!--#include virtual="/ASPSamp/Samples/srcform.inc"-->
</BODY>
</HTML>
```

The Mortgage.Info object referenced in the previous CreateObject method is a version of the Mortage Internet application rewritten to produce HTML output. Since HTML uses table tags instead of tabs, the AmortTable method is modified to produce the correct output, as shown in Listing 31.20.

Listing 31.20   MortInfo.CLS—An ActiveX Component Available to ASP

```
' Mortgage.Info -- MortInfo.Cls
Option Explicit
' Module-level variables.
Dim msPrinciple As Single
Dim msRate As Single
Dim miMonths As Integer
Dim msPayment As Single

Public Function Payment(sPrinciple As Single, sRate As Single, iMonths As
➥Integer)
    ' Calculate the payment
    msPayment = Format(PPmt(sRate / 1200, 1, iMonths, -sPrinciple, 0) + _
        IPmt(sRate / 1200, 1, iMonths, -sPrinciple, 0), "Currency")
    ' Share these variable with Amort
    msPrinciple = sPrinciple
    msRate = sRate
    miMonths = iMonths
```

Part
IV

Ch
31

continues

Listing 31.20   Continued

```
    ' Return the payment.
    Payment = msPayment
End Function

Public Function AmortTable() As String
    Dim Index As Integer
    Dim strAmort As String
    ' Text for column headings.
    strAmort = "<table><tr><td>Month</td><td>Principle</td>" & _
        "<td>Interest</td></tr>"
    ' Write table.
    For Index = 1 To miMonths
        strAmort = strAmort & "<tr><td>" & _
            Index & "</td><td>" & _
            Format(PPmt(msRate / 1200, Index, miMonths, -msPrinciple, 0),
            ➥"Currency") & _
            "</td><td>" & _
            Format(IPmt(msRate / 1200, Index, miMonths, -msPrinciple, 0),
            ➥"Currency") & _
            "</td></tr>"
    Next Index
    ' Return the information.
    AmortTable = strAmort & "</table>"
End Function
```

From Here...

In this chapter, you learned how to use the Internet controls included with Visual Basic. You also learned how to access databases stored on IIS servers using database replication and Active Server Pages.

Active Server Pages can access ActiveX components installed on IIS servers. Visual Basic can create these ActiveX components and also ActiveX *documents* that run on client machines within Internet Explorer. For more information on these and related topics, see the following chapters:

■ Chapter 30, "Creating Internet Application in Visual Basic," describes how to create ActiveX documents that can be loaded from an Internet or intranet site to run on a client machine within Internet Explorer.

■ Chapter 20, "Using Classes to Create Re-usable Components," describes how to create ActiveX components that provide objects to other applications.

Optimization and Advanced Programming Techniques

32 Advanced Control Techniques   759

33 Advanced Form Techniques   787

34 Advanced Code Techniques   809

35 Accessing the Windows API   839

36 Designing Windows Applications   879

CHAPTER 32

Advanced Control Techniques

Controls are the core feature of Visual Basic that makes it a true Rapid Application Development (RAD) tool. The ability to visually lay out the placement of controls is what makes user interface design so easy in Visual Basic, but it's not the only control-related feature that simplifies the life of a Win32 programmer.

This chapter includes several techniques that I use to make the most of controls in Visual Basic. However, there are hundreds more techniques missing. The main purpose of this chapter is to help you think in a new way about the powerful things you can do with ordinary VB controls, and to help you remove your reliance on third-party controls. ■

Use control arrays to simplify your code

We'll show you how to reduce the amount of duplicate code in your applications by using control arrays.

Learn how to master some of the more advanced Windows common controls

You will learn how to write reusable code to simplify the use of the Windows common controls such as the treeview control.

Extend existing controls by modifying window styles and adding hooks

Discover how to add features and events to standard VB controls using the Win32 API.

Using Control Arrays

By now it is likely that you have written several hundred lines of code to deal with controls, but have you ever stopped to see how you could improve this code?

When making optimizations with controls, the first thing you should consider are control arrays. Control arrays give you the power to dynamically add and remove controls at runtime, as well as having one event handler for all of the controls in an array. Since most controls in a control array perform a similar task (such as option buttons), it is quite handy to write a few lines of code that will work with any control in the array.

Menu and Control Array Techniques

The `ControlArray.frm` sample demonstrates some basic techniques of control arrays using labels and menus (yes, menus are controls in VB). This sample loads a menu and label control array with a list of files for a selected directory. Every time the user switches directories, the control array is reset back to its default setting. Figure 32.1 shows a sample of what `ControlArray.frm` looks like after the `cmdBuildArray` button has been clicked for the selected directory.

FIG. 32.1

`ControlArray.frm` demonstrates control array techniques using menus and labels.

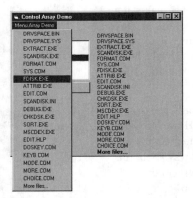

Listing 32.1 shows how to build a dynamic label and menu control array when the user clicks a button.

Listing 32.1   CONTROLARRAY.FRM—The *cmdBuildArray_Click* Event Demonstrates How to Load and Display a Control Array

```
'*********************************************************************
' Builds the control array for the current path in the dir control.
'*********************************************************************
Private Sub cmdBuildArray_Click()
    Dim strFileName As String
    Dim intIndex As Integer
    Dim intNewHeight As Integer
    Static intOrigHeight As Integer
```

```
'******************************************************************
' Get the original height of the form -- once
'******************************************************************
If intOrigHeight = 0 Then
    intOrigHeight = Height
End If
'******************************************************************
' Get the first filename from the path in the dir control
'******************************************************************
strFileName = Dir(dirPath.Path & _
    IIf(Right(dirPath.Path, 1) = "\", "", "\") & "*.*")
'******************************************************************
' Loop while dir is returning files
'******************************************************************
Do While Len(strFileName)
    '**************************************************************
    ' If intIndex > 0, then create a new control under the prev
    '**************************************************************
    If intIndex > 0 Then
        Load lblControlArray(intIndex)
        With lblControlArray(intIndex)
            .Move .Left, lblControlArray(intIndex - 1).Top + _
                lblControlArray(intIndex - 1).Height
            .Visible = True
        End With
        Load mnuArrayItems(intIndex)
        mnuArrayItems(intIndex).Visible = True
    End If
    '**************************************************************
    ' Stop at twenty and let the user know there were 20 files
    '**************************************************************
    If intIndex = 20 Then
        mnuArrayItems(intIndex).Caption = "More files..."
        With lblControlArray(intIndex)
            .Caption = "More files..."
            .Font.Bold = True
        End With
        Exit Do
    '**************************************************************
    ' Otherwise set the caption and find the next file
    '**************************************************************
    Else
        lblControlArray(intIndex) = strFileName
        mnuArrayItems(intIndex).Caption = strFileName
        strFileName = Dir
        If Len(strFileName) Then intIndex = intIndex + 1
    End If
Loop
'******************************************************************
' If the dir was empty, then notify the user in the first label
' and menu
'******************************************************************
If intIndex = 0 Then
    lblControlArray(0) = "No files found!"
    mnuArrayItems(0).Caption = "No files found!"
```

continues

Listing 32.1   Continued

```
'*****************************************************************
' Otherwise, resize the form
'*****************************************************************
Else
        '*****************************************************************
        ' Height of the title bar and border
        '*****************************************************************
        intNewHeight = (Height - ScaleHeight)
        intNewHeight = intNewHeight + lblControlArray(intIndex).Top
        intNewHeight = intNewHeight + lblControlArray(intIndex).Height
    End If
    '*****************************************************************
    ' If the new calculated height > original height, then resize
    '*****************************************************************
    If intNewHeight > intOrigHeight Then
        Height = intNewHeight
    '*****************************************************************
    ' Otherwise resize to the default
    '*****************************************************************
    Else
        Height = intOrigHeight
    End If
    '*****************************************************************
    ' Disable the cmdButton until the user changes directories
    '*****************************************************************
    cmdBuildArray.Enabled = False
End Sub
```

When using control arrays, there are several important concepts to remember. They are:

- You must create the first element of your control array at design time. This can be done quite easily by setting the Index property of your control to 0 (zero).

- Although you can add and remove control arrays at runtime, you can't unload the first element of your control array at runtime. This means you should always check for the first index in the control in loops.

- When new items in the control array are created (using Load) they take on the same properties (Caption, Top, Left, and so on…) as their parent, with one exception. Their Visible property equals False. This gives you the opportunity to change the new control's properties and move it to a new location before displaying it.

- Items cannot be added to a menu control array from a parent menu's Click event. For example, in ControlArray.frm, you can't load new menu items from the mnuArray_Click event.

- Each control in the control array is a separate window as far as Windows is concerned, so don't go overboard. Too many controls on a form can have a significant impact on the performance of your application, so use good judgment. For example, ControlArray.frm is the perfect example of what *not* to do in a "real world" application. A list box would have been more efficient than a control array. However, the purpose of this example is simply to demonstrate control array techniques on an unknown set of variables.

The code in Listing 32.2 demonstrates step 2 (listed previously) about how to shrink the control array without accidentally trying unload the first element.

Listing 32.2   CONTROLARRAY.FRM—*dirPath_Change* Demonstrates How to Unload a Control Array

```
'*********************************************************************
' Unload the control array every time the user changes the directory
'*********************************************************************
Private Sub dirPath_Change()
    Dim ctl As Control
    '*************************************************************
    ' Iterate through the controls collection unloading the labels
    ' and menus
    '*************************************************************
    For Each ctl In Controls
        If ctl.Name = "lblControlArray" Or ctl.Name = _
            "mnuArrayItems" Then
            '*************************************************
            ' If the index > 0 then unload it
            '*************************************************
            If ctl.Index Then Unload ctl
        End If
    Next ctl
    '*************************************************************
    ' Clear the first menu & label and re-enable the command button
    '*************************************************************
    mnuArrayItems(0).Caption = ""
    lblControlArray(0) = ""
    cmdBuildArray.Enabled = True
End Sub
```

The code in the `mnuArrayItems_Click` event following is a simplistic example of how using control arrays for menus can save you from having to write a lot of duplicate code. If you didn't have an array of menu items, the following code would have to appear in 20 separate click events, and you would have to display and hide each menu item based on the selection of dirPath.

```
'*********************************************************************
' Display the menu caption when a menu item is clicked
'*********************************************************************
Private Sub mnuArrayItems_Click(Index As Integer)
    MsgBox mnuArrayItems(Index).Caption, vbInformation
End Sub
```

Can you think of some real world examples of where menu control arrays might be a real code saver? How about a Most Recently Used (MRU) menu? Perhaps the most common application is in the Window menu of an MDI application. The following code was taken from `MDIChild.frm` in the next chapter:

Part

V

Ch

32

```
'*********************************************************************
' If you set your indexes of your Window menu properly, you can save
' yourself some code. I was careful to make sure my Window menu items
' indices were equivalent to the possible values for the Arrange
' method.
'*********************************************************************
Private Sub mnuWindowItems_Click(Index As Integer)
'    MDIParent.Arrange Index
End Sub
```

It is my humble opinion that you should always use control arrays for menus, since it is much more readable to have all of the code for a series of similar menu items (such as the Edit menu items) together.

Another more practical use for control arrays are with option buttons. I'm always amazed to see the complicated maze of code that people create to handle something as simple as option buttons. However, the average VB programmer is either unfamiliar (or uncomfortable) with control arrays, so they don't honestly see a better way to use option buttons. The code in Listing 32.3 demonstrates how easy it is to use control arrays with option buttons.

Option Button Techniques

Listing 32.3 OPTDEMO.FRM—Option Buttons Were Made for Control Arrays

```
'*********************************************************************
' OptDemo.frm - Demonstrates how to use a option button control array
'*********************************************************************
Option Explicit
'*********************************************************************
' Val(<parent frame>).Tag returns the index of the currently selected
' option button. We'll use this information to display the caption of
' the currently selected option button.
'*********************************************************************
Private Sub cmdCurButton_Click()
    Caption = optButtons(Val(fraParent.Tag)).Caption & " is selected!"
End Sub
'*********************************************************************
' Set the value of the initial option button (which fires the click
' event for that index)
'*********************************************************************
Private Sub Form_Load()
    optButtons(0).Value = True
End Sub
'*********************************************************************
' Store the index (or some other useful data) of the currently
' selected option button in the frame containing the option buttons
'*********************************************************************
Private Sub optButtons_Click(Index As Integer)
    optButtons(Index).Container.Tag = CStr(Index)
End Sub
```

In Listing 32.3, you'll notice a couple of neat tricks. The first is that we did not use a global variable to hold the index (or value) of the currently selected option button, but instead we used the `Tag` property of the frame that contains the buttons. Using the `Tag` property saves on memory resources because VB has already allocated memory for the `Tag` property, so why not use it?

The second trick is that we don't perform any actions in the `optButtons_Click` event. Instead, we only make a note (in the container Frame's tag) of which option button is selected. It is usually considered a poor programming practice to perform a specific action in direct response to clicking an option button. Being the good programmers that we are, we defer our "action code" in response to a more appropriate time (such as in response to the click of something like an OK button).

Applying Windows Common Controls Techniques

The common controls are a great feature of Windows 95 and Windows NT 4.0 because they prevent programmers from spending a great deal of time building user interface elements like progress bars and toolbars. They also promote consistency across a wide range of applications, which is a big win for the end-user. However, Microsoft knew that in order for these controls to gain wide acceptance among the development community, these controls would have to support a great amount of flexibility. After all, what good is a common TreeView control if you couldn't add (or remove) pictures? Therefore, Microsoft was careful to include a tremendous amount of frequently requested features in these controls. The disadvantage to this approach is that the controls are a little more difficult to use than controls we grew up with in previous versions of Windows (like the ListBox or TextBox controls).

In this section, I demonstrate how to accomplish some "simple" features that your users expect, using common controls, which aren't quite so simple to use.

Using a Progress Bar in Your Status Bar

Frequently, I have had people ask me how to use a progress bar in the status bar control as many Microsoft applications do. The first time I heard this question I sort of chuckled to myself, because I thought "how hard could it be?" With this in mind, I sat down and proceeded to demonstrate this task, but soon realized that this was not as trivial as I had expected. Figure 32.2 shows that this task can be done.

The major obstacle you face is that the status bar can't be a container for other controls, so you'll have to fake your users into believing that your progress bar control is embedded. This would be an easy task if the status bar stayed in a fixed location, and if it didn't have those darn panels. The `Form_Load` event in Listing 32.4 demonstrates how to initially set up your progress bar and the `Form_Resize` event demonstrates how to make sure your control always stays with its "parent" status bar.

Part

V

Ch

32

FIG. 32.2
Progress Bar Demo -
See, it can be done!

Listing 32.4   PROGDEMO.FRM—Progress Bar Control Demo

```
'****************************************************************
' Sets the initial values and puts controls in place
'****************************************************************
Private Sub Form_Load()
    stbStatus.Panels(2).Alignment = sbrCenter
    '****************************************************************
    ' Set the ScaleMode to pixels so we can type "- 2" below
    '****************************************************************
    ScaleMode = vbPixels
    '****************************************************************
    ' Size the progress bar to the height of the statusbar minus two
    ' pixels, change the appearance to flat, and make sure it has
    ' the highest ZOrder.
    '****************************************************************
    With pbrProgBar
        .Height = stbStatus.Height - 2
        .Appearance = ccFlat
        .ZOrder vbBringToFront
    End With
End Sub
'****************************************************************
' Reposition the progress bar every time the form is sized
'****************************************************************
Private Sub Form_Resize()
    With stbStatus
        pbrProgBar.Move .Panels(1).Left, .Top + 2, .Panels(1).Width
    End With
End Sub
```

The *TreeView* and *ListView* Controls

Now that we've simplified using the progress bar control with the status bar control, let's move on to something a bit more challenging. How about those controls you'd love to have in all your apps, but are too frustrated to use. Yes, I'm talking about the dreaded TreeView and ListView controls.

The Treeview control is the most fantastic control included in the common controls provided by Windows because it does a great job of displaying complex tree structures in a way that is easy for users to understand. It's also great because it saves you from having to implement this complex control yourself! However, the downfall is that because this control is responsible for displaying complex data, it requires a complex set of features to accomplish this task. The listview control is the same way. They are further complicated by the fact that the folks in Redmond went a little overboard with the object-oriented structure of this control. This means that sometimes simple tasks (such as adding or clearing items) are a lot more complex than they need to be.

The first thing you need to do is prepare your controls by adding a root node to the treeview control, and your column headers to the listview control. In our example, we will be creating a simple registry program. Yes, I know this is another technology that strikes fear into new VB programmers, but hopefully you will learn how to master both of these beasts through this example. Registry.vbp, shown in Figure 32.3, demonstrates our registry program in action.

FIG. 32.3

Registry.vbp demonstrates a good use of the TreeView and ListView controls.

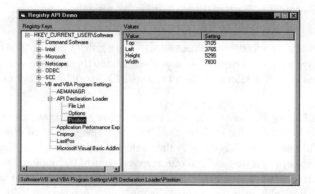

Listing 32.5 begins by creating the root node by adding a new element to the Nodes collection of the treeRegistry control. Next, we load our child nodes by using a helper routine called BuildTree (discussed later). Finally, we add our listview headers by adding new elements to the ColumnHeaders collection of the lvwRegistry control.

Listing 32.5   REGISTRY.FRM—Setting Up the *TreeView* and *ListView* Controls

```
'*********************************************************************
' Create the node, load the initial subkeys and set the column headers
'*********************************************************************
Private Sub Form_Load()
    '*************************************************************
    ' Create the root node
    '*************************************************************
    Dim nodRoot As Node
    Set nodRoot = treRegistry.Nodes.Add( , , , _
        "HKEY_CURRENT_USER\Software")
    '*************************************************************
    ' Add the initial subkeys from "HKEY_CURRENT_USER\Software"
    '*************************************************************
    BuildTree nodRoot, HKEY_CURRENT_USER, "Software"
    '*************************************************************
    ' Add the list view column headers
    '*************************************************************
    Dim clmHeader As ColumnHeader
    Set clmHeader = lvwRegistry.ColumnHeaders.Add( , , "Value", _
```

continues

Listing 32.5 Continued

```
        lvwRegistry.Width / 2.5)
    Set clmHeader = lvwRegistry.ColumnHeaders.Add(, , "Setting", _
        (lvwRegistry.Width - clmHeader.Width) - 45)
End Sub
```

That wasn't too bad, but the real work in Listing 32.6 is done in the BuildTree procedure. Next, we'll discuss how to load the treeview and listview controls using the BuildTree and LoadListItems routines. Both of these routines use a similar technique, but are quite different due to the structure of the controls.

The *BuildTree* and *LoadListItems* Procedures Take a deep breath. The code samples for these controls are a little complex, but if you single step through the BuildTree and LoadListItems shown in Listing 32.6 and Listing 32.7, you'll have a better idea of how to use these beasts.

BuildTree, in Listing 32.6, takes a parent node, a subkey string (such as Microsoft\Office), and loads the child keys from that registry item into the treeview control. However, the hard part is getting the child keys, which is done by the GetRegKeys function. This function returns a variant array of subkeys that we load into our treeview control by looping through the array. Examine the following code (or single step through Registry.frm) to see what is really happening in this code. For now, skip over the GetRegKeys function, since we won't discuss that function until a later chapter.

Listing 32.6 REGISTRY.FRM— *BuildTree* Loads Subkeys from a Variant Array

```
'******************************************************************
' Loads the subkeys of a registry key into the treRegistry control
'******************************************************************
Sub BuildTree(nodRoot As Node, HKEY As Long, strSubKey As String)
    Dim i As Integer
    Dim vntArray As Variant
    '******************************************************************
    ' You must declare a node in order to create a new node
    '******************************************************************
    Dim nodNewItem As Node
    With treRegistry
        '******************************************************************
        ' Set the tag to the full path less the hKey string
        '******************************************************************
        nodRoot.Tag = strSubKey
        '******************************************************************
        ' Get the keys to add to the tree
        '******************************************************************
        vntArray = GetRegKeys(HKEY, strSubKey)
        '******************************************************************
        ' Add the child keys to the registry
        '******************************************************************
        For i = LBound(vntArray) To UBound(vntArray)
```

```
            Set nodNewItem = .Nodes.Add(nodRoot, tvwChild, strSubKey _
                & "\" & vntArray(i), vntArray(i))
        Next i
    End With
    '****************************************************************
    ' Sort the node
    '****************************************************************
    nodRoot.Sorted = True
End Sub
```

Notice that for each item in the array we add a new node by simply adding a new element to the Nodes collection of the treeRegistry control, as we did earlier for our root node. Once we have finished loading our child notes, we sort them by setting the sorted property of the parent (or root) node to True.

In Listing 32.7, we use a similar technique. GetRegKeyValues returns the values of the registry key passed in using the HKEY and strKey parameters. Since we only show the values for the given key, we start by clearing out any existing list items using the Clear method. Next, we load the list from the array as we did earlier, with one exception. GetRegKeyValues returns a multidimensional array that contains a value and setting. What we will do is put the first dimension in the value column when the new ListItems element is added to the collection, then we'll put the setting in the settings column using the SubItems member of the collection.

Listing 32.7 REGISTRY.FRM—*LoadListItems* Loads a *ListView* Control from a Variant Array

```
'****************************************************************
' Loads the values for a key into into lstRegistry
'****************************************************************
Private Sub LoadListItems(HKEY As Long, strKey As String)
    Dim i As Integer
    Dim vntArray As Variant
    Dim itmNewItem As ListItem
    With lvwRegistry.ListItems
        '****************************************************************
        ' Always clear the list before reloading
        '****************************************************************
        .Clear
        '****************************************************************
        ' Don't stop for errors
        '****************************************************************
        On Error Resume Next
        '****************************************************************
        ' Get the values and settings
        '****************************************************************
        vntArray = GetRegKeyValues(HKEY, strKey)
        '****************************************************************
        ' If any error besides ERRBASE + 5 occured, then tell the user
        '****************************************************************
        If Err.Number And Err.Number <> ERRBASE + 5 Then
```

Part

V

Ch

32

continues

Listing 32.7   Continued

```
            MsgBox Err.Description, vbExclamation, Err.Source
            Err.Clear
            Exit Sub
        End If
    '*****************************************************************
    ' If here, then values were found so load them in the list
    '*****************************************************************
    For i = LBound(vntArray, 1) To UBound(vntArray, 1)
        '*************************************************************
        ' If the value = 0 then its the default value
        '*************************************************************
        If vntArray(i, 0) = "" Then vntArray(i, 0) = "(Default)"
        '*************************************************************
        ' Add the value to the list
        '*************************************************************
        Set itmNewItem = .Add(, , vntArray(i, 0))
        '*************************************************************
        ' Put the setting for the value in the settings column
        '*************************************************************
        itmNewItem.SubItems(1) = vntArray(i, 1)
    Next i
    End With
    '*****************************************************************
    ' Sort the newly added values (make sure lvwRegistry.Sorted = True)
    '*****************************************************************
    lvwRegistry.SortKey = 1
End Sub
```

Again, you'll notice that we sort the listview similar to the way we sorted the treeview control. You add all of your items, *then* you set the SortKey property equal to the key you want to sort. Now that you have seen *how* we load the keys into these controls, let's look at a couple routines that use this code.

Populating Controls in Response to an Event   When I first learned to program in Windows (version 3.0), one of the controls I liked most was the listbox control. It's a great control for displaying a list of information, so I frequently included it in my programs. I quickly learned that it was a good idea to load these controls with all of their data in the *Form_Load* event, so the user would never see my program adding items to the list. After all, loading the list in advance didn't slow down my app that much, and once the app was loaded, the user never had to wait for these lists to be populated. However, when I first used the treeview control, I made the mistake of treating it like a listbox. That is, I loaded all of the keys during the Form_Load event. For small applications, this wasn't a problem, but when I tried this with the registry, it took my form over a minute to load!

Shocked by this, I began to wonder how my app could be so slow compared the regedit.exe. Then it hit me; why am I loading *all* of the keys in advance? Why not just load the top-level keys, and load the others as needed? After all, most subkeys don't contain more than about 20 keys, so the keys should be loaded so fast that the user couldn't even see them being loaded.

After making some modifications to my program, I found that my theory was correct. Delayed loading helped my program to start faster, and loading subkeys on demand was so fast (even on a 486SX), that there was no reason for me not to do it. Now I had an optimized program that only displayed the keys that were of interest to the user, so a lot of unnecessary calls to Nodes.Add were eliminated.

Anytime you use the treeview control in your app, always keep this lesson in mind. Make sure you are only loading the top-level keys. Unless you have a large number of items under your top-level keys, you shouldn't waste time loading them. Listing 32.8 shows how I implemented this delayed loading in `Registry.vbp`.

Listing 32.8   REGISTRY.FRM—Responding to Node *Click* Events

```
'*********************************************************************
' Load the subkeys and settings (if necessary) when a node is clicked
'*********************************************************************
Private Sub treRegistry_NodeClick(ByVal Node As ComctlLib.Node)
    Dim strSubKeyPath As String
    '*********************************************************************
    ' Add the subkeys (if any) when a node is clicked
    '*********************************************************************
    LoadSubKeys Node
    '*********************************************************************
    ' Get the subkey path from the tag
    '*********************************************************************
    strSubKeyPath = Node.Tag
    '*********************************************************************
    ' If there is a backslash in the node tag, then...
    '*********************************************************************
    If InStr(strSubKeyPath, "\") Then
        '*********************************************************************
        ' Load the values for the selected node
        '*********************************************************************
        LoadListItems HKEY_CURRENT_USER, strSubKeyPath
        '*********************************************************************
        ' Put the subkey path in the status bar
        '*********************************************************************
        StatusBar.Panels(1) = strSubKeyPath
    '*********************************************************************
    ' Otherwise the selected node is the root
    '*********************************************************************
    Else
        StatusBar.Panels(1) = Node
    End If
End Sub
```

Part
V

Ch
32

When the user clicks a node, I first load the subkeys for the selected node. This happens quickly, so it gives the user something to look at while I'm loading the values and settings for the selected key. This strategy helps the user to perceive that my application is fast, even if I have to load a large number of settings and values. After all, users want something to happen immediately when they click a node, so that is what we give them.

Another optimization occurs in the LoadSubKeys routine. This code loads only the subkeys, if they haven't already been loaded. It does this by checking to see if any text appears in the tag for the current node. I do this because BuildTree assigns a value to the tag property of the parent node when it finishes loading the child keys. If the keys need to be loaded, I extract the subkey path and load the child keys.

Listing 32.9   REGISTRY.FRM—Loading Subkeys in a *TreeView* Control

```
'*********************************************************************
' Checks to see if the subkeys need to be loaded. If they do, then
' this routine builds the appropriate parameters for BuildTree and
' calls that function to load the subkeys into treRegistry.
'*********************************************************************
Private Sub LoadSubKeys(nodCurrent As Node)
    Dim strSubKeyPath As String
    Dim intWhere As Integer
    '*********************************************************************
    ' If the current node has already been loaded, then exit
    '*********************************************************************
    If Len(nodCurrent.Tag) Then Exit Sub
    '*********************************************************************
    ' Get the path of the current node
    '*********************************************************************
    strSubKeyPath = nodCurrent.FullPath
    '*********************************************************************
    ' Locate the first backslash
    '*********************************************************************
    intWhere = InStr(strSubKeyPath, "\")
    '*********************************************************************
    ' Modify strSubKeyPath to NOT include HKEY_CURRENT_USER\
    '*********************************************************************
    strSubKeyPath = Mid(strSubKeyPath, intWhere + 1)
    '*********************************************************************
    ' Don't stop for errors
    '*********************************************************************
    On Error Resume Next
    '*********************************************************************
    ' Add all of the child keys that are under the current node
    '*********************************************************************
    BuildTree nodCurrent, HKEY_CURRENT_USER, strSubKeyPath
    '*********************************************************************
    ' If any error besides ERRBASE + 5 occured, then tell the user
    '*********************************************************************
    If Err.Number And Err.Number <> ERRBASE + 5 Then
        MsgBox Err.Description, vbExclamation, Err.Source
        Err.Clear
    End If
End Sub
```

One disadvantage to this optimization is that if the user adds a new child key *after* I've loaded my list, then they don't see the new child key in my treeview control. However, this is an acceptable shortcoming because it would be too inefficient to constantly reload these children keys all of the time. A more realistic feature would be to either force the user to reload manually (as regedit.exe in Win95 does), or to flag the node to be refreshed at a user-defined interval (say every minute).

Now that you have had a chance to learn more about a couple of the Windows common controls, I suggest you experiment with some of the other controls not discussed here. Consider writing reusable code to help simplify common tasks with these controls, as we did with BuildTree. Another suggestion would be to create a new version of BuildTree so that it works with any type of key (such as files or database structures), not just registry keys. Maybe create a set of routines to simplify building a toolbar. The most important thing is to look at the complex aspects of these controls as a challenge to write great reusable code, but try to have fun while you're doing it.

Writing Frankentrols

By now, you have certainly run into some limitations with some of the controls in Visual Basic that have forced you to purchase third-party controls. If so, you've probably also been frustrated by the reliability and distribution nightmares associated with these controls. Have you ever wished that you could just add one or two minor features to a standard Visual Basic control, so you didn't have to depend on less reliable OCXs? If so, then this section is for you.

I'm a firm believer that you can and should do as much programming in VB without a dependency on external controls. That is not to say that I have anything against third-party controls. It's just that I feel more comfortable writing the code myself. That way, if something goes wrong, I don't have to wait for the next bug-fix release to come out. I also don't have to worry about my users having the correct version of the control installed on their machine. The way I get around this problem is to use the Windows API to modify the standard VB controls to include the features I want, but Microsoft left out. I call these controls *Frankentrols* (derived from Frankenstein Controls).

Visual Basic 5.0's addition of the AddressOf operator allows you to enhance your controls like never before (as shown in Figure 32.4). You can finally write a callback function that allows you to intercept messages being sent to a window, so you can have an opportunity to respond to events that standard VB controls do not expose. Like always, you can also use the Win32 APIs to enhance the appearance of standard controls by adding or removing style bits to and from any control. WndLong.vbp demonstrates some of these techniques by demonstrating how to transform an ordinary picturebox control into a movable sizable child window that supports drag and drop from Explorer.

FIG. 32.4
Once a picture box, now
a Frankentrol—It's Alive!

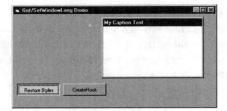

Brief Window Styles Background Information

Behind the scenes when you run your VB application, VB creates all of the controls on your form using the properties you set at design time. Many of these properties are more readable names for the window styles VB passes to the `CreateWindow` Win32 API call. Most of the VB names are similar to their Win32 equivalents. For example, the `Border` and `ClipControls` properties are called WS_BORDER and WS_CLIPCHILDREN, respectively. Others aren't so obvious. For example, WS_THICKFRAME in the Win32 API is equivalent to setting the `Borderstyle` property of a form to `Sizable`. This can make the process of figuring out which styles you need to accomplish a given task a little more difficult, but not impossible. The best ways to figure out which styles you need to accomplish a given task are:

- Use the Find Window feature in Spyxx.exe (included in the tools directory on the VB5 CD) and view the Styles tab to see what styles are applied to a specific window.

- Look in the Win32 API reference help file under the topics of `CreateWindow` and `CreateWindowsEx`. These topics describe each style in detail.

It is beyond the scope of this book to discuss all of the details of Windows styles. However, additional information on this topic can be found in the *Microsoft Developer's Network Library* and in *Visual Basic Programmer's Guide to the Win32 API* by Daniel Appleman.

Adding New Styles to a Control

To change the style bits of a control, you need to use the `SetWindowLong` Win32 API call. However, you should only append your new style to the existing styles of a control; otherwise, you will have to include all of the styles you want to use in your `SetWindowLong` call. You can find out what the current styles are for a given control by using `GetWindowsLong`.

Once you have the existing styles, you should append your styles by using the `Or` operator with each style you want to append. You can also toggle a style by using the `Xor` operator. The `UpdateStyle` routine shown in Listing 32.10 is a helper routine that allows you append or toggle the standard and extended styles of control.

Listing 32.10 WNDLONG.BAS—*UpdateStyle* Changes the Appearance of Your Controls

```
'**********************************************************************
' Allows you to update the sytles of window AFTER a window has been
```

```
' created. However, the caller is responsible for testing to see
' if there are any negative side effects of doing this.
'*******************************************************************
Public Sub UpdateStyle(ctl As Control, ByVal lngNewStyles As Long, _
    Optional blnExtended As Boolean, Optional blnToggle As Boolean)
    '*******************************************************************
    ' Predefine the Win32 constants required to change style bits
    '*******************************************************************
    Const GWL_STYLE = (-16)
    Const GWL_EXSTYLE = (-20)
    '*******************************************************************
    ' Variables
    '*******************************************************************
    Dim lngGWLType As Long        'Extended or Standard style bits?
    Dim lngOrigStyle As Long      'Get's the original style so Gets
                                  'changes can be ADDED to the existing
                                  'styles.
    '*******************************************************************
    ' Find out which bits should be modified
    '*******************************************************************
    lngGWLType = IIf(blnExtended, GWL_EXSTYLE, GWL_STYLE)
    '*******************************************************************
    ' Get the current bits
    '*******************************************************************
    lngOrigStyle = GetWindowLong(ctl.hWnd, lngGWLType)
    '*******************************************************************
    ' Xor toggles, so if the bits are set the will be cleared. If they
    ' are cleared, then they will be set.
    '*******************************************************************
    If blnToggle Then
        lngNewStyles = lngOrigStyle Xor lngNewStyles
    '*******************************************************************
    ' Or always sets the bits
    '*******************************************************************
    Else
        lngNewStyles = lngOrigStyle Or lngNewStyles
    End If
    '*******************************************************************
    ' Peform the requsted changes
    '*******************************************************************
    SetWindowLong ctl.hWnd, lngGWLType, lngNewStyles
    '*******************************************************************
    ' Raise a custom error if this call fails
    '*******************************************************************
    If Err.LastDllError Then
        Err.Raise ERRUPDATESTYLE, "UpdateStyle", CStr(Err.LastDllError)
    End If
    '*******************************************************************
    ' VB won't display changes from UpdateStyle properly using the
    ' InvalidateRect or UpdateWindow APIs, so we have to resize the
    ' control to reflect the changes.  Therefore, we will use this
    ' variable to restore the control to its original size.
    '*******************************************************************
    Dim sngOrigWidth As Single
```

Part

V

Ch

32

continues

Listing 32.10   Continued

```
'****************************************************************
' This is a VERY ugly hack, but it's the only reliable method I
' could find to make sure the window was updated properly. This
' code resizes the control, then restores it back to its original
' size.
'****************************************************************
With ctl
    sngOrigWidth = .Width
    .Width = .Width + .ScaleX(10, .Container.ScaleMode, vbTwips)
    .Width = sngOrigWidth
End With
End Sub
```

Although the code for UpdateStyle appears to be long, it is straightforward. Simply get the existing style using GetWindowLong, and append or toggle the new style using SetWindow-Long. If SetWindowLong fails, then raise an error, otherwise refresh the control to display the changes.

Listing 32.11 demonstrates how to toggle a sizable border and caption to a picture box using UpdateStyle with standard styles, as well as how to toggle the WS_EX_ACCEPTFILES extended style. This code is designed to toggle the styles when the check box control is checked, and to restore the control to its previous state when the check is cleared.

Listing 32.11   WNDLONG.FRM—The *chkStyle_Click* Event Demonstrates How to Use *UpdateStyle*

```
'****************************************************************
' Demonstrates how to use UpdateStyle
'****************************************************************
Private Sub chkStyle_Click()
    '****************************************************************
    ' Win32 constants used by this event. WS_EX_ACCEPTFILES is already
    ' defined in basYourCode with the other drag & drop API calls, but
    ' you could just declare it here if you prefer.
    '****************************************************************
    Const WS_BORDER = &H800000
    Const WS_CAPTION = &HC00000
    Const WS_THICKFRAME = &H40000
    '****************************************************************
    ' Toggle these styles on each call
    '****************************************************************
    UpdateStyle picWnd, WS_THICKFRAME, False, True
    UpdateStyle picWnd, WS_EX_ACCEPTFILES, True, True
    '****************************************************************
    ' Toggles the active state of picWnd. This means that if chkStyle
    ' is checked, picWnd's caption will appear the same as any other
    ' active window.
    '****************************************************************
    FlashWindow picWnd.hwnd, True
```

```
    '********************************************************************
    ' If chkStyle is checked then add a caption to picWnd and update
    ' chkStyle.Caption
    '********************************************************************
    If chkStyle Then
        UpdateStyle picWnd, WS_CAPTION
        chkStyle.Caption = "Restore Styles"
        '****************************************************************
        ' This is required to put text into picWnd's new caption
        '****************************************************************
        SetWindowText picWnd.hwnd, "My Caption Text"
    '********************************************************************
    ' Otherwise restore everything back to normal
    '********************************************************************
    Else
        UpdateStyle picWnd, WS_CAPTION, , True
        UpdateStyle picWnd, WS_BORDER
        chkStyle.Caption = "UpdateStyle"
    End If
End Sub
```

In addition, two API calls are used, `FlashWindow` and `SetWindowText`. Since VB never intended a picture box to have a title bar, we need to make the picture box look like an active window and give it a caption. We use these APIs to accomplish this task, but this brings up an important point. Although `UpdateStyles` shows you how to apply new styles, you may still have to find the API call(s) to "set" the value(s) of the newly applied style (such as the caption in this example). With this in mind, it's always a good idea to have the Win32 help file available when working with styles.

Callbacks and Function Pointers Explained

While UpdateStyle offers some neat ways to extend your controls, using Get/SetWindowLong is nothing new to VB programming. However, there is much more that we can do to our Frankentrols using Win32 callbacks. Although an advanced discussion about callbacks and event handling in Windows is beyond the scope of this book, I'll discuss a few basic concepts that are essential to understanding the remaining material in this chapter.

A callback is a windows term for a function pointer. A function pointer can be thought of as a variable that refers to a function instead of some value. This implies that you can use function pointers the same way you use variables, which is mostly true. The difference is that when you pass a variable to a function, your purpose is to provide input for some given task or calculation. However, when you use a function pointer, the purpose is to tell the function you are calling to execute a given function.

For example, say you were writing some generic function called `Sort`. The main purpose of `Sort` is to sort an array of values of any data type. Two of the fundamental features of any sort routine are the ability to swap and compare values. This means that `Sort` would need to know how to swap and compare your data. Since the way you swap and compare a user-defined type is different from the way you swap and compare an integer, you would need special functions called `Swap` and `Compare` to handle different data types.

Part

V

Ch

32

This means that if you want your sort code to apply to arrays of any type, you would need to have a way to "tell" Sort which version of Swap and Compare to use. The way you accomplish this is by using function pointers. For example, the following pseudo code (this means that this code won't work in VB) shows how Sort might work with function pointers:

```
Function Sort(anyArray() As Any, Swap As Function, Compare As Function)
Function SwapIntegers(...)
Function SwapRectangles(...)
Function CompareIntegers(...)
Function ComparRectangles(...)
Sub Foo()
    Dim r(5) As RECT
    Dim i(5) As Integer
    LoadIntAndRectArrays r, i
    Sort r, AddressOf SwapRectangles, AddressOf CompareRectangles
    Sort i, AddressOf SwapIntegers, AddressOf CompareIntegers
    PrintResults r, i
End Sub
```

By using function pointers, we can use the same Sort function with both integers and rectangles because we provided a pointer to functions that can compare and swap these data types. This eliminates the need for us to write special functions called SortRectangles and Sort-Integers in addition to our special Swap and Compare functions.

Although it would be great if we could do everything listed in the previous pseudo code using VB5, we can't. VB5 allows us to use the AddressOf operator to pass a pointer to a function that is defined in a BAS module only. What's more, VB5 doesn't give us a way to use the function pointer in VB code to call our function pointer. This means that function pointers are only useful with API calls. This leads me back to where we started, which were Win32 callbacks.

Many APIs in Win32 perform some task where the caller might want to perform some special action during the execution of the call. One such task is a Win32 callback called Enum-Windows. EnumWindows is called by passing in a function pointer and an optional argument. After you make this call, Windows enumerates through all of the currently loaded Windows. During this enumeration, Windows "calls" the function you passed in as the first argument to EnumWindows each time it finds a new window. This gives your program the opportunity to do some specific task (such as printing a list of loaded windows) with all of the windows it finds. This is a classic case of a callback because Windows "calls" your function during the execution of an API call.

Now that you have a better understanding of callbacks, it's time to describe the most important callback in Windows programming—the WndProc (or Windows Procedure). The WndProc is a special function pointer given to windows at the time a window is created that tells Windows where your "event handling" code is located. This way, every time Windows gets an event for your window, it can call your custom WndProc so that your program can respond to that event.

In VB, the WndProc isn't exposed directly, but you use it everyday. Events in VB such as the Form_Load or Click events, are all events that reside in the WndProc. VB just does a good job at hiding the messy details from you. However, it is during the process of "hiding the messy details" that VB exposes some shortcomings for the sake of simplicity. While this makes VB easy to use initially, it can make VB a little more complicated when you decide you want to respond to an event that VB hasn't exposed to you. To get to this hidden code you must give a control or form a new WndProc that points to your new WndProc. In addition, your code, must call the original WndProc so that the control or form has the opportunity to execute its default behavior (such as executing code in exposed events like the Click event).

The concept of giving a window a new WndProc is called subclassing or hooking. There are subtle differences between the two terms, but for this discussion, I will use them interchangeably. Subclassing gives you the control to intercept all windows messages sent to a window, and optionally respond to these messages. Your response could be one of the following:

- Ignore the message and pass it along to the original WndProc
- Intercept the message, perform a special task, and then pass it along to the original WndProc
- Intercept the message and prevent the original WndProc from responding to it by not calling the original WndProc

The last alternative is the most dangerous, because VB might have some internal code that does some internal action in response to a message that you intercept. If you prevented that message from being processed by its original WndProc, odd behavior or even a GPF could result. Therefore, it is recommended that you use great caution when using the code we are about to discuss.

Windows Hooks in Pure VB

The code discussed in this section comes from two modules. The first module, called WndLong.bas, contains some reusable code for hooking and unhooking a single window in your application. This code assumes that you have a Public callback function called WndProc defined in a Visual Basic module. The second module, called YourCode.bas, contains your callback and code specific to your hook implementation. This code is resuable only for adding Explorer drag-and-drop support to a window, and it requires that WndLong.bas (or an equivalent) is loaded in your project.

CreateHook* and *Unhook   CreateHook is used to create a hook for a given window. It uses SetWindowsLong with the GWL_WNDPROC flag to establish the hook, and it uses GetWindowsLong to retain a pointer to the original WndProc. The concept of creating a hook using Get/SetWindowsLong isn't much different than changing the style of a window as we did earlier in UpdateStyle. The major difference is that we must pass a pointer to a callback function when creating the hook, and we must restore the original WndProc (or Unhook) before terminating our application. If you fail to unhook a hooked window, a GPF will occur.

> **WARNING**
>
> WndLong.bas uses SetWindowsLong to demonstrate the basic concept of hooking a window. However, this method doesn't support multiple hooks, and is subject to crashing your application if more than one hook is created on a single window. Therefore, you should use the SetWindowsHookEx in your application.

Part
V

Ch
32

The best way to understand how CreateHook and Unhook work is to read the comments and examine the code in Listing 32.12. This code has been commented to explain each line of code, so be sure to read each line carefully.

Listing 32.12   *WNDLONG.BAS*—WndLong.bas Defines Your Hook Routines, *CreateHook* and *Unhook*

```
'*********************************************************************
' Constants and API declarations required for G/SetWindowLong and
' subclassing.
'*********************************************************************
Private Const GWL_WNDPROC = (-4)

Private Declare Function GetWindowLong Lib "user32" Alias _
    "GetWindowLongA" (ByVal hWnd&, ByVal nIndex As Long) As Long

Private Declare Function SetWindowLong Lib "user32" Alias _
    "SetWindowLongA" (ByVal hWnd As Long, ByVal nIndex As Long, _
    ByVal dwNewLong As Long) As Long

Public Declare Function CallWindowProc Lib "user32" Alias _
    "CallWindowProcA" (ByVal lpPrevWndFunc As Long, ByVal hWnd&, _
    ByVal Msg As Long, ByVal wParam As Long, lParam As Long) As Long
'*********************************************************************
' Pointers to the original WndProc and window handle of the hooked
' window
'*********************************************************************
Private mlngPrevWndProc As Long
Private mhWnd As Long
'*********************************************************************
' Custom error constant for UpdateStyle
'*********************************************************************
Public Const ERRUPDATESTYLE = vbObjectError + 5000
'*********************************************************************
' Never expose your private data members for write access, so return
' requests for the original WndProc as a read-only property
'*********************************************************************
Public Property Get OriginalWndProc() As Long
    OriginalWndProc = mlngPrevWndProc
End Property
'*********************************************************************
' Subclasses (or Hook's) a window
'*********************************************************************
Public Function CreateHook(hWnd As Long) As Boolean
    '*********************************************************************
    ' For simplicity's sake, CreateHook doesn't support multiple hooks,
    ' so we should make sure a hook doesn't already exist
    '*********************************************************************
    If mlngPrevWndProc Then
        MsgBox "CreateHook doesn't support multiple hooks!", vbCritical
        Exit Function
    End If
    '*********************************************************************
    ' Get and store the address of the current WndProc for hWnd
```

```
'*********************************************************************
mlngPrevWndProc = GetWindowLong(hWnd, GWL_WNDPROC)
'*********************************************************************
' If we couldn't get the address of the current WndProc, then
' reset mlngPrevWndProc and Assert
'*********************************************************************
If Err.LastDllError Then
    mlngPrevWndProc = 0
    Debug.Assert False
    Exit Function
End If
'*********************************************************************
' Create the hook. This code assumes you have a public function
' called WndProc that exists in another module, but CreateHook
' should have a long parameter that contains the address of your
' custom WndProc. For clarity's sake, I have hard-coded this value.
'*********************************************************************
SetWindowLong hWnd, GWL_WNDPROC, AddressOf WndProc
'*********************************************************************
' If the hook failed, then Assert
'*********************************************************************
If Err.LastDllError Then
    Debug.Assert False
'*********************************************************************
' If you got here, then everything worked so return true
'*********************************************************************
Else
    mhWnd = hWnd
    CreateHook = True
    Debug.Print "Hooked!"
End If
End Function
'*********************************************************************
' Restores the WndProc of a window to its original WndProc
'*********************************************************************
Public Sub Unhook()
    '*********************************************************************
    ' If no hook exists, then exit immediately
    '*********************************************************************
    If mlngPrevWndProc = 0 Then Exit Sub
    '*********************************************************************
    ' Restore the original WndProc
    '*********************************************************************
    SetWindowLong mhWnd, GWL_WNDPROC, mlngPrevWndProc
    '*********************************************************************
    ' If this action failed, then Assert (and prepare for a GPF)
    '*********************************************************************
    If Err.LastDllError Then
        Debug.Assert False
    '*********************************************************************
    ' Otherwise print Unhook in the immediate pane
    '*********************************************************************
    Else
        Debug.Print "UnHooked!"
    End If
End Sub
```

You'll notice that both CreateHook and Unhook both assert if an error occurs and print status messages to the immediate pane when everything works properly. This is useful only when you are debugging your application in the VB environment. In an EXE, a failure in your hook code will likely results in a GPF, so error messages aren't of much use. Keep this in mind when you are developing your own hook applications.

> **WARNING**
>
> NEVER use the stop button on the VB toolbar to end your program while you have open hooks. The stop program ends your program immediately, which prevents any cleanup code you may have to Unhook your window. Terminating a program without unhooking first will crash your app and VB.EXE.

The code in Listing 32.13 shows how to use CreateHook and Unhook in a check box control. If the chkHook is checked, then the hook is created. If it is unchecked, then picWnd is "unhooked."

Listing 32.13   WNDLONG.FRM—The *chkHook_Click* Event Shows How to Use *CreateHook* and *Unhook*

```
'**********************************************************************
' Demonstrates how to use CreateHook and Unhook
'**********************************************************************
Private Sub chkHook_Click()
    '**********************************************************************
    ' If hooked, then update chkHook.Caption
    '**********************************************************************
    If chkHook Then
      chkHook.Caption = IIf(CreateHook(picWnd.hwnd), "Unhook", "Fail")
    '**********************************************************************
    ' Otherwise restore chkHook.Caption
    '**********************************************************************
    Else
      Unhook
      chkHook.Caption = "CreateHook"
    End If
End Sub
'**********************************************************************
' If there is an open hook, you had better Unhook before closing or else
' you crash.
'**********************************************************************
Private Sub Form_Unload(Cancel As Integer)
    If chkHook Then Unhook
End Sub
```

As an extra safety precaution, the Form_Unload event (shown previously in Listing 32.13), makes sure to Unhook picWnd if it is still hooked when the user tries to end the program. You should always include this very important feature in your applications that use hooks. Remember that ending a program with an open hook will result in a GPF.

Implementing Explorer Drag and Drop in Your Custom Hook   Now that you know how to create a hook, you have to write some cool code to do something while you are hooked. One idea is to add support for Drag & Drop to your hooked control. In YourCode.bas, we'll intercept the WM_DROPFILES message and load a global array with the files dropped on our hooked control. We'll also force our picture box control to repaint itself, so it can display a list of the files that were dropped on it (from its Paint event). Figure 32.5 shows our Frankentrol, picWnd, after files have been dropped on it from Explorer.

FIG. 32.5

picWnd after files have been dropped on it from Explorer.

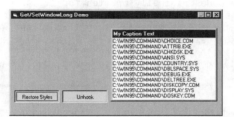

Listing 32.14 shows what our custom WndProc looks like. The most important part of this code lies in the actual declaration of our WndProc. Our WndProc takes a window handle (Long), a message (Long), a long value or wParam, and a pointer in the lParam (Long). The first three parameters are safe to use with VB. The last parameter, the lParam, is a little more dangerous because this parameter can contain a pointer to anything. It could be a string, a numeral, a structure, or even a function pointer. You don't know what it will be unless you look it up in the Win32 API. What's more, you can't treat it like any specific data type other than a pointer, because you could corrupt this value when passing it to CallWindowProc. For example, if you knew that the lParam was a string when Msg = x, and you wrote your WndProc to be ByVal lParam As String. Since VB would convert this pointer into to a string for you, that would corrupt this value before you had a chance to pass it through to CallWindowProc. Therefore, I recommend you always treat this parameter as a pointer, and rely on code elsewhere in your program to make use of this pointer. In addition, always pass it by reference and not by value. Passing it in ByVal dereferences this pointer, which again causes you to send invalid data to your CallWindowProc.

Listing 32.14   YOURCODE.BAS— *WndProc* is an Example of a Typical Custom *WndProc* Function

```
Public Function WndProc(ByVal hWnd&, ByVal Msg&, ByVal wParam&, _
    lParam As Long) As Long
    '****************************************************************
    ' All messages are longs, but are referred to by their predefined
    ' #defines in the API docs. It's usually a good idea to mimic
    ' these defines in your code as Consts. In this case we will be
    ' intercepting the WM_DROPFILES message, so we should predefine
    ' it somewhere in this module.
    '****************************************************************
    Const WM_DROPFILES = &H233
```

continues

Listing 32.14   Continued

```
'*********************************************************************
' If the current message is WM_DROPFILES we will call a helper
' routine that will do something with this message.
'*********************************************************************
If Msg = WM_DROPFILES Then ProcessDroppedFiles hWnd, wParam
'*********************************************************************
' I prefer to forward ALL messages to its original WndProc so it
' will execute the code originally written for it. When I do this,
' I must return the value of CallWindowProc as my return value.
' If I wanted to intercept a message, then I would set WndProc
' equal to 0 and NOT call CallWindowProc.
'*********************************************************************
WndProc = CallWindowProc(OriginalWndProc, hWnd, Msg, wParam, lParam)
End Function
```

One final thing you'll notice is that the return value of WndProc is the return value of CallWindowProc. Your WndProc should do this for all messages it passes on to the original WndProc. If you want to intercept a message entirely, then you should return 0 and not call WndProc. This informs Windows that you have processed this message, and that no additional default message handling should occur.

In our WndProc function, we kept our code simple by passing values from the intercepted message off to the ProcessDroppedFiles code. This is exactly what VB does internally, so ProcessDroppedFiles can now be thought of as an Event for the picWnd control. The code in this event is our "event handler", and it appears in Listing 32.15.

Listing 32.15   YOURCODE.BAS—*ProcessDroppedFiles* is an Event Handler for Your Intercepted Message

```
Private Sub ProcessDroppedFiles(hWnd As Long, hDrop As Long)
    Const MAX_PATH = 260        'Maximum path size as defined by Windows
    Dim lngNumFiles As Long     'Number of files dropped
    Dim strFile As String       'Name and path of the current file
    Dim lngCharsRet As String   'Number characters returned
    Dim i As Long               'Iterator
    '*********************************************************************
    ' Find out how many files were dropped
    '*********************************************************************
    lngNumFiles = DragQueryFile(hDrop, &HFFFFFFFF, vbNullString, 0)
    '*********************************************************************
    ' If no files were dropped, then exit
    '*********************************************************************
    If lngNumFiles < 1 Then Exit Sub
    '*********************************************************************
    ' Adjust lngNumFiles for a zero based array
    '*********************************************************************
    lngNumFiles = lngNumFiles - 1
    '*********************************************************************
    ' Resize the array to hold all of the dropped files
```

```
'*****************************************************************
ReDim vntWndProcResults(0 To lngNumFiles)
'*****************************************************************
' Load the array with the file names and paths
'*****************************************************************
For i = 0 To lngNumFiles
    '*************************************************************
    ' You must size your buffer in advance, so size it to MAX_PATH
    '*************************************************************
    strFile = Space(MAX_PATH)
    '*************************************************************
    ' Windows requires that you extract each element from its
    ' internal array one at a time, so that's what we will do.
    ' The return value is the number of characters in the return
    ' string, less the null terminator.
    '*************************************************************
    lngCharsRet = DragQueryFile(hDrop, i, strFile, Len(strFile))
    '*************************************************************
    ' Keep everything to the left of the null terminator
    '*************************************************************
    strFile = Left(strFile, lngCharsRet)
    '*************************************************************
    ' Add the string to our internal array
    '*************************************************************
    vntWndProcResults(i) = strFile
Next i
'*****************************************************************
' Free the memory allocated by the system to hold the filenames
'*****************************************************************
DragFinish hDrop
'*****************************************************************
' Repaint the window so it can display the filenames
'*****************************************************************
InvalidateRect hWnd, ByVal 0&, True
End Sub
```

This code simply loads a global variant with an array of the files that were dropped on picWnd. When this code finishes loading the array, it calls InvalidateRect on the picWnd to force it to repaint itself. The code following in Listing 32.16 shows how picWnd responds to paint events.

Listing 32.16 WNDLONG.FRM—The *picWnd_Paint* Event Paints a List of Files Dropped onto *PicWnd*

```
'*****************************************************************
' Print the contents of vntWndProcResults in picWnd
'*****************************************************************
Private Sub picWnd_Paint()
    '*************************************************************
    ' If vntWndProcResults is an array...
    '*************************************************************
    If VarType(vntWndProcResults) And vbArray Then
        Dim intUBound As Integer
```

continues

Listing 32.16 Continued

```
        Dim i As Integer
        '****************************************************************
        ' Clear the current contents and reset CurrentX and CurrentY
        '****************************************************************
        picWnd.Cls
        '****************************************************************
        ' Cache the upper bound of the array
        '****************************************************************
        intUBound = UBound(vntWndProcResults)
        '****************************************************************
        ' Print the contents of the array on picWnd
        '****************************************************************
        For i = LBound(vntWndProcResults) To intUBound
            picWnd.Print vntWndProcResults(i)
        Next i
    End If
End Sub
```

Every time picWnd gets a paint event, it checks to see if the global variable, vntWndProcResults (defined in YourCode.bas), contains an array. If it does, then files have been dropped on picWnd, so it paints a list the file names that were dropped on it.

That's it! You've survived the scary complex subject of Win32 callbacks, so you are now ready to write your own version of YourCode.bas (for use with WndLong.bas) in your own application.

From Here...

I hope that this chapter has helped you to look at tools you have *within* VB to further extend your applications. With the concepts discussed in this chapter, you now have the information you need to begin extending your use of the standard controls in Visual Basic, and removing your dependency on third-party controls. The topics discussed in this chapter are only the tip of the iceberg. I could write several more chapters on this subject, but the essential concepts are here. It is now up to you to move forward with them by experimenting on your own.

■ For more information about window styles and callbacks, consult the Win32 SDK (available from Microsoft).

■ To learn cool tips and tricks with forms, the Win32 API, and advanced code techniques, read the next three chapters.

CHAPTER 33

Advanced Form Techniques

By now, you probably think that you have mastered everything there is to know about forms. However, there are a couple tips and tricks that you might not have discovered yet. The purpose of this chapter is to demonstrate some techniques that you might not have discovered or might not have optimized. After completing this chapter, you should be able to apply new form techniques that make your programs more robust. ■

Create persistent forms

Make persistent forms that save their position and restore them when they are loaded.

Write an optimized MDI application

Learn some neat tips and tricks on how to develop an optimized multiple document interface application.

Develop a custom form for use with multimedia applications

Learn how to add hotspots, hyperlinks, and multimedia elements to your VB forms.

Saving Window Positions

Many people want to save the position of their forms at runtime so that they can restore them to their previous state. To address this problem, the WindowPosition() routine shown in Listing 33.1 provides a reusable module that can work with any form.

Listing 33.1   WINPOS.BAS—WinPos.bas Saves and Stores the Position of a Window

```
'*********************************************************************
' Saves or restores the window position for a form
'*********************************************************************
Public Sub WindowPosition(frmName As Form, blnSavePostion As Boolean)
    Dim strWinPosKey As String
    Dim strAppName As String
    '*********************************************************************
    ' Use the product name if it exists, otherwise use the exe name
    '*********************************************************************
    strAppName = IIf(Len(App.ProductName), App.ProductName, App.EXEName)

    With frmName
        '*********************************************************************
        ' This function is only designed for "normal" windows, so
        ' exit when the form is minimized or maximized.
        '*********************************************************************
        If .WindowState <> vbNormal Then Exit Sub
        '*********************************************************************
        ' Use the form name and a descriptive string to make it easy
        ' for the user to find these values in the registry
        '*********************************************************************
        strWinPosKey = .Name & " Startup Position"
        '*********************************************************************
        ' Save the current settings,...
        '*********************************************************************
        If blnSavePostion Then
            SaveSetting strAppName, strWinPosKey, "Height", .Height
            SaveSetting strAppName, strWinPosKey, "Width", .Width
            SaveSetting strAppName, strWinPosKey, "Left", .Left
            SaveSetting strAppName, strWinPosKey, "Top", .Top
        '*********************************************************************
        ' ...or restore the settings (center the form if not found)
        '*********************************************************************
        Else
            .Height = CSng(GetSetting(strAppName, strWinPosKey, _
                "Height", .Height))
            .Width = CSng(GetSetting(strAppName, strWinPosKey, _
                "Width", .Width))
            .Left = CSng(GetSetting(strAppName, strWinPosKey, _
                "Left", (Screen.Width - .Width) / 2))
            .Top = CSng(GetSetting(strAppName, strWinPosKey, _
                "Top", (Screen.Height - .Height) / 2))
        End If
    End With
End Sub
```

WindowPosition() takes a pointer to form and a save/restore flag (called blnSavePosition). The calling form simply passes in a pointer to itself for the first argument, and a Boolean for the second argument. If this argument is True, the routine saves the current form position in the registry. If it is False, WindowPosition() retrieves the last (or default) values from the registry and repositions the form.

Notice how the WindowPosition() routine uses the product name (if available) as the parent key to store the values for the window position. Next, the routine uses the form name along with the string "Startup Position" to create an easy-to-recognize key to hold the window settings. Two forms can't have the same name in the same project, so this approach ensures that users never have a name conflict in the registry. The only other important part of this code is the following line:

```
If .WindowState <> vbNormal Then Exit Sub
```

This line is important because if your resizable form is minimized or maximized, you don't want to save the form's size or move the form. If you did, you would encounter one of two possible problems:

- If you saved the size of minimized form and applied the size to a form whose WindowState property is vbNormal, you would give the form an unusable size.
- If you tried to move a maximized form, you would get an error.

To avoid these problems, you simply ignore the minimized and maximized cases. However, you could modify WindowPosition() to include a WindowState key in the registry. This modification would enable your version of WindowPosition() to support the restoring of windows to their minimized and maximized window states. This routine doesn't include this code, however, because you should load windows only in the vbNormal state.

While writing WINPOS.BAS, you might also include code that centers a form to the screen or to a parent (or owner) form. Initially, you might think that adding such code doesn't make much sense, because Visual Basic now includes the StartupPosition property. However, this property is limited. StartupPosition works only when a form is loaded, so if you want to center a form after loading it, you have to do it yourself. Because it is common to hide forms instead of unloading them, there are several cases in which you have to center a form yourself. The code in Listing 33.2 demonstrates how to do so.

Part
V

Ch
33

Listing 33.2 WINPOS.BAS—The *CenterForm()* Routine

```
'*********************************************************************
' Centers a form to the screen (default) or to a parent form (optional)
'*********************************************************************
Public Sub CenterForm(frmName As Form, Optional frmCenterTo As Form)
    With frmName
        '*********************************************************
        ' If frmCenterTo wasn't provided, then center to screen
        '*********************************************************
        If frmCenterTo Is Nothing Then
            .Move (Screen.Width - .Width) / 2, _
```

Listing 33.2 Continued

```
            (Screen.Height - .Height) / 2
    '********************************************************
    ' Otherwise center to frmCenterTo (useful for dialogs)
    '********************************************************
    Else
        '********************************************************
        ' If the child is larger than the parent, then center
        ' to the screen.
        '********************************************************
        If frmCenterTo.Width < .Width Or _
            frmCenterTo.Height < .Height Then
            CenterForm frmName
        Else
            .Move frmCenterTo.Left + (frmCenterTo.Width - .Width) / 2, _
                frmCenterTo.Top + (frmCenterTo.Height - .Height) / 2
        End If
    End If
End With
End Sub
```

The code in CenterForm() is fairly straightforward because if the optional argument isn't provided, it centers the form to the screen. If the argument is provided, the routine quickly checks to ensure that the child is smaller than the parent. If frmCenterTo is smaller than frmName, the routine centers the form to frmName. Otherwise, the routine centers the form to the screen. Figure 33.1 shows a child form that CenterForm() has centered to its parent window.

FIG. 33.1

CenterForm() also supports centering forms to their parent.

On the book's Web site at **http://www.quecorp.com/sevb5**, LASTPOS.VBP demonstrates how to use the code in WINDOWPOS.BAS using several different types of forms. LASTPOS.FRM, shown in Listing 33.3, contains code that you can copy and paste into any project that includes WINPOS.BAS.

Listing 33.3   LASTPOS.FRM—LASTPOS.FRM's *Load()* and *Unload()* Events

```
'****************************************************************
' Sets the initial window position and size (centered on the first
' start).
'****************************************************************
Private Sub Form_Load()
    WindowPosition Me, False
End Sub
'****************************************************************
' Saves the current window position before the form is destroyed
'****************************************************************
Private Sub Form_Unload(Cancel As Integer)
    WindowPosition Me, True
End Sub
```

The concept is simple. If your form is loading, restore your previous position by passing `False` to `WindowPosition`. If your form is unloading, save your window position by passing `True`.

Simplifying MDI

Even if you haven't already had to do so at some point in your programming career, you'll eventually have to write an MDI application. Although programming MDI applications isn't any more difficult than the programming that you are already accustomed to, it does require you to think in a new way.

When writing an MDI application, you need to keep several important concepts in mind:

- Each new child window that is loaded consumes memory. Having memory-intensive child windows causes your application to drain memory quickly, so keep the amount of code and the number of controls in your child windows to a minimum.

- If your child and parent windows have the same menu commands (such as File, Open or File, Exit), keep the code in the parent. Then your child form's menu click events should simply call the parent's menu click event for all shared code.

- Change all your menu click events from private to public, so your child and parent windows can share these events.

- Avoid using the name property of your child form. Instead, your child forms should use `Me` (or nothing at all), and your parent form should use `ActiveForm`.

- Put all invisible controls (such as a common dialog control or image list) on the MDI parent form. Then all your child windows share these controls without consuming extra memory.

Strict adherence to these rules both simplifies your code and improves your MDI application's performance. This section demonstrates these concepts in a simple MDI application. The application shown in Figure 33.2 is designed to be the skeleton framework for your own MDI application, so feel free to use this project as a starting point to suit your specific needs.

Part
V

Ch
33

FIG. 33.2
The MDI form array
demo application.

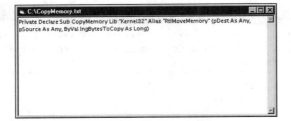

The MDI Parent

The MDI parent form is the "keeper" (or container) of the child windows, so it is responsible for creating new children. Along this duty, the parent also commonly keeps track of the number of child windows that it has created. In addition, the parent usually holds shared user interface elements such as toolbars and status bars.

Listing 33.4 shows the code used to maintain and expose the window count. WindowCreated() and WindowDestroyed() are called by the child windows in their Form_Load and Form_Unload events, respectively. ChildWindowCount() is a public property that enables the child windows to find out how many children are loaded.

Listing 33.4   MDIPARENT.FRM—MDIParent.frm Contains the Shared Code for the Application

```
'******************************************************************
' MDIParent.frm - Demonstrates some basic concepts on how an MDI parent
'    form should behave in an MDI application.
'******************************************************************
Option Explicit
Private mintChildWinCount As Integer
'******************************************************************
' Returns how many child windows have been created
'******************************************************************
Public Property Get ChildWindowCount() As Integer
    ChildWindowCount = mintChildWinCount
End Property
'******************************************************************
' Called when a window is created to increment the window counter
'******************************************************************
Public Sub WindowCreated()
    mintChildWinCount = mintChildWinCount + 1
    UpdateButtons True
End Sub
'******************************************************************
' Called when a window is created to decrement the window counter
'******************************************************************
Public Sub WindowDestroyed()
    mintChildWinCount = mintChildWinCount - 1
    UpdateButtons mintChildWinCount
```

```
End Sub
```

Notice the call to UpdateButtons in Listing 33.4. This private helper routine enables and disables toolbar buttons. If children exist, the toolbar buttons are enabled. When the last child unloads, WindowDestroyed() decrements mintChildWinCount to 0, which causes UpdateButtons to disable the toolbar buttons.

The most important code in MDIPARENT.FRM is the file menu click event code. This code is responsible for creating windows, opening files, and terminating the application. Because all these actions on the MDI parent file menu are also on the child form's File menu, you make this event public as shown in Listing 33.5.

Listing 33.5 MDIPARENT.FRM—Handling Menu Click Events

```
'*********************************************************************
' File menu handler for the MDI form when no windows are displayed.
' In this demo, the child windows will have a menu just like this,
' so we will make this Public so the children can call this event.
'*********************************************************************
Public Sub mnuFileItems_Click(Index As Integer)
    Select Case Index
        '*********************************************************************
        ' File New - Create a new child form, then display it.
        '*********************************************************************
        Case 1
            Dim frmNew As New frmChild
            frmNew.Visible = True
        '*********************************************************************
        ' File Open - Prompt the user for a file name, then load
        '     it into the child window (in OpenFile) if the user didn't
        '     press Cancel in the dialog.
        '*********************************************************************
        Case 2
            On Error Resume Next
            With cdlg
                .Flags = cdlOFNFileMustExist
                .Filter = "Text Files (*.txt)|*.txt|All Files (*.*)|*.*"
                .ShowOpen
            End With
    If Err <> cdlg.cdlCancel Then OpenFile cdlg.filename
        '*********************************************************************
        ' Index 3 is the separator, so don't do anything.
        '*********************************************************************
        'Case 3
        '*********************************************************************
        ' File Exit - Terminate the application
        '*********************************************************************
        Case 4
            Unload Me
```

```
        End Select
End Sub
```

When the user clicks the File New menu, the line `Dim frmNew As New frmChild` creates a new instance of the child form. However, this line doesn't really create the new form. The application actually creates the form when it accesses one of the form's properties or methods. Therefore, the line `frmNew.Visible = True` creates the form. After creating the form, the application sets the `Visible` property to `True`, which displays the form.

 TIP

Forms created using `New` are hidden by default, so remember to display them by setting `Visible` to `True`.

The File Open code (Index = 2) in Listing 33.4 simply displays an Open dialog box in which the user can supply a file name. If the user doesn't click the Cancel button, the application opens the file using the `OpenFile()` routine. The last item in the select statement is Index 4, which represents the File Exit case. This case is an easy one because the proper way to terminate an MDI application is to unload the MDI form.

> **CAUTION**
>
> Avoid using the `End` statement to terminate your applications. `End` terminates your application immediately, which prevents your `Form_Unload()` events from executing.

As mentioned earlier, the `OpenFile()` routine is responsible for opening a text file and loading it into a text box on your child form. Listing 33.6 shows the routine's code, which is quite simplistic and includes no basic error handling for such cases as testing for files greater than 44K under Windows 95. However, the code does provide a basic example of how to load a file into a text box, which suffices for this application.

Listing 33.6 MDIPARENT.FRM—Shared Code

```
'**********************************************************************
' Code shared among the child windows should be put in either a
' module or the MDI parent form.  This OpenFile code will be used
' by all of the children, so we will keep it in the MDI parent form.
'**********************************************************************
Public Sub OpenFile(strFileName As String)
    Dim strFileContents As String
    Dim intFileNum As Integer
    '**********************************************************************
    ' Get a free file handle
    '**********************************************************************
    intFileNum = FreeFile
    '**********************************************************************
    ' Open the file
    '**********************************************************************
    Open strFileName For Input As intFileNum
```

```
'*****************************************************************
'  Put the contents of the file into the txtData control of
'  the child form. This code will fail if the file is too
'  large to fit in the text box, so you should include
'  additional error handling in your own code.
'*****************************************************************
With ActiveForm
    .txtData.Text = Input$(LOF(intFileNum), intFileNum)
    '*****************************************************************
    ' Set the caption of the child form to the file name
    '*****************************************************************
    .Caption = strFileName
End With
'*****************************************************************
' Always close files you open as soon as you are done with them
'*****************************************************************
Close intFileNum
End Sub
```

Notice that the OpenFile() routine simply loads the file into the text box on the active window by referencing the ActiveForm property. You can safely assume that this text box is the correct location to load the file, because the active menu always refers to the active form. The user can open a file through the menu (even if he or she is using the toolbar), so you can always assume that any actions that you perform in your menu event handlers should apply to the active form.

The MDI Child

Now that you understand the MDI parent form's responsibilities, this section explores how the child should behave in this parent/child relationship. As mentioned earlier, child forms are responsible for calling the WindowCreated() and WindowDestroyed() methods of the MDI parent form. Listing 33.7 demonstrates how the child performs this task from the Form_Load() and Form_Unload() events. In addition, the child window sets its initial caption based on the MDI parent ChildWindowCount property. Although this technique is good for this example, you might want to make your algorithm for setting your initial caption a little more complex. What do you think would happen if you had three windows, closed the second window, then created a new window? How could you avoid this problem?

Part

V

Ch

33

Listing 33.7 MDICHILD.FRM—Child Forms Should Only Contain Event Handling Code

```
'*****************************************************************
' MDIChild.frm - Demonstrates some basic techniques on how an MDI child
'    window should behave.
'*****************************************************************
Option Explicit
'*****************************************************************
' When a new form is created, it should call the WindowCreated function
'  in the MDI parent form (which increments the window count in this
```

continues

Listing 33.7   Continued

```
'*case). It should also set its caption to distinguish it from other
' child windows.
'*********************************************************************
Private Sub Form_Load()
    MDIParent.WindowCreated
    '*****************************************************************
    ' This works, but it has a fatal flaw.
    '*****************************************************************
    Caption = Caption & " - " & MDIParent.ChildWindowCount
End Sub
'*********************************************************************
' Make sure txtData always fills the client area of the form.
'*********************************************************************
Private Sub Form_Resize()
    txtData.Move 0, 0, ScaleWidth, ScaleHeight
End Sub
'*********************************************************************
' Let the MDI parent know that this window is being destroyed.
'*********************************************************************
Private Sub Form_Unload(Cancel As Integer)
    MDIParent.WindowDestroyed
End Sub
```

One minor detail that you might have noticed in this code is the `Form_Resize()` event. This code ensures that the text box control always covers the form's entire client area. The code works with any control, so you can use it in your own applications.

Another important concept mentioned previously is that your child forms should use event handlers of the parent menu whenever possible. Listing 33.8 contains the event handlers for all the menus that MDICHILD.FRM uses.

Listing 33.8   MDICHILD.FRM—Menu Event Handlers

```
'*********************************************************************
' Since the child File menu is identical to the MDI parent file menu,
' we should avoid duplicate code by calling the parent's mnuFileItems
' click event.
'*********************************************************************
Private Sub mnuFileItems_Click(Index As Integer)
    MDIParent.mnuFileItems_Click Index
End Sub
'*********************************************************************
' The options menu is unique to the child forms, so the code should
' be in the child form or a separate BAS module.
'*********************************************************************
Public Sub mnuOptionsItems_Click(Index As Integer)
    '*****************************************************************
    ' Don't stop for errors
    '*****************************************************************
    On Error Resume Next
```

```
'*********************************************************************
' Show the color dialog (since all menu items here need it)
'*********************************************************************
MDIParent.cdlg.ShowColor
'*********************************************************************
' If the user clicks Cancel, then exit
'*********************************************************************
If Err = cdlCancel Then Exit Sub
'*********************************************************************
' Otherwise set the color based on the value returned from the dlg
'*********************************************************************
Select Case Index
    Case 1 'Backcolor...
        txtData.BackColor = MDIParent.cdlg.Color
    Case 2 'Forecolor...
        txtData.ForeColor = MDIParent.cdlg.Color
End Select
End Sub
'*********************************************************************
' If you set the indexes of your Window menu properly, you can save
' yourself some code. I was careful to make sure my Window menu items'
' indices were equivalent to the possible values for the Arrange
' method.
'*********************************************************************
Private Sub mnuWindowItems_Click(Index As Integer)
    MDIParent.Arrange Index
End Sub
```

The first menu is File, which is identical to the parent form, so you simply call the mnuFileItems_Click() event in the parent for default processing. The second menu is Options, which appears only in the child form, so you write your implementation code in the event handler. However, you make this event handler public so that it can be accessed by the toolbar control, which resides on the parent form. In addition, you use the common dialog control on the parent for your code, which displays the Color dialog box.

 If any menu item on your child form requires more than 12 lines of code (excluding Dim statements, comments, and white space), you should move that code to a shared module or into the parent form. This prevents your code from consuming too much free memory every time a new form is added.

Finally, the Window menu applies only to child forms (although it is the parent form that is responsible for this menu). By carefully creating your menu control array indices, you can write the implementation code for this menu using only one line of code.

Creating Multimedia Forms

Ask ten people to define the term *multimedia forms* (or *windows*), and you'll probably get ten different responses. For the purposes of this discussion, a multimedia form is a form that has a nonconventional user interface which incorporates a combination of high-resolution graphics, rich text, sound, and video. Examples of Microsoft programs that use multimedia forms are Encarta, Bookshelf, and Money. Although the success of a multimedia form depends on a great graphic design, there are other technical challenges that only the programmer can resolve. Items such as nonconventional menus, playback of video and sound, hotspots, and tips are all challenges that you, the programmer, must address. The purpose of this chapter is to explain some of these techniques so that you can create great multimedia applications.

The Multimedia Form

The multimedia form shown in Figure 33.3 is a simple example that demonstrates several popular features found in most multimedia applications. It contains the following multimedia elements:

- Transparent GIFs (see Ski World in Figure 33.3).

- A hotspot that you can click to activate an Internet Explorer hyperlink to Yahoo! In the form, this hotspot appears on the the skier's face.

- Background wave file sound playing in an infinite loop using a timer.

FIG. 33.3
Multimedia forms are easy in Visual Basic.

- High resolution "wallpaper" for the form using the `Picture` property.
- Tooltips and a rich text description window.
- A nonconventional menu that supports playing an AVI file on a picture box.

Listing 33.9 begins with some form-level declarations, and then continues with the `Form_Load()` and `SetupMenu()` procedures. These two subroutines are responsible for setting up the initial hotspots. In addition, the `Form_Load()` event starts the background sound if the current machine has a wave-playing device installed.

Listing 33.9 MULTIMEDIA.FRM—The Key to Getting Your Hotspots to Work Properly Is Correct Initialization

```
'**********************************************************************
' MultiMedia.frm - Demonstrates some basic techniques typically found
'    in multimedia applications.
'**********************************************************************
Option Explicit
'**********************************************************************
' PtInRect is a great API to use for "hit testing"
'**********************************************************************
Private Declare Function PtInRect Lib "user32" (lpRect As RECT, _
    ByVal X As Long, ByVal Y As Long) As Long
'**********************************************************************
' Our form changes its caption depending on the location of the mouse,
' so we'll define the default caption in advance
'**********************************************************************
Private Const CAPTION_DEFAULT = "Ski World Rocks!"
'**********************************************************************
' Set a URL for the hotspot hyperlink, and create an IE object
'**********************************************************************
Private Const URL_YAHOO_SKIING = _
                    "http://search.yahoo.com/bin/search?p=Skiing"
Private mclsIExplore As New clsInternetExplorer
'**********************************************************************
' Our app has a hotspot and a nonstandard menu, so we need to define
' form-level rects that describe their location for hit tests that
' will be done in the Form_Mouse* events.
'**********************************************************************
Private mrctHotSpot As RECT
Private mrctMenu As RECT
'**********************************************************************
' Prepares the form for initial display
'**********************************************************************
Private Sub Form_Load()
    '**********************************************************************
    ' Most of our code assumes pixels, so set the default scalemode
    ' up front
    '**********************************************************************
    ScaleMode = vbPixels
    '**********************************************************************
    ' We positioned the picAVI control where we want our hotspot to
    ' be at design time, so we should load its position into the
    ' hotspot rectangle. When loading the form, we need to move our picAVI
    ' control where it really needs to be to display our AVI.
    '**********************************************************************
  With picAVI
        mrctHotSpot.Left = .Left
        mrctHotSpot.Top = .Top
        mrctHotSpot.Right = .Left + .Width
        mrctHotSpot.Bottom = .Top + .Height
        .Move 180, 7
    End With
    '**********************************************************************
    ' Defines and paints our demo menu
    '**********************************************************************
```

continues

Listing 33.9   Continued

```
    SetupMenu
    '******************************************************************
    ' Loads the RTF control with some mock data
    '******************************************************************
    rtfDescription.LoadFile App.Path & "\multimedia.rtf"
    '******************************************************************
    ' If this machine can play wave files, then begin the background
    ' sound on an infinite loop by using a timer
    '******************************************************************
    If CanPlayWaves() Then
        tmrBackgroundSound.Enabled = True
        mnuHiddenItems(2).Enabled = True
    End If
End Sub
'******************************************************************
' Sets the hotspot boundary for the menu and prints it in dark blue
'******************************************************************
Private Sub SetupMenu()
    Dim sngTextWidth As Single
    Dim sngTextHeight As Single
    '******************************************************************
    ' Define our menu caption as a constant, since we will only
    ' support one static menu
    '******************************************************************
    Const MENU_CAPTION As String = "Menu Demo"
    '******************************************************************
    ' Get the size of the menu caption
    '******************************************************************
    sngTextWidth = TextWidth(MENU_CAPTION)
    sngTextHeight = TextHeight(MENU_CAPTION)
    '******************************************************************
    ' Right-align the menu to the form (5 pixels from the right edge)
    '******************************************************************
    CurrentX = ScaleWidth - (sngTextWidth + 5)
    '******************************************************************
    ' Define the position of the menu for later hit testing
    '******************************************************************
    With mrctMenu
        .Left = CurrentX
        .Top = CurrentY
        .Right = .Left + sngTextWidth
        .Bottom = .Top + sngTextHeight
    End With
    '******************************************************************
    ' Turn AutoRedraw on so we don't have to put this code in the
    ' Paint event
    '******************************************************************
    AutoRedraw = True
    '******************************************************************
    ' Print the menu caption in dark blue
    '******************************************************************
    ForeColor = QBColor(1) 'Dark Blue
    Print MENU_CAPTION
End Sub
```

After setting up your initial hotspots and loading and positioning your controls, you are ready to display the form. You should do so quickly enough that the wave file begins at the same time as the form appears. Immediately displaying cool graphics and playing sound gives your multimedia application a high-impact introduction.

 TIP If your form is quite large and takes a while to start, you might consider a small multimedia splash screen. This splash screen could start your background music and display a spiffy logo or graphic.

Hit testing works by checking to use the PtInRect() API function to check whether the mouse pointer is within the rectangle in the mouse events. The Form_MouseDown() event displays a menu if the user clicks the menu hotspot. The Form_MouseMove() event changes the caption and cursor if the user moves into the hyperlink hotspot. If the user clicks the skier's face, the Form_MouseUp() event opens the skiing search page from Yahoo! in Internet Explorer. You can accomplish all of this quite easily just by using the PtInRect() API function. The code in Listing 33.10 demonstrates these hit-testing techniques.

Listing 33.10 MULTIMEDIA.FRM—Hotspot Testing and Event Handling

```
'*********************************************************************
' If the user clicks within our menu with the left button, then
' display it
'*********************************************************************
Private Sub Form_MouseDown(Button%, Shift%, X As Single, Y As Single)
    If Button <> vbLeftButton Then Exit Sub
    If PtInRect(mrctMenu, X, Y) Then
        PopupMenu mnuHidden, , mrctMenu.Left, mrctMenu.Bottom
    End If
End Sub
'*********************************************************************
' If the user moves over our hotspot, then change the caption
' (if necessary)
'*********************************************************************
Private Sub Form_MouseMove(Button%, Shift%, X As Single, Y As Single)
    If PtInRect(mrctHotSpot, X, Y) Then
      If Caption <> URL_YAHOO_SKIING Then Caption = URL_YAHOO_SKIING
      MousePointer = 99
    Else
      If Caption <> CAPTION_DEFAULT Then Caption = CAPTION_DEFAULT
      MousePointer = 0
    End If
End Sub
'*********************************************************************
' If the user clicks our hotspot, then open the URL
'*********************************************************************
Private Sub Form_MouseUp(Button%, Shift%, X As Single, Y As Single)
    If PtInRect(mrctHotSpot, X, Y) Then
        mclsIExplore.OpenURL URL_YAHOO_SKIING
```

continues

Listing 33.10   Continued

```
    End If
End Sub
'*********************************************************************
' Our sample menu plays a video or stops playing the background sound
'*********************************************************************
Private Sub mnuHiddenItems_Click(Index As Integer)
    Select Case Index
        Case 1 ' Play Video
            PlayVideo
        Case 2 ' Stop backround sound
            StopPlayingWave
            tmrBackgroundSound.Enabled = False
    End Select
End Sub
```

Listing 33.10 also includes the menu's event handler. You create this menu on the form at design time, hiding the top-level menu item (mnuHidden). This way, the user can take advantage of the menu, but cannot see it on the main form. When the user clicks the left button on the form within the hotspot, the Form_MouseDown() event's the PopupMenu() method displays the menu. When displayed, the menu works just like an ordinary menu, so the menu-handling code is the same.

As you can see in Listing 33.11, you keep the code that handles the audio and video media to a minimum. Both of the subroutines listed depend on other reusable modules to play the media, but the form actually selects the media to play.

Listing 33.11   MULTIMEDIA.FRM—Media-Handling Code in Forms Should Be as Simple as Possible

```
'*********************************************************************
' We play our background continuously by playing the wave file
' asynchronously from a timer event. This allows the user to perform
' other operations while the sound is playing.
'*********************************************************************
Private Sub tmrBackgroundSound_Timer()
    '*****************************************************************
    ' You MUST set the interval to the number of millseconds it takes
    ' to play the wave file. You can find out how long a wave file is
    ' in seconds by using the sound recorder utility that comes with
    ' Windows. Convert the seconds to milliseconds and set that value
    ' here.
    '*****************************************************************
    If tmrBackgroundSound.Interval < 17320 Then
        tmrBackgroundSound.Interval = 17320
    End If
    '*****************************************************************
    ' Play the sound ASYNCHRONOUSLY
    '*****************************************************************
    PlayWaveFile App.Path & "\multimedia.wav", True
```

```
End Sub
'*****************************************************************
' Stops playing the background sound (failure is ignored)
'*****************************************************************
Private Sub Form_Unload(Cancel As Integer)
    StopPlayingWave
End Sub
'*****************************************************************
' Plays an AVI file in a picture box, then hides the box when it's done
'*****************************************************************
Private Sub PlayVideo()
    Dim blnPlayingWave As Boolean
    '*************************************************************
    ' See if the background sound is playing
    '*************************************************************
    blnPlayingWave = tmrBackgroundSound.Enabled
    '*************************************************************
    ' Stop playing the wave before displaying the video
    '*************************************************************
    If blnPlayingWave Then
        tmrBackgroundSound.Enabled = False
        StopPlayingWave
    End If
    '*************************************************************
    ' Display the window, play the AVI, then hide it again
    '*************************************************************
    With picAVI
        .Visible = True
        PlayAVI picAVI, App.Path & "\multimedia.avi"
        .Visible = False
    End With
    '*************************************************************
    ' Restore the background sound immediately by setting its interval
    ' to one and enabling the timer again
    '*************************************************************
    If blnPlayingWave Then
        tmrBackgroundSound.Interval = 1
        tmrBackgroundSound.Enabled = True
    End If
End Sub
```

Notice in the `PlayVideo()` function that you are careful to interrupt the background audio (if it is playing) while playing the video, and then restore it when the video is complete. This is important, because the continuity between different media playing can give your application a more professional appearance.

Most of the code in the listing is basic Visual Basic programming, with the help of some media helper functions. The one exception is the `Form_Unload()` event. Although this event contains only one line of code, it plays an important role. It ensures that the wave file stops before the program terminates. Without this event, the wave file would play until the end of the file because you chose to play it asynchronously. You should always stop a media from playing before you terminate your application.

Playing AVIs in a Picture Box

Most Visual Basic programmers have already learned how to play AVI in a picture box using Visual Basic's MCI control. But why use this 140K-plus OCX when you can do it with the API? Using the mciSendString() API function, you can play virtually any media that Windows supports. This section explains the code required to play an AVI in your multimedia form as shown in Figure 33.4.

PLAYAVI.BAS, shown in Listing 33.12, begins with some declarations required by this module and the PlayAVI() function. The remaining code for this module is intentionally omitted from this listing, but is available on the book's Web site located at **http://www.quecorp.com/ sevb5**. PlayAVI() begins by doing a simple check to ensure that a valid AVI file was passed. If so, the AVI file opens. After each of the mciSendString() calls, the function checks whether mciSendString() failed. If it fails anywhere along the way, you exit the function and return the error string.

FIG. 33.4

Why use controls when you can use the API to play videos?

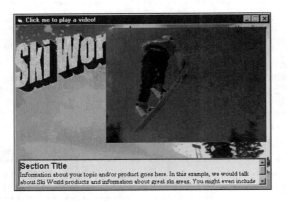

Listing 33.12   PLAYAVI.BAS—the *PlayAVI()* AVI Function Makes It Easy to Play AVIs

```
'*********************************************************************
' PlayAVI.bas - Plays an AVI in a picture box using the multimedia API
'*********************************************************************
Option Explicit
'*********************************************************************
' Declare types and API's required by this module
'*********************************************************************
Public Type RECT
        Left As Long
        Top As Long
        Right As Long
        Bottom As Long
End Type

Private Declare Function mciSendString Lib "winmm.dll" Alias _
```

```
       "mciSendStringA" (ByVal lpstrCommand$, ByVal lpstrRetStr$, _
       ByVal uRetLen As Long, ByVal hwndCallback As Long) As Long

Private Declare Function mciGetErrorString Lib "winmm.dll" Alias _
       "mciGetErrorStringA" (ByVal dwError As Long, ByVal lpstrBuffer$, _
       ByVal uLength As Long) As Long
'***********************************************************************
' Plays an AVI file in a picture box
'***********************************************************************
Public Function PlayAVI(picTarget As PictureBox, _
       ByVal strAVIName As String) As String

       Dim strAlias As String
       Dim strRect As String
       Dim rctResize As RECT
       Dim lngError As Long
       '***********************************************************************
       ' If the AVI file is not provided or found, then exit
       '***********************************************************************
       If strAVIName = "" Or Len(Dir(strAVIName)) = 0 Then
           PlayAVI = strAVIName & " was not found!"
           Exit Function
       End If
       '***********************************************************************
       ' Put the AVI file name in quotes (required for long file names)
       '***********************************************************************
       strAVIName = """" & strAVIName & """"
       '***********************************************************************
       ' Open the AVI and give it an alias called strAlias
       '***********************************************************************
       lngError = mciSendString("open " & strAVIName & " alias strAlias", _
           vbNullString, 0, 0)
       If lngError Then PlayAVI = GetMCIError(lngError): Exit Function
       '***********************************************************************
       ' Set the target window using the alias and the window hWnd
       '***********************************************************************
       strAlias = "window strAlias handle " & picTarget.hWnd
       lngError = mciSendString(strAlias, vbNullString, 0, 0)
       If lngError Then PlayAVI = GetMCIError(lngError): Exit Function
       '***********************************************************************
       ' Force the target window to realize the palette of its background
       ' window. If you don't do this, then you'll see ugly palette
       ' flashes in 256 color mode.
       '***********************************************************************
       lngError = mciSendString("realize strAlias background", "", 0, 0)
       If lngError Then PlayAVI = GetMCIError(lngError): Exit Function
       '***********************************************************************
       ' Get the size (in pixels) of the AVI in the form of a string
       '***********************************************************************
       strRect = Space$(128)
       lngError = mciSendString("where strAlias destination", strRect, _
           Len(strRect), 0)
       If lngError Then PlayAVI = GetMCIError(lngError): Exit Function
       '***********************************************************************
       ' Convert the AVI size string into a rect value
```

Part
V

Ch
33

continues

Listing 33.12   Continued

```
'***************************************************************
rctResize = ParseStrToRect(RTrim(strRect))
'***************************************************************
' Since we are using pixels, set the parent's scalemode to pixels
'***************************************************************
picTarget.Container.ScaleMode = vbPixels
'***************************************************************
' If rctResize contains valid data, then resize picTarget
'***************************************************************
If rctResize.Right > 0 Then
    picTarget.Width = rctResize.Right - rctResize.Left
    picTarget.Height = rctResize.Bottom - rctResize.Top
End If
'***************************************************************
' Refresh the container to avoid ugly painting problems
'***************************************************************
picTarget.Container.Refresh
'***************************************************************
' Play the AVI file synchronously
'***************************************************************
lngError = mciSendString("play strAlias wait", vbNullString, 0, 0)
If lngError Then PlayAVI = GetMCIError(lngError): Exit Function
'***************************************************************
' Close the AVI file
'***************************************************************
lngError = mciSendString("close strAlias", vbNullString, 0, 0)
If lngError Then PlayAVI = GetMCIError(lngError): Exit Function
End Function
```

After opening the AVI, you assign the picture box's hwnd to the window, so the window knows that you want to play the AVI in the picture box. Next, you set the picture box palette to match the container's palette so that no palette conflicts occur that might cause the form display to look ugly while you play the AVI. Next, you get the AVI's size and then resize the picture box to hold the AVI. Finally, you refresh the form (to show the resized picture box properly) and play the AVI synchronously. After the AVI finishes playing, PlayAVI() closes it.

Playing Wave Files

No great multimedia application is complete without sound. Although your applications can play sound using such formats as MIDI and CD Audio, wave files are still the most popular format used today. No multimedia example would be complete without mentioning how to play wave files in your application, so this section discusses a small subroutine called PLAYWAVE.BAS.

The PLAYWAVE.BAS module, shown in Listing 33.13, contains one method to determine whether the current machine has a wave playback device installed, and a second function that plays a wave file. The `CanPlayWaves()` function simply calls `waveOutGetNumDevs()` to find out how many wave device drivers are installed. If one or more is installed, the current machine can play wave files (even if the user can't hear them because he or she has turned off the speakers).

Listing 33.13   PLAYWAVE.BAS—Playing a Wave File Is Easy with
PlayWaveFile()

```
' *****************************************************************
' PLAYWAVE.BAS - Plays a wave file.
' *****************************************************************
Option Explicit
Private Declare Function PlaySound Lib "winmm.dll" Alias _
    "PlaySoundA" (ByVal lpszName As String, ByVal hModule As Long, _
    ByVal dwFlags As Long) As Long
Private Declare Function waveOutGetNumDevs Lib "winmm.dll" () As Long
' *****************************************************************
' Returns True if wave files can be played on the current machine
' *****************************************************************
Public Function CanPlayWaves() As Boolean
    CanPlayWaves = waveOutGetNumDevs()
End Function
' *****************************************************************
' Plays a wave file
' *****************************************************************
Public Function PlayWaveFile(strFileName As String, _
    Optional blnAsync As Boolean) As Boolean
    Dim lngFlags As Long
    ' *************************************************************
    ' Flag values for dwFlags parameter
    ' *************************************************************
    Const SND_SYNC = &H0           ' Play synchronously
    Const SND_ASYNC = &H1          ' Play asynchronously
    Const SND_NODEFAULT = &H2      ' No default sound event is used
    Const SND_FILENAME = &H20000   ' Name is a file name
    ' *************************************************************
    ' Set the flags for PlaySound
    ' *************************************************************
    lngFlags = SND_NODEFAULT Or SND_FILENAME Or SND_SYNC
    If blnAsync Then lngFlags = lngFlags Or SND_ASYNC
    ' *************************************************************
    ' Call PlaySound to play the wave file.
    ' *************************************************************
    PlayWaveFile = PlaySound(strFileName, 0&, lngFlags)
End Function
' *****************************************************************
' Stops playing the current wave file
' *****************************************************************
Public Function StopPlayingWave() As Boolean
    Const SND_PURGE = &H40
    PlaySound vbNullString, 0&, SND_PURGE
End Function
```

Part
V

Ch

33

The PlayWaveFile() function plays a wave file in either synchronous or asynchronous mode. (If you tend to confuse the two terms *synchronous* and *asynchronous*, remember that *synchronous* means that your code stops executing until the file has finished playing.) In this example, you need to play the file asynchronously because you want to enable the user to use the application while the wave file plays in the background.

The final function in this module is StopPlayingWave(), which stops playing an asynchronous wave file immediately. To prevent the wave file from playing after your application terminates, you need to use this function when you unload your form.

From Here...

Now that you have learned some new techniques to apply to your forms, you ought to review your current applications to see whether you can find places to apply them. Programmers can easily overlook form techniques, which is a big mistake. Forms are the most important part of your application because they are your application's connection to the user. Your form is the package in which you are presenting your code. Your program can be the best application on the planet, but if it is plagued by poor form design, your users will be less likely to use it. Don't let poor forms ruin your masterpiece. Apply the techniques described in this chapter and elsewhere in this book to make your applications more robust.

To learn about related topics, see the following sources:

- For more examples of form techniques, consult Chapter 28 "Integrating Visual Basic with Mail, Schedule, and Exchange."
- For assistance with form design, read Microsoft Press' *The Windows Interface Guidelines for Software Design.*
- For information on advanced animation techniques, read Microsoft Press' *Animation Techniques in Win32.*

CHAPTER 34

Advanced Code Techniques

This chapter contains a collection of advanced programming samples that demonstrate some advanced features that only a few Visual Basic programmers ever discover. These techniques and features aren't anything new, but are frequently overlooked. In fact, some of the techniques shown in this chapter, such as sorting, haven't been done in Visual Basic because its executables couldn't be compiled into native code. Now that Visual Basic has overcome this limitation, there is virtually no reason to use any language besides Visual Basic to write your entire application. ■

Make the most of variants and ParamArrays

You will learn when and how to use variants and ParamArrays in your code for maximum flexibility and the least amount of duplicate code.

Apply advanced computer science techniques

Learn how to apply basic computer science concepts such as searching, sorting, and linked-lists using pure VB code.

Manipulate bits and bytes

In a sample application that graphically maps the values of DWORD, you'll learn the basics of bit manipulation in Visual Basic.

Starting Simple

Although this chapter is titled "Advanced Code Techniques," this section discusses a couple of techniques that aren't very "advanced." Instead, they are useful code techniques that most Visual Basic programmers never really take advantage of in their own programs. By applying the techniques that this section discusses, you can save yourself from writing a lot of duplicate or unnecessary code. If you are already familiar with the techniques described in this section, you should skip it and move on to the section "Applying Computer Science Techniques in Visual Basic."

Taking Advantage of Variants

Visual Basic 2.0 first introduced variants as a "one-size-fits-all" data type. Variants can hold any of the data types used in Visual Basic, plus any array of these data types. Therefore, variants are extremely flexible and powerful. However, this flexibility comes at a price: performance. Behind the scenes, a variant is actually a user-defined type with a member for each data type that Visual Basic supports. This structure consumes a minimum of 16-bytes for variants with numbers, and 22-bytes (plus the length of the string) for variants with strings. Therefore, you waste a lot of memory when you put a 2-byte integer in a 16-byte variant, or a 1-byte string in a 23-byte variant.

The moral to this story is that you should never use variants out of laziness. Whenever you use a variant, you should have a good reason for doing so. One such reason occurs when you have a function for which you need to return an array. Another case is in a simple function that needs to support all data types. The latter case is the true purpose for variants: flexibility. Thus, you usually shouldn't use variants as global or static variables, nor use them in loops. However, if you have a good knowledge of how to use variants, you can add some great features to your applications and shared modules.

The code in this section comes from VARIANT.FRM (see Figure 34.1). This program offers a simple demonstration of some cool variant tricks. The code begins with Listing 34.1, the `PrintVariant()` function, which is designed to print the contents of almost any variant data type (except multidimensional variant arrays) on VARIANT.FRM.

FIG. 34.1
VARIANT.FRM shows
`PrintVariant()` at
work.

Listing 34.1   VARIANT.FRM—the *PrintVariant()* Function Prints Variants of Almost Any Data Type

```
'*********************************************************************
' Prints the contents of variant to the form, even if it's a single-
' dimension variant array
'*********************************************************************
Private Sub PrintVariant(vntInput As Variant)
    '*****************************************************************
    ' If vntInput is an array...
    '*****************************************************************
    If VarType(vntInput) And vbArray Then
        Dim i As Integer
        Dim intUBound As Integer
        '*************************************************************
        ' Always cache your upper bounds
        '*************************************************************
        intUBound = UBound(vntInput)
        '*************************************************************
        ' Loop through the array and print the value of each element
        '*************************************************************
        For i = LBound(vntInput) To intUBound
            Print "Index" & Str(i) & " = " & vntInput(i)
        Next i
    '*****************************************************************
    ' Otherwise, it must be a single value...
    '*****************************************************************
    Else
        Print vntInput
    End If
End Sub
```

The key to this code is that it first checks whether `vntInput` contains an array. If it does not, the `PrintVariant()` function passes it to the `Print()` method. If `vntInput` is an array, the code prints the array by looping from its lower boundary to the array's upper boundary. Notice that you do not assume that the array starts with zero or one, because this would certainly cause the function to fail. However, you do assume that the user won't pass in a multidimensional array, so `PrintVariant()` is certainly not foolproof.

Listing 34.2 demonstrates a simple example of handling multidimensional arrays. This demonstration is also imperfect, but it does work with any two-dimensional array. The major limiting factor preventing you from writing a function that prints a multidimensional array with any number of dimensions is that there is no way to determine the number of dimensions in an array. In addition, you would need to create a loop dynamically for each dimension, which is impossible to do at runtime.

Part
V

Ch
34

Listing 34.2   VARIANT.FRM—Printing Multidimensional Variants

```
'*******************************************************************
' Demonstrates how to use a multidimensional array returned as a variant
' from a function
'*******************************************************************
Private Sub cmdPrintMultiDim_Click()
    Dim vntArray As Variant
    Dim intRow As Integer
    Dim intCol As Integer
    Dim intMaxRow As Integer
    Dim intMaxCol As Integer
    Cls
    '*******************************************************************
    ' Retrieve the multidimensional array...
    '*******************************************************************
    vntArray = CreateMultiArray(3, 3)
    '*******************************************************************
    ' Cache the upper bounds of each dimension of the array
    '*******************************************************************
    intMaxRow = UBound(vntArray, 1)
    intMaxCol = UBound(vntArray, 2)
    '*******************************************************************
    ' Loop through the first dimension
    '*******************************************************************
    For intRow = LBound(vntArray, 1) To intMaxRow
        '*******************************************************************
        ' Loop through the second dimension and print the contents
        '*******************************************************************
        For intCol = LBound(vntArray, 2) To intMaxCol
            Print vntArray(intRow, intCol)
        Next intCol
    Next intRow
End Sub
'*******************************************************************
' Shows the results of using the plus operator with a string and
' a numeric value when using variants
'*******************************************************************
Private Sub cmdVariant_Click()
    Cls
    '*******************************************************************
    ' Prints a numeric value using PrintVariant (notice how the string
    ' 1 was added to 100 instead of being concatenated)
    '*******************************************************************
    PrintVariant "1" + 100  ' = 101, not 1100
End Sub
'*******************************************************************
' Demonstrates how to return a multidimensional array from a function
'*******************************************************************
Private Function CreateMultiArray(intRows%, intCols%) As Variant
    Dim strReturn() As String
    Dim i As Integer, j As Integer
    '*******************************************************************
    ' Build the array based on the sizes provided by the caller
    '*******************************************************************
```

```
        ReDim strReturn(0 To intRows, 1 To intCols) As String
        '******************************************************************
        ' Iterate through the rows
        '******************************************************************
        For i = 0 To intRows
            '**************************************************************
            ' Load each element of the array with some default values
            '**************************************************************
            For j = 1 To intCols
                strReturn(i, j) = "Row" & Str(i) & " Col" & Str(j)
            Next j
        Next i
        '******************************************************************
        ' Return the array
        '******************************************************************
        CreateMultiArray = strReturn
    End Function
```

CreateMultiArray() is a simple function that creates a two-dimensional array based on the size requested by the caller. The function loads the array with bogus data and returns it to the caller.

The two command button click events shown in Listing 34.3 demonstrate how flexible variants can be. These click events pass a variety of different data types to the PrintVariant() function to show how flexible it really is.

Listing 34.3   VARIANT.FRM—Using *PrintVariant()* with Different Types of Variants

```
'**********************************************************************
' Builds a variant array with nonconventional lower and upper
' boundaries and sends this array to PrintVariant to print it to the
' form.
'**********************************************************************
Private Sub cmdVntArray_Click()
    Dim strArray(92 To 104) As String
    Dim i As Integer
    Cls
    '******************************************************************
    ' Build an array with an unusual lower bounds
    '******************************************************************
    For i = 92 To 104
        strArray(i) = "Item " & CStr(i - 91)
    Next i
    '******************************************************************
    ' Notice how PrintVariant can print this array without failing
    '******************************************************************
    PrintVariant strArray
End Sub
'**********************************************************************
' Demonstrates the flexibility of the Array function and variants by
' passing in a variety of objects to PrintVariant for further
```

Part
V

Ch
34

continues

Listing 34.3   Continued

```
' processing.
'****************************************************************
Private Sub cmdVntArray2_Click()
    Dim Excel As Object
    Cls
    '****************************************************************
    ' Put the path to the windows directory in the text box
    '****************************************************************
    Text1 = Environ("windir")
    '****************************************************************
    ' Set the path of the file list box to the windows directory, and
    ' select its first item
    '****************************************************************
    File1.Path = Text1
    File1.ListIndex = 0
    '****************************************************************
    ' Don't stop for errors (in case Excel isn't installed)
    '****************************************************************
    On Error Resume Next
    '****************************************************************
    ' Create an Excel application object
    '****************************************************************
    Set Excel = CreateObject("Excel.Application")
    '****************************************************************
    ' If CreateObject failed, then print everything except Excel
    '****************************************************************
    If Err.Number Then
        PrintVariant Array("One", 2, vbNull, Font, Text1, File1, _
            Menu1, Name)
    '****************************************************************
    ' Print everything, including the default property of the Excel
    ' object. Also be sure to close Excel before the End Sub.
    '****************************************************************
    Else
        '****************************************************************
        ' Notice the wide variety of objects that will print using
        ' the PrintVariant command! Notice how the default value of
        ' all of the objects (Font, Text1, File1, etc.) are printed.
        '****************************************************************
        PrintVariant Array("One", 2, vbNull, Font, Text1, File1, _
            Menu1, Name, Excel)
        Excel.Quit
    End If
End Sub
```

Listing 34.3 uses the Array() function, which takes a variable number of arguments (VB does this internally by using ParamArray) and returns a variant array of the results. This example passes a string, an integer, a null, a font object (the font property of VARIANT.FRM), Text1's text property, the File1 list's first item, a menu item's value property, the form name, and (if possible) an Excel OLE Automation object's caption property. Now that's flexible. When you need flexibility, always keep variants in mind. When you need optimal performance (such as loops), always try to use the smallest data type possible.

ParamArray: the King of Flexibility

If you've already used `ParamArray`, feel free to skip this section. If you haven't, this section is going to be a real treat for you. `ParamArray` is perhaps one of the best features added to Visual Basic 4.0, because it finally enables you to write a function that can take an unknown number of arguments (from zero to infinity). Other languages have long offered this feature to programmers, but it is still rather new to Visual Basic. Because `ParamArray` simply converts into a variant array the arguments passed to your function, it is simple to use. Listing 34.4 shows an example of the use of `ParamArray`.

Listing 34.4   PARAMARRAY.BAS—ParamArray.bas Demonstrates How to Use *ParamArray()*.

```
'*********************************************************************
' Demonstrates how to use ParamArray
'*********************************************************************
Public Sub ParamArrayDemo(ParamArray vntArray() As Variant)
    Dim intMax As Integer
    Dim i As Integer
    '*********************************************************************
    ' If no arguments were passed, then exit
    '*********************************************************************
    If IsMissing(vntArray) Then Exit Sub
    '*********************************************************************
    ' Cache the upper boundary of the array
    '*********************************************************************
    intMax = UBound(vntArray)
    '*********************************************************************
    ' Init i with the lower boundary, and loop through all elements
    '*********************************************************************
    For i = LBound(vntArray) To intMax
        '*********************************************************************
        ' Display some information about the values passed in
        '*********************************************************************
        MsgBox CStr("Input: " & vntArray(i)) & vbLf & _
            "VarType: " & CStr(VarType(vntArray(i))) & vbLf & _
            "TypeName: " & TypeName(vntArray(i)), vbInformation
    Next i
End Sub
```

The `ParamArrayDemo()` subroutine takes an unknown number of arguments. If no arguments are passed to it, it does nothing. Otherwise, it iterates through the array displaying a message box for every argument passed in. Each message displays the item passed in, as well as some information about it. This application doesn't use any forms, so the starting point for it is `Sub Main()`, which simply passes in five different data types:

Part
V

Ch
34

```
'********************************************************************
' Entry point for this windowless application
'********************************************************************
Private Sub Main()
    '****************************************************************
    ' Call the demo sub using values of different data types.
    ' Feel free to try some of your own!
    '****************************************************************
    ParamArrayDemo 1, "2", 3&, 4!, 5#
End Sub
```

The call to `ParamArrayDemo` displays five message boxes that tell the user which types of values were passed. Feel free to experiment with this code to see what happens when you use different data types and numbers of arguments.

Applying Computer Science Techniques in Visual Basic

Although this chapter is far from being a Computer Science (CS) textbook, applying some common CS principles to Visual Basic is useful. Writing algorithms that search and sort, creating and using linked lists, and manipulating bits are all fundamental concepts of every good CS curriculum. However, most CS textbooks apply these techniques using such languages as C or Pascal. In fact, most books written about Visual Basic ignore this subject completely. Although this section isn't designed to teach you these fundamental concepts, it does show you how to apply them in Visual Basic.

Getting Started with Searching and Sorting

Although it has been possible to write searching and sorting algorithms in Visual Basic since version 1.0, the fact that Visual Basic code was interpreted rather than native code led most people to program the algorithms in other languages, because searching and sorting require a large number of operations that simply bogs down even the best of interpreters. However, with the capability to compile to native code (introduced in Visual Basic 5.0), you can write these algorithms in Visual Basic without paying a significant performance penalty. In fact, the performance of these algorithms in Visual Basic is now comparable to other languages such as C, C++, and Pascal. This section focuses on two of the most popular algorithms for searching and sorting: the binary search and QuickSort.

N O T E The code in this section derives from samples found in both other Microsoft languages and *Hardcore Visual Basic* by Bruce McKinney (Microsoft Press, 1995). The examples in this section take the best features from all these samples and formulate them into a more reusable set of code. ■

Writing Generic Helper Functions In almost every code module that you will ever write, you are certain to code a few private helper functions that make your core functions more readable. For this searching and sorting module, SORTSEARCH.BAS, you must have two helper functions to avoid hundreds of lines of additional or duplicate code.

The Compare() and Swap() functions shown in Listing 34.5 provide a data type independent mechanism for comparing and swapping variables. Neither of these functions is complex, but their role in the success of the binary search and QuickSort algorithms is essential. Even the smallest bug in either function causes the algorithms to fail, so you must code them carefully.

Listing 34.5   SORTSEARCH.BAS—Searching and Sorting Helpers

```
'*********************************************************************
' SortSearch.bas - Routines to allow you to search and sort through
'   variant arrays
'*********************************************************************
Option Explicit
'*********************************************************************
' Option Compare Text allows the searches and sorts to ignore
' case. Comment out this line if you wish to have case-sensitive
' searches and sorts.
'*********************************************************************
Option Compare Text
'*********************************************************************
' Same as StrComp, but applies to variants
'*********************************************************************
Private Function Compare(vntItem1 As Variant, _
                         vntItem2 As Variant) As Integer
    '*********************************************************************
    ' If less than, then return -1
    '*********************************************************************
    If vntItem1 < vntItem2 Then
        Compare = -1
    '*********************************************************************
    ' If greater than, then return 1
    '*********************************************************************
    ElseIf vntItem1 > vntItem2 Then
        Compare = 1
    End If
    '*********************************************************************
    ' Otherwise do nothing, which returns zero (indicating that they
    ' are equal)
    '*********************************************************************
End Function
'*********************************************************************
' Swaps two variants in place (since we are passing ByRef)
'*********************************************************************
Private Sub Swap(ByRef vntItem1 As Variant, ByRef vntItem2 As Variant)
    '*********************************************************************
    ' Dim a temp value to hold the original value of vntItem1
    '*********************************************************************
    Dim vntTemp As Variant
    '*********************************************************************
```

continues

Part
V

Ch
34

Listing 34.5   Continued

```
      ' Store vntItem1 in a temporary variable
      '*********************************************************************
      vntTemp = vntItem1
      '*********************************************************************
      ' Set vntItem2 equal to vntItem1
      '*********************************************************************
      vntItem1 = vntItem2
      '*********************************************************************
      ' Set vntItem2 equal to the temporary variable
      '*********************************************************************
      vntItem2 = vntTemp
End Sub
```

Compare() is a data type independent version of Visual Basic's StrComp() function. It compares two variants. If the first item is less than the second item, it returns –1. If the first is greater than the second, Compare() returns 1. Otherwise, the function returns zero to indicate that the two variants are equal. Swap() simply takes a reference to two variables and swaps them in place. Nothing fancy goes on in these functions, but as you'll see, these functions are the core of your searching and sorting routines.

Notice that Listing 34.5 begins with some definitions in the General Declarations section of the SORTSEARCH.BAS module. The most significant one is Option Compare Text. This definition tells Visual Basic that you want to ignore the case of strings in the Compare() function. If you decide that you want your searches and sorts to be case-sensitive, you should comment out this line of code. In addition, you could rewrite your Compare() function to support both case-sensitive and case-insensitive comparisons.

Searching with *BinarySearch()*   The concept of a binary search is to use a sorted array to find a specific value, using a divide-and-conquer mechanism. Because the array is sorted, you begin by checking the middle value with the item for which you are searching. If the search item is less than the middle item, you reapply this algorithm to the array's lower half, and so on. However, for this function to work, the array must be sorted.

Listing 34.6 begins by ensuring that the user has actually passed an array to the function. When working with variant arrays, you must always double-check to make sure that the caller doesn't try to pass a simple variant. Next, you make the all-important check of the blnIsSorted optional argument. Optionally, the caller sets this flag to tell you that vntArray is already sorted, so you shouldn't try to sort it again. If the caller doesn't set this value or if it is False, you sort the array using the QuickSort algorithm.

Listing 34.6   SORTSEARCH.BAS—Binary Searching

```
'*********************************************************************
' Performs a binary search for vntFind on a variant array, and
' sorts the array if the call doesn't set blnIsSorted = True
'*********************************************************************
```

```vb
Public Function BinarySearch(vntArray As Variant, _
    vntFind As Variant, Optional blnIsSorted As Boolean) As Integer
    '*****************************************************************
    ' Dim integers for the high, low, and mid points of the array
    '*****************************************************************
    Dim intHigh As Integer
    Dim intLow As Integer
    Dim intMid As Integer
    '*****************************************************************
    ' Make sure vntArray really is an array
    '*****************************************************************
    If VarType(vntArray) And vbArray Then
        intLow = LBound(vntArray)
        intHigh = UBound(vntArray)
    '*****************************************************************
    ' If it is not, then exit (returning a not found result)
    '*****************************************************************
    Else
        BinarySearch = -1
        Exit Function
    End If
    '*****************************************************************
    ' If the array isn't sorted, then sort it (otherwise your binary
    ' search will likely fail)
    '*****************************************************************
    If Not blnIsSorted Then QuickSort vntArray
    '*****************************************************************
    ' Enter into an infinite loop (because we'll exit the loop within
    ' our case statement)
    '*****************************************************************
    Do
        '*****************************************************************
        ' Set the mid point of the half you are currently searching
        '*****************************************************************
        intMid = intLow + ((intHigh - intLow) \ 2)
        '*****************************************************************
        ' Compare the mid point element with the element you are
        ' searching for, and act accordingly based on the return
        ' value from Compare
        '*****************************************************************
        Select Case Compare(vntFind, vntArray(intMid))
            '*****************************************************************
            ' vntFind was found, so return the index and exit
            '*****************************************************************
            Case 0
                BinarySearch = intMid
                Exit Function
            '*****************************************************************
            ' vntFind is in the lower half, so set intHigh to the
            ' mid point and repeat the search
            '*****************************************************************
            Case Is < 0
                intHigh = intMid
                '*****************************************************************
                ' If intLow is equal to intHigh, then the item was
```

continues

Listing 34.6   Continued

```
                    ' not found, so exit
                    '*********************************************************
                    If intLow = intHigh Then Exit Do
                    '*********************************************************
                    ' vntFind is in the upper half, so set intLow to the
                    ' mid point plus one and repeat the search
                    '*********************************************************
                Case Is > 0
                    intLow = intMid + 1
                    '*********************************************************
                    ' If intLow is greater than intHigh, then the item
                    ' was not found, so exit
                    '*********************************************************
                    If intLow > intHigh Then Exit Do
            End Select
        Loop
        '*********************************************************
        ' Item not found, then return a value less than the LBound
        '*********************************************************
        BinarySearch = LBound(vntArray) - 1
    End Function
```

The remaining code applies the concepts of the binary search algorithm by using the Com-
pare() function to compare two items to each other. If the search finds the item, its index is
returned. If not, you return a value that is one less than the given array's lower boundary to
indicate that the search did not find the item. This algorithm is a simple yet efficient way to find
a given element in an array. Later in this section is a demonstration of this function that uses an
array that the user provides.

Sorting with *QuickSort()*   Many sorting algorithms have been developed by many great computer scientists, but perhaps the most popular algorithm ever written is QuickSort. In its simplest form, QuickSort is a sorting algorithm that accomplishes a relatively fast sort by using
the CS concept of recursion. Although versions of QuickSort exist that don't rely on recursion,
the form shown in this section is the most common. The downside to using recursion in a
sorting algorithm is that each recursive call consumes space on the stack, which limits the
number of elements that can be sorted to the available space on the stack. In testing this code,
I sorted an array of 10,000 strings without running out of stack space, so the function should
suffice for most of your sorting needs.

Like the BinarySearch() function, QuickSort() begins by ensuring that vntArray is actually
an array (see Listing 34.7). After doing so, the function checks whether the array contains
more than two elements. If vntArray contains only two elements, the function does a simple
comparison, performs a swap (if necessary), and exits.

Listing 34.7 SORTSEARCH.BAS—Sorting with *QuickSort()*

```
'*********************************************************************
' Sorts a variant array using the QuickSort algorithm
'*********************************************************************
Public Sub QuickSort(vntArray As Variant, _
    Optional intLBound As Integer, Optional intUBound As Integer)
    '*********************************************************************
    ' Holds the pivot point
    '*********************************************************************
    Dim vntMid As Variant
    '*********************************************************************
    ' Make sure vntArray really is an array
    '*********************************************************************
    If (VarType(vntArray) And vbArray) = 0 Then Exit Sub
    '*********************************************************************
    ' If optional args weren't provided, then get the default values
    '*********************************************************************
    If intLBound = 0 And intUBound = 0 Then
        intLBound = LBound(vntArray)
        intUBound = UBound(vntArray)
    End If
    '*********************************************************************
    ' If the LBound is greater than the UBound, then there is nothing
    ' to do, so exit
    '*********************************************************************
    If intLBound > intUBound Then Exit Sub
    '*********************************************************************
    ' If there are only two elements in this array, then swap them
    ' (if necessary) and exit
    '*********************************************************************
    If (intUBound - intLBound) = 1 Then
        If Compare(vntArray(intLBound), vntArray(intUBound)) > 0 Then
            Swap vntArray(intLBound), vntArray(intUBound)
        End If
        Exit Sub
    End If
    '*********************************************************************
    ' Dim the indices
    '*********************************************************************
    Dim i As Integer, j As Integer
    '*********************************************************************
    ' Set your pivot point
    '*********************************************************************
    vntMid = vntArray(intUBound)
    '*********************************************************************
    ' Loop while lower bound is less than the upper bound
    '*********************************************************************
    Do
        '*********************************************************************
        ' Init i and j to the array boundary
        '*********************************************************************
        i = intLBound
        j = intUBound
        '*********************************************************************
```

continues

Part
V

Ch
34

Listing 34.7 Continued

```
            ' Compare each element with vntMid (the pivot) until the
            ' current element is the less than or equal to the mid point
            '*************************************************************
            Do While (i < j) And Compare(vntArray(i), vntMid) <= 0
                i = i + 1
            Loop
            '*************************************************************
            ' Compare each element with vntMid (the pivot) until the
            ' current element is the greater than or equal to the mid point
            '*************************************************************
            Do While (j > i) And Compare(vntArray(j), vntMid) >= 0
                j = j - 1
            Loop
            '*************************************************************
            ' If you never reached the pivot point, then the two elements
            ' are out of order, so swap them
            '*************************************************************
            If i < j Then Swap vntArray(i), vntArray(j)
        Loop While i < j
        '*************************************************************
        ' Now that i has been adjusted it the above loop, we should swap
        ' element i with element at intUBound
        '*************************************************************
        Swap vntArray(i), vntArray(intUBound)
        '*************************************************************
        ' If index i minus the index of intLBound is less than the index
        ' of intUBound minus index i, then...
        '*************************************************************
        If (i - intLBound) < (intUBound - i) Then
            '*************************************************************
            ' Recursively sort with adjusted values for upper and lower
            ' bounds
            '*************************************************************
            QuickSort vntArray, intLBound, i - 1
            QuickSort vntArray, i + 1, intUBound
        '*************************************************************
        ' Otherwise...
        '*************************************************************
        Else
            '*************************************************************
            ' Recursively sort with adjusted values for upper and lower
            ' bounds
            '*************************************************************
            QuickSort vntArray, i + 1, intUBound
            QuickSort vntArray, intLBound, i - 1
        End If
End Sub
```

If after all of the initial tests the function still determines that the array must be sorted, you apply the sorting algorithm. Examine the code in Listing 34.7 for details on each step of this algorithm.

Using *BinarySearch()* and *QuickSort()* Now that you have written your algorithms, it's time to put them to use in an example. This example uses a text box with a default list of strings. When the user clicks the search or sort command buttons, you apply the appropriate algorithm and display the results in a read-only rich-edit text box. Figure 34.2 shows the result of a search for the word Texas.

FIG. 34.2
Searching and sorting with SORTSEARCH-DEMO.VBP.

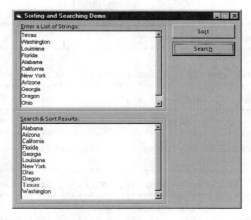

 To keep things simple, Listing 34.8 omits some of the window management helper code. However, so feel free to view this code along with the entire sample in the SORTSEARCHDEMO.VBP project on the book's Web site (**http//www.quecorp/sevb5**).

Listing 34.8   SORTSEARCH.FRM—SortSearch.frm Demonstrates How to Use the Code Found in SortSearch.bas.

```
'*******************************************************************
' SortSearch.frm - Demonstrates how to use basSortSearch
'*******************************************************************
Option Explicit
'*******************************************************************
' Prompts the user for a string to search for, and searches for that
' string based on the list in txtInput
'*******************************************************************
Private Sub cmdSearch_Click()
    Dim vntArray As Variant
    Dim strFind As String
    Dim intFoundIndex As Integer
    Dim blnSorted As Boolean
    '***********************************************************
    ' If any text is in rtfResults, then the list has already been
    ' sorted
    '***********************************************************
    blnSorted = Len(rtfResults.Text)
    '***********************************************************
    ' Load the sorted list if it is available
```

continues

Listing 34.8 Continued

```
'******************************************************************
If blnSorted Then
    vntArray = LoadStringsIntoArray(rtfResults.Text)
Else
    vntArray = LoadStringsIntoArray(txtInput)
End If
'******************************************************************
' Prompt the user for a search string
'******************************************************************
strFind = _
    InputBox("Enter the item to search for:", "Search", vntArray(0))
'******************************************************************
' If no input was provided, then exit
'******************************************************************
If Len(strFind) = 0 Then Exit Sub
'******************************************************************
' Search for strFind in the array of strings (and sort only if
' the array is not already sorted)
'******************************************************************
intFoundIndex = BinarySearch(vntArray, strFind, blnSorted)
'******************************************************************
' If not found, then tell the user
'******************************************************************
If intFoundIndex < LBound(vntArray) Then
    MsgBox "Item not found!", vbExclamation
End If
'******************************************************************
' Update the RTF control with the sorted array. If the search
' item was found, it will be highlighted in bold red.
'******************************************************************
LoadArrayIntoRTF rtfResults, vntArray, intFoundIndex
End Sub
'******************************************************************
' QuickSort the list in txtInput and put the results in rtfResults
'******************************************************************
Private Sub cmdSort_Click()
    Dim vntArray As Variant
    '******************************************************************
    ' If rtfResults is not empty, then the list is sorted, so exit
    '******************************************************************
    If Len(rtfResults.Text) Then
        MsgBox "The input values are already sorted.", vbInformation
        Exit Sub
    End If
    '******************************************************************
    ' Load the list in txtInput into an array
    '******************************************************************
    vntArray = LoadStringsIntoArray(txtInput)
    '******************************************************************
    ' Sort the array
    '******************************************************************
```

```
      QuickSort vntArray
      '********************************************************************
      ' Display the sorted array in rtfResults
      '********************************************************************
      LoadArrayIntoRTF rtfResults, vntArray
End Sub
```

Both the cmdSearch_Click() and cmdSort_Click() events are similar in that they extract their arrays from input that the user provides in a text box. After the events apply their algorithm, the rtfResults control displays the results. The cmdSearch_Click() event differs slightly from cmdSort_Click() in that it performs a special check to see whether the array is already sorted. If the array is sorted, the sorted elements are in the rtfResults control. Otherwise, the cmdSearch_Click() event gathers the unsorted elements from the txtInput control. This information is used later when the call is made to the BinarySearch() function to tell it whether the array being passed is already sorted.

The cmdSort_Click() event simply sorts the values in the text box and puts the results in the rtfInput control. The cmdSearch_Click() event also puts a sorted array into the rtfInput control, but also highlights the element for which you were searching if the event finds the element. To do so, the event uses a special series of code in the LoadArrayIntoRTF() method (which this chapter doesn't show).

Going a Step Further with Linked Lists

The example in this section demonstrates the CS concept of a doubly linked list using Visual Basic classes. This concept already exists in Visual Basic in the form of collections, and this code should give you a better idea of how collections work. In addition, this implementation enables you to extend the concept of collections by writing your own doubly linked list that supports features not found in standard collections.

Creating the *Item* Object and Helper Functions   The example's class object, Item, shown in Listing 34.9, is a simple class that contains only the members for the object and the pointers to the next and previous items in the list.

Part
V

Ch
34

Listing 34.9   ITEM.CLS—Item.cls Contains the Object that Will be Used in Our Linked List

```
/********************************************************************
' Item.cls - This class is simply the data structure for a doubly
'    linked list.
'********************************************************************
Option Explicit
'********************************************************************
' Data members
'********************************************************************
Public strData As String
Public intData As Integer
'********************************************************************
```

continues

Listing 34.9   Continued

```
' Doubly-Linked List Pointers
'*************************************************************************
Public clsItemNext As clsItem
Public clsItemPrev As clsItem
```

By using a class module to create the object, you give yourself the flexibility to create as many data members as you want. However, you must modify your helper functions to support any additions or removal of data members from this class.

Now that you have an Item object, you need to write helper routines that enable you to build and navigate through the linked list. Listing 34.10 includes the InsertAfter() and RemoveItem() functions that are designed to add new elements to the list and remove existing elements. LISTHELPERS.BAS also includes an InsertBefore() function, but Listing 34.10 doesn't show it because it is virtually identical to the InsertAfter() function. Consult the LISTDEMO.VBP project for details on the implementation of the InsertBefore() function.

Listing 34.10   LISTHELPERS.BAS—Adding and Removing Elements

```
'*************************************************************************
' Inserts a new item in the linked list after an existing item
'*************************************************************************
Public Function InsertAfter(clsPrevious As clsItem, _
    Optional strData$, Optional intData As Integer) As clsItem
    '*********************************************************************
    ' If clsPrevious hasn't been initialized, then bail...
    '*********************************************************************
    If clsPrevious Is Nothing Then
        MsgBox "InsertAfter failed: Previous item was invalid", _
            vbExclamation
        Exit Function
    End If
    '*********************************************************************
    ' Create the new item
    '*********************************************************************
    Dim clsNewItem As New clsItem
    '*********************************************************************
    ' If the clsPrevious is the not the tail item, then the item after
    ' clsPrevious needs its clsItemPrev pointer set to the new item.
    '*********************************************************************
    If Not (clsPrevious.clsItemNext Is Nothing) Then
        Set clsPrevious.clsItemNext.clsItemPrev = clsNewItem
    End If
    '*********************************************************************
    ' Set the values for the newly created item
    '*********************************************************************
    With clsNewItem
        .strData = strData
```

```
            .intData = intData
            Set .clsItemPrev = clsPrevious
            Set .clsItemNext = clsPrevious.clsItemNext
        End With
        '********************************************************************
        ' Point the previous item to the newly created item
        '********************************************************************
        Set clsPrevious.clsItemNext = clsNewItem
        '********************************************************************
        ' Increment the item count
        '********************************************************************
        mintCount = mintCount + 1
        '********************************************************************
        ' Return a pointer to the newly inserted item
        '********************************************************************
        Set InsertAfter = clsNewItem
End Function
'************************************************************************
' Remove an item in the doubly linked list
'************************************************************************
Public Function RemoveItem(clsItemToRemove As clsItem) As clsItem
        '********************************************************************
        ' If a valid item was not passed, then bail...
        '********************************************************************
        If clsItemToRemove Is Nothing Then
            MsgBox "You can't remove an uninitialized item!", vbExclamation
        End If
        '********************************************************************
        ' If the item to remove is the tail...
        '********************************************************************
        If clsItemToRemove.clsItemNext Is Nothing Then
            '****************************************************************
            ' If Next = Nothing & Prev = Nothing, the last item in list!
            '****************************************************************
            If clsItemToRemove.clsItemPrev Is Nothing Then
                MsgBox "Can not remove the last item in the list!", _
                    vbExclamation
                '************************************************************
                ' Return a pointer to clsItemToRemove
                '************************************************************
                Set RemoveItem = clsItemToRemove
                Exit Function
            '****************************************************************
            ' Otherwise, remove the item and return a pointer to the
            ' previous item
            '****************************************************************
            Else
                Set clsItemToRemove.clsItemPrev.clsItemNext = _
                    clsItemToRemove.clsItemNext
                Set RemoveItem = clsItemToRemove.clsItemPrev
            End If
        '********************************************************************
        ' Otherwise, something must be after the item to remove...
        '********************************************************************
        Else
```

Part

V

Ch

34

continues

Listing 34.10   Continued

```
'***************************************************************
' If clsItemToRemove is the head, them remove the head and
' set a new head of the list.
' OPTIONAL: You may want to raise an error here
'***************************************************************
If clsItemToRemove.clsItemPrev Is Nothing Then
    Set clsItemToRemove.clsItemNext.clsItemPrev = _
        clsItemToRemove.clsItemPrev
    Set RemoveItem = clsItemToRemove.clsItemNext
'***************************************************************
' Otherwise clsItemToRemove is in the middle of the list...
'***************************************************************
Else
        Set clsItemToRemove.clsItemPrev.clsItemNext =
clsItemToRemove.clsItemNext
        Set clsItemToRemove.clsItemNext.clsItemPrev =
clsItemToRemove.clsItemPrev
        Set RemoveItem = clsItemToRemove.clsItemPrev
    End If
End If
'***************************************************************
' Decrement the linked list item count
'***************************************************************
mintCount = mintCount - 1
'***************************************************************
' Destroy the item to be removed
'***************************************************************
Set clsItemToRemove = Nothing
End Function
```

Although the purposes of these two functions are entirely different, the methodology used to accomplish their result is similar. When you add or remove an item to or from the list, you must manipulate the list's clsItemPrev and clsItemNext member variables. The AddItem() function points these members to the newly created item, whereas the RemoveItem() function points these members to the objects before and after the item being removed. When the operation is complete, both functions return a pointer to a valid object in the list. Closely examine both of these functions to see how various situations influence these functions' code paths.

The GetIndex() function is useful for retrieving a specific element of the collection (see Listing 34.11). You can retrieve the index by using any of the data members of Item as the index or "key." To retrieve the element, the function performs a linear search through the linked list until it finds the requested element. If GetIndex() finds no match, it returns Nothing.

Listing 34.11   LISTHELPERS.BAS—Retrieving a Specific Element

```
'***************************************************************
' Returns a pointer to a specific item in the list
'***************************************************************
```

```
Public Function GetIndex(clsStart As clsItem, Optional strData$, _
    Optional intData As Integer) As clsItem
    '******************************************************************
    ' If the user didn't tell us where to start, then bail...
    '******************************************************************
    If clsStart Is Nothing Then Exit Function
    '******************************************************************
    ' If the user didn't tell us which item to select, then bail...
    '******************************************************************
    If intData = 0 And strData = "" Then Exit Function
    '******************************************************************
    ' Dim a pointer for iterating through the linked list
    '******************************************************************
    Dim clsCurItem As clsItem
    '******************************************************************
    ' Set the pointer to the item the user told us to begin with
    '******************************************************************
    Set clsCurItem = clsStart
    '******************************************************************
    ' Linear search through all items in the list
    '******************************************************************
    Do While Not (clsCurItem.clsItemNext Is Nothing)
        With clsCurItem
            If .intData = intData Or .strData = strData Then
                '******************************************************
                ' Return a pointer to the found item and exit
                '******************************************************
                Set GetIndex = clsCurItem
                Exit Function
            End If
            Set clsCurItem = .clsItemNext
        End With
    Loop
    '******************************************************************
    ' Check the data members of the last item in the list
    '******************************************************************
    With clsCurItem
        If .intData = intData Or .strData = strData Then
            '******************************************************
            ' Return a pointer to the found item
            '******************************************************
            Set GetIndex = clsCurItem
        End If
    End With
    '******************************************************************
    ' If not found, then return Nothing (by not doing anything)
    '******************************************************************
End Function
```

The key to the GetIndex() function is the capability to iterate through the linked list. To provide this capability, you create a pointer to the start item and traverse the list. You walk the list by setting the clsCurItem pointer to the clsNextItem member of clsCurItem until you reach the tail.

Using the Doubly Linked List   Now that you have defined the Item object and have the helper functions in place, you are ready to use your linked list. Listing 34.12 shows the linked list in action after a couple of operations have been performed on it. You should experiment with this sample to discover advantages and disadvantages of this linked list compared to arrays and Visual Basic collections.

Listing 34.12 shows one way to populate and destroy the linked list. Although this example is rather simple, it does highlight some of the challenges of using linked lists. The list initially begins with a head element and three additional objects. After you build the initial list, the mclsCurItem pointer points to the last item added to the list.

Listing 34.12   LISTDEMO.FRM—Building and Destroying the List

```
'**********************************************************************
' ListDemo - Demonstrates one way to build and use a linked list
'**********************************************************************
Option Explicit
'**********************************************************************
' Form-level pointers to the head and current item in the linked list
'**********************************************************************
Private mclsHead As New clsItem
Private mclsCurItem As clsItem
'**********************************************************************
' Builds the initial list, sets the head, and does some prep work
'**********************************************************************
Private Sub Form_Load()
    Dim i As Integer
    '******************************************************************
    ' Optional - label the head (helpful during debugging)
    '******************************************************************
    mclsHead.strData = "Head"
    '******************************************************************
    ' Set the current item to the head
    '******************************************************************
    Set mclsCurItem = mclsHead
    '******************************************************************
    ' Create three items to give the user something to play with
    '******************************************************************
    For i = 1 To 3
        Set mclsCurItem = _
                    InsertAfter(mclsCurItem, "Item " & CStr(i), i)
    Next i
    ... ' Code has been intentionally omitted from this listing
End Sub
'**********************************************************************
' Although VB is supposed to do cleanup, I feel better freeing the
' list myself. This is not a required element of this program.
'**********************************************************************
Private Sub Form_Unload(Cancel As Integer)
    '******************************************************************
    ' Let's be good citizens and free the list ourselves
    '******************************************************************
    Dim clsCurItem As clsItem
```

```
        Set clsCurItem = mclsHead.clsItemNext
        '*********************************************************************
        ' Remove all of the items in the list (printing the count in the
        ' Immediate window)
        '*********************************************************************
        Do While Not (clsCurItem.clsItemNext Is Nothing)
            Set clsCurItem = RemoveItem(clsCurItem)
            Debug.Print basListHelpers.Count
        Loop
End Sub
```

The Form_Unload() event demonstrates the concept of traversing the list to destroy all its elements. You specifically unload this list because you cannot rely on Visual Basic doing the proper cleanup of these objects itself.

After you create the initial list and load the form, the user is in control of the linked list. The user can add or remove any items by using the cmdInsertBefore and cmdRemoveItem command buttons. Listing 34.13 describes each of these controls' click events in detail.

Listing 34.13 LISTDEMO.FRM—Adding and Removing Items

```
'*************************************************************************
' Inserts an item in the list before the item specified by the user
'*************************************************************************
Private Sub cmdInsertBefore_Click()
    '*********************************************************************
    ' Get a pointer to the item that will be after the newly inserted
    ' item.
    '*********************************************************************
    Set mclsCurItem = GetIndex(mclsHead, , Val(InputBox( _
        "Enter a integer index:", "InsertBefore", _
        CStr(mclsCurItem.intData))))
    '*********************************************************************
    ' Insert the item in the list (using some generated default data)
    '*********************************************************************
    Set mclsCurItem = InsertBefore(mclsCurItem, "Item " & _
        CStr(basListHelpers.Count + 1), basListHelpers.Count + 1)
    '*********************************************************************
    ' If InsertBefore worked, then update the list box and labels
    '*********************************************************************
    If Not (mclsCurItem Is Nothing) Then UpdateFormItems
End Sub
'*************************************************************************
' Removes the currently selected item
'*************************************************************************
Private Sub cmdRemoveItem_Click()
    '*********************************************************************
    ' RemoveItem returns a pointer to another item in the list, so
    ' keep that value for further processing.
    '*********************************************************************
    Dim clsReturn As clsItem
    '*********************************************************************
```

Part

V

Ch

34

continues

Listing 34.13 Continued

```
    ' Don't let the user remove the head (optional)
    '******************************************************************
    If mclsCurItem.strData = mclsHead.strData Then
        MsgBox "You can't remove the head. Please select another item."
        Exit Sub
    End If
    '******************************************************************
    ' If there is more than one item in the list...
    '******************************************************************
    If basListHelpers.Count > 1 Then
        '**************************************************************
        ' Remove the current item and catch the pointer to the item
        ' returned by RemoveItem.
        '**************************************************************
        Set clsReturn = RemoveItem(mclsCurItem)
        '**************************************************************
        ' If clsReturn doesn't have an item in front of it, then it
        ' is the tail.
        '**************************************************************
        If clsReturn.clsItemNext Is Nothing Then
            '**********************************************************
            ' If nothing is before the item returned, then clsReturn
            ' is the last item in the list (which is the head)
            '**********************************************************
            If clsReturn.clsItemPrev Is Nothing Then
                Set mclsCurItem = Nothing
            '**********************************************************
            ' Otherwise set the current item to the 2nd to last item
            '**********************************************************
            Else
                Set mclsCurItem = clsReturn.clsItemPrev
            End If
        '**************************************************************
        ' Otherwise, set the current item to whatever is in front of
        ' clsReturn (because clsReturn could be the head)
        '**************************************************************
        Else
            Set mclsCurItem = clsReturn.clsItemNext
        End If
        '**************************************************************
        ' Update the list box and labels to reflect this change
        '**************************************************************
        UpdateFormItems
    End If
End Sub
```

Adding items is rather simple. You ask the user where to add the item and then let InsertBefore do the dirty work. Adding the new item updates the form-level pointer, mclsCurItem, to the current item in the list. If the item is added successfully, you update the display.

Removing items is a little more tedious because you have to test for special cases such as deleting the head or tail. After removing the item, you check to ensure that a valid pointer was returned. If the pointer is valid, you set the `mclsCurItem` variable to a valid object. Finally, you update the display to reflect the modified list's contents.

Twiddling Bits in Visual Basic

This section demonstrates some fundamental concepts of bit manipulation. Figure 34.3 shows the "bit-twiddling" program. This program provides a graphical display of the effects of setting bits and extracting words and bytes for larger values.

FIG. 34.3

HEXTOBIN.VBP demonstrates basic bit-manipulation techniques.

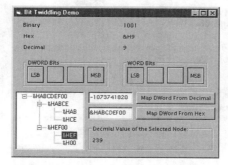

To break double words into words and break words into bytes, you need a module that performs these operations for you. The BITCONVERT.BAS module shown in Listing 34.14 does so by defining four of the most common bit-conversion functions used in the Win32 API. These functions might look familiar to you because just about everyone has had to write them at some time in his or her Visual Basic programming career. The functions in this listing are just one interpretation of how you should write them. You might have already written your own version; however, if you haven't, you'll want to include these functions as a basic part of your code library.

Part V

Ch

34

Listing 34.14   BITCONVERT.BAS—BitConvert.bas Demonstrates Some Common Bit Manipulation Techniques

```
'*******************************************************************
' BitConvert.bas - Extracts high and low bits from values
'*******************************************************************
Option Explicit
'*******************************************************************
' Get the low byte of a word
'*******************************************************************
Public Function LoByte(intWord As Integer) As Integer
    Dim intResult As Integer
    intResult = intWord And &HFF
    LoByte = intResult
End Function
```

continues

Listing 34.14 Continued

```
'****************************************************************
' Get the high byte of a word
'****************************************************************
Public Function HiByte(intWord As Integer) As Integer
    Dim intResult As Integer
    intResult = (intWord And &HFF00&) \ &HFF&
    HiByte = intResult
End Function
'****************************************************************
' Returns the lower 4 bytes of a DWORD
'****************************************************************
Public Function LoWord(lngDWord As Long) As Integer
    If lngDWord And &H8000& Then
        LoWord = &H8000 Or (lngDWord And &H7FFF&)
    Else
        LoWord = lngDWord And &HFFFF&
    End If
End Function
'****************************************************************
' Returns the upper 4 bytes of a DWORD
'****************************************************************
Public Function HiWord(lngDWord As Long) As Integer
    HiWord = lngDWord \ &H10000
End Function
```

All these functions apply the same concept of taking a larger value and returning half of the original bits. Examine the code to see how to perform this extraction, and experiment with them using the sample program. Because you use only signed values in Visual Basic, the return values for some of these functions might surprise you.

Listing 34.15 contains the code for the `picWord_Click` event. `picWord` is a control array of picture boxes that act like buttons for the purpose of setting and clearing bits. Figure 34.3 shows this control array in the word bits frame on the right side of the form.

Listing 34.15 HEXTOBIN.FRM—Toggling Specific Bits

```
'****************************************************************
' Toggles bits on and off (PictureBox acting as button)
'****************************************************************
Private Sub picWord_Click(Index As Integer)
    '****************************************************************
    ' A persistent variable to hold the WORD
    '****************************************************************
    Static sintBits As Integer
    '****************************************************************
    ' Maintain the state of the PictureBox in its tag
    '****************************************************************
    picWord(Index).Tag = Not CBool(picWord(Index).Tag)
```

```
'*******************************************************************
' Declare an integer to mask with sintBits
'*******************************************************************
Dim intMask As Integer
'*******************************************************************
' Get the mask for the bit button that was clicked
'*******************************************************************
Select Case Index
    Case 0 ' LSB
        intMask = &H1 '1
    Case 1
        intMask = &H2 '2
    Case 2
        intMask = &H4 '4
    Case 3 ' MSB
        intMask = &H8 '8
End Select
'*******************************************************************
' You toggle bits by Xor'ing them with their mask value
'*******************************************************************
sintBits = sintBits Xor intMask
'*******************************************************************
' Draw raised or depressed depending on the setting of the bits
'*******************************************************************
Draw3DBorder picWord(Index), sintBits And intMask
'*******************************************************************
' Update the labels to show the different views of sintBits
'*******************************************************************
UpdateLabels sintBits
End Sub
```

When the user clicks one of the controls in this array, you use the Xor operator either to set or clear the bit. You then display the control as either up or down to indicate its current setting. After setting the bit and drawing the button, you populate the labels with a graphical representation of the current bit pattern.

To set a specific bit, your code must apply the Xor operator to a bit mask. Put simply, you mask with the "on" bit of the bit that you are trying to set. For example, if you want to toggle the first bit, your mask is 1; to toggle the third bit, your mask is 4. The code sample demonstrates this with a two-byte integer value (also called a WORD). HEXTOBIN.FRM also includes the source code for applying this same concept to a four-byte-long value (also called a DWORD).

Rarely in your Visual Basic programming life will you need to see the actual binary representation of a value. However, the whole purpose of the HEXTOBIN.FRM example is to present data in its hexadecimal, decimal, and binary equivalents. To convert a value into its binary equivalent, you must divide a quotient by two until you can no longer divide it, then use each iteration's remainder as the bit's value. Listing 34.16 performs this operation in a loop and sets each bit's value in a string that you return to the caller.

Listing 34.16   HEXTOBIN.FRM—*ConvertToBinary()* Displays a Value as Its Binary Equivalent

```
'*******************************************************************
' Converts a long into its binary equivalent and returns a string
' with spaces between every four bits
'*******************************************************************
Private Function ConvertToBinary(ByVal lngQuotient As Long, _
    Optional intBits As Integer) As String

    Dim strBinary As String
    Dim strReturn As String
    Dim i As Integer
    '***************************************************************
    ' If intBits isn't provided, then use the default of 4
    '***************************************************************
    i = IIf(intBits, intBits, 4)
    '***************************************************************
    ' Create a string that is large enough to hold the bits so we can
    ' use the Mid statement to replace the zeros with the real bit
    ' values.
    '***************************************************************
    strBinary = String(i, "0")
    '***************************************************************
    ' Loop while the quotient is not zero
    '***************************************************************
    Do While lngQuotient
        '***********************************************************
        ' The remainder is the bit value, so set this value in the str
        '***********************************************************
        Mid(strBinary, i, 1) = CStr(lngQuotient Mod 2)
        '***********************************************************
        ' Divide the quotient by 2 again
        '***********************************************************
        lngQuotient = lngQuotient \ 2
        '***********************************************************
        ' Decrement i, so we'll know which bit to set in strBinary
        '***********************************************************
        i = i - 1
    Loop
    '***************************************************************
    ' DWORDs can be hard to read, so add space between every four bits
    '***************************************************************
    For i = 1 To (intBits \ 4)
        strReturn = strReturn & Left(strBinary, 4) & " "
        strBinary = Mid(strBinary, 5)
    Next i
    '***************************************************************
    ' Return the neatly spaced binary representation of lngQuotient
    '***************************************************************
    ConvertToBinary = strReturn
End Function
```

This code begins by building a default zero-bit string. When you enter the loop, the `Mid()` statement sets each bit in place. After the loop, you check whether the bit string is a DWORD. If so, you add spaces after each bit so it is easier to read.

Listing 34.17 is similar to `ConvertToBinary()`, but a little simpler because Visual Basic already includes the `Hex()` function to convert a value to its hexadecimal equivalent. This code simply converts a value to its hexadecimal equivalent and pads it with leading zeros if necessary.

Listing 34.17 HEXTOBIN.FRM—Displaying a Fixed-Length Hexadecimal Value

```
'*********************************************************************
' Returns a hex string with leading zeros (if necessary)
'*********************************************************************
Private Function GetFixedHex(vntBits As Variant, Optional intBits _
    As Integer) As String

    Dim strResult As String
    Dim strHex As String
    '*****************************************************************
    ' If intBits wasn't provided, then assume 4 bits
    '*****************************************************************
    intBits = IIf(intBits, intBits, 4)
    '*****************************************************************
    ' Get the hex representation of the bits
    '*****************************************************************
    strHex = Hex(vntBits)
    '*****************************************************************
    ' If negative, then check to see if we need to remove leading F's
    '*****************************************************************
    If vntBits < 0 And Len(strHex) > intBits Then
        strHex = Mid(strHex, intBits + 1)
    '*****************************************************************
    ' Otherwise, add leading zeros (if necessary)
    '*****************************************************************
    Else
        strHex = String(intBits - Len(strHex), "0") & strHex
    End If
    '*****************************************************************
    ' Return the result with the VB hex prefix (&H)
    '*****************************************************************
    GetFixedHex = "&H" & strHex
End Function
```

This code enables your program to always display the hexadecimal value in an easy-to-read format. Because each hexadecimal value represents a byte, you ask the user how many bytes the result string should represent. In this way, you can determine how many leading zeros you might need to pad the string.

From Here...

 Although no single chapter can really do this chapter's topic justice, you should have learned enough new techniques to improve your own applications. Many more great examples are throughout this book that exist on **http://www.quecorp.com/sevb5**.

For information about related topics, see the following sources:

- For more advanced coding techniques, review the samples in Chapters 6 through 8.

- Hundreds of great samples are available on the Microsoft KnowledgeBase. You can browse the KnowledgeBase on the Microsoft Web site at **http://www.microsoft. com/kb/**.

- For advanced techniques with OLE Automation, consult the "Integration with Office" section earlier in this book.

CHAPTER 35

Accessing the Windows API

Microsoft added thousands of great new features in the Visual Basic 4.0 and 5.0 releases, but Visual Basic still lacks many features of the Win32 API. These omissions are intentional; because Visual Basic includes the functionality to call the API, not every API function needs to be part of Visual Basic. Another reason for these omissions is that each Win32 API that Visual Basic "wraps" causes the Visual Basic run time to grow longer. The longer the run time, the slower your applications are, and the longer it takes to load the run time when your application boots. Therefore, Microsoft's exclusion of many Win32 API functions is actually a wise decision, because it saves precious space in the Visual Basic run time for cool new features.

This chapter explains how to use some of the more useful API functions, but is far from a complete resource. No single chapter could do this subject justice, but this one should provide enough information to get you started. This chapter's goal is to turn you on to some of the neat things that you can do with the Win32 API. By using the API, you can write more advanced applications that are not possible in pure Visual Basic programming. Read on, and have fun playing with the examples. ■

Learn how to use functions from the Win32 API and DLL's

You will learn how to use several of the Win32 API functions and understand the declaration statements for them.

Write reusable objects that wrap groups of API functions

Most tasks accomplished using the API require a group of specific functions, so you will learn how to group these functions into reusable class objects.

Make the most of the Graphics Device Interface (GDI) in your application

Our `TransparentPaint()` example will show you how to use some common GDI functions to paint transparent bitmaps on to any window.

Master the registry API functions

Learn how to build a powerful class module that encapsulates the functionality of the most commonly used registry API functions.

Calling Basic API and DLL Functions

Although this chapter is not intended to teach you everything there is to know about accessing the API or writing declarations statements for use with DLLs, this section covers some fundamentals. However, this section assumes that you have already read the chapter "Calling Procedures in DLLs" in the *Visual Basic Programmer's Guide*. The information in this chapter is designed to complement the programmer's guide by demonstrating how to implement a variety of helpful API calls.

Calling *GetVersionEx()*

The best way to learn how to use (or call) a DLL is by example. The code in Listing 35.1 demonstrates how to use one of the most common Win32 API calls, GetVersionEx(). When you call this API function, it fills a user-defined type (UDT) called OSVERSIONINFO with information about the Windows version. Closely examine the code in this listing to see how to use this API call and its return values.

Listing 35.1   WINVER.BAS—*GetWindowsVersion()* Returns a Usable String Based on the Values Returned from *GetVersionEx()*

```
'************************************************************************
' Types, constants, and declarations required to get the Win version
'************************************************************************
Private Type OSVERSIONINFO
        dwOSVersionInfoSize As Long
        dwMajorVersion As Long
        dwMinorVersion As Long
        dwBuildNumber As Long
        dwPlatformId As Long
        szCSDVersion As String * 128 'Maintenance string for PSS usage
End Type

Private Const VER_PLATFORM_WIN32_NT = 2
Private Const VER_PLATFORM_WIN32_WINDOWS = 1

Private Declare Function GetVersionEx Lib "kernel32" Alias _
    "GetVersionExA" (lpVersionInformation As OSVERSIONINFO) As Long
'************************************************************************
' Returns a string suitable for displaying in a dialog box
'************************************************************************
Public Function GetWindowsVersion() As String
    Dim strOS As String
    Dim osvVersion As OSVERSIONINFO
    Dim strMaintBuildInfo As String
    '******************************************************************
    ' Many Win32 APIs have a first parameter that indicates the size
    ' of the structure (in bytes) so these structures will be portable
```

```
' to future OS versions or different systems (such as 64-bit
' systems or OSs). It is your responsibility to set this field
' prior to making the API call, and the Len function helps you
' to do that.
'*********************************************************************
osvVersion.dwOSVersionInfoSize = Len(osvVersion)
'*********************************************************************
' Get the version (exit if the GetVersionEx failed)
'*********************************************************************
If GetVersionEx(osvVersion) = 0 Then Exit Function
'*********************************************************************
' Get a string that represents the installed operating system
'*********************************************************************
Select Case osvVersion.dwPlatformId
    Case VER_PLATFORM_WIN32_WINDOWS
        strOS = "Windows "
    Case VER_PLATFORM_WIN32_NT
        strOS = "Windows NT "
    Case Else ' Impossible because VB doesn't run under Win32s
        strOS = "Win32s "
End Select
'*********************************************************************
' Get the major, minor, and build numbers and concatenate them
' to the OS name
'*********************************************************************
With osvVersion
    strOS = strOS & CStr(.dwMajorVersion) & "." & _
        CStr(.dwMinorVersion) & "." & _
        CStr(.dwBuildNumber And &HFFFF&)

    strMaintBuildInfo = Left(.szCSDVersion, _
        InStr(.szCSDVersion, Chr(0)))
End With
'*********************************************************************
' If this isn't a maintenance build (i.e., 4.xx.xxxx A)...
'*********************************************************************
If strMaintBuildInfo = Chr(0) Then
    GetWindowsVersion = strOS
'*********************************************************************
' Otherwise include the maintenance build info
'*********************************************************************
Else
    GetWindowsVersion = strOS & " " & _
        Left(strMaintBuildInfo, Len(strMaintBuildInfo) - 1)
End If
End Function
```

Part

V

Ch

35

This API call exhibits a common trait among many Win32 API calls in that it requires you to set the first member of the structure (dwOSVersionInfoSize) *before* calling the API function. This trait is new for Win32 and wasn't required in earlier versions of Windows. Microsoft added this trait to enable you to port the Win32 API to future processors without needing a new set of APIs. This means (in theory) that this chapter's Win32 code should work unchanged in the future when the desktop computer world moves to 64-bits.

Declaring API Functions

Now that you have seen how to use the `GetVersionEx()` API call in Visual Basic, this section shows how to make this API available to Visual Basic. To make a function call from an external source (such as a DLL or the Win32 API), you must write a declaration for this API in the General Declarations section. Here is what the declaration for `GetVersionEx` looks like:

```
Private Declare Function GetVersionEx Lib "kernel32" Alias _
"GetVersionExA" (lpVersionInformation As OSVERSIONINFO) As Long
```

To understand what this call really means, dissect it. The first three words, `Private Declare Function`, specify that you are declaring an external function for use only within the current module. The next word, `GetVersionEx`, when used with the `Alias` label, declares that you want to refer to this function in your Visual Basic code by using the word `GetVersionEx`. When you use `Alias`, this value could be anything. You could choose to call this value `MyGetWinVer`, for example.

The next two words, `Lib "kernel32"`, tell Visual Basic which library contains this function. (The library is a DLL, but use of the DLL extension is optional.) The next two words, `Alias "GetVersionExA"`, tell Visual Basic that whenever your program calls `GetVersionEx`, it should call the function `GetVersionExA` in KERNEL32.DLL. So far, the API call format we have been describing is similar to what you will see in most API declarations. The function, library, and alias names differ, but all these items appear in most API calls.

The next part of this call contains this function's argument list, `GetVersionExA`. It only has one parameter of type `OSVERSION` information that must be passed by reference (the default). Finally, the last two words, `As Long`, indicate that the function `GetVersionExA` returns a `Long` value.

Calling Functions in Other DLLs

Almost every document that you will ever read about using DLLs in Visual Basic will use the API DLLs as an example. At the end of these documents, the writer will explain how you can also grab these declarations out of the API Text Viewer program. Such documents give you a false sense of security because you depend heavily on the API Text Viewer for your API declarations. As soon as most programmers get a DLL (or new API) that doesn't appear in the API Text Viewer, they realize that they never really learned how to write a declaration themselves. Therefore, this section presents an exercise in which you look at the code for a small program and try to guess the API declarations.

Listing 35.2 uses two functions from a DLL that creates and resolves shortcuts. The functions, `CreateShortcut` and `ResolveShortcut`, are located in a DLL called SHORTCUT.DLL, and both return a `Long` value. Listing 35.2 retains all the comments and source code for this program, but the declaration statements are shown exclusively in Listing 35.3. Your mission (should you choose to accept it) is to examine the code in Listing 35.2 and figure out what the declaration statement should be. Write your declaration on a sheet of paper and compare it with the actual declarations in Listing 35.3. Good luck!

Listing 35.2 SHORTCUT.FRM—Using a Helper DLL to Manipulate Windows Shortcuts

```
'*********************************************************************
' Shortcut.frm - Uses Ronald R. Martinsen's shortcut.dll file to
'    create and resolve Windows 95 shortcuts.
'*********************************************************************
Option Explicit
'*********************************************************************
' Constant for the path of the shortcut file used for simplicity's sake.
' This isn't required.
'*********************************************************************
Private Const SHORTCUTPATH As String = "c:\Shortcut to Notepad.lnk"
'*********************************************************************
' CreateShortcut - Required function declaration to create a shortcut
' with the helper DLL.
'-------------------------------------------------------------------
' strSourceFile - File name of the target of the shortcut (can be a
'                   file, directory, or object)
' strLinkFile   - Name of the shortcut file on the disk (always use
'                   the LNK extension!!!!)
' strInitDir    - The current directory when the application starts*
' strArgs       - Command-line arguments (i.e., file name)*
' intCmdShow    - Determines how to display the window (use Shell
'                   function constants)
' strIconPath   - The location of the DLL or EXE with the icon you
'                   wish to use.*
' intIconIndex  - The index of the icon you wish to use (used only if
'                   strIconPath was supplied)
' * = use vbNullString for the default
' RETURNS       - Zero if the call worked, otherwise a SCODE HRESULT.
'*********************************************************************
<< DECLARATION GOES HERE >>
'*********************************************************************
' ResolveShortcut - Required function declaration to get the target
' path to a shortcut file.
'-------------------------------------------------------------------
' hWndOfYourForm      - The handle (hWnd property) of the calling
'                         window
' strShortcutFile     - File name of the shortcut
' strShortcutLocation - Return buffer for the path of the object the
'                         shortcut points to
' RETURNS             - Zero if the call worked, otherwise a SCODE
'                         HRESULT.
'*********************************************************************
<< DECLARATION GOES HERE >>
'*********************************************************************
' Create the shortcut in c:\
'*********************************************************************
Private Sub cmdCreateShortcut_Click()
    Dim strMessage As String
    '*********************************************************************
    ' Get the the path to the Windows directory
    '*********************************************************************
```

Part

V

Ch

35

continues

Listing 35.2   Continued

```
    Dim strWinDir As String
    strWinDir = Environ("windir")
    '****************************************************************
    ' Try to create a shortcut to notepad.exe. Build the err string
    ' if the call failed.
    '****************************************************************
    If CreateShortcut(strWinDir & "\notepad.exe", SHORTCUTPATH, _
        "c:\", vbNullString, vbMaximizedFocus, vbNullString, 1) Then
            ' Nonzero result, so notify the user that the call failed
            strMessage = "Unable to create a shortcut to Notepad. Check "
            strMessage = strMessage & "the source code parameters and try"
            strMessage = strMessage & "again."
    '****************************************************************
    ' Otherwise, the call worked, so tell the user
    '****************************************************************
    Else
        strMessage = "A shortcut to Notepad was created in c:\"
        '************************************************************
        ' Enable the resolve button now, since the file exists
        '************************************************************
        cmdResolveShortcut.Enabled = True
    End If
    '****************************************************************
    ' Display the success or failed message
    '****************************************************************
    MsgBox strMessage
End Sub
'********************************************************************
' Resolve the shortcut in c:\ (created in Command1_Click)
'********************************************************************
Private Sub cmdResolveShortcut_Click()
    Dim strShortcutTargetPath As String, strTemp As String
    '****************************************************************
    ' Build a buffer for the return string
    '****************************************************************
    strShortcutTargetPath = Space(260)
    '****************************************************************
    ' Make the call
    '----------------------------------------------------------------
    ' NOTE: If the TARGET (the return value) can't be found,
    '       then Win95 will display search dialog while it
    '       attempts to find it
    '****************************************************************
    If ResolveShortcut(hWnd, SHORTCUTPATH, strShortcutTargetPath) Then
        '************************************************************
        ' Nonzero result, so notify the user that the call failed
        '************************************************************
        MsgBox "Unable to resolve your shortcut", vbCritical
    Else
    '****************************************************************
    ' Trim the null terminator and display the results
    '****************************************************************
    strShortcutTargetPath = Left(strShortcutTargetPath, _
```

```
      InStr(strShortcutTargetPath, Chr(0)) - 1)
   MsgBox "Your shortcut points to " & strShortcutTargetPath, _
      vbInformation
   End If
End Sub
```

Listing 35.2 appears a bit long mainly because it includes many comments. In reality, this program is rather trivial. The essential function, CreateShortcut, simply takes the same values that you would normally see in a property page when creating a shortcut. ResolveShortcut is even simpler because you provide it with the path to a shortcut file, and it simply loads strShortcutLocation with the path to the file to which the shortcut references. This code features some common techniques for working with API functions that use strings, so pay close attention to the comments.

As promised, Listing 35.3 contains the function declarations for the CreateShortcut and ResolveShortcut functions. Were your declarations the same? If so, congratulations! If not, don't feel bad. Writing declarations can be a little tricky, especially if you've never programmed Windows in C.

Listing 35.3 SHORTCUT.FRM—The *CreateShortcut* and *ResolveShortcut* Function Declarations

```
Private Declare Function CreateShortcut Lib "shortcut.dll" _
   (ByVal strSourceFile$, ByVal strLinkFile$, ByVal strInitDir$, _
   ByVal strArgs$, ByVal intCmdShow%, ByVal strIconPath$, _
   ByVal lngIconIndex As Long) As Long

Private Declare Function ResolveShortcut Lib "shortcut.dll" _
   (ByVal hWndOfYourForm As Long, ByVal strShortcutFile As String, _
   ByVal strShortcutLocation As String) As Long
```

Thus concludes this crash course on writing declarations. If you are interested in learning more, Daniel Appleman's fantastic reference book the *Visual Basic Programmer's Guide to the Win32 API* (Ziff-Davis Press© 1996) covers this topic extensively. Every Visual Basic programmer should purchase a copy of this book, because it is the only resource that translates the Windows API into a form that Visual Basic programmers can use.

Getting Down to the Good Stuff

This section has an unorthodox title because it discusses API examples that I classify as "cool." None of these APIs is especially difficult to use, but all are extremely helpful to have in your sample code library. You start easy and graduate toward more complex use of the API in combination with advanced Visual Basic code techniques. Finally, you write the TransparentPaint() function, which is almost purely API programming in Visual Basic. All the listings in this section are rather large due to the complexity of the samples, but don't let that

Part
V

Ch
35

discourage you. Each sample is commented well enough that any intermediate programmer should be able to follow along.

Warming Up with the Memory Class

Instead of diving right into a complicated example, you first need to understand the memory class. Most programmers like to include basic memory information in their About boxes, but Visual Basic does not provide any method for doing so. If you want to know how much random access memory your machine has, you have to call the Windows API. Although this isn't a terrible inconvenience, many programmers have written duplicate code many different ways to accomplish the same objective. This section presents a useful, yet reusable, class for getting memory information.

Listing 35.4 is a memory class that prevents you from having to mess with the API. This class is structured so that you can easily add additional features.

Listing 35.4   MEMORY.CLS—Demonstrating How to Wrap an API Function into a Reusable Class Object

```
'*******************************************************************
' Memory.cls - This class takes a snapshot of the memory status and
'    provides the user with a simple interface to get common
'    information about the current memory status.
'*******************************************************************
Option Explicit
'*******************************************************************
' Win32 required user-defined type (or struct) and declaration
'*******************************************************************
Private Type MEMORYSTATUS
        dwLength As Long
        dwMemoryLoad As Long
        dwTotalPhys As Long
        dwAvailPhys As Long
        dwTotalPageFile As Long
        dwAvailPageFile As Long
        dwTotalVirtual As Long
        dwAvailVirtual As Long
End Type

Private Declare Sub GlobalMemoryStatus Lib "kernel32" _
        (lpBuffer As MEMORYSTATUS)
'*******************************************************************
' Private member variable which holds the current memory status
'*******************************************************************
Private mmemMemoryStatus As MEMORYSTATUS
'*******************************************************************
' Returns the number of bytes of available physical RAM (OK if zero)
'*******************************************************************
Public Property Get FreeMemory() As Long
```

```
        FreeMemory = mmemMemoryStatus.dwAvailPhys
End Property
'***********************************************************************
' Returns the number of bytes of RAM installed in the computer
'***********************************************************************
Public Property Get TotalMemory() As Long
    TotalMemory = mmemMemoryStatus.dwTotalPhys
End Property
'***********************************************************************
' Returns the number of bytes of virtual memory allocated by the
' operating system
'***********************************************************************
Public Property Get TotalVirtualMemory() As Long
    TotalVirtualMemory = mmemMemoryStatus.dwTotalVirtual
End Property
'***********************************************************************
' Returns the number of bytes of virtual memory available to this
' process
'***********************************************************************
Public Property Get AvailableVirtualMemory() As Long
    AvailableVirtualMemory = mmemMemoryStatus.dwAvailVirtual
End Property
'***********************************************************************
' Calls the operating system to find out the memory status at the
' time this object is created
'***********************************************************************
Private Sub Class_Initialize()
    mmemMemoryStatus.dwLength = Len(mmemMemoryStatus)
    GlobalMemoryStatus mmemMemoryStatus
End Sub
'***********************************************************************
' Updates this object with current memory status
'***********************************************************************
Public Sub Refresh()
    GlobalMemoryStatus mmemMemoryStatus
End Sub
```

This class simply wraps the GlobalMemoryStatus API function. When the class is created, the API call is made in the Initialize() event, so this class is ready for use with no additional initialization necessary. Your application needs only to create a new variable of this class and access the properties that satisfy your program's needs. The class includes a public method called Refresh() that updates mmemMemoryStatus, just in case you have a need to do so.

Listing 35.5 uses clsMemorySnapshot the way that it is designed to be used. An application should define a variable of this class only in the local subroutine or function in which you are using it. Then every time that your subroutine or function is called, you get the current memory information. MEMDEMO.FRM displays some of the properties from the clsMem object and includes a special note about the return value from the FreeMemory property.

Part
V

Ch
35

Listing 35.5   MEMDEMO.FRM—Demonstrating How to Use
clsMemorySnapshot

```
'*********************************************************************
' MemDemo.frm - Demonstrates how to use clsMemorySnapshot
'*********************************************************************
Option Explicit
'*********************************************************************
' Creates a clsMemorySnapshot object and displays the results
'*********************************************************************
Private Sub cmdGetMemoryStatus_Click()
    '*****************************************************************
    ' The efficent way to use clsMemorySnapshot is to create a new
    ' clsMemorySnapshot object every time you need to get the memory
    ' status, so that is what we will do.
    '*****************************************************************
    Dim clsMem As New clsMemorySnapshot
    '*****************************************************************
    ' Holds the current ForeColor of the form since we'll need to
    ' change it temporarily.
    '*****************************************************************
    Dim lngForeColor As Long
    '*****************************************************************
    ' Always clear the form before displaying new information
    '*****************************************************************
    Cls
    With clsMem
        '*************************************************************
        ' Print physical memory information
        '*************************************************************
        Print "Total Installed RAM", Format(.TotalMemory \ 1024, _
            "###,###,###,###,##0") & " KB"
        Print "Free Physical RAM", Format(.FreeMemory \ 1024, _
            "###,###,###,###,##0") & " KB";
        '*************************************************************
        ' Print an asterisk that stands out in bold red
        '*************************************************************
        Font.Bold = True
        lngForeColor = ForeColor
        ForeColor = RGB(255, 0, 0)
        Print "*"
        '*************************************************************
        ' Restore to the default settings
        '*************************************************************
        ForeColor = lngForeColor
        Font.Bold = False
        '*************************************************************
        ' Print virtual memory information
        '*************************************************************
        Print "Total Virtual Memory", Format(.TotalVirtualMemory \ 1024, _
            "###,###,###,###,##0") & " KB"
        Print "Available Virtual Memory", Format(.AvailableVirtualMemory _
            \ 1024, "###,###,###,###,##0") & " KB"
    End With
    '*****************************************************************
```

```
      ' Print a blank space, then print a comment in bold
      '**********************************************************************
      Print
      Font.Bold = True
      Print "* = It's okay (and common) for this number to be zero."
      '**********************************************************************
      ' Restore the form bold value back to False
      '**********************************************************************
      Font.Bold = False
  End Sub
```

By wrapping an API call in a class, you make it easy to use as a standard Visual Basic object in the `cmdGetMemoryStatus_Click()` event. Wrapping API calls is a great way to simplify the use of many of them, as well as to ensure their proper use. Not only does such wrapping make the API call easy enough for new Visual Basic programmers to use, it also promotes the building of an API object library shared among an entire programming team. You should use this technique as much as possible, and try to keep your classes as simple as possible. After all, to achieve the best performance, you need to remember that "less is more."

Using the API to Overcome Visual Basic's Limitations

Visual Basic is a great language because it is simple enough to enable an intermediate Windows user to learn how to write a Windows application. This simplicity is what has attracted so many programmers, and what enables programmers to write applications in weeks that would take months (or even years) in C. However, this simplicity comes at price. That price is that many Visual Basic functions were written for Visual Basic 1.0, when Microsoft envisioned Visual Basic as being only a hobbyist's programming language or a Windows batch language. No one anticipated that Visual Basic would emerge as the most common programming language for Windows, so many of the version 1.0 functions contain limited functionality. One such function is `Dir`.

Although `Dir` suffices for your fundamental needs, it falls short when you try to perform such actions as searching your hard drive for all the files with the extension BAK. The function falls short for a simple reason: It doesn't support nested calls. After recognizing this shortcoming, Microsoft wrote the WinSeek sample, which uses a file and directory list box control to overcome this limitation. However, this workaround is unacceptable. The spaghetti code in WinSeek is hard to follow, poorly commented, and too slow for even the most trivial tasks.

 The `FindFile` class, shown in Listing 35.6, overcomes the shortcomings of `Dir` and WinSeek. This class encapsulates an API function into a reusable object, which makes the API function as easy to use as a built-in Visual Basic function. `FindFile` also keeps things simple by including only a minimal amount of core functionality. This simplicity enables users of this class to write their own algorithms for such special tasks as searching an entire drive for a specific type of file. In addition to reviewing the source code and comments for this class in Listing 35.6, you should also open FINDFILE.VBP on the book's Web site at **http://www.quecorp.com/sevb5** and view this class in Object Browser. This exercise will help you to examine this class as an object, as well as a sample piece of code that wraps several Win32 API calls.

Part
V

Ch

35

Listing 35.6   FINDFILE.CLS—FindFile.cls is an Object that Encapsulates the File Search API's

```
'*********************************************************************
' FindFile.cls - Encapsulates the Win32 FindFile functions
'*********************************************************************
Option Explicit
'*********************************************************************
' Attribute constants which differ from VB
'*********************************************************************
Private Const FILE_ATTRIBUTE_COMPRESSED = &H800
Private Const FILE_ATTRIBUTE_NORMAL = &H80
'*********************************************************************
' Win32 API constants required by FindFile
'*********************************************************************
Private Const MAX_PATH = 260
Private Const INVALID_HANDLE_VALUE = -1
'*********************************************************************
' Win32 data types (or structs) required by FindFile
'*********************************************************************
Private Type FILETIME
        dwLowDateTime As Long
        dwHighDateTime As Long
End Type

Private Type WIN32_FIND_DATA
        dwFileAttributes As Long
        ftCreationTime As FILETIME
        ftLastAccessTime As FILETIME
        ftLastWriteTime As FILETIME
        nFileSizeHigh As Long
        nFileSizeLow As Long
        dwReserved0 As Long
        dwReserved1 As Long
        cFileName As String * MAX_PATH
        cAlternate As String * 14
End Type

Private Type SYSTEMTIME
        wYear As Integer
        wMonth As Integer
        wDayOfWeek As Integer
        wDay As Integer
        wHour As Integer
        wMinute As Integer
        wSecond As Integer
        wMilliseconds As Integer
End Type
'*********************************************************************
' Win32 API calls required by this class
'*********************************************************************
Private Declare Function FileTimeToLocalFileTime Lib "kernel32" _
    (lpFileTime As FILETIME, lpLocalFileTime As FILETIME) As Long
Private Declare Function FileTimeToSystemTime Lib "kernel32" _
    (lpFileTime As FILETIME, lpSystemTime As SYSTEMTIME) As Long
```

```
Private Declare Function FindFirstFile Lib "kernel32" Alias _
    "FindFirstFileA" (ByVal lpFileName As String, _
    lpFindFileData As WIN32_FIND_DATA) As Long
Private Declare Function FindNextFile Lib "kernel32" Alias _
    "FindNextFileA" (ByVal hFindFile As Long, lpFindFileData As _
    WIN32_FIND_DATA) As Long
Private Declare Function FindClose& Lib "kernel32" (ByVal hFindFile&)
'*********************************************************************
' clsFindFiles private member variables
'*********************************************************************
Private mlngFile As Long
Private mstrDateFormat As String
Private mstrUnknownDateText As String
Private mwfdFindData As WIN32_FIND_DATA
'*********************************************************************
' Public interface for setting the format string used for dates
'*********************************************************************
Public Property Let DateFormat(strDateFormat As String)
    mstrDateFormat = strDateFormat
End Property
'*********************************************************************
' Public interface for setting the string used when the date for a
' file is unknown
'*********************************************************************
Public Property Let UnknownDateText(strUnknownDateText As String)
    mstrUnknownDateText = strUnknownDateText
End Property
'*********************************************************************
' Returns the file attributes for the current file
'*********************************************************************
Public Property Get FileAttributes() As Long
    If mlngFile Then FileAttributes = mwfdFindData.dwFileAttributes
End Property
'*********************************************************************
' Returns true if the compress bit is set for the current file
'*********************************************************************
Public Property Get IsCompressed() As Boolean
    If mlngFile Then IsCompressed = mwfdFindData.dwFileAttributes _
                                And FILE_ATTRIBUTE_COMPRESSED
End Property
'*********************************************************************
' Returns the value of the Normal attribute bit for dwFileAttributes
'*********************************************************************
Public Property Get NormalAttribute() As Long
    NormalAttribute = FILE_ATTRIBUTE_NORMAL
End Property
'*********************************************************************
' Primary method in this class for finding the FIRST matching file in
' a directory that matches the path &¦or pattern in strFile
'*********************************************************************
Public Function Find(strFile As String, Optional blnShowError _
    As Boolean) As String
    '*********************************************************************
    ' If you already searching, then end the current search
    '*********************************************************************
```

continues

Listing 35.6   Continued

```
            If mlngFile Then
                If blnShowError Then
                    If MsgBox("Cancel the current search?", vbYesNo Or _
                        vbQuestion) = vbNo Then Exit Function
                End If
                '*****************************************************************
                ' Call cleanup routines before beginning new search
                '*****************************************************************
                EndFind
            End If
            '*********************************************************************
            ' Find the first file matching the search pattern in strFile
            '*********************************************************************
            mlngFile = FindFirstFile(strFile, mwfdFindData)
            '*********************************************************************
            ' Check to see if FindFirstFile failed
            '*********************************************************************
            If mlngFile = INVALID_HANDLE_VALUE Then
                mlngFile = 0
                '*****************************************************************
                ' If blnShowError, then display a default error message
                '*****************************************************************
                If blnShowError Then
                    MsgBox strFile & " could not be found!", vbExclamation
                '*****************************************************************
                ' Otherwise, raise a user-defined error with a default err msg
                '*****************************************************************
                Else
                    Err.Raise vbObjectError + 5000, "clsFindFile_Find", _
                        strFile & " could not be found!"
                End If
                Exit Function
            End If
            '*********************************************************************
            ' Return the found file name without any nulls
            '*********************************************************************
            Find = Left(mwfdFindData.cFileName, _
                InStr(mwfdFindData.cFileName, Chr(0)) - 1)
End Function
'*************************************************************************
' Call this function until it returns "" to get the remaining files
'*************************************************************************
Public Function FindNext() As String
            '*********************************************************************
            ' Exit if no files have been found
            '*********************************************************************
            If mlngFile = 0 Then Exit Function
            '*********************************************************************
            ' Be sure to clear the contents of cFileName before each call to
            ' avoid garbage characters from being returned in your string.
            '*********************************************************************
            mwfdFindData.cFileName = Space(MAX_PATH)
            '*********************************************************************
```

```
        ' If another file is found, then return it. Otherwise, EndFind.
        '****************************************************************
        If FindNextFile(mlngFile, mwfdFindData) Then
            FindNext = Left(mwfdFindData.cFileName, _
                InStr(mwfdFindData.cFileName, Chr(0)) - 1)
        Else
            EndFind
        End If
End Function
'****************************************************************
' A private helper method which is called internally to close the
' FindFile handle and clear mlngFile to end a FindFile operation.
'****************************************************************
Private Sub EndFind()
    FindClose mlngFile
    mlngFile = 0
End Sub
'****************************************************************
' Return the short name of a found file (default = long file name)
'****************************************************************
Public Function GetShortName() As String
    Dim strShortFileName As String
        '****************************************************************
        ' If no current file, then exit
        '****************************************************************
        If mlngFile = 0 Then Exit Function
        '****************************************************************
        ' Get the short file name (without trailing nulls)
        '****************************************************************
        strShortFileName = Left(mwfdFindData.cAlternate, _
            InStr(mwfdFindData.cAlternate, Chr(0)) - 1)
        '****************************************************************
        ' If there is no short file name info, then strShortFilename will
        ' equal null (because of the (- 1) above
        '****************************************************************
        If Len(strShortFileName) = 0 Then
            '****************************************************************
            ' If no short file name, then it's already a short file name, so
            ' set strShortFileName = .cFileNae.
            '****************************************************************
            strShortFileName = Left(mwfdFindData.cFileName, _
                InStr(mwfdFindData.cFileName, Chr(0)) - 1)
        End If
        '****************************************************************
        ' Return the short file name
        '****************************************************************
        GetShortName = strShortFileName
End Function
'****************************************************************
' Return the date the current file was created. If the optional args
' are provided, then they will be set = to date and time values.
'****************************************************************
Public Function GetCreationDate(Optional datDate As Date, _
    Optional datTime As Date) As String
```

continues

Listing 35.6   Continued

```
    If mlngFile = 0 Then Exit Function
    '************************************************************************
    ' If dwHighDateTime, then Win32 couldn't determine the date, so
    ' return the unknown string. "Unknown" is the default. Set this
    ' value to something else by using the UnknownDateText property.
    '************************************************************************
    If mwfdFindData.ftCreationTime.dwHighDateTime = 0 Then
        GetCreationDate = mstrUnknownDateText
        Exit Function
    End If
    '************************************************************************
    ' Get the time (in the current local/time zone)
    '************************************************************************
    With GetSystemTime(mwfdFindData.ftCreationTime)
        '********************************************************************
        ' If datDate was provided, then set it to a date serial
        '********************************************************************
        datDate = DateSerial(.wYear, .wMonth, .wDay)
        '********************************************************************
        ' If datTime was provided, then set it to a time serial
        '********************************************************************
        datTime = TimeSerial(.wHour, .wMinute, .wSecond)
        '********************************************************************
        ' Use datDate and datTime as local variables (even if they
        ' weren't passed ByRef in the optional args) to create a
        ' a valid date/time value. Return the date/time formatted
        ' using the default format of "m/d/yy h:nn:ss AM/PM" or
        ' the user-defined value which was set using the DateFormat
        ' property.
        '********************************************************************
        GetCreationDate = Format(datDate + datTime, mstrDateFormat)
    End With
End Function
'****************************************************************************
' Similar to GetCreationDate. See GetCreationDate for comments.
'****************************************************************************
Public Function GetLastAccessDate(Optional datDate As Date, _
    Optional datTime As Date) As String

    If mlngFile = 0 Then Exit Function

    If mwfdFindData.ftLastAccessTime.dwHighDateTime = 0 Then
        GetLastAccessDate = mstrUnknownDateText
        Exit Function
    End If

    With GetSystemTime(mwfdFindData.ftLastAccessTime)
        datDate = DateSerial(.wYear, .wMonth, .wDay)
        datTime = TimeSerial(.wHour, .wMinute, .wSecond)
        GetLastAccessDate = Format(datDate + datTime, mstrDateFormat)
    End With
```

```
End Function
'*************************************************************************
' Similar to GetCreationDate. See GetCreationDate for comments.
'*************************************************************************
Public Function GetLastWriteDate(Optional datDate As Date, _
    Optional datTime As Date) As String

    If mlngFile = 0 Then Exit Function

    If mwfdFindData.ftLastWriteTime.dwHighDateTime = 0 Then
        GetLastWriteDate = mstrUnknownDateText
        Exit Function
    End If

    With GetSystemTime(mwfdFindData.ftLastWriteTime)
        datDate = DateSerial(.wYear, .wMonth, .wDay)
        datTime = TimeSerial(.wHour, .wMinute, .wSecond)
        GetLastWriteDate = Format(datDate + datTime, mstrDateFormat)
    End With

End Function
'*************************************************************************
' Takes a FILETIME and converts it into the local system time
'*************************************************************************
Private Function GetSystemTime(ftmFileTime As FILETIME) As SYSTEMTIME
    Dim ftmLocalTime As FILETIME
    Dim stmSystemTime As SYSTEMTIME
    FileTimeToLocalFileTime ftmFileTime, ftmLocalTime
    FileTimeToSystemTime ftmLocalTime, stmSystemTime
    GetSystemTime = stmSystemTime
End Function
'*************************************************************************
' Sets the default values for private members when this object is
' created
'*************************************************************************
Private Sub Class_Initialize()
    mstrUnknownDateText = "Unknown"
    mstrDateFormat = "m/d/yy h:nn:ss AM/PM"
End Sub
'*************************************************************************
' Ends any open finds, if necessary
'*************************************************************************
Private Sub Class_Terminate()
    If mlngFile Then EndFind
End Sub
```

The FindFile class contains private declarations for everything that needs to be both an independent and complete object. Also, the class is about 60 percent faster than WinSeek. However, performance is not the only reason to use the FindFile class. It provides a wealth of information about each found file, and supports searching unmapped networked drives using Universal Naming Convention (UNC) paths.

FindFile is similar to Dir in that your first call specifies the search criteria, and subsequent calls retrieve the files that correspond to that search criteria. However, FindFile is different in that your first call is to the Find() method, and subsequent calls are to the FindNext() method. Your application should keep looping as long as FindNext() is returning strings, or until you are ready to begin the next search by calling Find() again.

Listing 35.7 demonstrates a simple use of the FindFile class. This function's purpose is to retrieve all the files in the current directory that satisfy a given search criteria. All the items found are loaded into a collection that the caller provides. Finally, this function returns the number of files that were added to the colFiles collection.

Listing 35.7   FINDFILE.FRM—Searching for Files in a Single Directory

```
'****************************************************************
' A simple routine that finds all of the files in a directory that
' match the given pattern, loads the results in a collection, then
' returns the number of files that are being returned.
'****************************************************************
Private Function FindFilesInSingleDir(ByVal strDir As String, _
    strPattern$, colFiles As Collection) As Integer
    '****************************************************************
    ' Create a new FindFile object every time this function is called
    '****************************************************************
    Dim clsFind As New clsFindFile
    Dim strFile As String
    '****************************************************************
    ' Make sure strSearchPath always has a trailing backslash
    '****************************************************************
    If Right(strDir, 1) <> "\" Then _
        strDir = strDir & "\"
    '****************************************************************
    ' Get the first file
    '****************************************************************
    strFile = clsFind.Find(strDir & strPattern)
    '****************************************************************
    ' Loop while files are being returned
    '****************************************************************
    Do While Len(strFile)
        '****************************************************************
        ' If the current file found is not a directory...
        '****************************************************************
        If (clsFind.FileAttributes And vbDirectory) = 0 Then
            colFiles.Add strFile ' don't include the path
        End If
        '****************************************************************
        ' Find the next file or directory
        '****************************************************************
        strFile = clsFind.FindNext()
    Loop
    '****************************************************************
    ' Return the number of files found
    '****************************************************************
```

```
      FindFilesInSingleDir = colFiles.Count
End Function
```

This function begins by creating a new clsFindFile object and building the search string. A call to the Find() method retrieves the first file, and the function retrieves subsequent files by looping until FindNext() no longer returns a value. If no files are found, FindFilesInSingleDir returns zero, and the function makes no changes to the colFiles collection. This function suffices for your basic needs, but isn't much better than Dir because it lacks support for searching subdirectories. However, this limitation is due to the implementation of the FindFile class, not a limitation of the class itself.

Listing 35.8 goes one step further by including support for searching subdirectories. The FindAllFiles() function overcomes the limitations of Dir and FindFilesInSingleDir, but is slightly slower than the previous function. Your application determines whether it really needs to search subdirectories, then calls the appropriate function. This way, you can obtain the results using the fastest method possible.

Listing 35.8 FINDFILE.FRM—FindAllFiles() Includes Subdirectories in Its Search, But Imposes a Small Performance Price

```
'*****************************************************************
' A complex routine that finds all of the files in a directory (and its
' subdirectories), loads the results in a collection, and returns the
' number of subdirectories that were searched.
'*****************************************************************
Private Function FindAllFiles(ByVal strSearchPath$, strPattern As _
    String, Optional colFiles As Collection, Optional colDirs As _
    Collection, Optional blnDirsOnly As Boolean, Optional blnBoth _
    As Boolean) As Integer
    '*****************************************************************
    ' Create a new FindFile object every time this function is called
    '*****************************************************************
    Dim clsFind As New clsFindFile
    Dim strFile As String
    Dim intDirsFound As Integer
    '*****************************************************************
    ' Make sure strSearchPath always has a trailing backslash
    '*****************************************************************
    If Right(strSearchPath, 1) <> "\" Then _
        strSearchPath = strSearchPath & "\"
    '*****************************************************************
    ' Get the first file
    '*****************************************************************
    strFile = clsFind.Find(strSearchPath & strPattern)
    '*****************************************************************
    ' Loop while files are being returned
    '*****************************************************************
    Do While Len(strFile)
        '*****************************************************************
        ' If the current file found is a directory...
        '*****************************************************************
```

Part
V
Ch
35

continues

Listing 35.8   Continued

```
        If clsFind.FileAttributes And vbDirectory Then
            '*********************************************************
            ' Ignore . and ..
            '*********************************************************
            If Left(strFile, 1) <> "." Then
                '*****************************************************
                ' If either bln optional arg is true, then add this
                ' directory to the optional colDirs collection
                '*****************************************************
                If blnDirsOnly Or blnBoth Then
                    colDirs.Add strSearchPath & strFile & "\"
                End If
                '*****************************************************
                ' Increment the number of directories found by one
                '*****************************************************
                intDirsFound = intDirsFound + 1
                '*****************************************************
                ' Recursively call this function to search for matches
                ' in subdirectories. When the recursed function
                ' completes, intDirsFound must be incremented.
                '*****************************************************
                intDirsFound = intDirsFound + FindAllFiles( _
                    strSearchPath & strFile & "\", strPattern, _
                    colFiles, colDirs, blnDirsOnly)
            End If
            '*********************************************************
            ' Find the next file or directory
            '*********************************************************
            strFile = clsFind.FindNext()
        '*************************************************************
        ' ... otherwise, it must be a file.
        '*************************************************************
        Else
            '*********************************************************
            ' If the caller wants files, then add them to the colFiles
            ' collection
            '*********************************************************
            If Not blnDirsOnly Or blnBoth Then
                colFiles.Add strSearchPath & strFile
            End If
            '*********************************************************
            ' Find the next file or directory
            '*********************************************************
            strFile = clsFind.FindNext()
        End If
    Loop
    '*****************************************************************
    ' Return the number of directories found
    '*****************************************************************
    FindAllFiles = intDirsFound
End Function
```

`FindAllFiles()` can search subdirectories mainly because it calls itself recursively. It does so by checking whether the current file is a directory. If so, the function makes another call itself using all the same parameters that the original caller passed in, with one exception: The `strSearchPath` parameter is modified to point to the next subdirectory to search.

Now that you have written the search routines, examine some of the code in FINDFILE.FRM (shown in Figure 35.1) that uses these search routines based on requests from the user of the search dialog box. Listing 35.9 shows how to perform this search based on the values that the user sets in the search dialog box. The code also plays a `FindFile` video during the search, to give the user something to look at during long searches.

FIG. 35.1
FINDFILE.FRM is a
Visual Basic version
of the Windows
FindFile dialog box.

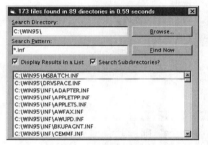

> **N O T E** When using this sample, the caption displays the number of files and directories found when your search completes. This value is correct, but might differ from the values that the MS-DOS `Dir` command and the Windows Find dialog box return. Both `Dir` and the Find dialog box use different mechanisms for counting the number of "files" returned, neither of which is completely accurate. Listing 35.9 uses a method that correlates to the value returned when you view a directory's properties in Windows Explorer. ■

Listing 35.9 FINDFILE.FRM—Choosing the Right Search Technique

```
'*********************************************************************
' Find matching files based on the contents of the text boxes
'*********************************************************************
Private Sub cmdFind_Click()
    '*****************************************************************
    ' Prevent the user from clicking the find button twice, and
    ' hide the browse button so the AVI can be seen
    '*****************************************************************
    cmdFind.Enabled = False
    cmdBrowse.Visible = False
    '*****************************************************************
    ' Give the user a video to watch (wasteful, but cool)
    '*****************************************************************
    With aniFindFile
        .Open App.Path & "\findfile.avi"
        .Visible = True
        Refresh
```

continues

Part
V

Ch
35

Listing 35.9   Continued

```
        .Play
    End With
    '********************************************************************
    ' Tell the user what you are doing and display an hourglass pointer
    '********************************************************************
    Caption = "Searching..."
    Screen.MousePointer = vbHourglass
    '********************************************************************
    ' Always clear before performing the operation (in case the list
    ' is already visible to the user)
    '********************************************************************
    lstFound.Clear
    '********************************************************************
    ' Perform the appropriate search
    '********************************************************************
    If chkSearchSubs Then
        SearchSubDirs
    Else
        SearchCurDirOnly
    End If
    '********************************************************************
    ' End the video, then restore the buttons and pointer
    '********************************************************************
    aniFindFile.Stop: aniFindFile.Visible = False
    cmdFind.Enabled = True
    cmdBrowse.Visible = True
    Screen.MousePointer = vbDefault
End Sub
```

This code simply controls the user interface, but doesn't actually do any searching. Instead, it determines which helper function to call based on the default value property of the chkSearchSubs control. The code uses this technique because the helper search functions are rather complex, so including in the click event would make this code difficult to read.

Listing 35.10 starts with the simple SearchCurDirOnly() helper routine. This routine simply calls FindFilesInSingleDir and loads the results from the colFiles collection into a list box (if necessary). That part of the code is simple enough, but the next routine, SearchSubDirs(), is a little more complicated. If the user wants to search for all the files with the extension TMP, you first must get a list of all the directories by calling FindAllFiles(). After creating this list of directories, you can search each of them for TMP files.

Listing 35.10   FINDFILE.FRM—Using the Results from the Find Functions

```
'********************************************************************
' Performs a simple search in a single directory (like dir *.*)
'********************************************************************
Private Sub SearchCurDirOnly()
    Dim dblStart As Long
    Dim colFiles As New Collection
```

```
'****************************************************************
' Begin timing, then search
'****************************************************************
dblStart = Timer
FindFilesInSingleDir txtSearchDir, txtSearchPattern, colFiles
'****************************************************************
' Adding items to the list is slow, so do it only if you have to
'****************************************************************
If chkDisplayInList Then LoadCollectionInList colFiles
'****************************************************************
' Tell the user how many files were found and how long it took _
' to find (and load) the files
'****************************************************************
Caption = CStr(colFiles.Count) & " files found in" & _
    Str(Timer - dblStart) & " seconds"
End Sub
'****************************************************************
' Performs a complex search in multiple directories (like dir *.* /s)
'****************************************************************
Private Sub SearchSubDirs()
    Dim dblStart As Long
    Dim colFiles As New Collection
    Dim colDirs As New Collection
    Dim intDirsFound As Integer
    Dim vntItem As Variant
    '****************************************************************
    ' Don't forget to add the search directory to your collection
    '****************************************************************
    colDirs.Add txtSearchDir.Text
    '****************************************************************
    ' If the user searches for *.*, then the search is simple (and
    ' much faster)
    '****************************************************************
    If Trim(txtSearchPattern) = "*.*" Then
        dblStart = Timer
        intDirsFound = FindAllFiles(txtSearchDir, "*.*", colFiles, _
            colDirs, , True)
    '****************************************************************
    ' Otherwise, things get sort of complicated
    '****************************************************************
    Else
        '****************************************************************
        ' First search to get a collection of all the directories
        '****************************************************************
        intDirsFound = FindAllFiles(txtSearchDir, "*.*", , colDirs, True)
        '****************************************************************
        ' Start timing now, since the last search was just prep work
        '****************************************************************
        dblStart = Timer
        '****************************************************************
        ' Search for the file pattern in each directory in the list
        '****************************************************************
        For Each vntItem In colDirs
            '****************************************************************
            ' Display the current search directory in the caption
```

continues

Part

V

Ch

35

Listing 35.10   Continued

```
        '****************************************************
        Caption = vntItem
        FindAllFiles CStr(vntItem), txtSearchPattern, colFiles
    Next vntItem
End If
'****************************************************
' Adding items to the list is slow, so do it only if you have to
'****************************************************
If chkDisplayInList Then LoadCollectionInList colFiles
'****************************************************
' Tell the user how many files were found in how many dirs and
' how long it took to find (and load) the files
'****************************************************
Caption = CStr(colFiles.Count) & " files found in" & _
    Str(intDirsFound) & " directories in" & Str(Timer - dblStart) _
    & " seconds"
End Sub
```

Notice that when each of the two routines listed previously complete, they display some basic results in the caption. This technique enables you to experiment with the FindFile program so that you can see that FindFile itself is quite fast, but loading the items into a list can be quite slow. When using the FINDFILE.VBP demo program, experiment with different types of searches, such as searching a networked drive using a UNC path. Try improving the program to support all the features that the Windows Find dialog box supports.

Going Graphical with the GDI API

One of the most complex features in the Win32 API are the Graphics Device Interface (GDI) API functions. Because these APIs are quite complicated, tedious, and prone to General Protection Faults (GPF), Microsoft excluded most of them from Visual Basic. Although the lack of GDI functions shelters you from the complexity and makes your programs more robust, it severely limits your ability to do the "cool" things that many users expect (such as transparent bitmaps). Visual Basic 4 alleviated this problem to some extent by providing such new features as PaintPicture and the ImageList control, but still fell short. Therefore, you eventually will have to call the GDI API functions from your application. This section demonstrates some of the more common GDI API functions by presenting a powerful function called TransparentPaint().

N O T E   The TransparentPaint() routine in this section is a Win32 version of Mike Bond's TransparentBlt code, which originally appeared in the *Microsoft KnowledgeBase KB* article number Q94961. TransparentPaint() adds many modifications to this code and includes a wealth of new comments. ▪

TransparentPaint(), as shown in Listing 35.11, treats a bitmap like an icon when you paint it on a surface. Unlike bitmaps, icons enable you to designate a part of them to be transparent. TransparentPaint() overcomes this limitation by enabling you to make all of a single color on a bitmap transparent. To accomplish this difficult feat, you must create a series of temporary bitmaps and do some painting in memory only. Although this abstract concept can be quite complicated, the comments in TransparentPaint() try to explain what is happening at each step.

Listing 35.11   TRANSPARENT.BAS—Transparent.bas Paints Bitmaps on Surfaces Using a Transparent Background

```
'*********************************************************************
' Paints a bitmap on a given surface using the surface backcolor
' everywhere lngMaskColor appears on the picSource bitmap
'*********************************************************************
Sub TransparentPaint(objDest As Object, picSource As StdPicture, _
    lngX As Long, lngY As Long, ByVal lngMaskColor As Long)
    '*****************************************************************
    ' This sub uses a bunch of variables, so let's declare and explain
    ' them in advance...
    '*****************************************************************
    Dim lngSrcDC As Long      'Source bitmap
    Dim lngSaveDC As Long     'Copy of source bitmap
    Dim lngMaskDC As Long     'Monochrome mask bitmap
    Dim lngInvDC As Long      'Monochrome inverse of mask bitmap
    Dim lngNewPicDC As Long   'Combination of source & background bmps

    Dim bmpSource As BITMAP   'Description of the source bitmap

    Dim hResultBmp As Long    'Combination of source & background
    Dim hSaveBmp As Long      'Copy of source bitmap
    Dim hMaskBmp As Long      'Monochrome mask bitmap
    Dim hInvBmp As Long       'Monochrome inverse of mask bitmap

    Dim hSrcPrevBmp As Long   'Holds prev bitmap in source DC
    Dim hSavePrevBmp As Long  'Holds prev bitmap in saved DC
    Dim hDestPrevBmp As Long  'Holds prev bitmap in destination DC
    Dim hMaskPrevBmp As Long  'Holds prev bitmap in the mask DC
    Dim hInvPrevBmp As Long   'Holds prev bitmap in inverted mask DC

    Dim lngOrigScaleMode&     'Holds the original ScaleMode
    Dim lngOrigColor&         'Holds original backcolor from source DC
    '*****************************************************************
    ' Set ScaleMode to pixels for Windows GDI
    '*****************************************************************
    lngOrigScaleMode = objDest.ScaleMode
    objDest.ScaleMode = vbPixels
    '*****************************************************************
    ' Load the source bitmap to get its width (bmpSource.bmWidth)
    ' and height (bmpSource.bmHeight)
    '*****************************************************************
```

continues

Listing 35.11   Continued

```
GetObject picSource, Len(bmpSource), bmpSource
'*******************************************************************
' Create compatible device contexts (DCs) to hold the temporary
' bitmaps used by this sub
'*******************************************************************
lngSrcDC = CreateCompatibleDC(objDest.hdc)
lngSaveDC = CreateCompatibleDC(objDest.hdc)
lngMaskDC = CreateCompatibleDC(objDest.hdc)
lngInvDC = CreateCompatibleDC(objDest.hdc)
lngNewPicDC = CreateCompatibleDC(objDest.hdc)
'*******************************************************************
' Create monochrome bitmaps for the mask-related bitmaps
'*******************************************************************
hMaskBmp = CreateBitmap(bmpSource.bmWidth, bmpSource.bmHeight, _
    1, 1, ByVal 0&)
hInvBmp = CreateBitmap(bmpSource.bmWidth, bmpSource.bmHeight, _
    1, 1, ByVal 0&)
'*******************************************************************
' Create color bitmaps for the final result and the backup copy
' of the source bitmap
'*******************************************************************
hResultBmp = CreateCompatibleBitmap(objDest.hdc, _
    bmpSource.bmWidth, bmpSource.bmHeight)
hSaveBmp = CreateCompatibleBitmap(objDest.hdc, _
    bmpSource.bmWidth, bmpSource.bmHeight)
'*******************************************************************
' Select bitmap into the device context (DC)
'*******************************************************************
hSrcPrevBmp = SelectObject(lngSrcDC, picSource)
hSavePrevBmp = SelectObject(lngSaveDC, hSaveBmp)
hMaskPrevBmp = SelectObject(lngMaskDC, hMaskBmp)
hInvPrevBmp = SelectObject(lngInvDC, hInvBmp)
hDestPrevBmp = SelectObject(lngNewPicDC, hResultBmp)
'*******************************************************************
' Make a backup of source bitmap to restore later
'*******************************************************************
BitBlt lngSaveDC, 0, 0, bmpSource.bmWidth, bmpSource.bmHeight, _
    lngSrcDC, 0, 0, vbSrcCopy
'*******************************************************************
' Create the mask by setting the background color of the source to
' transparent color, then BitBlt'ing that bitmap into the mask
' device context
'*******************************************************************
lngOrigColor = SetBkColor(lngSrcDC, lngMaskColor)
BitBlt lngMaskDC, 0, 0, bmpSource.bmWidth, bmpSource.bmHeight, _
    lngSrcDC, 0, 0, vbSrcCopy
'*******************************************************************
' Restore the original backcolor in the device context
'*******************************************************************
SetBkColor lngSrcDC, lngOrigColor
'*******************************************************************
' Create an inverse of the mask to AND with the source and combine
' it with the background
```

```
'*******************************************************************
BitBlt lngInvDC, 0, 0, bmpSource.bmWidth, bmpSource.bmHeight, _
    lngMaskDC, 0, 0, vbNotSrcCopy
'*******************************************************************
' Copy the background bitmap to the new picture device context
' to begin creating the final transparent bitmap
'*******************************************************************
BitBlt lngNewPicDC, 0, 0, bmpSource.bmWidth, bmpSource.bmHeight, _
    objDest.hdc, lngX, lngY, vbSrcCopy
'*******************************************************************
' AND the mask bitmap with the result device context to create
' a cookie cutter effect in the background by painting the black
' area for the nontransparent portion of the source bitmap
'*******************************************************************
BitBlt lngNewPicDC, 0, 0, bmpSource.bmWidth, bmpSource.bmHeight, _
    lngMaskDC, 0, 0, vbSrcAnd
'*******************************************************************
' AND the inverse mask with the source bitmap to turn off the bits
' associated with transparent area of source bitmap by making it
' black
'*******************************************************************
BitBlt lngSrcDC, 0, 0, bmpSource.bmWidth, bmpSource.bmHeight, _
    lngInvDC, 0, 0, vbSrcAnd
'*******************************************************************
' XOR the result with the source bitmap to replace the mask color
' with the background color
'*******************************************************************
BitBlt lngNewPicDC, 0, 0, bmpSource.bmWidth, bmpSource.bmHeight, _
    lngSrcDC, 0, 0, vbSrcPaint
'*******************************************************************
' Paint the transparent bitmap on the source surface
'*******************************************************************
BitBlt objDest.hdc, lngX, lngY, bmpSource.bmWidth, _
    bmpSource.bmHeight, lngNewPicDC, 0, 0, vbSrcCopy
'*******************************************************************
' Restore backup of bitmap
'*******************************************************************
BitBlt lngSrcDC, 0, 0, bmpSource.bmWidth, bmpSource.bmHeight, _
    lngSaveDC, 0, 0, vbSrcCopy
'*******************************************************************
' Restore the original objects by selecting their original values
'*******************************************************************
SelectObject lngSrcDC, hSrcPrevBmp
SelectObject lngSaveDC, hSavePrevBmp
SelectObject lngNewPicDC, hDestPrevBmp
SelectObject lngMaskDC, hMaskPrevBmp
SelectObject lngInvDC, hInvPrevBmp
'*******************************************************************
' Free system resources created by this sub
'*******************************************************************
DeleteObject hSaveBmp
DeleteObject hMaskBmp
DeleteObject hInvBmp
DeleteObject hResultBmp
DeleteDC lngSrcDC
```

Part
V

Ch

35

continues

Listing 35.11   Continued

```
    DeleteDC lngSaveDC
    DeleteDC lngInvDC
    DeleteDC lngMaskDC
    DeleteDC lngNewPicDC
    '*******************************************************************
    ' Restores the ScaleMode to its original value
    '*******************************************************************
    objDest.ScaleMode = lngOrigScaleMode
End Sub
```

To keep this code simple, Listing 35.11 omits the API declarations. However, they are available in TRANSPARENT.BAS on the book's Web site. This section doesn't explain what is happening during each step of `TransparentPaint()` because the explaination is already included in the comments of Listing 35.11. It also would be more difficult to follow this listing if it were broken into several smaller blocks. After reading the comments for this subroutine, you should single-step through the TRANSPARENT.VBP project on the book's Web site. This exercise will help you visualize what is happening at each step.

Although the code in `TransparentPaint()` is quite complex, using it is easy. Listing 35.12 loads a bitmap from a resource (using LoadResPicture) and uses `TransparentPaint()` to paint the bitmap on the form's upper-left corner. The last parameter, `vbGreen`, tells `TransparentPaint()` to replace any green bits in the bitmap with bits that match the form's background color. Figure 35.2 shows the result.

FIG. 35.2

TransparentPaint()
is a must for your
multimedia applica-
tions.

Listing 35.12   TRANSPARENT.FRM—Transparent.frm Shows How to Use the TransparentPaint Function

```
'*******************************************************************
' Transparent.frm - Demonstrates how to use basTransparent's
'   TransparentPaint using a bitmap from a resource file.
'*******************************************************************
Option Explicit
'*******************************************************************
' Gets a StdPicture handle by loading a bitmap from a resource file
' and paints it transparently on the form by using gray as the mask
' color.
'*******************************************************************
Private Sub cmdPaintTransBmp_Click()
    TransparentPaint Me, LoadResPicture(103, 0), 0, 0, QBColor(7)
End Sub
```

Try replacing the resource file in this project with your own resource file to see how `TransparentPaint()` works. Also, try using different mask colors, as well as the images from picture boxes. Now you never again will have to write an application that looks cheesy because it doesn't use transparent bitmaps.

Registry Revisited

Chapter 32, "Advanced Control Techniques," demonstrated how to use the TreeView and ListView controls in a small registry program called REGISTRY.VBP. The code in this section is from a module in that project called REGISTRY.BAS. This code is responsible for retrieving the values from the registry that were subsequently loaded into the TreeView and ListView controls. The listing in this section, like that of most sections in this chapter, is long because it includes the discussion of the code in the form of comments. Before and after each listing, the text includes some additional comments on the code, but the most important comments are in the listing itself. Because of the size of REGISTRY.BAS, this section's listing includes only some of the module's functions. However, you should examine all the code on the book's Web site (at **http://www.quecorp.com/sevb5**) so you can see that REGISTRY.BAS is perhaps the only registry module you'll ever need in your applications.

The most common interaction between Visual Basic programs and the registry is reading and writing strings to and from a specific or new key. Listing 35.13 contains two functions, `GetRegString()` and `SetRegString()`, that accomplish this task. In addition to setting registry strings, `SetRegString()` also creates new keys in the registry. If either of these functions fail, they raise a user-defined error. This way, your application can handle this error without notifying the user.

Listing 35.13 REGISTRY.BAS—*GetRegString()* and *SetRegString()* Read and Write Registry Strings

```
'*********************************************************************
' REGSITRY.BAS - Contains the code necessary to access the Windows
'                registration database.
'*********************************************************************
' GetRegString takes three arguments: an HKEY constant (listed above),
' a subkey, and a value in that subkey. This function returns the
' string stored in the strValueName value in the registry.
'*********************************************************************
Public Function GetRegString(HKEY As Long, strSubKey As String, _
                             strValueName As String) As String
    Dim strSetting As String
    Dim lngDataLen As Long
    Dim hSubKey As Long
    '*********************************************************************
    ' Open the key. If successful, then get the data from the key.
    '*********************************************************************
    If RegOpenKeyEx(HKEY, strSubKey, 0, KEY_ALL_ACCESS, hSubKey) = _
        ERROR_SUCCESS Then
        strSetting = Space(255)
        lngDataLen = Len(strSetting)
```

Part
V

Ch
35

continues

Listing 35.13   Continued

```
            '****************************************************************
            ' Query the key for the current setting. If this call
            ' succeeds, then return the string.
            '****************************************************************
            If RegQueryValueEx(hSubKey, strValueName, ByVal 0, _
                REG_SZ, ByVal strSetting, lngDataLen) = _
                ERROR_SUCCESS Then
                If lngDataLen > 1 Then
                    GetRegString = Left(strSetting, lngDataLen - 1)
                End If
            Else
                Err.Raise ERRBASE + 1, "GetRegString", _
                    "RegQueryValueEx failed!"
            End If
            '****************************************************************
            ' ALWAYS close any keys that you open.
            '****************************************************************
            RegCloseKey hSubKey
        End If
    End Function
    '****************************************************************
    ' SetRegString takes four arguments: an HKEY constant (listed above),
    ' a subkey, a value in that subkey, and a setting for the key.
    '****************************************************************
    Public Sub SetRegString(HKEY As Long, strSubKey As String, _
                                strValueName As String, strSetting _
                                As String)

        Dim hNewHandle As Long
        Dim lpdwDisposition As Long
        '****************************************************************
        ' Create and open the key. If successful, then get the data and
        ' then write it to the key.
        '****************************************************************
        If RegCreateKeyEx(HKEY, strSubKey, 0, strValueName, 0, _
            KEY_ALL_ACCESS, 0&, hNewHandle, lpdwDisposition) = _
            ERROR_SUCCESS Then
            If RegSetValueEx(hNewHandle, strValueName, 0, REG_SZ, _
                ByVal strSetting, Len(strSetting)) <> ERROR_SUCCESS Then
                Err.Raise ERRBASE + 2, "SetRegString", _
                    "RegSetValueEx failed!"
            End If
        Else
            Err.Raise ERRBASE + 3, "SetRegString", "RegCreateKeyEx failed!"
        End If
        '****************************************************************
        ' ALWAYS close any keys that you open.
        '****************************************************************
        RegCloseKey hNewHandle
    End Sub
```

Although these two functions accomplish different tasks, the methods that they use to accomplish their tasks are virtually identical. The user provides a predefined long constant HKEY value (such as HKEY_CURRENT_USER), a subkey (such as Software\Microsoft with no leading backslash), and a value to read from or write to. Both functions (using different registry functions) begin by opening the subkey, then read to or write from it. They both end by closing the key that they opened.

Listing 35.13 demonstrates a fundamental technique required during all coding with the registry. You must open and close subkeys before you can retrieve any values. Windows opens and closes the HKEY values, so you never have to worry about opening or closing them. This concept of opening and closing registry keys is repeated during every function in REGISTRY.BAS, so keep it in mind if you decide to write your own registry functions.

Listing 35.14 demonstrates this fundamental technique again using DWORD (or Long) values. The GetRegDWord() and SetRegDWord() functions enable you to read and write Long values to and from the registry. Because most registry values that you'll ever use are strings, the listing includes a conditional compilation argument in REGISTRY.BAS called LEAN_AND_MEAN. By default, this conditional compilation constant is undefined, so its value is zero. For this reason, all the code in the LEAN_AND_MEAN section is included in your application by default. However, if you want to write an application that doesn't take advantage of any of the functions in the LEAN_AND_MEAN section, you could edit your project properties and set the LEAN_AND_MEAN conditional compilation constant equal to 1. This prevents your executable from including this code, thus reducing the executable's size and memory requirements. All the remaining code in REGISTRY.BAS that appears in this section is part of the LEAN_AND_MEAN section that you can exclude from your application.

Listing 35.14   REGISTRY.BAS—Extended Registry Functions Using Conditional Compilation

```
'*********************************************************************
' Extended registry functions begin here
'*********************************************************************
#If LEAN_AND_MEAN = 0 Then
'*********************************************************************
' Returns a DWORD value from a given registry key
'*********************************************************************
Public Function GetRegDWord(HKEY&, strSubKey$, strValueName$) As Long
    Dim lngDataLen As Long
    Dim hSubKey As Long
    Dim lngRetVal As Long
    '*****************************************************************
    ' Open the key. If successful, then get the data from the key.
    '*****************************************************************
    If RegOpenKeyEx(HKEY, strSubKey, 0, KEY_ALL_ACCESS, hSubKey) = _
        ERROR_SUCCESS Then
        '*************************************************************
        ' Query the key for the current setting. If this call
        ' succeeds, then return the string.
        '*************************************************************
        lngDataLen = 4 'Bytes
```

Part
V

Ch
35

continues

Listing 35.14   Continued

```
        If RegQueryValueEx(hSubKey, strValueName, ByVal 0, _
            REG_DWORD, lngRetVal, lngDataLen) = ERROR_SUCCESS Then
            GetRegDWord = lngRetVal
        Else
            Err.Raise ERRBASE + 1, "GetRegDWord", _
                "RegQueryValueEx failed!"
        End If
        '****************************************************************
        ' ALWAYS close any keys that you open.
        '****************************************************************
        RegCloseKey hSubKey
    End If
End Function
'********************************************************************
' Sets a registry key to a DWORD value
'********************************************************************
Public Sub SetRegDWord(HKEY&, strSubKey$, strValueName$, lngSetting&)
    Dim hNewHandle As Long
    Dim lpdwDisposition As Long
    '****************************************************************
    ' Create and open the key. If successful, then get the data
    ' and then write it to the key.
    '****************************************************************
    If RegCreateKeyEx(HKEY, strSubKey, 0, strValueName, 0, _
        KEY_ALL_ACCESS, 0&, hNewHandle, lpdwDisposition) = _
        ERROR_SUCCESS Then
        If RegSetValueEx(hNewHandle, strValueName, 0, REG_DWORD, _
            lngSetting, 4) <> ERROR_SUCCESS Then
            Err.Raise ERRBASE + 2, "SetRegDWord", _
                "RegSetValueEx failed!"
    +   End If
    Else
        Err.Raise ERRBASE + 3, "SetRegString", "RegCreateKeyEx failed!"
    End If
    '****************************************************************
    ' ALWAYS close any keys that you open.
    '****************************************************************
    RegCloseKey hNewHandle
End Sub
```

The way that you read and write DWORD (or Long) values to and from the registry is almost identical to the method that you use for strings. The only difference is that instead of passing your string's or buffer's length to RegQueryValueEx() and RegSetValueEx(), you pass the number of bytes of memory occupied by a Long value. Because a Long value holds four bytes, you pass the number four.

The GetRegKeyValues() function, shown in Listing 35.15, enumerates through a given subkey in the registry and returns all its values and settings. This function loads the ListView control with all the values of the subkey selected in the TreeView control in REGISTRY.FRM. Although this function isn't extraordinarily difficult, it is long and complex given the nature of enumeration and multidimensional arrays.

Listing 35.15   REGISTRY.BAS—*GetRegKeyValues()* Demonstrates Registry Enumeration

```
'***********************************************************************
' Returns a multidimensional variant array of all the values and
' settings in a given registry subkey.
'***********************************************************************
Public Function GetRegKeyValues(HKEY&, strSubKey$) As Variant
    Dim lngNumValues As Long        ' Number values in this key

    Dim strValues() As String       ' Value and return array
    Dim lngMaxValSize  As Long      ' Size of longest value
    Dim lngValRetBytes As Long      ' Size of current value

    Dim lngMaxSettingSize As Long   ' Size of longest REG_SZ in this key
    Dim lngSetRetBytes As Long      ' Size of current REG_SZ

    Dim lngSetting As Long          ' Used for DWORD

    Dim lngType As Long             ' Type of value returned from
                                    ' RegEnumValue

    Dim hChildKey As Long           ' The handle of strSubKey
    Dim i As Integer                ' Loop counter
    '*******************************************************************
    ' Exit if you did not successfully open the child key
    '*******************************************************************
    If RegOpenKeyEx(HKEY, strSubKey, 0, KEY_ALL_ACCESS, hChildKey) _
        <> ERROR_SUCCESS Then
        Err.Raise ERRBASE + 4, "GetRegKeyValues", _
            "RegOpenKeyEx failed!"
        Exit Function
    End If
    '*******************************************************************
    ' Find out the array and value sizes in advance
    '*******************************************************************
    If QueryRegInfoKey(hChildKey, , , lngNumValues, lngMaxValSize, _
        lngMaxSettingSize) <> ERROR_SUCCESS Or lngNumValues = 0 Then
        Err.Raise ERRBASE + 5, "GetRegKeyValues", _
            "RegQueryInfoKey failed!"
        RegCloseKey hChildKey
        Exit Function
    End If
    '*******************************************************************
    ' Resize the array to fit the return values
    '*******************************************************************
    lngNumValues = lngNumValues - 1 ' Adjust to zero based
    ReDim strValues(0 To lngNumValues, 0 To 1) As String
    '*******************************************************************
    ' Get all of the values and settings for the key
    '*******************************************************************
    For i = 0 To lngNumValues
        '***************************************************************
        ' Make the return buffers large enough to hold the results
        '***************************************************************
```

continues

Listing 35.15 Continued

```
    strValues(i, 0) = Space(lngMaxValSize)
    lngValRetBytes = lngMaxValSize

    strValues(i, 1) = Space(lngMaxSettingSize)
    lngSetRetBytes = lngMaxSettingSize
    '***************************************************************
    ' Get a single value and setting from the registry
    '***************************************************************
    RegEnumValue hChildKey, i, strValues(i, 0), lngValRetBytes, _
        0, lngType, ByVal strValues(i, 1), lngSetRetBytes
    '***************************************************************
    ' If the return value was a string, then trim trailing nulls
    '***************************************************************
    If lngType = REG_SZ Then
        strValues(i, 1) = Left(strValues(i, 1), lngSetRetBytes - 1)
    '***************************************************************
    ' Else if it was a DWORD, call RegEnumValue again to store
    ' the return setting in a long variable
    '***************************************************************
    ElseIf lngType = REG_DWORD Then
        '***********************************************************
        ' We already know the return size of the value because
        ' we got it in the last call to RegEnumValue, so we
        ' can tell RegEnumValue that its buffer size is the
        ' length of the string already returned, plus one (for
        ' the trailing null terminator)
        '***********************************************************
        lngValRetBytes = lngValRetBytes + 1
        '***********************************************************
        ' Make the call again using a Long instead of string
        '***********************************************************
        RegEnumValue hChildKey, i, strValues(i, 0), _
            lngValRetBytes, 0, lngType, lngSetting, lngSetRetBytes
        '***********************************************************
        ' Return the Long as a string
        '***********************************************************
        strValues(i, 1) = CStr(lngSetting)
    '***************************************************************
    ' Otherwise, let the user know that this code doesn't support
    ' the format returned (such as REG_BINARY)
    '***************************************************************
    Else
        strValues(i, 1) = REG_UNSUPPORTED
    End If
    '***************************************************************
    ' Store the return value and setting in a multidimensional
    ' array with the value in the 0 index and the setting in
    ' the 1 index of the second dimension.
    '***************************************************************
    strValues(i, 0) = RTrim(Left(strValues(i, 0), lngValRetBytes))
    strValues(i, 1) = RTrim(strValues(i, 1))
Next i
'*******************************************************************
' ALWAYS close any keys you open
```

```
'*****************************************************************
RegCloseKey hChildKey
'*****************************************************************
' Return the result as an array of strings
'*****************************************************************
GetRegKeyValues = strValues
End Function
```

The `GetRegKeyValues()` function is unique among most functions that you've ever used or written because it returns a multidimensional array containing the values in the first dimension and the settings in the second dimension. This gives the calling function the flexibility to use the values returned from this function in any manner that it chooses. However, the caller is responsible both for checking to ensure an array was returned (in case there were no keys) *and* for treating the results from this function as a two-dimensional array.

`GetRegKeyValues()` begins, like every function in REGISTRY.BAS, by opening the subkey, but then does something unique. It calls a helper function (not shown) called `QueryRegInfoKey()` that returns some helpful information about the subkey. `QueryRegInfoKey()` simply wraps a registry function called `RegQueryInfoKey()` that provides information about the subkey, such as how many values it contains and the length of the longest value and setting. This information helps you determine whether to begin the enumeration, how large an array you need, and how large the string buffer needs to be. After you receive this information, you are ready to begin the enumeration.

During each iteration of the enumeration, you set all your string buffers. Next, you attempt to retrieve the value and setting as strings. If the setting is a string, you trim any trailing nulls. If the setting was a `DWORD`, you make the call again, this time passing a `Long` value and a buffer size of four bytes. After retrieving the `DWORD`, you convert it to a string and load it into the array. If the setting is neither a string nor a `DWORD`, you load the array with a special string that tells the caller that the return value is in an unsupported format.

You repeat the enumeration for all the values and settings. When you finish, you close the key that you opened and return the two-dimensional array by its name. The caller gets a variant return value that contains this two-dimensional array.

REGISTRY.BAS describes the remaining functions in detail. You should read this program's comments and experiment with each of the functions. The book's Web site located at **http://www.quecorp.com/sevb5** also includes some examples that demonstrate how to use each of REGISTRY.BAS' functions in REGISTRY.FRM's `Form_Load()` event. These functions are at the end of the `Form_Load()` event and are commented out. Feel free to use them in REGISTRY.FRM, in Visual Basic's immediate pane, or in a separate application to see how each of the REGISTRY.BAS functions work.

Callbacks Revisited

Chapter 32, "Advanced Controls Techniques," describes in detail how to use callbacks. Because this subject is complex, this section provides another example. If you didn't read the last section of Chapter 32, "Writing Frankentrols," you should do so now. The information in this section simply picks up where the last example left off.

Part
V

Ch

Listing 35.16 demonstrates how to use the EnumWindows API call. EnumWindows takes a function pointer and a pointer to a value that you want to pass to your function pointer. In turn, it iterates through the Windows task list, calling your callback function during each iteration. CALLBACK.BAS contains the callback function and some helper routines that enable you to print a list of visible windows on a form.

Listing 35.16   CALLBACK.BAS—Callback.bas Demonstrates How to Use Callbacks in VB

```
'******************************************************************
' Callback.bas - Demonstrates how to do callbacks in VB
'******************************************************************
Option Explicit
'******************************************************************
' EnumWindows takes a function pointer (AddressOf your callback
' function) and an lParam argument (can be a pointer to anything you
' would like sent to your callback function)
'******************************************************************
Private Declare Function EnumWindows Lib "user32" _
    (ByVal lpfn As Long, lParam As Any) As Boolean
'******************************************************************
' There are a lot of windows loaded that are never visible, so
' I usually use the IsWindowVisible API call to filter out only the
' top-level windows the user sees
'******************************************************************
Private Declare Function IsWindowVisible Lib "user32" _
    (ByVal hWnd As Long) As Long
'******************************************************************
' I use the following APIs to get the captions and class names of the
' visible windows
'******************************************************************
Private Declare Function GetWindowText Lib "user32" Alias _
    "GetWindowTextA" (ByVal hWnd As Long, ByVal lpString As String, _
    ByVal cch As Long) As Long

Private Declare Function GetWindowTextLength Lib "user32" Alias _
    "GetWindowTextLengthA" (ByVal hWnd As Long) As Long

Private Declare Function GetClassName Lib "user32" Alias _
    "GetClassNameA" (ByVal hWnd As Long, ByVal lpClassName$, _
    ByVal nMaxCount As Long) As Long
'******************************************************************
' This is a callback function. Notice how the function is declared
' as Private. This private flag applies only to VB, not to Windows,
' so it is okay to declare your callback functions as Private if you
' don't want them to be accessible in external modules. Also notice
' how we used the lParam pointer to pass as a form to our callback
'******************************************************************
Private Function CallBackFunc(ByVal hWnd As Long, _
    lParam As Form) As Long
    Dim strhWnd As String * 8
    Dim strClass As String * 20
    '******************************************************************
```

```
    ' If the window is visble, then print some information about it
    ' on the lParam form
    '********************************************************************
    If IsWindowVisible(hWnd) Then
        strhWnd = "&H" & Hex(hWnd)
        strClass = GetWindowClassName(hWnd)
        lParam.Print strhWnd & strClass & GetWindowCaption(hWnd)
    End If
    '********************************************************************
    ' Return False only if you want to stop EnumWindows from calling
    ' this callback again
    '********************************************************************
    CallBackFunc = True
End Function
'************************************************************************
' Returns the caption of a window
'************************************************************************
Private Function GetWindowCaption(hWnd As Long) As String
    Dim lngCaptionLen As Long
    Dim strCaption As String
    '********************************************************************
    ' Get the length of the caption and add 1 to account for the
    ' null terminator
    '********************************************************************
    lngCaptionLen = GetWindowTextLength(hWnd) + 1
    '********************************************************************
    ' Allocate your buffer to hold the caption
    '********************************************************************
    strCaption = Space(lngCaptionLen)
    '********************************************************************
    ' Get the caption and return the characters up to (but not
    ' including) the null terminator
    '********************************************************************
    lngCaptionLen = GetWindowText(hWnd, strCaption, lngCaptionLen)
    GetWindowCaption = Left(strCaption, lngCaptionLen)
End Function
'************************************************************************
' Get the class name using the same techniques described above
'************************************************************************
Private Function GetWindowClassName(hWnd As Long) As String
    Dim strClassName As String
    Dim lngClassLen As Integer
    lngClassLen = 50
    strClassName = Space(lngClassLen)
    lngClassLen = GetClassName(hWnd, strClassName, lngClassLen)
    GetWindowClassName = Left(strClassName, lngClassLen)
End Function
'************************************************************************
' Print some headers and call EnumWindows to print the window info
'************************************************************************
Public Sub CallbackDemo(frmName As Form)
    frmName.Cls
    frmName.Print "Handle" & "  Class Name", "Window Caption"
    frmName.Print "------" & "  ----------", "--------------"
```

continues

Listing 35.16 Continued

```
     EnumWindows AddressOf CallBackFunc, frmName
End Sub
```

CallBackFunc() begins with the callback function, which is declared as private. It is private because you don't call this code anywhere in your Visual Basic application. However, the private qualifier doesn't affect Windows' ability to call this function. Each time that this function is called, you check whether the current window is visible. If it is, you print its hwnd, class name, and window caption on the form passed in as the lParam of EnumWindows. Finally, you always return True. If you want to end the enumeration, you return False from the callback function. You might do this if you use EnumWindows to find a specific window. After finding the window for which you were searching, you can stop the enumeration.

GetWindowCaption() and GetWindowClassName() simply encapsulate a couple of API functions to make your callback routine as simple as possible. Because both of these functions are retrieving strings from an API function, they both build string buffers before the API call and trim the null terminator after the API call.

The last function in Listing 35.16 is perhaps its most important: the public CallbackDemo() method. This method is the public interface to your application and is responsible for calling EnumWindows and printing the results on the form that you provide when you call CallbackDemo().

Figure 35.3 shows the callback function at work in CALLBACK.FRM. Listing 35.17 demonstrates how to build this task list. By using the Me keyword, you pass in a reference to the form where you make the call.

FIG. 35.3

EnumWindows is great for creating a task list.

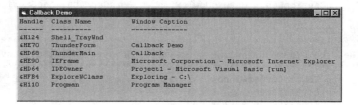

Listing 35.17 CALLBACK.FRM—Callback.frm Shows How Easy It Is to Use Our Callback Module

```
'****************************************************************
' Callback.frm - Demonstrates how to use basCallback
'****************************************************************
Option Explicit
'****************************************************************
' Updates the form with the current window list every time it gets
' a paint event
'****************************************************************
```

```
Private Sub Form_Paint()
    CallbackDemo Me
End Sub
```

Because windows are always being added and removed, you put your call to `CallbackDemo()` in the `Form_Paint()` event. Creating or removing windows usually causes the form to be re-painted, so this technique enables the form to contain the latest visible window list.

From Here...

Now that you've had a small taste of what the Win32 API can do for you, it's time to experiment on your own. Take the samples in this chapter apart and use them in your own applications. Experiment, extend, and optimize them for your own code library. You'll find that once you get the hang of writing Visual Basic programs that leverage the power of Win32, your dependency on third-party controls will decrease markedly. Can you think of any controls that you currently have that you could replace with code in this chapter? If so, begin reworking your program right away.

For information on related topics, see the following sources:

- For more examples of using Win32 API calls, read Part IV, "Integration Visual Basic with Other Applications," and Part V, "Optimization and Advanced Programming Techniques."

- For assistance with translating the API functions to Visual Basic, you should get a copy of Daniel Appleman's *Visual Basic Programmer's Guide to the Win32 API* from Ziff-Davis Press.

- For more samples of applications that use the Win32 API, browse the book's Web site at **http://www.quecorp.com/sevb5**.

Part
V

Ch
35

CHAPTER 36

Designing Windows Applications

Visual Basic was created to allow programmers to write "real apps, real fast." Prior to the release of Visual Basic 1.0, writing a Windows application was hard work, requiring a lot of very low-level programming knowledge just to get a simple window to appear. Visual Basic removed this level of "under the hood" complexity by automating a good deal of the difficult nuts and bolts programming that was required to write even the simplest of Windows applications. Procedures—such as creating and placing windows, selecting fonts by which to output text to a control, or defining an event, such as a button click—while very difficult things to do in a low-level language such as C, are relatively simple in Visual Basic.

However, although VB frees the programmer from the more mundane chores of Windows programming, it does not relieve the programmer from the responsibility to follow good software design and programming practices in day-to-day activities.

An analogy can be drawn here between a programmer to Visual Basic and a cabinetmaker to power tools. While a power tool can make the labor of cabinetmaking easier, mere possession of the tool does not guarantee that the cabinetmaker will make a good cabinet. The utilization of the tool is only as good as the cabinetmaker's ability to

"User centered" software development process

This chapter shows you how to write programs that take into consideration the needs and preferences of the user, first and foremost.

Consistent and effective graphical interfaces

Learn how to design interfaces that are predictable and easy to learn and use.

Improved user perception of your programs

Learn to make programs that are responsive and error tolerant.

Avoid programming pitfalls

Learn techniques that will make your code easy to understand and easy to maintain.

make and follow a schematic, select the appropriate materials, and execute the fundamental skills of cabinetmaking.

The same can be said of writing programs in Visual Basic. While Visual Basic is a very powerful and easy-to-learn tool, the programs that are made in Visual Basic are only as good as the design and implementation skills of the programmer, as well as his day in and day out programming practices.

While Visual Basic makes programming easier, it does not necessarily make programmers better. ■

Implementing a "User Centered" Software Development Process

Imagine that you are the head of a major Hollywood movie studio. A good portion of your responsibilities is to decide which films to fund and which to avoid. One day, two enterprising filmmakers approach you about investing in their films. Both filmmakers want to make an action/adventure film about a handsome archeologist off in search of treasure. You interview them both. The first filmmaker gives you a general verbal idea about how the film will go. The second filmmaker tells you how the film will go by showing you a series of scene sketches (storyboards), shows you a script of the movie, presents an estimated budget for production costs as well as a detailed shooting schedule, and has on hand a market study analyzing the intended audience's likes, dislikes, and viewing history. Given that neither filmmaker has the stature of a Steven Spielberg or Penny Marshall, which one are you inclined to fund?

Most likely you would fund the second one. Why? Because she has a clear grasp of what she wants to do, who she wants to do it for, and how she wants to do it.

The same can be said about making software. Being an effective software developer means having a clear idea of *what* program you want to write, *who* you want to write it for, and *how* you want to do it. Many times, paying attention to the needs, expectations, and habits of the user of the software is often a trivial afterthought in the software development process. This tendency is self-defeating because, in most cases, intrinsic ease of use determines the long-term success of your code.

The process of software development can be broken up into three phases, as listed in Table 36.1.

Table 36.1   The Three Phases of Software Development

Phase	Activity
Pre-Production	Determine user
	Analyze user needs and usage style
	Determine features set
	Prioritize features

Phase	Activity
	Create specification
	Create schematic of program
Production	Divide work among programming group
	Code and build
	Debug
	Perform usability tests
	Correct bugs and address usability issues
Post-Production	Prepare online help and end-user manuals
	Document program for future maintenance
	Prepare program for deployment
	Evaluate program and process for future versions

Understanding the activities and dynamics of each of these phases is important to the overall efficiency of your development effort and the quality of your end product.

The Pre-Production Phase

The Pre-Production phase of developing a Windows application is where your product is defined and specified. In pre-production, you draw up the blueprint upon which your product is built. You also decide what the purpose of the product is, what its features are, and, of those determined features, which version of your product will implement a given feature set.

In pre-production, you create a user profile. For instance, you determine if your intended users are comfortable with Windows, thus requiring little elementary support. If your users have never used a computer before, your program will require a good deal of on-screen instruction.

Localization issues are also identified during this phase. Will your product be released in US English? Will it require UK English as well? Will you eventually be releasing in French, Japanese, or Arabic? These are important issues to consider, and you will do well addressing them at the beginning of the development process where change is cheap, rather than at the end of the process where change is very, very expensive.

 It is always most cost effective to correct a mistake or make a change to a program feature in the Pre-Production phase. For example, let's say that you are asked to write a clock program for a client. Your client decides that she wants to have an alarm feature in the program. Adding the alarm at this point is a fairly simple, inexpensive modification. All you need to do is change the specification. However, let's say that your client decides to have the alarm feature added while the project is in post-production. Adding the feature at that point becomes costly in terms of time and money. The program must be respecified, recoded, retested, and redocumented.

The Production Phase

The Production phase of the development process is where you take the product specification prepared in pre-production and turn it into code. In addition, you create media and other resources that your code might require. In this phase, you determine the optimal language in which to code.

> **N O T E** That this is a book on Visual Basic, for all intents and purposes, the optimal language *is* Visual Basic. However, keep in mind that this might not always be the case. Even VB has its limitations and misapplications. If you are working within a group of programmers, production is where you divide up the work and do build control. ■

System testing, the process of testing code for bugs, usability, and compliance to specification is also done within the Production phase. There are two schools of thought concerning testing methods, and both are worth mentioning here.

One method of testing is called waterfall testing (see Figure 36.1). In the waterfall method, the testing process is considered to be separate from the programming part of the software development process. Waterfall testing first requires that all the code that needs to be written to satisfy a specification is created. Then, that code is sent to the tester for testing. After the testing is complete, the results are sent back to the coders to make the necessary code corrections and modifications.

The other method is called iterative testing (see Figure 36.2). In iterative testing, testing is considered to be part of the programming process. As the programmer completes a discreet set of procedures, he is continually sending his completed work to the tester for inspection and response. While the iterative method might seem like nothing more than a lot of waterfall tests, it is not. In the iterative testing method, the tester is included in and consulted about the development process from as early as the Pre-Production phase. In the waterfall method, the tester is brought in well towards the end of the Production phase. Both methods work, and both methods have their virtues and shortcomings.

> **N O T E** A *build* is the process of taking all of the pieces of code that each member in a programming group is working on and compiling those pieces into one program. It works like this: Imagine that you are part of a group that is writing the alarm clock app talked about in the preceding tip. Your job is to write the code that makes a sound at a given time. Another member of the group is charged with writing the part of the program that reports the time. And another member of your group is writing the graphical interface. At the end of the work day, you turn your code over to a buildmaster. The other members of your group do the same. The buildmaster then takes the code, composes it into a single source project, and compiles it into a single .EXE. The buildmaster documents the particulars of the build—time, parts, contributors, and so on—and then sends that .EXE on to Quality Assurance (Q/A) for testing. ■

FIG. 36.1
Waterfall testing requires that most testing take place at the end of the Production phase.

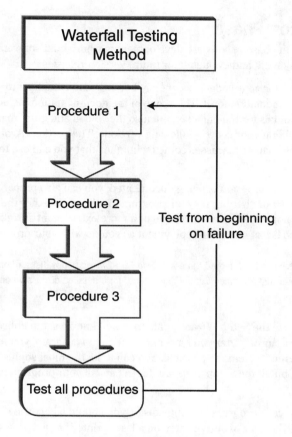

FIG. 36.2
Iterative testing requires that testing take place throughout the Production phase.

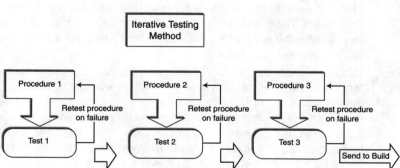

The Post-Production Phase

The Post-Production phase of software development is where built software is documented, prepared for deployment, and evaluated for future version releases.

Documentation   After your code is acceptably bug free and compliant to specification, you must write the documentation for it. The scope of the documentation includes not only the online help and manuals for the end-user, but also the "blood and guts" manuals for the people who will be maintaining your code in following versions. The section "Avoiding Programming Pitfalls" later in this chapter discusses some techniques that you can use to make your code easier to document.

Deployment   As your program is being documented, you can also prepare it for deployment. Deployment is the act of distributing your program to others. Whether the deployment be modest, such as a floppy disk in an envelope, or a more extravagant shrink wrap release, you should put as much effort into your deployment as you do with your programming.

N O T E   Visual Basic can be deployed three ways: via CD-ROM, on floppy disks, or on a network. See Chapter 32, "Advanced Control Techniques," for a detailed discussion on creating Setup programs. ▪

First, you need to use the Setup Wizard or another well known setup utility to create a Setup program for your program. After you have made the Setup program, you must thoroughly test it on as many different systems as possible. You can write the most sophisticated piece of software in the world, but, if the Setup program doesn't install your program properly, your labor is lost.

If you are shipping your program on floppy disks, you should label each disk clearly, avoiding hand written labels in favor of ones printed on a laser printer or by a professional printer. In Visual Basic, it is not at all unusual to have programs that require more than one floppy disk for deployment. Tagging with "X of Y disks" on the disk labels is good practice. For an end user, there are few things more frustrating than trying to install a piece of software only to find out that you are missing a disk.

 T I P   "X of Y disks" tagging is good practice when numbering floppy disks for deployment. In X of Y disk tagging, the number X stands for the particular disk number, while the number Y represents the total number of disks in the deployment set. For example, if my deployment set totals five disks, the first disk is labeled "1 of 5 Disks," the second disk is labeled "2 of 5 Disks," and so on with the last disk labeled "5 of 5 Disks." By doing this, the end user knows exactly how many disks he should have in his deployment set at all times, even if the deployment is only a one disk set.

If space permits, put installation instructions on the disk label. Offer a clear, noticeable note in the deployment package informing the user what to do in the event of difficulty. These things are important and have a definite impact on how the quality of your work is perceived.

CAUTION

Files copied from CD-ROM to hard disk have a default file attribute of READ ONLY. You cannot write to them. This can cause problems if your program is deployed with files which require write access—for example, .INI or database files. When testing your deployment, check to make sure that your Setup program removes the READ ONLY file attribute from the files it copies from CD-ROM.

Evaluation and Future Versions   At the end of every software development process is a period when you look over what you have done to determine how to do it better on the next version. Next version? That's right, because most software gets revised, no matter how small the project. As you were coding your project, without a doubt you came across problems. And, as you solved these problems, you probably said to yourself that the next time you did this, you would do so and so, in such and such a way. Mistakes are things from which we learn, and you will do well to apply what you have learned from your errors to a future version.

Most software is developed under strict time constraints. No person or enterprise can take forever to produce a functional piece of code. As a result, it often is not possible to implement every specified feature into a given release. Therefore, planning to implement features over progressive versions is a viable development strategy.

The evaluation of "real life use" of your code happens in the Post-Production period. The true test of a software product's effectiveness and usability is the test of time. No laboratory condition can ever adequately anticipate every nuance of user interaction. It is only by deploying your program, supporting your program, and eliciting the end users' responses and suggestions for future improvements that you can realistically and accurately evaluate what works and what doesn't.

Creating Consistent and Effective Graphical Interfaces

Imagine that you have run out of coffee. Luckily, there is a gourmet coffee store within driving distance. You get in your car, put the key in the ignition, turn the key, and nothing! Your car won't start. As you are pounding the steering wheel, one of your neighbors comes by and, seeing your distress, offers to lend you her car. You gladly accept her offer. She gives you the keys and a few instructions such as, "It's an automatic and full of gas, so you shouldn't have any problem."

You get in your neighbor's car. You look for the ignition on the steering column—after all, that's where it is on your car. But it's not there. You search for it and finally find it on the center console. You put the key in and turn the ignition. The car starts. You try to put the car in gear, but what you thought was the gear shift turns out to be the emergency brake. You finally find the gear shift and get the car in gear. You start to drive. At an intersection you try to signal left, but what you thought was the turn signal turns out to be the windshield wiper control. You pull off to the side of the road and reach into the glove compartment for the owner's manual. The only problem is what you thought was the glove compartment turns out to be the air bag. You finally find the owner's manual. You open it up. It is written German. You don't read German. You give up. The car is just too hard to drive.

What does this parable have to do with creating consistent and effective graphical interfaces? Well, think of it this way: Software programs are like cars, the more predictable and sensible they are to use, the easier it is to get where you want to go.

Although the Windows operating system has standardized a whole lot about graphical user interface design, and VB has made programming for Windows a whole lot simpler, there is still a good deal of unpredictable use of Windows components (menus, buttons, list boxes, combo boxes, and so on) as well as an intuitively inconsistent amount of variety among Windows programs. This inconsistency defeats the fundamental purpose of the graphical user interface paradigm—to make operating a computer a more productive, enjoyable, less frustrating experience for the user.

Do not think that providing a consistent, predictable graphical interface for your program requires that you forego creativity or uniqueness in your design efforts, or that your product will be less distinguishable from other programs.

Making a Well-Designed Form

Although making a form in Visual Basic is a simple thing to do, making a well-designed one is not that easy. Making a good form is more than inserting controls and programming events. To make a well-designed form, you should understand what the function(s) of a particular form is, how it is going to be used, when it is going to be used, and how it relates to the other forms within a given program.

 Let's take a look at the form, frmSettings (frmESet.frm), in Figure 36.3. (This form is in the project, EvilJot.vbp, which is on the books Web site.) The purpose of this form is to set the display attributes for another form. This form suffers from a number of poor design choices that prevent it from effectively achieving its full functionality.

FIG. 36.3

An example of a poorly designed Display Settings form that fails to adhere to standard user interface layout convention.

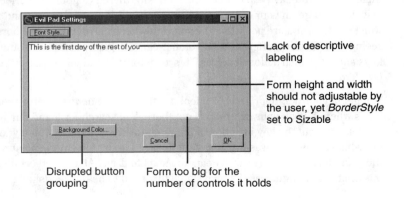

The first item for correction is the choice of setting the form's BorderStyle to Sizeable. Should the user resize the form (see Figure 36.4) either by intention or mistake (double-clicking the title bar is not an uncommon accident), the form does not resize or reposition the controls to accommodate the new form size. Forms that are sizable are generally used in instances where the user needs a window of varying size to accomplish something—for example, Word's documents window or Paint's drawing window. The correction to this problem is to set the form's BorderStyle to Fixed Single or Fixed Dialog.

FIG. 36.4

The controls are not resized or repositioned when the form is resized. The form's *BorderStyle* should be set to Fixed Single or Fixed Dialog.

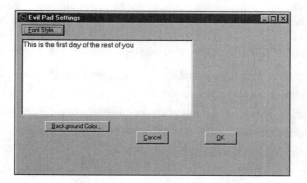

Notice the initial size and location of the form. It completely covers the form whose attributes are to be set. This can easily confuse the user. To remedy this flaw, the form should be repositioned so that when it appears, a portion of the form to be affected is showing.

Notice, too, that the form suffers from poor, almost non-existent, descriptive labeling. The designer is assuming that the user will intuitively know what this form is about, what the function of the label control is, and how each button affects the overall program.

Probably the bigger cause for concern with regard to this form's design is the almost arbitrary use of space and the inconsistent placement of buttons and labels on the form. When it comes to the size of a fixed size form (that is, a dialog box), the rule of thumb is "less is best." You want to allow the form to take up no more real estate then it needs, but not make it so small that controls are congested, and control text and captions are illegible.

You should also organize the placement of controls according to functionality. In the frmSettings form, separating the buttons Font Style from the Background Color is confusing and causes a lot of extra mouse movement activity, which is not necessary. Positioning the Font Style and Background Color together in one group and the OK and Cancel buttons in another creates distinct areas of functionality that the user will find more organized and memorable.

Taking into account the things discussed here, take a look at Figure 36.5. This is an illustration of the improved form, frmSettngs (frmSet.frm), which is part of the Visual Basic project, goodjot.vbp. Notice the reduced size of the form, the change of the form's BorderStyle, the reorganization of the form's buttons, and the inclusion of a frame to provide a sense of functional unity and descriptive labeling.

FIG. 36.5
An improved Display
Settings form enhances
functional effectiveness.

Designing Menus   Making consistent, effective menus is about being able to follow some
pretty straightforward design guidelines and being able to organize the intended functionality
of your menus consistently and concisely. Following are a few high-level guidelines and suggestions that will enable you to make professional looking menus that meet the user's expectation:

- Follow standard Windows layout convention: File, Edit, View, and so on
- Group menu items logically and concisely
- Use separator bars to group related functionalities in a drop-down menu
- Avoid redundant menu entries
- Avoid menu bar items without drop-down menus
- Don't forget to use the ellipsis(…) to denote menu entries that activate dialog boxes

Follow Standard Windows Layout Convention for Menus   Windows has been around for a
long enough period of time that its installed base of users has developed a certain expectation
about how Windows applications should work and look. One of the areas where user
expectation is extremely strong is the layout of the menu bar. Take a look at Figure 36.6. In this
example, the designer of this menu has chosen to breach standard Windows menu bar layout
convention. Conventional expectation is that the menu bar item File comes first in a menu bar,
followed by Edit. This design reorders the menu bar item order to Edit, then File. This change
forces the user to have to relearn a habitual menu navigation method. This unconventional
reordering of the menu bar will probably cause the user to experience initial confusion. In this
case, there is little to be accomplished and possibly a good deal to be lost by not conforming to
the de facto Windows convention.

FIG. 36.6
Re-ordering the
standard Window menu
bar is not always a good
idea.

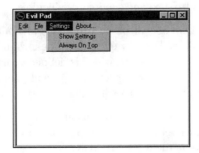

Part
V

Ch
36

Group Menu Items Logically and Concisely   Referring to Figure 36.6, notice that the illustrated menu bar item Settings has only two sub-items: Show Settings and Always on Top. These two sub-items can be moved to the File drop-down menu. Doing this condenses the menu bar without affecting the functionality or accessibility of the moved items.

Use Separator Bars to Group Related Functionality in a Drop-Down Menu   After the Show Settings and Always on Top drop-down menu items have been moved to the File menu (see Figure 36.7), they can be grouped together by putting a separator bar before and after the items.

FIG. 36.7

The File menu has the Setting and Always on Top menu items consolidated into it. Notice the use of separator bars to group the functionality.

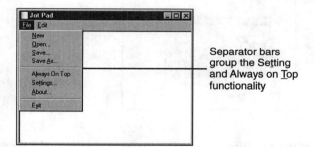

Separator bars group the Setting and Always on Top functionality

Avoid Redundant Menu Entries   While it's always a good idea to offer the user multiple ways of performing the same behavior within your program—for example, clicking Copy in the Edit menu or striking the Ctrl+C keys to copy selected data to the Clipboard—it is not good practice to have a given functionality appear in more than one place with your program's menu. Nor is it a good idea to have the same menu caption appear in more than one place in your program doing two different actions. In Figure 36.8, notice that the caption Settings appears both in the File menu and as a menu bar entry, Settings. Also notice that when you click the Settings menu item in the File menu, the Setting dialog box appears. When you click the Settings menu bar item, the Settings drop-down menu appears. This is bad business. Having the caption Settings in two different areas of the program's menu will not only confuse the user, but having two different behaviors attached to each caption will confound her.

FIG. 36.8

Notice that the Settings menu item appears in the File drop-down menu and on the menu bar. This is a confusing design choice.

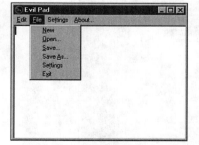

Avoid Menu Bar Items Without Drop-Down Menus   If you find yourself in a situation where you have a menu bar item without any sub-items, you might want to rethink your design decisions (see Figure 36.9). An orphan menu bar item has the behavior of a button. If that sort of behavior is what you want, then you should use a button control to achieve that given functionality. A better solution is to move the orphan menu bar item to be a sub-item of another menu bar item that groups a similar set of functions.

FIG. 36.9
Menu bar items should
not invoke dialog boxes.
They should invoke
drop-down menus.

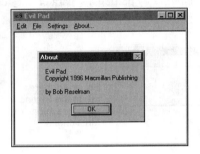

Don't Forget to Use the Ellipsis(...) to Denote Menu Entries that Activate Dialog
Boxes   When an ellipsis appears next to an item in a drop-down menu, it means that clicking that menu item makes a dialog box appear. Many people unfamiliar with designing Windows application for general or enterprise wide use frequently forget to use it. Using the ellipsis when the situation warrants adds to the professionalism of your application.

Offering Choices

When it comes time for a user to make a decision within your program, it is usually more efficient to provide a set of choices from which to select (see Figure 36.10). Selecting choices reduces the risk of error due to typing mistakes. Also, providing a choice sets the range of acceptable entries.

FIG. 36.10
Selecting a typeface
from a list of available
fonts is easier for the
user than typing in a
selection.

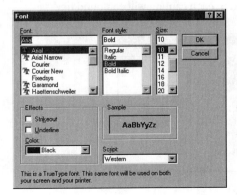

ListBox versus ComboBox   Visual Basic provides two powerful control types: the list box and the combo box.

A list box allows the user to view a list of all available choices before, during, and after the time a selection is made. A list box allows no user input. The user can only input data by selecting from a list. This can be a drawback should the user need to input data that the program does not provide. Another drawback of the list box is that it requires a good deal of window space to be useful. A list box that shows only two or three items can appear cramped and awkward.

When window space is at a premium, a combo box can be a better design choice. The combo box has three styles: drop-down combo, simple combo, and drop-down list (see Figure 36.11). Drop-down combo boxes display a drop-down list that also permits typed-in user input. The simple combo style shows an input box above a list, almost like a list box with a text box above it. The drawback of using the simple combo style is that, like a list box, it requires a good deal of window space to be effective. The third style, the drop-down list style is similar to the simple combo. However, the drop-down list does not allow the user to type in any input.

FIG. 36.11

The different styles of a Combo Box—Dropdown combo, Simple combo, and Dropdown list.

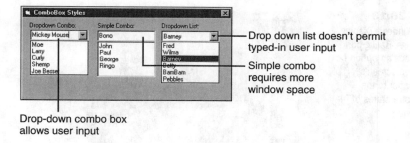

Overusing list boxes and combo boxes can also harm an application's performance. If a list box or combo box lists too many items, the control can increase the load time of the form to which the control belongs. You can reduce the number of items in a list by finding out what the actual limits are. Does a user need all the states in the United States, or only the ten with which the company normally does business?

Option Boxes versus Check Boxes   To present a fixed number of choices, use the check box and option box controls. A check box gives the user two choices only: on or off, implemented or not implemented. For example, the Windows Explorer View, Option dialog box uses the check box to indicate whether to Display the Full MS-DOS Path in the Title Bar or not (see Figure 36.12). An option box presents the user with a fixed list of exclusive choices. For example, the Windows Display Settings, Appearance tab uses an option box to set a screen's wallpaper to the exclusive states of Tile or Center (see Figure 36.13).

FIG. 36.12
You can use check boxes to allow the user to make mutually inclusive choices.

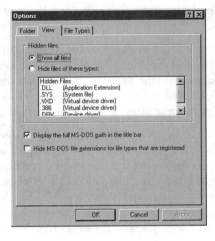

FIG. 36.13
The Windows Display Settings, Background tab uses an option box to set a screen's wallpaper to the exclusive states of Tile or Center.

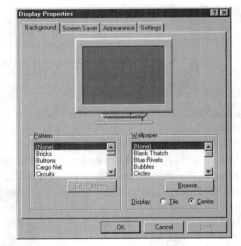

CAUTION

If your application uses more than one form and you expect the user to terminate your application by using the control box of any of the forms, make sure to add the End command to the Form_Unload event of the given form. Failure to do so can result in having your application remain active in memory even though no windows are visible.

Improving User Perceptions of Your Programs

When users click an icon, they like to see something happen. Unless the application appears to take some kind of action, some users become confused and begin to suspect that the program doesn't work. Users might perceive an application with many forms as "slow" because it is constantly loading and unloading the forms. This loading and unloading also confuses users and creates a performance problem.

Whether an application is "slow" or "fast" is a matter of the user's perception. If users see something happening on-screen while an application is executing, they perceive the application as "fast" rather than "slow." The techniques described in this section help you to create "fast" applications.

Load Time   If you load all of a program's forms at program startup, they will appear more quickly when the application calls them. Although this slows the application's performance at program startup, the application's runtime performance is much faster. Simply load all the forms that belong to an application by using the load method. This method places the forms in memory where they are invisible to the user.

This technique works well for applications with a small number of forms (up to five). For applications with more forms, you might use this technique for similar groupings of forms. For example, an accounting payroll application might load all the forms associated with displaying employee information during an employee data-entry session.

The *Sub Main* Subroutine   The Options dialog box (which you display by choosing Tools, Options), has a Project tab that enables you to change the startup form to Sub Main. To take advantage of this setting, you need a module with a Main subroutine. This frees you from having to keep any startup routines within a form's load event.

The Sub Main subroutine is an excellent place for all the startup code required at startup time. For example, the Sub Main subroutine might contain code for checking the application's path. You might place a splash screen on-screen while the subroutine checks this path.

Splash Screens   One way to deal with lengthy program startups is to display a splash screen during load time. A splash screen is a borderless form that displays information about the application and its designer. Many commercial applications, including Microsoft Word and Excel, display splash screens at program startup. A splash screen provides the user with visible proof that something is happening.

Avoiding Programming Pitfalls

Whether you are a member of a team of programmers or are a programmer working on your own, your code will have to be maintained either by you or others. And, as hard as it was getting that certain function to work right after hours of debugging when you first wrote it, you or a team member will probably find it a lot harder to figure out what you did in that function six months down the line when it comes time to improve and enhance it. However, while it might be hard, it doesn't have to be horrendous. If you take certain precautions and use foresight, you can make the preparation time needed to maintain your code reasonable and relatively painless.

Programming Readable Code

The most important thing that you can do toward making your code easy to maintain is to make it readable—not only to yourself but also to others. If another programmer cannot read your code, he wastes precious time figuring out exactly what the program does and how. Readable code gives others a quick, intuitive "feel" for how your program works. Also, readability has a definite impact on how your code is perceived within the professional community. Those who have to modify your code will be grateful for the efforts you made on their behalf.

Using Visual Basic Constants

Visual Basic enables you to write code with numeric values to specify how an object should behave. This capability makes writing code easier, but makes reading the code harder afterwards. The solution is to use global constants that represent these values. Code that uses constants is much easier to read. You no longer have to add a CONSTANT.TXT file to your Visual Basic projects as you did with versions of Visual Basic prior to version 4.0. Microsoft includes global constants in the support files, so you no longer have to add the constant file to use the constants.

Some programmers are proud that they can read code without the help of constants. Unfortunately, not all programmers are capable of doing so, including some who might need to read your code. By using the Visual Basic global constants, you make your code more readable to all programmers, even those who cannot read code as easily. Even if you are capable of reading code without constants, using constants still makes your code easier to read, especially if you tend to forget what you have done and why. For example, which of the following code lines is more readily understandable:

```
FORM1.SHOW 1
```

```
FORM1.SHOW vbModal
```

When you read code that uses the constants, you do not have to remember what each value means. The code is more readable.

Commented Code

Writing commented code is a pain, but reading uncommented code, even if you wrote it yesterday, can be an even greater pain. Trying to figure out the logic of the code on-screen is time consuming. Taking the time to put in comments, on the other hand, saves you time in the long run. There's an old saying among programmers: "You can never comment too much!" Imagine trying to read and understand the meaning and use of the code in Listing 36.1 without the comments.

Listing 36.1   36List01.TXT—A Program that Searches the Tag Property of Each Control and Displays the Appropriate Database Field Information in Each Control

```
' The following routine searches through all the controls
' on a form and checks each control's TAG property.
' If the tag property is a field name, this routine loads
' the current field's value into that control.

Sub LoadFormData (WndName As Form, dyn As Dynaset)
Dim Cntl%, FieldName$, Result$, N%, i%

Screen.MousePointer = vbHOURGLASS

'Search through all the controls on the indicated form
For Cntl% = 0 To WndName.Controls.Count - 1
  FieldName$ = WndName.Controls(Cntl%).Tag
  If TypeOf WndName.Controls(Cntl%) Is OptionButton Then

    ' Find the value of this field and store in the appropriate
    ' option button control
    N% = Abs(dyn(FieldName$))
    If WndName.Controls(Cntl%).Caption = "YES" Then
        WndName.Controls(Cntl%).Value = N%
    ElseIf WndName.Controls(Cntl%).Caption = "NO" Then
        WndName.Controls(Cntl%).Value = Abs(N% - 1)
    End If

  ElseIf TypeOf WndName.Controls(Cntl%) Is ComboBox Then

    If dyn(FieldName$) <> Null Then

      ' Format the current field's value
      Result$ = dyn.Fields(FieldName$)
      ' Find the field's value in the current combo box
      For N% = 0 To (WndName.Controls(Cntl%).ListCount - 1)
        i% = WndName.Controls(Cntl%).ListIndex + 1
        WndName.Controls(Cntl%).ListIndex = i%
        If Len(WndName.Controls(Cntl%).Text) <> 0 Then
          Exit For
        End If
      Next N%
    End If

  ' If the control is a text box
  ElseIf TypeOf WndName.Controls(Cntl%) Is TextBox Then

    ' If the current field's value is blank then skip
    If dyn(FieldName$) <> Null Then

      ' Store the formatted value in the text box
      WndName.Controls(Cntl%).Text = dyn.Fields(FieldName$)
```

continues

Listing 36.1   Continued

```
      End If
    End If
  Next Cntl%

  Screen.MousePointer = vbDEFAULT

  End Sub
```

Listing 36.1 contains the subroutine `LoadFormData`. You could reference this subroutine in the `load` event of any form. Simply provide the name of the `dynaset` containing the data, position the table at the appropriate record, place the names of the fields that you want in the appropriate control's tag property, and run this routine. In instances where you cannot use `Bound con-trols`, this routine works amazing well. Notice that the use of `vbHourGlass` and `vbDefault` makes it clear what the program is doing to the `mousepointer`.

Use Descriptive Naming

Visual Basic allows you to use up to 255 characters to name a variable, sub, or function, and 40 characters to name a control. You can take advantage of this feature to make your code easier to understand by giving your variable, function, and controls names that reflect their identity, purpose, function, or position. Listing 36.2 shows an example of using descriptive naming to make your code more readable.

Listing 36.2   36List02.TXT—Example Using Descriptive Naming for Variables and Controls

```
Private Sub cmdChoices_MouseDown(Index As Integer, ➥
                                 Button As Integer, ➥
                                 Shift As Integer, ➥
                                 X As Single, ➥
                                 Y As Single)
    Dim i%
    '"The pressed button typeface will be set according to the option,
➥opFontFace
    'value set

    'Set the old font (the gf prefix denotes global to form) so it can
    'reset on MouseUp
    gfOldFontFace$ = cmdChoices(Index).Font
    'Adjust for the new font setting
    If opFontFace(0) = True Then
        cmdChoices(Index).Font = opFontFace(0).Caption
    Else
        cmdChoices(Index).Font = opFontFace(1).Caption
    End If

    'Query to option buttons and set the caption case
    'for the button depressed
```

```
    For i% = 0 To 2
        Select Case i%
        Case 0
            If opFontCase(i%).Value = True Then ↦
                cmdChoices(Index).Caption = ↦
                UCase(cmdChoices(Index).Caption)
        Case 1
            If opFontCase(i%).Value = True Then ↦
                cmdChoices(Index).Caption = ↦
                LCase(cmdChoices(Index).Caption)
        Case 2
            If opFontCase(i%).Value = True Then ↦
                cmdChoices(Index).Caption = gfOldFontCase$(Index)
        End Select
    Next i%
End Sub
```

From Here...

Designing an effective Windows application requires more understanding and planning than just putting controls on a form. Implementing a user-centered software development process helps you design cost effective, user-friendly applications that work well and are easy to deploy and revise.

An application's appearance is as important as what the application does. A poorly thought-out application interface detracts from the application's usefulness because users focus on the bad interface rather than what it does. Be careful how you organize controls and menus. Also be careful to ensure that your program complies with and responds to the user's expectations.

Have consideration for those who will maintain your code after you are through with it. Comment your code thoroughly. Use constants and descriptive naming.

To find information on related topics, see the following chapters:

■ For more information on the toolbar and status bar, see Chapter 32, "Advanced Control Techniques."

■ To find out more about MDI and SDI applications, see Chapter 33, "Advanced Form Techniques."

Index

Symbols

3-D CheckBox control, 296

3-D Panel control, 296

A

-a switches, availability, 501

About class, 594-597

**About dialog boxes,
creating, 592-594**

**AbsolutePosition property,
321-322**

Access, 610-634
Connect property, 390
databases
controlling, 370-373
creating, 273
dialog boxes, displaying, 606

accessing
classes
limitations, 177
from programs, 182-185
databases, 190-193
with RDO, 411-412
external databases, 388-394
remote applications, 501
Visual Basic, menu bar,
18-19

**action queries, 216-217,
357, 361-362**

statements
DELETE, 357-358
INSERT, 358
troubleshooting, 329

actions, 49
multiple events, 88
user input, 111

Activate
event, 56-57
method, 685

**activation OLE, controls,
433-436**

ActiveX
classes, adding modules,
488-495
Control Interface Wizard,
512, 524-528
controls, 17
creating, 15, 512-522
DLLs, 17
projects, 470
Document DLL template
icon, 714
documents, creating, 15
EXE, 17
objects
refining, 491-496
running, 490-491
terminology, 442

ActiveX .EXE, projects, 470

**ActiveX Components dialog
box, 718**

Add button, 236

**Add Class Module
command (Project menu),
489**

**Add Data Source dialog box,
406**

Add Drivers dialog box, 405

Add Field dialog box, 271

**Add File command (Project
menu), 168**

Add File dialog box, 168

**Add Form command
(Project menu), 164, 739**

Add function, 332

**Add Index dialog box,
272-273**

Add method
collection objects, 485-486
Outlook, 680

**Add Module command
(Project menu), 163, 165**

**Add Procedure command
(Tool menu), 159**

**Add Procedure dialog box,
158, 179**

**Add Project command (File
menu), 521**

**Add Property Page
command (Project menu),
528**

Add Tab command, 22

Add Watch command
(Debug menu), 150

AddField method,
EasyDAQ, 614-615

Add-In Manager command
(Add-Ins menu), 524

Add-In Manager dialog box,
524

add-ins
ActiveX Control Interface
Wizard, 524-528
building, with classes, 175
classes, 168
code modules to projects,
165
controls
control toolbox, 22
to forms, 59
fields, 275
forms, 168
to programs, 164-165
hotkeys and shortcuts,
creating menu bars, 97-99
indexes, 274
indexes to tables, 272-273
modules, 168
projects, 470
properties to classes,
178-181
records, 330
tables, 270-272, 274
tabs, control toolboxes, 22
Visual Data Manager, 364

Add-Ins menu commands
Add-In Manager, 524
Visual Data Manager, 364,
398

adding browser
applications, 738-741

AddItem ListBox method,
70

addition, operators,
128-129

Additional Controls dialog
box, 523

AddLevel procedure, 542

AddNew method, 330

AddOrEditRecord method,
617-619, 626-628

addresses (IP), finding, 721

AddSlide method, 637-638

aggregate functions (SQL
SELECT statements),
353-354

aliases, assigning (SQL
SELECT statements), 343

Alignment property, 64

ALL predicates, SQL
SELECT statements,
343-344

ALTER TABLE (DDL
statement), 359

Alter Table query, 275

AND operator, BETWEEN
predicate, 351

ANSI committee, 40

API (application program
interface), 404

APIs, 845-877
calling functions, 840-845
declaring, 842
GetVersion(), 840-841
functions
GlobalMemoryStatus,
847
GDI (Graphics Device
Interface) functions,
862-867

Append method, 259

Application class Excel,
601-606

applications
browsers
as add-ins, 738-741
creating, 734-741
Internet Explorer,
736-738
chat, creating, 746-749

classes, adding modules,
488-495
compatibility
checking, 548
maintaining, 545
components, viewing
names, 476-477
creating, 229-232
adding essential
functions, 231-232
database navigation,
230-231
form setup, 229-230
debugging, 540
designing for Windows 95,
443
editions, creating, 550
entries, de-registering,
553-554
Internet
activating, 722-723
creating, 714-717
passing data to servers,
729-731
preparing for network
transmittal, 717-721
security, 723-725
user documents (moving
between), 725-726
user documents (passing
data between), 726-728
Internet Information Server
(IIS), creating, 751-756
loading time, 582
lockups, splash screens,
579-580
MDI
child form, 587-590
Excel, 577
Microsoft
integrating, 693-696
non-OLE or DDE
supporting, 696-712
OLE Automation, memory
requirements, 647
opening linked objects, 435
ports, 493
Registry, registering,
460-464

running
  creating new objects, 542-543
  retrieving objects, 544
single-use, lost references, 534-535
source code, choosing, 607
starting (testing), 544
three-phase development, 880-885
  post-production phase, 884-886
  pre-production phase, 881
  production phase, 882
versions
  adding information, 548-549
  code-compatibility, 548-549
Web pages, VBScript, 567-568
Word, 648-650

appointments (forms), Outlook, 667

arguments
  Code, 433
  HeightNew, 422
  KeyValue, 538
  verbnumber, 434
  WidthNew, 422

array handling, VBScript, 564

arrays
  controls, 760-765
    imgTools, 650
    menu techniques, 760-764
    option button techniques, 764-765

ASP (Active Server Pages), 751
  Internet Information Server applications, 751-756

objects, 753-754
  VB-created objects, 754-756

assignment statements, 127

Attach button, New Attached Table dialog box, 400

Attach method, 699

attaching
  external tables, 396-401
  tables
    Access, 400-401
    DAO, 397-398
    with Visual Data Manager, 398-400

attachments, Outlook, 675-678

Attachments command (Utilities menu), 399

AttachToMessage method, Outlook, 675-677

authentication, Internet applications, 723-725

Authenticode Security Technology dialog box, 724

Auto Statement Builder, 16

AutoActivate property, 433-434

automation, *see* remote automation

Automation servers,
  building with classes, 175
  OLE, connecting to, 684-688

AutoSize property, 63

availability
  -a switches, 501
  -p switches, 501

Avg aggregate function, 353

AVI files (picture box playback), multimedia forms, 804-806

B

BASIC, background of, 38

Basic property, initializing, 481

batch languages, 561

BEGINTRANS statement, recovering deletions, 358

behavior (properties), controlling, 44-48

BETWEEN predicates, 350-351
  (WHERE clauses), 348

BinarySearch() function, searching and sorting, 818-820

binding, Excel, 576

bit manipulation, CS programming techniques, 833-837

blnAdd parameter, AddOrEditRecord method, 617

BOFAction property, 284

Bookmark property, 320-321

bookmarks, troubleshooting, 321

Boolean variables, 121

BorderStyle form property, 51, 64
  controls, 53

bound controls, 226-229, 291-296
  adding to forms, 227-228
  combo boxes, 292
    data bound, 293-294
  data bound grids, 295
  DataField property, 228-229
  DataSource property, 228-229

list boxes, 292
data bound, 293-294
third party, 296

BoundColumn property, 294

breakpoints, coding, 154

browsers
applications
browsers as add-ins, 738-741
creating, 734-741
Internet Explorer, 736-738
FTP, creating, 742-746
scripting languages, declaring, 565

bugs, eliminating, 144-156

BuildTree procedure, 768-770

built-in dialog boxes, 111-117
Color, 116-117
File, 112-114
Filter property (specifying file types), 114
opening and saving files, 113-114
Font, 114-116
Print, 117

built-in support, remote automation, 498

BulletListItem property, 639

buttons
Attach (New Attached Table dialog box), 400
creating, Access, 629-630
form setup, 235-236
View Code, 166
writing event procedures, 85
View Object, 166

byte variables, 121

C

C, 41

C++, 41

calculated fields
controls, labels, 341
creating, (SQL SELECT statements), 340-341

calculation queries, 327-328

Call keyword, procedures, 161

CallbackDemo( ) method, 876

CallBackFunc( ) function, 876

callbacks, 873-877
frankentrols, 777-779

calling statements, parameters, 161

Caption property, 63, 223
forms, 44

Caption settings (forms), 230

cascading
deletions, tables, 213
updates, tables, 213

Case statements, 138

cboContact procedure, 628

cDataAccess class, 191-192

Change events, Slider control, 518

changes, rejected, 213

character-range lists, LIKE predicate, 349

chart control, 16

chat applications, creating, 746-749

Check Box control, 21

check box controls user choices, graphical interfaces, 891-892

CheckBox control, 68-69

checking remote automations, 501-502

child forms, Excel, 587-590

child tables, 252-254

child windows, MDI, 795-797

Circle method, creating control interfaces, 515

Class Builder, 474-475

class modules, new, 176

class objects (MAPI), sending mail, 678-681

class types OLE objects, 419-420

Class_Initialize event, 473, 700

classes, 473-474
About, 594-597
accessing
from programs, 182-185
limitations, 177
actions, performing, 181
add-ins, building, 175
adding, 168
Application, Excel, 601-606
building, 176-185
cDataAccess, 191-192
cPrint class, 185
creating, 471-475
collections, 484-488
EASYDAO.CLS, 611
events, 177
adding, 181-182
exposed, OLE server interfaces, 601-606
FindFile, 849, 855-877
functions, 175
global, 471
hierarchies, 487
initial variables, setting, 189
initializing, 189
modules
adding, 488-496
calling form events, 489
public, 496

multiUse, 471
naming, 476-477
object-oriented
    progamming,
    implementing, 175
objects, 181
    comparing, 471
    enhanced printer,
    186-189
OLE Automation servers,
    175
organizing, 487
private, Standard .EXE, 470
properties
    adding, 178-181
    setting, 177-178
reusable, 470-471
Set statements, 473
singleUse, 471
statements, Dim, 474
uses, 175-176, 190-193
VolumeControlConstants,
    518
see also controls

**ClearAll procedure,
630-631**

**Click event, Web pages,
566**

**client applications, creating
Pool Demos, 507**

**client machines, running
remote applications, 501**

**ClipArt Gallery miniserver,
689**

Close button, 236

**clsExchangeData object,
707, 711**

**clsPowerPoint object,
636-644**
    extensibility, 637

cmd_Click procedure, 629

**cmdBack event procedure,
735**

**cmdCreate_Click event,
Outlook, 672**

**cmdGetMemoryStatus_
Click( ) event, 849**

**cmdNext event procedure,
735**

**cmdSearch_Click( ) event,
825**

**cmdSend_Click event,
Outlook, 680**

cmdSort_Click( ) event, 825

COBOL, 79-82
    design history, 33
    to Visual Basic, 32

Code argument, 433

**Code command (View
menu), 85**

code compiler, 15

Code Editing window, 148

code window, 25

codes
    functions, 158-163
    maintenance, 893-897
        commented code,
        894-896
        descriptive naming,
        896-897
        readable code, 894
    modular construction,
    158-163
    modules, adding, 165
    native compiling, 170
    P-code, compiling, 170
    procedures, 158-163

coding breakpoints, 154

collection, VBScript, 564

collections, 484
    classes, creating, 484-488
    Controls, 484
    creating grouping actions,
    485-486
    Forms, 484
    objects, 485
        built-in properties and
        methods, 485-486
        organizing, 487-488

properties, 485
Recipients, Outlook, 570
Shapes, 639

Color dialog box, 116-117

**Column to Sort By combo
box, 235**

**COM (Component Object
Model), 646**

**Combo Box control, 21,
292**
    data bound, 293-294
    user choices, graphical
    interfaces, 891

ComboBox control, 72-73

**Command Button control,
21**

**command-line parameters,
500**

**Command1_Click event,
Excel, 575**

**CommandButton control,
58**

commands
    Add-Ins menu
        Add-In Manager, 524
        Visual Data Manager,
        364, 398
    databases (Visual Basic),
    258-260
    Debug menu, Add Watch,
    150
    Edit menu, Find Key, 551
    File menu
        Add Project, 521
        Get External Data, 396,
        400
        Make, 170, 522, 717
        New, 568
        New Project, 512, 714
        Open, 715
        Open Database, 364
        Save Registration File,
        551
    Form menu, View Code, 568
    Help menu, Search
        Reference Index, 27

Insert menu, User Form, 523

multiple, If statements, 134-135

program, 302

in programs, 276

Project menu
Add Class Module, 489
Add File, 168
Add Form, 164, 739
Add Module, 163, 165
Add Property Page, 528
Components, 22, 167, 413, 514, 734
Project Properties, 512
Properties, 473, 476, 488, 490, 495
References, 166, 474, 542, 736
Remove, 739
Remove File, 168

Script menu, Event, 569

Start menu, Control Panel, 404

Tools menu
Add Procedure, 159
Design Outlook Form, 568
Procedure Attributes, 478, 495

Utilities menu, Attachments, 399

View menu
Code, 85
Debug, 148
Options, 724
Watch Window, 149

commented code, code maintenance, 894-896

CommitTable method, EasyDAQ, 614-615

common controls, 765-773
progress bars, 765-766
TreeView and ListView, 766-773

BuildTree and LoadListItems procedures, 768-770
control event responses, 770-773

Common Dialog control, 58

CommonDialog control, 111-117
Color dialog box, 116-117
File dialog box, 112-114
Filter property (specifying file types), 114
opening and saving files, 113-114
Font dialog box, 114-116
Print dialog box, 117
ShowPrinter method, 117

communication
ODBC (Open Database Connectivity), 404-408
RDC, 412

Compare( ) function, 817, 820

comparing early binding, late binding, 502

comparison operators
JOIN clauses, 345
WHERE clauses, 348

Comparison predicates, WHERE clauses, 348

compatibility, checking, 548

compiling
programs, 170-171
VBScript, 564

Component Object Model, *see* **COM**

Component page (Project Properties dialog box), 548

Components command (Project menu), 22, 167, 413, 514, 734

Components dialog box, 22, 167, 243, 413

components of projects, managing, 166-168

Compose Mail dialog boxes, 667
Outlook, 678

computer science programming techniques, 816-837
bit manipulation, 833-837
linked lists, 825-833
doubly linked lists, 830-833
Item object, 825-829
searching and sorting, 816-825
BinarySearch( ) function, 818-820
generic helper functions (writing), 817-818
QuickSort( ) function, 820-822

conditional loops, true conditions, 142-145

conditions
multiple, accepting, 351
While, 143

Connect property, 281
accessing databases, 389

Connect property settings, 389-390

connections, OLE automation servers, 684-688

constants
code maintenance, 894
declaring, 563
public, enumerations, 483-484
variables, 125-127
creating your own, 126-127
supplied constants, 126
VBScript, 563, 564

constructing codes, modular, 158-163

container controls (OLE), displaying MS application objects, 693-696

containers, 45

Contents, help system, 27

context-sensitive, help system, 28

control, data, 206

control flow, VBScript, 564

Control Panel command (Start menu), 404

control toolbox
adding controls, 22
tabs, adding, 22
toolboxes, 21-22

ControlBox form property, 52

controlling
behavior of properties, 44-48
program startups, 168-169

controls, 57-61
.OCX, starting projects, 512-513
actions, CommandButton control, 74
ActiveX, creating, 15
ActiveX Control Interface Wizard, 524-528
adding to forms, 59
arrays, 760-765
menu techniques, 760-764
option button techniques, 764-765
Borderstyle form property, 53
bound, 226-229, 291-296
adding to forms, 227-228
combo boxes, 292
data bound combo boxes, 293-294
data bound grids, 295
data bound list boxes, 293-294

DataField property, 228-229
DataSource property, 228
list boxes, 292
third party, 296
chart, 16
CheckBox, 68-69
common, 765-773
progress bars, 765-766
TreeView and ListView, 766-773
CommonDialog, 111-117
Color dialog box, 116-117
File dialog box, 112-114
Font dialog box, 114-116
Print dialog box, 117
ShowPrinter method, 117
compiling, 522
control toolbox
adding, 22
creating, 512-522
customizing, 24
Data, 280-285
advantages, 280
limitations, 280-281
other database formats, 281-285
data, 222-225, 286-291
adding to forms, 223
BOFAction property, 284
changing properties, 286-287
DatabaseName property, 224-225
EOFAction property, 285
Error event, 290
find and seek operations, 296-297
methods, 290-291
option buttons, 297-298
optional properties, 285
recordsets, 287-288
RecordSource property, 225
SQL statements, 363
tables and snapshots, 283-284
Validate event, 289

databases, restrictions, 370
de-registering, 554
defined, 14
events, adding, 517-519
frankentrols, 773-786
adding new styles, 774-777
callbacks and function pointers, 777-779
hooking, 779-786
window styles, 774
grouping (collections), 485-486
imgHold image, 650
initializing, 516-517
interfaces, drawing, 514-515
Internet, 741-749
creating chat applications, 746-749
creating FTP browsers, 742-746
label, calculated fields, 341
lists, 69-73
ComboBox control, 72-73
ListBox control, 69-70
managing, 167
methods, adding, 517-519
Microsoft Access, 523
Microsoft Office, 522-523
MSFlexGrid, 16
multiple, handling with single procedures, 86-87
new, 16
OLE
activation, 433-436
Picture property, 431
OLE Container
Excel, 577-590
Word, 648-663
OOP, 13
organizing, 20-22
projects, 470
properties
adding, 517-519
adding design-time, 519-521
setting and retrieving values, 59-61

Property pages, 528-530
registering, 523
resizing, 515
running
    project groups, 521-522
    under development,
    521-522
runtime, 517
scaling, (OLE objects), 427
Slider, 514
StartupPosition property, 54
text, 62-67
    Label control, 62
    RichTextBox control,
    65-69
    TextBox control, 64-65
three-dimensional effect,
    adding
    (Word), 652-653
Volume, 513
Web pages, 566
WebBrowser ActiveX, 734,
    741

Controls collection, 484

conversion, VBScript, 564

**CopiesToPrinter property,
244**

copying, databases, 219

**Count aggregate function,
353**

Count property
collection objects, 486
collections, 485

counter loop, 140-142

cPrint class, 185

**CREATE INDEX (DDL
statements), 360**

**Create method, EasyDAQ,
614-615**

**CREATE TABLE (DDL
statement), 359**

**CreateDatabase method,
258**

CreateEmbed method
class types, 419-420

creating OLE objects at
    runtime, 418

**CreateField method, 258,
265**
EasyDAQ, 614-615

**CreateHook (hooking),
779-782**

CreateIndex method, 265
EasyDAQ, 614-615

CreateIndex methods, 258

**CreateItem method,
Outlook, 667**

**CreateLink method, creating
OLE objects at runtime,
418**

**CreateLocalTask method,
Outlook, 667**

**CreateMultiArray() function,
813**

CreateObject function
GetRunningObject
    procedure, 544
multiuse objects, 536-537

CreateObject method, 755

**CreateQueryDef method,
268**

**CreateRecordset method,
613-614**

CreateRelation method, 267

**CreateShortcut function,
845**

**CreateTable method,
614-615**

**CreateTableDef method,
258**

creating
ActiveX controls, 15
ActiveX documents, 15
applications, 229-232
    adding essential
      functions, 231-232
    database navigation,
    230-231

    form setup, 229-230
    Internet Information
      Server (IIS), 751-756
browser applications,
    734-741
chat applications, 746-749
client applications
    Pool Demos, 507
constants, 126-127
databases, 248-260
    with Access, 273
    with Visual Data
      Manager, 269-273
databases with other tools,
    269-273
dynasets from dynasets, 307
forms, automatically,
232-236
functions, 158-162
graphical interfaces, 885-893
    forms, 886-890
    user choices, 890-892
    user perceptions, 892-893
indexes, 265-266, 324-325
Internet applications,
    714-717
menu bars, 93-99
    adding hotkeys and
      shortcuts, 97-99
    main item setup, 94
    menu item code
      (writing), 99-100
    modifying menu
      structure, 97
    multiple level menus,
      95-97
multimedia forms, 797-808
pop-up menus, 102-103
    activating the menu, 103
procedures, 158-162
    Sub statement, 158

programs, distributable,
169-171
queries, 268-269
relations, 267-268
remote applications,
    requirements, 498

remote logging services, remote automation services, 729-730
snapshots, 309
tables, 260-264, 356
tables with Queries, 264

cross tab reports, 239

Crystal Reports
control, 243
setting properties, 245-246
setup, 243-244
starting, 238-240
Report Expert, 239
selecting data fields, 240-241

currency variables, 121

custom controls, *see* **ActiveX controls**

Custom Controls dialog box, 413

customizing
controls, 24
database structure, 273-276
databases, with SQL, 275-276
fields, 272
forms, 24
multiple records, 325-329
toolbars, 16, 25
windows, 25

D

DAOs (data access objects), 206, 610-632
external database, accessing, 389-392
RDO similarities, 409-411
tables, attaching with, 397-398

data
control, 206
importing
with Access, 396

external databases, 394-396
with programs, 395-396
timing, 394-395
integrity, 203
normalization, 251-252, 257-258
organizing, 249-255
source, ODBC, 404-409
types, Jet Engine, 205
validation, 214-216

Data Access Object libraries, troubleshooting, 303

data bound combo boxes, 293-294

data bound grids, 295

data bound list boxes, 293-294

data control, 22, 58, 280-291
BOFAction property, 284
changing properties, 286-287
control, 58
EOFAction property, 285
Error event, 290
external databases, accessing, 393
optional properties, 285
RDC similarities, 412
recordsets, 287-288
SQL statements, 363
tables and snapshots, 283-284
Validate event, 289
action parameter values, 289

data controls, 222-225
adding to forms, 223
DatabaseName property, 224-225
find and seek operations, 296-297
methods, 290-291
option buttons, 297-298
RecordSource property, 225

data dictionary report sources, 240

data fields (selecting), Report Expert, 240-241

data file report sources, 240

Data Form Wizard, creating forms automatically, 232-233

data keys, relating tables, 207

data manipulation language, *see* **DML**

Data property, EASYDAO.CLS, 611

data types
variants, 810-815
ParamArray function, 815-816
VBScript, 564

data-definition language, *see* **DDL**

Data-Definition-Language Statements, *see* **DDLs**

DatabaseName property, 224-225, 282-286
external databases, 390-391

databases, 198-201
access, 190-193
controlling, 370-373
multi-user, 369
adding essential functions, data access application, 231-232
adding tables to, 264
changes, rejected, 213
classes, EASYDAO.CLS, 611
commands (Visual Basic), 258-260
copying, 219
creating, 248-260
with Access, 273
with Visual Data Manager, 269-273
creating with other tools, 269-273

customizing, with SQL,
275-276
DBMS, 201-203
design, implementing,
258-269
design requirements, 248
designing, 248-258
    child tables, 252-254
    data normalization,
    251-252
    key activities, 248-249
    lookup tables, 252-254
    objectives, 248
    organizing data, 249-255
    organizing tables,
    254-255
    tables, 249-250
elements, 200
engines
    controls, 370
    functions, 203
    Jet, 610
    manipulative statements,
    337
    specifying source, 342
exclusive uses, 370-371
external
    accessing, 388-394
    data, importing, 394-396
    data control, 393
flat-file, 198
indexes, 255-257
    multiple-key expressions,
    256-257
    searching with, 255
    single-key expressions,
    255-261
integrity, 207-216
Internet access, 749-751
management, Access, 610
multiple, retrieving
    information from, 343
navigating, data access
    application, 230-231
objects, 206
on-screen information,
310-312
opening, 303-310

performance, 254-255
queries, 257-258
RDO, accessing, 411-412
registration
    debugging, 539-540
    editions, 550
relational, 198
repairing, 621
restricting, access to tables,
    371-372
sources, creating forms
    automatically, 233-235
SQL, 335
    statements, 367
structure, customizing,
    273-276
tables, 304-305
    multiple, 343
    SQL, 336
Visual Data Manager, 364

**DataField property,
228-229, 287, 294**

**DataField settings (forms),
230**

**DataSource property, 228,
294**

**date statements, VBScript,
564**

date variables, 121

**dbDenyRead
(OpenRecordset method),
371**

**DBEngine, objects, 206,
408-414**

**DBMS (database
management systems),
201-203**
    advantages, 202-203
    elements, 203
    queries, 216-219
    query language, 216

DCOM 95, installing, 498

DDE, VBScript, 564

**DDL, (Data-Definition
Language), 218, 335**

**DDLs (Data-Definition-
Language Statements),
359**
    limitations, 359
    statements
        creating tables, 360
        defining indexes, 360-361
        defining tables, 359-360

**de-referencing, remote
applications, 503**

Deactivate event, 56-57

**Debug command (View
menu), 148**

**Debug menu commands,
Add Watch, 150**

debugging, 540
    code maintenance, 893-897
        commented code,
        894-896
        descriptive naming,
        896-897
        readable code, 894
        VB constants, 894
    databases, registration,
    539-540
    DLLs, in-progress, 542
    environment, 148
    errors, trappable, 481
    Immediate window, 152
    in-progress, 540-542
    objects, 532-540
        cross process access,
        542-544
        multiuse, 533-534,
        537-538
        single-use, 533-534
        subordinate, 538-539
        variables, 532
    platforms, target, 544-545
    programs, 144-156
    remote applications, 502
    SQL, queries, 364
    Sub Main procedure,
    540-542
    VBScript, 564
    Watch window, 149
    Wizards, creating, 622-625

decisions
statements, 133-139
False conditions, 135-137
If, 133-135

declaration, VBScript, 564

declaration statements
objects, creating, 183
public variables, 178-179

declarations
collections, 485
events, changing
procedures to public, 489
methods, 478-479
options, 336
PARAMETERS, 356-357
parameters, 336
properties, 478-479
shared, storing, 578-579
variables, 121-124
explicit, 122
fixed-length strings,
123-124
implicit, 122-123

**defining field objects,
261-263**

Delete button, 236

**DELETE FROM,
manipulative statements,
337**

Delete function, 332

**Delete method, 274,
331-332**
troubleshooting, 274

**DELETE statement (SQL),
357-358**

deleting
fields, 275
indexes, 274
queries, 268-269
records, 331-332
relations, 275
tables, 274
cascading of, 213

**deployment, post-
production phase, 884**

DESC keyword, 352

**Description line (Object
Browser), documenting
objects, 495**

**descriptive naming, code
maintenance, 896-897**

**Design Outlook Form
command (Tools menu),
568**

designing
applications for Windows 95,
443
databases, 248-258
child tables, 252-254
data normalization,
251-252
key activities, 248-249
lookup tables, 252-254
objectives, 248
organizing data, 249-255
organizing tables,
254-255
tables, 249-250

**determining values of
variables, 149-152**

**development environment,
new features, 15**

Dial method, 491
phone number argument,
adding, 491-492

**DialNumber procedure,
492**

dialog boxes
About, creating, 592-594
ActiveX Components, 718
Add Data Source, 406
Add Drivers, Add button,
405
Add Field, 271
Add File, 168
Add Index, 272-273
Add Procedure, 158, 179
Add-In Manager, 524
Additional Controls, 523
Authenticode Security
Technology, 724

built-in, 111-117
Components, 22, 167, 243,
413
Compose Mail, 667
Outlook, 678
Custom Controls, 413
Drivers, 405
Edit Formula, 241
Edit Watch, 151
File Open, Outlook, 678-680
Finished, 718
General Options, 24
Import, 396
Information, creating, 581
Input, 110
Insert Object, 418
Insert Procedure, 179
Internet Distribution
Location, 717
Link, 400
Network, 721
Networking, 721
New Attached Table, 399
New Project, 17, 714
New Report, 238
Options, 51, 124, 717, 722,
724, 893
Procedure Attributes, 478,
495
Project Properties, 170, 473,
548
Properties, 59, 223, 283, 294
References, 166
Outlook, 673
Remote Connection Details,
731
Safety, 718
Safety Level, 722
Select Database, 406
Select Interface Members,
524
Select Project, 717
SQL, 364
Table Structure, 271-272

Dim statement, 258
classes, 474

dimensions, twips, 20

directories
preventing dragging,
450-451
Tools/RegistrationUtilities,
523

**Directory List Box control,
21, 58**

Display method, 696

displaying, forms, 55-56

**displays, controlling (OLE
objects), 421-429**

**DISTINCT predicates, SQL
SELECT statements,
343-344**

**distributable programs,
creating, 169-171**

**division, operators,
129-131**

DLL (dynamic link library)
files, 16

**DLLs (Dynamic-link
libraries)**
calling functions, 840-845
GetVersion(), 840-841
de-registering, 554
debugging in-progress, 542
Excel, 592-607
objects, registering, 551
projects, 470

**DLLSelfRegister function,
551**

**DML (data manipulation
language), 335**
queries, 216-218

Do loops, 142-145

dockability, 16

**documentation, post-
production phase, 884**

documents
ActiveX, creating, 15
custom properties (Word),
663

pretty-printing, (Word),
662-663
projects, 470
user
moving between
(Internet applications),
725-726
passing data between
(Internet applications),
726-728

**Documents.Add method,
Word, 648**

**Documents.Open method,
Word, 648**

double variables, 121

**doubly linked lists,
830-833**

DoVerb method, 434, 696

Drag Handles method, 49

dragging and dropping
directories, preventing,
450-451
files, 448-452
manual operations, 444-448
OLE (Object Linking and
Embedding), 443
Automatic Setting, 443

Draw miniserver, 689

drill down reports, 239

**Drive List Box control, 21,
58**

drivers, ODBC, 404
accessing, 405

Drivers button, 405

Drivers dialog box, 406

**DROP INDEX (DDL
statements), 360**

**DROP TABLE (DDL
statement), 359**

**Duplicate Definition errors,
496**

Dynamic-link libraries, *see*
DLLs

dynasets, 306-308, 336
advantages, 306
creating from dynasets, 307
definition, 306
disadvantages, 306
SELECT statements,
362-363
setting up, 306-308
tables, accessing, 371

E

e-mail
clients, Outlook, 664, 673
forms, Outlook, 667

early binding
Excel, 576
late binding, comparing, 502
speed, 502

**EASYDAO.CLS database
class, 611**

**Edit Formula dialog box,
241**

Edit function, 332

Edit menu, 19, 93

**Edit menu commands, Find
Key, 551**

Edit method, 330-331

Edit Watch dialog box, 151

editing
fields, 275
indexes, 274
records, 330-331

**editions, creating
applications, 550**

elements
databases, 200
DBMS, 203

eliminating bugs, 144-156

embedded objects
activation, controlling,
433-436
basing on a file, 419
creating, 419

saving, 436
see also OLE objects

enabling
properties, 46
remote applications, server files, 498-499

encapsulation, 13, 174
program segments, 175

engines
databases, functions, 203
Microsoft Jet, 203-206

enhanced printer objects
classes, setting up, 186-189
properties, 187

enumerations
(Enum), 484
public constants, 483-484

EOFAction property, 285

Equation class type, 419

Equation Editor miniserver, 689

Error event, data controls, 290

Error statements, Property Let procedure, 481

errors
debugging programs, 144-156
defining, Volume control, 518
handling, VBScript, 564
loops, 140
OLE, 466-468
polling for, 467-468
trappable, 467
remote automation, 502-503
trappable, 481

evaluation, post-production phase, 885

Event command (Script menu), 569

event-driven programming, 11-12

events
adding to controls, 517-519
adding to classes, 181-182
calling forms, 489
Change, Slider control, 518
class modules, 177
Class_Initialize, 473, 700
Class_Terminate, 700
Click, Web pages, 566
cmdCreate_Click, Outlook, 672
cmdGetMemoryStatus_Click(), 849
cmdSearch_Click(), 825
cmdSend_Click, Outlook, 680
cmdSort_Click(), 825
Command1_Click, Excel, 575
control reponses, 770-773
data control
Error, 290
Validate, 289
defined, 14
dragging operations, 445-448
dropping operations, 444-445
event-driven programming, 77
Form_Load, 708
Form_Unload(), 831
handling, 82-87
handling objects, 185
Initialize, 516, 699
PowerPoint, 636-637
Load and Activate, 56-57
LostFocus, 628
models, 79-82
Mouse_Down, Word application, 650-651
Mouse_Up, Word application, 650-651
ObjectMove, 430
OLECompleteDrag, deleting moved text, 446
OLEGiveFeedback, changing mouse pointer, 448

OLESetData, retrieving large items, 447
OLEStartDrag, dragging text off forms, 446
OnComm, 494
procedures
handling multiple controls, 86-87
public, 489
ReadProperties, adding design-time properties, 519
Resize, 421-422
causes, 422
resizing controls, 515
sequences, 87-89
determining event order, 88-89
multiple action events, 88
system-initiated, 83-85
Terminate, PowerPoint, 636-637
txtMultiBugs_Change, 629-630
Updated, 433
user-initiated, 84-85
Web pages, 566
webView_Command State Change, 735
WriteProperties, adding design-time properties, 519

events (procedures), writing, 85-86

Excel
collections, object hierarchies, 487-488
controls, OLE Container, 577-590
DLLs, 592-607
forms, child, 587-590
importing from, 634
MDI parents, 582-587
OLE Automation, 574-576
macro recorder, 574-575
tips, 576
projects, XLCONT.VBP, 590
splash screens, 579-580
SQL statements, creating, 364

Web site, 608
XLM macro language, 558

Excel Close method, 435

Excel.Chart class type, 419

Excel.Chart.7 class type, 420

Excel.Sheet class type, 420

Excel.Sheet.7 class type, 420

Exchange, MAPI, 673

ExchangeData method, 703

ExchangeData object, 699

Exclusive property, 285

EXE projects (controls), running, 521-522

executables, 559

Execute method, 744
queries, 219

execute method, action queries, 361

execute methods, SQL statements, 367

explicit declarations, 122

Explorer Drag and Drop (custom hooks), 783-786

exponents, operators, 131-132

exposed classes, OLE server interfaces, 601-606

expressions
multiple-key, 256-257
single-key, 255-261

external databases
accessing, 388-394
data control, 393
tables, attaching, 396-401

F

False conditions
statements, 135-137
Not operator, 135-136

feedback
(user) event-driven programming, 78

Field, objects, 206

field object, defining, 261-263

field properties, setting, 263-264

field-level validation, 214

fields
adding, 275
calculated, 340-341
customizing, 272
defining, 338-342
deleting, 275
editing, 275
form setup, 235
naming, 341-342
selecting, 338-339
updating, multiple, 359
values, comparing, 344

File dialog box, 112-114

File edition (objects), 548

file input/output, VBScript, 565

File List Box control, 22, 58

File menu, 19, 93

File menu commands
Add Project, 521
Get External Data, 396, 400
Make, 170, 522, 717
New, 568
New Project, 512, 714
Open, 715
Open Database, 364
Save Registration File, 551

File Open dialog boxes, Outlook, 678-680

File version (objects), 548

FileLen (files), checking, 421

Filename property, EASYDAO.CLS, 611

files
checking, 421
DLL, 16
dragging and dropping, 448-452
.EXE, testing VB Terminal application, 490-491
libraries, object, 560
multiple, accessing, 597-601
naming, application editions, 550
objects, saving OLE, 436
.OCX
compiling controls, 522
controls, 512
OLE
reading, 451
reading objects, 437
saving, 451-460
OUTLINE.EXE, 551
PUBLIC.BAS, 649-650
.REG, 551
creating, 551-553
registering, 553
selecting multiple, 450
Setup Wizard types, 720
SETUP.LST, 551
specifying types, Filter property, 114
storing multiple objects, 452-458

filter property, setting, 322-323

filters, configuring, 348-351

financial functions
VBScript, 565

find and seek operations, data controls, 296-297

Find Key command (Edit menu), 551

Find methods, 314-317

Find() method, 857

FindAllFiles() function, 857, 859

FindFile class, 849, 855-877

FindNext() method, 856

FindRecord method, 619-620

Finished dialog box, 718

First aggregate function, 353

fixed-length strings, 123-124

flat-file, databases, 198

Font dialog box, 114-116

Font form property, 52

Font property, collections, 488

FontBold control property, 115

FontItalic control property, 116

FontName control property, 115

FontSize control property, 115

FontStrikethru control property, 116

FontUnderline control property, 116

For Each...Next statement, collections, 484

For loops, 140-142

foreign keys, *see* data keys

Form menu commands, View Code, 568

Form_Load event, 708

Form_Unload() event, 831

forms, 44, 50-51
 adding, 168
  to programs, 164-165
 adding bound controls, 227-228
 adding controls, 59
 adding data controls, 223
 button setup, 235-236
 Caption property, 44

controls, running, 521
creating
 automatically, 232-236
 graphical interfaces, 886-890
customizing, 24
data-entry, 234
displaying, 55-56
events
 calling, 489
 changing procedures to public, 489
field setup, 235
files, 168
grouping (collections), 485-486
MDI child, FRMWORD.FRM, 653-656
mdiOLE, 650
multimedia
 AVI file playback, 804-806
 creating, 797-808
 wave file playback, 806-808
objects
 displaying, 503
 initializing, 503
OLE, displaying objects, 422-423
Outlook, 667-672
parent, MDI, 792-795
PPTDemo, 644
properties, 51-55
removing, 168
scroll bars, adjusting procedure, 426
setup, data access application, 229-230
startups, setting, 169
text, dragging off, 446
VBScript, 565

Forms collection, 484

FORTRAN, 79-82

forward-only recordsets, 310

Frame control, 21,58

frankentrols, 773-786
 adding new styles, 774-777
 callbacks and function pointers, 777-779
 hooking, 779-786
  CreateHook and Unhook, 779-782
  Explorer Drag and Drop (custom hooks), 783-786
 window styles, 774

Friend declarations, 478-479

Friend keyword, 479

FRMWORD.FRM, (MDI child form), 653-656

FROM clause (SQL SELECT statements), 342

FROM clauses, 343

FTP browsers, creating, 742-746

function pointers, frankentrols, 777-779

Function restrictions, 370

functions
 Add, 332
 aggregate (SQL SELECT statements), 353-354
 API, 840-845,
  declaring, 842
  GDI (Graphics Device Interface) functions, 862-867
  GetVersion(), 840-841
  GlobalMemoryStatus, 847
 BinarySearch(), searching and sorting, 818-820
 CallBackFunc(), 876
 codes, 158-163
 Compare(), 820
 CreateMultiArray(), 813
 CreateObject
  GetRunningObject procedure, 544
  multiuse objects, 536-537

CreateShortcut, 845
creating, 158-162
databases, engines, 203
Delete, 332
DLL, 840-845,
    GetVersion(), 840-841
DLLSelfRegister, 551
Edit, 332
FindAllFiles(), 857, 859
generic helper
    Compare(), 817
    Swap(), 817
    writing (searching and
        sorting), 817-818
GetIndex(), 828
GetObject, 533
GetRegDWord(), 869
GetRegKeyValues(), 870,
    873
GetRegString(), 867
GetVersion(), 840-841
GetWindowCaption(), 876
GetWindowClassName(),
    876
helper, Excel, 578
InsertAfter(), 826
MsgBox, returning values,
    107-109
ParamArray, 815-816
PrintVariant(), 811
programming interface, 203
QueryRegInfoKey(), 873
QuickSort(), searching and
    sorting, 820-822
Registry, 464
RegQueryValueEx(), 870
RegSetValueEx(), 870
RemoveItem(), 826
ResolveShortcut, 845
scope of, 162-163
SearchCurDirOnly(), 860
SetRegDWord(), 869
SetRegString(), 867
SpellCheck, 648
storing, 163
toolbar, 19-20
TransparentPaint(), 845,
    862

UpdateStatus, 649-650
VerifyRequiredField,
    626-628

G

**General Options dialog box,
24**

**General tab (Project
Properties dialog box),
490**

**generic helper functions
(writing), searching and
sorting, 817-818**

**Get External Data command
(File menu), 396, 400**

**GetArrayData method,
EasyDAQ, 615-617**

GetData method, 748
    EasyDAQ, 615-617
    GetControlData, 615-617

**GetDatabase property,
EASYDAO.CLS, 611**

**GetFieldValue method,
619-620**

GetIndex() function, 828

GetObject function, 533

**GetObject property, Excel,
576**

**GetRecipients method,
Outlook, 672**

**GetRegDWord() function,
869**

**GetRegKeyValues()
function, 870, 873**

**GetRegString() function,
867, 870**

**GetRunningObject
procedure, CreateObject
function, 544**

**GetVersion() function,
840-841**

**GetWindowCaption()
function, 876**

**GetWindowClassName()
function, 876**

**GetWorkspace property,
EASYDAO.CLS, 611**

global classes, 471

**global data, objects,
multiuse, 537-538**

**GlobalMultiUse setting
(Instancing property), 533**

**GlobalSingleUse setting
(Instancing property), 533**

GoToSlide method, 639

Graph miniserver, 689

graph reports, 239

graphical interfaces
    creating, 885-893
        forms, 886-890
        user choices, 890-892
        user perceptions, 892-893

grid data-entry forms, 234

grids, forms, 24

GROUP BY clause
    functions, aggregate, 354
    (SQL SELECT statements),
        355

H

**HAVING clause (SQL
SELECT statements), 355**

HeightNew argument, 422

Help, getting, 27-29

Help menu, 19, 94
    commands, Search
        Reference Index, 27

help system
    Contents, 27
    context-sensitive, 28

helper functions, Excel, 578

hierarchies
creating, 594-597
objects, 487-488

HighlightWindow method, 706

hooking frankentrols, 779-786
CreateHook and
Unhook, 779-782
Explorer Drag and Drop
(custom hooks),
783-786

Horizontal ScrollBar control, 58

Horizontal Scrollbar control, 21

hotkeys
adding, creating menu bars,
97-99
defined, 18

I

Icon form property, 52

icons
ActiveX Document DLL
template, 714
message, 105
Program Manager,
registering, 462-467

identifiers, unique, 211

If statements, 133-135
multiple commands, 134-135
single-line, 134

Image control, 22, 58

imgHold image control, 650

imgTools control array, 650

imgTools(Index) picture property, 650

implementing, database design, 258-269

implicit declarations, 122-123

Import dialog box, 396

importing data, 396
with Access, 396
Jet
(database engine), 610
DAQs, 610-632
external databases, 394-396
OLE Automation,
communicating, 632-635
with programs, 395-396
SQL statements, 366,
creating, 364
tables, attaching, 400-401
timing, 394-395
Wizards, creating, 622-625

IN predicates, 350
(WHERE clauses), 348

inclusive searches, BETWEEN predicate, 350

Index, objects, 206

Index property, 284

indexes, 255-257
adding, 274
adding to tables, 272-273
creating, 265-266, 324-325
defining, 360-361
deleting, 274, 361
editing, 274
multiple, updating, 325
multiple-key expressions,
256-257
primary, troubleshooting,
265
searching databases with,
255
setting, 324
single-key expressions,
255-261
troubleshooting, 257

information, on-screen, 310-312

Information dialog boxes, creating, 581

inheritance, 13, 174

Initialize event, 516, 699
PowerPoint, 636-637

initializing
classes, 189
objects, forms, 503

INNER clauses (SQL SELECT statements), 345

input
user, 109-111
actions (determining),
111
Input dialog setup, 110

Input dialog box, 110

INSERT INTO, manipulative statements, 337

Insert menu commands, User Form, 523

Insert Object dialog box, 418

Insert Procedure dialog box, 179

INSERT statement (SQL), 358

InsertAfter() function, 826

InsertObjDlg method, creating OLE objects at runtime, 418

installing
DCOM 95, 498
objects, 550-553
remote automation servers,
731

instances (remote applications), de-referencing, 503

Instancing property
accessing classes, 177
debugging objects, 533
declarations, 478-479
settings, 470-471

Integer data type, VBScript, 562

integer variables, 121

integrating, Microsoft applications, 693-696
non-OLE or DDE
supporting, 696-712

integrity
data, 203
database, 207-216
referential, 212

interface programming functions, 203

interfaces
Access, 610
controls
drawing, 514-515
Word, 653-656
graphical, creating, 885-893
PowerPoint, 636
user, Outlook, 667

interfacing
forms, 24
Visual Basic, 17-25

internal variables, defining, 186-187

Internet
applications
activating, 722-723
creating, 714-717
passing data to servers, 729-731
preparing for network transmittal, 717-721
security, 723-725
user documents (moving between), 725-726
user documents (passing data between), 726-728
controls, 741-749
creating chat applications, 746-749
creating FTP browsers, 742-746
database access, 749-751

Internet Distribution Location dialog box, 717

Internet Explorer, browser applications, 736-738

Internet Information Server (IIS)
creating applications, 751-756

objects, 753-754
VB-created objects, 754-756

Internet Transfer control (Inet.OCX), 741-749
creating FTP browsers, 742-746

InvokePrettyPrint macro, 663

IP addresses, finding, 721

Item method
collection objects, 486
collections, 485, 487

Item object, linked lists, 825-829

J

JavaScript, 562

Jet
(database engine), 610
DAQs, 610-632
DDLs, 359
queries, increasing speed, 366
SQL statements, action queries, 361

Jet Engine, data types, 205

JOIN clauses, 345-346
(SQL SELECT statements), 344

JOIN condition
indexes, 366
(SQL statements), 339

K

key fields (tables), relationships, 344

keys
hot, 18
shortcut, 19

KeyValue argument, 538

keywords
DESC, 352
Friend, 479

L

Label control, 21, 58

label controls (fields), calculated, 341

Label text control, 62

languages
BASIC, 38
batch, 561
C, 41
C++, 41
choosing, 571-572
COBOL, 33
DDL, 218
DML, 216-218
Excel, XLM macro, 558
macro, 558
ODBC, 404-408
RDC, 412
Windows programming debate, 41

Last aggregate function, 353

late binding
Excel, 576
remote applications, debugging, 502

LEFT clauses (SQL SELECT statements), 345

libraries
compatibility, maintaining, 545
object
Outlook, 664
viewing in Outlook, 571
type, 559-561
MAPI, 673-675

LIKE predicates, 349
(WHERE clauses), 348

Line control, 22, 58

Line method, creating control interfaces, 515

line methods, Word,
652-653

Link dialog box, 400

linked lists, CS
programming techniques,
825-833
doubly linked lists,
830-833
Item object, 825-829

linked objects
activation, controlling,
433-436
creating, 420-421
opening, 435
saving, 436
updating, 432-433
see also OLE objects

list box controls
data bound, 293-294
properties, 293-294
user choices, graphical
interfaces, 891

ListBox control, 58, 69-72,
292

ListField property, 294

listing reports, 239

listings
2.1 COBOL.TXT—A
COBOL Program Uses
Lots of Text, 34-35
2.2 The Visual Basic Code
that Augments the
Window's Operation, 36
3.1 Richtext.frm—
Assignment Statements to
Set Text Properties, 66-67
3.2 OptDemo.frm—If
Statements Determine
Option Button Selection,
68
4.1—AgeCheck.txt Code
to Verify the Age Entered,
78
4.2—MenuSel.txt One
Way COBOL Can Handle
the User's Menu Selection,
80

4.3—IFExampl.txt The IF
Statement Takes Care of
the User's Menu Selection,
80
6.1—CostEst.Txt Cost
Estimation Using
Multiplication and Division
Operators, 130-131
6.2—Mailing.txt String
Concatenation Used in
Mailing Labels, 132-134
6.3—Credit.txt Making
Decisions in Code, 135-136
6.4—FalseIf.txt Handling a
False Condition, 135-136
6.5—
Handicap.txt Handicap
Calculation Using
Conditional Statements,
136-138
6.6—GradesIf.txt Grade
Distribution with Multiple
If Statements, 137-138
6.7—Payroll.txt Payroll
Calculation with Select
Case Statement, 138-139
6.8—
CaseElse.txt Handling
Invalid Input with Case
Else, 139
6.9—ForLoop.txt Using
For Loops to Initialize
Variables, 140-141
6.10—ExitFor.txt Exiting a
Loop Early, 141
6.11—
DoLoop.txt Processing
Database Records with a
Do Loop, 142-143
6.12—Authors.txt Using
Do Until to Process a
Database, 144
7.1 FuncTest.txt—A
Function Averaging Two
Numbers, 162
8.1 Triggering an Event in
Your Class, 182

8.2 Declaring the Private
Variables of the Class, 186
8.3 Properties of a Class
Are Defined by Property
Procedures, 187-188
8.4 A Public Procedure
Defines the Output
Method of the cPrint
Class, 188-189
8.5 Setting the Initial
Value of Variables, 189
8.6 Setting the Margins of
the Output Device, 190
8.7 The cDataAccess Class
Property and Method,
191-192
8.8 Accessing the
cDataAccess Object, 192
10.1 Program Statements
Placed in the Click Event
of Command Buttons to
Add Capabilities, 231
11.1 Defining a Database
Object and Creating a
Database, 259
11.2 Creating Field Objects
and Setting Poperties, and
Adding Indexes to the
Table, 261-262
11.3 Adding Fields to the
Table Definition, 262
11.4 Creating Index Objects,
Assigning Properties, and
Adding Indexes to the
Table, 266
11.5 Specifying a
Relationship Between Two
Tables Using the Relation
Object, 267
12.1 Setting or Changing
the DatabaseName and
RecordSource Properties
of a Data Control at
Runtime, 287
12.2 Procedures Let You
Reuse Code Easily,
288-290
12.3 Data Checking in the
Validate Event, 290

12.4 Populating the List with the AddItem Method, 292

12.5 Use the Seek or Find Method to Search for a Specific Record, 297

13.1 How to Create a Simple Dynaset, 306-307

13.2 How To Set the filter and sort Properties of a Dynaset and Create a Second Dynaset from the First, 308

13.3 Create a Snapshot in Much the Same Way You Create a Dynaset, 309

13.4 Placing the OpenDatabase and OpenRecordset in the Form_Load Event, 311

13.5 Assigning Data Fields to the Display Properties of the Form's Controls, 311

13.6 Assigning Move Methods to Navigation Command Buttons to Make Them Work, 313-314

13.7 How to Move Through Selected Records in a Dynaset Using Find Methods, 315

13.8 Creating a Dynaset with a Filter Condition, 316

13.9 Using the Seek Method to Find a Specific Record in a Table, 317-318

13.10 Varying Results Are Obtained Using Different Seek Operators and Index Orders on a Tab, 319

13.11 Using a Bookmark to Return to a Specific Record in a Recordset, 320

13.12 Storing Multiple Bookmarks in an Array, 321

13.13 Absolute and Percent Position Are Other Ways to Move in a Recordset, 322

13.14 Two Methods for Creating a Filtered Dynaset, 323-324

13.15 Creating a New Index and Setting the Index Property, 325

13.16 Using Calculation Queries to Determine Information About Data in the Recordset, 327-328

13.17 Using Action Queries to Perform Operations on Multiple Records, 329

13.18 Using AddNew and Update to Add a Record to the Recordset, 330

13.19 Using Edit and Update to Change the Data in a Record, 330-331

13.20 Using Delete to Remove a Record from the Recordset, 332

13.21 Using Transaction Processing to Handle Multiple Changes to a Database as One Group, 334

14.1 Selecting Fields from Multiple Tables in a SQL Statement, 340

14.2 Creating a Variety of Calculated Fields with the SELECT Statement, 341

14.3 Naming the Field, 342

14.4 Retrieving Information from More than One Database, 343

14.5 Using a Table Alias to Cut Down on Typing, 343

14.6 Obtaining Unique Records with the DISTINCT or DISTINCTROW Predicates, 344

14.7 Examples of the Three JOIN Types, 346

14.8 A WHERE Clause Performing the Same Function as an INNER JOIN, 347

14.9 Comparison Operators Used with Many Types of Data, 349

14.10 Use the LIKE Predicate for Pattern-Matching, 350

14.11 Using the BETWEEN Predicate to Check an Expression Against a Range of Values, 351

14.12 Combining Multiple WHERE Conditions with AND or OR, 351

14.13 Specifying the Sort Order of the Output Dynaset, 352

14.14 Using Aggregate Functions to Provide Summary Information, 354

14.15 Using the GROUP BY Clause to Obtain Summary Information for Record Groups, 355

14.16 The HAVING Clause Filters the Display of the Selected Group Records, 355

14.17 Using the INTO Clause to Save Information to a New Table, 356

14.18 Using the INSERT INTO Statement to Add a Group of Records to a Table, 358

14.19 Using the UPDATE Statement to Change Field Values for Many Records at Once, 359

14.20 Using the ALTER TABLE Statement to Add or Delete a Field from a Table, 360

14.21 Create Several Types of Indexes with the CREATE INDEX Statement, 361

14.22 Run SQL Statements with the DatabaseExecute or QueryExecute Method, 362

14.23 Using the Create Methods to Retrieve the Records Defined by a SELECT Statement, 362-363

15.1 Use dbDenyWrite to Prevent Others from Updating Tables While You Are Working with Them, 372

15.2 Use the Read-Only Option to Prevent Users from Modifying Data, 372

15.3 Set the Recordset's LockEdits Property to Choose the Record Locking Method, 375

15.4 To Gaining Access to a Secured Database, 376

15.5 You Can Perform Security System Maintenance Using Commands from Visual Basic, 378

15.6 You Can Add Encryption to Your Database Using the CreateDatabase or CompactDatabase State, 379

15.7 Determine Which Locking Method Is in Effect When an Error Occurs, 384

16.1 ClubXprt.Txt—Data Access Methods Also Handle External Database Files, 391-392

16.2 ClubImpr.Txt—Importing External Data Using the Data Access Objects, 395-396

16.3 Attach.txt—Easily Attach External Tables with Code, 398

17.1 RDOSampl.txt—Access Information in an ODBC Data Source Using the RDO Methods, 411

18.1 Getting Filenames to Create Linked Objects, 420-421

18.2 Procedure for Adjusting Scroll Bars, 426

18.4 Opening Objects Within An Application, 435

18.5 Use Excel's Close Method to Deactivate an OLE Workbook Object that is Open Within the Excel Application, 435

18.6 DocClose method to Deactivate Objects, 436

18.7 Containing References to OLE Automation Objects, 437

18.8 Referencing the WordBasic OLE Automation object, 438

18.9 WordBasic methods, 438

19.1 Using OLEDragOver to Drop Text on a Form, 445

19.2 Using the OLEDragDrop Event to Display Text Dropped on a Form, 445

19.3 Starting a Manual Drag with the OLEDragMethod, 445

19.4 Using the OLEStartDrag Event to Drag Text Off a Form, 446

19.5 Using OLECompleteDrag to ed Text Delete Moved Text When the Drag Completes, 447

19.6 Defer Time-Intensive Operations to OLESetData, 447

19.7 Using OLEGiveFeedback to Change the Mouse Pointer, 448

19.8 Using the DataObject's Files Collection, 449

19.9 Modifications to Listing 19.8 to Handle Multiple File Selections, 450

19.10 Using GetAtter to Prevent Directories from Being Dragged, 450-451

19.11 Using the ReadFromFile Method, 451

19.12 Using the SaveToFile Method, 452

19.13 Getting a Temporary File Name, 453-454

19.14 Creating a File Header for OLE Storage, 454

19.15 Writing an OLE Object to a File, 455

19.16 Updating the File Header, 456

19.17 Saving All OLE Objects to a File, 457

19.18 Moving the File to Its Permanent Location, 458

19.19 OpenForBinary and OpenForRandom Support Procedures, 458

19.20 Reading an OLE File Header, 459

19.21 Retrieving an Object from the File, 460

19.22 Loading All Objects, 460

19.23 Registering the OLE File Type, 462

19.24 Checking Registration Entries on Start-Up, 465

19.25 Polling for OLE Errors, 467

20.1 Math.cls—A Simple Class, 471-472

20.2 Using the Math Class, 472

20.3 Math.BAS-Scoping Rules for Objects, 472

20.4 TestMath.BAS— Using the Math Class, 474

20.5 CompMath.CLS— Adding a Default Property, 478

20.6 Keyboard.CLS—The Keyboard NumLock Property, 479-480

20.7 Using the NumLock Property, 480

20.8 System.CLS-Read-Only Properties, 480

20.9 Read-Only Property Errors, 481

20.10 Document.FRM-Read/Write Object Property, 482-483

20.11 Document.BAS— Main( ) Creates a Document Object and Adds Some Text, 484

20.12 A Simple Enumeration (Enum), 484

20.13 Forms-Built-in Collections, 484

20.14 Grouping Actions, 486

20.15 The cmdClear Procedures Clears All the Text Boxes in the Collection, 486

20.16 VTERM.CLS—Adding a Phone Number Argument, 492

20.17 VTERM.CLS-Phone Number Arguments, 492

20.18 VTERM.CLS— Adding a PortOpen Property, 493

20.19 VTERM.CLS— Adding a SendLine Method, 493-494

20.20 VTERM.CLS— Create a TrapText Property, 494

20.21 VTERM.CLS — Create a Text Property, 495

21.1 Objects, Initializing and Terminating, 503

21.2 SimpleThread Pools, 506

21.3 Thread Pools, Procedures, 507

22.1 Initializing Controls, 516

22.2 Changing the sound volume, 517

22.3 Creating a Value Property, 517-518

22.4 Volume.CTL-Error Code Definitions, 518

22.5 Volume.CTL-Raising an Event, 518-519

22.6 Volume.CTL-Adding a Design-Time Property, 519

22.7 Volume.CTL-Adding a Speaker Property, 520-521

22.8 ActiveX Control Interface Wizard, 528

22.9 Property Page Wizard, 529

22.10 Volume.PAG-Changing the Property Page, 530

23.1 Creating a Lost ReferenceDim mobjNumber, 535

23.2 Showing Lost References to Excel, 535

23.3 Incorrect Initialization, 536-537

23.4 One-Time Initialization, 537

23.5 Creating a Secure Method, 539

23.6 Use a Main Procedure for In-Process Testing, 541

23.7 Debugging OUTLINE.VBP Cross-Process, 543

23.8 The GetRunningObject Procedure, 544

24.1 Registering a DLL at Start-Up, 551

24.2 Registering the OUTLINE application, 552-553

24.3 Removing Registration Entries, 554

25.1 Greetings Routine Is Compatible, 559

25.2 VB Code Works in VBScript, 562-563

25.3 Defining Variables for Missing Constants, 563

25.4 SIMPLE.HTM, 566

25.5 VBSCRIPT.HTM, 566

25.6 A Complete VBScriptApplication in a Web Page, 567-568

25.7 OUTLOOK.VBS—The VBScript Version, 570

26.1 Recording Code in Excel, 574-575

26.2 PUBLIC.BAS—Shared Procedures and Declaration, 578-579

26.3 SPLASH.FRM-Calming User Crash Fears, 579-580

26.4 INFO.FRM— Information Dialog Boxes, 581

26.5   MDIOLE.FRM—An MDI Form, 582-587

26.6   EXCEL.FRM—In an MDI Application, 587-590

26.7   SAMPLE.XLS—Supporting Code in Excel, 590

26.8   ABOUTBOX.FRM—A Generic About Box, 592-594

26.9   ABOUT.CLS-Creating Object Hierarchies, 594-597

26.10 COMMON.BAS—Modules, 597-601

26.11 APP.CLS—An Exposed Class Interface, 601-606

26.12 SHOWABOUT.TXT, 607

27.1   EASYDAO.CLS-A Simple Database Class, 611

27.2   EASYDAO.CLS-Using DAO Objects, 612

27.3   EASYDAO.CLS—Opening a Database, 612-613

27.4   EASYDAO.CLS—CreateRecordset, 613-614

27.5   EASYDAO.CLSMethods, 614-615

27.6   EASYDAO.CLS-Returning Records, 615-617

27.7   EASYDAO.CLS-Adding or Editing Records, 617-619

27.8   EASYDAO.CLS—Record Navigation, 619-620

27.9   EASYDAO.CLS—Repairing Databases, 621

27.10 BUGS.FRM—Creating Wizards, 623-625

27.11 BUGS.FRM—NavigatePages, 625-626

27.12 BUGS.FRM—UpdateData, 626-628

27.13 BUGS.FRM—User Validation, 628

27.14 BUGS.FRM—Event-Handling Routines, 629-630

27.15 BUGS.FRM—Data Manipulation Routines, 630-631

27.16 ACCESS.FRM—Access OLE Automation, 632-634

27.17 POWERPNT.CLS—The Core of clsPowerPoint, 636-637

27.18 POWERPNT.CLS-Extending clsPowerPoint, 637

27.19 POWERPNT.CLS—Working with Slides, 637-638

27.20 POWERPNT.CLS—Working with Text, 638-639

27.21 POWERPNT.CLS—Working with Shapes, 640

27.22 POWERPNT.CLS—Working with Slide Shows, 641

27.23 PPTDEMO.FRM—clsPowerPoint, 643

28.1   SPELLER.FRM—OLE Automation with Word, 646-647

28.2   PUBLIC.BAS, 649-650

28.3   MDIOLE.FRM—The MDI Parent, 650-651

28.4   MDIOLE.FRM—The MDI Form, 651-652

28.5   MDIOLE.FRM—The Paint Event, 652

28.6   MDIOLE.FRM-Adding 3-D effects, 653

28.7—FRMWORD.FRM   An MDI Child Form, 654-656

28.8   PRETTYPRINT.BAS Code Module, 657-661

28.9   PRETTYPR.FRM, 662-663

28.10 OUTLOOK.CLS—Sending Mail and Appointments, 664-667

28.11 OUTLOOK.FRM-Outlook Class Objects, 668-672

28.12 MAPI.CLS-MAPI Objects, 673-675

28.13 ATTACHMENTS.CLS—The Attachments Class, 676-677

28.14 MESSAGE.FRM-Sending Mail, 678-680

29.1   TALK.FRM—Establishing a Connection with TextServer, 685

29.2   TALK.FRM—Sending and Receiving Text to and from TextServer, 686

29.3   FRMTALK.FRM—Using TextServer's ReplaceAll Method, 686

29.4   FRMTALK.FRM—The LoadText Procedure, 687

29.5   TALK.FRM—The RegisterTextServer Procedure, 687-688

29.6   MINISERV.FRM—Determining Which Miniservers Are Available, 690-692

29.7   FRMOBJECT.FRM—FRMOBJECT.FRM Takes Advantage of Some Available OLE Servers, 695

29.8   EXCHANGEDATACLS—An Object Designed to Manually Exchange Data Between Windows, 696-698

29.9   EXCHANGEDATACLS—The ExchangeData Object Properties, 699

29.10 EXCHANGEDATA.CLS—Attach Is Really a Custom Class_Initialize Event Requiring Arguments, 700

29.11 EXCHANGEDATA.CLS—The Class_Terminate Event as a Helper Method, 700

29.12 EXCHANGEDATA.CLS—StartCapture Initiates the Window-Tracking Code, 701

29.13 EXCHANGEDATA.CLS—The Move Method Highlights the Current Window, 701-702

29.14 EXCHANGEDATA.CLS—EndCapture Stops Tracking and Exchanges the Data, 702

29.15 EXCHANGEDATA.CLS—ExchangeData Exchanges Data Differently, 703

29.16 EXCHANGEDATA.CLS—Returns All the Strings from a List as a Single String, 704

29.17 EXCHANGEDATA.CLS—If All Else Fails, Try WM_GETTEXT and WM_SETTEXT, 705

29.18 EXCHANGEDATA.CLS—HighlightWindow Contains Only API Drawing Calls Written in VB, 706-707

29.19 STUBBORN.FRM—Declarations and Initialization Code, 707-708

29.20 STUBBORN.FRM—The Paint Event Draws a Pointer on the Form, with Instructions, 709-710

29.21 STUBBORN.FRM—The Mouse Events Simply Call clsExchangeData to Do the Real Work, 710-711

29.22 STUBBORN.FRM—Using SendKeys to Integrate with Other Applications, 711-712

31.1 WebBrowser.FRM Navigating to URLs Using the WebBrowser Control, 735

31.2 WebBrowser.FRM Updating the Caption Once Navigation Completes, 735

31.3 WebBrowser.FRM—Enabling/Disabling Forward and Back Commands, 736

31.4 WebBrowser.FRM—Resizing the Browser, 736

31.5 WebTool.FRM—Connecting to Internet Explorer Events, 737-738

31.6 WebAddin.VBP—Modifications for the VB WebBrowser Add-in, 739

31.7 WebAddin.VBP—Making the VB WebBrowser Add-In More Useful, 740

31.8 FTPBrowse.FRM—Using the Internet Transfer Control, 743-744

31.9 FTPBrowse.FRM—Detecting Events in the Internet Transfer Control, 744-745

31.10 FTPBrowse.FRM—Using a Timer to Wait for Requests to Complete, 745-746

31.11 Chat.FRM—Using the Winsock Control, 746

31.12 Chat.FRM Connecting to Another Computer with Winsock, 747-748

31.13 Chat.FRM Transferring Data with the Winsock Control, 748

31.14 Chat.FRM—Reinitializing the Winsock Control, 748

31.15 Chat.FRM—Tracing Winsock Events, 749

31.16 InetBiblio.FRM—Retrieving a Database Using the Internet Transfer Control, 750

31.17 InetBiblio.FRM Synchronizing Changes to a Database Over the Internet, 751

31.18 Biblio.ASP—Retrieving a Database Using Active Server Pages, 751-752

31.19 Biblio.ASP—Using ActiveX Components from ASP, 754-755

31.20 MortInfo.CLS—An ActiveX Component Available to ASP, 755-756

32.1 CONTROLARRAY.FRM—The cmdBuildArray_Click Event, 760-762

32.2 CONTROLARRAY.FRM—dirPath_Change Demonstrates How to Unload a Control Array, 763

32.3 OPTDEMO.FRM—Option Buttons Were Made for Control Arrays, 764

32.4 PROGDEMO.FRM—Progress Bar Control Demo, 766

32.5 REGISTRY.FRM—Setting Up the TreeView and ListView Controls, 767-768

32.6 REGISTRY.FRM—BuildTree Loads Subkeys from a Variant Array, 768-769

32.7 REGISTRY.FRM—
LoadListItems Loads a
ListView Control from a
Variant Array, 769-770

32.8 REGISTRY.FRM—
Responding to Node Click
Events, 771

32.9 REGISTRY.FRM—
Loading Subkeys in a
TreeView Control, 772

32.10 WNDLONG.BAS—
UpdateStyle Changes the
Appearance of Your
Controls, 774-776

32.11 WNDLONG.FRM—
The chkStyle_Click Event
Demonstrates How to Use
UpdateStyle, 776-777

32.12 WNDLONG.BAS—
WndLong.bas Defines
Your Hook Routines
CreateHook and Unhook,
780-781

32.13 WNDLONG.FRM—
The chkHook_Click Event
Shows How to Use
CreateHook and Unhook,
782

32.14 YOURCODE.BAS—
WndProc Is an Example of
a Typical Custom
WndProc Function,
783-784

32.15 YOURCODE.BAS—
ProcessDroppedFiles Is an
Event Handler for Your
Intercepted Message,
784-785

32.16 WNDLONG.FRM—
The picWnd_Paint Event
Paints a List of Files
Dropped onto PicWnd, 786

33.1 WINPOS.BAS—
WinPos.bas Saves and
Stores the Position of a
Window, 788

33.2 WINPOS.BAS—The
CenterForm() Routine,
789-790

33.3 LASTPOS.FRM—
LASTPOS.FRM's Load()
and Unload() Events, 791

33.4 MDIPARENT.FRM—
MDIParent.frm Contains
the Shared Code for the
Application, 792

33.5 MDIPARENT.FRM—
Handling Menu Click
Events, 793-794

33.6 MDIPARENT.FRM—
Shared Code, 794

33.7 MDICHILD.FRM—
Child Forms Should Only
Contain Event Handling
Code, 795-796

33.8 MDICHILD.FRM—
Menu Event Handlers,
796-797

33.9 MULTIMEDIA.FRM—
Hotspot Initialization,
799-800

33.10 MULTIMEDIA.FRM—
Hotspot Testing and Event
Handling, 801-802

33.11 MULTIMEDIA.FRM—
Media-Handling Code in
Forms Should Be as
Simple as Possible,
802-803

33.12 PLAYAVI.BAS—the
PlayAVI() AVI Function
Makes It Easy to Play
AVIs, 804-806

33.13 PLAYWAVE.BAS—
Playing a Wave File Is
Easy with PlayWaveFile(),
807

34.1 VARIANT.FRM—the
PrintVariant() Function
Prints Variants of Almost
Any Data Type, 811

34.2 VARIANT.FRM—
Printing Multidimensional
Variants, 812-813

34.3 VARIANT.FRM—
Using PrintVariant() with
Different Types of
Variants, 813-814

34.4 PARAMARRAY.BAS—
ParamArray.bas
Demonstrates How to Use
ParamArray(), 815

34.5 SORTSEARCH.BAS—
Searching and Sorting
Helpers, 817-818

34.6 SORTSEARCH.BAS—
Binary Searching, 818-820

34.7 SORTSEARCH.BAS—
Sorting with QuickSort(),
821-822

34.8 SORTSEARCH.FRM—
SortSearch.frm
Demonstrates the Code in
SortSearch.bas, 823-825

34.9 ITEM.CLS—Item.cls
Contains the Object that
Will Be Used in Our
Linked List, 825-826

34.10 LISTHELPERS.BAS—
Adding and Removing
Elements, 826-828

34.11 LISTHELPERS.BAS—
Retrieving a Specific
Element, 828-829

34.12 LISTDEMO.FRM—
Building and Destroying
the List, 830-831

34.13 LISTDEMO.FRM—
Adding and Removing
Items, 831-832

34.14 BITCONVERT.BAS—
Some Common Bit
Manipulation Techniques,
833-834

34.15 HEXTOBIN.FRM—
Toggling Specific Bits,
834-835

34.16 HEXTOBIN.FRM—
ConvertToBinary()
Displays a Value as Its
Binary Equivalent, 836

34.17 HEXTOBIN.FRM—
Displaying a Fixed-Length
Hexadecimal Value, 837

35.1 WINVER.BAS—
GetWindowsVersion( )
Returns a Usable String
from GetVersionEx( )
values, 840-841

35.2 SHORTCUT.FRM—
Using a Helper DLL to
Manipulate Windows
Shortcuts, 843-845

35.3 SHORTCUT.FRM—
The CreateShortcut and
ResolveShortcut Function
Declarations, 845

35.4 MEMORY.CLS—
Demonstrating How to
Wrap an API Function into
a Reusable Object, 846-847

35.5 MEMDEMO.FRM—
Demonstrating How to
Use clsMemorySnapshot,
848-849

35.6 FINDFILE.CLS—
FindFile.cls Is an Object
that Encapsulates the File
Search API's, 850-855

35.7 FINDFILE.FRM—
Searching for Files in a
Single Directory, 856-857

35.8 FINDFILE.FRM—
FindAllFiles( ) Includes
Subdirectories in Its
Search, 857-858

35.9 FINDFILE.FRM—
Choosing the Right Search
Technique, 859-860

35.10 FINDFILE.FRM—
Using the Results from the
Find Functions, 860-862

35.11 TRANSPARENT.BAS—
Transparent.bas Paints
Bitmaps on Transparent
Backgrounds, 863-866

35.12 TRANSPARENT.FRM—
Transparent.frm Shows
How to Use the
TransparentPaint
Function, 866

35.13 REGISTRY.BAS—
GetRegString( ) and
SetRegString( ) Read and
Write Registry Strings,
867-868

35.14 REGISTRY.BAS—
Extended Registry
Functions Using
Conditional Compilation,
869-870

35.15 REGISTRY.BAS—
GetRegKeyValues( )
Demonstrates Registry
Enumeration, 871-873

35.16 CALLBACK.BAS—
Callback.bas
Demonstrates How to Use
Callbacks in VB, 874-876

35.17 CALLBACK.FRM—
Callback.frm Shows How
Easy It Is to Use Our
Callback Module, 876-877

36.1 36List01.TXT—
Searching Tag Properties
for Control Database
Fields, 895-896

36.2 36List02.TXT—
Example Using
Descriptive Naming for
Variables and Controls,
896-897

lists
character-range, LIKE
predicate, 349
controls, 69-73
ComboBox, 72-73
ListBox, 69-72

ListView control
Windows common controls,
766-773
BuildTree and
LoadListItems
procedures, 768-770

control event responses,
770-773

literals, VBScript, 564

Load event, 56-57

**Load statement, displaying
forms, 55**

**load time (user
perceptions), graphical
interfaces, 893**

**LoadCombos procedure,
622-625**

**LoadListItems procedure,
768-770**

**LoadPage procedure,
630-631**

**logging services, remote
automation services**
calling, 730-731
creating, 729-730

long variables, 121

lookup tables, 252-254

loops, 140-144, 326-327
conditional loops, 142-145
counter loop, 140-142
errors, 140
For loops, 140-142

LostFocus event, 628

M

macro languages, 558

macro recorder
Excel, OLE Automation,
574-575
Word, 648

macros
calling, Word, 662-663
InvokePrettyPrint, 663
Word, 656-661

mail label reports, 239

**maintenance, applications,
545**

Make command (File menu), 170, 522, 717

Make tab (Project Properties dialog box), 549

managing
components of projects, 166-168
controls, 167
project, 157-171
references in programs, 166

manipulative statements, 336-337

MAPI, 673-680
class objects, sending mail, 678-681
libraries, type, 673-675
SDK, Web site, 673

MaskedEdit control, 296

master/detail data-entry forms, 234

math operators, 127-132
addition and subtraction, 128-129
exponents, 131-132
multiplication and division, 129-131

Max aggregate function, 353

Max property, Slider control, 514

MaxButton form property, 52

MDI (Multi-Document Interface windows), 15, 791-797
applications
child form, 587-590
FRMWORD.FRM, 653-656
Excel, 577
child windows, 795-797
parent form, 792-795
Excel, 582-587
Word, 650-651

MDial_Click event procedure, 491-492

MDIChild form property, 52

MDIForm_Load procedure, 651-652

mdiOLE form, 650

memory class, 846-849
APIs, 846-849

menu bar (Visual Basic), accessing, 18-19

menu bars
controlling programs, 92-101
creating, 93-99
adding hotkeys and shortcuts, 97-99
main item setup, 94
menu item code (writing), 99-100
modifying menu structure, 97
multiple level menus, 95-97
optional settings, 100-101

Menu Editor, 94
creating pop-up menus, 102-103

menus
designing graphical interface forms, 888-890
Edit, 93
File, 93
Help, 94
pop-up, creating, 102-103
Tools, 94
View, 93
Window, 94

message boxes, updating users, 103-109
message icons, 105-106

methods, 48-49
Activate, 685
Add
collection objects, 486
collections, 485
Outlook, 680
AddField, EasyDAQ, 614-615
adding (to controls), 517-519
AddNew, 330
AddOrEditRecord, 617-619, 626-628
AddSlide, 637-638
Append, 259
Attach, 699
AttachToMessage, Outlook, 675-677
CallbackDemo( ), 876
Circle, creating control interfaces, 515
class actions, 181
collections, 485
CommitTable, EasyDAO, 614-615
Create, EasyDAO, 614-615
CreateDatabase, 258
CreateEmbed, creating OLE objects at runtime, 418
CreateField, 258, 265
EasyDAO, 614-615
CreateIndex, 258, 265
EasyDAO, 614-615
CreateItem, Outlook, 667
CreateLink, creating OLE objects at runtime, 418
CreateLocalTask, Outlook, 667
CreateObject, 755
CreateQueryDef, 268
CreateRecordset, EasyDAO, 613-614
CreateRelation, 267
CreateTable, EasyDAO, 614-615
CreateTableDef, 258
creating, 477-483
data control, 290-291
declarations, 478-479
default, assigning, 477-478
defined, 14
Delete, 274, 331-332
Dial, 491
Display, 696
Documents.Add, Word, 648

Documents.Open, Word, 648
DoVerb, 434, 696
Edit, 330-331
Excel Close, 435
ExchangeData, 703
Execute, 744
execute
  action queries, 361
  SQL statements, 367
Find, 314-317
Find( ), 857
FindNext( ), 856
FindRecord, 619-620
for relating tables, 207-211
GetArrayData, EasyDAO, 615-617
GetControlData, EasyDAO, 615-617
GetData, 748
  EasyDAO, 615-617
GetFieldValue, 619-620
GetRecipients, Outlook, 672
GoToSlide, 639
HighlightWindow, 706
InsertObjDlg, creating OLE objects at runtime, 418
Item
  collection objects, 486
  collections, 485, 487
Line, creating control interfaces, 515
line, Word, 652-653
Move, 312-314
Move n, 314
MoveFirst, 619-620
MoveLast, 619-620
MoveNext, 619-620
MovePrev, 619-620
Navigate, 741
objects, 184
oleobject.CreateEmbed file [, type], 418
oleobject.CreateLink file, 418
oleobject.InsertObjDlg, 418
OpenDatabase, 303
OpenDB, EasyDAQ, 612-613

OpenRecordset, 305-306
  dbDenyRead, 371
  SQL statements, 362-363, 367
OpenRecordset method, accessing tables, 371
printer objects, enhanced, 188
properties, comparing, 493
Quit, 535, 575
  Excel, 576
  Word, 648
Range, collections, 488
rdoRegisterDataSource, 408
ReadFromFile, 437
  reading OLE files, 451
ReadProperty, 519
RegisterDatabase, 408
Remove
  collection objects, 486
  collections, 485
Repair
  EasyDAO, 612
  repairing databases, 620-621
ReplaceAll, 686
Run, Word, 663
RunSlideShow, 641, 644
SaveToFile, 436
  saving files, 451
ScaleX, 708
ScaleY, 708
Seek, 317-320, 324
SendAppointment, Outlook, 667, 672
SendData, 748
SendLine, 491, 493
SendMail, Outlook, 667, 673-675, 680
SetSlideTransition, 641
Sheets, collections, 487
Show, Load statement, 55
ShowAboutBox, Excel, 607
ShowPrinter, CommonDialog control, 117
StartCapture, 700
TransferDatabase, 634

TransferSpreadsheet, 634
TransferText, 634
Update, 331, 433
UpdateData, 626-628
vs. properties, 49-50
WindowCreated( ), 795
WindowDestroyed( ), 795
WordBasic, 438
Workbooks, collections, 487
WriteProperty, 519
MFC (Microsoft Foundation Classes), 684
Microsoft
  applications
    integrating, 693-696
    non-OLE or DDE supporting, 696-712
  Developers Network, Web site, 681
  OLE miniservers, 689-693
Microsoft Access controls, 523
Microsoft Developer's Network, *see* **MSDN**
Microsoft Excel
  GetObject, 535
  lost references, displaying, 535
Microsoft Jet
  engines, 203-206
  history, 204-205
  security features, 204
Microsoft KnowledgeBase, Web site, 644
Microsoft Mail
  MAPI, 673
Microsoft Office
  controls, 522-523
  .OCX, 512
  SQL statements creating, 364
  Web site, 608, 644, 681
Microsoft Word, *see* **Word**
Min aggregate function, 353

Min property, Slider control, 514

MinButton form property, 52

MinimizeAll procedure, 484

miniservers, OLE, 689-693

mobjBasic object variable, 481

mobjExcelSheet variable, 437

models, events, 79-82

modems, SendLine method, 493

modular construction, codes, 158-163

modules
adding, 168, 488-495
classes
building, 176-185
calling form events, 489
creating, 176, 471-473
events, 177
naming, 476-477
objects, 181
properties, setting, 177-178
public, 496
codes, adding, 165
declarations, storing, 578-579
Excel, 597-601
files, 168
procedures, storing, 578-579
removing, 168
Word, pretty-printing, 656-661

mouse pointers, changing defaults, 448

Mouse_Down event, Word application, 650-651

Mouse_Up event, Word application, 650-651

MouseDown procedure, 710

MouseMove procedure, 710

Move Handles method, 49

Move methods, 312-314

Move n method, 314

MoveFirst method, 619-620

MoveLast method, 619-620

MoveNext method, 619-620

MovePrev method, 619-620

MSACCESS.EXE, *see* **Access**

MSDN
(Microsoft Developer's Network)
Web site, 644

MSDraw class type, 419

MSFlexGrid control, 16

MsgBox functions, returning values, 107-109

mthTest variable, 472

multi-use objects
optimizing
multithreaded
applications, 504-506
restrictions, 506
remote applications,
performance, 503-504

MultiLine property, 65

multimedia forms
AVI file playback, 804-806
creating, 797-808
wave file playback, 806-808

multiple action events, 88

multiple commands, If statements, 134-135

multiple controls, handling with single procedures, 86-87

multiple forms, working with, 164-166

multiple level menus, creating menu bars, 95-97

multiple-key expressions, 256-257

multiple-tier, ODBC drivers, 404

multiplication, operators, 129-131

multithreaded applications
features, 506
multi-use objects,
optimizing, 504-506
pausing, 507
project properties, setting,
507
thread pools, 506

multiUse classes, 471

multiuse objects
global data, 537-538
initialization, 536-537
subordinate object,
debugging, 538-539

MultiUse setting (Instancing property), 533

N

name properties, 46-48

Name property, 227
object variables, debugging,
532
Outlook, 570
Slider control, 514
Volume control, 513

naming variables, special identifying characters, 123

native code compiler, 15, 170

Navigate method, 741

NavigatePages procedure, 625-626

navNoReadFromCache flag, 741

Network dialog box, 721

Networking dialog box, 721

networks, preparing Internet applications, 717-721

New Attached Table dialog box, 399

New command (File menu), 568

New Project command (File menu), 512, 714

New Project dialog box, 17, 714

new projects, types, 17-18

New Report dialog box, 238

normalizing, data, 257-258

NOT operator, BETWEEN predicate, 350

Note-It class type, 419

Note-It miniserver, 689

O

object
defined, 14
hierarchies, creating, 594-597
libraries, Outlook, 664

Object Browser
Description line, documenting objects, 495
type libraries
VB/VBA compatibility, 559
viewing, 559-561
VolumeControlConstants, 518

object libraries, type libraries, comparing, 560

object linking and embedding, *see* **OLE**

Object property, 435, 437

object variables, 121

object-oriented programming, 174-175
implementing with classes, 175

ObjectMove event, 430

objects

ActiveX
adding modules, 488-495
refining, 491-496
running, 490-491
applications, testing
starting, 544
ASP (Active Server Pages), 753-754
VB-created, 754-756
classes, comparing, 471
clsExchangeData, 707, 711
clsPowerPoint, 636-644
extensibility, 637
collections, 485
built-in properties and methods, 485-486
creating, 542-543
DAOs (data-access objects), 206
DBEngine, 408-414
deactivating, 435-436
debugging, 532-540
cross process access, 542-544
lost references, 534-535
multiuse, 533-534
single-use, 533-534
variables, 532
default names, 46
developing, 183-184
declaration statements, 183
Set statements, 183-186
dropping and dragging automatically, 444-448
embedded
basing on a file, 419
creating, 419
events, handling, 185
ExchangeData, 699
field, defining, 261-263
getting rid of, 185
grouping (collections), 485-486
hierarchies, 485, 487-488
identifying prefixes, 47
initializing forms, 503
installing, 550-553

instances, tracking, 485
libraries
maintaining compatibility, 545
viewing in Outlook, 571
linked
creating, 420-421
updating, 432-433
linked lists
doubly, 830-833
Item, 825-829
methods, 184
documenting, 495
multiuse
global data, 537-538
initialization, 536-537
subordinate objects, 538-539
naming, 476-477
OLE
activating for editing, 434
class types, 419-420
controlling displays, 421-429
creating at runtime, 418-421
editing, 439
enabling scrolling, 423-426
enabling zooming, 427-429
moving at runtime, 429-430
reading, 437, 459-461
retrieving, 436-437, 458-461
saving to files, 436
scaling to fit controls, 427
sizing at runtime, 429-430
sizing windows, 422-423
storing, 436-437
OLE Automation
debugging, 539-540
retrieving, 437-439
organizing, (collections), 487-488
printer, enhanced properties, 187

printers, enhanced, classes, setting up, 186-189
Private, 538
properties, 45
    creating, 481-485
    documenting, 495
PropertyBag, 519
providing, remote applications, 502
QueryDef, 268
recordset, properties, 322-325
Relation, 267
retrieving, 544
Selection
    Word, 648
similar, grouping, 485
standard prefixes, 46-47
startup, Sub Main, 517
storing multiple, in single files, 452
TableDef, 258
    attaching tables, 397
    defining, 261
terminating, forms, 503
type libraries, 560
uninstalling, 553-554
unrecognized, troubleshooting, 439, 496
Useful Class, 592-608
variables, Excel, 576
VBScript, 565
versions, 548-550
    creating, 548-549
word wrapping, 185

ObjectVerbCount property, 696

ObjectVerbs property, 434

OCX
controls, 513
files
    compiling controls, 522
    starting projects, 512-513

ODBC
data source, 404-409
drivers, 404
    accessing, 405
    types, 404

ODBC (Open Database Connectivity), 404-408

ODBC database servers, SQL statements, 367

ODBC DataSources, importing from, 634

OLE(Object Linking and Embedding), 174
Automation, closing objects, 435
see also ActiveX
automation servers, building, 175
    connecting to, 684-688
container control, displaying MS application objects, 693-696
controls, 58
    activation, 433-436
    Picture property, 431
dragging and dropping, 443
Automatic setting, 443
errors, 466-468
    polling for, 467-468
    trappable, 467
files
    reading, 451
    saving, 452-460
objects
    activating for editing, 434
    class types, 419-420
    controlling displays, 421-429
    creating at runtime, 418-421
    deactivating, 435-436
    editing, 439
    enabling scrolling, 423-426
    enabling zooming, 427-429
    moving at runtime, 429-430
    reading, 437, 459-461
    retrieving, 436-437, 458-461
    saving to files, 436

scaling to fit controls, 427
sizing at runtime, 429-430
sizing windows, 422-423
storing, 436-437
servers
    interfaces, 601-606
    Microsoft miniservers, 689-693
storage files, headers, 454
time-outs, 466-468

OLE Automation
Access, communicating, 632-635
applications, memory requirements, 647
Excel, 574-576
    macro recorder, 574-575
    substituting for DLLs, 592-607
    tips, 576
objects
    retrieving, 437-439
    debugging, 539
Word, 646-648
    optimizing performance, 656-667
    tips, 648

OLE Container control
Excel, 577-590
Word, 648-663

OLE Control, 22, 296

OLE Messaging, see MAPI

OLECompleteDrag event, 446

OLECONT.VBP, 649-650

OLEDragMode property, dragging and dropping, 443

OLEGiveFeedback event, changing mouse pointer, 448

oleobject.CreateEmbed file, [type] method, 418

oleobject.CreateLink file method, 418

oleobject.InsertObjDlg

method, 418

OLESetData event,
retrieving large items, 447

OLESize.VBP (project),
creating, 423

OLEStartDrag Event, 446

on-screen information,
310-312

OnComm event, 494

OOP (object-oriented
programming), 12-13
controls, 13

Open command (File
menu), 715

Open Database command
(File menu), 364

Open Database Connectivity
(ODBC) standards, 307

Open property, 715

OpenDatabase method, 303

OpenDB method, EasyDAO,
612-613

opening
attached tables, 401
databases, 303-310
files, File dialog box,
113-114
objects, 435
tables, 305

OpenRecordset method,
305-306
dbDenyRead, 371
SQL statements, 362-363,
367
tables, accessing, 371

operators
comparison
JOIN clauses, 345
WHERE clauses, 348
False condition, Not,
135-136
math, 127-132
addition and subtraction,

128-129
exponents, 131-132
multiplication and
division, 129-131
string, 132-133
VBScript, 565

optimizing
multiuse objects
multithreaded
applications, 504-506
restrictions, 506
remote applications, 507-508
single-use objects, 507-508

option box controls (user
choices), graphical
interfaces, 891-892

Option Button control, 21

option button techniques,
control arrays, 764-765

option buttons, data
controls, 297-298

option explicit statement,
variables, 124-125

OptionButton control, 58

Options command (View
menu), 724

options declarations, 336

Options dialog box, 51,
124, 717, 722, 724, 893

Options property, 285

OR operator, BETWEEN
predicate, 351

Oracle, SQL, 335

ORDER BY clause
dynasets, 363
(SQL SELECT statements),
352

Organization Chart
miniserver, 689

organizing
controls, 20-22
data, 249-255
tables, 254-255

OUTLINE.EXE file, 551

Outlook, 664-672
attachments, 675-678
class objects, 664-667
forms, 667-672
interfaces
user, 667
object, libraries, 664
objects, viewing library, 571
VBScript, 568-571

P

-p switches, availability, 501

P-code compiling, 170

Package class type, 419

Paint.Picture class type,
419

Paradox, Connect property,
390

ParamArray function,
815-816

parameters
blnAdd, AddOrEditRecord
method, 617
calling statements, 161
command-line, 500
declarations, 336
passing, Word, 662-663
procedures, 161
SaveChanges
Quit method, 575
Word, 648
SQL statements, 356-357
vntFieldPipeValue,
AddOrEditRecord method,
617

parent forms, MDI,
792-795

Parent property, object
variables, debugging, 532

pausing
multithreaded applications,
507
programs, 154-156

PercentPosition property, 321-322

performance
databases, 254-255
remote applications
multiuse objects, 503-504
single-use objects, 503-504

phantom instances (remote applications), problems, 503

Picture Box control, 21

picture boxes (AVI file playback), multimedia forms, 804-806

Picture property
creating control interfaces, 515
(OLE control), 431

PictureBox control, 58

platforms (target), testing, 544-545

pointers, changing defaults, 448

PointMode property, 699

polling for errors, OLE, 467-468

polymorphism, 13, 174

Pool Demos (client applications), creating, 507

pop-up menus, creating, 102-103

PortOpen property, 491, 493

positioning, record pointers, 312-322

positions
of forms, 44
twips, 20
window, saving, 788-791

post-production phase
three-phase software development, 884-886

deployment, 884
documentation, 884
evaluation, 885

PowerPoint, 635-644
objects, clsPowerPoint, 636-644
slides, adding, 637-638

PPTDemo form, 644

pre-production phase, three-phase software development, 881

predicates, 348
SQL SELECT statements, 343-344

prefixes, identifying objects, 47

PrepareForm procedure, 696

preserving (variables), procedures, 163

PrettyPrint.dot template, 656

previewing reports, 241

primary keys, *see* **data keys**

Print dialog box, 117

printer objects, enhanced
methods, 188
properties, 187

PrintVariant() function, 811

private classes, Standard .EXE, 470

Private object, 538

private procedures, 162

Private setting (Instancing property), 533

Procedure Attributes command (Tools menu), 478, 495

Procedure Attributes dialog box, 478, 495

procedures
accessing, by multiple files, 597-601

AddLevel, 542
cboContact, 628
ClearAll, 630-631
cmd_Click, 629
codes, 158-163
creating, 158-162
defined, 14
DialNumber, 492
event
handling multiple controls, 86-87
writing, 85-86
GetRunningObject, CreateObject function, 544
LoadCombos, 622-625
LoadPage, 630-631
MDial_Click event, 491-492
MDIForm_Load, 651-652
MinimizeAll, 484
MouseDown, 710
MouseMove, 710
NavigatePages, 625-626
parameters, 161
PrepareForm, 696
properties, 477
creating, 179-193
types, 178-179
Property Get, 479
creating object properties, 481
Property Get Basic(), 481
Property Let, 479-480, 519
errors, 481
Property Let Basic, 483
Property Let Basic(), 481
Property Set, creating object properties, 481
Property Set SetBasic(), 481
RegisterTextServer, 687-688
ReturnToExample(), 590
running, 161
scope of, 162-163
SearchTree, 542
SetBasic(), 481
SetObject(), 483
SetupForm, 622-625
shared, storing, 578-579
storing, 163
Sub, 157-171

Sub Main
  debugging, 540-542
  testing applications start-up, 544
Sub statement, creating, 158
variables, preserving, 163
VerifyRequiredField, 630-631

processing, transaction, 333-334

production phase, three-phase software development, 882

program (startups), controlling, 168-169

program commands, 302

Program Manager (icons), registering, 462-467

programmatic controls, 370

programming, 10-16
  APIs, 845-877
    memory class, 846-849
    overcoming VB limitations, 849-862
  callbacks, 873-877
  code maintenance, 893-897
    commented code, 894-896
    descriptive naming, 896-897
    readable code, 894
    VB constants, 894
  computer science techniques, 816-837
    bit manipulation, 833-837
    linked lists, 825-833
    searching and sorting, 816-825
  event-driven, 11-12, 77
  interface, functions, 203
  loops, 140-144
  multi-user, 369-370
  object-oriented, 174-175
  OOP, 12-13
  Registry, 870-873
  variables, 120-127

programs
  accessing classes, 182-185
    creating objects, 183-185
  commands in, 276
  compiling, 170-171
  controlling with menu bars, 92-101
    creating menu bars, 93-99
    menu item code (writing), 99-100
    optional settings, 100-101
  debugging, 144-156
  distributable, creating, 169-171
  new forms, adding, 164-165
  pausing, 154-156
  references, managing, 166

progress bars, Windows common controls, 765-766

progress updates
  informing users, 103-109
    displaying messages, 104-106
    message icons, 105-106
    returning values (MsgBox function), 107-109

project groups (controls), running, 521-522

project managing, 157-171

Project menu commands
  Add Class Module, 489
  Add File, 168
  Add Form, 164, 739
  Add Module, 163, 165
  Add Property Page, 528
  Components, 22, 167, 413, 514, 734
  Project Properties, 512
  Properties, 473, 476, 488, 490, 495, 522, 548
  References, 166, 474, 542, 736
  Remove, 739

Remove File, 168

project properties (setting), multithreaded applications, 507

Project Properties command (Project menu), 512

Project Properties dialog box, 170, 473, 548

project window, 24

projects
  changing, 488-489
  classes, 473-474
    adding modules, 488-495
    reusable, 470-471
  components, managing, 166-168
  controls, 582
    starting .OCX, 512-513
  creating OLESize.VBP, 423
  EXE, running controls, 521-522
  naming, 476-477
  properties, Instancing settings, 470-471
  types of, 17-18
  USEFUL.VBP, 592-594
  XLCONT.VBP, Excel, 590

properties
  AbsolutePosition, 321-322
  adding, 178-181
    (to controls), 517-519
  adding to classes, 178-181
    Property Procedures, 178-183
  Alignment, 64
  AutoActivate, 433-434
  AutoSize, 63
  Basic, initializing, 481
  behavior, controlling of, 44-48
  BOFAction, 284
  BorderStyle, 64
  Borderstyle controls, 53
  BoundColumn, 294
  BulletListItem, 639
  Caption, 63, 223

classes, 177-178
collections, 485
Connect, 281
   accessing databases, 389
controls, setting and
   retrieving values, 59-61
CopiesToPrinter, 244
Count
   collection objects, 486
   collections, 485
creating, 477-483
   read-only, 480-481
   read/write, 479-480
   write-only, 480-481
Crystal Reports, setting,
   245-246
Data, EASYDAO.CLS, 611
DatabaseName, 224-225,
   282, 286
   external databases,
     390-391
DataField, 228-229, 287, 294
DataSource, 228, 294
declarations, 478-479
default, assigning, 477-478
defined, 14
design-time, adding, 519-521
documenting, 495
Enabled, 46
EOFAction, 285
Exclusive, 285
fields setting, 263-264
Filename, EASYDAO.CLS,
   611
filters, setting, 322-323
Font property, 488
forms, 51-55
GetDatabase,
   EASYDAO.CLS, 611
GetObject, Excel, 576
GetWorkspace,
   EASYDAO.CLS, 611
imgTools(Index) picture,
   650
Index, 284
Instancing
   accessing classes, 177
   debugging objects, 533

ListField, 294
Max, Slider control, 514
methods, comparing, 493
Min, Slider control, 514
MultiLine, 65
Name, 46-48, 227
   debugging object
     variables, 532
   Outlook, 570
   Slider control, 514
   Volume control, 513
Object, 435, 437
objects, 45, 181
   creating, 481-485
ObjectVerbCount, 696
ObjectVerbs, 434
OLEDragMode, dragging
   and dropping, 443
OLEDropMode, dragging
   and dropping, 443
Open, 715
Options, 285
Parent, debugging object
   variables, 532
PercentPosition, 321-322
Picture
   (OLE control), 431
   creating control
     interfaces, 515
PointMode, 699
PortOpen, 491, 493
printer objects, enhanced,
   187
procedures, 477
PropertyPage, 528
Public
   accessing classes, 177
   Volume control, 513
Readonly, 285
recordset objects, 322-325
RecordsetType, 286
RecordSource, 225, 284, 286,
   337, 363
ReportFileName, 244
RowSource, 293
Saved, Excel, 575-576
ScrollBar, 65
SelBold, 66
SelectionFormula, 244

SelFontName, 66
SelFontSize, 66
SelItalic, 66
SelStrikeThru, 66
SelUnderline, 66
ShapeText, 639
SizeMode, 421-422
sort, setting, 323-324
Speaker, 520-521
StartupPosition, controls, 54
SystemDirectory, 480
Text, 65, 491, 494, 699
   Editor object, 536
TickFrequency, Slider
   control, 514
TrapText, 491, 494
UpdateOptions, 432
Value, assigning defaults,
   477
values, 184
   retrieving, 180
   setting, 179
   versus methods, 49-50
Visible, 46
Visible property, 738
WordWrap, 63

**Properties command
(Project menu), 473, 476,
488-490, 495, 522, 548,
739**

**Properties dialog box, 59,
223, 283, 294**

**Property Get Basic()
procedure, 481**

**Property Get procedure,
479**
   creating object properties,
   481

**Property Let Basic
procedure, 483**

**Property Let Basic()
procedure, 481**

**Property Let procedure,
479-480, 519**
   errors, 481

Property Page Wizard, 529

Property pages, controls, 528-530

Property Set procedure, creating object properties, 481

Property Set SetBasic() procedure, 481

PropertyBag object, 519

PropertyPage property, 528

providing (objects), remote applications, 502

public
classes modules, 496
events, procedures, 489

public constants, enumerations, 483-484

public procedures, 162
class actions, 181

Public properties, adding (to controls), 517-519

Public property
accessing classes, 177
Volume control, 513

public variables, declaring, 178-179

PUBLIC.BAS, 649-650

PublicNotCreatable setting (Instancing property), 533

Q

queries, 257-258
action, 216, 329, 357, 361-362
DELETE statement, 357-358
INSERT statement, 358
troubleshooting, 329
Alter Table, 275
calculation, 327-328
compiling, 366
creating, 268-269
creating tables with, 264
DBMS, 216-219
deleting, 268-269
DML, 216-218
Execute method, 219
Non-Jet Databases, 219
repetition, 219
retrieval, 217-218, 362
SQL, 336
optimization, 367

Query Builder (VDM), 365

query language, DBMS, 216

QueryDef
creating, 362
objects, 206
SQL statements, 337

QueryDef object, 268

QueryRegInfoKey() function, 873

QuickSort() function, searching and sorting, 820-822

Quit method, 535, 575
Excel, 576
Word, 648

R

RAM (OLE Automation), memory requirements, 647

Range method, collections, 488

RDC (remote data control), 412-413
data control similarities, 412
setting up, 413-414

RDO (Remote Data Objects), 409-412
DAO similarities, 409-411
databases
accessing, 411-412

rdoRegisterDataSource method, 408

read-only properties, creating, 480-481

read/write properties, creating, 479-480

readable code, code maintenance, 894

ReadFromFile method, 437
reading OLE files, 451

reading, OLE objects, 459-461

Readonly property, 285

ReadProperties event, adding design-time properties, 519

ReadProperty method, 519

Recipients collection, Outlook, 570

record pointers, positioning, 312-322

record-level validation, 215

records
adding, 330, 617-619
deleting, 331-332, 357
editing, 330-331, 617-619
grouping, 354-355
moving from one to another, 312-322
multiple, customizing, 325-329
navigating, 619-620
retrieving, 336, 615-617
sorting, configuring, 352
sources, creating forms automatically, 233-235
SQL, manipulative statements, 337
SQL SELECT statements, eliminating, 344
updating, 331

Recordset, objects, 206

recordsets, 322-325
AbsolutePosition property, 321-322
adding records to, 330
Bookmark property, 320-321

creating, 363
data control, 287-288
dynasets, 336
forward-only, 310
four types of, 304
loops, 326-327
PercentPosition property, 321-322
snapshots, 309
tables, 345
accessing, 371

RecordsetType property, 286

RecordSource property, 225, 284, 286, 337, 363

references
applications, single-use, 534-535
avoiding, 543
EASYDAO.CLS, 611
programs
managing, 166

References command (Project menu), 166, 474, 542

References dialog box, 166
Outlook, 673

referential integrity, 212

Refresh button, 236

Refresh method, data controls, 291

.REG files, 551
creating, 551-553
registering, 553

REGEDIT.EXE, 687

RegisterDatabase method, 408

registering
applications in Registry, 460-464
Program Manager, icons, 462-467
remote applications
procedures, 499
purpose, 499

RegisterTextServer procedure, 687-688

registration databases
debugging, 539-540
editions, 550

registration files, *see* **.REG files**

Registry, 870-873
applications
registering, 460-464
removing entries, 553-554
functions, 464
objects, installing, 550-553

registry files (features), remote applications, 498-499

REGOCX32.EXE utility, 554

RegQueryValueEx() function, 870

RegSetValueEx() function, 870

REGSVR32.EXE utility, 554

rejected changes, 213

relating, methods for tables, 207-211

Relation object, 267

Relation object variable, 267

relational databases, 198

relations
creating, 267-268
deleting, 275
troubleshooting, 268

remote applications
accessing Visual Basic environments, 501
creating, 498
debugging, purpose, 502
instances, de-referencing, 503
late binding, 502
objects, providing, 502

optimizing, 507-508
performance
multiuse objects, 503-504
single-use objects, 503-504
phantom instances, problems, 503
registering
procedures, 499
purpose, 499
running client machines, 501
server files, enabling, 498-499

remote automation
built-in support, 498
definition, 497
errors, 502-503

remote automation servers
installing, 731
logging services
calling, 730-731
creating, 729-730

remote automations, checking, 501-502

Remote Connection Details dialog box, 731

Remove command (Project menu), 739

Remove File command (Project menu), 168

Remove method
collection objects, 486
collections, 485

RemoveItem ListBox method, 70

RemoveItem() function, 826

removing
forms, 168
module, 168

Repair method
databases, repairing, 620-621
EasyDAO, 612

repetition, queries, 219

ReplaceAll method, 686

Report Expert
Preview Report button, 241
Save button, 242
selecting data fields, 240-241

ReportFileName property, 244

reports, 237-242
cross tab, 239
Crystal Reports
Report Expert, 239
selecting data fields, 240-241
starting, 238-240
drill down, 239
graph, 239
listing, 239
mail label, 239
previewing, 241
running, 242-246
Crystal Reports control, 243
saving, 242
sources
data dictionary, 240
data file, 240
SQL, 240
standard, 239
summary, 239
top n, 239

required-field validation, 216

Resize event, 421-422
resizing controls, 515

Resize events, causes, 422

ResolveShortcut function, 845

restrictions
(database), 370
multiuse objects, optimizing, 506

retrieval queries, 217-218, 362

retrieving OLE objects, 458-461

ReturnToExample() procedure, 590

reusable classes, 470-471

Rich Text Format, *see* **RTF**

RichTextBox control, 296

RichTextBox text control, 65-69

RIGHT clauses (SQL SELECT statements), 345

ROLLBACK statement
deletions, recovering, 358

RowSource property, 293

RTF (Rich Text Format), 66

Run method, Word, 663

running
procedures, 161
remote applications, client machines, 501

running reports, 242-246
Crystal Reports control, 243-246
setting properties, 245-246
setup, 243-246

RunSlideShow method, 641, 644

runtime
controls
initializing, 517
responding to change, 517
OLE, creating objects, 418-421

Rushmore (optimization), 366

S

Safety dialog box, 718

Safety Level dialog box, 722

Save Registration File command (File menu), 551

SaveChanges parameter
Quit method, 575
Word, 648

Saved property, Excel, 575-576

SaveToFile method, 436
saving files, 451

saving
files, File dialog box, 113-114
multiple objects to single files, 452-458
OLE, objects to files, 436
OLE files, 451-460
report, Report Expert, 242
window positions, 788-791

ScaleX method, 708

ScaleY method, 708

scope of
functions, 162-163
procedures, 162-163

Script menu commands, Event, 569

scroll bars, adding OLE objects, 423-426

ScrollBar property, 65

Search Master Index, 27

Search Reference Index, 27

Search Reference Index command (Help menu), 27

SearchCurDirOnly() function, 860

searching
BETWEEN predicate, 350
CS programming techniques, 816-825
BinarySearch() function, 818-820
generic helper functions (writing), 817-818
QuickSort() function, 820-822
databases, with indexes, 255

SearchTree procedure, 542

security
Internet applications,
723-725
VBScript, 562
see also databases,
controlling access

**security features, Microsoft
Jet, 204**

**Seek method, 317-320,
324**

SelBold property, 66

**SELECT, manipulative
statements, 337**

**select case, statements,
137-140**

Select Case statement, 651

**Select Database dialog box,
406**

**Select Interface Members
dialog box, 524**

**SELECT INTO statement,
358**

**Select Project dialog box,
717**

SELECT statement
databases, multiple tables,
343
recordsets, creating, 363

SELECT statements
data sources, specifying,
342-343
dynasets, 362-363
fields
defining, 338-342
naming, 341-342
selecting, 338-339
filters, configuring, 348-351
functions, aggregate,
353-354
parameters, 356-357
PARAMETERS declaration,
356-357

predicates, 343-344
queries, retrieval, 362
records, grouping, 354-355
snapshots, 362-363
sort conditions, 352
(SQL), 337-357
defining fields, 338
tables (creating), 356
tables, relationships, 344-347

Selection object, Word, 648

**SelectionFormula property,
244**

SelFontName property, 66

SelFontSize property, 66

SelItalic property, 66

SelStrikeThru property, 66

SelUnderline property, 66

**SendAppointment method,
Outlook, 667, 672**

SendData method, 748

**SendLine method, 491,
493**

**SendMail method, Outlook,
667, 673-675, 680**

sequences
event, 87-89
determining event order,
88-89
multiple action events, 88

**server files, enabling remote
applications, 498-499**

servers
OLE
interfaces, 601-606
Microsoft miniservers,
689-693
OLE automation,
connecting to, 684-688
building, 175
passing data to (Internet
applications), 729-731
remote automation
calling remote logging
services, 730-731

creating remote logging
services, 729-730
installing, 731

**Set statement, Property Let
Basic procedure, 483**

Set statements
classes, 473
objects, creating, 183-186

SetBasic() procedure, 481

SetFocus method, 49

SetObject() procedure, 483

**SetRegDWord() function,
869**

**SetRegString() function,
867**

**SetSlideTransition method,
641**

setting
filter properties, 322-323
form startups, 169
indexes, 324
optional field properties,
263-264
project properties
multithreaded
applications, 507
sort properties, 323-324

setting up
dynasets, 306-308
RDC, 413-414

Setup Wizard, 717
file types, 720

SETUP.LST file, 551
.REG files, registering,
553-554

**SetupForm procedure,
622-625**

Shape control, 22, 58

Shapes collection, 639

ShapeText property, 639

**Sheets method, collections,
487**

shortcut keys, 19, 99
creating menu bars, 97-99

ShowAboutBox method, Excel, 607

ShowPrinter method, CommonDialog control, 117

Simple Combo combo box, 73

single record data-entry forms, 234

single variables, 121

single-key expressions, 255-261

single-line If statements, 134

single-tier, ODBC drivers, 404

single-use applications, references, 534-535

single-use objects
optimizing, 507-508
remote applications, performance, 503-504

singleUse classes, 471

SingleUse setting (Instancing property), 533

sites
Web
Excel, 608
MAPI SDK, 673
Microsoft Developers Network, 681
Microsoft KnowledgeBase, 644
Microsoft Office, 644
MSDN, 644
Office, 608, 681
VB Scripting Edition, 572
VBScript, 563
web, www.quecorp.com, 541, 559

size, forms, 44

SizeMode property, 421-422

Slider control, 514,
initializing, 516-517

slides
adding (PowerPoint), 637-638
transition times, specifying, 641

snapshots, 309, 362-363
advantages, 309
creating, 309
data control, 283-284
disadvantages, 309

software
three-phase development, 880-885
post-production phase, 884-886
pre-production phase, 881
production phase, 882

sort conditions, configuring (SQL SELECT statements), 352

sort property, setting, 323-324

sorting
CS programming techniques, 816-825
BinarySearch( ) function, 818-820
generic helper functions (writing), 817-818
QuickSort( ) function, 820-822

SoundRec class type, 419

Speaker property, 520-521

speed, early binding, 502

SpellCheck function, 648

Speller program, 646

spelling checker (Word), 646-647

splash screens, 579
user perceptions, graphical interfaces, 893

SQL
(Structured Query Language), 336
commands
controlling record range, 348
customizing databases with, 275-276
databases, 335
dynasets, 336
functions, aggregate, 353-354
optimization
compiling queries, 366
queries, 367
optimizing, 366-367
indexes, 366
queries, 336
debugging, 364
statements, 335-359, 361-363
Access, 366
creating, 363-366
creating QueryDef, 362
data control, 363
data manipulation language, 335
data-definition language DDLs, 359-361
DELETE, 357-358
executing action queries, 361-362
INSERT, 358
manipulative, 337
naming, 337
parameters, 356-357
passing to other databases, 367
retrieving records, 336
SELECT, 337-357
UPDATE, 359

SQL dialog box, 364

SQL report sources, 240

SQL Server, 335
importing from, 634

SQL statements, **327-329**
  action queries, 329
  calculation queries, 327-328

Standard .EXE, **17**
  projects, 470

standard prefixes, objects, **46-47**

standard reports, **239**

standards, Open Database Connectivity (ODBC), **307**

Start menu commands, Control Panel, **404**

StartCapture method, **700**

starting
  Excel, 576
  projects, .OCX controls, 512-513
  Visual Data Manager, 364

startup objects, Sub Main, **517**

StartUpPosition form property, **52**

StartupPosition property, controls, **54**

startups
  forms, setting, 169
  program, controlling, 168-169

statement builder, **16**

statements, **127-139**
  assignment, 127
  declaration, 183
  DELETE, 357-358
  Dim, 258
    classes, 474
  displaying forms
    Load, 55
    Unload, 55
  Error, Property Let procedure, 481
  False conditions, 135-137
    Not operator, 135-136
  For Each...Next
    collections, 484

If, 133-135
  multiple commands, 134-135
  single-line, 134
INSERT, 358
manipulative, 336
math operators, 127-132
  addition and subtraction, 128-129
  exponents, 131-132
  multiplication and division, 129-131
multiple-condition, 351
select case, 137-140
SELECT INTO, 358
Set, 183-186
  Property Let Basic procedure, 483
SQL, 327-329, 335-359
  action queries, 329
  calculation queries, 327-328
  manipulative, 337
  SELECT, 337-357
Structured Query Language (SQL), 255
UPDATE, 359

status updates, informing users, **103-109**
  displaying messages, 104-106
  message icons, 105-106
  returning values (MsgBox function), 107-109

StDev aggregate function, **353**

StDevP aggregate function, **353**

storing
  functions, 163
  procedures, 163

string variables, **121**

strings
  comparisons
    LIKE predicate, 349
  fixed-length, 123-124

operators, 132-133
VBScript, 565

Structured Query Language (SQL) statement, **255**

Structured Query Language, see **SQL**

styles
  creating, Word, 656-661
  window
    adding new, 774-777
    frankentrols, 774

Sub Main
  controls, initializing, 517
  Main, 169

Sub Main procedure
  debugging, 540-542
  testing applications start-up, 544

Sub Main subroutine (user perceptions), graphical interfaces, **893**

Sub procedures, **157-171**

Sub statement (procedures), creating, **158**

subordinate objects (multiuse objects), debugging, **538-539**

subroutines (queries), action, **357**

subtraction, operators, **128-129**

Sum aggregate function, **353**

summary reports, **239**

supplied constants, **126**

Swap() function, **817**

syntax checker, **145-146**

syntax errors
  debugging programs, 144-156
  syntax checker, 145-146

system-initiated events, **83-85**

SystemDirectory property, 480

T

Table Structure dialog box, 271-272

TableDef object, 206
attaching tables, 397
defining, 261

TableDef objects, 258

tables, 249-250
Access, attaching with, 400-401
access, restricting, 371-372
adding, 270-272, 274
adding databases to, 264
adding indexes to, 272-273
advantages, 305
aliases, assigning, 343
attached, opening, 401
child, 252-254
clauses
JOIN, 345-346
WHERE, 346-348
creating, 260-264
SQL SELECT
statements, 356
creating with Queries, 264
DAO, attaching with, 397-398
data control, 283-284
databases, 304-305
defining, 359-360
deleting, 274, 360
deletions, cascading, 213
disadvantages, 305
external, attaching, 396-401
lookup, 252-254
methods for relating, 207-211
multiple, databases, 343
naming, 356
opening, 305
organizing, 254-255
records, deleting, 357

recordsets, 345
relationships, setting, 344-347
SQL, 336
and Index Sort Orders
Yield Different Results, 319
manipulative statements, 337
Mode of a Snapshot, 309
updates
cascading, 213
Visual Data Manager
attaching with, 398-400

tabs
control toolboxes
adding, 22

target platforms, testing, 544-545

tasks, forms Outlook, 667

templates
PowerPoint, 644
PrettyPrint.dot, 656
Word, 656-661

Terminate event, PowerPoint, 636-637

terminating, objects, forms, 503

testing, in-progress, 540-542

text
controls, 62-67
Label, 62
RichTextBox, 65-69
TextBox, 64-65
dragging, 446

Text property, 65, 491, 494, 699
Editor object, 536

TextBox control, 58

Textbox control, 21

TextBox text control, 64-65

TextServer
Activate method, 685

OLE automation servers, 684
ReplaceAll method, 686

third-party bound controls, 296

thread pools, multithreaded applications, 506

three-phase software development, 880-885
post-production phase, 884-886
deployment, 884
documentation, 884
evaluation, 885
pre-production phase, 881
production phase, 882

TickFrequency property, Slider control, 514

time statements, VBScript, 564

time-intensive operations, deferring, 447

timeouts, OLE, 466-468

Timer control, 21, 58

Tool menu commands, Add Procedure, 159

toolbars
creating (Word), 650-651
customizing, 16, 25
functions, 19-20
status bar, updating, 651
three-dimensional effect, adding, 652
ToolTips, 20

toolboxes, control toolbox, 21-22

Tools menu, 94

Tools menu commands
Design Outlook Form, 568
Procedure Attributes, 478, 495

Tools/RegistrationUtilities directory, 523

ToolTips, defined, 20

top n reports, 239

**transaction processing,
333-334**
  deletions, recovering, 358

**TransferDatabase method,
634**

**TransferSpreadsheet
method, 634**

TransferText method, 634

**TRANSFORM, manipulative
statements, 337**

**TransparentPaint() function,
845, 862**

trappable errors, 481

**TrapText property, 491,
494**

**TreeView control, Windows
common controls,
766-773**
  BuildTree and
    LoadListItems procedures,
    768-770
  control event responses,
    770-773

troubleshooting
  action queries, 329
  applications, multi-user, 370
  bookmarks, 321
  creating public class
    modules, 496
  Data Access Object
    libraries, 303
  Delete method, 274
  displays, 439
  errors
    Duplicate Definition, 496
    trappable, 481
  events, Resize, 422
  indexes, 257
  object libraries, 545
  objects
    OLE Automation, 439
    unrecognized, 439
  OLE Automation
    Excel, 576
    Word, 648

  OLE objects, editing, 439
  primary indexes, 265
  relations, 268
  variables, 316
  see also debugging
  see also SQL optimization

**true conditions, conditional
loops, 142-145**

twips, 46
  defined, 20

**txtMultiBugs_Change event,
629-630**

type libraries, 559-561
  features, remote
    applications, 499
  MAPI, 673-675
  object libraries, comparing,
    560

U

Unhook (hooking), 779-782

unique identifiers, 211

Unload event, 56-57

**Unload statement,
displaying forms, 55**

**/UNREGSERVER switch,
553**

**UPDATE, manipulative
statements, 337**

Update button, 236

Update method, 331, 433

**UPDATE statement, (SQL),
359**

**UpdateControls method,
data controls, 291**

Updated event, 433

**UpdateData method,
626-628**

**UpdateOptions property,
432**

**UpdateRecord method, data
controls, 291**

**updates (tables), cascading
of, 213**

**UpdateStatus function,
649-650**

updating
  multiple indexes, 325
  records, 331

**Useful Class object,
592-608**

**USEFUL.VBP project,
592-594**

**User Form command
(Insert menu), 523**

**user interfaces, Outlook,
667**

user restrictions, 370

user-initiated events, 84-85

users
  documents
    moving between
      (Internet applications),
      725-726
    passing data between
      (Internet applications),
      726-728
  feedback, event-driven
    programming, 78
  improving perceptions,
    graphical interfaces,
    892-893
  input, 109-111
    actions (determining),
      111
    Input dialog setup, 110
  offering choices, graphical
    interfaces, 890-892
  progress and status updates,
    103-109
    displaying messages,
      104-106
    message icons, 105-106
    returning values
      (MsgBox function),
      107-109
  user-initiated events, 84-85

utilities
REGOCX32.EXE, 554
REGSVR32.EXE, 554

Utilities menu commands, Attachments, 399

V

Validate event (data controls), action parameter values, 289

validation
data, 214-216
field-level, 214-215
record-level, 215
required-field, 216

Value property, defaults, assigning, 477

values, comparing (tables), 344
functions, 161
of variables, determining, 149-152
properties, 179, 184
retrieving, 180
setting, 179
setting and retrieving, 59-61
returning, MsgBox function (user updates), 107-109
vbOLEChanged, Code argument, 433
vbOLEClosed, Code argument, 433
vbOLERenamed, Code argument, 433
vbOLESaved, Code argument, 433

Var aggregate function, 353

variables
constants, 125-127
creating your own, 126-127
supplied, 126
debugging, 532

declarations, 121-124
explicit, 122
fixed-length strings, 123-124
implicit, 122-123
defining, VBScript, 563
Excel, 576
internal, defining, 186-187
mobjBasic object, 481
mthTest, 472
naming, special identifying characters, 123
option explicit statement, 124-125
procedures, preserving, 163
programming, 120-127
public, declaring, 178-179
Relation object, 267
troubleshooting, 316
types of, 120-121
values of, determining, 149-152

Variant data type, 562

variant variables, 121

variants, 810-815
ParamArray function, 815-816

VB
(Visual Basic)
porting, 563
VBA
code-compatibility, 559
comparing, 558-561
differences in language definitions, 558
shared features, 558
versions, choosing, 571-572

VB Scripting Edition, Web site, 572

VB Terminal
ActiveX objects
refining, 491-496
running as, 490
class module, creating, 489
.EXE file, testing as, 490-491

VB4, Instancing property equivalents, 533

VB5, object variables, debugging, 532

VBA (Visual Basic for Applications), features not in VBScript, 564-565

VBA type library, predefined constants, 562-563

VBE (Visual Basic Editor), 558

vbOLEActivateAuto (AutoActivate setting), 434

vbOLEActivateDoubleClick, (AutoActivate setting), 434

vbOLEActivateGetFocus (AutoActivate setting), 434

vbOLEActivateManual (AutoActivate setting), 434

vbOLEAutomatic (UpdateOptions setting), 432

vbOLEChanged value, Code argument, 433

vbOLEClosed value, Code argument, 433

vbOLEFrozen (UpdateOptions setting), 432

vbOLEManual (UpdateOptions setting), 432

vbOLERenamed value, Code argument, 433

vbOLESaved value, Code argument, 433

vbOLESizeAutoSize, (ScaleMode setting), 422-423

vbOLESizeAutoSize (SizeMode property settings), 421

vbOLESizeClip, (ScaleMode setting), 422

vbOLESizeClip (SizeMode property settings), 421

vbOLESizeStretch, (ScaleMode settings), 427

vbOLESizeStretch (SizeMode property settings), 421

vbOLESizeZoom
(ScaleMode settings), 427
(SizeMode setting), 427

vbOLESizeZoom (SizeMode property settings), 421

VBScript, 561-571
forms, 565
missing VBA features, 564-565
Outlook, 568-571
security, 562
variables, defining, 563
Variant data type, 562
VBA type library, 562
predefined constants, 562-563
Web pages, 562, 565-568
application, 567-568
Web site, 563

verbnumber argument, 434

VerifyRequiredField function, 626-628

VerifyRequiredField procedure, 630-631

versions, creating (objects), 548-549
information, adding, 548-549

Vertical ScrollBar control, 21,58

View Code button, 166
writing event procedures, 85

View Code command (Form menu), 568

View menu, 93

View menu commands
Code, 85
Debug, 148

Options, 724
Watch Window, 149

View Object button, 166

Visible, properties, 46

Visible = True statements, Excel, 576

Visible property, 738

Visual Basic
ActiveX controls, creating, 15
ActiveX documents, creating, 15
Application Wizard, 17
background of, 37-40
BASIC, 38
code, 38-39
code editor, 39
controls, .OCX, 512
database commands, 258-260
GUI, 39-40
interface, 17-25
introduction, 9-29
menu bar, 18-19
new features, 15-16
programming, 119-156
toolbar, functions, 19-20

Visual Basic environments (remote applications), accessing, 501

Visual Basic Help Topics, 27

Visual C++ controls, .OCX, 512

Visual Data Manager, 364-365
(Add-in), 364
Query Builder (VDM), 365
starting, 364
tables, attaching, 398-400

Visual Data Manager (Visual Basic), creating databases with, 269-273

Visual Data Manager

command (Add-Ins menu), 364, 398

Visual FoxPro controls, .OCX, 512

vntFieldPipeValue parameter, AddOrEditRecord method, 617

Volume control, 513
events, adding, 517-519
methods, adding, 517-519
properties
adding, 517-519
Speaker, 520-521

VolumeControlConstants class, 518

W

Watch Window command (View menu), 149

wave files, playback (multimedia forms), 806-808

Web browsers, *see* **browsers**

Web pages
VBScript, 562, 565-568
application, 567-568

Web sites
Excel, 608
MAPI SDK, 673
Microsoft, Developers Network, 681
Microsoft KnowledgeBase, 644
Microsoft Office, 644
MSDN, 644
Office, 608, 681
VB Scripting Edition, 572
VBScript, 563
www.quecorp.com, 541, 559

WebBrowser ActiveX control, 734, 741

WebLog.TLB, 731

WebLog.VBR, 731

webView_CommandStateChange event, 735

WHERE clause, 351-368
DELETE statements, 357
dynasets, 363
fields, updating multiple, 359
functions, aggregate, 354
HAVING clause, comparing, 355
indexes, 366
(SQL SELECT statements), 344, 346
(SQL statements), 339

While condition, 143

WidthNew argument, 422

wild cards, LIKE predicate, 349-350

wild-card parameter
(SQL statements), 338

Window menu, 94

window styles
adding new, 774-777
frankentrols, 774

WindowCreated() method, 795

WindowDestroyed() method, 795

Windows
32-bit
OLE Automation memory requirements, 647
applications, multi-user, 370

windows
child, MDI, 795-797
customizing, 25
saving positions, 788-791
sizing (OLE objects), 422-423

Windows 95
applications, designing, 443
common controls, 765-773
progress bars, 765-766

TreeView and ListView, 766-773

Windows NT
common controls, 765-773
progress bars, 765-766
TreeView and ListView, 766-773

Windows Task Manager (remote automations) checking, 501-502

WindowState form property, 52

Winsock control (Winsock.OCX), 741-749
creating chat applications, 746-749
creating FTP browsers, 742-746

Wizards
ActiveX Control Interface, 512
ActiveX Control Interface Wizard, 524-528
creating, 622-625
NavigatePages procedure, 625-626
Property Page, 529

Word, 646-648
controls
interface, 653-656
OLE Container, 648-663
documents
custom properties, 663
enabling pretty-printing, 662-663
macro recorder, 648
macros, 656-661
calling, 662-663
objects, Selection, 648
OLE Automation
optimizing performance, 656-667
tips, 648
parameters, passing, 662-663
Speller program, 646
spelling checker, 646-647

VB code module, pretty-printing, 656-661

word wrapping, objects, 185

Word.Document class type, 419

Word.Document.7 class type, 419

Word.Picture.7 class type, 419

WordArt class type, 419

WordArt miniserver, 689

WordBasic methods, 438

WordDocument class type, 419

WordWrap property, 63

Workbooks method, collections, 487

Workspace, objects, 206

WOSA (Windows Open System Architecture), 404

WRITE statement, COBOL and FORTRAN, 79

write-only properties, creating, 480-481

WriteProperties event, adding design-time properties, 519

WriteProperty method, 519

writing
event procedures, 85-86
menu item code, 99-100

www.quecorp.com, 541, 559
CLASSEX.VBP file (enhanced printer objects), 186

X

XLCONT.VBP project, Excel, 590

Y-Z

ZOrder, SetFocus, 49

ZOrder method, 49

Check out Que® Books on the World Wide Web
http://www.quecorp.com

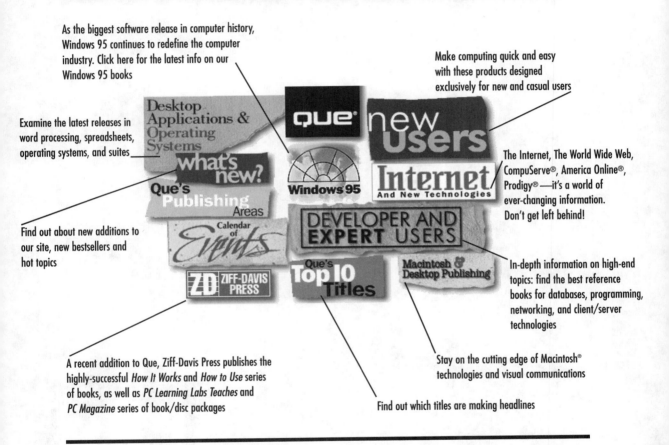

As the biggest software release in computer history, Windows 95 continues to redefine the computer industry. Click here for the latest info on our Windows 95 books

Make computing quick and easy with these products designed exclusively for new and casual users

Examine the latest releases in word processing, spreadsheets, operating systems, and suites

The Internet, The World Wide Web, CompuServe®, America Online®, Prodigy® —it's a world of ever-changing information. Don't get left behind!

Find out about new additions to our site, new bestsellers and hot topics

In-depth information on high-end topics: find the best reference books for databases, programming, networking, and client/server technologies

A recent addition to Que, Ziff-Davis Press publishes the highly-successful *How It Works* and *How to Use* series of books, as well as *PC Learning Labs Teaches* and *PC Magazine* series of book/disc packages

Stay on the cutting edge of Macintosh® technologies and visual communications

Find out which titles are making headlines

With 6 separate publishing groups, Que develops products for many specific market segments and areas of computer technology. Explore our Web Site and you'll find information on best-selling titles, newly published titles, upcoming products, authors, and much more.

- Stay informed on the latest industry trends and products available
- Visit our online bookstore for the latest information and editions
- Download software from Que's library of the best shareware and freeware

MACMILLAN COMPUTER PUBLISHING USA
A VIACOM COMPANY

Technical
---- **Support:**

If you need assistance with the information in this book or with a CD/Disk
accompanying the book, please access the Knowledge Base on our Web
site at **http://www.superlibrary.com/general/support**. Our most
Frequently Asked Questions are answered there. If you do not find the
answer to your questions on our Web site, you may contact Macmillan
Technical Support **(317) 581-3833** or e-mail us at **support@mcp.com**.